MISSION SURVIVAL

MISSION SURVIVAL

The people of Israel's story in their own words: from the threat of annihilation to miraculous Victory

EDITED AND COMPILED BY
RUTH BONDY
OHAD ZMORA
RAPHAEL BASHAN

W. H. ALLEN
LONDON
1968

TO THE SEVEN HUNDRED ISRAELIS
WHO IN JUNE 1967 WILLINGLY
GAVE UP THEIR LIVES, SO THAT
ISRAEL WOULD SURVIVE.

AMERICAN-ISRAEL PUBLISHING COMPANY, LTD. BAT YAM, ISRAEL
PRINTED IN ISRAEL BY E. LEWIN-EPSTEIN LTD. BAT YAM, ISRAEL
FOR THE PUBLISHERS W. H. ALLEN & COMPANY
ESSEX STREET LONDON WC2
491 00839 2

Contents

CONTENTS

CONTENTS

Introduction

THE WAR BETWEEN ISRAEL AND EGYPT, JORDAN AND SYRIA LASTED only six days, but it may take generations and volumes to evaluate its full impact. It passed like a storm and left in its wake a completely changed Middle East, a different balance of power, new borders, amazed and stunned people and a trail of death. Wars which drag on and on, as wars usually do, allow the people involved enough time to comprehend their meaning and their implications, but six days (and the actual fighting was over in 118 hours), give no one time to catch his breath and to realize what has happened. When the cease-fire was signed on the 12th of June and the guns fell silent, the Israelis "were as in a dream," and so were the Arab nations concerned—except that their dream was of a different kind.

Gradually Israel's people asked themselves: How did it happen? How could we have changed so quickly from a nation on the verge of annihilation to victor over three armies, almost three times as strong in equipment and more than twice our number of men? What gave us this victory—the training of Zahal? The willingness to die? The superiority of the Israel Air Force? The fighting spirit? The inferiority of the Arab soldier? Divine Providence? Jewish stubbornness? Lack of choice?

This book tries to answer this crucial question, not through an analysis of military strategy (this has to be left to the experts and will occupy them, no doubt, for a long time to come) but through the eyes and lips of those who took part in the war, who saw it unfold, who bear witness to history in the making—soldiers, pilots, commanders, field-surgeons, children in border settlements and worried mothers in the towns, prisoners of war and Arab youth in the Old City, kibbutz members under Syrian fire, and widows of the fallen.

These are the stories of some outstanding battles of the Six-Day War, in Jerusalem, in Sinai, on the Syrian Heights, seen not as a confrontation between weapons of different power and make, but as a clash of men, who fought and feared, dared and hoped, were wounded and died. The Israeli army is built on reserves. All the men between the ages of 18 to 45 are called to arms, a fact which gives it the special character of a real "people's army," a name atrociously misused nowadays. Many Israeli journalists and writers participated in the war, some as army correspondents and others as regular combatants, and these are their impressions, during the days of tension preceding the war, the war itself and its aftermath, written from a standpoint of personal involvement.

It is no secret that one of the reasons for the superiority of the Israeli army is the quality of its leadership (its officers and commanders do not spur their men: "Forward!" but call to them: "Follow me!") This book presents portraits of some of the outstanding personalities of this war, interviews with them, their speeches and the summing up of their experiences. Some of them, such as Defense Minister Major-General Moshe Dayan or the Chief-of-Staff, Major-General Yitzhak Rabin, are famous names by now; others—the commander of the paratroops who fought in Jerusalem, the four generals of Sinai, or the builders of the Israel Air Force, are little known abroad, but in the eyes of the people of Israel they are symbols of bravery and heroes. Since the struggle in the international arena is a direct outgrowth of the actual fighting (and Israel must be one of the few countries in history that had to fight as hard for the right to exist in peace as in war) we have included the address of Abba Eban, Israel's Foreign Minister, before the United Nations on June 19, now a classic example of diplomatic utterance.

While the war lasted less than a week, the time span covered by this anthology is three months, from the celebrations of Israel's Independence Day on the 15th of May and the closing of the Straits of Tiran a few days after to the administrative unification of Jerusalem, the spasmodic gush of population from West Bank to East Bank and vice versa, and the stationing of UN observers on both sides of the Canal. We have included in this book articles, stories, and small items illuminating big events, from all daily and weekly papers appearing in Israel, which, in contrast to the size of the country even in its new boundaries, are rather numerous; material from bulletins put out by the various military units in the field, letters written by soldiers, transcripts of press conferences with commanders of the three fronts plus a chronology of events to simplify orientation.

This was a unique war in many respects—swift and, in a way, old-fashioned, in that personal courage still counted more than the push of a button. We have tried to catch its special character through its human features—the volunteers looking for work, the helicopter pilot in love with his profession, the Jew of Jerusalem meeting his Arab neighbor over the fence for the first time after 19 years. It is our fervent hope that this may be the last anthology about the last war for Israel, for ages to come.

The Editors

Words and Meanings

TERMS

Al-Fatah	—Syrian marauders
Fedayyin	—Egyptian marauders
Halacha	—Jewish law as officially codified
Kibbutz	—Collective labor village
Kiddush	—Prayer sanctifying symbols of food (bread, wine)
Kumzits	—"Come and sit" around a campfire
Magen David Adom	—"Red Shield of David" disaster service
Mishnah	—A code of Jewish law derived from Scripture
Moshav	—Cooperative labor village
Sabra	—"prickly pear"—a native-born Israeli
Shalom	—peace, hello, good-bye, well-being
Torah	—Bible, specifically Five Books of Moses
Uzi	—Israel-made sub-machine gun
Western Wall	—of Solomon's Temple area
Zahal	—("Zva Hagana le-Yisrael") Israel Defense Army

MEASURES

25 *millimeters*	=1 inch
1 *meter*	=39 inches
8 *kilometers*	= 5 miles

MILITARY RANKS

Segen-Mishne	—2nd Lieutenant
Segen	—1st Lieutenant
Seren	—Captain
Sgan-Aluf	—Lieutenant-Colonel
Aluf-Mishne	—Colonel
Aluf	—Brigadier-General
Rav-Aluf	—Major-General (usually the C-o-S)

REMARKS

Most of the dates given in this book appear as they are used in Israel: June 5, 1967 is 5.6.67 (the day precedes the month).

Chapter One

The Gathering Storm

ISRAEL AND NEIGHBORING COUNTRIES

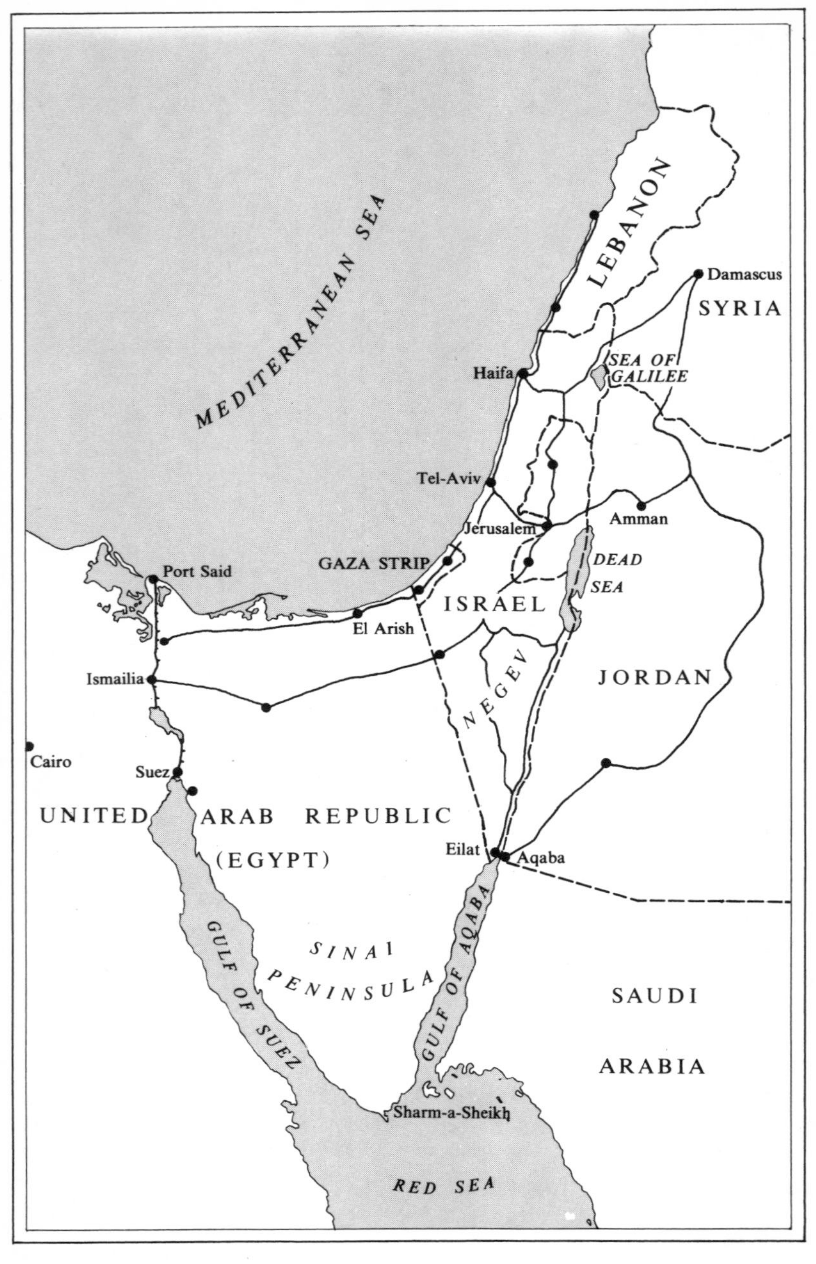

ARAB INSTIGATION AGAINST ISRAEL, WHICH HAD BEEN GOING ON FOR 19 years—on the radio, press and television—was one of the mainstays of the regimes in Egypt, Syria, Jordan and Iraq. Arabic-speaking Israeli citizens, as well as the Arab citizens of the State, could listen for 19 years to vulgar abuse, murderously provocative speeches, and incendiary slogans of revenge, any time they turned their sets to an Arabic-speaking Middle East station. The Israelis listened to the streams of invective, to the fantastic exaggerations and lies pouring forth from the broadcasting stations in Cairo, Damascus, Amman and Baghdad, with a mixture of amazement and contempt. But the citizens of those countries swallowed the poison, and their young generation was fed and bred on it. If the diplomats in the world capitals, who always urged Israel to keep calm in view of Nasser's "moderation," had listened to just one of the daily broadcasts of the Voice of Cairo, they would have understood the real trends in the Arab world.

But these were not just idle words. The Arab leaders promised their peoples that the day of revenge was drawing close. On May 8th, 1960, Nasser proclaimed in Mansura: "The treachery with which we always had to contend did not prevent us, 800 years ago (the time of the Crusaders) from reconquering Jerusalem, after it had been in enemy hands for 88 years. Nothing will prevent the Arab nations from attaining their wish, from stamping out treachery and imperialism, and reconquering the Holy Land, as we have done 800 years ago." On May 18th, 1962, Nasser said at a session of the Egyptian Government: "We will launch total war at the right moment. I will not agree to start incomplete military activities, but when we initiate war, I want to be certain of our ability to win." Two weeks later, on June 2nd, 1962, he proclaimed: "Our military budget amounts to over two billion Egyptian pounds. Our army is the strongest. We really want action, and we are not speaking just for inner consumption!"

On February 7th, Nasser said in an interview given to an Indian paper: "There is no avoiding war in Palestine. As long as Israel exists, war is bound to break out." On March 8th, 1965, he declared at Assiut: "When we enter Palestine, the soil will not only be covered with sand; it will be drenched with blood!"

In 1967, the Egyptians stopped trying to hide their intentions. On May 17th, the commentator of the Egyptian radio station "Saut-Al-Arab" proclaimed: "The whole country of Egypt, with its entire human, economic and scientific potential, is ready to launch a total war against Israel." The following day, a commentator of the same station broadcast this declaration: "The only language Israel understands is a total war which will put an end, once and for all, to Zionist existence." On May 19th, the Voice of Cairo broadcast: "We are ready to launch now a fierce battle, in order to prevent the imperialists and the UN forces from protecting Israel. We are expecting this war—and we shall win!"

Other Arab states followed suit. Syria broke all records of savagery; its broadcasts and its press called daily to "kill, crush, burn and destroy the Zionist viper's nest." On May 24th, the Syrian paper *Al-Ba'ath* demanded "to erase Israel from the face of the earth." The Syrian President, Al Atassi, called in a speech at the central committee of the Workers' Union "to burn Israel's interests, and to destroy the country." Radio Damascus broadcast in May: "The annihilation of Israel is indispensable to the freedom and honor of the Arab nation."

The Iraqi paper *Al Manar* wrote on May 30th: "The question is not whether the Zionist enemy has a right to the Gulf of Akaba or not; the question is whether Israel has a right to exist at all." Radio Amman bragged that day: "Hussein, the military leader, has moved his headquarters to the front, in order to be together with his brave soldiers. In due time they will crush Israel, and God bless that time!"

As Egyptian forces poured into Sinai and the Straits of Tiran were blocked, the mouthpieces of Arab propaganda rose to a hitherto unheard of pitch of hysterical bellicosity. On May 25th, the Voice of Cairo broadcast: "Our forces are perfectly ready—we are prepared to sink any Israeli vessel which will try to pass the Gulf of Akaba." Next day, the Egyptian radio announced: "We know that the blockade of the Gulf of Akaba is a *casus belli.* Israel has two alternatives, either of which is drenched in her own blood. Israel can either strangle in the Arab economic and military noose, or be shot to death by the Arab forces surrounding her on the south, north and east."

Gamal Abdel Nasser decided to dispense with diplomatic niceties, and in the speech he held at the House of Representatives at the end of May, he declared: "We have restored the situation in Sinai to the point it stood before October of 1956. We are going to restore the situation in Palestine to the point it stood before 1948!" He asked Parliament to invest him with emergency powers, and his request was granted. On May 28th, Nasser declared at a well-attended press conference in Cairo: "If Israel wants war, let it be! We will choose the place and the time, and we will say to her: Go ahead!"

Israelis were certain that Nasser's speeches were no mere slogans. He would not be satisfied with the blockade of the Straits and the concentration of troops in Sinai. Apparently, the time had come to put in practice the "theory" he had preached for years: the extermination of Israel.

As tension in the Middle East mounted and approached its climax, and assumptions and theories about the coming events multiplied, Mohammed Hassnein Heykal, editor of the Egyptian paper Al Ahram *and Nasser's personal friend, who often served as the Egyptian ruler's mouthpiece, openly and unequivocally voiced Egypt's true intentions. Heykal's article (most of which follows) was published on May* 26*th.*

It is difficult to write about current events, especially when the pace and depth of these events is storm-swift.

It is simple to write about what actually did happen; this is merely commenting on the events and analyzing them. Nor is it difficult to write about the future, since the future is infinite and each day has its morrow.

The real problem is to discuss what is taking place when it is happening. This depends on the hands of the clock, for minutes and even seconds may count. The gravity is further compounded when the theme of the discussion deals with matters of life and death.

I am convinced that an armed clash between Egypt and the Israeli foe is inevitable. This armed clash may break out at any time and anywhere along the lines separating the Egyptian armed forces from those of the Israeli foe on land, at sea and in the air, in an area extending from the northern Gaza Strip to the southern point of the Gulf of Akaba at Sharm-a-Sheikh.

In the impending clash, the most significant elements are the psychological factor and its impact on the balance of power in the Middle East. For Israel, passage through the Gulf of Akaba is more vital than ever. Israel is now undergoing a rude awakening from an all-night carousal and drunken stupor. The sources of German reparation payments have run dry. There have been grants and contributions, but Israel has already drawn a good deal from this well. Even if its current economic crisis should obtain relief from unforeseen sources, especially with the aid of propaganda, it is certain that many people in the West are already disgusted with this entity, which cannot lead a normal life—like an infant which refuses to grow.

Israel has been placing much hope in its trade with East Africa and Asia. All of this trade has been passing through the Red Sea and the Gulf leading to the port of Eilat. Many plans have been drawn up to expand this trade. There are also oil-flow arteries. Israel has laid two pipelines to transport Iranian oil to the Haifa refineries. There have also been some vague dreams about digging another canal, between Eilat and the port of Ashdod, to compete with or replace the Suez Canal.

These are important issues which Israel cannot ignore. In my opinion, however, these will not be the determinants in the Israeli reaction to a closing of the Gulf of Akaba.

The decisive issue is the psychological one. Closing the Gulf of Akaba to Israeli shipping and to Israel-bound strategic materials, even in non-Israeli ships, will signify that the Arab world, represented by Egypt, has for the first time succeeded in changing, by the use of force, a situation which had been forcibly imposed upon it.

There may be other reasons for advocating that the Arab struggle be conducted as it has been in the past. We can argue that Palestine had been sold out by the British to the Zionists; this is true. We can say that the UN has defaulted; this is true. We can point out that the Arab reactionaries, from Jordan's King Abdullah to Saudi Arabia's King Feisal, conspired against Palestine; this is true. We can claim that imperialism, represented by the armed forces of Britain and France, forced upon us this entity known as Israel; this is true. We can state all of these things, yet the sole unvarnished truth is that Israel has always been imposed on the Arabs by force. The Arabs did not have the power to oppose this with force and to replace it, before the world, with conditions which would reflect Arab rights and interests.

Israel has always based its existence, security and future on force. The philosophy of its leadership is that only fear will thwart the Arab. This is where Israeli terrorism reaches its peak. From the Israeli viewpoint, all of the events set forth above were aimed at achieving one goal—to convince the Arabs that Israel can do everything and that we can do nothing, that helplessness is an inborn Arab trait and that we must therefore accept the situation as it stands.

The weakness in the Israeli philosophy lies in its assumption that two or even three million Israelis can impose their will on a sea of 80 million Arabs.

For many wearisome years, the Arabs have lacked a rallying point around which they could set things in their proper place.

This is the first time that the Arabs can challenge Israel's efforts to shape things by force, in a direction synonymous with Arab rights and interests. Allowing Israel passage through the Gulf of Akaba was a fact imposed on the Arabs by the force of imperialist arms. The closing of the Gulf to Israel, this week, is a different fact, this time imposed by the force of Arab arms and assured by them. As far as Israel is concerned, this fact constitutes the most serious issue.

The question is, therefore, not merely of the Gulf of Akaba itself but of the entire philosophy behind Israel's security, the basis of its existence since its birth. This necessarily leads to the inevitable conclusion that there is no avoiding an armed clash between Egypt and the Israeli foe. We must expect that the first blow will be delivered by the enemy. Then will come the second blow, which we shall strike, an effective blow with the most telling results imaginable.

The glorious days between May 14th and 23rd marked the change in the situation and the balance of power in the Middle East.

Although the broad front of Arab unity had been impaired by the failure of Arab summit conferences—and, with this failure, the inability to defend the Arab states bordering on Israel—this was something over which Egypt had no control. Egypt can be in control, however, of another objective, namely the readying and solidification of its own armed forces. Egypt has therefore been placed on a footing of preparedness. This was the first point in Egypt's strategy during the ten glorious days. The second was the complete surprise which attended Egypt's act. Apparently—and now it seems almost certain—the anti-Egypt forces—imperialism, Arab and Israeli reactionaries—believed their own propaganda about the weak state of Egypt to the very end; people at times become the victims of their own fabrications. This is precisely what must have happened, else how can we understand Israel's consistent provocation of Syria, up to the point of declaring that its forces would attack Damascus?

The Israeli threat to Syria, and the real intentions behind it, have forced this unexpected situation, to which Egypt had to give immediate reply. But while this situation came as a surprise, it was countered by the decisive and forceful Egyptian stand and its wonderful leadership. Egypt was not prepared for this specific situation; it had been preparing for everything and anything.

Now these were the events of the ten glorious days, one after another, taken in considered steps:

The decision to live up to the defense pact with Syria, transmitted by Egypt's Chief of Staff, Mahmoud Fawzi, in his five-hour flight to Damascus; the request by letter from Mahmoud Fawzi to the commander of the United Nations Emergency Force to remove his men from the Egypt–Israel boundary line; immediate deployment of Egyptian armed forces in all the evacuated positions along the border; the demand by letter from Egypt's Foreign Minister, Mahmoud Riad, to UN Secretary-General U Thant, that the UNEF be completely removed from Egypt and Gaza; the occupation of Sharm-a-Sheikh at the approach to the Gulf of Akaba; the order to close the Gulf of Akaba to Israeli shipping and to non-Israeli ships carrying strategic materials to Eilat; strong rejection of any US intervention. These steps had the support of an armed force unequaled in the annals of the Middle East, from the standpoint of size, preparedness and fighting spirit.

This has had two results. The invasion of Syria was rendered impossible because all of the enemy's forces had to be shifted to the south in order to confront the poised Egyptian deployments.

The situation imposed by the Anglo-French invasion of 1956 has undergone a change. This means that even at this stage the Egyptian strategy has worked and has achieved its objective, namely, to dispel the plot to invade Syria, plus another valuable goal—the deployment of Egyptian forces to confront Israel directly, and the closing of the Gulf of Akaba to Israel.

Is this chapter closed?

No, it has only begun. Israel cannot pass over in silence and accept with equanimity everything which has transpired until now. Israel must react. The next step is up to her. We must expect that she will strike the first blow.

By the use of force, Egypt has attained its goals, at this stage, without the actual use of weapons. We must now wait for the next stages: Will Israel attack, and, can the second blow which we shall strike, hold good for all time.?

Mohammed Hassnein Heykal: "No Avoiding War"; *Al-Ahram,* 26.5.67

A week after Israel's celebration of her 19*th birthday, the wheels of history started spinning with lightning speed.* 100,000 *Egyptian soldiers and about* 1,000 *tanks were moved east, to Sinai and the Israeli frontier. Arab political activity broke all previous records: following a confrontation between Nasser and the UN Secretary General, U Thant, the UN Emergency Forces evacuated their bases along the Israeli border and at Sharm-a-Sheikh. Egyptian and Palestinian forces replaced them. But the acts of provocation culminated with Nasser's declaration about the blocking of the Straits of Tiran.*

Israel was not asleep, and reacted immediately with partial mobilization of its reserve forces.

His parents opened the door and said: "Avraham, they were here twice from the Army. They left you a notice."

Only moments earlier, Avraham Lazar had been in the thick of an argument about student council elections in the Beer-Sheba University Institute. As he crossed the fragrant lawn in the warm evening, his mind was on the lab work he had to prepare, the physics problems, the English lessons.

During the night hours he rode in the mobilized pick-up truck all around the city, knocking on doors, rounding up others. He went to the staging grounds of his own armor unit. The lab and the lessons were forgotten. In their stead he went to the enlarged under-roof area and set about taking care of the Centurion tank—his to command in the reserve corps.

Over the past weekend Avraham was joined by large numbers of other reserve men from all over the country, in response to the swift call-up. The call found them at work, at home, in the movies, in the synagogue. Moshe Abramov was just coming out of evening prayers when his son came running toward him, shouting with open excitement: "Daddy, Daddy, the Army!" That entire evening Moshe Abramov kept speculating where he would be reciting the morning prayer on the next day. He recited it in a large camp in the south, with a makeshift congregation.

It was quite a common sight, during the night hours last weekend—groups passing from house to house, knocking on doors, talking to sleepy figures in pyjamas on the other side of the half-open door. At times the reception was livelier. "Come on in and have some coffee. I've been expecting you." Then, knapsack on back, on to the staging ground, still in civilian clothes. Transport via public conveyance, or tracks bearing the yellow label on the windshield: "Mobilized Equipment."

In the cities, villages and settlements, the "soldiers-on-leave-11-months-of-the-year" streamed with their knapsacks to their staging grounds. Rarely did the recruiters come across a sour face. In fact, many of the reservists welcomed the call as though they were being invited to hold a reunion—which, in a sense, it was going to be. Daily worries, livelihood, family, studies—all were put into deep-freeze by the tension of the moment.

Members of an old-time armor unit gathered at a public park in the center of Tel-Aviv, slapped each other on the back, exhibited the novelties they brought to this new reserves call-up. Zohar Koren brought a small gas range which he had picked up on his last trip to Europe. The biggest hit and object of envy was Moshe Zolreich's battery-operated midget fan ("I usually keep it in the car.")

The caravans of recruits drew the attention of the populace. At Ofakim, a group of children gathered by the highway and threw wild flowers at the columns of cars and trucks that went past. In Lydda, two elderly women came up to the parked trucks at midnight and kept murmuring: "God bless you! Good luck!"

The phones at reserve unit headquarters didn't stop ringing. "Don't you want me? How come I haven't been called?" Men showed up at the meeting places, fully-equipped, without having been summoned. One of the Sinai Campaign veterans accused the reservist "brass" of not having called his unit at all.

They were all over the south, these reservists, digging trenches, taking care of their weapons, checking new equipment, getting briefed in the command tent, with telephone linesmen crawling in and out. The maps set up against the tables were marked with arrows, colored circles, green lines running tangent to red ellipses.

In a well-camouflaged tent hard by the side of a stifling-hot hillock, somewhere in the Negev, General Yisrael Tal explained the deployment of his forces in the sector to an interested group of listeners: Prime Minister Levi Eshkol, Chief-of-Staff General Yitzhak Rabin, and Commanding General of the Southern Command Yeshayahu Gavish, who were touring of the far-flung units.

Several dozen miles away, at a spot no less hot, Lieutenant Zvi (33, a successful Tel-Aviv lawyer) discussed the social welfare problems facing the veteran motorized infantry battalion. Many of the old-timers in the battalion, he pointed out to the battalion commander, had been associated with it for over 14 years. Up to that moment, some 97 percent of the reservists had reported for duty, among them several men who had left their families practically destitute. They had not complained, he said, but had simply and quietly reported their situation, then went on with their work of unloading boxes of ammunition for medium machine-guns.

Zvi himself had received his call-up notice via telephone in his spacious office. He switched off the air-conditioner, got into his car, stopped off at his home, then drove on to the unit base "to save time. The court cases will hold; after all, quite a few clients have also been called up . . ."

At the base in the south, Sergeant-Major Yosef Eisen was busy doing something entirely unwarlike. He was taking advantage of the first free moments in 48 hours to immerse his tired feet in a large ex-biscuit can which he had filled with water plus a large dash of salt. "Good for your blood circulation," he assured his snickering comrades.

In another reservist unit, the men, already settled, were now awaiting new orders. In the meantime they began planning their "social life." "After all," pointed out Levi Oushieff, "who knows how long we'll be staying here. We have to see to it that things don't get too boring." Levi was the official jester of the unit; all along, he did it well, and he knew it. But there were more serious things which demanded attention. In one of the tents, next to the bulletin board and its pages of briefing about the sector and call-up information, some of the fellows set up an attractive Synagogue Ark. Strangely enough, men who usually stayed away from religious services at home now began to edge toward the Ark. "In crisis," said machine-gunner Shlomo Ochion, "we are all good Jews."

"The fellows around here," said a senior officer of the armored corps, "know well why they had been called, and they are truly prepared to do everything to achieve peace. Their morale, you might say, is Double A-1."

Yadin Dudai: 11-Month Vacation Ended; *Bamahane,* 23.5.67

★

It is like an airfield, a railway station or a port. Citizens pass by, bags in hand early in the morning, dressed just like worthy, decent citizens going off to respectable places. These citizens, a precise cross-section of all classes within the community, are due to be transformed into veteran soldiers within a few hours.

Take the car. Off to the destination. Distribution of equipment, distribution of arms. General strip-tease on a stretch of blasted heath. The company directors, drivers, butchers, teachers, engineers, open the army pack. They strip off the civvies, put on battle-dress, tighten the belt. Into the civilian cases and bags go the civvies. Then the cases and bags are closed, to be opened on release.

Invariably the stout fellow gets the thin pants, the lanky one the short bags. A lively barter trade begins. Fat hunts for thin who has received fat man's trousers. Tall hunts for short who has received giant pants. The strip-tease ends and the reserve battalion prepares to leave, by company, platoon, section, officers and all, according to the ranks of the echelon.

In a shady corner the section commander gets to know his men. He introduces himself. His job—teaching future teachers. He asks the other section members who they are.

One is a shutterer. Another runs a laundry. A third is an engineer. The fourth is a factory manager. The fifth an agent. The sixth a student, the seventh yours truly, the eighth the section boss.

No time for small talk. They start out.

The battalion moves towards its objective.

From the packs come the scouting-tents. We split into two's. Each pair puts up a tent. The grass is cleared during the incidental digging. The ground is covered with an extra blanket. By noon the battalion has taken up positions and is entrenched and prepared.

The field rations arrive. We eat from tins.

By evening we shall know one another properly, duties will be allocated, the military spit-and-polish brought up to date.

After the exhausting refresher drill there are more field rations in the evening. There's tea and a standard spirit lamp. The mess-tin is placed on the tiny flame. Tea is brewed.

A last cigarette and the sleep of the dead.

The transistor is the center of life. It has priority over almost every other activity. At each fresh news program we gather round and listen tensely. Naturally we know all the news by heart. But there's no telling.

There's no discussing the news, hardly a single remark. No time. When there will be, people will almost certainly be back home again. After a back-breaking set of exercises with intervals for a smoke, at the meals and in the brief leisure before falling asleep, we begin to get to know each other.

What haven't we got here!

The company commander is a university lecturer. The factory manager in my section spent a period of 16 years with the U.S. State Department. The engineer is a Palmah veteran and Yitzhak Rabin was his platoon commander. Our platoon commanders are younger than their men.

Absolute readiness without appeal. No grumbling, no sick-parade. Fitness—what can be said about fitness? We do our best. Men who have seen three wars, who have sons and daughters about to graduate from secondary schools, try to run like youngsters; to crawl, to march, to do everything they could do so well. It is very hard to get such men to do impressive exercises, but nobody even dreams of asking it of them.

Among them are fighters who have not forgotten the rules. You see this by the way they hold the sub-machine guns, the way they look after their arms.

We have a big Turk and a small Turk. They speak Ladino to one another and laugh all the time. The big one is a giant; fat, with hands like oar-blades. He was the king of the moaners when we were in peacetime. But on the range they all came to look at the miracle—a shot group of 2.5 centimeters. In the grenade drill we set up a can as target. He flings best, hitting the tin. He has a daughter aged 18. His physical fitness is AA.

The little Turk is the company joker and a first-class shot. He has such a special kind of humor that I can't even describe it.

Anyone who is sent on guard duty goes out. Anyone assigned to clean the latrines does it with dry efficiency. Yesterday our section cleaned the latrines of the battalion. Nobody said he didn't like the job. (Pardon this example, but it is most instructive.)

There is any amount of preparedness. And no tricks about it. But there are no shouts of encouragement in the style of the football field. These men have already seen wars, and after all here they are, and they need no patriotic encouragement. And maybe the whole of the State has changed for that matter too, and nowadays there is a more responsible attitude towards this thing they call war. War is not a slogan but a reality of sacrifice and blood. And certainly there is no need here for any encouragement from behind the lines, or nationalist warming up and brain-washing. What has to be done is going to be done, quite dispassionately.

There is much security in the knowledge that they are all here in the lines, and there is an absence of the nervousness of the city, the uncertainty as to what may happen. Now anything may happen.

Once the men have re-established the routine of preparedness they begin to talk. One thinks of the situation this way, another differently. But the discussions are friendly. One likes Eshkol, the other Ben-Gurion. One says we have to declare war, the other that we have to weigh and exhaust all possiblities. There are some who claim that Ben-Gurion would have proclaimed war long ago. Others say that he would not have moved either without backing. There are those who argue that if Eshkol should succeed in avoiding war he will obtain a majority at the next elections. Here people speak openly and freely about everything. To me it seems that the debates are conducted at a higher level than in the Knesset, for instance. These are serious people here.

I asked the little Turk what he thought about the argument. He said that this argument was good since everybody could say what he was thinking. I asked him if he was for war. He said that nobody who has a wife and children is going to be happy about a war. But if it's necessary and there is no choice . . . I have not heard anybody talking contemptuously about the enemy. But they all agree that Israel cannot be defeated.

The battalion command notifies us that there will be an evening for local artists.

As it turns out there are plenty. There are actors, there is a jazz pianist, there is the conductor of a synagogue choir who is himself a cantor; there are guitarists, singers, and in general all the talents you can want. It turns out that there is even a well-known literary critic who can write a review of the performance. Somebody wonders how all these artists reached a single unit. Why wonder when many of those mobilized belong to the Tel-Aviv area?

It will be an interesting evening.

It turns out that everything is possible and that we remember quickly. The truth is that in the bosom of Nature it is possible to rest from routine worries by immersing ourselves in a different routine. The equipment and the kit-bag become part of the body, so that one is taken by surprise and feels too light without it. When it is all over maybe they will all become materialists again, worrying about car, apartment, job, and getting ahead. And what is wrong with that? What has happened now proves that if necessary every peace-time materialist, every citizen in slippers, can transform himself into a battling animal with the awareness, fitness and capacity for doing what is required of him; and an important part of the concept of capacity is contributed by the concept of preparedness.

See you again.

Amos Kenan: In the Field; *Yediot Aharonot,* 26.5.67

The first week of preparedness was over. The second week came, and nothing happened in Israel except for the additional mobilization. The Middle East was in the spotlight of world attention, and political activity in the Arab States became increasingly more febrile. The UN talked, argued, promised and soothed, but the noose tightening around Israel's neck made tension in the country unbearable.

There are 12 hours to our timepiece but no zero, and the hours therefore crawl along as though the hands were made of lead. At six o'clock come the news headlines, at seven the news in detail, one hour later the spot news, at ten o'clock the "Light Band" newscast, at 11:30 a.m. the special edition, plus the 1:00 p.m. (noon, officially) news and at 2:00 p.m. the news review. The "Long Wait" clock moves around in this fashion until midnight. During the night, in the middle of slumber, we look at the luminous dials, just to see what time it is. On the next day it's the same story, each hour with its news, though nothing is new. Everything, newswise, is cut and dried. One waits, discusses, worries, complains.

Then, after the lonely hours have gone down the drain, there comes the awful fear that zero hour has been obliterated in Israel. Watchmaker! We have lost an hour.

A person who doesn't know what to do with himself must be active. The way to thwart helplessness is to keep busy—to distribute envelopes, to chauffeur the activists, to prepare shelters, dig trenches, learn first-aid, bake cookies for the soldiers, paste paper strips on the windows—anything is better than waiting and doing nothing. One should do something—take pictures down from the walls, knit caps, count the stars in their constellations—only not come in conflict with spare time.

We know which are the important and the decisive acts, but since it is beyond us to perform them, we turn to the trivial—to polish the globe of the kerosene lamp, buy coarse salt, fill a pail with water, prepare two bandages and the white ointment to apply to wounds, cut black paper, obey orders, make assumptions, do drills, make up rules of conduct, set down plans—all these are good for coping with the "long wait."

It's difficult to comprehend the change. Only two weeks earlier we were busy head-over-heels—the job, the house, social obligations, keeping things neat and in place, dinner for eight and premieres. Winter things had to be moth-balled and that membership in the swim club had to be renewed; the sofa pillows should be dry-cleaned and letters answered and the bookcase put in order. Everything to be done, without procrastination. All these things were certainly not unimportant originally, since we spend half our lives doing them. But now, for a brief period, our well-tempered daily schedule has lost its equilibrium. We shall yet go back and note down in our pocket diary scores of important matters which must be done on one and the same day—except that the pages for the month of May will remain empty, a memorial to the long wait for the invasion which never made it.

As soon as the first news reached us about the withdrawal of the UNEF, we knew that life would never shrink back to its former confines. Even when things are as they should be, life does not retrace its footsteps; it is only that the distance between and the path leading from one day to the next are so minute that one is not aware of them, like those icebergs which, every year, move several millimeters southward. But now we know that, regardless whether life will return, it will not be to the place whence it left. Even when we go back to our homes, our jobs and offices, hairdressing salons and coffee shops, we shall never be as we were prior to the two weeks of eternity.

On first thought you said to yourself: Three wars—that's enough. There has to be some cut-off point. Thrice we have experienced the clamp around the heart, the day war came, and this (it seems to us) should be enough for one lifetime. On second thought we reasoned: What, really, is the difference between three and four? So we are not to be the generation to live serenely and dwell peacefully under our vine and figtree. And it's good that we knew this while we lay on the grass in the shade of the figtree, with an apple and a book and the fragrance of blossoms in the air—that we didn't take things for granted, such as unlimited hot water and chilled wine in a sparkling glass, a drawer full of shoes arranged in orderly rows and a home brilliantly illuminated. Ours is a generation which receives gifts on a lend-return, temporary and until-further-notice basis.

Cassandraism has never been a popular profession. He who predicts trouble just when everyone is feeling comfortable, when the cash register is jingling. the car is zooming along and salaries are mounting—and the prediction does not come true—is the soul of wickedness, who delights in preventing others from enjoying themselves. If he turns out to be right and the black hour does strike, what gratification can he have? His vindication is his punishment. What sense is there in saying: "See? I told you so!" If you did not set fire to yourself as did the Buddhist monks, then you were remiss in not doing everything you could to prevent the prophecy from coming true. The trouble with us war didacts is that we possess a long memory which goes back to September 1938, to a pretty and bustling city called Munich. We remember the Czech soldiers, poised to go forth in defense of the homeland; we remember the good faith of teachers and parents, of law-abiding and disciplined and courteous people, all of whom said: "The cultured nations will not be party to this." Nor, they were sure, would the world stand aloof; on the contrary, they maintained, the world would come to their aid. We, on our part, surmised that the last illusions about the democracies lending a hand in distress had been burned in the crematoria, that at least we had found this lesson in the ashes of the millions—never to place any stock in promises or protestations of friendship, but to learn to live alone. But no! Cambridge taught Oxonian English and ancient Persian and how to live like a gentleman, but the deeds of Lord Runciman were not part of the curriculum.

We have often said that we shall never forget, but we have forgotten. Now that we are biting our lips and clenching our fists, we again promise ourselves: "This lesson we shall remember today, tomorrow, the next day, next year. Let us not have prophets of comfort and the ways of pleasantness. And if we begin forgetting, someone will be there to remind us."

It is unbelievable but true. The quiet, tanned and dusty fellows in the wide-brimmed headgear in the Negev and the rapacious animals at the canned goods shelves in the supermarkets are members of one people, perhaps of the same family. Anonymity is the pitfall of the dwellers in the large city. They are responsible for the nation, but the latter is not posted at the entrance to the store. If the vultures were to be photographed with their shopping bags sagging down to the floor, or if they were to feel the eyes of a dozen friends upon them, or if they would have to give an account before friends whose opinions they value, many of them would doubtlessly hold back. If it were to be publicized that Yankel Zuchmir has bought ten cans of beef tongue, 18 cans of sardines (four of them in piquant tomato sauce), and 10 pounds of rice (which is already the playground for those cute little black bugs), then shame would have outweighed gluttony. Most of us, in ordinary times, are fairly nice; not because we are righteous and pure of heart, but we are simply afraid of jeopardizing our status in the society in which we live, even if this status is miniscule. To remain a person of integrity in the midst of anonymity takes the kind of discipline and character which cannot be shopped for in the supermarket.

Now comes the shining hour, the "every-dog-has-his-day" of the small neighborhood groceries, those with the sack of flour in the corner and the herring barrel near the counter. This is their revenge on that efficient technology which sought to sweep them away from the scene. How you flock back, you adherents of hygiene, of selection and time-saving; how you come back now, like prodigal sons, to the counter, the bread knife and olive tin, to the grocer, the little businessman. Here justice reigns (perhaps with a bit of pull), certainly not the jungle and not the battlefield; each customer and her bottle of cooking oil, each with her box of *matzot;* (not in their rosiest dreams did the "Rishon Letziyon Matzot Company" expect to dispose, in May, of their surplus from the preceding Passover). The past two weeks have taught us many things, not the least of which is the doctrine of the neighborhood grocery. Therefore, Mr. Greenspan, wouldn't you please forgive us our transgressions and take us back into your little family circle.

The difference between the sexes becomes pronounced once more; the men go to their stations and the women remain at home. Something in the faces of the soldiers, in the manner of their walk, in their hands on their hips, seems to say: "It was difficult to leave home, but now that we did, it is for the best." Gone is the struggle for a living, mortgage, loan, arguments about seniority, the manager's prodding, the noisy next-door neighbors; all those irritating minutiae are now far beyond the pup-tents. The men are happy when the families come out to visit them on the Sabbath, but when the day draws to an end and the time comes for the good-byes, it is even more difficult. They shouldn't have come. This is not their territory. It is only in this little Israel that the difference becomes all fouled up, since the home front is often closer to the frontier than is the military encampment.

Glory be to Alexander Graham Bell, of blessed memory, inventor of the telephone which binds us together with its wires. In the evenings the wives stay at home, in deep solitude, and wait for the call that may come; perhaps he will be able to get to a public telephone, or slip a note into somebody's pocket, or has met an acquaintance who is now back in the city. But then, whoever feels the heavy-hearted need to let off steam, to yell at someone picks up the receiver and dials. The phone rings and you hurry to answer it; perhaps something has changed, perhaps this marks the end to waiting.

The Fifth Grade is having its Bible exam ("Compare the episode of the poor man's lamb with that of Naboth's vineyard"); the Eighth is preparing for matriculating. The radio carries a talk on sugar-beet blights and a lecture on the history of the Greek epic. The press tells about the "Encounter" episode and about the CIA and the "Economic Forecast for the '70's." The ads advise you to acquire a Saab on easy terms and to "reveal the beauty of your hair with Lanol Shampoo." The show must go on, except that the audience finds it hard to concentrate.

When you read, in the foreign press, the commentaries of the military analysts and the international law experts and the Middle East savants, who weigh with Olympic calm the possible development of events inside Israel—whether this or that or the other is likely to transpire—you feel yourself rebelling. After all, the subject under discussion is people, life, *our* life, our children. But then, we too, had indulged in academic discussions of the war in Vietnam and the state of things in Yemen; when all is said and done, you cannot empathize with the entire world! And now we are again the center of attraction. Again our dozing press office is filled with reporters hungry for news and television crews with equipment stretching from Metulla to Eilat. We are the stage, we are the actors and we are paying to see the show.

Whoever passes away at this time, be he a person of stature, departs without impressive death notices and eulogies. Whoever enters matrimony at this time, does so without receptions ("post-poned for unforeseen reasons until further notice.") Whoever dips his hand into the till at this time will not be making the headlines. Even the controversial post-mortem issue is dead. Where are they all? They are far away, on the other side of that fine, clinging, penetrating, abrasive desert dust.

When the tourists first began to pack their bags, you saw them milling about in the lobbies of the luxury hotels ("Harry, where's your camera?" . . . "Harry, you haven't forgotten the plane tickets, have you?") and you felt proud. This was the difference. When we were still citizens of the Mosaic faith elsewhere in the world and saw evil times in the offing, we always had the problem of leaving or staying. Now we have no such problem; we are here to stay. And they didn't have to flee in haste, to cancel concerts, forego tours of the countryside, take a chance of losing cameras. They had nothing to fear. We are waiting, with full confidence, for the maritime powers to come to our aid.

Modern zoologists have come to the conclusion that, among living creatures, the sense of ownership of property, of territory, of a parcel is a drive no less powerful than sex. Groups of monkeys fight over territory, birds sing over it, armies fight to possess it. This concept, which a month ago was for us a subject of academic interest, has now received a novel significance. Over this small parcel of land, an infinitesimal spot on the world map, an insignificant area, we are prepared to fight with a love which is helpless, senseless, illogical, truncated, a kind of a primitive love, blind and painful—and we do not even care to camouflage it. We don't care if we are trite or sentimental, as long as we are not shamed.

The entire country is worried. In the large, silent and dimmed city the concern is for the mobilized, and in the pup-tents the concern is for the family back in the city. The home front is concerned for the border settlements, and the villages are worried about Jerusalem. People are worried about those in Eilat or on the high seas. The expression "See you again" has suddenly acquired a significance which we had never noticed previously. It is no longer an accepted fact but a promise, an aspiration. "*Shalom*" is still being said in an off-hand way. That "*Shalom* means peace" we have long forgotten, and no one is going to convince us now that *shalom* means compromise.

Ruth Bondy: The Long Wait; *Dvar Hashavua,* 2.6.67

Hussein flew to meet Nasser, exchanged kisses with him at the airport, and all the bitterness of years of mutual vituperation seemed to have vanished: both men signed a military pact. The Jordanian Army was put under Egyptian military command, Egyptian commando troops were flown to Jordan, Egyptian units were moved from Yemen to Sinai, the Iraqi Army moved toward the Israeli frontier, Syria reinforced her forces on the Golan Heights, Lebanon threatened, Algeria promised help, and even Kuwait sent soldiers to help Nasser. Still, Israel did not stir. The restlessness of Israeli citizens could be felt on every street at the rear, in every military camp on the dunes of the Negev. The Chief-of-Staff, General Yitzhak Rabin, addressed the troops in his sober and thoughtful way:

Two weeks have passed since Zahal went on full alert, following the concentration of Egyptian forces in eastern Sinai and the closing of the Straits of Tiran.

The mobilization, armament and preparation stages put us to a major test in achieving full preparedness with dispatch, dexterity and thoroughness. The entire army—all branches, departments and divisions—passed this test, attaining results far beyond what had been planned and expected.

Troops and war plans, however, are but part of the means by which a state pursues its security policies and even its military policies.

We now find ourselves in a situation where our military might and the readiness to activate it are intertwined with political developments. The two facets, the military and the political, are dependent on each other and complement one another. Military preparedness lends strength to political undertakings and increases the probability of their success.

The transition from one area to the other is likely to be sharp and sudden. This consideration bids us persist in preparing for immediate action.

We have the power not only to check aggression but also to defeat the forces of the enemy on his own soil, on condition, however, that we do not indulge in the illusion that the danger has passed or has diminished, and that we maintain patience and endurance while remaining on the alert. I know that this is not a light request; the emotional strain on a fighter who is asked to wait under high tension is not less than on a soldier who is called upon to storm an enemy position.

To you on the home front—the parents, wives and children whose dear ones, having been called to the colors, have left their homes and are now standing guard in all the sectors of Israel, I say: "I see your sons, husbands and fathers every day on my tours of the units. I want to send all of you collective regards from them all. Their spirit is steadfast, they are confident in their own strength, and they are doing their job most commendably."

I am sure that Zahal and the border settlements have no peers in the wonderful manifestation of esprit de corps, the fellowship of the fighting men, and the fighting spirit. You can trust them completely, without reservations. They will stand up to any foe, fulfill every task, hold on to any position.

And you men of Zahal, be worthy of the unqualified trust which the nation has placed in you. Be strong and of good courage.

Major-General Y. Rabin: "Zahal Can Check Aggression," 1.6.67

Other commanders also tried, each in his own way, to explain the situation to the soldiers and ask them for something which seemed even more difficult than fighting: self-restraint. The commander of a paratroop unit told his soldiers:

It is possible that the enemy of today is not the same enemy as of 10 years ago. His weapons are not the same, nor does his army now include those who had suffered the defeat at that time. However, just as the Jews have not changed in 2,000 years, neither have the Egyptians changed in 10. I believe that we are facing the same Arabs, with the same deep chasm between officers and soldiers, with the same inferior fighting spirit, with the same tendency to disintegrate the moment something goes awry with their planning. We must therefore put pressure upon them, overwhelm them, allow them no respite, confound them despite the difference in numbers. The moment we outstrip their pace of offense and aggressiveness, they will crumble as did their brothers 10 and 20 years ago. We shall encounter shifts and waits, but we must maintain high morale, preparedness and poise. Our pent up tension will find release, and when it does, it will come with a burst of power which no obstacle will be able to contain.

I wish all of you patience, and, when we go forth—success!

In a field bulletin: Paratroop Commander to his Men; 28.5.67

Author and correspondent Yael Dayan, General Moshe Dayan's 28-*year-old daughter, wrote a letter from the southern front to a friend in London. Yael, whose father called her back from a European tour when tension started mounting, was mobilized and posted as military correspondent at the headquarters of a division.*

You should see me now. High boots, white with dust, khaki uniform, canteen and knife in belt, and a wide-brimmed desert hat. My skin is brown-black and smothered with dust—and I don't think I ever felt better.

The Egyptian trenches are within sight and our soldiers are in touch and the border is like a question mark, though straight, wondering what the next moment will bring.

Ten days in the field now, the heat at times unbearable, the food very average. Everywhere there is white dust; sandstorms turn the dust into whirlpools in the air which mould scenery and the faces into one large screen of yellow, all just waiting.

Waiting is harder than war. Like a spring ready to go, a trigger left unpressed, the whole machine is tense, keeping the morale high is a problem. This is my job now.

I go from unit to unit, reservists and regulars, talking, explaining and strengthening the pride of this extraordinary army which is bound to win.

A strange feeling, a woman in the army. Living conditions in the field now are nil: small tents, field showers, dug-in holes for lavatories.

And yet, none of the girls preferred to go back north, though they were given the choice. They are here as secretaries, nurses, supply clerks, dealing with communications and the like.

We can handle arms if necessary and we walk around like the men, with helmets and sub-machine guns, but this is not the point.

A girl in a unit is a touch of home. She combs her hair in the evening when the dust goes down, she rubs cream on her cheeks, she makes coffee, she looks in the mirror, she asks the soldier about his children, she has a smile ready: and, above all, she is there to help.

The girls are not destined for fighting, though trained for it the way the men are. If they are in a frontier village, they are bound to be involved in the defense of it, and they are armed for this.

But here we are of most help in freeing men for combat by ourselves doing all the other jobs that have to be done.

This is a people's army in the full sense of the phrase. Mostly, the men are husbands and fathers away from home: they are not professional soldiers, and their motivations are abstract patriotism and a sense of duty.

A woman around is a link between all that is familiar for them and all that is foreign and new.

Yael Dayan: In the Front Line; *Sunday Telegraph, London,* 28.5.67

The US Government, like other governments, had no illusions about the situation in the zone and the future developments. The following announcement is typical of many other advertisements published at that time in the Israeli press:

Due to the current situation all American citizens are advised to depart from Israel via the first available commercial transportation. This notice applies to *all* American citizens and is not limited solely to those who do not have essential business in the country.

Americans should make their own travel arrangements directly with commercial transportation companies or travel agents. No assurance can be given that the US Government will be able to provide transportation if the situation should suddenly deteriorate further. All Americans are therefore urged to act now.

Americans who do not have valid passports should get in touch with the American Embassy in Tel-Aviv or the American Consulate-General in Jerusalem.

Second Warning: Important Notice; American Embassy, 5.6.67

But not all American tourists heeded the advice of their Embassy about leaving Israel.

The El Al spokesman yesterday announced that of 400 tickets paid for abroad by relatives of foreign citizens in Israel, 70 percent of the latter have informed the company that they have no intention of leaving the country.

According to a Tourism Ministry source, the following cable was sent from a Tel-Aviv Post Office yesterday by an American girl, aged about 20, to her family in New York:

"Situation very bad. Am staying here where I belong."

In Jerusalem, a young English student, an Orthodox boy, who had been spending the past year working as a clerk in a Jerusalem office, had several weeks ago given his employer a month's notice of his intentions to resign as he planned to return to England. He was due to leave next week. Yesterday, he went to his employer and asked to withdraw his resignation. He said:

"I've enjoyed Israel when everything was quiet and pleasant. I don't think I ought to leave when Israel is in trouble." He said he had gone to the Army Recruiting Office to volunteer, and asked his employer whether he might continue at his job pending his call-up.

An 83-year-old American Jew from Washington, D.C., Dr. Julius Dohany, a lawyer and former Government official, arrived in Israel last week for his first visit. Dr. Dohany, who was a pre-war Zionist leader in Yugoslavia, was overwhelmed by Israel, and a few days after his arrival here he told a local acquaintance: "Trouble or no trouble, I'm staying here. I'm cabling my wife to join me."

They Chose to Stay; *Jerusalem Post,* 24.5.67

In the meantime, Zahal was completing its mobilization. The regular army and the reservists were massed on Israel's frontiers, ready to strike. The Israeli nation was absolutely certain that if this army were called to fulfill its supreme duty—to fight for the survival of the State—nothing would stand between the army and victory. One of the architects of Zahal is a quiet and modest man, named Yitzhak Rabin.

Once upon a time, as the story goes, in the good old days, the Cadoorie soccer team played a game against Mas'cha, and the scoring stood at 0:0. Exactly one minute before the end of the match, Yitzhak Rabin jumped, hit the ball head-on, scored a goal, and Cadoorie won 1:0. Karniel Jr. from Mas'cha said at that time: "Wow! This Rabin's sure got a head on his shoulders!"

The incontrovertible fact that Yitzhak Rabin does have a head on his shoulders became evident at a very early age. When he was three and a half years old, the well-known kindergarten teacher from Tel-Aviv, Haskina, met his father Nehemiya and told him: "Listen, Nehemiya, I was almost despairing of your son. I couldn't get him interested in anything. He was always aloof, kept to himself, and didn't play with the other children. Today I read the children a story. Yitzhak, as usual, was keeping apart. When I had finished reading, I asked him: 'Yitzhak, did you understand anything?' And he answered quietly: 'Yes, everything!' 'What did you understand?' I wanted to know. And he told me the whole story by heart, from the beginning to the end. You could have knocked me down with a feather!"

Yitzhak Rabin was a man of principles ever since his youth. The story goes that when he started studying at the School for Workers' Children, he had quite mediocre marks in spelling in third grade. The renowned teacher Eliezer Smolli called his attention to that fact. Eight-year old Yitzhak Rabin answered quietly, as usual: "Listen, Smolli, every child studies the way he wants at this place, and I wouldn't advise introducing new ways!"

Yitzhak Rabin was born in Jerusalem, and he has deep feelings for the Holy City. His father, Nehemiya Rabin, came to the country with the soldiers of the Jewish Legion. His mother, Rose Cohen, was an extraordinary person, an admired figure in the workers' community in the country. She was a strong-willed woman, with great personal charm. The old-timers of the Old City still remember "Sister" Rose, who used to go from house to house during the riots of 1920, giving comfort, bolstering up morale, taking care of the needy—and distributing arms. People say that he takes after her in determination, in uprightness and resoluteness. When the Rabin family moved to Tel-Aviv and Yitzhak finished elementary school, he was sent to study farming at Cadoorie. His talents became immediately apparent: he excelled at his studies, and was awarded a prize by . . . the High Commissioner, Harold MacMichael. His father Nehemiya says: "When he graduated from Cadoorie I received a letter from the headmaster, Mr. Fiat, inviting me to the graduation ceremony. We attended the ceremony, Israel Guri, Shraga Netser and myself. Afterwards we sat and talked with the staff, and the headmaster, Fiat, told me: 'As a rule, I want my students to be farmers. But Yitzhak is an exception. I will try to get him into the Berkeley University in California. I am quite convinced that he will be accepted without entrance examinations, if only he would make a slight effort in English. You, Nehemiya, must help him!' And Rosenberg, the chemistry teacher, said on that occasion: 'In all the years I have been teaching, I never knocked at night on the door of the headmaster, Mr. Fiat. But when I read Yitzhak's graduation composition, I couldn't restrain myself, and I had to call at the headmaster's at midnight to share my feelings with him!'"

But fate did not decree for Yitzhak Rabin to study at Berkeley. Yigal Alon, platoon commander at Cadoorie, noticed the quiet blond boy, sturdy and blue-eyed. He gave him his military chance. Afterwards there were the days of the Palmah, the striking force of the Hagana. Yitzhak finished a course for platoon commanders and went through his fire baptism—cutting out a Lebanese frontier outpost, held by Vichyites, which entailed a march of 35 kilometers in one night. The task was completed flawlessly, without any losses. Yitzhak Rabin was appointed head of the course for platoon commanders at Joara. The days of the Second World War came, and his father says: "He was in a quandary. The people who joined the Brigade became national heroes, Yitzhak told me, while we, the people of the Palmah, are made to look like deserters." I told him: "Listen, Yitzhak! I heard Yitzhak Sadeh at a chat around the fire, and he said the following: 'The British have British soldiers, the French have French soldiers. The British fight for Britain, and the French for France. We need our own soldiers!'"

In 1944, Rabin headed a daring operation which entailed breaking into the Atlit Refugee Camp and releasing the refugees. He covered their retreat until the last refugee had disappeared on the road to Bet Oren. When summing up this operation, he said, as tersely as ever. "The planning and the execution were not bad."

Later on, he walked into the British Police Center at Jenin, disguised as an electrician, in order to carry out reconnaissance and scouting activities, but on his way back to the base, his motorcycle collided with a heavy truck, and Yitzhak Rabin was seriously injured in his leg. He spent a long time in a cast. On the "Black Saturday" of June 29th, 1946, when the British searched every house with a list of names, they found him and transferred the Chief-of-Staff to be, with his leg in a cast, to Latrun. When he needed medical care, he used to be sent, under escort of a jeep with a machine-gun, to Gaza Hospital.

The War of Independence found Yitzhak Rabin serving as Deputy

Commander of the Palmah Brigade "Har'el." At 26 years of age, he took part in all of the bitter, bloody battles: in the opening of the road to Jerusalem, the battle of Sha'ar Hagai, Sheikh Jerrah, Katamon, and the desperate efforts to break into the Old City. Later on Rabin went south, as Operations Officer of the Southern Front, under the command of Yigal Alon. The story goes that at that time, the Israeli forces were attempting an assault on Uja el Hafir. The Palmah scouts learned that there was an ancient, hidden path, leading from Halutza through Rouheiba and Wadi Abiyad to Uja. An engineering officer was dispatched to examine the path and submit a report. His report was: "Not a chance!" Alon sent Rabin for an additional inspection. Rabin returned and summed up his opinion in a terse and laconic sentence which became a classic of its kind: a military credo of his. Yitzhak Rabin said: "It is difficult—but possible!" The result: Uja el Hafir was conquered.

There is no doubt that history repeated itself in Rabin's case, and the circle started during the War of Independence was closed this week. Rabin was one of the people present at a meeting between Yigal Alon and the Sudanese Brigadier, Tahah "The Tiger," from the Faluja Pocket. Alon made it clear to Tahah that his men were surrounded on all sides, and the sooner he surrendered, the better. When the terms of surrender were drawn a young Egyptian captain named Gamal Abdel Nasser, who had kept silent and apart throughout asked permission to speak up and said: "May I ask something of the Israeli representatives?" "Go ahead!" Tahah answered. Nasser asked: "Is this badge of a sword and wheat-stalks which you wear on the collar, the badge of the Palmah?" "That's right," replied Alon, "it is the Palmah badge." Nasser smiled sadly and concluded: "In that case, everything is clear!"

It seems that his memory was not good enough. This month, his armies received a third reminder on the subject from the Israeli Defense Forces, under the command of the man who was present at that meeting: Yitzhak Rabin.

After the War of Independence, Rabin was appointed Chief of Operations of the General Staff. In 1952 he attended the Army Staff College in Great Britain. Among his innovations in Zahal: the whole high command must go through a paratroop course. In 1956 he was put in charge of the most "problematical" border, and appointed Commander of the Northern Zone; later on, he was made Chief of the Staff Department.

The Chief-of-Staff is a handsome man, rugged, broad shouldered, with a candid expression. He has a high forehead, blond-reddish hair, and a scattering of freckles which make him look younger than his 45 years. His speech is sometimes slow, but always quiet, terse and to the point. His thinking is quick, deep, incisive. He has light blue eyes, and he looks you straight in the face. He is not smooth, evasive nor flexible—his personality exudes the inner calm of a man who believes in what he is doing. His usual attire: a well-ironed uniform, open at the collar, with the general's stars on his epaulettes, and silver paratroops' wings on his chest. His office: simple, efficient and compact. A desk, a few small armchairs for visitors, maps on the walls. On the bookcase shelves: volumes of encyclopedia, strategy books, airplane models made of burnished copper. In a corner on a table: a vase with roses.

High officers who work with the Chief-of-Staff and are in daily contact with him, say that he is a man of balanced thought, of independent and original conception, endowed with a great talent for coordinating the various factors integrating the military composition. One of them told me: "Yitzhak has a phenomenal memory. He is a walking encyclopedia on every subject. We have a joke at the General Staff, that in case the electronic computer breaks down, there is nothing to worry about as long as Yitzhak Rabin is around. He searches for every detail of every question. When an arms acquisition is to be made, he studies minutely the smallest mechanical and technical differences between the various types of tank. He is capable of pointing out the advantages and drawbacks of the diesel engine as compared to the gasoline engine. He knows exactly the life-span of all gun barrels used by Zahal. When he was Deputy Chief-of-Staff, he went on a trip to France in order to examine the 'AMX-30' tanks. The Frenchmen said: 'His expertise in armor is such, as if he were a born tankman!'"

One of his closest aides says: "He takes no nonsense! You can't sell him nor sweet-talk him into anything. He wants precise data; he studies them, examines and compares. He is a demanding boss, and not an easy man to work with. Yitzhak is quite capable of asking you: 'For how many days will our ammunition stretch?' You give him the information, and he answers in that quiet way of his; 'I am afraid you are wrong by so many shells!' Somebody at the General Staff has already said: 'This expertise of Rabin's will be the end of me!'"

Yitzhak Rabin knows Zahal inside out. He is extraordinarily meticulous and thorough about everything. There is a joke making the rounds of the high command: the most expert Chief of Department at the General Staff is the Chief-of-Staff himself! He is very patient, extraordinarily persistent, and he has an immense capacity for work. People who know him say that he is not bound by any conventions. He is always looking for new and original solutions, adapted to our specific military problems. He has great political acumen, and he is perfectly aware of the fact that every border incident has immediate political repercussions. Yitzhak Rabin is the man who developed the conception according to which a maximum of results must be achieved with a minimum of means and the least political embroilment. He also propounded the theory according to which an Israeli shot is unlike any other shot in the world. There is a great difference, from the point of view of international repercussions, between a machine-gun, mortar or tank, when used in retaliation raids. I was told that before almost every retaliation raid he would brief the field commanders, so that they would know precisely the intentions of the higher command in this particular operation.

The Chief-of-Staff is always found where decisions are to be taken. For instance: when the fighting was going on at Um Katef and Abu Agheila, he flew down there, met the commanding officers and the zone commander, and helped them solve their problems. At week's end he was with the commander of the Northern Zone, ready to solve any problem as it arose. When he was offered a brief tour of the West Bank, he answered: "Leave me alone! The war is not over yet, and I must be where decisions are needed!" All through the war he slept on a cot at his office, answering the telephone himself. He only dropped in at home once or twice.

He has a great regard for human life. One of the main elements of his considerations is: "What is the price? How many lives is it going to cost?" He recently flew in his helicopter to a point removed about 80 kms. from Beer-Sheba. As he landed, several officers came running and told him that there were three severely wounded soldiers, and if they were not immediately removed to a hospital, their lives would be endangered. The Chief-of-Staff called off his tour, put his helicopter at the disposal of the wounded, and waited three hours for its return. When he was invited to a gala concert in Jerusalem celebrating the victory, he answered crossly: "Today, while soldiers are being killed, I am not going to sit in a concert hall!"

Palmah-bred Yitzhak Rabin does not stand on formalities in his relations with his subordinates. At the General Staff sessions, the generals call him by his first name, but anybody coming into his office salutes him. He keeps correct relations with his co-workers. He is not vindictive, nor does he hold a grudge; he resents mistakes, but always gives full backing. When there is a snag, he demands its immediate rectification. He tells the person responsible for it: "Look here, you botched this thing up; but I am in charge of Zahal, therefore I am responsible for this mistake!" He dislikes speeches, but is quite able to lecture for an hour on a complicated matter without referring to notes. He speaks then in long but perfectly lucid sentences. When war erupted, he met pilots about to fly missions and told them: "I have so many things to tell you, but I can't find the words to do it. Allow me to paraphrase Churchill and tell you: 'never was the fate of so many hanging on the ability and courage of so few.' The way you fight will determine the fate of the nation and of the State!"

Yitzhak Rabin is sensitive about other people's feelings. When he has to relieve somebody of his duties, he looks for a way to give him the news with the most tact and the least offense.

The Chief-of-Staff hates cocktail parties, gala dinners and ceremonies. His acquaintances say: he is a thoroughly honest man, and any kind of pretension is foreign to his nature. In times of stress he has nerves of steel, but then he smokes heavily. During the war he went through dozens of cigarette packs, chain-smoking all the time, and often asked people around him in the War Room, the headquarters and advance posts for a cigarette.

The Chief-of-Staff swallowed nearly every book written on the Second World War. People say that in this field he is a walking encyclopedia. He has no special religious feelings, but he is on excellent terms with the Chief Army Chaplain, General Goren. When somebody suggested that the whole staff should say the afternoon prayer at the Wailing Wall, the Chief-of-Staff took it up enthusiastically. Surprising as it may seem, Yitzhak Rabin admires Ben-Gurion; with certain reservations and objections, but still—he admires him. When the Palmah was dispersed, Rabin was summoned to a meeting with Ben-Gurion on the evening of the great protest rally. The Prime Minister kept him, talking on and on.

Finally Yitzhak Rabin stood up and said: "Excuse me, but I must leave now." "Where are you going?" asked Ben-Gurion. "To the rally," was Rabin's reply. He took his place on the rostrum with the rest of the Palmah commanders, and was reprimanded for disobeying an order.

Another man he admires is his teacher, Eliezer Smolli. They say that the day he was appointed Chief-of-Staff he "reported" to Smolli. Rabin admitted, on one of the rare occasions he exhibited emotion in public: "Eliezer Smolli, his living example and his wonderful lessons, were of an immense influence for me and my friends. Many of the things he taught me are still part of me. His science lessons taught me first of all to sense the surroundings. We did not study indoors, but outdoors, surrounded by Nature. He proved to us that Nature is a living, breathing, talking thing. He taught us to understand Nature, to understand why a certain plant grows on a slope and strives for the sun, while another plant tries to hide in the summer. His lessons made a deep impression on me. They gave me a feeling for outdoors, a love for the country and anything connected to it. My childhood, which is one of the most beautiful periods of my life, will always be related to a big shack standing in a depression surrounded by sand dunes. This shack is where the School for Workers' Children in Tel-Aviv was lodged at the time. Nowadays there is a public park at the place. The shack was grey and dilapidated; hot in the summer and cold in the winter, but we loved it; we loved its peculiar atmosphere. Smolli perpetuated our experiences in that shack in his book 'Children of the Beginning.' I was one of those children!"

No one has ever heard Yitzhak Rabin telling an off-color joke, and a high officer may lose all of his standing with Rabin if he tells a dirty joke in his presence. He dislikes liquor and ties, but likes chocolate, (especially milk and almonds) and sweets. He is fond of sport and swimming, and his favorite hobby is taking pictures and movies. Somebody asked him this month: "Well, Yitzhak, what about your pictures?" And he answered: "Believe me, I even forgot where I put away the camera!"

Yitzhak Rabin is basically an introverted and reserved person. He does not exteriorize his feelings. He is very restrained, a man of true modesty and humility, and he talks very quietly. Sometimes he even seems shy. That is nothing new. The following story about him is typical: When Yitzhak Rabin married his wife, Leah, the wedding was attended by Israel Galili, Yitzhak Sadeh, Yigal Alon, and other Palmah commanders. Rabin was standing under the canopy, wearing a hat, embarrassed because of the religious ceremony, which he could not follow very well. When the rabbi, who was half an hour late, started intoning the benedictions in his best voice, Rabin told him: "Please, sir, not so loud! Not so loud!" When the ceremony was over, he went over to his brand-new bride and told her very earnestly: "Leah, let me tell you, that this is the very last time I'm getting married!"

His wife Leah is a loyal helpmate. Leah Rabin is a teacher by profession. These days she takes care of the wounded in the hospitals. Among the hundreds of checks pouring daily into the Ministry of Defense, one stood out by its originality. The sender wrote: "I enclose all my savings, in the amount of 505 Pounds. Please use the 500 Pounds to celebrate on the day of victory, and five Pounds to buy flowers for the wife of the Chief-of-Staff."

Yitzhak Rabin has a very clear idea about the nature of the Israeli soldier, and the way he differs from the Arab soldiers. Rabin said: "The Arab countries defined themselves as being in a state of war with Israel, and they proclaimed that their aim is to exterminate us. They are making their preparations with this aim in mind. The question is, when will war break out. Consequently, we must be constantly prepared. We must be ready at any time. As to the feelings our soldiers harbor toward the enemy, I think there is a great difference between both sides of the frontier. The Arab countries have a definite purpose: the annihilation of the State of Israel. They proclaim this purpose, and teach it. In order to do it, they instill in their soldiers a feeling of hatred towards us. It is a simple and clear educational aim: in order to take something away from somebody, you must promote a feeling of hatred which will justify the plunder. With us, the situation is different. We do not intend to despoil anybody. I don't know anyone in Israel who aims to conquer Damascus or Cairo in order to rule them. Therefore, we have no need to inculcate hatred, even though most of the Arab nations wish to destroy us. I am convinced that most Arabs, and not only their leaders, are full of hatred toward Israel. The Israeli soldier has first and foremost a feeling of love. He loves his country and the hopes of his nation. In loving what is ours, he gets the strength to resist anybody trying to take it away from us."

I asked him several years ago: "Nasser proclaims very often

that he intends to defeat Israel in one crushing blow. What do you think of that?" The Chief-of-Staff answered calmly: "I am certain that Israel cannot be defeated with one blow. I am certain that we must take great pains to prevent Israel from being defeated with one blow. The main problem is the following: how to avoid being caught by surprise, how to be always prepared. The key to this is in our own hands. If we do what has to be done, if we invest what has to be invested, we shall prevent Nasser from doing it. Suppose the Egyptians want to attack us from the air. They might do it. The question is not whether they can take this decision, but the results they are likely to get. If we are prepared every day, every hour, they won't find it worthwhile to try it." I asked him then: "To what degree have the Egyptians absorbed the immense Russian equipment they had received?" He had foresight enough to say in 1964: "Generally speaking, I would say that all the Russian equipment has been absorbed, or is being absorbed. This applies to all types of airplanes, starting from MIG-21 fighters and TU-16 bombers, transport planes and helicopters. It applies to the SA-2 surface-to-air missiles, and surely it applies to ground equipment, tanks, guns, as well as naval equipment—destroyers and missile carriers. Of course, you must define first what you mean by absorption. There are many ways of absorbing equipment. You can shoot, move, transport, fly. This is one way of doing it. You can also exploit the equipment to the utmost, bringing to bear all the technical and objective properties of the weapon. I am sure that the Egyptians are capable of using the Russian equipment, but I very much doubt that they know how to exhaust thoroughly all the possibilities of this first-rate equipment. It is not at all the same thing. There is an enormous difference between both ways."

Nevertheless, he never underestimated the enemy. He always had a certain regard for King Hussein, and he adroitly analyzed Nasser's shrewd moves. Last Friday, when he arrived at the northern front, several drivers ran to him and announced gleefully: "General Rabin! Haven't you heard? Nasser resigned!" Yitzhak Rabin did not react. He told his party: "It is only a ploy. He'll be back." Later on he asked who was suggested as Nasser's successor. He was told, that it was Zakaria Mohieddin. Rabin told them immediately all about Mohieddin, his background and his political leanings.

The Chief-of-Staff has seen many a battle, but Jerusalem is deeply impressed in his soul. He will never forget the battles of 1948 to open a road to the capital. The Chief-of-Staff says: "Many were killed in the battle for the opening of the road. Half the battalion was gone. The exhausted, wounded fighters complained bitterly: 'Why is there no more ammunition? Why should we be exposed to fire, traveling in open tracks?' I told them: 'All right, anybody who doesn't like it, doesn't have to escort any more convoys! But nobody gave up his right to be killed in order to keep the road to Jerusalem open'."

He also remembers the battles of Beit Mahsir: "Half of the Gadna youths sent as reinforcements were immediately killed by the Jordanian shelling. The fortified positions kept changing hands. Five days of terrific fighting. One of the worst days of my life. Finally, the Arabs retreated. Why? Because the one who has the more spirit and the longer wind is always the one to win!" And Yitzhak Rabin sums up as follows: "The war of 1948 must not happen again. This is not the way to wage war. At that time I vowed that if I survive the war, and I stay in charge of security matters, I'll do everything in my power to avoid fighting that way again!"

This is what he vowed—and he kept his pledge.

Raphael Bashan: He Kept the Pledge of 1948; *Ma'ariv*, 13.6.67

In spite of the mobilization of Zahal, the period of May 15*th to June* 5*th,* 1967, *was one of the darkest in the history of the State of Israel. The country was on its own. Israel had the sympathy of the world, but lacked any real support, while the surrounding Arab States were brandishing the flaming sword of annihilation and every passing hour seemed to be an hour lost. The feeling shared by many people at that time was expressed in an article by Moshe Shamir, one of the foremost Israeli writers.*

May 1967. The 19th summer. Suddenly this has happened. This. What is happening now. What is happening now with the speed of hours and minutes and the terrifying slowness of week after week, of delay after delay.

Two separate sets of shocks. The shocks of military preparedness and the spiritual awakening of the whole people; urgent, swift and sharp. And on the other hand, as in slow-motion nightmare, a horror suffused with the sleeping pills of the leadership.

After the economic slowdown a security slowdown has been imposed upon us. The economic slowdown was difficult but maybe,

maybe it has been fruitful. Maybe, indeed, the security slowdown has been fruitful as well. And that fruit we shall eat. We are eating it already. It is bitter and opens the eyes very wide.

For nothing is certain and no forecast is well-founded. But one thing is beyond every possibility of doubt. This country is no longer going to be what it was.

And maybe that is a good thing. For that reason, maybe, the month of May '67 in our history is going to link up with May '48 and October '56.

There are few occasions in history when a whole nation wakes up in a single moment. When they open eyes together, quiver and understand together and close ranks together with that understanding. This is what happened in the second half of May 1967 to the Jewish people in the State of Israel.

During the years we have been saying: "This can't go on very long." We were referring to the inflated and unorganic economic well-being, the exaggerated self-assurance, the State and institutional —and private—extravagance, the general pleasure in the *dolce vita* with its amusement at all costs, amid all classes and sections of the people.

Now it has happened at last. First an economic crisis which displayed vast areas of sub-surface insecurity in the fields of economics, society, morality and education. And now, at a single blow, in the political field.

The economic crisis told us the truth about the bread we eat. The security and political crisis has told us the truth about the air we are breathing. The bread is not assured. It has to be freshly made every day. That applies to every nation. The time has come to recognize that it also applies to us.

The air is not assured. It has to be secured every day afresh. That applies only to our nation, of all those upon the face of the earth. It is no use complaining. The time has come to recognize this for a fact.

By means of three swift maneuvers Nasser has deprived us within a single week of almost all the political supports of our security. Within a single week he has been transformed from a political and military bankrupt to the most respected "big boss" in the region. Within a week he has erased all the inner Arabian disputes, gathered all his neighbors under his wings, slapped the United Nations in the face, brought U Thant and the Security Council to their knees, spat on the United States, and thrust his spear-point between our eyes. And there is nothing left for us except to pride ourselves on not even twitching an eyelid.

At the time these lines are being written nobody in the world knows how things will develop. Not the chief actor nor his producer with the Stanislavsky technique, not one of the public, and certainly not the second chief actor who plays the part of Hamlet in the uniform of the Israel Defense Forces. Who knows? Maybe there will be "an improvement in the situation." Maybe one or an other formulation, one or an other political point of view, will somehow lead to matters arranging themselves so that it will be possible to go on living and exporting and holding the 20th Anniversary Celebrations of the State of Israel in a quiet atmosphere. Yet even if Nasser is compelled to carry out a full-scale retreat, these days will not be blotted out from our hearts and awareness, nor will their lesson be forgotten. This State will never again be what it was.

We have eaten the bitter fruit and our eyes are wide open.

Not that anything new has been revealed. The old, the constant, the true, have been laid bare with cruel force. All the cosmetics of those who were consciously trying to calm us have been washed away, and the stitches of the permanent patchers-up have ripped asunder. The fat of illusions has melted, along with the convenient pamperings, and the mist and fog of expert and so highly authoritative prophets has evaporated into thin air.

We have been forcibly brought under the X-rays of history. We have been forcibly stretched out on the X-ray table. They have engaged in a fluoroscopy. The cold skeleton, the likeness of the bare bones of veritable truth, have been placed before us. Maybe we should be grateful for this.

If it is not too late, if there is still time, we can look around.

And what will we see? Why, we see the old truth we knew: Between us and death stands only Zahal. Zahal alone.

No international guarantees, no agreements, no law and justice, no United or maybe Untied Nations, no friendly powers and not even these, those or other political interests. After 20 years of independence and two historic victories we once again see, eye to eye, how extermination is taking its first steps towards our borders; how the Arab Golem is beginning to move upon our home, directed and guided by the Muscovite Dictatorship which has succeeded in identifying itself to the very last with the most dreadful associations of Hitlerism, even though it has not forgotten to thrust beneath the tongue of its Golem the holy name of Socialism.

This we have seen and so has all the world. The Russian reaction may be astonishing in its severity, but not in its essence. Russia is in essence the ally of violent dictatorial regimes. Like calls to like, Russia stands together with Nasser for all kinds of geo-political reasons, but fundamentally because here it has to deal with a regime that holds its people in a slave camp. Russia feels at home with such regimes. It is incapable of achieving contact, agreement and cooperation with democratic systems. It can find no common language with a regime where there is public opinion, which reckons with the press, where governments replace one another and considerations of justice, logic or morality have weight. Russia's only ally in the West is the dictator on the Seine. Russia cannot bear the very existence of democracy because any contact with it has the effect of corrosive acid on any non-democratic regime, including its own. For in a democracy there are instruments for examining the truth, and there is a demand for that commodity. And truth is Enemy Number One of Soviet Russia.

Here is one point about which we have absolutely and finally sobered up. Yet even more important are the shocks of the new sobriety regarding ties and friends in the West. I could never manage to be enthusiastic about De Gaulle. About the French press, yes; about French public opinion. But how many children's throats can be protected with the aid of newsprint? England and America shifted a couple of ships in the Mediterranean and the Red Sea. What has come out of it except, in the best of cases, a cloudier and more sinuous formulation for the process of strangling us, degrading us and preparing the background for liquidating us?

These are the facts in all their cruelty. Any negotiations with Nasser now are a warrant for our extermination at this or some other timing. Every appeasement is surrender. Every word with him is the abandoning of Israel. The Israel Army has to act. The Army must produce its power and absolute superiority and put them in action. This tragic fact, that the truly peace-loving people has to go to war, serves more than anything else to awaken us.

Every nation in the world has an army. Every nation in the world knows that, in the last resort, its life and peace depend on its army. For a long time we deluded ourselves into believing that we as well, like most peoples in the world, did not have to put our army in operation in order to make the enemy think twice. What has happened during these last few days has made it clear to us that we have no political card at all. We have no space for maneuvers. We do not even have room for "play," as the garage men say; that is, some limited leeway in order to gain time, for an opportunity of maneuvering and shifting.

During the War of Liberation there was an armored lorry that used to travel along the road to Jerusalem. A phrase was scribbled on it in chalk. It is a phrase that has again become very relevant: "Victory or Death."

Moshe Shamir: No Way Back (I); *Ma'ariv,* 30.5.67

The citizens of the State of Israel demanded the immediate creation of a National Union Government, but the party wheels ground slowly. The public demand to appoint Moshe Dayan, the man who seemed the most suitable choice for this task in these turbulent times, as Minister of Defense, met with the opposition of the old-timers in the establishment. Their opposition was mainly based on the fact that Moshe Dayan is one of the leaders of Rafi, a splinter party of Mapai, which Ben-Gurion had founded as an opposition party in 1965, *after having led Mapai, Israel's major party, for many years. But popular pressure increased: giant advertisements appeared in the newspapers, bearing the signatures of hundreds of public figures, and demanding Moshe Dayan's appointment as Minister of Defense. On June* 1*st, as the political skies of the Middle East were darkening and the Israeli citizens were losing their forbearance, the National Union Government was established following a fierce political battle. Moshe Dayan received the Defense portfolio, and two new Ministers from the rightist party Gahal, Menahem Begin and Joseph Sapir, were added to the Government. Soldiers and civilians alike received the news about Dayan's appointment with a sigh of relief. David Ben-Gurion and Menahem Begin, mortal enemies for a quarter of a century, embraced and kissed in public. The imminent danger had unified the people of Israel as it had never been unified since the creation of the State. All eyes were directed to Dayan:*

Moshe Dayan, the Minister of Defense, known as the "Hawk of the Desert" and the "Enfant Terrible of the Middle East," was in his boyhood a quiet young man. When the editors of *Ma'ariv Lanoar* asked him to participate in a series of articles on the theme "When

I was 16," he replied, with his characteristic barbed humor, "all I can tell you is that I always helped my parents, took good care of my sister, and was an all-round good boy."

His father, Shmuel Dayan, one of the founders of Degania, corroborates this self-evaluation in a letter he wrote to his wife Deborah in the hospital: "My dear! I found our son Mosinka very well, playing with the children, happy, and not coughing so much. He wanted to know right away 'How is Mama?' I told him about your health and gave him some goodies. He ate with the other children, had his dose of quinine and went to bed. Then he wanted to know whether you had a good bed. In his sleep he murmured 'Chocolate, candy . . .' In the evening I bathe him. He comes to me gladly, puts his little arms around my neck. My heart weeps for him, and my warm tears drop onto the face and eyes of our dear child. I drop off to sleep at his side."

He was named *Moshe,* perhaps symbolically, after Moshe Barsky, the first man to die in Degania. Barsky was murdered by Arabs in the fall of 1914, on the road between Degania and Menahemia, while on his way to bring medicine to a sick comrade. Six Arabs fell upon him, and he fought them off until he was shot in the back.

Says Dayan: "My father once asked me to do something, and I refused. He became angry, thrust me into a large chicken-coop in the yard and said, 'You'll stay here until you change your mind.' The darkness frightened me; it was cold, and I kept hearing all sorts of strange noises, but I did not give in. After a few hours my father let me come out."

What is Moshe Dayan like today? What are the characteristics, thoughts and habits of the new Minister of Defense? Conversations with his friends and associates from various periods provide a profile.

His basic attribute: an extraordinary knack for leadership. He determines the environment, is never subject to it. Some of his processes are not understandable while they are taking place, but to him they are part of an entity and have a logic of their own. More than once he has caused some surprise by severing contact with ideas, people, posts. Even greater was the surprise when it became evident that his actions constituted long-range planning, for which the step in question gave him a more advantageous point of attack. One thing is certain—he is an original personality, unconventional, despises conformity, shies away from the colorless, disdains set opinions. Whenever he is reminded that "one doesn't do that," his invariable reply is, "I do."

Dayan has an unusual sense of timing, and is endowed with sharp intuition about matters and developments in the future. In April of 1964 he drew the wrath of the Prime and Defense Minister when he made this statement in public: "The friendship with France has not been impaired, it is true. But it is even more true that while France was at war with Algeria we were joined in a struggle against a common enemy, and it was natural for France to send us tanks and planes to carry on the war on our front. But this situation no longer exists." The Prime Minister quickly commented that the statement had been made "on the personal responsibility and opinion of the Minister of Agriculture," and that it in no way reflected the opinion of the Government as of December 1963.

While everything seemed peaceful, Dayan declared, at a conference of southern *moshavim* (workers' settlements) which took place at Kfar (Village) Warburg: "International acknowledgment of Nasser's right to meddle in Algeria or Yemen is a political fact which bids us expend much effort on the advancement of our status in the world, even if we are not in a state of emergency and are not subjected to daily infiltration and marauding." In January of 1965 he warned: "There is no doubt but that Zahal's capacity to discourage attack is the decisive factor in the present disposition of the Arab states not to annihilate Israel. This does not mean, however, that the Arabs will do nothing to create incidents which might lead to war between themselves and Israel. There are many differences between a situation wherein the Arab states open hostilities against Israel, shell her cities, infiltrate her territory in order to destroy her, and that in which Israel sends its forces to operate on sovereign Arab soil. Rulers of Arab states can shy away from inaugurating a war with Israel and at the same time initiate action which might induce Israel to attack them. This policy may well be based on the premise that nations who might come to Israel's aid in the first instance would not be willing to do so in the second. Nor is this the sole consideration."

In the same month of 1965 Dayan said further: "We must maintain at all costs the status quo between ourselves and the Arab states—not merely the status quo in terms of physical territory but also in reference to the limits of what we shall endure and what we shall not endure. Every concession on our part in this area will invite a process of deterioration and the renewal of hostile acts against us; this deterioration will become more difficult to arrest the longer it goes on."

In our conversation toward the end of 1965, Dayan repeated his well-known stand on the UNEF (United Nations Emergency Force): "As far as the Egyptian border is concerned, I would prefer not having them there; they are of no value to us . . . Egyptian sovereignty over the Sinai Peninsula is not being challenged; we must therefore look at the presence of the UNEF there as being strictly temporary. This arrangement is bound some day to be terminated, either because the UN will decide to abolish it, or because Abdul Nasser might not wish, for certain reasons, to have it continue. Then a new crisis will in all probability again erupt in the matter of free sea passage to Eilat. Egypt will not be able to overlook the paradox of its belligerent declarations and the free passage of Israeli ships. We might have avoided this crisis, had Egyptian forces gone in, when we withdrew from Sinai, in return for an agreement to free passage."

Today it is generally admitted that in the matter of his visit to Vietnam, Dayan also proved his far-sightedness by "two chess moves forward," as he put it. In those days, when he was being attacked on all sides, he said to me in an interview: "I am not going to Vietnam in order to judge which of the two sides is right, but I am deeply interested in studying the situation and understanding it. The war in Vietnam is now being conducted with conventional weapons and on a local scale. I think we have much to learn from this war and from the manner in which it is being waged. I am not contemplating, at this moment, a return to Zahal, but, as others are doing, I expect to continue thinking, speaking and writing, and at times also participating in making security decisions. I therefore feel impelled to look into the development and use of arms and into tactics which can be illuminating for us. Don't forget that the last war in which I took part was the Sinai Campaign, and that was ten years ago. At that time we were limited to certain equipment. Since then Zahal has acquired and will continue to acquire additional and more modern arms—helicopters, planes, tanks. I therefore think that it's just as important to check on the war in Vietnam as it is to view the annual maneuvers of Zahal."

What is his work schedule like? How does he get along with his advisers? Those who know him best say that he subscribes to the "Emphasis" method, rather than to the "Train." The difference is this: "Train" methodologists plug along from six in the morning until midnight, stop at every bureaucratic station, do everything themselves. "Emphasists" like Dayan work during limited hours, set the tone, decide policy, determine the objectives, and leave the execution to people they can trust.

A fighter by nature, Dayan speeds up the pace, drives forward, fights tooth and nail for everything which looks right to him—it doesn't matter what, whether the allocation of irrigation water for agriculture to the north and the south, which at the time aligned the entire kibbutz movement against him, the "Marbek" and "Moneymaker" affairs, population dispersal, the abolition of barns maintained on the outskirts of urban centers, or basic questions dealing with security and political life. Dayan is not much concerned with the popularity of his "current image"; he stresses the cumulative effect of his ideas and acts. It is interesting to note that Dayan's success as Minister of Agriculture was a major factor in the decision of the kibbutz and settlements representatives in Mapai institutions to support his choice as Minister of Defense.

He is not a publicity hound. He doesn't ask that everything written about him be red-pencilled every morning, for his attention. He doesn't care about criticism, as long as he is not misquoted and the facts are not distorted. When he has something to say he picks up the phone and says it straight, in his own name. When he has nothing to say, or when the timing isn't right. he shuts up like a recalcitrant clam. His associates have often tried to instill in him a more positive attitude toward the press and a greater appreciation of public relations. One of them, who had been to the USA, enthusiastically told Dayan about a press conference given by the late President Kennedy—fresh, lucid, informative. Replied Dayan: "Far be it from me to minimize the value of the Kennedy press conferences, yet this man lost everything on one card in the Bay of Pigs episode and regained it on one card in forcing the removal of Soviet missiles from Cuba. Long after the brilliant Kennedy press conferences are forgotten, these two acts will still be remembered. It's deeds that count."

When Dayan delves into any problem, he does not go for psychological probing. He once said: "I am not interested in *why* the opposing side thinks as it does; what I want to know is *what* it is thinking, what are its real intentions." He thinks clearly, decides quickly, is daring in his decisions, independent in his calculations, full of surprises and resourcefulness, as though he would never reveal to anyone what he really has in mind—until the very end. One of his friends once likened him to a submarine; "it proceeds beneath the surface and tells you its location only from time to time, when it chooses to raise its periscope." At the negotiations table his diplomacy is realistic, lucid, purposeful, thought out to the last detail—like a strategic campaign. These attributes came to the fore during the negotiations with King Abdullah and when he headed the delegation to discuss the armistice with Jordan in Rhodes.

The bargaining tactics of Dayan are well illustrated by the following episode. In 1955 he went to the USA with Engineer Blass to discuss with the Americans the scheme for the apportionment of the Jordan waters among the countries of the region. Blass regarded this particular scheme as calamitous. In the concluding session at the Israel Embassy in Washington, Dayan said: "I suggest that we tell the Americans that we agree to the scheme. We shall in this way win on two counts: one, we won't be in conflict with the United States, and two, the Arabs will then refuse to accept it." And that's exactly how it turned out. The Israelis announced their acceptance; the Arabs automatically rejected it, and the scheme died aborning.

In direct contrast with the rumors consistently spread about him by Arab propaganda media, Dayan does not have "an appetite for hating Arabs." His estimate of the Arabs is considerate, objective and direct, without the slightest touch of hypocrisy or obsequiousness. He once told me in an interview: "You want to know whether it was I who coined the saying 'I look at the Arab problem through my lower gunsight.' It's a smart saying, but it isn't mine. Avraham Yaffe said it. Actually, my reaction to the Israeli Arabs is a very positive one. I met Arab farmers and Bedouins in my youth and I learned to respect them. Take the Arab farmer. He gets up at three in the morning, works like a mule, without quotation marks; he has an open heart and lives off the toil of his hands and the fruits of his land. While I was the Minister of Agriculture I tried to get close to them. I sat with Arab olive growers, tobacco and vegetable growers, listened to their problems and tried to help them. When deep dissension arose between the Government and the Arab villages in the Bet Netofa Valley, where the canal for the National Carrier was being dug, I went straight to the site of the trouble, met with a score of hostile and bitter sheikhs and told them: 'Honorable

Sheikhs! I have come here to study the situation of the affected villages, as though they were Ein Harod or Nahalal. I do not go along with the theory that the Arabs should be told what they would like to hear, and that patriotism should be left to Tel-Aviv.'" Dayan's approach to the Arabs in Israel was always realistic. He always contended that these Arabs should be given the same privileges and should assume the same responsibilities as the other citizens of the State. Military rule was called for only to handle known or potential lawbreakers.

In Dayan's younger days, he became friendly with an Arab constable named Ahmad Jabr, who was in charge of the region, along with a handful of Jewish supernumerary policemen. Jabr defended Nahalal during the riots, and even taught the young boys there how to make a spear out of a stick with a nail driven through one end. Known among the Arabs as a friend of the Jews, Jabr was captured by the Arab maraudung bands during the War of Independence, imprisoned in Jenin, escaped, and is now living in Um el-Fahm village. His son, following in his footsteps, is serving with the Israel constabulary.

At the time that Dayan was serving as Minister of Agriculture, he learned that an Arab agronomist in his employ was planning to emigrate from Israel because he felt that he was being deprived of his rights on account of his origin. Dayan got into his car, drove to the agronomist's home in Galilee, sat with him for many hours and induced him to remain. Thereafter, he used to invite him to his office for consultations to get his ideas and opinions.

Dayan's sense of humor is unique—open and direct, variegated, unexpected, and at the same time sharp, barbed and devastating. He reacts quickly and phrases his retorts in such way as to disarm his adversary completely and place him on the defensive, in the poorest light possible. When he was Minister of Agriculture, he was called upon to defend the "Moneymaker" tomato-growing scheme in the Knesset. "Gentlemen of the Knesset," he said, "I intend to speak on behalf of the 'Moneymaker' scheme to my very last drop of tomato juice." On the occasion of the opening of the Ministry's regional office in Beer-Sheba, he told a story about a clever Bedouin who, when asked for his opinion about farming in the Negev, replied: "When there were no rains, we once used to say 'Everything is in the hands of Allah!' Today, when there are no rains, we say 'No matter! Allah is great! We are receiving drought subsidies!'"

And Dayan continued with a touch of his particular brand of irony: "Should you ever feel like striking or demonstrating, don't waste time or energy to come to Tel-Aviv; just give me 24 hours' notice and I'll come here to Beer-Sheba. What's more, if you'd be feeling like smashing windows, I'd be willing to bring along window panes from the Ministry."

Dayan can and does use his well-honed humor to slaughter any number of "holy cows." At a ceremony held to mark a change of "top brass" of "Mekorot," he startled the audience by intimating that a paratroop unit could, in half a day, accomplish as much as did the "Hashomer" (Jewish watchmen's organization in Palestine prior to World War I) in all of its vaunted history. Shortly after the Sinai Campaign he was asked to give a public lecture on the lessons to be derived from it. He replied: "It is not for me to say what led up to the Sinai Campaign. As for future repercussions, it is too early to prophesy. Regarding the situation between the past and the future, every child knows it, and I have nothing to add." At Eilat Beach, he and his Ministry of Agriculture director, Gad Yaacobi, were seen skipping stones atop the water; Dayan simply wanted to show Kfar Vitkin-born Yaacobi that Nahalal kids could throw stones better.

Dayan always had great disdain for party hacks and politicians in general. When he was still on Mapai's Board of Elections, he was approached by a delegation which demanded that its members be given assured election spots on the Party ticket for the Knesset. Replied Dayan: "Sorry, all the seats are taken. Standing room only!" When the Mapai approved his candidacy for Minister of Defense, one of the Party's central figures came up to him and said, in a patronizing manner: "You see, Moshe, we have finally got you to be Defense Minister." To this Dayan reportedly replied: "The main reason for it is the Egyptian army, but you also had a share in it."

Dayan can be cordial and sympathetic. When he was still a student at the Hebrew University in Jerusalem, he received a letter from Kibbutz Nirim, written by Amir, a third-grader of the "Almond" Group, on behalf of that cubscout-like association. He replied: "My greetings to you, children. Many thanks for your letter and the invitation to visit you at Nirim. I shall certainly come. Last time I was there, it was to inspect the shelters. Now I, too, am a student, first year, and my teachers bother me and insist that I do a lot of homework, and if I don't get a sunstroke from walking around without a hat, I'll get it from all this homework, and this is worse. I am glad that you chose the name "Almond" for your group, because in your region once grew beautiful almond trees, and I am sure they will grow there again. When I was a boy, I wrote a poem to my little sister, and part of it I still remember. I am enclosing it in return for Na'ava's beautiful poem about the almond tree. If you wish, ask your teacher to punctuate it. I didn't do it because my punctuation is terrible. Sincerely, Moshe Dayan."

Abroad, Dayan has been known to advance where other Israelis fear to tread. In 1957, when he and Shimon Peres were on the way back from Burma, they stopped overnight in New Delhi but found all the hotel rooms taken by the British Prime Minister Harold MacMillan and his entourage. "Listen," said Dayan to the desk clerk, "you go to Mr. MacMillan and tell him that, downstairs, you have Moshe Dayan, the man on whose account he is now Prime Minister. Have him arrange to give up a room for me." The clerk hesitated, then went up and came back, amazed beyond measure: "They have evacuated a room for Your Excellency the General."

Again, in Teheran, he went on a tour of the famous Bazaar. Someone identified him, and immediately, a crowd of many hundreds was following him. "What are they saying?" asked Dayan of his companion, Meir Ezri, Israel's minister to Persia. "They are saying," returned Ezri, "'Here is the Jew who beat the Arabs.'"

Whenever complicated or controversial matters appear on the agenda, Dayan says to his aides: "Gentlemen, this is the program. Let the difficulties speak for themselves."

When his friends ask him about the state of his health, he replies, "Medium and holding" if he is feeling well, "Medium minus" if he is not.

Dayan is not given to reminiscing. He avoids talking about the "good old days" of the brigade, meetings of commanders around a campfire replete with the steaming coffee and roast lamb. He is also reticent about the decade since the Sinai Campaign. People close to him explain this by noting that Dayan dislikes maintaining his public image on the basis of past records. At the same time, he does not disregard the importance of the past. For many years, he has been keeping a diary of things that really interest him. No one has ever gotten a glimpse of its contents.

Dayan is not given to frequent displays of emotion, but he still is deeply moved by personal acts of courage on the battlefield. This accounts for his strong ties with the paratroops. He happened to visit Nahal-Oz a day before Roy Rutenberg's wedding, chatted with him and was very favorably impressed with the young man. The next day, he learned that Roy had been brutally murdered by marauders from the Gaza Strip. He immediately went back to Nahal-Oz and, weeping at the graveside, read a eulogy which he had written.

Dayan is very considerate of human life. Military men who know him emphasize the importance of this point in his tactical and strategic planning. During the period of reprisal action, he was greatly distraught by the fact that despite the sacrifices made in each action of this kind, the result wound up with nothing achieved; "you break through, tear down, destroy—and go back to your base." In planning the Sinai Campaign, he repeatedly and angrily stressed the fact that shelling of Gaza would invariably invite attacks on the Jewish rural settlements along that border.

Dayan is sensitive to the life and problems of the man in the ranks, he who crouches in the trenches and "eats sand." He loves to visit the units, talk with the men, check on their morale, find out what they are thinking. Once, when he was Chief-of-Staff, he was told by a group of soldiers that they could get nothing to eat when they returned from night drills. Dayan immediately issued an order that these men were to receive hot tea and jam. He then made surprise visits at those hours to see that his orders had been fully followed. When he found that another unit had no sugar, he aroused the quartermaster from his sleep and ordered that a sack of sugar be sent to that unit.

No one has ever heard Dayan shout. Generally, he is reserved, and even his sharpest remarks are spoken in disciplined tones. His nature is described by friends as being "anti-environmental"; when all the others are nervous, tense and at the snapping point, Dayan is as cold as ice. On the other hand, when the sentiment in the environment is one of smugness, lethargy, conformity, he becomes stormy and aggressive, especially when he has the feeling that the public is content with sitting back, enjoying the "fleshpots" and hearing good news only.

He likes to build his people up. He spreads authority around, shows interest only in the core of things, hates managerial duties.

"Count me out of administration," is one of his favorite expressions. Still, while he delegates authority, he keeps the end of the rope in his hands. He never shifts the blame for failure onto his men; his back is broad enough to bear it. He is said to be less careful than he should be in choosing assistants. When he discovers this to be the case, he wastes no time on formalities, looks into the matter and takes decisive action.

Dayan likes to encourage his men, to compliment them, verbally and in writing, for tasks carried out quickly and efficiently. Jokingly, at times, he issues left-handed compliments, as he did when he sent a note to one of his close assistants in the Ministry of Agriculture who had written a speech for him which he later delivered before the Knesset: "I read, not badly, the pretty good speech, which you wrote." He hates blandishments, hypocrisy, false modesty; if he suspects that someone is trying to buy him with honeyed compliments, he cuts that person down to size at once. He likes to surround himself with challenging people, even though he may not take their advice; Dayan is known as a tough person to advise. He comes to meetings with ideas already thought out and thoroughly calculated. When his assistants propose something new which he himself has not thought of, he says: "Let it go for now." The next time the idea is presented, he will already have chewed on it and, if he likes it, he accepts it. He never agrees with an idea simply because it has been drummed into him. He is known to break off conversations in the middle, rather than to allow their boredom to continue to the bitter end. He prefers "no" to "perhaps." Once he has reached a decision, it is impossible to budge him, even an inch. Ben-Gurion once said to him: "People say you are tough." Returned Dayan: "You know what it says in the Bible about the sons of Zeruiah, who helped David establish the kingdom—'the sons of Zeruiah were tough.'"

Dayan is tough, often impatient with people; when he cannot stand someone, he doesn't waste a minute on him. He never maintains contact with people for the sake of courtesy alone. If he has no interest in certain people, he simply ignores them.

There are many unknown aspects to Dayan's character, personality and habits; dark corners into which his image doesn't reach. He has a deep and abiding association with agriculture and the tilling of the soil. Despite attractive offers, he has consistently refused to sell his land in Nahalal; "it's a part of my own body," he says. For the past few years, his farm has been worked by his son, Ehud.

Dayan's fingers are strong and stubby—the fingers of a real farmer.

His close friends say that Dayan has the soul of a poet. He once used to write poems and barbed verses.

His literary talent comes to him from his mother, Deborah. He is a great admirer of the poet, Nathan Alterman, calls him "Nathan the Wise" and knows many of his poems by heart. Unlike politicians, he always manages to read, write, dabble in archaeological excavations. He isn't afraid to be alone with himself, doesn't need the company of friends to think, contemplate and make decisions. While writing "Sinai Diary," he shut himself up in his home for four months, going out only to refer to Zahal historical documents. Archaeology is said to be an escape, for him, from the stormy reality which surrounds him, but others maintain that he has a scholarly approach to the subject, is familiar with its literature, and is able to identify the exact stratum of any discovery which is brought to his attention.

Like his mentor, David Ben-Gurion, Dayan does not have intimate friends, although he has a tremendous circle of acquaintances, and, if he chooses, he can be the center of attraction anywhere. He neither smokes nor drinks. As for food, his friends say: "If he has an appetite, he will eat anything, and generally, he has one." He loves his sons, Assaf and Ehud, and drops in on his daughter, Yael, in Athens, whenever he goes abroad. Some time ago, he happened to be in Athens, just when the revolution took place. A Greek officer who happened to catch sight of him, exclaimed: "General, I had no idea that you were mixed up in this one."

Dayan is a great admirer of Churchill, is quite familiar with his writings and quotes him frequently. He also thinks very highly of Generals Montgomery and Wingate. At one time, he was also an admirer of Dr. Ralph Bunche ("a high-level intellectual and moral force"); his current opinion is not known. He speaks and writes a fine English, which he learned, basically, while imprisoned for two and a half years in Acre fortress. He also began learning French, but had to give it up for lack of time.

He is not religious and is not a believer, but he has a positive attitude toward the truly observant. "I believe in believers," is his summation of the matter. When the Rabbi of Klausenberg and his adherents came to settle in Israel (Dayan was Minister of Agriculture at that time), he said: "Even if this *aliyah* will present certain problems, I am all for it, since it will lead the way in bringing over here the centers of Judaism in the United States. We must give preference to discussions with the religious here, not those remaining in large centers abroad." When Dayan was imprisoned in Acre, he was found one day, surrounded by the other prisoners, reading to them the Biblical Portion of the Week, the story of Jacob and Rachel.

Dayan is completely free of fear. Those close to him insist that all episodes which have taken place in his life have imparted to him a mystical immunity to hurt. This may be the reason for his impatience in time of battle. He dislikes to be behind the lines and wait for reports, and chooses to go up to the front.

He once told me: "During the Sinai Campaign, when we had no report from Sharm-a-Sheikh, I flew to A-Tur. We took two trucks from the Italian firm working in the area, rode some 150 kilometers to Sharm-a-Sheikh. The road was empty. All along the way, we passed Egyptian soldiers in retreat. We were completely exposed. Any Egyptian could have wiped us out. It wasn't the most comfortable feeling in the world." I asked him: "Has anyone ever made an attempt on your life?" "Once," he replied quietly. "During the reprisal raids, a grenade was thrown at my car, but it exploded under the wheels."

I asked him about fear. "Let's analyze it," he returned. "Fear is a matter of instinct with a physical reaction in its wake. One is afraid of the dark, another shrinks back at the sound of a bullet and bows his head when hears it. This is the advantage I have over others—I don't bow my head."

Raphael Bashan: "I Don't Bow my Head"; *Ma'ariv,* 6.6.67

At a press conference held on June 3rd by the Minister of Defense, Moshe Dayan, for 400 television, radio and press correspondents from all over the world, he parried the flood of questions in brilliant and mordant style, giving no hint about Israel's intention for the future. When a newspaperman asked whether it was true that Israel had relinquished the military initiative because of hesitations and delays, Dayan answered: "If you mean that we relinquished the initiative because we didn't launch an attack or start war—then you are right. But if you mean that we have missed our chance even if war breaks out later on—then I am afraid that I can't share your opinion." In answer to another question, General Dayan said: "In case of war, I wouldn't want American or British men to die for us.

and I don't think we need them." When he was asked whether the Egyptians might use long-range missiles, Dayan replied: "They may try." Hundreds of the most renowned correspondents in the world, gathered in Tel-Aviv, did their best to bait the new Minister of Defense and elicit sensational declarations or some kind of information. In vain. Finally, a foreign correspondent asked him: "Is time a factor acting for or against Israel?" General Dayan said: "I don't believe that nations live with a stop-watch in their hands. I can't conceive of a situation in which a country 'stops playing the game' when something goes wrong. There are better situations and worse situations. The question is, what you do with your time. It is possible that in a month we'll find ourselves in a better situation, if we use our time to improve it."

Several correspondents drew their conclusions, and left Israel for their countries of origin. Two days later, the date was June 5th.

For three weeks, soldiers had been massed by the tens of thousands in the desert, in the blazing sands, in the mountains, drinking tepid water, eating combat rations, expecting letters from home, listening on their transistor radios to the news broadcasts, and tensely watching the enemy poised on the frontiers.

Wadi Nitzana. A God-forsaken strip of scarred and lacerated earth, stricken sterile by the sun and bleach-whipped by the wind, stubbed with protruding basalt rock and bone-dry brush patrolled by venomous yellow scorpions. One hour after dawn the temperature is at 100 degrees. The night is icy cold, and when the sandstorms come, don't bother looking for cover.

No one knows exactly how long we have been shrivelling here in the trenches. Time is beyond count. Most of the watches have been finely ground to a halt by the sand and dust. Five centuries from now, someone mutters, archaeologists will be digging us out with bulldozers. We'll look fine then; the desert sand preserves the petrified indefinitely.

Each new day of trench-digging begins at four, before dawn. Half-paralyzed, I slowly crawl out of my sleeping bag. My left arm and leg refuse to move. A mattress of stone may delight a fakir, perhaps, but for my muscles it's the end. Nearby one of the fellows screws his head around to the east and groans, through clenched teeth: "Sun, I hate you!" Overhead, a flight of buzzards is holding an ominous air show.

A stocky sergeant, face jaundice-yellow with sand, takes a tepid gulp from his canteen. "Today, my fellow-combatants," he rasps, "we shall be entertained by a group of renowned artists—a Cuban mandolin orchestra, a magician, and a Negro chanteuse. We shall also have the pleasure and delight of being interviewed by 'Kol Yisrael' on our candid and outspoken opinion of Nasser." He spits the water out in disgust. Ever since we got here, we haven't seen anybody looking like an artist. We're beginning to believe that these heralded star appearances before the troops is just deceptive Egyptian propaganda.

Shaving time. One nut douses himself with lotion; to the others he is a candidate for the mental ward. Then the rumor factory gets going. Every rumor is taken most seriously, even the one that a battalion of elephants had been airlifted to fight the Egyptian tanks. The men clean their weapons. Someone remarks, just like that and without being asked, that a black snake had spent the night with him in his sleeping bag. "It didn't rattle, and even if it did, it wasn't poisonous." We all congratulate him.

Breakfast. Rumor has it that the battery cook is a chef with a dozen diplomas, all of them from abroad, and that his specialty is roast squab. We don't have squab here, and you really can't expect him to do much with buzzards and vultures. As for the diplomas, they can't say too much for a chef who comes up daily with tea, eggs and tomatoes, in that order of frequency. The tea is full of sand. Each of us will wind up with a quarry in his gall-bladder.

And so begins another day, at the end of which we shall be slightly less sane than the day before. We are a tiny cog in the tremendous military machine emplaced on the Egyptian frontier, a minute flag pricked into the large-scale command map. We don't know a thing of what is going on, and it's this not knowing which keeps eating away at our entrails. We listen to all the newscasts, in every language but Turkish and Bulgarian, but they are all vague and don't lessen the apprehension. The Battalion Commander pays us a visit, but he doesn't know much more than we do. We are told something about the Egyptian array facing us. Somebody figures out that if the muzzles of all the Egyptian artillery pieces were to be welded end to end, they'd make a pipeline long enough to bring water from the Sea of Galilee to the Sahara Desert. All of us agree that if the Egyptians have our unit's position down on their maps, may the Almighty preserve us.

You don't have to be an economist to be able to estimate the cost, per day, of this war-under-wraps. From the trenches, we can see the thousands of vehicles, half-tracks and tanks, rolling by; the cost of the fuel, let alone the maintenance expense, must be up in outer space. Plants all over the country are idle. This we know because most of their workers are with us, in this endless desert. A small, poor country can't take this forever. And the days keep rolling along. The Foreign Minister departs, the Foreign Minister arrives; Johnson says this, Johnson says that; an aircraft carrier sails, drops anchor somewhere, and that's all.

We lie in the sparse shade of the camouflage netting, imbedded in the sand like so many mummies. Pink noses vie with purplish ones. Lips are dry, cracking apart. When you first came here, you buttonholed the nearest fellow with half an ear and sounded your opinion off about matters of strategy and/or the beauties of the desert. Should you dare open your mouth in that vein now, you'd be tied to the bore of a muzzle looking at the business end of a tank-piercing shell. If you want to listen to the news, take your transistor and drag yourself beyond the dunes. Most of the men have developed an allergy to news and suffer skin eruptions after every broadcast.

We swat the huge flies about us, listlessly. They say that one such fly lost its way and landed at a military air base. It was being serviced with fuel and ammunition when someone suddenly discovered that it didn't have a bomb rack. Well, so much for that. We play poker with sticky marked cards, munching in the meantime on wafers which cause lasting heartburn. The card players cheat, which makes the game more interesting. The chess players wind up losing the plastic pieces in the sand, but "Uzi" bullets make fair substitutes. Then we do crossword puzzles which someone had already solved. We also fashion planes out of paper and hold mock air battles. Our mirages (small "m") are similar: a bathtub, white tablecloth, a discotheque. Those who receive mail from home are openly envied by the others. We have a guessing pool: When do we get home? The hopeless optimists say—by Rosh Hashana, or, in about four months.

Yisrael Saposnikov, artillery commander, comes from Tel-Aviv and is an enterprising chap. Right in the middle of the desert he sets up a barber shop equipped with makeshift shaving instruments. His customers emerge with skulls which shine like spotlights. All of us are yellow with dust; the baldies look like Buddhist monks. A night watchman who met them has not yet recovered from the shock.

The hatred for the foe is intense, subdued but evident. The Egyptians are the ones who brought about our being here, to shrivel away in the desert sun, to choke in the dust and sandstorms. There is also scorn for this enemy, who couldn't take his defeat like a man but must brag himself into believing that he had won the 1956 deal. There's a hearty respect for the weapons the Egyptians have, but none for the men who operate them. "To this very day," says Yosef Kahlon, a motor mechanic from Ashkelon, "I hold it against the Engineers Corps for what they did to us in the Sinai Campaign. They were clearing a mine field, and the Egyptians were trying to shell them. Being Egyptians, they miscalculated the distance, and their shells landed in our area, although the Egyptians didn't even know we were there."

I asked him how badly they were hit.

"We had no casualties. The Egyptians forgot to remove the caps from the detonators. That particular page must have been missing from their artillery manual. Anyway, not a single shell exploded."

"Then why hold anything against the Engineers?"

"It's the idea. What if our enemies were not the Egyptians?"

On the whole, the lighter side of things doesn't get far here. We are not young army regulars whose youth can offset any situation. Our outfit is made up of reservists. The men are burdened with families and worries. Their breath comes hard and their bones creak. The wife of one is pregnant; the child of another has the measles. Problems and worriers broil together in the sun, nerves are as taut as telegraph wires. Every now and then one of us would get up and wordlessly go off, beyond the dunes, to digest his daily dose of depression, by himself and on his own. An unintended nudge which, in a bus back home, would have earned the offender no more than a juicy "You ass, you," gets here a ferocious glare and clenched fists.

That we are comparatively sane is something we owe our Battery Commander, A., he with the chiseled features of a Roman senator. Every time he opened his mouth, I expected him to orate in Latin and exhort his legions to storm the gates of Carthage. A. is a senior official in the Ministry of Agriculture in Beer-Sheba who, through no fault of his own, became the chieftain of this desert area. He wears shapeless trousers distinguished by their multitude of patches and a shirt of unknown color. He sleeps with us in the trenches, plays dominoes (not too badly) and chess (miserably). He stands in line for mess, with all the others, and eats from the same greasy plate while squatting on the sand like an Oriental. He has a thing about anyone roving around unarmed; any man caught in this state, he has promised, will have bow-ties made out of his insides.

In contrast with A., who is indistinguishable from the lowliest private, we have a picture of the spic-and-span Egyptian officer with an orderly to polish his buttons. You are thankful that you have A. on your side and that the Egyptian officer and his orderly are on the other.

Our last night in Wadi Nitzana had all the usual earmarks—bitter cold and a howling wind. We kept squirming, half-frozen, in our sleeping bags. Sleep was impossible. Raoul Nitzan of Holon did a bit of magic, lit a fire and passed coffee around in empty tin cans. I shall always be indebted to him for that coffee.

In the morning we heard the booming of cannon, but we didn't attach any special meaning to it. Every once in a while the artillery units would hold maneuvers with live ammunition on useless targets. Somewhat dejected, we prepared for another day of digging trenches.

Just at that moment A. returned from the battalion command headquarters. His eyes were gleaming, but his tone was cold and unemotional. He looked at us quietly, then said: "Climb aboard your vehicles. We're pulling out."

Eli Teicher: Blazing Sands; *Dvar Hashavua,* 23.6.67

Chapter Two

A People Goes to War

*V*OLUNTEERS WERE ALMOST AS BUSY AS HIGH-LEVEL POLITICIANS *during the grim days that followed so hard upon their merry-making on Independence Day; those Israelis who have not been called up for active service or Haga (Civil Defense), and foreigners who chose to share Israel's fate, scurried from pillar to post to proffer their services.*

"I am registered on every list in town," one girl student told me forlornly, "the Town Major, City Hall, Hadassah Hospital, Magen David Adom (Israel's Red Cross), the Civil Defense—absolutely everywhere. But one needs pull to get accepted. Have you got any pull?"

Democracies work in strange ways. Few of us realize how much we are left on our own, to make our decisions about life, even in these socialized days. When President Nasser moved with such startling speed, the average citizen found himself alone and bewildered in a hostile world, trying with his puny resources to withstand mighty empires on the march. How was he to express his upsurge of patriotism?

The country's leaders, with more urgent problems on their hands, gave no guidance during the first 48 hours. It is no wonder that the ordinary woman, left to her own devices and thinking along her traditional lines, worried about how she was going to feed the family, and so precipitated the shopping spree.

But human beings are astonishingly resilient; in remarkably short time the feeling of being alone passed. Israelis and friends from abroad, who had not succumbed to the first panic, started to get together to plan their personal answers to the warmongering dictators.

Trudging along the volunteering beat, I went late one night to the Town Major's office. A most charming staff-sergeant was receiving visitors with patience and a smile, notwithstanding the fact that her eyes shone with the brightness of near-exhaustion. I awaited my turn. First she sent three *yeshiva* students off to bake bread at a local bakery. A young woman with a car had her name, address and telephone registered.

When I asked what kind of work volunteers could do, she said they could help pregnant women, women with large families, crippled children, and other such families, where the departure of the man for the wars had created intolerable burdens; they could help distribute food to these people over the first chaotic days; they would keep supplies moving.

"We are really going to use everybody," she assured me. "It takes time to organize. But volunteers will get all the work that they want, I promise you."

Up at Hadassah I found a score of American girl students, chattering away feverishly while they rolled bandages. Mrs. Zmira Baker, of Ya'al, the Helping Hand of Hadassah, is putting volunteers to work. But apparently the supply, so far, exceeds the demand.

On a bright Sabbath morning, I drove three girl volunteers, who had served during national service in a military-agricultural Nahal unit at Kfar Aza, down to that kibbutz, which borders the Gaza Strip, to offer their services. On the way down I stopped at a full-service petrol station to fill up with petrol, but was told that there was none to be had. When I reached the Sha'ar Hanegev station, run by the 11 kibbutzim of the area adjoining the Strip, I asked the veteran kibbutznik in charge diffidently if he had petrol for sale. He looked at me in amazement, and wondered: "What on earth do you think I sell here?"

While he was filling the tank, I asked for his opinion of the crisis. His eyebrows shot upwards. "What crisis?" he retorted.

At Kfar Aza I learned that there, too, volunteers needed pull to be taken. Dozens of hopeful applicants had been streaming to the border kibbutzim to show their mettle. Only volunteers who had been on the kibbutz, or had other valid claims, were being accepted.

When I had last been on the settlement some years before, it had been rather a forlorn one, which suffered from many economic and social ills. The original founding group had left. But, I was told, two Nahal groups had fused, harmoniously; farming was booming;

there had been wonderful rains—a little too much, perhaps, but that was an error of the Lord's in the right direction; all was right in the world, apart from such minor irritants as that moustachioed man from lower Egypt. Why are so many dictators hairy in the upper lip?

A kibbutz has immense advantages over the city in time of crisis: the individual does not have that agonizing sense of personal responsibility for his future, of having to make the right rendez-vous with destiny in the nation's hour of trial. I sat in the room of the dairyman, Dobush, with his wife Avital, while their nine-month-old child surveyed us intently.

"Two members of our kibbutz are on *shlihut* (mission) in France." Dobush told me, while he poured cold drinks. "They wrote to us that they saw the crisis on television. First they saw Egyptian tanks hurtling through Sinai. Then the commentator asked rhetorically: Where are these tanks aimed? And the film switched to show the new dining-room and houses of Kfar Aza."

It was certainly hard to imagine any more peaceful or attractive spot than Kfar Aza on a sunny Sabbath day. Children in singlets and shorts played around the houses; the gardens glowed with color. In the new dining-hall, we ate an excellent lunch; girls sent on cooking courses had obviously learned to infuse spice and taste into their meals.

Dobush, the son of a professor of biochemistry, tends to be somewhat didactic: he gave me an excellent lecture on the state of agriculture at Kfar Aza. So many dunams of cotton, irrigated and unirrigated; so many acres of citrus; so many acres of field crops; so many cubic meters of water. My head spun with information while I devoured mashed potatoes. Remembering that I was on an assignment, I kept trying to bring him back to the threat from his Egyptian neighbors.

"We'll be all right," he said, impatiently. "Of course one of our problems is that none of us was here before the Sinai Campaign, so we don't know what it was like in the days of the *fedayun* (saboteurs). We have had ten years of comparative peace. The Arabs work right up to the border; so do we. I've often tried to speak to them. One, a young man, said that we are all right personally, but that we had robbed them of their land, and should give it back to them. I tried to argue with him logically, but all he would say was that we must first give back the land, and then we could talk. When I tried to pull him further into argument, he started to talk about how pretty our girls are."

At that, the Arab had something. What were relations like with the UNEF soldiers?

"They fluctuated. At one time, they used to come across to join in our festivals, but two years ago that stopped. We used to send them milk and dairy products. When we chatted at the border, they were always friendly."

Had the UNEF really guarded the border? Would there be any point in stationing them on Israel soil, as had been suggested somewhere?

Avital gave the answer, indignantly. "Of course not—we are not threatening the Arabs. In any case, the real protection was that Nasser was accepting UN decisions; the UNEF symbolized this. For instance, they could not stop infiltrators who came to steal."

Dobush laughed. "They used to steal the string from round the bales. For some reason, they value string in Gaza. So one night we left a great pile of string on the border as a present to them, hoping they would leave our bales intact. They took the pile—and the string from the bales as well."

After lunch we climbed Kfar Aza's decrepit look-out post, carefully placing our feet so as not to break the weather-worn planks. Avital said rather sadly, "We haven't had to use this during all these years."

We looked across as delighful and pastoral a scene as one could imagine: green fields of cotton and sugar-beet, yellow lands covered with field crops lay stretched out below us. Dobush pointed out the vacated UNEF posts and the water-tower of Gaza. The only sign of war was a trench being dug near the post.

We watched a tractor at work on the Israeli fields, and *fellahin* (Arab peasants) patiently digging with hoes on the Arab side of the border. The peace seemed complete.

"Isn't it a pity?" sighed Avital.

Philip Gillon: Go Anywhere; *Jerusalem Post,* 2.6.67

Dismay was the first reaction of world Jewry to the developments in the Middle East, followed by deep anxiety, then by a grim determination to do everything to prevent the Arabs from carrying out their threat—to wipe Israel off the map. Apparently the Jews themselves were astounded by the power of their own emotions; up to this hour of trial, many of them were unaware how closely their souls were attached to Israel's fate. The eagerness to serve Israel in its darkest hour found expression on many levels—personal volunteering for military service, raising funds, organizing demonstrations and direct intercession with heads of state, gathering signatures on petitions and letter-writing and, to the neglect of everything else, following radio, TV and press accounts of whatever was happening in or around Israel. American Jewry was shaken to the very depths of its being.

Up to the very last moment we were afraid they would not come. That they would not march. That they would not identify themselves in public. We knew by experience that there was a good basis for the doubts. American Jews do not enjoy participating in Jewish demonstrations. They are good and devoted Jews, to be sure. They have always given and always will give money for charity, and they devote hours and evenings of their precious time for communal requirements. But to get them out into the street, to join them up in a procession of Jewish masses—that was out of the question. A few organizations tried and failed. In most cases our Jewish brethren prefer to behave as though they were far away in Europe. There has been no success in collecting 100,000 Jews for a protest meeting in a Jewish city like New York. Not even for the silent and silenced Jews of Russia. The organizers never succeeded in attracting 20,000 people to Madison Square Garden for their sake. That was the reason why they have never celebrated a Jewish National Day in this metropolis until now. Other national minorities arrange celebrations of that kind every year. There is an Irish day, Italian day, Polish day, Chinese day, Greek day. Even the Germans have a day of their own. Only the Jews have never had one. The Jewish leaders were afraid of a flop. They thought our people would never respond, would never turn up.

This year we learnt that they are not to be judged so negatively. This year they came to the meeting-place. They came in their masses. Men and women, elders with long beards and free-thinking youngsters, schoolboys and their teachers, Yeshiva students and engineers, members of Zionist youth movements and students who have hitherto had the habit of revolting against their Jewishness. In thousands and tens of thousands they came to Riverside Drive by the Hudson, in order to march for Israel and identify themselves with those who fought for her.

Why should this year be different from all other years? This year they had heard the answer given on their behalf in Israel: Never again will the Jewish people be enslaved to Pharaoh in Egypt or to any other king in any other land. The crisis on the frontiers of Israel and Arabia was what brought about this great wonder in the USA as well. In actual fact we may be able to say one day that the Lord did us a favor when he hardened the heart of Nasser. Slumbering forces of love awakened here on his account. Some say that even in 1948 and 1956 there was no such awakening as this one. Not even during the War of Independence and the Sinai Campaign did the volunteer spirit reach such dimensions amid US Jewry. Never did it feel itself so linked to the fate of Israel as now.

In the synagogues days of prayer were proclaimed. University students organized to fly eastward if they should be summoned to help the war effort there. Hundreds of young men thronged all the Israeli Consulates of the continent, and stated that they were prepared to leave for Israel at once at their own expense. It would be hard to find a Jewish family here that has not done something for the Jewish State. So and so has bought Bonds; someone else has sent 10 telegrams to the White House and Congress members. A third has raised funds for the UJA.

The assimilationists among us have forgotten their complexes. The anti-Zionists in our midst, including the members of the notorious American Council for Judaism, have decided not to publicize their "ideology" at this time. Well-known intellectuals, who had hitherto had the habit of displaying a neutralist and objective attitude towards Israel, now telephone me a dozen times a day, asking apprehensively: "What's the news? What can be done? How can we help?"

This reaction calls for inquiry. After all, it is not the first time that the State of Israel has been in distress. It has already experienced grave crises. Serious dangers have confronted it more than once. It has already faced the enemies who have long proclaimed their plan to blot it from the face of the earth. Why have the Jews become so excited this particular time? How can one explain the difference that has come about in their souls, and their sudden identification with Israel, during this present crisis in particular? How to account for it?

For after all, unlike 1948 or 1956, every American Jew has other worries to disturb him. There is the Vietnam War, the Race Problem, the question of relations with Gentiles. How could he have abandoned all these and responded with every bone in his body and all his heartstrings to something happening on a distant front, where his children are not to be found and which does not affect his immediate interests? How is it that this time he has actually come to the Great March and the other marches that demonstrated the solidarity of New York Jewry with Israel?

Furthermore: Unlike the past, it is impossible to claim that the Jewish awakening is due to propaganda on the part of those Israeli institutions which engage in propaganda and information. This time it was unnecessary to spur or prod public opinion. Everybody who reads the papers, everybody who listens to the news broadcasts by radio and television, has become transformed somehow or other into a propagandist in his own field, within his own limits, after his own way. The development in itself is what has electrified the Jews here. Each one of them saw himself as a partner responsible for what was happening in Jerusalem and the Negev. Nasser's impudence was a counter-weight to 20 years of energetic Zionist, Israeli, Jewish propaganda. During these 20 years United States Jews learnt from their spiritual and political leaders that the State of Israel and the People of Israel are a single entity. Only now did they believe and understand that this indeed is so.

The Jews of America now understand that Nasser's war is not directed against Israel alone; it aims at the entire Jewish people. The same applies to Moscow's policy. When Nasser speaks of "total war" he means a Third Destruction. The same applies to those who support his wars. They know well that the Jewish people today cannot permit itself to see the beginnings of Redemption destroyed and burnt from without. They know well that if, heaven forbid, anything should happen to the renewed Jerusalem, then many Jews including those who do not live there would not hold out any longer. How many such calamities can a people experience in a single generation? Nasser and his friends know well that if they succeed in fulfilling their dream this time, many Jews will perish and take their own dream with them to the grave.

But the Jews also know this. It seems to me that it is the first time this thought has penetrated into their consciousness. Maybe it is because they heard Feisal of Saudi Arabia telling the television correspondent that the Arabs have made up their minds to liquidate Israel once and for all. Maybe they have revolted against the hypocrisy of the rulers of the USSR, who permit themselves to mock at human intelligence when they put the blame on Israel. Every child in the street knows that the crisis is due to Nasser, and he himself admits it. Yet Nikolai Fedorenko at the UN, and his masters in the Kremlin, denounce the "aggression" of Israel. Nasser mobilizes military forces and sends them to Sinai. Nasser entrusts the frontier to Shukeiry's gangs. Nasser closes the Straits of Tiran. And Moscow yells that Israel is to blame. Should we not conclude from this that the heads of Soviet Russia have decided that if they help Nasser they can also solve their own problem, the one affecting the Jews in their Soviet country?

That is why the Jews of the United States have mobilized as one man behind the State of Israel. They understand what is involved. And they also understand the ultimate significance of the game. That is why they are so deeply disturbed. That is why they are concerned. That is why they are ready for battle. Tell them what to do, for they will do everything. Ask money of them and they will give it. Send a call to the young men, tell them that Israel requires them, and a volunteer movement will arise such as our history has never seen in recent generations.

The Jews of America have come to understand that they belong to a people that does not need, and is unable, to rely on strangers. For that reason they wish to prove that Israel has to and is entitled to rely on them.

Eliezer Wiesel: The Huge Procession; *Yediot Aharonot,* 2.6.67

For many American Jews, fund-raising on behalf of Israel has become almost second nature. This time, however, challenged by the threat to Israel's very existence, the readiness to raise such vitally-needed funds surpassed all expectations. In two weeks' time, from the commencement of the crisis to the outbreak of war, a total of $100,000,000 *was gathered in the United States, an amount which would ordinarily have taken several years to raise.*

The Defense Ministry in Tel-Aviv did not have the only operations room during the Six Day War. There was another such room in New York: headquarters of the United Jewish Appeal. While no one was sticking pins on maps, a battery of several dozen telephones, telex machines, and mounds of corned beef and pastrami sandwiches kept this headquarters instantly and constantly in touch with its officers in the field. When the fury of "battle" was over, the UJA's Special Emergency Campaign had collected more than three times the sum it had allocated to Israel in 1948.

"Here's how it worked," said the UJA's Executive Chairman, Rabbi Herbert Friedman, who was "Chief-of-Staff" of the entire operation.

"On Monday, May 29, we voted for the emergencey fund and immediately got to work raising money. A typical call, say to Harry X in Pittsburgh . . . 'Look, Harry, you know what's happening. Israel's going to be at war . . . Don't argue with me. I'm telling you this is what's going to happen. I want $500,000.'

"People were absolutely shocked. We began talking in millions. I asked the telephone company for 20 more phones. They said, all right; we'll be able to manage that two weeks from Thursday. I said I want them in two hours. And I got them.

"Within hours people were streaming in from all over the country. They just left their businesses and families and came to man the phones and collect money. They stayed for days, and worked non-stop. These were all money men themselves. By Thursday we had 20 such men.

"One of my staff people would sit next to the money man at the phone. He'd pull a card from the file . . . Y in New Orleans. 'Ask him a quarter million.' The money man would then call.

"Decisions on amounts of money that used to take weeks or months now took minutes. On Tuesday Finance Minister Pinhas Sapir and the Chairman of the Jewish Agency Executive, Aryeh Pincus, arrived. We installed them in our offices, and brought people in to see them.

"'*Kama?*' (How much?)' Sapir would ask me in Hebrew.

"'*Reva* (a quarter)', I'd tell him, and so it went.

"Then we put Sapir and Pincus and Golda (Meir, former Israeli Foreign Minister) and Foreign Minister Abba Eban and our own officers on video tape with special messages and sent them by plane or special messenger all over the country, and arranged speaking engagements for them. We sent out 120,000 letters to specially selected names taken from our computerized memory bank. And by the end of that week we had arranged for fund-raising meetings in almost every Jewish community in America."

The fund-raising operation culminated ten hectic days during which Rabbi Friedman decided that an Israel–Arab war was inevitable.

"On May 20 we got a cable from the Jewish Agency requesting $20 or $30 million right away. The cable reached me at 8:30 on

Saturday night in my office. I worked through to Sunday putting the apparatus into effect to start collecting past pledges. You see, at any moment we always have \$30–\$40 million in pledges outstanding. It's our 'accounts receivable.' People make pledges every year. Sometimes it takes two years or three before they fully pay a pledge. Thus there's always a constant flow of money.

"The same day I flew to Israel and as soon as I arrived on May 22, I saw Eshkol (the Prime Minister), Sapir, Pincus. Monday, Tuesday, Wednesday we had non-stop consultations. I was trying to understand the dimensions of the problem. The size of the possible war was unclear to me. All day Thursday and Thursday night I spent on the Sinai line with the army, familiarizing myself with the problems. But already on Monday, May 22, as soon as I had arrived and sensed the atmosphere, I was convinced there was no way out except war, and I never changed my mind.

"On Friday, May 26, I flew to Athens to meet Fisher (Max Fisher, UJA General Chairman), who was there on business before coming to Israel. I briefed him and we were back here Friday night. We met Eshkol, Rabin (Chief-of-Staff), Sapir, Arnon (Director-General of the Treasury), until 3 o'clock in the morning.

"And as soon as the meeting was over I started sending long telex cables to my boys in New York on what I wanted done. I called for a National Executive meeting for Monday noon, and we had everyone in New York at that time. I'm not the kind that cries wolf, and they knew it.

"By Saturday night we were back in New York, and I worked all day Sunday in the office. We invited the heads of all the Jewish organizations to attend the Executive meeting—Schwartz of the Bonds, Rabbi (Joachim) Prinz (Chairman of the Conference of Presidents of Major American Jewish Organizations), (Rabbi Israel) Miller (Chairman of the American Zionist Council), (Morris) Abram (President) of the American Jewish Committee."

But as Rabbi Friedman is quick to point out, it wasn't only the millionaires or the near-millionaires who suddenly and swiftly unlatched their coffers as never before. In Okmulgee, Oklahoma, a community of a few Jewish families, \$1,700 was raised. Deciding that this wasn't enough, they sold their tiny synagogue for an additional \$4,000 for the fund. (Several days later a more affluent New Yorker who had already donated \$7,500 heard about this, and sent \$4,000 to Okmulgee's Jews to buy their synagogue back.)

At Brandeis University a Jewish student from Brooklyn flew home the day before his final exams, withdrew savings of $2,500 for tuition, gave it to the fund, and caught a return plane in time for his exam.

Children collected money in apartment houses in the large cities. Grade schoolers sold lemonade on the streets. Cars, furniture, jewelry were auctioned. In Indianapolis a loan fund was established to enable people to give more than they had readily available.

In New York, a university professor sent in $25,000, his life savings, with a note saying: "You've got it all now," and a gas-station owner donated the deeds to his two stations.

Non-Jews, spurred with sympathy for Israel, contributed as well. Catholic Fordham University in New York donated $5,000. In Miami, Jewish and non-Jewish Cuban refugees matched each other dollar for dollar in a $50,000 drive.

An Irish policeman outside a synagogue rally in New Jersey gave $20. Christian families of Arab background sent in money from various cities. In St. Louis a Negro woman contributed $25 "from my heart, because some very fine Jewish people have been so kind to me." In Baltimore, when a Jewish driver offered to pay a Negro driver for minor accident damage, he was told to give it to the Israel Emergency Fund.

Soldiers in Vietnam, Jews and non-Jews, sent in part of their monthly pay packets. And from State College, Pennsylvania, Kevin Burns wrote: "I thought I would like to send a dollar. I'm only 11, and that's all I can afford. I hope the Arabs stop, and for good. I hope Israel gives it to them good! With best wishes.

"P.S. I think your cause is just."

Erwin Frenkel: Mobilizing the Millions; *Jerusalem Post,* 13.7.67

★

It was as though an electric current had coursed through the communities of the Diaspora. From Johannesburg to New York, from London to Los Angeles, hundreds and thousands of Jewish volunteers began streaming to railway stations, seaports and airports. Actually no official call had gone forth, asking them to come, nor did they know exactly to what task they would be assigned in Israel, on the brink of war. This was a spontaneous awakening of the Jewish heart, beating as one with the State of Israel from one end of the world to the other.

They arrived at Lydda Airport, day after day, in an ever-increasing stream. Excited, fired up, with only a knapsack on their backs and small valises in their hands, ready for any task. "Is Kibbutz Kfar Blum near the Syrian border?" asks a volunteer from Manchester. "That's right," answer the Jewish Agency people, who are handling the volunteers. The Manchester youth is not satisfied. "Are you sure that Kfar Blum is on the Syrian border, and not on the Lebanese?" Again he is assured that the Kibbutz is really and truly located on the Syrian border. "Wonderful," he exclaims. "That's what we came for!"

They came, in this ever-increasing stream, from every point on the globe—from the United States, Canada, Britain, South Africa, France, Belgium, Holland, Scandinavia, Brazil, Uruguay, Chile. Said New York-born Joe Templeman, an economics student at Brooklyn College: "When Nasser's troops began moving into Sinai, I knew that the situation was dangerous. The minute I heard that Israel was mobilizing, it was clear to me that the settlements would be short of working hands. I couldn't stay at home any longer. I went to the Agency offices and asked them to send me to Israel, right away."

Moira Robbins, pretty and 21, a model working in a large fashion house in Philadelphia, put it this way: "I heard on TV about the closing of the Straits of Tiran. I saw the ridiculous discussions in the Security Council, and even though I had never thought of getting to Israel, I felt that my place was here." Harvard Berhard, a 20-year-old student of English literature from Toronto, Canada, said: "I am not a Zionist, but as a Jew I couldn't rest while Israel would be fighting for its life. I understood that I had to be here, right away."

The same sentiments were shared by Benjamin Virobnik, 16, perhaps the youngest of the volunteers to come to Israel. Benjamin, a high school student in Brussels, said: "I told my mother that it wasn't right, that we should be in Belgium and view the tension of war on television." My mother was a bit afraid at first, but then she agreed. David Crock, a medical student at the University of Johannesburg, said: "I think that Israel is my country. First I shall finish my studies in South Africa, then I shall return for my advance work at the Hebrew University." A young girl of London, Michelle Valerie, says right out that she is prepared to live in Israel. She had once tried to settle here permanently, but couldn't make a go of it. Language difficulties. "But you can say," she tells the reporters at the airport, "that I am looking for work. If I find it I'll give you a written guarantee that I'll stay." Abraham Mutzani claims that he, too, is ready to try to remain in Israel, on condition that he finds work in his field—fashion design.

Swiss Rimon Kuttchy is one of the scores of non-Jewish volunteers who arrived at Lydda in the crammed planes. Why did he come? Said Kuttchy: "I have always been interested in Jewish problems and Jewish history. I am especially interested in the kibbutz. Perhaps Switzerland's attitude toward the Jews also had something to do with it. When I learned that Israel was in trouble, I first helped to raise funds, then I volunteered to come."

Another non-Jew is Mark Hong from Singapore. What induced him to come to help Israel? "I am studying economics in London," explained Mark, "I have Jewish friends. They told me that you are in great danger, and I have come to help you. My parents don't even know that I am here. I shall yet hear about it." At the Israel Consulate in Los Angeles appeared an American Indian of 26, who had served five years as a paratrooper in the U.S. Army and fought in Korea. He now offered his good services to Israel, and was ready to pay travel expenses out of his own pocket. Why to Israel? "I love to fight."

At Kennedy International Airport in New York, volunteers waited three days on end for space aboard a plane to Israel. In the London airport, the constabulary had to be called out to help maintain order among the hundreds of volunteers queuing up to grab any available space on Israel-bound planes. Scores of volunteers boarded planes at the Jan Smuts Airport in Johannesburg for the long hop to Tel-Aviv. On the "Voice of South Africa" radio program, a minister announced, in his sermon of the week: "We are now facing the war between Gog and Magog of which the Prophet spoke, the war which will be followed by the advent of the Messiah!"

The Editors: The Volunteers

If there be a spot, anywhere on the globe, where the term "people's army" has some validity, it is Israel. Zahal's emergency strength is built on reservists; all men up to 40 *and fit for service, regardless of profession, address, origin, educational level or family size, are called up on an equal basis. Dr. Amnon Rubinstein, lecturer in the law school of Tel-Aviv University and a well-known contributor to the daily* Ha'aretz, *served in the Six-Day War as troop commander. In an article written for the* N.Y. Times Magazine, *he describes the unique character of Israel's "people's army" and the way it operates.*

It all started Friday night, May 20. My wife and I were driving through downtown Tel-Aviv with two American visitors when we noticed small groups of men waiting beside their luggage on street corners, huddled together in the chilly spring air. "This is it," I said to my wife, "the call-up is on." I told my American friends that I would have to leave them and hurry home; the reserves were being mobilized—most probably I would be called.

All week long, news of Egyptian Army concentrations on the border had increased our apprehension. Radio Cairo had been outdoing itself with a stream of venomous threats to wipe out Israel and massacre the Jews. Finally, when Nasser ordered the UN Emergency Force out—and U Thant obliged—it was clear that Nasser meant business. A call-up was inevitable. The regular army alone could not defend the country against the huge, well-equipped Arab armies.

Driving home that night, I saw the first stage of the amazing process which, in the space of 48 hours, can turn a mass of civilians into a disciplined army and the whole country into one huge encampment. The streets were filled with people carrying suitcases, rucksacks, kitbags, bags of all sorts and sizes. They were all leaving their homes, heading toward various collection points where they would be picked up and carried off to unknown destinations. On Saturday morning usually bustling Tel-Aviv would awaken to find itself half-empty.

At home I found, pasted on the door, a red-lettered notice. Under the door a copy of the same notice had been shoved. It said:

"By virtue of the authority granted by law to the Minister of Defense, you are hereby drafted into emergency service. You are to report to your unit collection point at 05:00 with all your personal equipment."

The notice is part of what is known as a "quiet alarm." There are two methods of calling up the reserves—by broadcasting code words over the radio and by personal delivery of notices. Every reserve unit has a delivery team, whose job it is to know their comrades' addresses and to deliver the notices as speedily as possible. If the draftee is not found at home, the notice is pasted on his door.

In order to keep this call-up machinery oiled, exercises are held periodically. How often I had cursed this irritating and seemingly superfluous business of having to report to the collection point. This time it was different.

The "personal equipment" mentioned in the notice was already neatly packed and waiting in the closet, a prosaic reminder of the constant threat hanging over Israel. I had four hours to sleep.

At 4:30 a.m. my wife drove me to the collection point. The roads swarmed with men going to their respective collection points, by car and by bicycle, on foot, hitchhiking. There were men of various ages and conditions: married men and bachelors, youngsters recently released from regular service and older men, too. Israelis belong to the active reserves up to the age of 49, after which they go over to Civil Defense. There were young, unmarried women who serve in the reserves and in the regular army as well. And there were Orthodox men, distinguishable by their skullcaps, driving on the Sabbath although this is forbidden by religious precept. But this was a case of *Pikuach-Nefesh,* a matter of life and death, which set aside such prohibitions.

At the collection point, I found most of my men already arrived. By 5:10 o'clock, 92 out of the 95 called up had registered with the unit clerk. As we later found out, one of the three missing had been ill; he arrived at the front three days later. The two others were abroad.

The registration list, which our clerk filled out, was sent to headquarters. From all over the country, such lists were being forwarded to an electronic computer. Within a week of the call-up, the computer would arrange for payments to the family of every draftee. The civilian-turned-soldier would know that those dependent on him were being taken care of. The computer would also determine the percentage of those called up who were serving in the lines. Incredible as it may sound, it was close to 100 per cent.

In some units, the ranks were swelled by volunteers not called up in the first phase. In one paratroop battalion, the percentage was brought up to 110 per cent by determined volunteers who showed up and refused to go home. In another division, 4,000 volunteers appeared. They could not stay at home while their friends were mobilized.

Waiting for transport, we chatted, exchanged views, joked together. We knew each other well. For five years we had been meeting regularly.

Every reservist is liable to be called up in the course of the year:

privates for a maximum of 30 days, officers for as long as 37 days. These annual refresher courses are designed to keep us in trim and acquaint us with new techniques and arms, so that the unit can be put into immediate action, any day, any time. They are conducted by the regular army at one of its many training bases. This is our only point of contact with the regulars. Our place is within the framework of the reserves, and the division to which we belong is part of the civilian army.

Our unit is as heterogeneous, as varied, as interesting as the people of Israel. It includes *sabras* (native-born) and new immigrants, men of European origin (Ashkenazim) as well as those of Oriental extraction (Sephardim). Their Hebrew is rich in various accents, and they come from all walks of life. Some arrived in well-tailored suits and ties, others wore overalls.

There is a family atmosphere about the unit, enhanced by the difference in ages. The youngest soldier is Rachamim, a mechanic, tall, dark, 23. He has been with us only two years and is fondly referred to as "the boy." He is a typical *sabra;* a bit rough on the outside, he is happy-go-lucky, likes pop tunes (Nancy Sinatra's above all), dancing and having a good time. The oldest is Moshe, 51, a prosperous lawyer, Polish-born. He is past the active-service age but was allowed to stay in the unit after having insisted that he could still do his stint as quartermaster.

There is a family atmosphere but no family. Fathers and sons are not permitted to serve in the same unit, to avoid a double loss in case of action.

Finally our transport arrived: an urban bus, a tourist "guided tours" coach and a small van—all civilian vehicles. The army cannot move the reserves with its own transport. Hence it recruits civilian-owned vehicles, all of which must be registered with the army. The same system which mobilizes soldiers—notices and predetermined collection points—functions for vehicles. Sometimes the owners are assigned as drivers of their own vehicles; other times they leave the car at the collection point, and the recruited drivers take over. I was given such a car, a small delivery van, whose owner had left a note on the seat: "Take care of my pet. She is nice to those who handle her with care. She tends to heat up and likes to drink lots and lots of water. Hates brutal army trucks. Loves to stay away from fire. Otherwise, she is a reliable old cat."

This civilian transport lends a surrealist air to the army. Moving vans, still in their civilian paint, carry guns. Lorries (from which the signs, "Available for hire," have not yet been removed), ice cream vans, trucks, spew out mortars, munitions, weapons. Moving vans are also turned into mobile canteens; tenders are swiftly transformed into ambulances; buses move soldiers. It is a colorful army, made more bizarre against the backdrop of arid, monotonous desert scenery. (Later the cars would be camouflaged by the simple device of plastering them with desert mud.)

At 6 a.m. we started moving southward. The roads were jammed bumper to bumper, ordinary traffic of vehicles going from Tel-Aviv to the Negev. The atmosphere was gay. Children gathered along the roadside and waved enthusiastically.

Soon the heat began to be felt. Field shower-stalls were put up at intersections for those who could stop long enough. Mobile canteens dispensed soft drinks to sweating soldiers. Army comfort stations were assembled along the route. M.P.'s directed traffic; motor repair units were already posted along the roads to extricate broken-down vehicles. All these services were provided by the civilian army, run by men recruited just the day before.

At about 8 o'clock we reached the northern Negev and stopped for a drink at Ofakim, a development town populated by new immigrants—in this case, an odd mixture from North Africa and Rumania. It is a dreary little place, with those depressing rows of tenement blocks, all alike, which disfigure the face of Israel. The inhabitants work in the few local factories or in nearby areas; some live on the dole. Along its main street you can usually see men sitting on the sidewalk, gazing apathetically at the littered roadway.

This Saturday was different: the place was transformed. When we stopped, we were surrounded by women and children, their eyes alight with excitement. They rushed home, brought out food—sweet Moroccan cakes, Rumanian delicatessen, candies, pickles, lemonade, all were forced on us despite our protests. Two old men, on their way to synagogue, prayer books in hand, pushed their way through the milling crowd and began reading aloud a chapter from the Book of Psalms. The familiar words, "The Lord is my shepherd, I shall not want," were hardly recognizable through the sad, minor-keyed, oriental chant. I said to Reuven, my second in command, "This cannot be real. It must be an overdone, over-acted scene from a bad propaganda movie." Reuven, a quiet-mannered kibbutznik, remarked: "Bad taste, my friend, bad taste."

After half an hour we resumed our journey southward and by noontime reached our emergency depot. Every reserve unit has such a depot, containing all the equipment necessary to turn a group of soldiers into a fighting unit ready for combat. The depots are run by the regular army, whose job it is to keep the equipment at the ready. The stores are never used in peacetime, for training. They are opened only in an emergency, by special order, when the reserves are mobilized. Periodically, reserve officers and quartermasters are taken on a tour of inspection, so that they may be fully acquainted with the stocks. Our last visit there had been two months before; a waste of time, we'd thought. But now we knew exactly where each item was and could complete the issue of guns, munitions and equipment by the afternoon.

Soon we were wearing the plain, ill-fitting camouflage-patterned uniforms. A couple of days later, when we moved farther to the south, we looked very much alike. The desert dust, carried by afternoon winds, covered our clothes, skin, got into our hair. The professionals, clerks, merchants, farmers, the workers of yesterday, became desert rats in an incredibly short time—sunburned, dirty, rough. Some grew moustaches and beards, so that they resembled the Hebrew warriors of old.

The distinctions of civilian life, which only a few days before had ruled our lives, were replaced by new distinctions. Wealth lost its meaning. Rank—signifying authority and responsibility—took its place. The prosperous physician of the city took orders from a hitherto unemployed worker. Age distinctions swiftly disappeared. Middle-aged patresfamilias accepted the leadership of young officers who might have been their children. Profession and skill became irrelevant. Instead, a new talent mattered: the undefinable knack for living in the field, of securing comfort in eminently uncomfortable circumstances.

My sergeant-major, Yitzhak, has this gift. He turned up with a small rucksack, but it was an inexhaustible treasure trove of vitally necessary items. Everything needed for living in the open comes out of that bag—knife, flashlight, rope, first aid, desert goggles. Yitzhak (we call each other, officers included, by first names) is a soldier tried and true. He came to Palestine from Rumania, where the whole of his family died in a Nazi death camp. As a mere boy of 14, he managed to jump from the train taking him to the gas chambers. He spent two years hiding in the thick woods, stealing food, eating whatever he could lay hands on, living by his wits, an experience which made him a superman in the art of survival. He senses his way at night, alert to every suspicious noise. He is always on hand, opening bottle caps with his teeth, administering first aid, making a fire, recounting a story, telling off a grumbling soldier.

By contrast, our cook, who goes by the nickname of "Fatso," is the anti-soldier. He arrived with a jumbo-sized suitcase, which fell apart after three days. It is chock-full of a multitude of irrelevant items (an electric shaver, for example, where no current is available) but very few of the necessities. He keeps losing and borrowing things and is totally dependent on others' help. The first night we slept in the trenches he took out a pair of lurid silk pajamas and a small pillow, a sight that set us all roaring with laughter.

But all this was yet to come. We were still on our way southward. Our next stop was the Negev capital of Beer-Sheba. It was teeming with military, and its cafes did a brisk business; but the main attraction was a bus converted into a mobile post office, with 20 telephone lines serving soldiers eager to get into touch with their families and friends.

Inside the bus, there rose a cacophony of voices, each trying to rise above the others:

"I'm O.K. Everything will be all right."

"How're the boys? Yes, I'll come back soon. I promise."

"Well, actually it's so good that I'm considering staying in the reserves for good. Good company. Wonderful weather. Gorgeous scenery. No nagging wife. Food could be improved upon, but that's true at home, too, with your cooking."

"Please don't worry . . . please. . . ."

"No, don't send anything. Just write. Every day."

"A boy! No kidding? A boy, listen, it's a son! A son!"

Beer-Sheba itself was calm. Though it might well become the target of enemy bombardment, its inhabitants were alert but not alarmed. Women and older children were already digging air-raid trenches near the houses. A special service, run by volunteers, distributed cookies, books, gifts to soldiers. This was part of a special kind of mobilization of those staying behind—the mute, unsung effort of women left without husbands, children without fathers, parents without sons. In the next few days workers all over Israel would donate part of their earnings to the war effort, businessmen would pay their taxes in advance, children would sort and distribute mail, drivers would take hikers stranded by the shortage of public transport. The country, usually divided by political strife, suddenly forgot all divisions, all other issues, and united in its fight for existence.

There was, however, one exception to the rule of unity; the old-guard politicians were not always ready to let bygones be bygones. For two weeks, the popular demand to set up a national emergency Cabinet was resisted by fanatic leftist politicians. Meir Ya'ari, the 70 year-old leader of the leftist Mapam party, threatened to leave the Government if General Moshe Dayan, hero of the Sinai Campaign, were made Minister of Defense. He said such a step would be "a black day for the workers." But the people forced the old-time politicians to capitulate: a national government was finally established with Dayan as Minister of Defense. Political bickering could not dampen Israel's calm, enthusiastic response; besides, the danger was too obvious.

From Beer-Sheba we traveled south again, attached to an armored division, one convoy in an unending chain of traffic, all heading for the Negev. That night we placed our anti-aircraft guns in position and started digging into the hard soil. By morning, drenched with perspiration, we were ready for action. We were deployed near the Sinai border around a supply and munitions dump. Our task: to protect the dump, which served the armored division, against possible air attack.

Then started the long wait. The Government was waiting to see whether diplomacy could open the Gulf of Akaba to Israeli navigation. For an army of civilians, this was a difficult period. We had all left families, homes and businesses on sudden call. All of us believed that war was inevitable. (The odds in camp were 9 to 1 that the war would start before the end of May, and many lost money when May 31 went by without a shot being fired.) Obviously Nasser saw in the military pacts which he had signed with Jordan and Syria an opportunity to translate his dreams of conquest into action.

These were unusually quiet days. The mass movements of the army had been completed. We killed time by drilling, listening to news—we lived from one newscast to the other—and devouring the newspapers. We also played at war councils. In this army of civilians every soldier is a prime minister, weighing the pros and cons of every possible move, giving advice to Johnson, scolding de Gaulle, urging on Wilson. We had been supplied with free postcards, and these were, and still are, sent off by the hundreds, a paper bridge linking us with our families.

We woke up every morning at 3:30 so that by first morning light we would be ready for any surprise air attack. The hot days were like so many eternities, and the sun seemed never to move. At night we gathered around the fire (a blackout was not ordered until the war broke out), singing songs in Hebrew, Yiddish, Russian, English.

The star of these nights was Moshiko, who hails from Greece. He had fought through three wars—once with the Greek partisans against the Nazis, twice against the Arabs here. He knows the Negev like the palm of his hand; he was here in 1948, in the War of Independence, and again in 1956, in the Sinai Campaign. He is 49, has two sons and four grandchildren. His sons are in an armored division—somewhere.

Moshiko, old-time veteran that he is, knows how to live well, even in wartime. He brought with him a case of dry wine; he will not eat his dinner without a bottle. Every night his hearty laughter rings throughout the encampment, but occasionally he withdraws silently to a corner, staring mutely into the darkness. When he is gay, he entertains the men with "anecdotes" or a mock belly-dance—to the rhythm of hand-clapping, he moves through the hot, windless night air in a lazy, sensuous Greek dance.

Then, Monday, June 5, more than two weeks after the call-up, war started. We rose as usual at 3:30 and went through the routine of sitting and waiting, ready for instantaneous action in the silence of a chilly morning. It was going to be, it seemed, just another day of waiting until suddenly Yitzhak shouted: "Listen, listen!"

From afar, beyond the hills, we could hear the sound of distant, muffled drums—the sound of war. Within minutes, the sound grew into a familiar symphony of guns, mortars and planes. So this was it. War.

Our first feeling was one of relief. After the long tense days and endless nights, after the weeks of speculation, it had finally begun. The die had been cast. It was better than the anxiety, the uncertainty, the suspense.

But relief was accompanied by alertness. Within minutes now, an air attack was to be expected. The Egyptians had three airfields in the Sinai Peninsula, close to the front line. Doubtless they knew from air reconnaissance exactly where we were deployed. In anti-aircraft units, there is very little one can do to insure personal safety. One has to be at the gun, or very close to it, unsheltered, open to attack. The only defense is to shoot down the enemy. With their hundreds of Russian-made MIG's, the Egyptian Air Force posed a formidable threat, and not simply to our unit. A single plane could destroy the whole dump, cutting off essential supplies from our troops.

It would be a matter of minutes, seconds before they attacked—seconds in which our eyes pierced the blue Mediterranean skies, trying to find a tiny dot that would instantly grow into a menacing, death-spreading machine. A nonsensical refrain from a Beatles song stubbornly stuck in my mind:

We all live in a yellow submarine,
A yellow submarine, a yellow submarine.

Fifteen minutes passed. Half an hour. A whole hour of thudding hearts. And then I was summoned to headquarters. There an artillery liaison officer stood in the center of the tent; he winked at the battalion commander, sharing a common secret. When all the officers were gathered around, the liaison officer said: "I have good news for you. The Egyptian Air Force has been virtually destroyed. Our pilots report the destruction of 140 planes. Most runways in enemy airfields are out of use."

For a long moment there was silence, and then one of the officers stuttered: "But it's only 10 o'clock in the morning; it's too early." His protest broke the spell. We clamored for the details of the air force action, the first advance of our troops into Sinai, the fierce armored battle that was raging just a few miles away from us.

I drove back through the encampment, rushing from one crew to the other, shouting the good news, adding a warning that the state of "zero alertness" (readiness for immediate action) was still in effect and that enemy planes were still capable of action and were to be expected. The men could not leave their gun posts, but they had to give some expression to their mounting emotions; standing by their guns, perspiring under their steel helmets in the broiling sun, they hugged one another and shouted, "Mazeltov."

Slowly the day crept by—second after second—without an Egyptian plane in sight. The sound of war was receding. The front lines were moving away from us at an incredible pace, deep into the Sinai toward Egypt. By afternoon it was quiet, the silence broken only by helicopters delivering our wounded to a nearby field hospital.

The excitement and relief of the morning were now replaced by a feeling of disappointment, of being left out of things, almost forgotten. The timid, worried civilians of yesterday were eager for action, but the war was running away from us. Reports kept coming in, fantastic stories of incredible victories, while we were stuck in our encampment searching the skies, looking in vain for a single enemy plane.

For entertainment, we listened to Radio Cairo. It went on as if nothing had happened:

"Our glorious Arab troops, our unconquerable armies, are marching on Tel-Aviv. Haifa is already burning. Israelis are panicking. Where is General Dayan now? He is hiding in a shelter, the coward. Listen, you Jews. Run for your lives. We are coming to kill you one by one. We bring death and annihilation to the Zionist gangs. We are advancing everywhere. Where is your Prime Minister? In the shelter, with the Chief-of-Staff, the cowards."

Great roars of laughter greeted this mad version of Tokyo Rose, which would continue in the same vein while Israeli troops were occupying the east bank of the Suez Canal.

That night, exhausted by the excitement of doing nothing, I went to visit the wounded at the field hospital. In the big tent the smell of antiseptics, blood and anesthetics lay heavy. Only one man was groaning with pain; the rest were quiet. A nurse was bandaging one of the wounded. A young soldier motioned me over to him. He seemed incredibly young, a mere school boy. His beardless, smooth face was disfigured by an ugly wound which left him with only one eye. He asked for a cigarette, and I lit one and placed it between his lips, putting it in and taking it out for each puff since he made no move to do so himself. I didn't know what was wrong with his arms and dared not ask. I thought I had to say something, but I could not think of anything that would not sound hollow.

Outside, another helicopter landed, bringing more casualties to the adjacent operating tent. I kept holding the cigarette for the young boy. Finally he spoke in a clear, firm voice: "Tell them there's a dead man in that bed on my left. They'll need the bed soon." I rushed out to find someone; I couldn't take that tent any longer.

Outside, on the ground, lay the wounded on stretchers. A plump, dark-skinned officer was being carried into the operating tent, protesting all the while: "No, no. I'm all right. Take the others. Please. Please. Take the others first." On my way back to camp, I felt proud and ashamed at the same time—proud of being part of this people, this army; ashamed of being all in one piece.

The next day I went on a reconnaissance tour into Sinai, following in the wake of the armored division to which we were attached. It was not easy to catch up with the division headquarters. As Rachamim said, it was moving so fast, it would be in Vietnam the following week.

In Sinai, the scenery along the shell-torn road to Bir Gafgafa was a landscape of crushing defeat: smoking tanks; trucks twisted into surrealistic sculptures; piles of bodies, flies swarming over the already rotting flesh; corpses frozen by rigor mortis in odd poses, like a movie suddenly stopped; the corpse of an Egyptian driver in his seat, his hands clutching the steering wheel, his head leaning forward, his dead eyes staring at the burned-out convoy ahead of him; a dead Egyptian pointing his scorched hand upward; a dead camel in the middle of the road; a bicycle in the ditch; a shell set near a 25-pound gun, ready to be shoved into it; a goat wandering aimlessly near the blackened remains of a MIG. And all under a harsh, glaring sun blazing down upon a bleak desert.

I had been in the Sinai Campaign in 1956 and seen that Egyptian defeat. It was nothing compared to this debacle. Here was the army that only yesterday was to wipe Israel off the map and drive us into the sea. Yet it was not a scene to give one joy. This was the enemy, but these dead soldiers had been human beings. The sight of their forlorn bodies was a sad monument to Nasser's folly.

But the war was not over, not yet. In the evening, on our way back, this time through the freshly taken Gaza Strip, we stopped for refueling at Rafiah, on the border separating Sinai from the strip. Near a small railway station stood a bloodstained, empty half-track, and not far from it lay the bodies of nine Israeli paratroopers. They had been killed minutes before our arrival. A Fedayun, a member of the gangs of marauders trained by the Egyptians for guerilla warfare inside Israel, had thrown a hand grenade into the half-track. He had been hiding on the roof of the railway station, lying there all day long in the sun, waiting for his opportunity. His one hand grenade had killed all nine boys on the spot.

They lay there on the ground as if resting from a hard day's work. A small transistor radio lay near them; it was still on. A frightened soldier knelt beside them, sobbing. From the radio came the sound of music (I think it was an overture to one of von Suppe's operas) and then a commercial extolling the glories of some brand of instant coffee.

The Fedayun was held at gunpoint near the station building, his hands tied behind his back. He looked around him with glazed, indifferent eyes; then he was blindfolded and taken to the prisoners' camp. We rode silently back through villages in the Gaza Strip. White rags were hung out everywhere to signify surrender.

On Thursday, June 8, our battery moved to a new encampment at Bir Gafgafa, 90 kilometers from the Suez Canal, site of an armored battle in which more than 100 Egyptian tanks had been destroyed. It was the fourth day, but the war with Egypt was virtually over. There were still local pockets of resistance here and there. Shots were still being exchanged on the roads. Some Egyptian stragglers, probably unaware of the scale of the defeat, fought a lost battle. But the majority were either surrendering or trying to reach the Canal on foot, unhindered and sometimes even assisted by the Army, so long as they gave up their arms without resistance.

On Friday, we placed our guns into position near divisional headquarters. That day we took about 700 prisoners of war. They came down from the hills, barefoot, dirty, exhausted. In the daytime they were helpless, harmless. But after sunset, the stragglers could become dangerous. The night before, three Israelis guarding their stranded tank had been attacked and murdered by Egyptian soldiers. Their mutilated bodies, the male organs cut off and placed in their mouths, were found beside the tank. Some of the men were thirsting for revenge. I had to talk to them, to calm them down. Our ways are different from those of the enemy, I told them. The order against mistreating prisoners of war in any manner would be rigorously enforced.

One of our prisoners was taken by Menahem, a thin, sickly-looking oldster, who arrived on Saturday morning with the supply convoy. He was the antithesis of a soldier, out of place in the desert and bewildered by the sights around him. That morning, however, he found a Russian automatic rifle and carried it proudly around with him, clinging to this new status symbol and swaying under its unaccustomed weight. He was still carrying his gun when he went a bit out of the camp to relieve himself. Suddenly, in front of him, he saw an Egyptian soldier clad only in underwear. Before Menahem could recover from the shock, the Egyptian threw himself on the ground, kissing Menahem's feet and begging for his life in all but unintelligible Arabic. Heaving with excitement, Menahem ordered him to get up and led him back into camp, pointing the rifle at the prisoner's back. The Egyptian, once he realized that his life was to be spared, stuck his tongue out and gestured to show that he was thirsty. Menahem gave him some water. The Egyptian swallowed avidly, then smiled and shouted: "*Ya'ish* (Long live) Dayan," "*Ya'ish* Eshkol"—adding a curse on Nasser for good measure.

This was the customary coin in which Egyptian prisoners paid for water and food. It did not mean a thing, as we well knew. Behind the smiles, one could occasionally discern a swift flash, a spark of hatred that could easily flare into murder and revenge. We knew this well, from bitter experience. To Menahem, however, this was a day of glory, and he told the story to all and sundry, proudly displaying the Russian rifle. Later he was shocked to learn from another soldier that his potent rifle lacked bullets.

Now the excitement has subsided. The men have already started grumbling. We grumble about the bad food and the weather; we grumble about the flies, which appear in the early morning out of nowhere, wage a ferocious war on us, then disappear mysteriously at nightfall. We curse the desert and its sandstorms, which cover us with dust and bring from afar the stench of dead bodies. We don't have enough fresh water and haven't had a shower for weeks. Moshiko says that Nasser has really won the war—by removing his army from this blasted desert and leaving us stuck here, in the wilderness.

We long to go back home, to return to our families and civilian life. And yet, some are afraid of this return to old routines. It will not be easy. We'll not soon forget the exhilaration, the glory, the enthusiasm, the fears, the hopes, the faces of the dead, the eyes of the wounded, the laughter of lost friends, the days in which our hearts beat as one.

While I write, the men are making an evening meal of their rations. As I watch them from my tent, I keep thinking: "Surely, this is the strangest of armies. Its face is that of our whole people. It is an army of individuals, but there is hardly any need for disciplinary action. It is an army which always wants to go back home but which can fight like lions if necessary. Surely, there have never been soldiers like these civilians."

Dr. Amnon Rubinstein: Sinai Diary; *N.Y. Times Magazine,* 2.7.67

Zahal must solve general problems which engage every army in the world, plus some others which arise when the army consists of men of the Jewish faith. On the eve of the war, Zahal's Chief Chaplain, Brigadier-General Rabbi Shlomo Goren, received hundreds of requests from religious servicemen for legal decisions raised by the emergency.

Question: Is it permitted to travel on the Sabbath during an alert?

Answer: Travel for security purposes, i.e., to safeguard people's lives, in a military or a civilian area, and taking measures to prevent any damage whatsoever to the above-mentioned by an enemy or infiltrators, is permitted on the Sabbath. In case of travel for security purposes permitted on Sabbath, no special effort should be made to assign it to a non-religious person, but, in the measure that security demands it, it should be done by anyone so ordered by the commanders in charge.

At the same time, a soldier who carries out a security task permitted on the Sabbath should not desecrate the Sabbath by performing other acts which are not essential for security. He should say the benediction over the wine, say grace and otherwise observe the Sabbath as it should be.

Question: Is it permitted to eat without first washing the hands when the quantity of water is limited and when on duty on the field or in time of emergency?

Answer: Referring to a law written in the Mishnah, we have reason to believe that our soldiers are exempt from washing hands, since our encampments are subject to relevant laws in the Mishnah.

Question: Is it permitted to go out for ambush by vehicle on the Sabbath?

Answer: Going out for ambush on Sabbath against infiltrators entering our borders, even though it is clear that their purpose may be robbery rather than murder, is regarded as action designed to save human lives, and is, therefore, permitted on the Sabbath according to Halacha. Soldiers who go out for ambush on Sabbath Eve while it is still daylight should sanctify the Sabbath before going out for the ambush, even before sunset, since it is permitted to sanctify the Sabbath when necessary, even in the afternoon, an hour and a quarter before sunset. They should also say the benediction over the wine or bread, before going out. If they could not do so before going for ambush, they should sanctify on their return, if it is still night and before dawn. And if they could not sanctify at night they should do it on the following day after prayer, at the Sabbath meal, and recite the Sabbath Eve kiddush, except "Vayechulu," which is not recited at day-time.

Question: Is there a legal duty to recite some prayer before battle and in time of war?

Answer: The Torah commands us to pray and beseech God before going out to battle, though there is no definite prayer for this occasion.

It is possible to compose a special text of prayer which will express the emotions of the heart, the purpose of the war, and the belief in God's salvation for His people and land.

Question: Is there any obligation to blow trumpets before a battle?

Answer: We find in the Torah a special version of prayer for times of war; to blow, to shout, to cry out to the heavens by trumpets, which replaces spoken prayers, as mentioned in the Torah, the Book of Numbers, Chapter 10, Verse 9:

"And when ye shall carry on war from your land against the foe who oppresses you, ye shall blow trumpets and ye shall be remembered by the Lord your God, and ye shall be delivered from your enemies."

Chief Chaplain Rabbi Shlomo Goren: Wartime Regulations

Although call-up of reservists was over, many still remained on the home front. These men refused to contemplate the unattractive prospect of staying at home, at a time when Israel's forces were arrayed along the borders.

Ladies and gentlemen, tension is running high. Are the shelters in order? Have you prepared food? War may break out any moment now, a civil war between those who have been called up and those who haven't been.

In a democratic country, you see, there should not be partial mobilization. This is a social injustice which arbitrarily differentiates between citizens of the same weight, age, height and I.Q., between the virile male and the has-been.

In the course of one week, the country was divided into a superior breed and an embittered inferior breed. The hatred seething between the two camps can be dangerous. The situation can't be allowed to go on like this. A decision must be taken immediately.

I was happy to hear that the men left behind at home, thirty-year-olds turned into have-beens, are seriously organizing themselves.

They have set up defense lines against the attacks of children on the street, neighbors, wives, acquaintances, mistresses, business partners and friends, who spring on them a poison-shell like, "Not called up yet, eh?" or "What, you still here?"

One protective measure of proven effectiveness is to hide at home. I know 500 young men who haven't left their homes for a week. Why, do you think, is everything deserted—the streets, the theaters, the discotheques? Because of those who have been called up? No. Because of those who haven't been called up.

But how long can you hide at home, without sunlight, without friends, without even a hamburger. And this leads us to the important chapter on "How to Stop an Attack Outdoors."

The best defensive system is the method of the "recruit on his way." A fellow toted an unwrapped parcel under his arm for a week. The parcel contained a khaki shirt and pants. He took it to the swimming pool, to the movies, to the café. No one asked questions.

A similar system is camouflage. That is, wearing a real khaki uniform to mislead the enemy.

A certain landscape architect is the father of the high-level strategy system. This system was born three days ago, when the architect went out for a walk, as usual, and a breath of fresh air at his café.

Suddenly he felt 50 pairs of perfectly cosmeticized eyes riveted on his stomach. The architect immediately turned on his defense mechanism, although no one had said a word. "If I'm still around, it means that the situation is not serious. Nothing is going to happen, believe me."

One of the more sophisticated systems is the Baby-sitter approach. The has-been says with an apologetic chuckle, "I got to keep the girls amused on the home front."

The Patriotic system: "What's the matter, haven't I done enough? Let these youngsters do their share. They were handed the State on a silver plate. At 14 I was in the War of Independence. I fought in Sinai and at the Syrian front. I am through with war. Excuse me a moment, please, I must call Colonel Yoske and ask him why they haven't called me up yet. Must have slipped his mind."

The IBM system: "Why? Because I changed my telephone number, that's why. As a matter of fact, I also changed my quarters, changed my surname into a Hebrew one, and they also have another secretary at the recruitment office. Everything is bedlam."

The Economic system: "The Tel-Aviv front needs me. I am the mainstay of the local economy. No improvised jobs in the Negev for me. I have never been unemployed. There always was a job for me."

High Policy system: "Why should I suffer the sand-storms in the Negev for nothing? There isn't going to be war, anyway. Just a drill. Nasser is a logical man, after all. Most of his army is in Yemen. He knows a confrontation with Zahal won't enhance his prestige. He hasn't forgotten the lesson of Sinai. And then, he's got enough economic problems in Egypt. Every year there are a million new mouths to feed. Why should he want war now?"

The Self-Deprecatory system: "What good will an old man like me be to Zahal? 35 next month. Look at me; am I the Army type? I would be just so much dead weight. I am an invalid, an unproductive element. Anything I touch falls to pieces. All thumbs. I'll be of more use to Zahal if they don't take me."

The Savior-of-the-Country system: "Well, really, do I look like a desk-bound type? I don't care about preparations, ordnance and things like that. This is for the youngsters. The commando troops are called at the very end, to save the country."

The most shattering defense system is the Surprise tactic: "Of course I haven't been called up yet. I must wait. I am in the booty brigade!"

Ziva Yariv: The Inferior Breed; *Yediot Aharonot,* 26.5.67

The Druses, an Arab community of a different (not Moslem) and secret faith, are scattered throughout Syria, Lebanon and Israel. For many centuries they suffered under harsh Moslem rule. Since the War of Independence, the Druse community in Israel has thrown in its fate with Israel's. Known for generations as fearless fighters, the Druses are the only Arab-speaking, non-Jewish group in Israel to be conscripted. When the crisis arose and Druses of call-up age had not yet been mobilized, the leaders of the community called to the Israeli authorities: "Take us into service, at once."

In the Galilean village of Yarcha, the Druses wait in the shade of the stone houses for the call to arms. Radios are on at full blast. The Druse Member of the Knesset, Sheikh Djaber Mu'adi, declared that the Druse community would turn out in full force to serve in Zahal. In a call to the Druse citizens to display loyalty to the State, the sheikh from Yarcha wished Zahal victory. After his speech his followers from all parts of the Galilee came to him so that they could shake hands with him and to express their preparedness to join in the campaign.

The broad-shouldered Druse sheikh was pleased: "The Druses were very happy with my speech. Many people rang me up to tell me that they haven't heard such strong words for a long time. The Druse community is strong and ready. Only the Arab members of the Knesset left the hall of the Knesset when I spoke. They still greet me, but their looks belie it."

The only one who came to shake his hand was the Arab Member of the Knesset from Nazareth, Sa'if a-din al-Zuabi. "This is my way," he told the Druse sheikh, "I am not changing it and I don't care if I have opposition. I am sticking with the Jews to the end."

Sheikh Djaber Mu'adi was quick to ask the Government "that the Druse citizens be given arms. We are ready."

"I am a little surprised at Nasser. If he wants leadership over all the Arabs, this doesn't matter to us. But if he wants to isolate the State of Israel, this is an evil intention. It is a sign that he wants war—there is no other meaning. If there will be war, too bad for him. It won't take much time before we'll be in Cairo. But our soldiers—they're soldiers; our tank corps are tank corps; and our officers—they're officers. And on their side—they're only ready over the radio.

"The Russians can prepare a lot of arms for them. That's good for us. Anyway, everything will come to Israel. No matter what, the world can be told that we, the Druses, are ready, ready to give our lives for Israel, for our country."

The chime clock sounded faintly in Sheikh Djaber Mu'adi's room. The dignitaries of the community sit along the gigantic mirrors, set in their carved wood frames, and quietly discuss the situation. The "War Council" of the white bearded elders, their turbans are white, with a red crown at the top. They are experienced in war; they have no doubt as to which side they are with in these fateful moments.

Slipping bead after bead of the *Masbaha,* the amber string of beads through their fingers, the elders of the tribe talk it over. They have wonderful patience and unlimited faith in Israel's ability to overcome her problems.

Sheikh Djaber Mu'adi sums up and the elders nod their heads: "Our blood is red like the blood of the Jews. Our hearts beat like theirs and our lives are dedicated to your State because it is also our native land."

Zvi Elgat: The Druses Wait for Orders; *Ma'ariv,* 26.5.67

Hundreds of Israeli newsmen, as well as foreign correspondents from abroad, were keyed up for the advent of the imminent war—which nevertheless took its time in arriving. The only alternative for the gentlemen of the press was to buttonhole the recruits and subject them to interviews. The recruits were also on edge because of the seemingly interminable waiting, but they were grateful that they didn't have to experience the tension gripping the home front.

"When I heard that the situation was getting serious, I cut my vacation short and returned to the unit. I threw my things into the knapsack, and left home in a hurry, to ease the goodbyes. Now here I am, awaiting orders."

Dan Amit, the reservist, was all confidence and optimism, even though the circumstances didn't warrant it. The rumbling of tanks could be heard in the distance; a kind of rattling of chains, dull thuds and the creaking of straining steel. The smell of war was in the air—and here he sat opposite me with his green eyes and rugged face and smiled, completely self-confident.

Yesterday he was working as a postal clerk in Beer-Sheba; today he is a combat soldier. 39 years old, and he is still a combat soldier. His face is gray with dust, and lack of sleep rings his green eyes with dark circles. But to me he does not look tired, in spite of the outer signs of fatigue. He acts like a man who has just emerged from the shower, fresh and energetic. The broad-rimmed khaki hat sits on his head with easy nonchalance, its strap dangling behind his ear.

He is not a big man, but when he puts on his uniform he exudes a kind of strength. His face is tanned, his hair iron-gray and his lips are pressed into a thin line, zipper-tight.

"How did you get used to the new situation?"

"When I heard that the party is starting, I was on vacation. I canceled all vacation plans and left for the unit. 'Why did you come? Go home. We'll call you,' they said. They called me that evening, and I was ready. I had already packed my knapsack with the shaving gear and a change of clothes; I now kissed my wife, Irith (11) and Eiyal (9), and left quickly. I said goodbye to the new car too. I bought it and didn't even have the opportunity to drive it."

"Did the children cry?"

"My elder daughter had seen me leaving for reserve duty before. She took it now like the other times. She doesn't realize yet that this time it's slightly different. The younger son didn't understand very clearly what's going on. He somehow got it into his head that I've gone to find a turtle for him. When I was already at the door, he called out: 'Daddy, when you come back, bring the turtle.'" Dan Amit chuckles. "So now I must bring back a turtle."

"Is this the only thing that worries you?"

"What is there to worry about? I wasn't worried when I was wounded, in one of the border incidents before the Sinai Campaign. I took the worst then. What else is there to worry about? When I am with the boys, I never worry!"

"What happened in that incident?"

"I was doing reserve duty, and was with a unit patrolling the border along the Gaza Strip. Suddenly, an Egyptian patrol opened heavy fire on us. A bullet got me in the leg, and I was left in the field, all alone, for three hours. It was no picnic, I can tell you, but I wasn't afraid. I could see the boys, 200 meters away, on the hillside. They couldn't come close to me, because of the heavy fire that was being poured on us. So I lay there, in the open field, with bullets of all sorts whistling over my head. I remember thinking that if it weren't for the danger and if that wounded foot of mine weren't giving me trouble, I would have found the whole thing entertaining . . ."

"And the outcome?"

"Very simple. After three hours our half-tracks managed to get to me and rescue me."

"And the leg?"

"It was not too pleasant, but we made it. They wanted to downgrade my health-rating and transfer me to a service unit."

"Well?"

"You think I am out of my mind? Leave the boys just because of some slug in the foot? I refused!"

"Are you that much attached to the unit?"

"And how! You should have been at the reunion this week. All the boys were there. That was really something! You know how it is: 'Hi! What's new? How's life treating you? How's business? The wife? The kids?'—all the routine questions. And then we get down to gossip: who got divorced, who got married, who got rich and who got poor. And then, the stories around the fire, reminiscences and jokes and laughter, and all of a sudden you may curse and shout at the top of your voice all the profanity you wouldn't think of uttering at the office. Well, that's that. A man's world. Once in a while, it's wonderful."

Dan Amit fell into a reverie. Then he woke up with a start, like a man caught at some offense.

"Just one moment, though. Don't misunderstand me. I am not an adventurer nor anything like that. On the contrary, I like peace and quiet. I am the type who likes to sit in his slippers, listen to the radio and play with the children, or take a walk in the country. But I also like the army; it's because of the army that I am able to do all that, in peacetime. It may sound like 'Zionism,' like exaggerated patriotism. Still, this is the way I see it. For me, the mobilization order is like a reminder of an old debt. And this is a debt I pay willingly, because I consider it a privilege. If I'm still a combat soldier, it means I'm O.K.

"Of course, there's a difference. In the Independence War I was an 18-year-old bachelor, without a family, without any worries. In the Sinai Campaign I was married and the father of a baby. Now I am the head of a family: a wife and two kids. This changes your outlook a little, you know.

"In a certain way, perhaps I do feel a greater burden of responsibility than before, because of the knowledge of what I have to lose and whom to take care of. But all this is offset by the feeling that in time of trouble, I have someone whom to protect. You might say, perhaps, that I grew more serious than before, but not, by any means, more fearful."

"Do you hate Nasser?"

"I don't hate anybody. There are people I like better and there are people I like less, but I don't hate anybody. Of course I would prefer to live in decent neighborly fashion with them. But in the present situation, when he keeps uttering those threats of his, I would hardly say that I'm crazy about him. You can't choose your parents, nor your brothers, as you know. In our case, I think we can't choose our neighbors either. You have to make the best of what you have, and act according to circumstances. There's a French saying about a beautiful thorny plant, delightful to look at but hard to touch, because it's prickly. That's Zahal, all over. Nasser has many virtues as a politician, but he also suffers from a serious shortcoming—a weak memory. The fact is that he has forgotten that saying."

"Were you ever in close contact with Egyptian soldiers?"

"Sure! During the Sinai Campaign."

"What did you think of them?"

"The Egyptians are strong only in numbers. They also have a

reputation for being noisy. It reminds me of the man who was walking in the dark and singing at the top of his voice, to drive away his fear. The same is true of Cairo Radio. I know, from my experience in previous battles with the Egyptian Army, that their ordinary soldier is not too keen on war. He doesn't even hate us so terribly, and generally speaking, he doesn't understand why his leaders send him here to die. The Egyptian soldier, like any other soldier, wants to live in his own country. That's why he isn't trying so hard in Yemen either, in my opinion."

"What about the Palestinian refugees?"

"Well, they certainly hate us. But we remember them from the time preceding the War of Independence. We can assume they haven't changed much. Their wild rabble always runs for dear life when faced with real strength. Of course it's very dangerous having them right on the border now, but—it may yet turn out for the best. If I were in their shoes. I would keep shouting *'Abu-Ali'*—make a lot of noise, that is—but I wouldn't budge . . ."

Dan Amit does not strike any poses. No political agent has brainwashed him. He expresses his thoughts with convincing frankness and exudes self-confidence. I thought that perhaps I should ask for a transfer to his unit. In that burning heat, in some remote place of the country, in the noise of barracks full of the smell of sweat, the smoke of cigarettes and the fumes of fuel; in the midst of prewar preparations, surrounded by quartermasters bustling about and supply trucks raising clouds of dust; when no one knows what and when and where and why and how—he is not worried by anything!

"Come now," I said. "Does nothing really worry you? Nothing at all?"

"You want the truth?" he asked in a feeble voice, as if he was breaking down under the interrogation. "The truth it, I am terribly worried about this situation. A friend of mine went abroad two weeks ago. I promised I would water his flower garden. Do you think they'll keep until I come back? What's going to happen? Who is going to water the flowers?"

Uri Porat: I'm a Combat Soldier; *Yediot Aharonot*, 26.5.67

A major problem, during the long days of waiting, was the maintenance of contact between recruit and family. Army mail was slow; opportunities of getting to a phone were rare. The chief communication channels were the newspapers, which were delivered regularly to the encampments. Entire pages in the dailies were devoted to two-way regards. Behind each message was its own unique story.

To Joseph, Menashe, Gabriel, Michael and Raphael Boshri and brothers-in-law Alexander and Joseph—from father and the family.

*

To Zvi Hai—You have a son. Lily and the baby are well.

*

To Menahem Shitreet—Take care of yourself. From your loving wife and family.

*

To Makhlouf and Nissim Avitan—The family hopes you will come back safely. From father and particularly from Ayal and Haim.

*

To Geddi and Danny Rosenstadt—The baby is being given the name Yaron Immanuel. Mother leaves hospital at the end of the week. From Bracha and Micky and the Rosenstadt, Gansel and Hagis families.

*

To Gideon David—Contact your partner. Urgent. Isaac David.

*

To Avshalom Rassabi—Edith's operation has been deferred for a week. Don't worry. Your loving wife Aliza.

*

To Zohar Lakovsky—A son has been born to you. Everything in order at home.

*

To Ephraim Megrakar—Hope you will reach hospital to see the son born to you. From Ruhama.

*

To Oded and Avigdor Sofer—The children have already recovered. From David.

*

To Joseph Biton—Have not yet sold the apartment but have already arranged with the painter. Your son feels well. From your wife Miriam.

Greetings to Soldiers; *Various Papers*

Weapons were "at ease" during the days of preparedness, but the onslaught of gift parcels, candies and cakes went on unabated. The servicemen were bombarded with a bewildering assortment of garments (which they couldn't wear), toiletries (which they couldn't use), foodstuffs and sweets of all kinds (terrible on the uniforms). Up to the neck and gasping, they cried: "Enough, enough!"

The armor commanders are very busy indeed. That is natural. They hardly manage to get home. They are not the only ones, but the wives of the armor commanders have united to establish contact and display their enthusiasm for their husbands and the armor troops. In a certain southern city 10 wives of armor commanders got together and baked 100 cakes, which they sent to their husbands and the soldiers under their command.

The unit commander is holding a meeting. The door is closed and the discussions are very grave indeed. Maximum concentration. All of a sudden the door opens and a corporal belonging to the unit enters carrying a parcel in cardboard. The commander's face grows stern. He does not like being bothered about trifles or things that are not directly connected with the matter under discussion.

"What's that, corporal?" he asks.

"A cake," says the corporal.

"What?!!" roars the commander in a blaze. "Is Roval sending cakes already?"

"A cake from your wife," says the corporal.

The package is opened and out of it emerges a huge apricot cake.

The commander grins. So do the other commanders. Ah! Wives, children, family are preserved in the heart all the time, a precious treasure. But the perils of war, the preparations for victory, drove their dear ones even deeper into hiding there. And lo and behold! The wives have remembered and openly expressed their love of their menfolk and their trust in them.

The commander's face brightens. A smile splits it in two. He bangs his two fists on the map-covered table. "Lads!" he shouts. "A cake! Who wants cake?"

The commander cuts it up. Each receives a slice with an apricot perched on it. They eat the cake and enjoy it. Silently. The family—the thing which together with the Homeland is the reason for all the preparations, all the readiness and will to fight—fills the distant room which is so constantly surrounded by whirling pillars of dust.

Then they laugh, slap one another on the back and praise their womenfolk. The corporal leaves with a cardboard plate on which are slices of cake sent to the soldiers of the unit. Out in the dust and sand the tousled-headed soldiers in full equipment stand with festive slices of cake in their hands.

In this way the hundred cakes make their way to the unit. Under the camouflage net of the tent they eat strawberry cake with a pink cream. In the shadow beside the half-track they eat chocolate cake. The gunner of the Centurion licks the cream of the almond cake off his fingers.

The cakes of the tank commanders are only part of the expression of the link and the love between the rear and the army in front. Day after day, by direct ways, indirectly, by messengers, the soldiers receive gifts from home, clean underwear, razor blades, cigarettes, sweets, drinks and cakes.

And one of the commanders remarks: "When a tank crew sets out to fight and it's equipped not only with marksmen and ammunition, but with fresh cakes from home as well—then there's nothing in the world that can stop it."

Shabtai Tevet: Wives of the Commanders; *Army Press Release,* 31.5.67

Military regulations provide that the place where a specific soldier is to be found must be kept secret, even from the family. Nevertheless, despite the secrecy, the encampments scattered throughout the country suddenly became besieged by parents, wives, children, brothers and sisters who wanted to know whether Uzi, Danny, Uri or Benny were stationed there. On the Sabbath, when the home front went forth to visit the encampments, the entire country seemed to be arrayed not for war but for a gigantic national picnic.

At first a solitary car appeared. The father, bald and heavy-set; the mother, bright-eyed and eager. "Do you know Amos?" they asked the soldier at the entrance.

"You his father?" the soldier asked. "All right, drive straight ahead to that big tree. You'll find him there."

The car turned and drove along the hard dirt road to the open field where the army unit, called up on the previous night, had set up its encampment.

Later came a motor scooter, driven by a helmeted girl. "I am looking for Yoram; he's a captain," she said. The soldier's eyes dropped to her wedding ring. "I'm his wife," she confirmed. "All right," returned the soldier, not unaware of her charms. "Drive on to the tree and inquire there."

Hardly had the captain's wife moved on when another car appeared. A couple and two children. "We're looking for Ya'acov, Sergeant Ya'acov."

The soldier snorted. "What's going on here, reunification of families?" He relented with a smile. "O.K. Drive to that tree over there and ask again."

Civilian vehicles kept on arriving in a thin but endless stream. The news had made the rounds of the homes: The unit's staging grounds are close to the city, right by the highway. Worried mothers and wives rushed to make up parcels of sandwiches and goodies, of a sweater left behind and another pair of socks, just in case. None came empty-handed. Some even went back home and returned with more—like the driver of the pick-up truck who drove to a nearby settlement and returned with cases of fruit juice, or the meat market man who came with a heap of broiled chickens.

At night the parking field turned into a campfire site. Servicemen and their families sat around the dozen bonfires. All the refreshments had been gathered into a common pool, and now women and girls moved in the crowd, passing around pieces of chicken, cake, oranges, apples. The mood grew lighter, happier.

"Shmulik, bring out the accordion."

A thin soldier with a huge accordion materialized out of the darkness. Two or three opening chords, and the songs began to rise into the air. Bottles of brandy passed from hand to hand. "Really, Mama, what's going on? Since when have you become a brandy drinker?" Mama was not fazed. "It's *lehayyim,* for everybody's safe return."

The night wore on. More and more families joined the throng, and many a child could be seen perched on his soldier-father's lap.

Close to midnight an order came to bring the party to a close. The long line of cars began leaving the field, accompanied by waving of farewell from the servicemen.

On the very next morning, the meat market man went to his place, loaded a crate with meat and sausages and sped off to the staging ground; the boys should have something good to eat until their kitchen was set up. To his amazement he found that the tents of yesterday had disappeared, as though they had never existed. Only the ashes of the bonfires and the empty cartons and bottles remained, the remnants from the good time of the preceding night.

M. Savar: The Great Campfire; *Ma'ariv,* 29.5.67

Chapter Three

The Fifth of June

WHEN THE FIRST AIR-RAID WARNING SOUNDED, AT 7:55 A.M. ON June 5, most of the people (those who had not been called up) were at their places of work or on the way there. School children were sliding into their seats and housewives were putting their establishments in order. Despite the three long weeks of waiting, the first reaction was rather bland; just a test, perhaps. Or maybe some fool had pushed the wrong button. Only a few proceeded immediately to the shelters, as a matter of form. It was only some 20 minutes later, when the advertisements on the "Kol Yisrael" second band were interrupted and the announcer read the official communique about the outbreak of war, did Israel's citizenry learn that the hour had come.

The spokesman for Zahal made the following announcement:

From the morning heavy battles are taking place in the southern area, between Egyptian armored and air forces and Zahal forces which advanced to stop them. The Egyptian forces opened air and land attacks this morning. Egyptian armored forces advanced at dawn across the Negev and our forces went out to meet them. At the same time a large number of Egyptian air jets which were approaching the coast of our country were seen on radar screens. A similar effort was made in the Negev area. The Israel Air Force went out to meet the enemy and air battles were begun which are continuing at this minute.

Aharon Megged, a prominent Israeli author, reflecting sentiments of the nation, wrote on the outbreak of war:

Steadfast and confident, totally mobilized, the nation listened to the first thunder of artillery, the first air raid sirens.

The nation has been readied for this, now several weeks. It has been prepared for many years, ever since it laid the first foundation stones of Gedera, Rosh Pina, Degania and Tel-Hai.

The nation is united as never before in its history, and stronger than ever.

This is not a new situation. It is the old one, pitched to a higher key. The nation is therefore undismayed.

In 1920, a handful of settlers stood off a mob of Arab marauders. In 1929—in Hulda, Beer-Tuvia, Kfar Uria—hundreds stood up to thousands. In 1936 and 1939 we already numbered in the hundreds of thousands, but threatening us was an inflamed Arab population thrice our number. In the War of Independence, seven states and their armies were arrayed against our small but heroic units, but ours were armed with the deathless weapon of the indomitable spirit.

Today, the forces of the enemy are stronger, larger, better armed. We, too, are at least by that much stronger. As they were unable to best us then, so will they not do it now.

This is as clear as this soil is solid: Much blood will be shed and much destruction will take place, but it is impossible to vanquish a fighting nation, bound to its land and home, to the birthplace of its heritage, its sole haven on the face of the earth.

Our armed forces will be accompanied not only by armor, aircraft, artillery and seapower, but also by the spirit of this ancient land, by the tongue of the Book to which it gave birth, by the memory of the seers whose prophecies this Book has recorded, the heroes who died for it, the legends, the songs, the love for what has been achieved here in the past 70 years, with sweat and blood, with noble spirit, inspired by the best in human aspirations, and striving toward labor and peace.

With our armed forces will go the love of this people, ingathered from many dispersions, a people with the impress of generations-long suffering on its countenance and the wounds of the latest holocaust still raw in its flesh, a people whose remnant found its way here, seeking peace and rest.

With our forces will go everything that we hold dear, everything which we have drawn from the wealth of this soil—the rocks, the books, the trees, the children, the sagas, the legends.

All these are possessed of great power, stronger than the hatred of the foe, than its vengeful drive, its savagery.

Aware of the absolute righteousness of our cause, and aware of them who come to throttle us, to trap us in their deadly snare, who threaten us day and night with annihilation and who now move to make good their threat, we now have no alternative but to rise against this foe, to shake him off our body and to deal him a blow from which he will never recover, deal it with all the force of our will to survive.

Hence the steadfastness. Hence the confidence.

Aharon Megged: Steadfast and Confident; *Lamerhav*, 6.6.67

The very last thing this soldier did before going out to battle was to write to his mother.

This letter was written on that Monday, in the early hours of the morning. During the war and after it the mother held on to her youngest son's letter as to a good luck charm. She was left alone at home and at work. Her elder son had been mobilized and her husband had also gone to war.

The three of them returned home safely. It is thanks to the letter—"good luck charm," said the mother.

Monday, 5/6/67

Dear Mother:

I can imagine your situation. I, too, listen to the news over the radio. For the time being I am still stationed at a pine-grove somewhere in the center of the country. Dear mother, be steadfast and have faith in Zahal. We have strength and power and we shall not yield! I know you want father and me at home, but here I would like to explain something to you. Mother, this is our opportunity, mine and Yossi's (Dad has done enough) to decide our own fate and our right to live in this land. I shall act wholeheartedly but carefully and without meaningless ardor. Even though you never regarded me as being a serious person, at times I can be that too. I would not be willing at a time like this to sit at home while all the soldiers of our army are fulfilling their duty.

Meanwhile, there is nothing to worry about. We do nothing and wait. We are fed well, feel well and hope to be home soon and hold a homecoming party, which you will prepare.

In case I shall not be able to write in the near future, please do not worry. I shall be running short either of time or writing paper.

Again I repeat—don't worry. Everything will turn out fine, and we will be there to celebrate our victory.

Look after yourself. Give my regards to Yossi and Ruth. Tell them I can't write to them because I don't have writing paper. I hope that they won't be angry with me.

Your loving son,
Asher

A Letter to Mother; *Al Hamishmar*, 26.6.67

Trained by experience, the border kibbutzim were prepared for long sessions underground. As prescribed, the children and their supervisors went down into the shelters, while their mothers went about doing the work assigned to them.

Today we went down with the children to the shelters. We had known that this moment would come and it came on a regular clear morning on the second day of the week. The children asked if this was practice or war. And we refused to believe that it was really war. "I want peace!" shouted one. "I want peace!"

Later the mail came. Letters from soldiers, newspapers. This morning nothing was more ancient than this morning's newspaper. Later we tried to convince them, the little ones, that they should sleep a little. But they only wanted to sing, to play, to yell, to eat. After each newscast they demanded that we tell them what had been said on the radio. When we hesitated they said: "Then at the time of the next newscast we'll yell so that you won't be able to listen."

We told them that the war had broken out and that it was far away from us, somewhere far away. But in the afternoon they heard, together with us, the sounds of the shelling in the neighboring kibbutz. At the same time we sang together their hit songs: "Kol Hakavod" (All Honor) and "Zrayim shel Mastik" (Chewing-gum Seeds), until the sound of cannon was silent, apparently because of the muses. When we arranged them carefully, each child in his corner on his wooden bunk, tier on tier, just like in 1956, suddenly our hearts constricted because we saw names written on the plates, names of our small children who, in the the days of Sinai, spent their time on these wooden bunks in this shelter. Omri, Nimrod, Nurit, Ofra—were written on the bunks. We settled the children, however, for their afternoon naps in the exact places where their brothers had lain in 1956 to the sound of shelling. But they did not want to sleep.

And we—we also could not. We already knew, we had heard what was going on and where it was going. And after the tension this was an excitement of happiness, of overflowing emotions which did not let us rest.

Carmela Lachish: I Want Peace!; *Al Hamishmar,* 6.6.67

The first hours of the war caused general confusion. The home front was rent with air-raid sirens, on the war front the well-oiled military machine moved forward, but no one actually knew what was happening. Every transistor was surrounded by avid listeners, but the hourly news broadcasts were maddeningly indefinite. At 10:30 *a.m. came the message from Major-General Moshe Dayan to the men of Zahal.*

Soldiers of the Israel Defense Forces: At this hour, we do not yet have accurate reports on the position in the battles which are taking place on the Southern Front. Our planes are engaging in heavy combat with the enemy planes and our land forces have gone out to silence the Egyptian artillery which is heavily bombarding our villages opposite the Gaza Strip, and to halt the Egyptian armored forces which are trying in the first stage to cut off the southern part of the Negev.

General Murtagi of Egypt, commander of the Arab forces in Sinai, has sent a radio message to his soldiers and told them that the eyes of the whole world are turned towards them to see the results of their holy war, and called upon them to conquer by strength of arms and the unity of their brotherhood the stolen land of Palestine.

Soldiers of the Israel Defense Forces: We do not aim at conquest. Our own aim is to frustrate the attempt of the Arab armies to conquer our country, and to sever and crush the ring of blockade around us. The Egyptians have enlisted the aid and have taken under their command the Syrian, Jordanian and Iraqi forces. They have also been joined by units from Kuwait and Algeria.

They are more numerous than we, but we shall beat them. We are a small people but a brave one, seeking peace but ready to fight for our life and our country. The home front will no doubt have to bear suffering, but the supreme effort will be demanded of you, the soldiers, of the fighters in the air, at sea and on land, of those in the trenches and in the border villages, and of the attackers in the armored columns.

Soldiers of Israel's Defense Forces, in you today we repose our hopes and our confidence.

Major-General Dayan's Broadcast to the Nation; 5.6.67

Most of the nation was optimistic, believing wholeheartedly that Zahal would in due course emerge victorious. But even the most sanguine did not dare dream that, within the span of a single week, the war would begin and end with a victory so overpowering and decisive—without cities lying in ruins, without thousands dead and myriads wounded. This kind of history doesn't repeat itself, said many to themselves, and it is impossible that we should repeat the achievement of the Sinai Campaign, and as swiftly. 16 *long hours passed before the first victory announcements were made public. During these hours the question was not "Will we win?" but "At what price victory?" Several weeks before the war, Moshe Dayan, then a member of the Knesset and prior to his appointment as Minister of Defense, wrote an article analyzing the factors behind Zahal's prowess and superiority and describing the stuff of which Jewish fighters are made. In view of the events that followed, the article points up the author's far-sightedness. It also answers the questions asked repeatedly by Israelis and foreigners: "What* is *the secret of Zahal's strength?"*

The State of Israel came into being in war. Its fighters, soldiers and civilians alike, routed the soldiers of the Arab armies which attacked from the north, east and south. After the State was established the clashes did not cease; in these, too, Israel had the upper hand.

What is the source of Israel's strength? Technical superiority? Organizational efficiency? Moral supremacy? (And what exactly is the meaning of "moral supremacy"?)

Exactly what is it that makes it possible for Israel today to overcome her enemies, as David overcame Goliath?

It might be well to begin with a few remarks concerning the nature of the struggle of David and Goliath. David was not the innocent, emotional type who charged into battle armed by his faith alone, willing to risk his life without first making a few relevant calculations. He was a shrewd and careful fighter, this David—not only the full-grown king who subdued his neighbors and expanded his country's borders, but also David the shepherd, the "youth ruddy and of a fair countenance." First he made a very careful inquiry as to what reward awaited the man who would best

Goliath. Then he tried on the conventional weapons—the brass helmet, the coat of mail, the sword—and rejected them, saying he had had no experience with them. Only then did he go into battle—carrying a staff, five small stones, and a sling.

Who knows what the outcome would have been had David gone forth to duel Goliath with a sword! By deciding in favor of stones, David did not retreat but, as a matter of fact, secured an advantage in weapons. Goliath did not have a bow, so that he could not hit David from a distance. David exploited this situation, and with his sling he sent a stone crashing into Goliath's forehead. In other words, David fought Goliath not with inferior but with superior weapons. His feat consisted not in the fact that he was a little man ready to go out and fight a powerful enemy, but in that he succeeded in finding a weapon which gave him, the weaker man, the advantage.

The Bible also tells us of David's spiritual qualities. To be sure, he declared that "God saves not with sword and spear, for the battle is the Lord's." But his faith did not express itself in reliance on miracles; he was also guided by faith in his own strength. David knew that one should not ignore the value of strength. He had grappled with the bear and the lion and had overcome them. He had behind him experience which told him that there is no such thing as a "lost war." There were, to be sure, fighters of little faith, and there were wrong ways of waging war; but whoever was ready to fight with all his might would find ways of overcoming the lion, the bear, and Goliath too.

The Bible does not tell us very much about Goliath. We are told only about his physique—he was a powerful giant. Still, it is possible to learn something about his character from the equipment he carried. His entire body was wrapped in armor: brass helmet, coat of mail, greaves of brass to protect his shins and knees, a shield borne before him by his armor-bearer. I don't know if we can deduce from this that Goliath lacked courage, but there is no doubt that he was very concerned about his body and did his best to shield it from harm.

This defense conception—a kind of walking Maginot Line—had a very ponderous outcome, literally speaking. Goliath's brass coat of mail weighed something like 125 pounds, and his spear had an iron head which weighed about 15 pounds. Add to this the brass helmet, the brass greaves, the spear, and the sword. Altogether Goliath carried something like 160 pounds of armor. A very impressive fortress indeed. But whether this was an efficient war machine is quite a different matter. In a defensive battle Goliath, in all his brass, might have won. But he certainly was not capable of maneuvering and moving briskly. (The Bible points out that David "hasted and ran . . . to meet the Philistine" while Goliath "arose, and came and drew nigh.") But perhaps Goliath didn't want to move. Perhaps it wasn't enough that the armor protected Goliath; Goliath also hid behind the armor, leaving it to the metal to do the fighting.

I have dwelt at some length on the different aspects of the Battle of Elah Vale not because I object to the symbolism which later generations have attached to it. On the contrary, there is nothing that symbolizes the Israeli fighters of our time better than the battle of David and Goliath. What needs to be stressed here is that David did not forego arms for spirit, and did not rely on the Lord God of Hosts alone to do battle for him, but rather sought and found a way of fighting which gave him a military advantage over Goliath. But this approach to combat hinges on one thing: only he who "has the spirit of God in him" can employ it. It is the fighting approach that makes for daring, fearless men.

Victory in war can be achieved only through military advantage, and moral superiority must find military-technical expression if it is to carry any weight in battle.

The team commanding the Israel Defense Forces today is the "third generation" since the establishment of the State. By this I mean the young commanders—the company commanders, the platoon commanders, the submarine crews and the combat pilots; they who lead their squads in actions on the other side of the border and they who lead the assaults on enemy positions. So many of them fall in action, and in their kitbags you find black roses rather than marshals' batons. The generation that preceded them led the Defense Forces units in the reprisal raids of 1954–56 and in the Sinai Campaign, and in the generation before that were the leaders in 1948, in the War of Liberation.

The period between generations in the Israel Defense Forces is about ten years, a time span in which most of the commanders are replaced. During this period the veterans overcome the law of gravity and rise up to the top, while the younger generation takes command of the fighting units.

But time isn't the only element separating these generations.

In the course of ten years political, technical and social changes take place, arms and equipment improve (especially in the air force), the enemy grows stronger, and, above all, society undergoes transformations. The young people entering the armed forces are a product of civilian society, and until they put on that uniform it is the air of the street—*esprit de rue*—that they breathe. The prevailing spirit today is different from that of 1956, just as Israel of the Sinai Campaign was no longer the old Palestinian Jewish community of 1948. This is not the place to discuss the influence of the improvements or changes in armament on the character of the armed forces. I will only speak of the correlation between society and the spirit of the armed forces—*esprit de corps*.

Despite the great changes which have taken place in the Israeli populace in the last 20 years, I think that the morale—the fighting spirit—of the young commanders in the armed forces today is not inferior to that of their predecessors, to the morale of the armed forces in Sinai or in the War of Liberation. On the contrary, it seems to me that today's commanders are better fighters than their predecessors were. In other words, the young men of 1948 were, to be sure, the products of a more idealistic age than the present one, and in the tests of day-to-day civilian life they proved themselves less materialistic than the youth of today—the "Espresso Generation." But this does not apply to the military sphere. For all their pursuit of comforts—cars, luxury apartments, higher salaries, and all that goes with it—a pursuit that is much more intense in this country today than it was in the 'forties, the number of commanders in the forefront and calling to their soldiers "Follow me" (they do it in an undertone; shouting is done only by top-sergeants on the parade ground), is greater today than it was in the Israel Defense Forces of 1948, and even of 1956.

The reason for this is that, over the years, there has crystallized in the Israel Defense Forces a strict and binding approach to the duties and responsibilities of a commander. It is an uncompromising military conception. An officer cadet may be from a kibbutz, or may have grown up in the home of a real estate speculator, but when he undertakes to be an officer in the Israel Defense Forces he knows—and accepts without reservations—that this means setting a personal example, and with his own body carrying out the battle mission together with and usually in the lead of his men.

The fighting spirit of the Israeli soldiers is the fruit of a tree rooted in and nourished by the various layers of Israel's renaissance going back more than a hundred years.

The educational approach of the Israel Defense Forces—the prescription of "shalts" and "shalt nots," the insistence that commanders fulfill their responsibilities—all this forged a fighting spirit, but this was not created out of nothing.

The "Return to Zion" of our time, in the broadest sense of the term, is almost by definition a fighting people's movement—a national-pioneering liberation movement, a movement of idealists whose members, whether they themselves came here or whether they are native-born of parents who had come here from the Exile, are *a priori* prepared to be a minority struggling for the attainment of its objective.

The pioneering spirit, the readiness to volunteer and to personally implement the aims of Zionism, were the educational basis of the renascent Jewish life in this country. Agricultural settlement, Jewish labor, Jewish self-defense, the Hagana, the Jewish Brigade in World War II—all of this came on a voluntary basis, against the background of a readiness to sacrifice one's private life in the cause of the revival of Jewish life in the homeland of the Jewish people.

Furthermore, there were activities of a civilian character which, in their nature and spirit, were in effect acts of "conquest." The stockade settlements and the settlements in the Negev which were established in the wake of the White Paper, which in effect banned Jewish settlement, constituted, politically speaking, a colonizing offensive; militarily speaking, they were battle outposts. More than a mere physical expression, i.e., setting up fortifications, getting equipment and arms, and training people—this development was shaped by the spirit of the settlers. They saw the fight to defend their land as no less a part of their mission than building up a farming economy and cultivating the soil.

And it was not merely a matter of psychological preparedness; repulsing Arab attacks was a part of the day-to-day life of the Jewish community here from its very first day. There was not a single part of the country where the Arabs did not strike out at the Jews, and every few years there were disturbances. (At first the Arab attacks were called "raids," and then they were called "disturbances"—the disturbances of 1921, the disturbances of 1929, the disturbances of 1936.) These attacks, however, not only did not discourage the Jews, but even when the defenders were forced to abandon their settlements, the attacks served to spur the development of Jewish strength. As Arab hostility grew, the determination of the Jews to fight for their rights also grew.

Now a fighting spirit needs practical channels of expression. The first *Shomrim* (Jewish guardsmen) and settlers learned their fighting theory from the Arab inhabitants. The farmers would get up at 3 o'clock in the morning to feed their cattle their mash of legumes. (Today, Palmyra, the dainty queen of the dairy at Kibbutz Sarid, who produces 12,000 litres of milk a year, doesn't get the care that plow-oxen received 60 years ago.) The Jewish guardsmen imitated their neighbors: they donned *keffiyes* on their heads, wrapped themselves in *abbayes,* and cultivated handlebar moustaches with a ferocious upsweep.

Even though the Jewish guardsmen were courageous and daring, they were far from achieving ascendancy over their foes. Among the Arab thieves and the Arab guardsmen there were also fearless boys, and the "technology" of the noble Arab steed, the *Abu-Hamseh* (rifle which took a magazine of five bullets), and their technical know-how—familiarity with the paths of Wadi Fijas—did not give the Jewish guardsmen any advantage over the Arabs.

The superiority of the Israeli fighter over the Arab did not begin to show till later, when the clashes took place in collective frameworks (defense of the Jewish community) and in military units, requiring a combination of intelligence, know-how, and high-quality fighting ability.

I do not believe that the main expression of the superiority of the Jewish soldiers in their encounters with the Arab soldiers was in "the few routing the many." First of all, the calculation is not that simple. We are accustomed to saying that in the War of Liberation, Israel defeated seven Arab states that attacked her. To the extent that one is counting states, this is correct.

Egypt, Syria, Iraq, Jordan, Lebanon, Saudi Arabia and Yemen declared a war of conquest against Israel. In the end they were forced to halt their campaign and to retreat. But if we consider not the number of states but the number of fighting units, then it is doubtful whether, in the last stages of the War of Liberation, the Arab forces arrayed against Israel enjoyed numerical superiority everywhere. The same applies to the Sinai Campaign. Here, too, a distinction must be made between the Egyptian troops on the Sinai front, who outnumbered the Israeli troops engaged in the campaign, and the number of troops who actually took part in engagements. (Of course, it may be argued that this shows the inferiority of the Arabs, in that they are incapable of putting in the field all the military might latent in a population of 50 million. But this argument does not alter the fact that, in the wars between the Israeli and the Arab armies, the Arab soldiers did not always outnumber the Israelis.) The fighting ability of the Israel army and the fighting spirit of its soldiers are noteworthy in their own right and not only in comparison with those of the Arabs. The Arab states have certain basic faults and shortcomings which prevent their armies from going to war as they should. But the strength of the Israel army is not only relative. It is not a result of the weakness of the Arabs. The way Israeli soldiers volunteer for dangerous tasks, the eagerness of the young recruits to be assigned to the paratroops and to special units in order to do their full share in battle, the practice of commanders leading their units in charges—all of this puts the Israel Defense Forces on a high fighting level, without any relation whatsoever to the shortcomings of the Arab armies.

Furthermore, in most of the engagements that have taken place between Arab and Israeli forces since the War of Liberation, relative numbers were not a decisive factor. The air engagements were largely between individual pilots or between pairs. These engagements in the Sinai Campaign and since have all ended up with Israeli victories. In the reprisal actions, too, the test was not of numbers. The main problems confronting the Israeli units were the long trek on foot to the site of the engagement, the undetected approach to the enemy outpost, the swift and coordinated action during the charge, and the man-to-man battle inside the outposts and in the trenches. Success in these actions depended on courage, battle acumen, and readiness to risk life itself for one another. In these instances, merely increasing the number of the soldiers would not have made the difference. The test was one of quality and not of quantity.

The factors today guiding the actions of the Israel army are altogether different from what they were before the establishment of the State. Not only has the status (army instead of underground organizations), organization and equipment changed, but the conception as well; from the fundamental approach of defense, the Israel Defense Forces have adopted an increasingly offensive conception.

To be sure, the Israel army is still known officially as the "Defense Forces," but it is not a defense army. It is, in the positive sense of the term, an aggressive, hard-hitting army in tactical conception and, above all, in spirit. The last two "generations" have functioned exclusively in an aggressive framework. Never once did they array themselves for a defensive battle. The Sinai Campaign, the reprisal actions and the raids across the border were offensive actions plain and simple; educationally speaking, this was of crucial importance. A defensive battle can be fought even when morale is not particularly high, there being no choice left but to defend one's self, back to wall, defended by fortifications and by the premeditated, automatic use of the different arms. But an offensive—charging into the enemy's trenches, capturing his outposts and attacking his units—cannot be waged without a high fighting spirit. Moreover, in offensive fighting, especially of small units—platoons and companies—the commander must also be the leader, a locomotive pulling his men along with him.

This aggressive spirit applies not only to actions that have actually been carried out but also to the psychological preparedness of the Defense Forces. Israel's borders, and most of the areas beyond them, lack natural demarcations, such as wide rivers or tall mountains, and they are not even delineated by artificial fortifications. Even in wartime the Arab armies cannot create hermetic "ocean-to-ocean" front lines such as was done in Europe. The fact that the area is a relatively easy one to move across and is relatively short in fighting corps and fortifications, invites offensive tactics and provides scope for daring sweeps into enemy territory, flanking moves, and deep penetrations.

The clearest technical expression of the new aggressive conception which has replaced the defensive one is the absence of fortifications and fences along the country's borders. Even though Israel's policy—accepted by the army without reservations—is, politically speaking, fundamentally a defensive one, those responsible for the Israel Defense Forces have all through the years avoided committing themselves to the defensive. Their reaction to Arab challenges has always been to strike back, to hit the enemy's bases, to carry the war into Arab territory—certainly not to huddle behind defensive shelters. The Israeli soldier sees the concept of "war with the Arabs" as one of attack on the static positions of the units of an Arab army. The problems confronting the Israeli soldier are how to cross the Jordan River; how to traverse the Wilderness of Sinai; how to clear the mines defending the Arab outposts; how to breach the fence; how to silence the machine-gun positions. Fenced fortifications, trenches, and defensive fire are, generally speaking, the trade-mark of the Arab armies. The Israeli soldier thinks of himself in terms of charging, parachuting, movement of armored vehicles, and night patrols.

On the face of it, none of this is very important. It may be said that when war comes, reality will shatter all the theories as to who will do what in battle. But it just isn't so. These theories—the spirit by which an army lives, faith in one's strength, and unhesitating readiness to charge and conquer—decide the outcome of a war more than many important physical factors.

I have no fear that this will sound like so much highflown talk; for the truth is that our young men spend their youth and young adulthood (by this I mean something between the ages of 10 and 30) in a kind of state of intoxication, as though propelled by a powerful melody playing inside them. They are imbued with a powerful (what we seasoned adults call "unbalanced") faith in their strength, with a sense of mission, a mission that is not a duty but a privilege—the privilege of being the first, the trail-blazers, the defenders, the bearers of the plow and sword of the Jewish people. Above all, they are possessed with an unbridled love for their land—the Negev, Galilee, the Wilderness of Sinai, the "Red Rock" of Petra and Wadi Ze'elim in the Arava, the desiccating *hamsin,* the black, star-studded nights, with love for their unit comrades, for Tami and Anat waiting back home, for the lights of the settlements behind them as they cross the border.

The source of this feeling is variegated. It includes the greatness and the failures of Jewish history. It combines a reaction to the negative image of the Exile "wandering Jew" with pride in belonging to a people of great spiritual might, a martyred people adhering to its faith in spite of persecutions and Inquisitions. And above all, it has the living Bible and the State of Israel. In these two elements they possess what their parents did not—a sense of the normalcy, the sovereignty, the reality of their Israeli citizenship, and the direct link with the Bible, with the Israelites who lived on their land in Judaea and Samaria in the time of the Judges, and the House of David. For them the blighted Gilboa, the cool waters from the well of Bethlehem, the craggy playground of the mountain goats in the Wilderness of Ein Gedi are not legends of 3,000 years ago. They are the landscape of their lives, the ground under their feet. The paths along which David fled from Saul, and Samson's romantic road to

Timna are the paths they follow on reprisal raids and on patrols.

The paratroop commanders—Arik, Davidi, Mota (themselves of the flesh and bone of this generation)—have succeeded in capturing this spirit and shaping a fighting regimen to match. Retreat, regardless of how desperate the situation, never came into consideration. (The blood-drenched Battle of the Mitla Pass in the Sinai Campaign, which no other unit of the Israel Defense Forces was equipped to fight, is an example of this.) Killed and wounded men are never abandoned in the field, even when their removal involves danger and further losses. Wounded men who would scent that an action was coming up would walk out of their hospitals, and soldiers who had completed their national service would leave their civilian jobs in order to join the operation and "give the boys a hand." The terms "too risky," "outnumbered," or "impossible" have been stricken from the lexicon.

If I had to pick a prototype of the Israeli soldier out of all the fighting men I have known, I would pick Meir Har-Zion. Of course, he is not the "typical Israeli soldier." The typical is the of average, while Har-Zion is head and shoulders above them all; this is to say that he is a typical Israeli fighter, except that he does the job better than the rest. Far better. He is a superior scout, a bold charger, a shrewd fighter, stubborn, uncompromising. He is best portrayed not by adding superlatives to his name but by describing his actions, his forays across the border, the raid on Hebron on that snowy day, the capture of the Syrian positions in the Kinneret operation and the Battle of er-Raha'awe—the engagement in which he was seriously wounded.

What is special about Har-Zion is the quality found in some measure in all the members of his generation, the combination of the tough and daring soldier who even relishes battle, and the poetic soul; the red-bereted paratrooper and the farmer deriving satisfaction from his dull, exacting toil. This seeming paradox is actually an expression of identical aspirations, qualities nourished by the same spiritual source. The Har-Zion who lives with his wife and children in an isolated house near the Crusader fortress of Kaukab el-Hawa and finds purpose in breeding cattle is not the Mr. Hyde of some Dr. Jekyll fighting-man. The aspirations and motives which drive him to join the paratroops are the same which make him devote himself to back-breaking toil in the steep ravines of the Jordan Valley.

I assume that not only I, but anybody who has followed one of

Meir Har-Zion's operations considers him an outstanding fighter, a model battle leader. But I must confess that in picking him as the Israeli soldier *par excellence,* I have in mind not only his fighting image—tall, brawny, curly lock hanging down on his brow, shy smile covering up tension and fatigue. I vividly recall my first meeting with him, a meeting which had nothing to do with war.

I think it was in 1954. We were touring the Egyptian border near Be'erotayim. Lying around were corpses of some camels that had been shot in an engagement with Bedouins in a recent action. On one of the cadavers, a few hundred meters from us, was perched a large black bird. I wanted to take a shot at it. I knelt and raised my rifle. Before I could take aim, somebody pulled my arm and snapped at me: "What are you doing? That's an eagle!"

I turned around. Before me stood the leader of the patrol squad—Meir Har-Zion. I don't recall whether I was already Chief-of-Staff or still Chief of Operations. In any case, having a rifle pulled from my hands by a corporal was not really the accepted military tradition.

Har-Zion explained to me that only 30 braces of eagles were left in the country, and they had to be preserved from extinction. In the area there were two eagles that nested on a steep cliff, where foxes and wildcats could not get at the young eagles.

We rode up to the cliff. When we were near, we got out of the command car and stealthily started to make our way to the eagles' rock. But the nesting eagle noticed us and soared into the sky.

A long time has passed since that meeting. If I would now have to find that spot where the eagles were nesting, I wouldn't be able to do so. But one part of that scene has always remained etched in my memory—an eagle soaring up with heavy but graceful wing-beats, spiralling upward, circle and up, circle and up, and Har-Zion leaning on his rifle and following the eagle with his eyes. Not a glance of curiosity, not even a glance of wonderment, but a "professional," scrutinizing glance, seeking to take in every detail, in order to learn from it.

Moshe Dayan: The Fighters' Spirit. Courtesy of *Israel Magazine.*

Chapter Four

The Sky is Not the Limit

IN TWO HOURS AND FIFTY MINUTES THE EGYPTIAN AIR FORCE HAD been destroyed, in the skies, on airfield runways, in the Sinai Desert and along the Nile. It took the IAF another hour to deal a crushing blow to Syrian and Jordanian air strength. By the afternoon of June 5 complete air supremacy had been achieved; the skies, as airmen say, were clean.

The Six-Day War was, for the IAF (Israel Air Force), a baptism of fire. In the War of Independence, Israel had a few obsolete planes. During the Sinai Campaign, the French air force provided part of the umbrella for Israel's skies, while, at the same time, French and British planes were hammering Egypt itself. This time, the Israeli pilots had ample opportunity to prove their claim that "the best to the Air Force." Architect of the IAF, builder of its image, its commander and moving spirit for many years (until his appointment as Chief of Operations of the Zahal General Staff) is Brigadier-General Ezer Weizmann. "Ezer," nephew of the late Dr. Chaim Weizmann, first President of the State of Israel, is a unique individual: colorful, tough-talking, with extraordinary influence over those under his command. This interview, held several years ago, when General Weizmann was still commander of the IAF, points up the validity of his approach, his analyses, beliefs and foresight, as vindicated by the war in June of 1967.

Why beat around the bush when, with the Commander of the Air Force, Brigadier Ezer Weizmann, you can get right to the point? Everybody knows that.

I asked: What did the Air Force have in mind when it coined the slogan: "The best to the Air Force?"

Ezer Weizmann (speaking with supersonic speed): Let me give you a little introduction. Flying is an all-around challenge—intellectual, physical, psychological. I can't think of another occupation which calls for so much concentration plus precise, clear thinking as does flying. Every tiny move has to be planned, understood, and perfectly executed. A pilot is under constant physical and psychological pressure. He lives in a world of unusual dimensions: he breathes oxygen, wears special clothing and a special helmet, relies on a complex engine and complicated electronic and hydraulic systems, is at the mercy of various strange whims of the air. Do you think the boys go up there just in order to cruise around at 40,000 feet and show how clever they are? I think that a pilot today is no less a pioneer than they who once drained the swamps. *(slowly)* Until a few years ago the whole thing wasn't understood too well—partly through our own fault. In the early years of the State, many people were sure that the Israel Air Force was completely "Anglicized." They simply wouldn't believe that those pilots up there were Jewish boys. What can you do? That's the way they looked at it. Then another school of thought developed. These people were convinced that an Air Force man was a kind of space-extrovert, roaming around up there in the clouds, stunt-flying just for the fun of it, wing-loose and fancy-free. But when we said "The best to the Air Force," we meant to say to parents, to teachers, to our top-notch youth: Flying is a good thing. We've built up a good force, well-organized, professional, full of fighting spirit. Whoever wants to cast his lot with a good thing, to give the best that's in him—let him join us! Today we have fellows with 3,000 hours in the air, professionals who can compete with any air force in the world.

Question: What do you think of the Egyptian, Syrian and Iraqi air forces? On the one hand, hardly a week goes by that there isn't some news about their getting more Russian equipment, and on the other hand, we keep hearing how bad the Arab pilots are.

Weizmann (weighs every word): The hardest thing for an army in peacetime is to size up the enemy accurately. You're always caught between two extremes: the tendency to over-estimate the enemy's ability, and the sub-conscious inclination to down-grade him a bit. The problem is to arrive at a dispassionate, balanced estimate. The press, with all due respect, may be able to give a quantitative evaluation, but for objective reasons it can't give you a thorough military analysis. By this I mean *(counts on his fingers)* an assessment of the different classes of weapons and their potentials, organization, maintenance, the quality of the regular manpower, the level of the enemy's intelligence. So much for the intellectual. Now, to the point *(warms up to it):* I happen to be one of those Jews who believe wholeheartedly that we can stand up to the Arabs. Fact: two million people surrounded by 40 million hostile people—and they go right on building, developing. And this isn't just some insignificant enemy who's here today and gone tomorrow. *(emphatic)* It'a a real enemy! The fact is that the two million are superior. The moment I stop believing that, I'll quit the Air Force. Some of our own people question the quality of our next generation. *(aroused)* I don't believe that Israeli youth is undergoing a crisis! I just don't believe it *(tone like a sonic boom)!* Our young people are terrific! I know them—they come to me! Our boys and girls are among the best in the world. *(settles back in his rocker)* When I think of my generation, the generation that set up the State and all that went with it . . . Didn't we have shirkers, blowhards, swindlers, and just plain no-goodniks? *(relaxes)* Sometimes I have the feeling that in some respects, the generation of the '60's is better than we were. But let's get back to the Arabs. Let's begin with Egypt. It's true that they've managed to get a lot of good equipment in the last couple of years. They got the MIG-21, a good plane. There's no way of knowing absolutely in what ways it's better or worse than the Mirage, because they haven't met each other yet—*(between clenched teeth)* something our pilots are eagerly looking forward to check if they get the chance. In any case, the MIG-21 is in a class with the Mirage. My personal opinion is that the Mirage is a better plane. The Egyptian Air Force also has S.A.-2 ground-to-air missiles, which are like the Nike-Ajaxes but not at all like our Hawks. The Egyptians have expanded and improved their radar network, they've improved their bases, and they're training more pilots all the time. All in all, you can say that the Egyptian Air Force is better today than it was in 1956. But the Israeli Air Force of today is also a better one. I hope that much is clear. Now quantitatively the Egyptians are ahead of us—they've got more planes, more installations, more manpower. The big question is *(counts every word)* what all this adds up to qualitatively. Now note this down: I think that we're letting ourselves be taken in too much by the notion that in the end, technology will tip the scales in war. In other words, you've got an Ouragan, and he's got a MIG-21—it's all settled; he wins. I say that it's the human element that will clinch the outcome. The way the craft is operated, the way the ammunition is used, the way everything is maintained—all this is a product of a man's thinking, his personal qualities, his character;

all this is still a deciding factor, and will remain so for a long time to come, in actual fighting. And all the more so in the air. For example: I'm not at all sure that the Russian experts are a pure and unadulterated blessing for the Egyptians. What do they teach them? They teach them what they themselves learned in Russia. These tactics aren't always applicable to the Sinai wastes. Our biggest satisfaction—if it's proper to speak of destructive power in terms of positive creation—is that our organization, our fighting methods, our system of maintenance are mainly the product of thinking which is derived from the experience of our own Air Force. I'm one of the last products of the Royal Air Force still in service here. At the time a loud wail went up: What's going to happen to us when the RAF men leave the Air Force? What's going to happen? Nothing happened! Everything is going along fine! Now you may ask: So what are you learning in France? We're learning how to handle specific aircraft. Organization and operational concepts are our own brainchild.

Question: What do you think of the level of the Egyptian pilot?

Weizmann: (thinks hard) I don't want to say that the Egyptian pilot is some sort of an ineffectual, indolent, half-baked creature or anything like that. I'm sure they have some clever, intelligent and capable men. But this profession *(voice rises)* called flying might better be called an art. Flying is an art that calls for a high degree of self-discipline. And the Israeli pilot is made of such stuff that he will put up a better show in a dog-fight than the Egyptian. There's a tremendous difference between flying an airplane and operating it as a weapon. I'm sure that anybody of average intelligence can fly a Mirage; it's a pleasure to drive such an airplane *(goes through a few piloting motions)*. The question is how the pilot handles himself in a plane-to-plane battle in the air; whether he gets the maximum out of this weapon; whether he can make split-second, hairbreadth calculations at supersonic speed. Every touch of the lever has to be calculated. You're shooting away at a moving target. Even a Mirage has its limitations. *(takes off again, climbing steeply)* You've got to know how to fly the plane to its limits, to move the lever precisely, to work the radar, to calculate and decide on the nose: timing, range, target, weather—and to knock out the enemy! *(in full battle action)* You press! You squeeze! You've got no more juice left in you! But you're an Israel Air Force man, and you're far and away better than the Egyptian. That's a fact *(his fists lets the table know it)*. Of course,

I'm speaking of the average. Sure, it can happen on a particular day that the pilot is having his Day of Genius and ours is suffering his Day of Mediocrity. But on the average, we've got it all over them.

Question: What's the score in the air battles between us and the Egyptians since Sinai?

Weizmann: Since Sinai we've had 12 air encounters with the Egyptians. Two of their planes were downed and 12 badly damaged.

Question: What about ours?

Weizmann: Ours? What an insult! Zero. Except for a Super-Mystère that got a bullet in the tail and has long since recovered. The Egyptians have repeatedly made big noises about having knocked out an Israeli airplane, but they've never been able to produce the evidence. All they've been able to show is some reserve fuel tanks, which fighter planes sometimes jettison in order to lighten their load. Why did we beat them in 12 encounters? It's no accident. *(full speed ahead)* The Israeli pilot pushes to the end. The problem with our people is to tell them when to stop. Sometimes I feel like a soccer referee blowing the whistle to call "Offside." Here we have a very strict policy. There are no two ways about it. We decide very carefully whom to keep. In the past year I've grounded three pilots because I didn't think they were physically fit for combat flying. *(heartily)* We've got men here—thinking men, good men, intelligent; they like theater, music and all the rest of it—but the main thing is that we're training them for just one thing—it may sound a bit heroic: We're training them for victory! No, I'm not ashamed of the word: Victory! In our day-to-day life we spend time wondering whether there will be a showdown between us and the Egyptians, whether Nasser is a major or a minor enemy. Here we know one thing: If the time comes, we shall have to win. Our pilots are trained to operate by day and by night, in fog, in the dark, in fire and water. An Israel Air Force man knows: That's a MIG out there—knock it down! Wipe it out! Rip it to shreds! You're going up against an enemy—get on top of him and don't come back till you've smashed him to bits! Our boys love their equipment. A pilot who doesn't believe in his craft, for any reason, will stop flying it. *(with the cunning of an expert)* He'll find a thousand reasons for switching planes. In the Air Force we've never yet forced anyone to fly.

In the middle of the Air Force Commander's room is a long, brooding table. Large-scale maps; shiny model planes; the picture of a smiling boy standing beside a Sturman plane, and in his face you can see that he already knew then that one day he would be commanding the Air Force. Beside the Brigadier's black swivel chair is an intercom that keeps humming away mysteriously. It beeps. He pushes a switch. A voice says: "Are you alone, Chief?" He: "No, there's a newspaperman here, Raphael Bashan of *Ma'ariv.*" Laughter in the background. He says: "S.O.B.'s. Laughing at me, eh? What's up?" Voice: "This, that, and the other." Brigadier Weizmann: "We'll talk about it later." He pushes another switch. "Yosske, don't move from there, I'll be needing you soon." Beep. The Chief Engineer reports something about runways.

Ezer Weizmann is . . . Ezer Weizmann; a special kind of man, prototype of a certain clearly defined type of Israeli. Well-groomed moustache, close-cropped hair, candid, full of charm when called upon to exude it and aggressive when necessary, sharp-spoken, never hesitating to put things in no uncertain terms, sometimes in a vocabulary not used by polite society. And sometimes he comes up with biblical expressions like "I placed my soul in my palm," or "And should I perish, then perish I should." In military vernacular, he "lives his subject." Or rather, in his case, he flies it. When Ezer Weizmann speaks of the Air Force, it seems to you that in just a second he's going to go soaring through the window, grab the first Mirage, and off—wham!

He is a strict disciplinarian. He scorns ceremony and social amenities and makes no bones about it. After work, he is one of the boys—not as a commander doing a favor to his subordinates, but as an equal among equals; someone to whom the others look up and come with their problems. He is always bursting with energy, and there is a bit of boyish mischief in him, as well as daring and courage which he likes to cover up by pretending to be an extrovert. He belongs to that colorful class of persons around whom there develop sagas, anecdotes and jokes, true and apocryphal. And one suspects that Ezer Weizmann relishes every bit of it. The kind of stories they tell about him! For example, once upon a time he allegedly had the idea of setting up a company that would fly fresh flowers from this country to Europe. In order to prove that it was possible, he flew an old crate from London to the Zionist Congress in Basle. They say he's the only pilot in the Israel Air Force who wears glasses; once, while he was bombing a column of Egyptian armor in Sinai, his glasses steamed up and he had trouble finding his way back. He is also supposed to have a thing about ships. Why? Because he's never had the opportunity of attacking one. There's a standing order at headquarters: Whoever sights an enemy ship approaching the Israel coast is to notify Ezer immediately. He has developed a sharp Israel Air Force "lingo" which is a combination of tremendous self-confidence and merciless self-criticism. He will frequently ask his subordinates: "Well, and how's the best air force in the Middle East this morning?" Or he will say: "Please—don't fly less than 30,000 feet above my wing. You're liable to bump into my morale."

His hobbies: going up in his ancient Spitfire ("I took her up yesterday—it's heavenly!"); listening over and over again to recordings made of dog-fights, listening again and again to the refrain: "I see the enemy to starboard! I'm breaking to port! Approaching! I'm on top of him! Knocked him out! Going for Number Two!"

Question: Do you think a Pearl Harbor is possible in our region?

Weizmann: (unequivocally) No. And I'll tell you why: If you mean—here you are sitting with the Air Force Commander, and he's telling you all kinds of grand and glorious stories, and all of a sudden: Boom! Boom!—the Egyptians are here dropping bombs, and you thumb your nose at Ezer Weizmann and say: Well, they've fixed you!—No, that could never happen. Wars don't start that way any more. On the other hand, there have been many wars in which the armies went into battle unprepared. Had I gone to a strategist before the Sinai Campaign and told him we have such and such airplanes, and so many pilots with X flying hours, and so many tanks, and that the day after tomorrow we're going to attack the Egyptians—do you know what he would have said? He'd have said we're insane! I think that if Nasser decides to attack us it won't be just to bite off a piece of Eilat, but to annihilate us. And this means making preparations, and it means massing troops in Sinai. Whatever happens, if there's war *(decisive)* it'll have to be short. Each side will want a decision in a minimum of time. I think some people here have the wrong idea about the distances between us and them. From Gaza to Tel-Aviv it's —snap!—three minutes. Cairo to Tel-Aviv: 20 minutes. And the same holds the other way, of course. Here I want to go off course for a minute and point out that our persistent claim to the world that we need defensive weapons is 100 percent justified. An air attack on us is not a matter of conquest, but of "to be or not to be."

A beep on the intercom. Weizmann lifts the switch: "It's you, is it?

In a little while, O.K.?" Then to me: "He's a terrific boy. Chief of Operations. Married; two kids. We're all one big family; that's because we believe in what we're doing. We've always got to be on our toes; we always face new challenges, new objectives. And the spirit of comradeship is high. How do you test how a soldier is going to stand up in battle? Are you going to set up a little war for him? In the Air Force you find out soon enough; sending a man up in a plane means putting a man through what is pretty damn close to battle conditions. *(completely confident)* I have not the slightest doubt when I say to you that we've got the best boys in the country! *(emphatically)* I know every one of them—and when I say I *know* them, I mean I know them!"

Question: Are Air Force men attracted to civilian aeronautics?

Weizmann: (a study in disgust) That sort we regard as having been spun out by centrifugal force. We've got nothing against them—but we don't want any of their favors. Anybody who wants to leave—let him go to El Al, let him carry 100 passengers on the Lydda–US route, let him collect his 2,000 pounds a month, and may he have a long and happy life. But whoever wants excitement, new challenges, class Double-A-De-Luxe satisfaction, and—I'm not ashamed to say it—on top of it all also wants to be a pioneer, then he's welcome to the Air Force. Training one pilot costs us—costs you *(his finger completes the identification)* half a million. And if the fellow picks himself up and goes to the civilian market—well, if you call that logic, then it beats me what logic is!

Raphael Bashan: A Pilot is Born; *Ma'ariv*, 29.4.63

At 8:00 *a.m. on the day war broke out, as the IAF went into battle, IAF Commander Brigadier-General Mordecai Hod sent the following message to his units:*

"Urgent. From Air Force Commander 050800 to all fighting units. Members of the Israel Air Force:

"The impudent and malicious Egyptian foe has raised his hand to destroy us. The Air Force, clenched fist of Zahal, has its orders. We are taking off for battle. The third link in the chain of our struggle for independence and freedom, in the historic land of our birth, is about to be forged. The triple thread of 1948, 1956 and 1967 shall not be snapped. The spirit of Israel's warriors throughout the generations will be with us in battle—the immortal courage of Joshua bin-Nun's men, the stalwarts of David, the Maccabees, the valiant fighters in the War of Independence and the Sinai Campaign. This spirit will be our source of strength and inspiration as we engage the Egyptian foe, the threat to our security, our sovereignty and our future. In his smashing defeat we shall find peace and security for ourselves, for our children and for generations yet to come. Aloft, then! After the enemy! Smite him to oblivion and destroy his fangs! Scatter him through the desert, so that Israel may forever dwell secure in its land."

General Hod's Message to IAF Units; 5.6.67

IAF pilots fulfilled the orders of their Commander quite literally. Within the span of three hours they knocked out the air forces of Egypt, Syria and Jordan, and did not overlook Iraq. They achieved the first condition for victory—air supremacy. The accounts of the IAF's success, based as this success was on joint planning, years of training, excellent equipment, resourcefulness and first-rate ground crews are, nevertheless, the stories of individuals. As in the theater, many labored behind the scenes, but on the stage only the stars appeared. All attention was centered on the lonely heroes up in the sky—the pilots.

"You're going to meet the best pilots of the best squadron of the whole Middle East," the squadron commander, himself one of the best known pilots of the Air Force, told me, while the champagne bottles that stood lined up in a row on his desk bore witness to the number of enemy planes he had accounted for in dog-fights.

When I asked him why not the best squadron in the whole world, he replied with a smile that they're unassuming people.

It's Friday today, and to the visitor from outside everything seems quiet and relaxed, as if there had never been a war. Only the outcrop of red sirens on the roof of the headquarters building reminded me that this was where the best pilots of the whole Middle East took off on their raids, and that here, in this green oasis of peace cut up by grey tarmac runways, time is measured in minutes broken up into seconds and fractions of seconds.

Lieutenant Menahem caught his whole enormous bag within one day, the Wednesday of the war. That morning he had been called at 3:50—by mistake—and went on alert at 6:30, waiting for take off orders. That day, the main assignments were air-to-ground attacks to bomb enemy forces. At 6:30 he got his orders to take off in the direction of the Canal.

"When we approached the area, we were informed that there were

MIG's harassing our forces. We went down low to search for them. That was near Romani. While we were circling, Number One discovered four MIG-19's flying around below us. We came down on them. Number One stuck onto the tail of the last one and brought him down, then he took on the third and brought him down too. Then he made room for me. Meanwhile, the two others had discovered us and turned round to fight us. I had a short battle with them. At a given moment I was sitting on the tail of the last one and gave him a short burst, but missed. Apparently my sights had gone wrong. I continued chasing him until I was in a convenient position for shooting, fired without using the sights, and hit him with one of my bursts. We turned round and rolled over in honor of our victory.

"Then we waited for the next assignment.

"At noon I went on alert inside the plane. I sat around for two hours until I got orders to take off, again in the direction of the Canal. We were given advance information that IL-28's were attacking our forces, with MIG-21's giving cover. We raced to the Canal. When we came near the Canal Zone, I discovered an IL-28 flying over the sea in the direction of Israel. That made me mad. The cheek—not to fly to Sinai where the army was, but to Israel to bomb civilian targets. I told Number One, and we turned fast in his direction. I reached him first. He started shooting at me from a range of a thousand yards, with his rear cannon. The IL-28 has a crew of three. At first he shot without aiming, but then he improved and things became different. I gave him a short burst from far away to try and silence him, but I must have missed. I came closer. At 500 yards I opened up with a longer burst. His tail blew up, but he continued flying, turned to the beach, got stuck in the sand, and exploded. Immediately afterwards we set course for the Canal again, and one minute later Number One discovered the cover. You can put that "cover" in inverted commas. I think it was a formation of four. That is all we want, to meet enemy planes. Just let them come, and it will be all right. While turning in their direction, I saw one of the MIG's at a distance of one kilometer. Neither of us had the tactical advantage over the other. I shed my spare fuel tanks, turned in the direction of the MIG, and within 15 seconds I was sitting on his tail. I put him in my sights and gave a short burst at 250 yards. I saw the hit straightaway. The explosion was very strong. The plane broke up and the pieces fell all over the area."

Lt. Menahem has a long account to settle with the Arabs, though he is only 22 years old and one of our youngest Mirage pilots ("I took a short-cut to the Mirage. After one year and four months as a pilot I was already flying Mirages. Excellent plane"); 22 years ago, a few days before Menahem was born, his father, who was a member of the Watchmen's Association, was murdered at night by Arabs, in an orange grove not far from the base where the son he never knew is serving. Menahem is a fourth-generation Israeli and a graduate of the "Kfar Hayarok" Agricultural School. In this short war, the first time he came under fire, he settled part of his long account: he bombed airfields in Jordan and Syria, and ground targets in Sinai and again in Syria, and brought down three enemy planes in air fights.

Edith Zertal: Story of a Long Day; *Bamahane,* 5.7.67

★

He zoomed down from the heavens and came into the room.

"What's doing up there, Major Ron?"

"Hu-ha! Plenty!"

"And what's the latest?"

"Coming right up!"

I looked into the blue eyes of Flight Commander Ron for some reflection of the black smoke rising from hundreds of planes, in flames from Cairo to Damascus, from Amman to Iraq. I saw none. He had left it all behind, and his blue eyes reflected an effervescent flame within him.

But Ron is not altogether at peace with himself. You see it in the blond, unruly hair which seems to reject the crown of glory placed on his head by his feats of valor. His cheeks are flushed, and there is no mistaking the sincerity of his indignation.

"It's not right—definitely not right. We would be much closer to reality if we were to put aside the rainbow colors and see the gray shadows. Any praise that is due should go to every commander in the armored corps, the infantry, to every paratrooper and commando, no less than to the pilot. Say the word 'pilot,' and people think that he takes off from mid-air. Not at all. For the pilot, the sky begins on the ground, literally. His feats are the result of a complete organization—the ground crew, the plane itself, the firing power, the control center behind the radar. Not that I want to gloss over our own deeds, in destroying the enemy bases and shooting down their planes in aerial combat, but if we succeeded, in three hours, in knocking off the Egyptian air force, the largest among Arab air arms, it was also because of the many hours of racking work put into our aircraft by the ground crews. Let's agree with the truth—they are the ones for first honors."

"Very well; but later, when you take off and retract your landing gear and find yourself up there alone, what sets you apart as a sky soldier?"

"That fact that he is up there all alone is, I think, the outstanding difference. On the ground, a soldier can become detached from his unit, but he still makes contact with it. In a fighter plane you are definitely on your own. It's not only that you have to do everything yourself—plot your course, follow it, make all the tactical calculations, operate your set of weapons. You have to keep yourself at a high pitch, repeating over and over 'I got to be better, I got to be better!' Better than whom? Better than yourself and the pilot you think you are. When paratroopers jump together, this common act keeps the pitch up. The presence of others—even though they are your comrades—is a spur to which you respond. Up there, in a plane, you have to talk yourself into being the best in the business.

"For the last 24 hours I made many sorties; here, there—the day will come when all the details will be known—but a real surprise awaited us at Gardaka air base, south of Sharm-a-Sheikh. We swept low, dropped our bombs on the ground installations, and prepared to go back when we suddenly discovered four MIG's trying to latch themselves on to our tail. There we were—four Mirages with limited fire power and just about enough fuel to get us back home, against four well-armed and fueled MIG's above their own field. Well, the battle was at low altitude and lasted exactly two minutes. Three MIG's were shot down inside the base area, in plain sight of the hundreds of Egyptians on the base, and the fourth crashed while trying to land. I mention this as an example of this 'got to be better' psychology of ours, which makes us extremely intent on the successful execution of our task. The high degree of our pilots' personal identification with their assignments, plus their handling of their craft and weapons, produces the combination which gets positive results."

"Have you ever come across the definition of a pilot as one who represents the sum of his people's culture and the handling of the control stick?"

"No, I haven't, but I fully agree with it. A good pilot is not merely a mixture of skill, resourcefulness, discipline and good judgment, but also, even primarily, an outgrowth of the spiritual values and the cultural level which had nurtured him. Inside the fighter plane, all of your emotional forces are compressed into concentrating on your objective; everything else becomes secondary. The measure of this concentration indicates the true fiber of the pilot's inner being, and this is something which no two-year flying course or a mere passing of tests can influence."

"Do you therefore think that there is some connection between the traditional values of our people and the quality of our Air Force?"

"This I cannot tell exactly, but I do feel there is a connection between our inborn Jewish tradition of self-sacrifice and the readiness on the part of every soldier of ours to sacrifice his life, if need be. There is a connection between the resourcefulness, the fighting spirit and comradeship-in-arms demanded from every soldier and the tradition of mutual responsibility which distinguishes our Jewish people. These are ingredients common to both."

"And this, in your opinion, is what gives our Air Force its superiority over its enemies?"

"Let's look at it from the viewpoint of the character of our foes. I have now seen all of their airmen in action—the Egyptians, the Jordanians, the Syrians. I can tell you that, even though we already had the feeling that our performance level is better than theirs, we were still amazed when we found out how right we were. I couldn't believe it even when I saw it with my own eyes. For instance, the simplest rules of battle formation are apparently strange to them. You can actually see how the other pilot shies away from taking risks, even calculated ones; he doesn't press the attack, and even when he is in the position to let go a burst, he seems to hesitate just long enough to miss the mark when he does shoot. This kind of a pilot can't get very far. Small wonder that, whenever their pilots sensed that they did not have the fullest possible advantage, they simply turned tail and fled—only to find *us* on *their* tail.

"Up there you have no choice; you can't afford to be second best. You are either the first or the last. If you don't outlast him, you will be down below. Up there, either his MIG explodes and you are happy, or your Mirage blows up and he is happy. I can tell you that we have been quite happy during these past 24 hours. Mind you, we don't rejoice because their planes and pilots fell.

I don't feel any particular hatred toward the enemy pilots—that's not the word. There is no personal enmity here, as when two women pull each other's hair. But as long as he is my country's enemy, he is mine as well. We don't go after the man in the pilot's seat. We go after that unit in the aggressive array of armament bent on destroying us and everything we hold dear. It's this array that we want to put out of business."

"What do you think of this formidable foe who, when he could no longer put planes into the sky, fresh-baked a rumor that an American–British air umbrella was protecting Israel?"

"We know about it and, believe me, when I heard it I was ashamed for them and insulted for myself. Let me explain. No matter how much we wish the enemy to be weak and that we come out on top, we still expect him to show some fighting spirit. not just go through the motions and beat it back to his base. Even if what he is fighting for is wrong, you still expect him to believe in his cause, enough to put up a fight. After all, belief in the righteousness of your cause is the only thing that can possibly justify war. But when even this is lacking, when you realize that you are fighting not men but some panicked creatures, you feel let down, even though this fact does not change reality. I am ashamed to be involved with such a foe, and I regret even more every drop of blood that we have to shed in such a conflict.

"When I hear the incessant playing of military marches over Cairo Radio, I feel proud that we have no need for parades, trumpet flourishes and marching songs to stimulate us to go forward. Just look at the way our armor has been cutting through Sinai! I am sure we are doing better with songs about our brave fallen ones. In this respect I think that we, the native-born *sabras,* are very much Jews. Our generation has been raised on the stories of the Ten Martyred Sages who were put to death by Rome for spiritual insubordination, and of the others who gave their lives in sanctification of God's Name, of the heroes of Massada. These are stories of heroism, not only of death. I myself become more highly charged—and a better fighter for it—when I think of all that innocent Jewish blood that has been spilled over the centuries. When I climb up to Massada or hear these stories, my Jewish soul ignites. This is the spark which keeps our generations going. As I feel it, I know that I am a link in the chain of heroism which is not yet at its end. I feel that I serve not only Zahal but the entire people."

"Are these terms—link in generations, the spark—something which was generated by the events of the past few weeks, or do you feel that way all the time?"

"I have always felt that way, but only deep inside. Today, when emotions spill over, this, too, comes to the surface. Still, when I am up in that plane—and that's most of the time now—I don't think about these things at all—not the people of Israel, not the eternality of the people, only about the enemy whom I am to engage. Just as he is thinking about me. Both of us know for sure that the best man will win. The cause for which you are fighting may make you *stronger,* but the *better* fighter is the one who maintains better control of his plane, presses the button at exactly the right second, and has himself in hand all the way. This will decide the outcome.

"Up there I forget everything—even that I have a wife and children. Below, I am a husband and the father of two children, who were with me at the base until a few days ago. Yesterday, as I was on my way to the plane, someone handed me a blank postcard. I wrote to my wife: 'Winning as usual. Morale high as always. Be seeing you.' There is little more that we, the pilots, can write. Our families live our lives with us 24 hours a day. They bear with love, even with gladness, the burdensome life at the base, having the din of the planes constantly in their ears and raising children within that strict military setup. They deserve all the credit in the world. And if we pilots are up there, enjoying clean skies and flying past our own boundaries unchallenged, it is because of the understanding spirit of our wives at home—which is really our first take-off base."

Geula Cohen: Interview with Ron; *Ma'ariv,* 9.6.67

According to conservative estimates, on the very first day of the war, the air forces of Egypt, Jordan, Syria and Iraq lost 374 *planes. The IAF, on that day, lost* 19 *planes. Information reaching the public by evening of June* 5 *listed* 8 *pilots dead and the others missing. As it was learned later, "missing" meant capture by the enemy for some, brutal murder by the enemy for others, and marvelous rescue from deep enemy territory for the rest.*

The four Mystères thundered down the steaming black runway and took off, one by one, just clearing the treetops, into the blue skies over the base.

The pilots, white helmets and oxygen masks tight, kept their eyes on the leader plane. It led them down, leveled off close to the ground and set a steady course to the southwest, toward Egypt.

It was eight o'clock in the morning, June the 5th—clear and beautiful as the sea below—the morning which everyone had been expecting, with mounting tension, since May the 16th.

The task assigned to blue-eyed, muscular Major Jonathan, Flight Leader—one of many such assignments given out that morning—was destined to decide the outcome of the entire war. He was to take his quartet of Mystères deep into Egyptian territory, to bomb the Fa'id Air Base, near Great Bitter Lake west of the Suez Canal. This was the assignment for which he and his men had been preparing for years. But now, flying towards the Canal a few yards above the surface, none of them could predict what the real action would be like.

They flew in this formation for half an hour, without communicating, until suddenly the wide runways of the Fa'id Base were streaking beneath them, runways with MIG's and Sukhoys lined up, uncamouflaged, and giant hangars lining the fringe of the field.

"One goes in," called Major Jonathan into his microphone. That was the only instruction he had to give; the other pilots knew exactly what each of them had to do. One second later, streaking at a speed of 500 m.p.h., the Mystères came at the field again, dropping their bombs one after another. Five minutes later, the air base was a mass of fire and smoke.

By the time that Major Jonathan completed his three strafing passes, there was only one MIG left on the field. "I'll take him." he announced. He flew in quickly, got the MIG in his sights, waited a moment, then pressed the button on top of his steering column. The MIG exploded immediately.

All at once, as he was pulling up through the mushrooming smoke, the Mystère rocked violently. Smoke filled the cabin, and Major Jonathan heard the first cracklings of flame somewhere behind the cockpit.

"I've been hit," he called into the microphone. "Bailing out." Now that he had decided on the emergency action, he was no longer tense. He switched off the ignition and began a long glide east, past Bitter Lake. "Any minute now," he told his companions. "This plane looks like it's for the hereafter."

"Got you," came the voice of the second in command. "Just tell us when you go."

Major Jonathan decided that whatever advantage he would gain from a bit more gliding might turn out to be disastrous. Notifying the others, he drew his arms and legs together and pulled the ejection lever. He managed to take a last look at the instrument board: altitude—1,300 feet. As his parachute opened he looked up, just in time to see his Mystère, now an orange ball of fire, pile into a cloud, blackening it with its smoke. Forgetting his situation for the moment, Jonathan wished he had his camera with him. A moment later he landed on the crust of the salt marshes, several kilometers from the Canal—the first of the Israeli pilots to abandon his craft on that day.

Half an hour later, the bell rang in the Operations Room of the Super-Perlon helicopter base. The Flight Commander picked up the phone, and a moment later he had his first assignment of the war and the first of its kind in the history of the Israel Air Force. He was to get one his helicopters into Egypt, past the radar network and the anti-aircraft batteries, to find and pick up Major Jonathan and return with him to the air base, flying low past the same radar and artillery.

The Six-Day War was then just one hour old.

The rescue operation itself could not take place before dark, and the assignment was not given out until several hours after the helicopter base had received its instructions. Four men were to take the Super-Perlon into Egypt: Captains Danny and Amos, Sergeant-Major Shmuel Rahmani and Major Yizhar, M.D. The four had already made two sorties that morning, evacuating wounded from Rafiah and El-Arish, under heavy fire, to the hospital in Beer-Sheba. Now they were to fly some 400 miles, into enemy territory, to find one man somewhere in the western sector of the Sinai Peninsula.

Captains Danny and Amos plotted the course, calculating range, altitude and the amount of fuel they would need. They discussed every technical detail, but not a word was said about their chances of making it there and back. They checked the equipment aboard the helicopter—life belt for a possible water rescue, communication apparatus, canteens, small arms, knives and flashlights. Some time later they were joined by the other two men, and the four climbed into the Super-Perlon, checked the instruments and rose into the air.

Major Jonathan could have been worse off then he was.

He had touched earth a few minutes after 8:30 in the morning, quickly freed himself of the parachute straps and checked his surroundings. For the moment he was completely alone. He proceeded to burn his code book, then gathered his pistol, knife and flashlight into one compact bundle. He was debating whether or not to take his food rations along, when, suddenly, a large flock of goats appeared some 500 yards away, followed by its shepherd. Jonathan dropped to the ground and waited until man and beast had disappeared, then rose, discarded his safety belt and headed east, toward the knee-deep sand dunes. Half an hour later, feeling the first pangs of thirst, he reached for his canteen—and swore in disgust. He had left the canteen along with the life belt.

He had covered some 20 kilometers, when he remembered that, for his situation, the instructions were to use the daylight hours for rest and the darkness for travel. He found a spot behind a low clump of brush and tried to sleep, but this didn't come readily. He lay drenched with perspiration, torn between hope and doubt. He was sure that the IAF would make every effort to find him, but the chances for success did not appear to him too bright. "At least they'll do everything to find me," he kept muttering to himself. Then, exhausted, he fell asleep.

Jonathan rose toward dusk and headed north, toward the distant highway. Here he intended holding up the first vehicle for some water, one way or another. He was only a kilometer from the highway—he could see lights moving—when suddenly he felt a sharp pain in his ankles. This meant the end to his forward progress. A cool wind was whipping up from the northeast. Jonathan dug a hollow trench in the sand and lay down on his back, keeping his eyes on the sky above him.

It may have been that the Egyptians were still under heavy shock from the disaster to their air force that morning; at any rate, the Super-Perlon made it to the Canal without being challenged. The darkness below was so thick that the lights of the ships could hardly be discerned. Captain Danny, at the navigating controls, directed the helicopter toward the spot where Major Jonathan had bailed out. "We should have no trouble spotting him in the morning," he remarked to the others, but he knew that it wouldn't be so simple. The slightest miscalculation on his part in tracking Major Jonathan's movements would cut down the time available for the search. And although the search party had been lucky in evading enemy detection, there was no guarantee that this luck would hold out indefinitely.

At this point the Super-Perlon had to fly low, if it hoped to achieve its mission.

At 10:30 p.m., Major Jonathan was awakened by a harsh whirring sound in the area. His mind at once shook off the wisps of slumber. "They've come for me!" He clambered out of the trench and searched the skies. A few kilometers to the east he could make out a dark shape circling about, some 40 meters above the sand. Excited as he was at the presence of his rescuers, he was still filled with admiration for their uncanny sense in following the direction which he had taken.

Jonathan jerked the flashlight out of the bundle, pressed the button, and began waving it vigorously above his head, in the code pattern. Immediately the helicopter veered sharply and came down in a gradual drop, light beam on. Jonathan placed himself directly in line with the beam. A moment later, the sand churned up by the blades whipped past his face. He ran forward, reaching the spot where the helicopter landed just as its door opened wide. Two pairs of hands lifted him inside the machine.

"Sit down," growled Shmuel, as Major Jonathan sought to shake everyone's hand. "Plenty of time for that later, when we get back."

They almost didn't make it back. The Egyptians had ample time to spot the craft. As the Super-Perlon began heading north, toward the open sea, it was caught momentarily in a criss-cross of searchlights. An instant later, two shafts of light arose from the ground, came up slowly until they had reached the altitude of the helicopter, then leveled off and came straight at it.

"Missiles!" yelled Danny. He and the others had thought that the bright objects were flares. Captain Amos immediately jerked the stick to the left and sent the helicopter into a steep drop, but not quite soon enough. A searing flash of light and an ear-splitting screech came into the cabin; one of the missiles had grated across the rear section of the craft, thrusting it downward.

"Brace yourselves," cried Dr. Yizhar. Amos saw the ground coming up at them. He wrapped himself around the stick and pulled. Slowly the helicopter righted itself and wobbled forward, rattling like a can in the wind.

Shmuel felt around the darkened instrument board. Nothing appeared to have been damaged. They continued flying shakily for about an hour, keeping low above the water. As they neared the Israeli coast, the voice of the checker in the control tower came through:

"What's the good word?" it asked, after identification had been established.

"We got Jonathan," replied Danny. "Good enough?"

Benjamin Landau: Bail-out Rescue; *Bamahane,* 5.7.67

Rescue of bail-out pilots was but one of the assignments given to the helicopters, in their first test under fire as a Zahal fighting arm. Commander Major Eliezer, known as "Cheetah," summarizes the achievements of the "choppers" entrusted to his overall care.

The helicopter base is like New York's Grand Central Station. People enter, come and go—paratroop commanders on their way to a briefing, newsmen hurrying to a press conference. The telephone doesn't stop jangling, people shout to each other down the entire length of the mezzanine. Opposite the staircase a yellow canary flickers in its cage. On the grass outside, weary pilots are stretching the fatigue out of their bones.

My interview with the Flight Commander began in the morning at the base and ended with a phone call in the evening. All along it was punctuated and riddled with interruptions: "Just one question, Eliezer . . . one minute more, Eliezer . . . take a look at the list, Eliezer . . . when will you finally be finished, Eliezer?" The helicopters are very busy.

"How is all this different from pre-war days?"

"Tremendously different. We always knew that our pilots are capable of doing a lot, but now we know that they can do more than we ever imagined. Yes, we did a good job. People with whom we worked give us a lot of credit. We did do a lot, more than we thought—more than we heard it was possible to do—I guess more than what the Americans have been able to do with helicopters in Vietnam. We did not copy their methods because our fighting situations are different, as are our tactics.

"Are the Americans considered to excel with helicopters?"

"They have a lot of them, at any rate. In Vietnam they have 1,700 late-model helicopters, 1967's, worth some two billion dollars. They send up hundreds of them at one time. In this, you see, we cannot compare ourselves with them."

"Do you read a great deal about Vietnam?"

"Everything that's published. What else do I read? Professional literature, all the foreign-language aviation weeklies and monthlies.

Many other texts, not necessarily dealing with my own profession but with other subjects as well—armor, military matters in general, war campaigns. I don't have much time for fine literature."

"How did the helicopters acquit themselves in this war?"

His elongated features lit up. "This was their first major test, and they came through beyond all expectations. We used only a few in the Sinai operation, mainly for rescue work. One of the conclusions we reached, for future reference, is that, in certain cases, transporting soldiers by helicopter is more convenient and efficient than para-jumping. There are no problems of wind or terrain. There are several paratroopers here who worked with us in the war; they would rather be airborne by helicopter than parachute, for tactical reasons. Our operation requires more instruments, detailed planning and coordination, but it also makes for enormous flexibility and speed, extreme mobility. A soldier's movements are not hampered by sand dunes or gullies or streams. Theoretically we can transport him 150 kilometers per hour. That's our speed. Helicopters have a tremendous potential."

"How do pilots like flying helicopters?"

"Flying-school training is geared to warfare. The fighter pilot gets the glory, but time is on the side of the helicopter, which performs a wide variety of tasks—airlifting soldiers, general transport, evacuating the casualties, patrol work and half a dozen others. It's really interesting to be a helicopter pilot. He is everywhere. He sees and hears many things because he is always working with other units. The time when pilots insisted on flying fighter planes only is behind us. The pilot soon falls in love with the helicopter. He likes the way it responds. A personal attachment is formed between the two. A fighter pilot drills within the same pattern. We are always learning something new, trying a new twist. There was a time when people thought that helicopters, because of their low speed, are for pilots who aren't allowed to fly jets because of medical restrictions. Experience has shown, though, that a helicopter pilot must be a hundred percent fit in every way: flying skill, health, ability to make decisions. You must have leadership qualities. You take off in one area and land in another, where you don't know what kind of a reception you'll get, whereas the fighter pilot always lands on the same runway. The helicopter pilot must operate independently over a long stretch of time. He must be mature, responsible, self-reliant."

"What is your pilot's most necessary attribute?"

"Love for his profession. Technical skill is secondary. I have come across many talented fliers who were grounded because they didn't show sufficient love for flying; they just weren't crazy enough about it. Of course, you can't do without high technical aptitude, intelligence and training. Courage? Well, courage is not so apparent in peace time, and you really can't evaluate a man's courage before the test comes. There are brave fellows whom you hardly notice, and there are brave extroverts. It's hard to judge beforehand."

"Did you suffer any losses?"

"We had no casualties at all, though we filled many tough assignments—some daring rescue operations, extricating fighter pilots from enemy territory. All of our men returned safely, some in damaged craft and leaking fuel tanks. We were pleasantly surprised to find that such a large craft, with so many moving parts, could take so much punishment. Some helicopters came back punctured like sieves, absolutely beyond repair—but they made it."

"Did you have an opportunity to observe Egyptian helicopter pilots in action?"

"They had huge helicopters—MI-6's, capable of transporting a load of 10 tons, or 80 combatants. Our own maximum is 40. But theirs is an awkward craft; besides, they didn't get to put it into operation. In a way, I am sorry we hit them so accurately. There wasn't one left for a souvenir. It would have made a fine exhibition piece."

"How did you get involved with helicopters?"

"I've been a Flight Commander since '59. Before that, I flew a fighter plane. There were two years in between, when I was an instructor in our flight school. My age? 33, this week."

Round face, square chin, black eyes with overhanging brows, serious gaze offset by a boyish grin, solid arms and quiet motions, a man who likes kids even if they are 23 and sport imposing beards. "My background? I was born in Jerusalem—at Hadassah on Mount Scopus, to be exact. Went to grammar school in Bet-Hakerem, then to a vocational school, where I took up draftsmanship and engineering."

"What was your ambition at that time?"

"I know that many give this answer, but I really decided to be a pilot when I was still quite young, back in the days of the War of Independence, when I saw Egyptian planes bomb Jerusalem. I chose my school subjects to fit this decision. For two years, after I became

16, I prepared to meet the requirements of the flying course. What did my parents say? For a while they had no inkling of the matter. When I did enroll for the course, they weren't enthused. Now they are proud. I went through training here, then went abroad for a short period to round out my studies. That was good for me. I was able to make comparisons, broaden my horizons. Frankly, however, I can say that the training which a pilot gets here is on just as high a level."

His men, outside, had already given me this information: Eliezer's brother, a paratroop officer in the regular army, had been killed a short while earlier, in this war. He was truly renowned for his fighting spirit. The entire Zahal knew him—all the commanders, including the Chief-of-Staff. He was commanding his company when he fell—an outstanding soldier in every respect. The third brother is also in Zahal. Armor. He had been attending university in the United States, and came back because of his brother's death. Since then he had been mobilized.

"Is this the home influence—three sons in the armed forces?"

"We are of Jerusalem stock. Quiet people, very much in love with our land. I was born in Jerusalem. My parents were raised there; both came from Turkey as children during the First World War. We never had military training. In fact, the folks kept putting pressure on us to quit the army and keep the school bench warm, but with us, love for our land always came first."

"Would you have wanted to continue studying?"

"I'd like to, but for the next two, three years I won't have time for it, for professional reasons. Still, if I do get the time in the future, I'd like to take up courses in social studies. This would have nothing to do with my present career, but to go study aerodynamics or some other subject connected with flying—that's for a young fellow setting out in life, when he can continue to engineering. At my age, no."

"Did you fly during the war, or were your duties on the ground?"

"I was Flight Commander. One of the things I learned was how to make my men operate under high tension and tough conditions. Though they hadn't been sleeping for days and nights on end, I had to keep them in check. They wanted to get back into action, again and again. I had to force them to rest—not that there was too much time for it, but at least four hours. Now they are coming up for weekend passes—their first vacation since 'Preparedness' began. Me? Just like anyone else. That's a Zahal tradition, in all branches. Command means responsibility, not special privileges."

"How about flying—is that a lifelong interest?"

"I've had no doubts here. Helicopters are prime operational instruments, an attractive combination of profession and hobby. I love flying; I already have 4,000 hours in the air. Recently, when we captured Golan Heights, I flew along the slopes of Mount Hermon. That was an unforgettable experience."

"What do you do during your free time?"

"I don't have much of it, but as much as I do, I like to spend with my family. I have three children; I keep their pictures hidden here, behind the desk. The older two are boys, six and four and a half. The youngest one is a girl. My wife is also of Jerusalem stock. Ours is a large family in Jerusalem, a whole clan. She managed to finish her studies in Economics and Government Administration, but now she is taken up with raising the children, right here on the base."

"Would you want to see your sons become fliers?"

"Well, by the time they are grown, there will be all sorts of strange objects flying around—space ships, air monsters. But if they make up their minds they want to fly, I'll be very happy."

Ruth Bondy: My Friends the Helicopters; *Dvar Hashavua,* 30.6.67

In the summer of 1966 *an Iraqi pilot defected to Israel, bringing along his MIG*-21, *the first to reach the West, intact. A study of this aircraft provided Israeli pilots with invaluable information about the weaknesses of the plane, which served as the core of Egypt's striking air power.*

Even discounting his particular feat in the war (his Super-Mystère brought down a MIG-21), Major Yalou is "quite something" in the Israel Air Force. Wherever he is, a good time is had by all. He is the life of the party, the hub of the "big wheels" when the gang gets together. Yalou is a fireball of *joie de vivre* and a fountain of native humor, a playful tornado who keeps everybody on the move.

At 32, Yalou is a veteran Super-Mystère pilot, "the first pilot out of Nes-Ziona," he grins, taking a humorous poke at his staid town, immediately adding, however, that his younger brother, Amnon, is also a pilot. Yalou brought to his flying apprenticeship a measure of mischief, and readily admits to being a better pilot than he was a student. He earned his wings piloting Mustangs and Spitfires. During the Sinai Campaign, his Mystère shot down two Vampires over Mitla Pass. Between then and a shift to the Super-Mystère, he taught in the Flying School. A few years ago, already a major in the IAF, Yalou almost terminated his flying career—he became ill. The IAF prayed for his recovery as the pious pray for the advent of the Messiah. "To sum it up," he says, "I went abroad, where they gave me the right pills, and I came back, fit as a jet." To prove it, he switched to a Mirage, went in for aerobatics, the Fouga, and now he is sole possessor of the distinction of having piloted the only Super-Mystère to bring down a MIG-21.

This was probably the first time in air history that these two planes flew at each other. The foreign correspondents I talked to after the war refused, at first, to believe it. Yalou himself was not aware of the uniqueness of his feat until several days later, when we met at his home in Nes-Ziona. His wife, Hassia, and two daughters were with us during the interview, and their eyes never left Yalou's broad, honest face. This was a treat for them.

"You can understand it," Yalou began. "Every pilot wants to bring down the enemy plane in battle. On the ground, the plane is an inanimate object which cannot react at all. Up there it comes to life; it breathes. Your gratification is even greater—though I don't wish it on anybody—when your own chances in the fight are practically nil. And that's what happened in the meeting between the Super-Mystères and the MIG-21's.

"On the first day of the War, we took off to attack a MIG-21 air base by the name of Teykel, located far in the mountainous area of northeastern Syria, a flight of 30 minutes plus and very difficult to navigate. We flew low and fast, in a four-plane formation. When we reached the base, we were surprised to see two MIG-21's circling above it. We had to switch from bombing to fighting. I ordered my No. 4 to draw the nearer MIG into a disadvantageous position. But the MIG was not decoyed easily. He went after No. 4 until he saw me coming at him. This sent him into a crazy pattern of aerobatics; he kept firing into the air like mad. I got him in my sights at about 150–200 meters and let go with three bursts. The first one hit his wing and sent him into a spiral dive. He parachuted from a height of about 150 meters, but I am pretty sure his parachute didn't open. In the meantime, Nos. 3 and 4 were engaging the other

MIG. They got him in the wing tips. The MIG began to roll over quickly—the pilot had lost control of the plane—then crashed. We saw no parachute. All this took about five minutes. The people below were certainly seeing a show, and we decided to add to the excitement. There was a MIG standing on the runway. I made one pass over it and turned it into a bonfire, while the other planes strafed the field clean. We returned without incident, as though the whole thing had been a practice drill."

"How did the Super-Mystère gain the advantage over the MIG's?"

"We maneuvered ourselves into a better position than they had," explained Yalou. "Besides, the moment their pilots saw us shooting at them, they were stricken with a nervous attack and lost all sense of judgment."

The Syrian assignment was not Yalou's first on that day. When he returned to his base, later that afternoon, wrung out and dripping, he took a brief hour's rest and went out again, this time to silence the Jordanian guns which were shelling Jerusalem from Sha'afat.

Yalou's toughest hour came when he flew to bomb the airfield at Inshas, in Egypt, near the summer palace of former King Farouk. "We ran into tremendous anti-aircraft fire. My No. 3 blew up right near me. My own plane was hit in the belly. I felt the plane dragging, and my chances of getting back to base didn't look too good. Several times I told my No. 2 that I might have to bail out and that he should make note of the spot. Had I been attacked, it would have been the end. Still, I managed to get back and land safely, and—listen to this—I took the same plane to Syria an hour later—that's how good our mechanics are."

Yalou doesn't go in for flowery description of IAF feats. "My men never think that any task can be beyond them. What's more, if one pilot does something outstanding, I practically owe it to the others to give them a chance to do likewise. In preparing for action, the fellows know exactly what they were up against, but they are always eager for more."

"How did you take it physically?"

"The high morale and the will to fly thrust all fatigue aside. I hardly slept at all, those six days and six nights. That awful fatigue came only later. The true significance of our victory also came to us some time afterwards. During the battle there were no emotions of fear, worry or confusion. We all enjoyed the stories which appeared in the foreign papers—the ones about our having a secret weapon, some kind of a bomb with a self-guiding apparatus. Nonsense. What we had was superior fighting quality, that's all."

"Do you happen to indulge, on the side, in a few superstitions?"

"Sure, why not? It doesn't do any harm if you let those things have a say. For instance, I—and many of the men—don't like to switch planes. We take what we are given as an act of fate. The few times I switched from my assigned plane to another I had problems with it."

"What was your feeling when you went out for your first sortie?"

"I felt like the student who is going to take his exam and feels sure that he will pass it. We have a saying that he who finds it tough during practice has it easy in battle, but he who finds practice easy usually has a hard time in battle. Our drill battles are so tough that it's no wonder we take off for the real thing with such confidence."

Tamar Avidar: Yalou's World Record; *Bamahane*, 5.7.67

Zahal Chief Chaplain, Brigadier-General Shlomo Goren, had composed a special prayer for pilots, invoking the Almighty to "save us from every foe lurking in the heavens and on the earth." Although the association of most Israeli pilots with the heavens is in the physical realm, there were some who folded the prayer leaflet and put it away in their flying jackets; if the prayer wouldn't help, neither could it do any harm. Their chief faith, however, was in their own ability which, coupled with the excellence of Israeli intelligence and the performance of the ground crews brought the IAF its glowing victory. General Hod made this interim review on the second day of the campaign and analyzed the triumph and its causes right after the war.

Today we tackled the Air Forces of Egypt, Jordan, Syria and Iraq. In this action about 400 enemy aircraft were destroyed.

The following are details of the enemy planes destroyed:

In *Egypt* about 300 planes: 30 heavy bombers of the Tupolev-16 type; 27 medium bombers of the Ilyushin-28 type; 12 fighter-bombers of the Sukhoy-7 type (which were only recently received by Egypt); 90 Mig-21 planes; 20 Mig-19 planes; 75 Mig-17 planes; and another 32 transport planes and helicopters. About 20 of these planes were destroyed in aerial combat.

In *Syria* 52 planes were destroyed: 30 Mig-21 planes; 20 Mig-17 planes; 2 Ilyushin-28 planes.

In *Jordan* 20 Hunter planes and 7 transport planes and helicopters were liquidated.

After a formation of *Iraqi* planes attacked Israeli settlements, we attacked Base H-3 in Iraq and destroyed 6 Mig-21 planes and 3 Hunter planes.

In the fighting we lost 19 pilots, of whom 8 were killed and 11 are missing. Some of these have been captured by the enemy. Their families have been informed. Details of our planes lost are: 4 Ouragans, 4 Mystères, 4 Super-Mystères, 2 Mirages, 1 Vautour, and 4 Fouga-Magisters.

Air Force Personnel! Our task is not yet over. The Air Force remains fresh and firm, ready to continue the activities which will ensure the victory of the Israel Defense Forces.

Brigadier-General Hod at Press Conference; 7.6.67

✶

Q.: How did the attack begin?

Gen. Hod: (exact) On the morning of June 5, the Egyptian Air Force was stationed at ten air bases: four in Sinai, three in the Canal sector, and three in the Cairo-South area. We waited until the Egyptian planes had landed for re-fueling, then attacked all ten airfields at once. *(gaily)* Two hours and fifty minutes later, I was able to notify the Chief-of-Staff that the Egyptian Air Force had been shattered, with more than three hundred of its planes destroyed.

Q.: What were the chief objectives of the operation?

Gen. Hod: There were two priorities: one, to eliminate the MIG's, which could have hampered our progress; two, to destroy the bombers. Before the war, I recall, someone asked me to what degree I could give assurance that Tel-Aviv wouldn't be heavily bombed. I replied: "I am confident that our Air Force can deal the Egyptian foe a mortal blow and then go on to joint operations with the other branches of Zahal."

Q.: What was the state of Egyptian air power following the IAF attack on June the 5th?

Gen. Hod: It was left in shreds—a few MIG-19's and MIG-17's, which were removed that same afternoon to Cairo International Airport, which we had not touched previously. After the transfer, however, we bombed this airfield as well, striking only at the military craft. Not a single civilian plane was hit *(hands me a photo)*. In the next three days the Egyptians launched pointless and desperate attacks with their remaining planes, in an attempt to slow down Zahal's advance and thus give the Egyptian forces in Sinai a chance to escape. These attacks not only failed in their objective but also caused further losses; on the second day, our fliers shot down nineteen planes, on the third—fourteen, and on the fourth—nine.

Q.: What targets did you hit in Cairo itself?

Gen. Hod: (very sure about it) From the beginning of the war to the cease-fire we didn't have a single civilian target. We were the only air force in the Middle East with unquestioned air supremacy. We could have flown anywhere *(emphatically)*. No one could have stopped us. But we restricted our attacks to military objectives only. It should be generally kept in mind that, in this war, two out of every three sorties made by our jet planes were in cooperation with ground forces. I say "cooperation" rather than "support" because the latter indicates help which the weak receives from the strong. Our ground forces were far from weak. I would say that the IAF is the spearhead of Zahal, and that it took part in all types of battles—in the air, on the ground, at sea. It's very difficult to wage war successfully without the advantage of air supremacy.

Q.: When and how did you take action against the air forces of Syria, Jordan and Iraq?

Gen. Hod: On the morning of June the 5th we had no evidence of any Syrian or Jordanian air activity similar to Egypt's aggressive acts. It was therefore decided that we would not begin hostilities in that sector.

Q.: What was the air strength of the Syrians, Jordanians and Iraqis?

Gen. Hod: Syria had about forty MIG-21's, forty MIG-17's, and a few bombers. Jordan had two flights of Hunters. The Iraqis had two flights of MIG-21's, a flight of Hunters and TU-16 bombers. Just before the war, they transferred a flight of MIG-21's from an airfield inside Iraq to Air Base 3-H on the Iraq–Jordan border.

Toward noon the Jordanians, Syrians and Iraqis began bombing points in Israeli territory. By this time, the Egyptian Air Force had already been taken care of, and we were free to turn our attention northward. Within an hour two-thirds of the Syrian Air Force had been demolished. The remaining planes fled to other airfields far inland, beyond our effective range, and abandoned the skies to us.

We also knocked out almost the entire flight of Iraqi MIG-21's stationed at the 3-H air base.

As we eventually found out, the Arab air forces had sliced up Israel among themselves somewhat as follows: The Egyptians were to take care of the territory from the southern border up to and including Tel-Aviv; the Jordanians and Iraqis were to handle the central part of the country up to Haifa; the Syrians were to mop up the north.

You will recall that a single Iraqi bomber had attacked Netanya. This puzzled us no end. What would a lone bomber be doing in Central Israel, without fighter protection? We had the answer when our two fliers who had been taken prisoner in Iraqi territory came back to us in a prisoner exchange deal. They told us that the Iraqis had ceaselessly interrogated them about the bomber they had sent to attack . . . Tel-Aviv. It turned out that the bomber pilot, a colonel in the Iraqi Air Force, had simply made an error and mistook Netanya for Tel-Aviv. He dropped three bombs there and was heading for Iraq with the other three, when he was shot down by an anti-aircraft battery in the Afula sector.

Q.: Which of the Arab fliers do you consider the best of the lot?

Gen. Hod: (appreciatively) The Jordanians were the best our fliers engaged in the air. When the two fliers I mentioned were returned from Iraq, they came back by way of Jordan, where they met and chatted with Jordanian fliers—not as conquerors and prisoners, but as professionals talking about their careers. The Jordanians were much taken with the personal gear our fliers carried; they touched the food rations and other items—like children. But they fought well.

Q.: And how would you compare the level of the other fliers with ours?

Gen. Hod: (decisively) I really think that today you won't find, in all the world, finer airmen than the IAF fliers. They passed one of the severest tests that any flier can be called upon to undergo. The results say that they rank with the finest airmen anywhere. Therefore, to compare any Arab flier with ours would be nonsense. There is just no comparison. The gap is much too wide. Now I don't mean to say that they didn't put up a fight, and I certainly don't imply that they made the war just child's play for us. Some of them fought well. The anti-aircraft fire from their bases, for instance, was very heavy and cost us some casualties.

It has been said that the Nasser–Hussein bit about the participation of U.S. planes on our side stemmed from the fact that the skies above Egypt were full of planes, and Nasser just couldn't believe we had so many. Of course, we didn't need a foreign umbrella and didn't have one. What happened was that the IAF attacked and fought at a rapid pace which very few among the world's air forces had ever achieved. *(gratified)* In Vietnam the maximum number of sorties in a day is two. Some of our fliers exceeded that by far. We operated during the four days of battle at a murderous pace and, if we would have had to, we would have continued further.

Q.: How many sorties, would you say, were made during the first day of the war?

Gen. Hod: Several thousand. Nor were the airmen the only ones who worked like demons. So did the mechanics and the ground crews. *(laughs)* After the war was over, several military attaches asked me, in amazement: "How did you ever do it? How much time did it take to service a plane from the moment it landed until it took off for the next assignment?" I replied: "Gentlemen, some time ago you attended an exhibition we put on for you, and you saw then, with your own eyes, how long the operation took." They thought I was joking. "Come now, General," they said. "We know all about it. The show was very well rehearsed." You will pardon me," I interrupted. "What you saw is actually how we operate." In fact, my ground crews broke all speed records for servicing planes in combat. There's a law of diminishing returns for planes which take part in the fighting. Our men ignored this law. Every plane which landed in a damaged state was repaired in jet tempo. There were no delays. The mechanics performed wonders, and the IAF came out of the war with its planes in ninety-nine point nine percent working shape. I wish to make note of still another achievement. During the war, the IAF was augmented by thousands of reservists. This meant a tremendous administrative burden which called for efficient operation of all services. *(marvels)* This Air Force worked like a Swiss watch. We had no problems—neither administrative, nor technical, nor operational, even when the Force was scattered over a wide area, east and west, from the Gulf of Solomon to the Suez Canal, from the border of Iraq to Damascus.

Q.: From your standpoint, how did the Sinai Campaign of 1956 differ from this war?

Gen. Hod: (analyzes precisely) Ezer Weizmann and I used

to be quite peeved when people would tell us: "Fine. We won the Sinai Campaign, but it wasn't the Air Force that did it. What kind of heroes would you have been, were it not for the English and the French?" The same people said, just before this war: "In the Sinai Campaign, the English and the French supplied us with an aerial umbrella. How do you expect to handle four Arab air forces all by yourselves?" There were people who wanted guarantees—or close to it—that the IAF would indeed be able to achieve what it said it could. But those familiar with the inner workings of the IAF were one hundred and one percent certain of its complete victory, all along. We who, together with the officers and men, have been sleeping, eating and dreaming "IAF," had during all these years but one goal—to prepare the IAF for the great test. We had not the slightest doubt as to the outcome.

True, never in my wildest dreams had I hoped for a victory in two hours and fifty minutes. I thought it would take us at least until nightfall. A foreign military attache asked me: "You say that you struck in response to an Egyptian act which took place earlier that morning. How can that be? For such a strike you would need at least six months of preparation." "Sir, you are right, but not quite," I replied. "We have been preparing for it for eighteen and a half years."

We fought and won all by ourselves. For the IAF, this war was what the War of Independence and the Sinai Campaign were for Zahal's ground forces. Now we, too, stood up to the test. This is infinitely important for the IAF's future and its image. *(confidently)* We shall be eating the fruits in the 'seventies and 'eighties. Our problem now is: Where are we heading, in this post-war period? What is in our sights?

Q.: What do you mean?

Gen. Hod: (explains) The flow of arms and equipment from the Soviet Union to Egypt is continuing. No Air Force can dare think of the next war, if and when it should come, in the terms of the past one. We must keep renovating, testing new theories, developing new techniques. War may come sooner or later than people think *(determined)*, but we must be ready.

Q.: The Egyptians claim that they still have plenty of airmen left.

Gen. Hod: That is not the issue. The question is how much morale can these airmen muster after the defeat of their force. Does it have *any* fighting spirit left? I wonder.

Q.: From the viewpoint of the Air Force, what significance is there to holding on to the Sinai Peninsula?

Gen. Hod: (concentrates) By holding on to it we prevent Egypt's springing a surprise attack on Israel by air. Sinai's air depth is sufficient to give us advance warning, to enable us to go out and meet the foe before he reaches his target. It enables us to engage him in battle above unpopulated areas. It prevents Egypt from surprising us by low flying. It places at our disposal all the advance air bases which had formerly been theirs. They will have to add sixteen minutes of flying time—and that's a lot!

Q.: The world press has made much of some secret weapon that you supposedly possess and which brought us victory.

Gen. Hod: (passionately) The only secret weapon is our men. When our nation is pushed to the wall, it rises up and lashes out tenfold. You hear a lot of talk about our young people—that they lack ideals, that they are empty and shallow, that they live in discothèques. Let me tell you something: These young people are better than we were at their age. They are ahead of us in education, devotion, grasp of things, span of knowledge. They are moved by a great love for the land of their birth, and they are prepared to lay down their lives for it. As for the Air Force, whoever serves with it, loves it intensely, from the officers to the last of the privates. *(very proudly)* This spirit is the secret weapon of Israel's people. It didn't come into being in one day, in the Air Force, and most of the credit for it should go to General Ezer Weizmann, who was in command of the Force for eight years. He built it up and breathed into it a special kind of fighting spirit. Ezer is the one who converted the Force from piston to jet, gave it its present format, and developed its operational efficiency. I inherited from Ezer an Air Force where all I have to do is maintain its standards and keep it clicking at the same tempo.

Mordecai (Mota) Hod, 40, is of medium height and easy-going manner, smokes a pipe and sports a moustache. A scion of the noted Fein family, pioneer settlers in Galilee, he was born and raised in Kibbutz Degania. During the Second World War he served in the Jewish Brigade—attached to the British Eighth Army—then went into the air branch of the Hagana. He had a hand in acquiring the first aircraft in Europe, climbed up each rung in the Israel Air Force ladder, from the very bottom to IAF Commander.

They tell about the time when the Kibbutz decided that Mota

should come back to Degania. IAF Commander Weizmann went to the Kibbutz, got its old-timers together and told them: "Comrades, if Mota doesn't remain in the Air Force, only people like me will remain—and look at me!" Mota stayed on. Today, whenever General Hod has to persuade kibbutzim to let their young people sign up for regular service in the IAF, he uses the same line: "If you don't let the young men do it, only people like me will be left there—and look at me!"

General Hod is described by his friends as being calm, quiet, reserved, a commander with the utmost confidence in his staff. "It's a pleasure to work with him." He himself loves the slogan: "I don't serve in the Air Force—I live there."

Q.: Many stories have been told about the valor of our fliers. Do you know any which have not yet been told?

Gen. Hod: Of the pilots who parachuted down to enemy soil, seven were extricated, in broad daylight and at night, always under heavy fire. *(emotional)* The helicopters did things difficult to describe. They rescued the pilots although they themselves had been hit, while their tanks were losing fuel, while the enemy was raking them with murderous fire. And don't forget, we're dealing with 100 octane fuel, where a single spark can blow up the plane.

There was the case of the senior commander in our Force who had parachuted down close to the Syrian positions on Golan Heights. Two helicopters, covered by four jets, went out to get him. The man had been hit by Syrian fire while coming down. He had a splinter in his head, a bullet in one leg and a broken bone in the other. He dragged himself up to a ridge to make it more difficult for the Syrians to get to him. It was touch and go every second—who would reach him first, the rescuers or the killers. *(happy)* We got there first.

There was the leader of a four-plane formation who was hit and lost altitude control. He kept after his target, got it, then executed a fantastic maneuver and landed safely. And I want to tell you about the "Piper" reconnaissance pilot who was on his way back from a grinding twelve-hour assignment when he spotted, on the ground, one of our pilots who had been forced to abandon his Super-Mystère. This was in enemy territory. He landed his "Piper" nearby, ready to help in any way he could; fortunately, a helicopter arrived and took the pilot aboard. On another occasion we had a mishap in a large bomb stockpile at one of our bases. A detonating cap had come loose on one of the bombs, and the entire business could have blown up sky high. Two ordnance men came in, didn't say a word, and set about taking the bomb apart. That took real courage.

Q.: You will no doubt be giving out a few dozen citations?

Gen. Hod:(shrugs) Why a few dozen? Five or six, perhaps. Bear in mind that citations are awarded only to men who showed bravery above and beyond the call of duty, and always while under enemy fire.

Q.: What do you propose to give to the pilot who downed four MIG's in the war?

Gen. Hod: He will get four certificates. We have four pilots who shot down three MIG's each, and quite a few who shot down one or two. Our final count is 452 enemy planes destroyed, of these 60 shot down in air combat.

Q.: Foreign military experts claim that the IAF could not possibly have used conventional methods only, and, as proof, they cite the fact that Israeli planes seemed to "smell out" the dummy planes from among the real ones in the Egyptian air fields.

Gen. Hod: Not at all. It was a matter of pure accuracy and expertise. We used conventional means: cannon, rocket bombs and relatively little napalm. We do not hold with the theory that the era of conventional means is past and that everything must now be electronic, automatic, complicated. Intricate equipment causes only confusion. Marksmanship and high-quality fire-power are part and parcel of our pilots' skill. Besides, we had taken photos while in combat, and these helped us to tell apart the dummy from the real thing.

Q.: Did the Egyptians employ missiles?

Gen. Hod: They did. They shot off plenty of missiles, but missed every time.

Q.: What did the war tell you about the Israel Air Force?

Gen. Hod: We have boiled down the reasons for its success to four: its ability to serve as a link for operation and control by all branches of Zahal; the minute planning that went into its own operations; the fighting spirit and thoroughness of execution, and first-rate intelligence information supply. The Air Force emerged from the war stronger, more solid. Its war was fought by young pilots who had received their wings only a few months earlier, as well as by veterans who had been away for over ten years and now returned as reservists. We also had pilots from all over the world. One came from a university abroad, on the very eve of the war, climbed into a Mystère, and when the fighting was over asked me for an immediate discharge, because his examinations were coming up in a few days.

I was flooded with hundreds of applications to serve. Pressure was put on us by men who had served in the IAF and were now beyond flying age, but they still wanted "to do something" in the Force. *(warmly)* And speaking about sacrifice, let me say a few words about the wives of the pilots. I find it difficult to describe how bravely they kept up with us, all these years, knowing full well what was going on and what might happen—but you couldn't tell it from their calm faces. I certainly cannot describe the reaction of the wives of the men who fell. You can imagine their grief. Still, somewhere within themselves they found the strength to tell me: "It really hurts. We have lost our husbands—and we shall no longer be part of the Air Force."

Raphael Bashan: How We Did It; *Ma'ariv,* 30.6.67

Chapter Five

Battle in the Desert

MAP OF SINAI

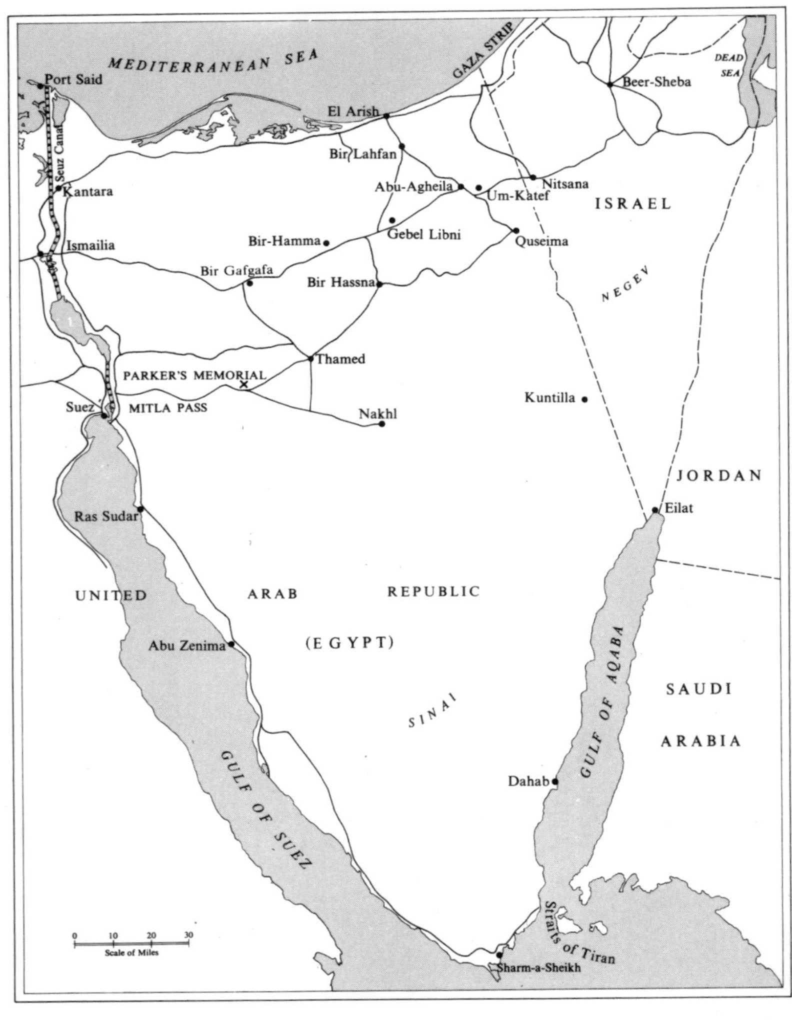

MEDITERRANEAN SEA
GAZA STRIP
DEAD SEA
Port Said
El Arish
Beer-Sheba
Seuz Canal
Bir Lahfan
Kantara
Abu-Agheila
Nitsana
Um-Katef
ISRAEL
Gebel Libni
Bir-Hamma
Quseima
Ismailia
Bir Gafgafa
Bir Hassna
NEGEV
Thamed
PARKER'S MEMORIAL
Kuntilla
Suez
MITLA PASS
Nakhl
JORDAN
Eilat
Ras Sudar
UNITED
ARAB
REPUBLIC
Abu Zenima
(EGYPT)
GULF OF AQABA
SAUDI
ARABIA
SINAI
GULF OF SUEZ
Dahab
0 10 20 30
Scale of Miles
Straits of Tiran
Sharm-a-Sheikh

THE SIX-DAY WAR STARTED IN SINAI WITH THE CONCENTRATION of Egyptian troops in the Peninsula and the blocking of the Straits of Tiran; it culminated in Sinai, and its fate was decided in Sinai. 11 years before, in 1956, Zahal had defeated the Egyptian Army in the course of 120 hours, and this was considered as one of the greatest achievements in the history of modern warfare. "Red Sheet" Operation was an improved repetition of the Sinai Campaign, a kind of Sinai Revisited. (The Israeli soldiers, who had had the experience of retreating because of international political pressures, joked: This time, the paratroops are taking along saplings to plant in the desert, so that ten years hence, when we have to conquer Sinai for the third time, there will be some shade in the wilderness.) Nevertheless, this war was different: different in intensity, in the daring and unusual fighting methods, and in its swiftness: within 87 hours, the Sinai Peninsula from the Suez Canal to Sharm-a-Sheikh had been taken by Zahal. Because of the rapid fighting, the course of the war could not be pieced together into a whole picture until the battles were over.

On June 12th, two days after the cease-fire had gone into effect, the Commander of the Southern Front, General Yeshayahu Gavish, met several hundred correspondents in Tel-Aviv, and told them about the battle:

First, I want to list the factors that led to the war. The Egyptians had deployed their land forces all along the border. They had diverted a large part of their forces they had in Yemen to Sinai. They had the advantage of numbers: Our strength was a little more than three division groups, against seven divisions of theirs. We did not have the benefit of the element of surprise: the enemy attacked first.

The beginning of the Egyptian offensive took the form of aircraft moving against Israel which was discovered by radar, of artillery fire on settlements along the border, and of a large armored force moving in the direction of our border in the Mitzpe Ramon sector.

There are three main routes through the Sinai Peninsula. One is the coastal road from Rafiah to the Canal, the second runs from Ketziot over Abu-Agheila to Ismailia, and the third over Kuntilla, Thamad and Nakhl to Port Fuad and Ismailia. In addition, there are a few linking roads.

Access to Sharm-a-Sheikh is mainly by air and by sea; there is also a single road along the west coast of the Sinai Peninsula.

Our operation had three objectives: First, to destroy the Egyptian army, that is to say, to break its strength once and for all; second, to take Sharm-a-Sheikh and open up the Tiran Straits for access by sea to Eilat; and third, as a condition for achieving the second objective, to occupy the whole Sinai Peninsula—for that is the only way to occupy Sharm-a-Sheikh.

The operation was carried out in three stages. In the first stage, our aim was to open up two main approaches to Sinai, and in the process to break up the forces holding the first line of defense. The second stage was to consist of penetration and pursuit in depth, with the aim of breaking down the second line of defense. In the third stage, we were to engage the enemy armored divisions in battle and destroy them.

The enemy, as I have said, had seven divisions, including two armored ones.

The first stage began when I received information at 8 o'clock in the morning that the enemy had begun his attack. We met him by means of a preventive attack on two routes at 8:15. Our one line of advance was by way of Khan-Yunis over Rafiah to El-Arish, and the other on the Ketziot–Abu-Agheila road. On either line we operated with one division group. At the same time, a third division group, advancing over dirt roads, penetrated into the center of the triangle formed by Gebel-Libni, Bir-Gafgafa and Bir-Lahfan. In addition to these division groups, we had two reinforced brigades in operation, one moving in the direction of Kuntilla, and the other advancing into the Gaza Strip from the south in order to occupy it. In this stage, which was concluded the next morning, we succeeded in defeating the 7th Division on the northern route, we took El-Arish and Abu-Agheila, and reached the center of the area with a whole division group. In addition, we occupied the whole of the Gaza Strip.

In the second stage, we advanced in order to break down the second line of defense, from Gebel-Libni to Bir-Hassna. The purpose of this attack was not only to break down the second line of defense, but also to force the enemy's armored divisions into a counter-attack, so that we could engage them in battle. The enemy's armored divisions did not attack. At this point, the division group of Brigadier Avraham Yaffe began to advance in the direction of Gebel-Libni and Bir-Hassna.

The division group of Brigadier Israel Tal, on the northern wing, broke through at Bir-Lahfan and, moving on at great speed, reached the Suez Canal just before dawn.

The division group of Brigadier Ariel Sharon moved into the maneuvering area between Quseima and Bir-Hassna and took Quseima.

The third stage was that of the tank battle. Our movements were designed to surround the enemy and force him to give battle. At this stage, the division group of Brigadier Tal arrived at Bir-Gafgafa and cut off the escape routes to the Canal. The division group of Brigadier Yaffe took the "Parker Monument" near the Mitla Pass and blocked the way to the south. Brigadier Sharon's division group took Nakhl and cut off the forces that lay in the eastern part of the Peninsula.

The enemy was forced to engage us in order to achieve a double purpose: to extricate himself and escape in the direction of the Canal, and to prevent our forces from reaching the Canal by the Ismailia, Jidi and Mitla roads.

The battle lasted the whole day and continued for several hours into the night. Something like 1,000 tanks were involved on both sides. The fighting was over by 10 p.m., and by three o'clock in the morning all our forces had reached the Canal.

On the day of the tank battle, airborne and naval forces reached Sharm-a-Sheikh. An additional land force arrived at Ras-Sudar via Mitla.

What are the results of the campaign?

The enemy has lost 700 tanks: 600 are destroyed, and another 100 taken undamaged. We have taken thousands of prisoners—we do not yet know exactly how many, but it is clear that tens of thousands of Egyptian soldiers are moving in the direction of the Canal.

We can say with certainty that four enemy divisions are a total loss, and the other three are broken even if part of them has escaped.

Among the equipment we have captured there are also a number of S.A.-2 ground-to-air missiles, which were found at a missile base between the Mitla Pass and the Suez Canal, all complete and ready for launching.

Our casualties are: 275 dead, 800 wounded and 61 tanks hit. The enemy has lost between 7,000 and 10,000 dead, and I do not know how many wounded. The wounded are in our hospitals.

In four days less five hours, an Israeli force of something like three divisions defeated and destroyed an army of seven divisions. This success was made possible by a number of factors:—

First: concentration of forces, speed of movement and keeping up the pace. For instance, we were able to concentrate a force stronger than that of the enemy wherever we wanted at the place and time of our choice. We kept up our impact and fought for four whole days, day and night, without interruption.

Second: Our commanders led in the fighting. A large part of our casualties are officers: company commanders, battalion commanders and even brigade commanders. This shows that the officers fought at the head of their troops, with the men following them. The fighting spirit was excellent, among the reserves as much as among the regular troops. Everyone fought in the knowledge and conviction that this was a fight for the life of the country; that was why morale was so good, the will to fight so great, and courage beyond anything we had expected.

We used unconventional methods of penetration in order to undermine the fighting power of the enemy from the beginning. An example is the way one of Brigadier Yaffe's brigades made its way into the center of the battlefield without having to fight at all.

Our support system (fuel, ammunition, repairs) was organized in a way which permitted our division groups to remain self-supporting for at least 72 hours. They needed no reinforcements until the last day.

Air space control was a particularly important factor in assuring freedom of movement and action. Air support was close: in each armor battle we used air support immediately before attacking the enemy armor.

Our Egyptian enemy's equipment was modern and of high quality. In general, the Egyptians fought well in defense, far less well on the move, and broke down when they had to keep up with our pace and with the moves we forced on them.

This war has been the war of the people, of the civilians who put on uniforms and fought the war with their body and spirit; and the victory is in the first place theirs.

To conclude, let me say this about the three commanders of the division forces: With three such generals one can go far.

Brigadier-General *Yeshayahu Gavish* at Press Conference; 12.6.67

General Yeshayahu Gavish, who had headed the fighting in the south, a territory three times bigger than the State of Israel, is a slim, blue-eyed, very courteous man. He speaks in a soft voice and chain-smokes constantly. He was born in Tel-Aviv in 1925, *went to farming school, and volunteered at* 17 *for the Palmah, the elite force of the Hagana. In the War of Independence he was Operations Officer at the Lydda front, and he saved the lives of the people of his unit when he kicked away a hand-grenade thrown at them by an Arab. After attending the Military College in Paris, he was appointed Head of the Staff Department at the General Staff. General Gavish knows the south like the palm of his hand: during the Sinai Campaign he served as Head of the Operations Department at the General Staff, which made him one of the planners of the Sinai Campaign. General Gavish has been serving for the past two years as Commander of the Southern Front; consequently he was in charge of the defense of the Israeli settlements bordering the Gaza Strip. A year ago he planned Zahal's greatest drill ever—the last drill before the war. This is the account of his personal experiences before and during the war:*

I returned from the opening ceremonies of Independence Day on May 14, at night. I think it was close to midnight when I received a phone call from the Chief-of-Staff. He said: "Listen, we have information that the Egyptian army is on its way into Sinai." At the moment I didn't know exactly what was going on, but I understood that the matter was far more serious than ever before. As far as I was concerned, this moment marked the beginning of the war. I returned to the Southern Command headquarters that same night. We set about drawing up our plans and preparing orders for the regular forces in the Southern Command. Later we issued the orders and deployed the forces in the area. I think that our forces were deployed along the line as of the night of May 15.

I now recall that our first reaction was the feeling that the Egyptians were sending troops into Sinai as a deterrent to some possible attack on our part. This was the primary phase of our military thinking. We were not worried by the situation, but we felt it necessary to safeguard the border, in a minimal measure, against all eventualities. Our basic conception, however, remained the same: Even should the Egyptians dispatch this or that number of troops, we would not be attacked.

Only a few days later it became evident that the Egyptian force was streaming into Sinai without letup and was beginning to represent an actual threat. This was no mere advance force but the Egyptian army in its full strength. At that point, of course, we began calling up our forces, deployed reserves as well, and set up divisional headquarters to plan the defense of the border. For us this was not a difficult operational problem, since Zahal had these plans all ready.

The third stage came when we began thinking in terms of active defense, that is, how to rout the Egyptian army if it should attempt to attack us, not only on the boundary line but beyond it, with the counter-attacks to take place deep in enemy territory.

When Egyptian strength in Sinai reached five to six divisions, it became patently clear that this threat was becoming one of the most serious ever to confront Israel. We began our period of waiting, while the Egyptians continued to pour troops into Sinai until their number reached about 100,000 men.

In retrospect, I think that Nasser had a twofold intention. The Egyptians felt that, unless they could outnumber us two or three to one, they could score no gains; to achieve this ratio they would have to put into the field at least seven divisions. We had also estimated that, unless Nasser had seven or eight divisions in readiness, he would have no chance.

I don't know what was his train of thought, but it is very possible, as we know from the testimony of many prisoners, that during the primary stage, Nasser intended to send enough troops into Sinai to bar freedom of action on our part, but with the eating came the appetite. When he blocked the Straits and realized that he was scoring impressive gains without war, he also understood that, in order to withstand possible action by Zahal, he would need all this force in Sinai, otherwise he could not hold up under an Israeli counter-attack.

I shall try to reconstruct the first day of the war. My staff officers and I were near an information center in an advance post along the Gaza Strip sector; this was at six in the morning. About 7:45 I received word that the Egyptian air force was aloft. Shelling began from the Strip toward our border settlements. An Egyptian division commanded by General Shazli was proceeding toward Mitzpe-Ramon, and our air force went out for counter-attack. At that moment I received a phone call from the Chief-of-Staff, in code: "The Knesset session is on." I then passed on to the division commanders the slogan for going into battle: "Red Sheet!" and added: "Ahead! Push on ahead!" From that point on, I felt as though I were in the center of major-scale maneuvers. All pressure and uncertainty now disappeared. We were in the war—and that was enough. From that moment on, the issue was: How will it go? We took another half-hour for checking things—whether the camouflage nettings had been lowered, whether the communications apparatus was working, whether all the units were in their assigned battle formations. From 8:15 on, I began getting reports from the divisional commanders that they were prepared to drive ahead. At that moment Division Commanding Generals Tal, Sharon and Yaffe received their orders to move forward. The general advance began, with our air force going ahead to crack the enemy artillery emplacements in Rafiah.

Did I have any estimate as to the probable number of dead and wounded? No, I had none. I never translated this in terms of figures, but I did know that it would entail hundreds of dead, but how many—I didn't even try to assess the meaning of this phase. As for the tank battles, we knew that we were going to face some 800 Egyptian tanks, and that it would cost us some two to three hundred tanks. Of course, 300 tanks means about 1,200 dead. I didn't think in terms of figures, however, but in terms of vulnerable armor.

I experienced no fear in the war. I must say that I was not in the actual fighting, although on three occasions I was close to enemy fire. Once in the Gebel-Libni sector, it turned out that the Egyptians had the location of my field headquarters. I was told by our men that they were planning to attack it from the air. We quickly lowered the camouflage netting, folded up the antennae, took two half-tracks, camouflaged them well, and drove into the gully, among the boulders. The Egyptian planes came, scoured the area, but didn't find us, since we were a good mile away. Then on the second day of the war, I was in a helicopter above Bir-Gafgafa, when suddenly two Egyptian Sukhoys came after us. Our pilot did a neat trick, dropping the helicopter almost down to the earth and thus evaded the jets. If the truth be told, I was more concerned about the sudden drop of the helicopter than about the Sukhoys.

The third occasion involved the Assistant Chief-of-Staff, General Haim Bar-Lev, as well. When we went to see General Tal, on his way to the Canal, we saw two MIG's diving at us, firing as they came. We had no choice but to drop to the ground. Anyway, this was my third war; why should I have felt any fright?

Many people ask me: What is the difference between the Egyptian soldier of 1967 and the Egyptian soldier of 1956? I think that the Egyptian soldier has improved since 1956; no doubt about that. He has improved in his fighting spirit. It took us a whole day to crack the Egyptian first line. We fought a full day in Rafiah and Khan-Yunis. It took us two days to achieve our objective in the Gaza Strip. This didn't happen in the Sinai Campaign, where the Egyptian forces crumbled in a matter of hours. You must bear in mind that ten years of regular army service improved the fighting morale and the quality of the Egyptian combatant. The fighting units which came from Yemen also had fighting morale. While they undoubtedly made progress, our own progress has been greater—and the gap between has grown. The Egyptian high command, I think, was in a troublesome dilemma with its Soviet military doctrine. Prisoners have told me that they did not agree with this doctrine and with the Soviet approach to the activation of large forces. Perhaps they didn't understand it, or simply didn't want to accept it. As far as activating large forces is concerned, I think that the Egyptian army is still very far from being capable of activating divisions and armies; its commands, staff officers and generals haven't mastered it. In the case of mobile armor, which is essentially the decisive element in battle, the Egyptian didn't dare make armored counter-attacks. Their prime concern was to extricate their forces from tight situations.

You want to know whether I believe in God. Let me say that I cannot tell you precisely whether I believe or not. But I can tell you this: Anyone who took part in this war had some faith in some unknown entity. Our chaplain distributed to the men a special prayer to be recited before going into battle. You will be amazed; not a single soldier left for battle without praying. Even the most hardened cynics prayed.

Gen. Y. Gavish: In a Military Publication of the Southern Command

Guns started roaring, and the soldiers hurried to the sergeant-major to give him their last letter before the battle. For many families, these were the last words in the handwriting of the son, the husband or the brother, who did not come back.

Just this minute our planes have begun the action of "softening up" the fortified position. The thunder of cannons interchange goes on.

All the commands of preparing for battle have already been given. And in the meantime he is bending over between the steel plates of the army transport, postcards on the stock of his rifle and he writes simple words to his loved ones. A few words which say something and a thousand which are not written. And for a moment the sender and his wife, his child, his beloved, his parents are in a world of their own. A sanctified minute.

The sergeant-major collects the letters and postcards from all the half-track crews. A few minutes later the order to move. On the back were only words, words of anxiety: "Don't do anything heroic. Get down into the shelters when there is an alarm. Look after the children. After yourself." Or: "Have you covered the big glass pane on the balcony?" And from war to peace: "When you grow up you won't have to fight." "You'll see, darling, that everything will turn out all right." "I'll be coming to hug you, my boy." "Enough blood has spilled on this soil." "You're already big enough, my daughter, to understand why father can't come to read you stories now."

The words are simple: "Father is guarding you." "Yes, we're afraid for a minute. Because we want to come back to you. And then we attack even more strongly—for the same reason." "I'm sorry that I didn't get to say Shalom."

And the card in which was written: "My dear children. I went to war to defend our country." And an opening to a postcard: "I am writing this on the soil of Sinai, under shelling." And a hurried ending: "I have to stop. We're moving." And always with love and kisses and regards. And one postcard with only five words: "We'll win. I love you."

A. Mossinson: Letter Before the Battle; *Army Press Release,* 6.6.67

The first ones to go off to battle in the south—after the pilots, that is—were the armored units, advancing at the Israeli "armor pace": swiftly, daringly, and using unorthodox methods. This prompted one of the biggest German newspapers to write, that "they advanced like Rommel; they won like Patton; and in addition, they kept singing all the way." Newspaperman Mordechai Barkai, a reserve major and now (after the war) Spokesman for the Ministry of Defense, served at the headquarters of the southern division. This is his account of the exploits of an armored battalion.

A patrol jeep sped to the head of the force. Sasson pushed himself into the front seat beside the machine-gun, his tall figure protruding like a third antenna. He waved his long arm: "Move!"

Tense feet pressed on the accelerator. The motors, roaring impatiently, belched forth sparks and explosions. The battalion shook itself and moved westward in two parallel columns. In one fell swoop the built-up tension, which had reached a scarcely bearable peak a few hours earlier, was dissipated.

Actually, this day had no beginning of its own. It was the continuation of the day before. The last set of battalion command orders had been drawn by Sasson after midnight, by the light of a lamp shining on the sector map, in a tent spread between two half-tracks. One after another it was O.K.'d by Arieh (tanks), Lapidot (tanks), Benno (tanks), Ze'ev (half-tracks) and Noam (patrol): "No problem; everything's tied up tight." They smoked cigarettes and drank strong coffee to overcome the deficit in sleep of the last 24 hours.

By dawn everything had been folded up with unbelievable speed, like a circus after its farewell performance. The nets disappeared, the packs were tied to the vehicles. Everyone was in a vehicle, all set to move.

"Are we moving, then?"

"Not moving."

"What's happening, dammit?"

Frustration and fatigue, which had been side-stepped by the feverish activity, again overcame the men. They slumped over their weapons. Eyes began to close. Here and there were preparations for breakfast. Someone had a transistor going.

The news: The price of gas is to be raised by 12 percent. Jewish groups throughout the world express their feelings of identification with Israel. The radio was turned off; no nerves to listen to it. A vengeful summer sun shone on the dozing armor battalion spread over the desert.

Suddenly someone heard the sound of jets. Others noticed them in the sky. An electric current brought the battalion to its feet. The cobwebs of sleep vanished. In no time at all everyone was aboard his vehicle. Without warning and without an order.

"Start the engines! Start the engines!"

The armor started the motors. Sasson, in his patrol jeep, drove to the head of the force; one hand holding a communication microphone and the other drawing, in the air, a circle that ended like a bolt into the blue.

"Move!"

The first sounds of explosion came a short distance ahead of the battalion vanguard. Shelling. Who and at whom? Clouds of smoke rose. Through them could be discerned the quick deadly flashes of fire of field cannon; the artillery barrage on the route along which the battalion was to penetrate into Sinai, along the Nitzana road.

The tanks quickly passed the battery artillery. The cannoneers followed them with open admiration and undisguised envy. Hands waved in encouragement. The black-and-white border posts, now unimportant and detached from any reality, were left behind.

The war had begun. Only at that moment it meant nothing whatsoever. The supporting artillery fire was far away and unreal, and the rumbling of the tracks filled the heavy, silent and oppressive emptiness. Eyes searched the skies which, perhaps, had never been so blue and clear. No one said this aloud but everyone thought about it to himself—

About their MIG's—

About their Tupolevs—

And about their Sukhoys.

Sasson was not at all concerned. Under the blue sky, surrounded by wasteland, he sat in his jeep as though it were an uncomfortable modern-style armchair, calm and content as if he were going out for a Saturday picnic. In his left hand was his signal microphone to the companies and to the brigade, and in his right hand, king-size "Pall-Mall." He was like an orchestra conductor, lightly and easily directing a wonderfully-trained orchestra which, as he knew very well, could conduct itself.

Wooden huts, with the blue of the UNEF, approaching. A red five-pointed star in the middle of the square and, on the walls of the huts, inscriptions of glory to Tito; these were the barracks of the Yugoslavian Emergency Forces in Egyptian Uja. Noam's scouts had already checked them. Empty. The battalion passed by without stopping. On the far horizon the oncoming post was painted: Tarat um-Bassis.

Arieh's tank company rolled forward at great speed in order to take up a covering position for Lapidot's and Benno's tanks, as they were fanning out for attack while on the move. When Arieh drew up to the covering position he did not stop but asked for and received permission to attack. The force of his drive swept the tanks past the post, without any opposition whatsoever. The rest of the tanks and half-tracks followed him over the sands to the roadsides, while the battalion command proceeded along the road itself.

Several yards before the edge of the post Sasson's jeep braked suddenly. "Stop!" Sasson roared into the microphone. The mines which he spied were scattered on the face of the road and along the shoulders, without any fencing and without any sign. With a sharp turn he drew aside all those who followed him and brought them by a detour to the rear slope from where, through his binoculars, he caught sight of the expected target farther along the road to the west—fenced, entrenched and well-fortified: Um-Tarpa.

Attack orders were given within seconds: Lapidot's tanks would give covering fire, Arieh's tanks would prepare to attack, Ze'ev's half-tracks would come from the left flank.

Forward!

Lapidot climbed with all of his tanks to the sandy "plait" and took up firing position on the high dunes. The Shermans opened fire. Arieh's armor, moving to cover, reached half-way to the target and there encountered the first enemy—four Russian T-34 tanks. Immediately upon contact, two of the four Egyptian tanks retreated to no-man's-land. The other two decided to fight. Precise artillery fire came from the flanks. Half of Arieh's forces took up positions with lightning speed. The other half was forced back and opened fire, joined by covering fire from Lapidot's tanks. No doubt that the two forces reacted instinctively and simultaneously. Israel, a platoon commander of Arieh's company, fired a shell at 1,800 meters. First bull's-eye. A shell from Lapidot's Sherman got the second bull's-eye at 1,750 meters. One tremendous explosion and then another. Red flames burst from the Egyptian tanks, followed by black clouds of heavy smoke which rose and spread rapidly. Excited voices gave out the good news of the double killing. Sasson sent his compliments and at the same breath—in a tone that is so unusual here—ordered: "Overrun them! Overrun them!" His order reached the tanks which were already speeding, while firing, towards Um-Tarpa.

Now Sasson went in front of the half-tracks of the armored infantry from the flank, urged them to reach the trenches quickly, and he, himself, at the head of the battalion command, drove his jeep along the narrow asphalt road, his voice overriding the tangle of voices coming over the signals instruments: "Go at them! Overrun them!" Belching fire, the tanks penetrated into the center of the position, grinding everything to bits under them. The armored infantry jumped from the half-tracks before they had come to a halt, leaped into the trenches with bursts from their Uzi's and throwing grenades. Um-Tarpa was crumbling. When the rest of the battalion was inside the encampment and it seemed that everything was over and done, the Egyptian artillery came to life. The position was in range, exact range. The shells fell like hail. The tanks, relatively protected, stood steadily, but the half-tracks, exposed from above, began to mill round and about the burning Egyptian vehicles. The young soldiers, tasting for the first time in their lives the flavor of a brutal shelling, put their helmeted heads next to the iron plates of their transport. Only Sasson—either instinctively or deliberately, it is difficult to know—stood upright in the command half-track, drew heavily on his perpetual cigarette, directed his driver in zig-zagging, and gave his opinion of the whole affair by a hand movement that is inimitable: "I couldn't care less about you, you so-and-so's!"

From the ammunition chambers and the gas tanks of the hit Egyptian tanks, trucks and cannon-carriers came constant explosions. But in the center of the post, in the fortified positions and in the trenches, all was silent. At 10:55, two hours after crossing the border, the armor battalion had racked up its first victory. From the far edges of the blue sky airplanes showed. Ouragans. Following them, a quadruplet of Fouga-Magisters. The jets passed over the battalion in low flight, tipped their wings in greetings of congratulations. From behind other half-tracks kept coming up. Brigadier-General Arik Sharon, the commander of the group, arrived. Officers of his party told about the first results of the air battle. 200 Egyptian planes had been destroyed on the ground and in the air. To put it briefly, the skies were ours!

According to our information, Um-Tarpa was to be only a warming up exercise. The real test were the gigantic defenses of Um-Katef, which extended to Abu Agheila on the west and almost as far as the edge of the Quseima dispositions on the south—hilly terrain fortified with impenetrable defenses, a hundred dug-in tanks and an enormous concentration of artillery. Taking Um-Tarpa, therefore, was no reason for a victory celebration. Some time after noon the tank company began to move forward, southwest, to make contact with Um-Katef. First Arieh's armor moved, took up positions and, at short range, began to look for targets. Lapidot's force, looking to give the cannon effective range, descended into the low-lying area of Baq'at-Katef, which was clear on all sides.

A howling sand-storm came up simultaneously with the first shots of the scouts. Sasson quickly became hoarse by repeating his order: "Look for anti-tank targets!" The raging sand-storm, the clouds of dust which the armored vehicles raised, the smoke of shooting and the sun blinded the tanks completely. For three long hours the armor blindly groped for its targets through the glaring haze curtain.

About 4:30 the sand-storm abated. The curtain of haze rose, visibility cleared and then, all at once, the battle began to rage. The enemy defenses consisted of a first and a second line, with dug-in tanks between, and behind them, more Egyptian cannon which fired rapidly. In the first five minutes Arieh's armor succeeded in turning two enemy tanks into burning torches. But the time for the assault itself was still to come. This became clear at nightfall. As the Egyptian artillery increased its barrage, Sasson ordered restraint: "Any tank which is not firing at a definite target is to take up a position."

In the waning daylight, Kuti, the commander of the adjacent brigade, came to see Sasson. His infantry was to attack the trenches at night and to clear them.

The Egyptian artillery barrage was becoming more severe. Craters began to pock-mark the area. The armor moved about in quest of hillocks for shelter against the barrage.

Later, when the darkness grew thicker, the enemy began to shower the area with flares for an effective artillery barrage.

At 10:30 p.m. Kuti's infantry force received orders to advance. It came up to the first line, and the fight in the trenches began. At the same time, the force of paratroops was dropped for a mission that was one of the most difficult in the whole war—to attack the Egyptian artillery positions at Arpan from the rear. They surprised the batteries, silencing them one after another; in so doing they, themselves, were caught in the fire and suffered heavy losses. At this stage, Arieh's tank platoon was ordered to break through into Um-Katef. The entire area in front of it was heavily mined, and Arieh had no choice but to invade via the only route, a narrow road which was under cross-fire. The first three tanks made it up the slope. However, the fourth tank hit a mine, and was not only put out of action but also blocked the road.

Without delay, a unit of sappers was rushed forward to work on clearing the minefield, while under deadly fire. The demolition officer was among the first to be wounded. In spite of it all, at the end of 45 minutes, the route was free for the entrance of the entire armor of the battalion. The rest of Arieh's tanks opened up an exchange with the Egyptian armor on the first line, while Lapidot's force attacked the second line on the slope and Benno's tanks joined him. After Ze'ev's half-tracks entered, all the fighting force of the battalion was inside the fortifications, but in complete darkness. Each tank and each half-track now became an independent fighting unit. What began as a battalion assault changed into a detachment attack on one of the two most fortified Egyptian centers in all of Eastern Sinai.

With the grey of dawn, the brigade commander, Motka, put into the battle another two armored battalions under the coordinating order of his second, Gideon. The Centurions broke through and joined up with the Shermans, which had burst their way through the defenses during the night. In the first light of day, jets of the Air Force dealt Um-Katef crushing blows. When they departed, a brutal battle developed between the combined Shermans and Centurions and the stubborn pocket of resistance of Egyptian armor which was consolidated in the south of the defenses. While the final struggle was raging in all its violence, helicopters appeared in the east. They penetrated the sea of smoke and tongues of flame, landed, gathered up wounded, rose and immediately after them other helicopters landed in an evacuation air lift—an operation of devotion and sacrifice, the sight of which touched the hearts of even the most hardened soldier. The battle of armor against armor began to reach its climax. The force under Gideon's command suffered losses, especially the Centurions. Half of the wounded were officers. But the Egyptian armor was destroyed, one after the other. The cannons shortened their range until it was suddenly discovered that Egyptian tanks were actually within the deployment of Sasson's battalion; they were hit from a distance of a hundred—even less—meters. The battle lasted four hours. In its final stages there was no longer a front and no line of attack. Only the last Egyptian tanks remained, doomed to destruction.

The Um-Katef campaign began at noon on June 5. Now, on the following day, close to eight o'clock, the Egyptian armor—cannons, vehicles and ammunition dumps—were in flames.

Sasson, cheeks covered with stubble and eyes red from dust and lack of sleep, sat in a jeep by the machine-gun, smoking and working on re-grouping his company. Lapidot, Arieh, Benno and Ze'ev—hoarse, faces caked with dust—moved about the armored cars in a personal supervision over the refueling, the reloading of ammunition, and general servicing.

The stories began to trickle in—about the behavior of the men in battle, the fighting of the crews, the enemy tanks destroyed, about the damage they themselves had sustained, about the wounds they had not reported.

Gabby, Arieh's second, had run into trouble. His tank had lost its signals apparatus, the machine-gun turret and part of the turret itself; but he, by himself, had knocked out seven Egyptian tanks. Benno, the commanding officer of the platoon, fared similarly. He was hit at close range. The crew got out safely intact and Benno, boiling with wrath, jumped into another tank, caught up with the tank which had hit him and destroyed it and, for good measure, several more. The victory was great—too great to be readily comprehended.

From here on, for almost two continuous days and nights, and until the final battle, the battalion spearheaded the war.

The process began on Tuesday, the third day of the week, and the second of the war, in the small hours of the afternoon. Even before the coming of darkness it was known that the Egyptian defenses in Quseima were crumbling. It was therefore decided to deal them a crushing blow from the air. When the enemy forces then scattered in all directions, they would be attacked from ambush and road blocks. In a hurried night session, by map and flashlight, Sasson explained to the seconds-in-command, by a simple wave of the hand, without elaborate planning, how to do away with any obstacle which they might encounter. The whole night the battalion waited impatiently for the Air Force to be done with its part and let the armor have a crack at the enemy. In the first light of morning, while the battalion was still shaking off the cold of the night and first sleep after two days and a night, the planes began their operation. Before an hour had passed the south-east horizon became split with columns of smoke. Now was the time! The battalion set out on its journey but quickly found itself in a quagmire of pitted and fissured loess soil.

Tanks and half-tracks strained forward, grinding out every meter. The entire battalion was enveloped in finely-ground white dust. Armor which was not equal to the situation had to be left behind. Finally the battalion was near the estimated retreat route of the Egyptians. But when it came in sight of the objective there was nothing left to ambush, nobody to attack; the Air Force had raked everything with fire and what remained had disappeared, thanks to the Egyptian art of flight. Kilometers of Egyptian vehicles, armored and others—smashed, scorched, burning—greeted the disappointed battalion. It drove parallel to the route, since the road itself was covered with burnt-out machines, exploded crates of ammunition, millions of bullets and shells, personal knapsacks and souvenirs familiar from Sinai Campaign ("Kadesh") days—the shoes thrown off to make travel across the sands easier. At the junction of the three routes, all the Zahal vehicles met for regrouping. A helicopter came down to gather the wounded. Within seconds it was stormed by thousands of soldiers taking advantage of the opportunity to send the first postcard of the war home. In the plain, transport planes parachuted down water containers from a low height.

"Where is Sasson?"

"Disappeared."

"Where?"

From a nearby Egyptian camp, deserted but not yet taken over by Zahal, a brand-new shiny Egyptian amphibious tank approached, swaying crazily and ploughing "figure eights" on the landscape. The soldiers who had handed in their letters left the helicopter and ran eagerly towards the newcomer. The applause given to the driver, Sasson, was not awarded even to stage star Topol—neither in London nor in Sinai.

The race with time, with the wide-open spaces and the retreating enemy, went on. Egyptian armor on the horizon was overtaken and destroyed by the spearhead tanks, without stopping the column. By nightfall several enemy vehicles were transformed into burning and exploding road signs, lighting up the darkness. Night stops for the battalion were for not more than two hours. Casualties resulted mainly from mines, the hidden form of combat at which this enemy was particularly adept.

Dawn came and, with it, the curtain rose on the last battle.

The order of the brigade commander, Motka, was couched in terms understood by all—to "race to Kal'at a-Nakhl, but fast, just so that we get there first."

"Yes, sir!" The race began. Tanks swallowed up distances like patrol jeeps. The route led past an Egyptian disposition in which everything pointed to a recent and hasty departure. The temptation to stop was exceedingly great—new T-54 tanks under camouflage nets, S.U.-100 mm. self-propelled cannons, batteries, amphibious armor and gigantic dumps of fuel and ammunition. But when it became clear that the disposition had been abandoned, the pace was maintained. Two or three times several tanks detached themselves from the flanks or dashed forward to knock off targets moving in the distance, without slowing up the momentum of the race. At six, on the morning of the fifth day of the week and the fourth of the war, the patrols reached the outskirts of the desert oasis of Kal'at a-Nakhl.

Forward! Speed was increased more vigorously. The column soon found itself in an alignment marked by Egyptian road markers; the fresh treads of the tires and tracks. By the wayside a herd of camels stood and happily devoured the rich vegetation. Around it several Bedouin women moved warily. The racing battalion, with all the clanging, evoked no more than haughty stares from the camels. The battalion went on in two columns, racing each other to the objective.

And there it was—Kal'at a-Nakhl. Tents, a water tower, a block of elongated buildings and a three-storey building, an exact copy of the Ministry of Housing headquarters in a development village. "Stop!" It was clear to everyone—even if it had not been clearly stated—that a-Nakhl was certainly deserted and, if so, it would get several salvos for the sake of appearances. The armor would then pass through and continue its speedy journey west, to the Parker Monument, through the Mitla Pass, not stopping until the track of the leading tank would paddle about in the waters of the Suez Canal. This was what everyone expected. Developments were otherwise.

When the spearhead reached effective range of a-Nakhl, two tank platoons deployed and fired the first salvo of shells.

No reaction.

The range was shortened, the tanks fired additional shells. Targets caught fire, clouds of smoke spread out and a tremendous fuel dump broke out into a reddish-black ball of flame which spread out and rose like the mushroom of Hiroshima.

Reaction—none.

Jets appeared from behind. The armor crews rushed to mark their vehicles with identification signs to prevent dangerous misunderstandings.

The signals apparatus delivered the instruction of the brigade commander to Sasson: "Secure yourself on the left flank!" This was instinct at work, but direct information could not have been more accurate. At the very same minute, two Egyptian tanks appeared on the left, at a range of approximately 2,000 meters, flanking the cannon of the spread-out Israeli armor.

"Fire!" The first tank managed to disappear into the area of a-Nakhl, the second was blown up by a direct hit.

There now developed not a battle but a slaughter. While the Air Force was still diving down on the more distant targets on the road leading to the Mitla Pass, an entire Egyptian armor brigade tried to escape with its life. Instead, it came within the deadly range of Sasson's armor and, as it turned out later, could not have been more completely demolished. It simply didn't know what had hit it. Arieh's tanks on the right, and those of Lapidot on the left, destroyed 15 Egyptian tanks within two hours. At this stage Motka activated the rest of his battalions in a pincer movement for combing the large Nakhl valley. This force destroyed the Egyptian brigade to the last vehicle. At noon, when the sun and the desert heat were at their peak, the tumult of battle quieted down. The tank corpsmen still did not know it, but they had written military history, not only in the fiery valley but in all of Sinai and in the annals of warfare.

This was not then the first time that this battalion had been under fire, nor its first time in Sinai. 19 years ago, in "Operation Ten Plagues," the battalion participated in the mopping-up of the Egyptian invasion in the south, and in Sinai ("Kadesh") it was almost the only battalion which had had the luck to battle the Egyptians armor-to-armor, to destroy their tanks and to pursue their crushed remnants up to the Canal.

So much for the battalion. As for its command: Sasson, the battalion commander, headed a group of half-tracks in the Sinai Campaign which took Abu Agheila and fought at Ruafa Dam, a battle which went into the history books and military manuals. Sasson's second, the bespectacled Uri, was in command of a tank platoon, and his half-track was one of the two armored vehicles which broke through the fortified dam itself. The seconds-in-command—Arieh, Lapidot, Benno, Ze'ev and Noam—had accumulated their battle experience only in the last few years, in the recurrent flare-ups on the former Syrian border. In the War of Independence they were small children, in the first Sinai war they were boys (their ages at the present: between 24–26). But their fighting has made them worthy of their elder brothers from the years of 1948 and 1956. They introduced their young crews to their baptism of fire and brought them out as battle-hardened tank corpsmen. The fighters of the battalion earned—in Um-Katef, in Um-Tarpa, in a-Nakhl—some of the most glorious laurels in the wreath of victory of Zahal in Sinai, achieved in what the corpsmen will always regard as the finest hour of their lives.

Mordecai Barkai: Breaking Through the Desert; *Dvar Hashavua,* 23.6.67

★

Yosef Mutsani and Amos Libereider crossed the border of Sinai this week and were privileged to have the contents of a water canteen poured over their heads in order to celebrate their third crossing of the Sinai border. Each of the three times, these two had crossed in a jeep together: in the Horev Campaign in 1948, the Sinai Campaign and now.

Avital Mossinson: The Third Time; *Army Press Release,* 6.6.67

Three divisions fought in Sinai, under the command of three generals: Yisrael Tal ("Tallik"), Avraham Yaffe, Ariel ("Arik") Sharon. Three magnificent, glorious commanders; each of them different from the others—in character, in physical appearance, in demeanor and in his way of fighting.

General Yisrael Tal ("Tallik"), commander of the armored forces that cracked the Egyptian lines, smashed the Syrian emplacements and overran the Jordanian positions, is a short, powerfully-built man with eyes of steel and a decisive voice, who himself looks like a small, stocky tank. He was born in 1924 to a farmer family in the Galilee Kvutza, Mahanayim. At the age of 16 he joined the Hagana. In the Second World War he volunteered for the British Army, served in the Jewish Brigade, and helped to organize the "illegal" immigration of Jewish survivors of the death camps from Europe to the Land of Israel. During the War of Liberation he was sent to Czechoslovakia, where he supervised arms shipments to Israel. When he returned he was appointed operations officer of the Northern Command.

Tallik slowly but steadily mounted the echelons of rank in the Israel Defense Forces. First he commanded the Infantry School. Then he held staff positions in the Instruction Division, and took a course for higher officers in England. After his return he was placed in charge of the Officers School.

His link with armor came suddenly and swiftly. After Operation Sinai, Moshe Dayan, then Chief-of-Staff, summoned him and said: "I have appointed you Assistant Commander of the Armored Forces. When are you prepared to transfer?"

"In another two or three weeks," answered Tal.

"No," said Dayan. "I mean, what time today?"

In the Israel Army, Tallik is reported to have an IBM brain. During his spare time he reads philosophy. He mastered the new field entrusted to him very swiftly indeed. From having been an infantry specialist he rapidly became the Army's "Mr. Armor."

General Tal showed himself a most thorough person, never relying on improvisation. He knows all tank types used by the Israel Army, to the very last screw. And in the case of Tallik this is no exaggeration. It is told that when he was appointed Assistant Commander of the Armored Forces in 1957, he simply hung up his uniform in the clothes cupboard and took a course for armor officers as a cadet from the ranks. Since becoming the Commander of Armor he has imbued his forces with a sense of precision and accuracy.

There are legends in the army about his thoroughness. It is said that when the forces received the first British Centurions, several leading officers came and complained of mechanical shortcomings and of defective braking in the new model. General Tal listened quietly to them and then asked: "Just a moment! Have you read the instruction book? (It had come together with the tanks from the factory.)—You haven't read it? Then go and read it and you'll know!"

The officers went off, studied the book of instructions and found the solutions to their problems. And the tanks ran as though they had been buttered.

Although he is one of the strictest commanders in the army, Tallik's door is always open to those under his charge. He is prepared to receive his men for conversation at all hours of the day. He listens to problems, he gives advice and guidance.

He is strict with his men, but far, far stricter with himself. His wife and two sons go to the beach by bus. The army car and driver, states General Tal, is intended for army use and not for private trips. In Tallik's headquarters guests are never offered more than cold water with raspberry juice in summer, and a cup of coffee in winter. General Tal has no "expense account." He pays for the raspberry juice and coffee from his own pocket. His men know this and respect him for it.

General Tal has given Israeli armor a new direction. He has shaped it, added drive and power to its force, introduced new and unfamiliar tactics. On Armor Day, which was held seven months before war broke out, he said in an interview:

"Considering the limited dimensions of the State of Israel, it will be necessary for the Israel Defense Forces, even in case of a defensive war, to transfer the locale of hostilities to enemy territory, and armor is the instrument best suited for the purpose. The region where the war may be fought is a typical tank arena, permitting the use of large-scale formations and the exploitation of all the powers of shock which are offered by armor. What characterizes Israel's principles of armor is that it is based on comprehensive exploitation of our higher-quality manpower."

The Six-Day War shows how correct he was.

The Editors

★

Military history is sometimes willing to repeat itself, or at least a step or two. During the Sinai Campaign, General Yaffe headed an unbelievable military operation: his brigade reached Sharm-a-Sheikh, at the southern end of Sinai—marching through the desert. In the Six-Day War he did it again: a reserve armored brigade under his command pushed on through seemingly impassable terrain—deep sand dunes—to the Egyptian rear at Bir Lahfan, caught the enemy by surprise, took its positions, and wiped out most of two Egyptian armored brigades which tried to relieve the besieged points.

He has been in the service of Israel's security for 30 years. In 1929 he volunteered for the Hagana and, years later, joined Captain Charles Orde Wingate's "Night Squads," whose operations, unorthodox but effective, saved the Jewish community in Palestine from the terrorism of Arab marauders. Like many other senior Zahal commanders-to-be, he served with the British Army during World War II. In the War of Independence he was in command of the battalion which took Acre and Nazareth. He then took his battalion south to the Negev and participated in "Operation-It's-a-Fact"—the conquest of Eilat.

Avraham Yaffe is a dedicated lover of nature. He roams about the country a great deal and is familiar with every trail and gully. After resigning from active service in Zahal in 1964, he was appointed to a post after his own heart—Director of the Nature Reserve Authority. It is said that, in the course of the long weeks prior to the Six-Day War, he spent hours studying special configurations of terrain in the south. One day he announced with great glee: "We have discovered a rare new specimen of scorpion." When the general appeared later at a press conference and analyzed the special characteristics of Israel's military reserves, he added, with a smile: "Instead of protecting Israel's nature reserves, I found myself commanding its military reserves."

Avraham Yaffe's entire household may be called "a fighting family." His daughter is a sergeant in Zahal. His son served under the father's command as a courier. His nephew is a captain in a Centurion unit. His wife, Aviva, is the sister of Leah Rabin, the wife of the Chief-of-Staff. When the family took count, it found that at least 15 of its members participated in the Six-Day War.

Broad-shouldered, built like a bear, Avraham Yaffe loves life and people, prefers good company and a witty anecdote. His best-known quip: "Of course I maintain a diet—lots of it." He is a teetotaler when it comes to alcohol and tobacco. His secret love is an oversize mug brimming with hot, hot tea.

When the country went on alert, this "retired" gentleman of 53 sought out the Chief-of-Staff and suggested: "It was fine to take off the uniform, but I still have 10 good years of Zahal left inside of it."

"So what would you like to do?" asked his brother-in-law.

"Whatever has to be done," replied the general. "I am prepared to go back as a brigade commander."

General Rabin agreed, and the veteran, commanding a division of reservists, smote the Egyptians hip on thigh. All of his former "boys," including Maurice, the brigade cook of Sinai Campaign days, volunteered to serve as soon as word got around that he was back in command. They were joined by Adina, the secretary of the Nature Reserve Authority, and Ethan, the general's chauffeur in private life.

The Six-Day War ended. The reservists went back home. As for General Avraham Yaffe, he is back in the bosom of nature, caring for birds and flowers, protecting rare animals from the inroads of indiscriminate hunters. His fifth war is now a matter of history.

The Editors

★

General Arik Sharon, whose division comprised armor, infantry, artillery, paratroops and engineering corps, performed one of the hardest and most complicated tasks of the Six-Day War: breaking into the Egyptian fortified district of Abu-Agheila, their "Maginot Line." General Sharon is unique as an Israeli fighter. He started his military career as platoon-commander during the War of Independence, and later on he took part in nearly every Israeli retaliation raid against Egypt, Syria and Jordan. He commanded special assault units, which undertook daring exploits across the frontier. During the Sinai Campaign he led the paratroops, who landed in impossibly difficult conditions at the Mitla Pass in Sinai, and prevented the Egyptians from sending reinforcements through this important artery to their troops in Sinai.

General Sharon is a tall man, round-faced, with almost completely white hair. In spite of his 38 years, he always addresses his men quietly, almost in a whisper, but his influence on the soldiers is almost magnetic, and under his command they are willing to attempt the impossible. Like Charles Wingate, whose personal example influenced many of the Israeli senior officers, General Sharon always carries with him a small Bible, which he often reads and quotes. When summing up the performance of his brigade in the Six-Day War, he quoted one of the Egyptian generals, who explained the defeat of his army as follows: "What are you supposed to do? These Jews never attack the way it is written in the books." Sharon never attacks the way it is written in the books. He always does the unexpected thing.

In time of battle, Arik keeps perfectly calm. Officers who fought at his side in the Six-Day War, in the bloody battles of Abu-Agheila, Um-Katef and Um-Shihan, said with frank admiration: "Arik never shouted; he was never upset, and he spoke with confidence-inspiring deliberation. You never make small talk with him, you never exchange views with him; when he feels like talking to you, he talks. In the course of the fighting we found ourselves several times in difficult situations—as when we pushed on to block the ways of retreat to the fleeing Egyptians. Our vehicles were exposed to fire, unprotected, and crowded together. As we were passing an Egyptian position, they opened hellish fire on us. Arik rose and stood on his seat, directing our fire. His whole body protruded from the car, as if he were trying to say: 'Look at me, boys! If this is the way I carry myself, you can do it too!'"

And his soldiers followed him all the way to the Suez Canal.

The Editors

The Mitla Pass had been a household word in Israel ever since the Sinai Campaign, when it was conquered in an extraordinarily daring attack by a paratroop unit under the command of Arik Sharon, suffering heavy losses. The Mitla Pass is 23 kilometers long. Control of either one of its entrances gives control of one of the few roads of access to the Suez Canal. One of the orders given to General Avraham Yaffe's division, with special mention referring to Colonel "Yeska"'s brigade, was "to hurry to the Mitla, to attack, to outflank and stop any enemy movement toward the Canal Zone, and to exterminate anybody trying to retreat through the Pass." The brigade reached the place much before the estimated time. The retreating Egyptians found the passage blocked, and all their attempts to break through failed. The result was that the Mitla Pass was turned into a shambles of armor, such as were uncommon even in the Second World War.

"It won't be an easy war this time," our officer said before we started moving. "We'll have many casualties, but we'll fight and we'll win. We're moving against enemy forces that are larger than ours and have more arms than we, and they are sitting in strong fortified positions. But we'll break through the enemy's lines, and we'll defeat him."

Our orders were to join up fast with a tank battalion that was moving against the Mitla Pass. Our battery was supposed to assist the tanks if infantry forces should turn up, and also to give cover to a fuel convoy that was on its way there. At that moment the battalion was moving towards Mitla on its last few drops of fuel and had already lost its maneuvering ability, because it could no longer spare the fuel for sideway moves.

We set out with seven vehicles: three Shermans that had been converted to guns, and four armored cars loaded with jerricans. At the last moment, we were joined by an Egyptian truck that we had captured at the beginning of the campaign.

Before the "Parker Monument" we had to stop for a moment to give fire cover to somebody. Meanwhile, the armored cars and the truck had disappeared round the corner. We didn't know where they had gone—to the right or to the left. Then we saw lights on the right, and we realized that that was where they were.

When we hurried after the lights, we realized that our armored cars had indeed gone that way, but that was not where the light came from: tanks, armored cars and trucks were burning all along both sides of the road and in the *wadi* below. As far as you could see, burning Egyptian vehicles were turning the night into day, with a noise that was a terrible symphony of destruction.

With considerable risk we made our way between the burning vehicles. Every few moments something exploded next to us with a sound of thunder and sparks flying everywhere. So we carried on for several kilometers through what had once been Egyptian companies and battalions of tanks and motorized infantry, till we came near Mitla. There it turned dark again. The fire was behind us, and we moved on once more in the light of our own headlights.

Suddenly, our tank ran into a truck full of soldiers. We looked at them from a distance of five paces. They were Egyptians, and they were armed to the teeth.

The Egyptians cheered when they saw us—and we opened fire with our "Uzis." *"Bas, bas!* (Stop!)" they shouted and tried to explain to us that they were "our people." They still thought that we were Egyptians as well. But they caught on immediately, and when they saw how few we were—6 against their 40—they jumped off the truck and attacked us. Our ammunition soon ran out, and the Egyptians tried to climb onto our tank and finish us off with their rifles. When we had no bullets left, we began to hit with the butts of our "Uzis" on the heads that stuck out and the hands that grasped the sides of our tank.

Twice they almost got far enough to use their rifles, but the silent battle went on. All one could hear were a few shouts, groans, and the dull sounds of butts on bodies. One of our men broke the butt of his "Uzi" and drew a knife. Suddenly, all at once, the attack petered out. The Egyptians who were still alive disappeared in the darkness. At that same moment, everything was lit up by a truck that had caught fire. Behind the last armored car we saw another truck. Someone was fast—too fast—and emptied a whole magazine into the driver's cabin. The glass splintered, and so did the steering wheel. The driver jumped out. It was the lieutenant who drove our captured Egyptian truck full of fuel. But the miracle that had worked for us all through the campaign held good. The lieutenant was safe and sound.

The tanks thirstily drank the fuel we had brought. We deployed between them. All that was left of the whole battalion were ten tanks, drawn up on the two sides of the Mitla Pass. The C.O. had put up loudspeakers between the tanks, and he himself had climbed a hill. Out of the loudspeakers, his orders resounded over the *wadi* with a strange sound. Suddenly, I realized that the C.O. was hoarse from giving orders and from being dead tired. That was what made his voice sound so strange, and at the same time so quietly confident.

Opposite, in the narrow pass between the mountains that was the only escape route for whole brigades of Egyptian tanks, troop-carriers and infantry, the latest Russian equipment was burning. Three of our tanks had taken positions on the right with their guns aimed at the Pass, and another three on the left. The remainder were aiming to the rear, so as to finish anything that managed to get by the first tanks; for the moment the enemy came near and got in between us, our tanks could not fire at him for fear of hitting each other.

Fire was burning ahead of us, lighting up whatever approached. From time to time, when the flames grew weaker, we would jump and drag more trucks into the pass and set them on fire, so that no one should enter the pass without our seeing him.

"Number ten!" The voice of the C.O. echoed through the *wadi*. "Two tanks approaching. The first is yours. Number nine, you take the other."

There was a noise of tracks biting into the sandy rock, of engines, and of flames crackling from half a dozen burning trucks. The Egyptian tanks came up fast—escaping from the death behind them into the death that was lying in ambush for them. We heard two shells leaving the gun barrels, and two deafening explosions.

"Sergeant-major!" the voice of the C.O. thundered.

"Three," came the answer.

"Write it down!" the C.O. ordered, and then, with something mocking in his hoarse voice: "The ledger is open and the hand is writing."

A group of half-tracks full of soldiers clattered up to the entrance of the gully.

"Sergeant-major, don't write that down! They're only troop-carriers. We only write down tanks."

I sat in the tank with nothing to do. I must have fallen asleep again. Suddenly, I was awakened by the thunder of the C.O.'s voice:

"Number two, another shell. If you don't hit him now, he'll get away to the Canal."

A terrible noise resounded behind us. The tank that had already gotten through was hit and went up in flames.

"Sergeant-major, how many?"

"41, Sir. The hand is writing."

All that morning we continued pouring fire on hundreds of vehicles that were streaming past from all directions: tanks, troop-carriers, trucks, command-cars, jeeps were lying around everywhere in frightening, glorious confusion. Sometimes we even called in the Air Force: the tanks that were galloping to their death were too large, and the pressure too heavy for our supply of ammunition.

Baruch Nadel: Night of Flames; *Yediot Aharonot,* 30.6.67

War does strange things to people: one person shrinks, the other seems to grow. Sometimes it singles out an ordinary soldier, who had never been considered much of a fighter, and turns him into a hero and a symbol. This is what happened to Sergeant Yossi Laffer, who served in an armored unit in General Tal's division:

At 6 a.m. on Tuesday, June the 6th, the armor concentrated at Rafiah received orders to advance. The objective was Gaza. Among the tanks that began thundering forward there was a group of "Pattons," headed by the commander's tank. As he gave his final instructions the C.O. silently prayed that his luck should not betray him again as it had the day before, when his tank had been hit by a shell and burnt in the height of the battle for Rafiah not far from the town. This morning he had received a fresh tank, and secretly congratulated himself for insisting that the new crew should include the same loader and signaler sergeant who had been with him yesterday. He's all right, he thought, he can be relied on.

Yossi Laffer, the loader and signaler in question, was already very busy. The unit roared ahead with guns blazing, destroying everything it met. Yossi listened tensely to the commander's objectives. He swiftly loaded the cannon, sent the shells straight at the targets. Several positions were discovered on the road and destroyed. Just before Khan-Yunis the company met a half-company of Stalin tanks. The Pattons swiftly deployed into assault positions, and the entire half-company was liquidated after a brief battle. Their unit advanced towards Khan-Yunis.

The commander's tank was the first to burst into one of the main streets. Yossi was busy loading a shell when the commander saw the trench dug across the roadway ahead of them. He waited for his officer to mark his target but heard only a great noise. The tank stopped.

Two shells were fired at them from one of the houses. Yossi did not know what had happened. As he loaded the shell his watch-strap slipped. He put the watch into his shirt pocket, after glancing at the time. It was a few moments before eight. He raised his head above the turret but saw nobody. A swift glance round showed that he was the only one left in the Patton. The rest of the crew had managed to jump out. He must have missed the order to abandon the tank.

And now began the private war of Yossi Laffer.

To begin with, he moved to the commander's position and placed himself beside the look-out instruments. He aimed at the building from which the two shells had been fired. It collapsed. Yossi was commending his marksmanship when opposite him, at a distance of about 400 meters, he noticed an armored troop-carrier advancing slowly on the left side of the street. Yossi sent a shell at it. It went up in flames. A lorry appeared in the distance, in the middle of the road. He promptly assessed it as 800 meters away. He loaded again and a black cloud of smoke mounted from the lorry.

Only then did he decide to inspect the position and check what had actually happened. He moved back to the driver's cabin and tried to put the tank in motion. It was useless. He stopped trying and felt happy when he found that he had at least succeeded in operating the motor for charging the accumulators. In that case, thought he, I can operate the communication set and the turret as well. He cautiously raised his head from the turret. The tank was tilted forward over the trench, with its two caterpillar tracks flung forward. So they had hit a mine.

There was silence nearby. In the distance could be heard the echoes of shots and explosions. Yossi clearly identified the sounds of the Uzis and the stronger rat-a-tat of automatic weapons. He assumed that the paratroops must be fighting within the town and the Russian Storm Rifles were returning fire. Before him stretched a long empty street. To his right ran a little alley. On both sides of the street were one- and two-storey houses. Several alleys ran together at the end of the street. A tall tower rose on the horizon.

Yossi crawled back into the tank. An unpleasant feeling ran through him. "How long can I hold out here?" he asked silently. The echoes of the distant shooting encouraged him. If they were shooting with light weapons it could not be so bad after all, said he to himself; and several millimeters of good stout steel were protecting him. He could not be hit by a bullet. Now he turned his head towards the remaining ammunition stacked in the tank and felt at ease. There were enough shells.

He took his watch out of his shirt pocket. It was almost 8:30. What should he do? He could leave the tank, enter one of the houses and hide. He could also stay in the Patton and do nothing, on the assumption that the Egyptians would see a damaged motionless tank and not pay any attention. Then he remembered the course for tank commanders. A tank was there. Ammunition was there. Then shoot. Go on fighting.

All of a sudden he began to feel apprehensive that a grenade might be flung at him from one of the two-storey houses. Better flatten out all the second storeys, he decided, and began to shift shells from the stock-pile to the gun. He loaded, aiming at the upper floors of the houses at the roadside and felt pleased as he saw the walls coming apart. They won't throw any grenades at me now; and he felt much better.

Each time he turned the turret the cartridge cases shifted and banged against his leg. He understood that this was because the tank was leaning forward in the trench. So he decided to fling each empty cartridge case out into the street. The noise of the fighting could be clearly heard. He listened hard in order to distinguish any concentration of shots from Russian Storm Rifles. When he identified a concentration point of the kind, he sent a shell in that direction. Each shell silenced a firing center. I may be cut off and alone, but I'm not out of the game yet, he thought, and was astonished at the cheerfulness that accompanied the thought.

Every few moments Yossi remembered to operate the motor for charging the accumulators and operating the communication set. That's very important, he thought. I have to make contact with the commander. But suddenly he remembered in alarm that the entire area behind the tank was dead ground as far as he was concerned. He could not see what was going on behind. He rose, took his Uzi, thrust his head out and swept the area behind him with several bursts. If the Egyptians did see that his tank still functioned, then at least let them believe that several men were there.

He casually brought his watch out of his pocket again. The time was 9:30. I haven't contacted the commander, he remembered, that's not in order. He saw that he had lost the microphone and began to search the reserve container. He did not find one in the first nor in the second, but only in the third. "This is the knocked-out tank," he reported, "this is the knocked-out tank." A tank commander must never mention his name. He began to think of some more suitable and easier means of identification and found it at last. "The Moshav lad speaking. The Moshav lad is alone in the tank," he broadcast. He waited a moment. For the fragment of a second there flashed through his mind the Nir-Israel moshav where he lived with his parents. Then he heard the familiar voice of the company commander. "They're coming to get you out. We'll get you out." The commander asked whether he had been hit and whether he was holding out. "Everything's in order," reported Yossi. "I'm holding out. It's all in order."

Now Yossi began to look for targets. For some reason he was annoyed at the tower rising on the horizon. It will be an interesting exercise, thought he, to bring the tower down. If anyone's up there, he won't find it pleasant. He went to the heap, pulled out a shell, and loaded it. A big hole appeared in the distant tower. He heard himself shouting: "Lovely! Excellent!"

Then he noticed several soldiers crossing the road at a run and entering one of the houses. He took a shot at it. After that he noticed that the windows of several houses were protected with stones. He took his sub-machine gun and sprayed the protected windows all along the street.

Interesting how much time has already passed, and he put his hand into his pocket. It was a little after 10. He noted, and not without some pride, that he was not afraid. He had no sense of fear. The commander had promised that they would get him away, so they would get him away. There was no doubt about it.

An Egyptian soldier again dashed across the road. Yossi shot a shell at the house where he hid. Suddenly he observed several civilians, including women and children, coming out of one of the houses and looking round. No point in having anything to do with them, he decided. So he merely shot a few rounds in the air in order to frighten them and drive them in.

Now he realized that every time he had to shoot a shell it meant a promenade in the tank. By a brief calculation he found each of these promenades was about four meters in length. So he decided to place several shells beside the gun and not to take a single shell each time.

He began to feel hungry. I'd like something good to eat, something light. He opened a combat ration, took out a tin of grape-fruit slices and drank some of the juice. Then he took the microphone. "Here's the damaged tank. Here's the Moshavnik. When are they coming to get me away?" he asked the commander. Instead of an answer he heard the commander ordering his next in command to get the Moshavnik away. But his joy did not last long. A few minutes later he heard one of the company's tanks reporting to the commander that he could not succeed in reaching the damaged tank. There were difficulties and he was returning.

Now he suddenly heard shots behind the tank. He raised his head and shot with his Uzi at the windows of the houses behind him. The shooting stopped. When it was almost 11 he began to feel very thirsty. He remembered the full water container fixed on the outer side of the tank. Very slowly he put his hand out and tried to undo the strap that surrounded the jerrican. After a few attempts he succeeded in releasing the container and brought it in.

While he was still gulping some water he heard feet running behind the tank. He put his head out once more. Egyptian soldiers were dashing across the road, seeking cover in the houses. He shot several bursts at them from the Uzi. Then he saw that he only had one clip of bullets left. He decided that from now on he would only shoot single shots. When he returned to his place at the command seat he saw a group of Egyptian soldiers entering one of the houses at the end of the street. Swiftly he loaded and hit the house. That's all past now, he thought, as he congratulated himself on his accurate fire.

What was the time? Almost 12. Time passes. Yossi opened a tin of corn. He was fond of corn. While chewing the kernels he saw through the periscope a number of Egyptian soldiers approaching the tank. He put down the tin, loaded a shell and fired at them. They jumped into one of the houses. He shelled it. Another group of Egyptian soldiers appeared. He shot a shell in their direction and they scattered. He tried to load another shell but couldn't. The shell would not go in. For the first time he was afraid. Something wrong with the cannon. It was unpleasant without the cannon.

Yossi took the microphone. "Here's the disabled tank. Here is the disabled tank. The big one is out of order. The big one's ruined."

A moment's silence. The company commander answered: "Hold out. We'll come to get you. Hold out. We'll get you." He put the microphone down and tried to repair the cannon, swinging it swiftly to one side and stopping it suddenly so as to jar it. The trick succeeded. The cannon unjammed. The shells could be loaded again.

A group of about 15 soldiers appeared near the burnt-out lorry. Yossi shot a shell at them. Several jumped into a house on the left. He felt more cheerful when he realized that they carried light arms. They won't succeed in hitting me with light weapons, he thought.

A figure appeared in the window of one of the houses not far from him. Yossi emerged again, shot one single shot and the man vanished. In the meantime he went on eating his corn, eating and watching through the periscope. He began to pay as much attention as he could to what was going on behind him. From time to time he climbed up to peep at the area behind, fire a single shot and pop back in again.

Now he saw a concentration of Egyptian soldiers. No doubt about it, they were beginning to pay attention to the tank and what he was doing. The soldiers hid behind the houses. Yossi inspected the shell container. There were still some but not many. He was not afraid but the situation was serious, beginning to be dangerous. Things were beginning to warm up. He aimed at the houses behind which the troops were hiding, and shot off one shell. Then he shot off a few bursts with the sub-machine gun. And again a shell followed by machine-gun bursts.

They began shooting at the tank. Yossi responded with shells. The shots at the tank became steadily stronger. Bullets hit the turret above Yossi's head. He was hit in a finger of his left hand, went down to the bottom of the tank and only then felt a pain splitting his chest. That's it, I'm hit. A bullet had struck the top of the turret and then ricochetted and hit him in the chest. He could hardly breathe for pain.

Yossi looked at his watch again. Two o'clock. Silly, thought he, to have to be killed just now, after having held out so long. Don't die, he began repeating to himself. Don't die. Don't die. He stretched his hand out to the case, pulled out a bandage, pulled off his shirt and bandaged his chest. In order not to lose blood he had better lie quiet on the floor of the tank. Not even budge. Outside there was a hellish fusillade falling on the tank. Bullets struck the turret and sparks fell on his uncovered belly. He tried to breathe deep, but it caused him fearful agony.

Now Yossi remembered that he had a grenade in his trousers' pocket. He rubbed his fingers over the grenade. I shan't fall into their hands alive. What did the Bible say? "Let me perish with the Philistines." If they'll mount the tank I'll use the grenade. I shan't surrender. They won't take me alive. He placed his tankman's helmet under his head and rested. Outside the firing continued. Once again he took hold of the grenade.

At this point he heard the voice of the commander giving orders to go out and relieve the disabled tank. This time he was sending a platoon to relieve him. Yossi heard the platoon commander reporting that they were meeting with difficulties but were advancing towards the tank.

Now Yossi decided that he must get himself up and fire the cannon. If I don't do it now I'm finished. I must. With a great effort he raised himself. He loaded the cannon and looked for a target. Calculating the trajectory of the bullets that were hitting the turret, he turned the gun on a neighboring house, shot and hit it. He loaded again and shot, loaded and sent off seven shells one after the other as though he were crazy. Only then did he suddenly remember that every shell weighed about 25 kilos (55 pounds). The wound was not bleeding but breathing was difficult. He couldn't breathe deeply.

There was silence after the volley of shells he had fired. Yossi sank to rest on the lower seat. He did not know how much time passed when he heard on his communication set that one of the tanks that had been sent to relieve him was close by. The tank was asking him to emerge and come over under cover of the dust and smoke of the houses that his shells had blown up. "We are 10 meters behind you," said the section commander. Yossi wished to inform him that he was wounded and couldn't move, but lost the microphone once more.

He could feel that if he did not come out at once they would reckon that he was not alive any more and would go their way. He took hold of the Uzi in one hand. With the last of his strength he emerged from the tank, climbed out of the turret and rolled himself down.

The unit commander, whose tank was the closest to the disabled one, at once understood that he was wounded. Yossi wanted to shout as much to him, but could not make a sound. The commander hurried to him. Yossi saw it was his good friend, who had gone through the same course for tank commanders.

They carried Yossi over to the tank, stretched him out on the floor, gave him water to drink, and the tanks made a dash at once for the Khan-Yunis railway station. "We've taken Gaza," someone whispered to him, and Yossi smiled, "Lovely."

All this time he kept himself conscious. He had once heard that a wounded man who becomes unconscious is endangering his life. After being shaken about from one place to another he reached the regimental assembly point. He remembers that the surgeon had a moustache and reassured him: "Everything will be O.K., there's nothing to worry about."

Late in the afternoon Yossi was placed on a pick-up truck leaving for the Beer-Sheba Hospital.

Yossi kept himself fully conscious. When they reached the point where the old signpost stands with the words "Frontier before you," Yossi told himself—I'm safe. I'm at home. For the first time that day he had a wonderful feeling. One of the orderlies accompanying him wanted to pull a curtain across the car window because of the blinding sun, but Yossi begged him: "No, no, I want to see the sun."

When they brought him into the hospital Yossi remembered the grenade in his trousers' pocket. He told the nurse about this and she dashed in alarm to the clothes stock in order to find it.

A few days later Aluf Mishneh Shmulik visited him and told him very simply: "Yossi, you're a hero!"

Shlomo Shamir: One-Man War; *Ha'aretz Supplement*, 21.7.67

His picture appeared on the Life *magazine cover, in all of the Israeli press, and in many newspapers throughout the world: face caked with dust and shaded by a beard-growth of several days, eyes bloodshot from sleeplessness, sun-baked skin, lines of stubbornness around the mouth—these became for hundreds of thousands of people the symbol of the fighting commander in the desert. Colonel Samuel ("Shmulik"), commander of an armored brigade under the order of General Yisrael Tal, is made—according to his commander— of tempered steel, of something different from ordinary flesh and blood.*

"Colonel," I said, "this time I won't let you off. I want to understand. How could one unit of armor have beaten eight Egyptian brigades? And the Egyptians fought back, at that, as you said yourself."

We were sitting in the mobile command post at Bir Gafgafa, with the red-hot desert all around us. The men, the crews of that legendary tank unit, were lying around under their tanks to get some shelter from the sun. We poured one bottle after another of boiling Egyptian Coca-Cola down our throats.

"How did it happen, Shmulik?"

The Colonel smiled. An infrequent smile on an unemotional face, and, as infrequent smiles tend to be, charming and good-natured. "It's just that we fought well."

I insisted. I wanted to get to the bottom of it. Of all the battle stories of Sinai, of all the miracles of the desert, the story of the record of this unit is the strangest; the unit that made its way from the north of the Gaza Strip to the Suez Canal in four days, fought eight or nine battles on the way, destroyed or captured something like 300 enemy tanks and thousands of troops—and all at the cost of no more than a couple of its own tanks and 70 of its men. But it was not only the record of the unit that made me seek out its commanding officer. I had always been curious about the man himself, ever since he told the story of the campaign he had fought to the journalists of Tel-Aviv, together with the other brigade commanders from Sinai. He was the man who finished his story by quoting what he had said to his men on the banks of the Canal: "I am proud to lead you, but I am a little ashamed to command you."

He does not look shy, this Shmulik, but not particularly daring either. He is certainly not the type of the field officer with a shock of hair and unwavering eyes. He is of average height, with a crew-cut and a hoarse voice. Only by talking with him at length and listening to him talking with his subalterns does one realize his speed of understanding, his precision of thought, his ability to decide and to command obedience.

All the officers and soldiers under his command respect and fear him. The contrasts of his personality confuse them, and they do not know what to make of him. He can keep his men at arm's length and at the same time give them a feeling of fatherly-comradely closeness. He has no compunction about giving a man 35 days detention for being slow with a salute or not buttoning his shirt up properly, but in battle he has a way of being always at the toughest spot and patting someone on the shoulder with a warm word of praise.

Suddenly you discover things about him no one has suspected. Everyone adds a dimension of his own to his personality: how he runs around in his jeep under fire as through he does not believe that bullets can hit, but insists that all his men keep their steel helmets on all the time; how he jumped down, three times during one battle, and finished off a well-entrenched enemy with his sub-machine gun. His officers are full of admiration for his versatility, his ability to size up a situation, to decide and act no less fast. He is a staff officer and field officer, commander and soldier, all in one.

Now that the fighting is over, he is again the martinet, the man who is about to put his soldiers on a diet of regular, exhausting routine training, even before the smoke that rises over his victory has blown away.

Shmulik loves his soldiers, but it is a love that does not spare the rod. His pride is evident in every look, in every word he speaks. He is like a man who has spent years making a complicated machine, and now at last has been able to operate it without a flaw. "You won't find crews that have more confidence in their weapons and in themselves, and that know more exactly what they have to do. Men who see their officers being shot to pieces and go on fighting. Tank crews that lay the dead bodies of their comrades in the tank and continue to advance and hit their targets. You should have seen—listen, you should have seen that—with what love, with what dedication they looked after their tanks. After a day of fighting they'd spend the whole night fueling and greasing and repairing what had to be repaired, and in the morning, without a moment's rest, they'd go ahead for another day's fighting. That's how it was, four days through, all the way to the Canal." Was that what made them win the war, courage and dedication? That is only part of the answer.

The Egyptian tanks were probably defeated by the unique tactics of fast frontal assault Shmulik used. Tank crews can fire at enemy tanks with deadly precision from a distance of hundreds of meters. There were such hits in the course of the fighting, more than once, but Shmulik made no system of them. The enemy artillery, he says, also knew how to use its guns. That kind of battle would have lasted for days on end and not given the desired results. The only way was to shock the enemy out of his wits by attacking at close range. That was a fighting method the Egyptians did not know and for which they had not prepared themselves. Their tanks remained helpless in their dugouts and were nothing but undercarriages for guns and targets for our men.

Shmulik paralyzed the enemy not only by frontal assault, but also by moving onward with undiminished momentum even before the battle was decided. His force did not deploy for battle, but was launched like an arrowhead that drove a wedge in the enemy front and carried on to new destinations, while the rearguard mopped up. So it could happen that on the first day, El-Arish was taken by only two companies of the whole force, while the remainder was still engaged with enemy forces in the Gaza Strip that had not yet been defeated. Actually, these two companies were cut off and encircled in El-Arish, since the Egyptians re-formed in El-Arish and had to be beaten all over again, in a drawn-out battle that will go down in history as one of the hardest and bitterest the unit has ever fought.

Uri Oren and Aviezer Golan: The Desert Was Tamed; *Yediot Aharonot,* 30.6.67

After the war, the armored brigade held a dress-parade in the desert. The parade was reviewed by the Chief-of-Staff, the Commander of the Armored Corps, and Colonel Shmulik, the C.O. of the brigade. The latter addressed his troops as follows:

"Our people, which knows what it means to fight for its life, has once more been forced to defend its existence, and this time steel has struck on steel and the enemy has suffered a decisive defeat.

You were the spearhead of the attack on the hard shell of the Egyptian army, the largest and most insolent of the enemy armies, in a merciless and bitter, but glorious and heroic fight. With storm, blood and fire we have broken through his fortified lines and destroyed his armor at Khan-Yunis, at the Rafiah lines, at Sheikh

Zuweid, at Jiradi and El-Arish, at Bir Lahfan and Bir-Hamma, and on the road full of blood and fire that leads to Ismailia.

Wherever we passed, we left behind us burnt-out skeletons, exploding tanks, and charred corpses. We looked death straight into the face, and he cast his eyes down.

We did not look back for dear friends who went up in flames with the steel of the tanks and trucks they rode in; we did not count the price in blood; in our burning anger we carried the thundering death of our armor into the heart of the enemy until he was totally defeated and we had liberated our people from the nightmare of immediate annihilation with which the cruel enemy had threatened it.

For we fought as Jews. We fought for our lives. We fought in anger.

The courage which the masses of our people revealed was more than we had foreseen; it is no mere chance that Israel exists. And indeed, Israel's victory will stand forever.

Friends, soldiers! You yourselves were not aware of your glorious courage; but when I saw how the tanks were pierced and went up in fire and the men carried on fighting inside them, I knew that man himself is the steel, and the armor is only metal.

Our witnesses are the 70 torches that burn here, for the 70 heroes we have left on the field of death, and twice as many wounded.

Our witness is the former unit command, that is no more but has been replaced from within the ranks in the course of the fighting. Our witness is the vanguard, that lost half of its strength but did not lose its impact—for our task was not easy.

Those who fell knew, and we all knew, what the price was and what we had to expect as we went into battle. We all went in readiness, in awareness of our mission, in the hope that all of us were building a better world for our children after us. We are ready for tomorrow, knowing that this time the enemy will not forget the anger of our armor.

In this war, the victory has been wholly yours. Be strong and of good courage, my brothers, heroes of fame."

The wind carries the commander's words straight to the hearts of the crowd. The guns thunder. The march-past of the armored brigade has begun.

Parents spill over onto the track. Mothers stretch out their arms to their sons who stand in the turrets of the tanks. Fathers run out of breath behind the half-tracks and call out to their sons. Girls run up to the tanks and call out to their boyfriends. Little children run after the tanks, shouting "Father!"

The whole large crowd runs along behind the tanks that speed on in clouds of dust colored red by the sinking sun.

By the evening, the first tank crews turn up to meet the large family. Brigadier Shmulik's son is asleep in his father's arms.

"He missed his father all the time," says his mother.

Colonel Shmulik: Address to the Troops; *Ha'aretz,* 7.7.67

When war erupted on the morning of June 5th, Captain Uri's unit was a nameless reconnaissance unit, but it belonged to a famous armored brigade (Shmulik's). This was a full-scale reconnaissance unit: jeeps, half-tracks, and a few tanks. And the men, of course. As evening came, the unit was decimated and crushed: in ten hours of continuous fighting it had lost half its men, all of its tanks, and nearly all of its vehicles; but it became a legend, a symbol of courage, of bravery and devotion.

This is Uri's story:

The first of our reconnaissance teams guided Pattons through the sands to Khan-Yunis. It was commanded by Lt. Joseph. The other teams accompanied a battalion of Centurions that got on the high-road south of Khan-Yunis and turned left, to Rafiah. We stayed behind the tanks until we were out of the town. Then we speeded up and put ourselves at the head of the column.

In Khan-Yunis there was hardly any opposition. The sight of the tanks had paralyzed the Arabs. If the infantry had marched in behind the tanks, the town might have been taken without a fight. But the infantry came only later. The tanks had taken a couple of turns through the street of the town, liquidated a few snipers' posts and were about to move out, when suddenly fire was opened from every roof and from behind every fence. Joseph was one of the first to be hit.

Our signals sergeant was a boy called Coby, who had never had any combat training or battle experience. But he did not get confused under fire, took command, got the men to leave the cars that had been hit, and made them take up defensive positions in one of the courtyards.

That unit remained pinned down in Khan-Yunis for hours before it could be brought out. Meanwhile, we raced on at the head of the

Centurions in the direction of the crossroads beyond Rafiah. I forgot to mention that we had only two companies of Centurions with us. The other two had been recalled to Khan-Yunis by the brigade commander to give support to the Pattons.

At the Rafiah crossroads we ran into all the fire in hell. Much has been said and written about those fortifications. They went on for miles in length and miles in depth, on both sides of the road. We were far ahead of the tanks, and we came under fire from all of them.

2nd Lt. Ya'acov Yarkoni of Na'an sat in the lead jeep. He was wounded in the arm from the first salvo. Other boys were hit, too. There was no cover at all on the road; to retreat was impossible, so there was only one thing we could do: attack. Yarkoni realized it, picked up his Uzi in his sound hand, and stormed the positions at the side of the road, with his unit following him.

The Egyptians in the trenches did not believe he would dare, and when they saw he did dare, they did not believe he would get safely across the mined strip on the side of the road. They stood there with half their bodies sticking up out of the trenches, and fired at us. But Yarkoni dared, and got through. He started straightaway to clear out the trench. 20 yards farther on, he was hit again, and fell.

You must understand: We hang very strongly together in this patrol unit, not only from the army, but way back from home. Most of the men are from kibbutzim and know each other from the youth movement. When Yarkoni fell, there was no need to ask for volunteers. His commander, Lt. Amos, drove straight through the mines with his jeep and pulled him out. But at the roadside the jeep caught a shell. One of our boys, "Muki" Yishvi from Giv'at Haim, went in with another jeep and brought a wounded man out. On his way back, he picked up yet another casualty. On the road, he saw one of our troop carriers burning, and brought out two wounded. He put them all in the jeep, but he had not driven a hundred yards when a shell fell next to him and two of the wounded fell out. He stopped under fire, put them back on the jeep, and brought them to the casualty station holding them with one hand and steering with the other.

Now listen to this. All four of them died within two days. This fellow "Muki" went out like a candle. It was as if each of them who died took away ten years of his life. Yes, he is with the unit, but it's no use trying, he won't talk to you.

Then the Centurions arrived and helped silence the fort.

At this point I was called back to guide a battalion of paratroops to the rear of Fort Rafiah, and the patrol unit reformed and carried on without me. This time only half a unit, under Lt. Eli, took the lead, and the other half followed at the end of the column, behind the tanks.

That was how we reached the next fort, Jiradi.

The Egyptians were not ready for such a rapid advance, and in their surprise they opened up with comparatively light fire. Uri Sand, the driver of the first jeep, was the only one who was wounded. He was put on a half-track, and the two companies of tanks broke through and drove on. But by the time the second part of the patrol unit arrived, the Egyptians were ready. One jeep caught a direct hit, and the three men in it were killed, including the only officer, 2nd. Lt. Shaul of Tiv'on. A half-track was hit and its crew took cover in the sand, next to the road. There was a sergeant among them, David Shuval from Einat, and he took charge; and as he was in charge, it was he who had to risk his life by running under fire to warn the main force that was coming up behind that they were running into an ambush.

He stopped the brigade commander's half-track out of range of the ambush, waited until the Pattons were deployed, and then returned to his men next to the disabled half-track, and started organizing the evacuation of the casualties. Meanwhile the Pattons had come up. One of them was hit and started burning. A boy called Nadav jumped on the turret and pulled the tank commander out, a lieutenant called Kahalani, who was wounded and in shock. I heard afterwards that Kahalani had gone back to the tank to save his men, and had not come out again.

Meanwhile, I had finished my assignment with the paratroops and raced on to catch up with my people. I arrived at the Jiradi ambush in the midst of the fighting.

I had a radio in my jeep and started signaling ranges to the guns.

Meanwhile, Shuval and some other men had got some 20 casualties together in four half-tracks. Shuval himself was wounded in one hand. I told him to join the casualties and get himself sent to the rear, but none of the half-track drivers knew how to get to the casualty station, which had meanwhile been set up at Sheikh Zuweid —an Egyptian strongpoint we had passed through almost without stopping.

I told Shuval to drive his jeep ahead of the half-tracks and show them the way. Do you know what he answered? He was afraid he had no driving license. But he went anyhow. On the way they had a rather frightening meeting: an SU-100 tank-destroyer suddenly emerged out of the sand a couple of hundred yards ahead of them. They were sure already that that was the end, and anyone who could stand on his feet jumped out of the half-track, but the SU-100 crossed the road and went on as if it had not seen them at all.

When they arrived at the casualty station, it was already dark. A lot of Egyptians had stayed in the trenches and started now to snipe at the medics. The result was general confusion, for the medics did not know what to do. The driver of one of the half-tracks, a corporal named Thomas Friedman, collected whoever could hold a rifle, set up a perimeter defense, and fought a small-arms battle with the Egyptians all through the night. In the morning they found many dead bodies there.

The reconnaissance unit was the first to enter El-Arish. That was Eli's force, the one that escorted the Centurions. They might have driven on, but they were out of destinations. Even in El-Arish they were scheduled to arrive after 24 hours, and the Centurions made it in eight; not many: 10 Centurions, a couple of half-tracks, and the jeeps of the patrol unit. They set fire to a few buildings, a fuel dump and some other things, and then discovered that they were running out of fuel and stopped driving around. They drew up on the square before the railway station and waited for us. We reached them at 2 o'clock in the morning, after the motorized infantry battalion of the brigade had cleaned out the Jiradi fortifications. We fueled up, reorganized, and in the morning we carried on.

Uri's patrol unit was not only first in El-Arish, but also the first of all IDF units to reach the Suez Canal. That was after three days and nights and 300 kilometers of incessant fighting, in which the brigade fought eight battles, broke through six enemy brigades, and finished off 150 tanks.

Since there was not enough fuel for our heavy vehicles, the brigade commander assigned the patrol jeeps to the race to the Canal. We were accompanied by six tanks, for which fuel was rounded up among the other tanks.

On the way, the convoy came across a number of enemy vehicles and shot at them. At the side of the road stood a T-55 that seemed to have motor trouble. The crew was trying to repair it. They were so far from expecting to find IDF vehicles so near the Canal that they signaled us to stop.

We dealt with that tank, and still another one. Then the jeeps climbed a little hill, drove past a crossroads—and saw the glint of the Canal in the moonlight. It was Thursday, half past three in the morning. The reconnaissance unit had come to the end of the road.

Aviezer Golan: The Anonymous Patrol; *Bamahane,* 11.7.67

It takes time to get used to the desert, to its beauty and cruelty. The city inhabitants learned it the hard way, in the course of several weeks.

Concepts alter in the desert. A handful of shabby huts serve as a landmark and are shown on the map in large lettering. The day begins early and drags on with a malicious sluggishness. By seven in the morning the sun is already blazing. It moves lazily towards its difficult peak-hours between eleven and two. In the afternoon the wind comes, but it brings dust clouds. The dust makes its way into the nostrils, the tent, the hair; into every hole and aperture. The wind also brings with it the stench of the bodies rotting in the heat. A powerful, sickening stench.

In the desert there is a new type of luxury: Water. Plain water and above all good, cold water, that can be drunk without fear of diarrhea. Water for a shower lies well on the other side of luxury. A real shower is just a wistful dream. Field showers have been set up at a number of points, using salt water with a high sulphur content. It is hard to soak oneself in this water and the hair of the head must not be wetted with it, otherwise it becomes a doughy, sticky mess of mud.

In spite of this the showers attract thousands of soldiers. Garments filthy beyond belief flutter off. The body looks strangely white compared to the swarthy faces and arms. By dint of the utmost effort a faint shadow of lather is produced. There is no need for towels. The hot dry air is the best towel, and in any case it is cleaner than the dirty towel.

The soldiers return to their cars and vehicles, clean for a little while. Within minutes they will be covered with dust and sand all over again. But now they feel more at ease and burst into song as they return to the desert routine.

Now you can look around and see the strength of the overthrown Egyptian Army, the size of its well-dug emplacements—so well dug that on occasion they did not even permit retreat. Cars, tanks, artillery are still to be found in their positions. You can see the flight frozen halfway, like a suddenly arrested film: the corpse of a driver in the lorry cabin, his hands still gripping the wheel and his head dropped forward. Trousers lying on a sewing machine—the repair was suspended by the sudden flight. A shell stands upright by the muzzle of an artillery piece, just about to be loaded. An assault formation of tanks that has frozen, scorched, burnt, broken up. Ownerless camels shamble slowly by. A twisted bicycle which arrived here somehow or other. A soldier must have tried to escape on it to the Canal.

Now at last you can pay attention and look at new-style weapons which are too numerous to count; at the armor and the artillery; the hundreds of sad-looking lorries; the gigantic airfields; the wealth of the poor Egyptian Army (mobile showers, mobile canteens with refrigeration machinery, splendid officers' clubs); the large and orderly camps; the well-camouflaged positions; the electric, water and telephone supplies. You can see all this but it is still hard to understand. How could all this fall, be crushed, be broken, collapse like a house of cards within two days?

You arrive to a desolate desert stretch. There is nothing at all that moves. You settle down in the silent landscape. Before you know where you are your enemies pounce upon you from somewhere or other in hundreds, thousands, and tens of thousands: The flies. Nobody can explain how they discovered you. Or what they had been living on until now before you arrive with your victuals. They swoop down upon you and make your day miserable.

Desert flies are different from flies behind the lines. They have an unbelievable capacity for suffering and persistence. No waving of the hands is going to drive them away. They will enter your mouth and nose without hesitation, make a landing within the tin of conserves of your battle rations, and dive down into the spoonful of water allocated to you. They will not permit you to sleep even a moment in the noonday heat.

At first you try to fight them. After several attempts resistance is weakened. You still engage in a number of actions while retreating, and finally surrender in despair. When a few days have passed you accept their existence and permit them to ramble at ease over your hands and face.

One consolation is left. These flies fight by day. As soon as the sun sets they vanish as swiftly as they appear. Where do they go? Nobody has yet discovered the mysterious camps to which they fly as evening falls, and from which they emerge next day with the first ray of sunlight.

Dr. Amnon Rubinstein: In the Desert; *Ha'aretz,* 20.6.67

Egyptian prisoners gave themselves up by the thousands to the Zahal units in Sinai. In the middle of the desert, hundreds of kilometers from the rear and from any settlement, there was no possibility to take them. Some of them were rounded up nevertheless, and some of them were given the means to continue their way to the Suez Canal, toward Egypt. The sight of the Egyptian soldiers, begging for a drop of water, ragged and bedraggled, abandoned by their commanding officers—who had been the first to take to their heels—was for many Israeli soldiers one of the most shattering sights of the war.

We were on a routine inspection in the Sinai Desert during the first days after the end of the war, when the remnants of the Egyptian army were straggling toward the Canal.

It was burning noon and the stifling air was drenched with the stench of decay. It seemed that the enemy dead were becoming more and more dead from day to day.

Our routine reconnaissance group consisted of five armed people with dry and burnt lips. The scorching sand which stuck to our faces gave us the strange look of wanderers in the desert. We thought about refreshing beer and a cold shower and pushed away the thought of the rotting bodies strewn around.

In the battle of Gebel-Libni we entered a deserted camp and stopped to take pictures by a luxurious hut which had shortly before been the officers' clubhouse. Still not being ready to leave, I stopped by a small tin hut. I thought I heard stifled groans from inside. I stuck my head through the open window. A cloud of flies settled on my face and a smell of decay reached my nostrils. Dimly I made out a figure of a man moving in the half-light and I quickly cocked my "Uzi."

"No! No!" A despairing cry came from within the hut.

I entered very carefully with my "Uzi" in my hand. On the floor, on a pile of filthy soiled rags lay an Egyptian soldier. His right foot was shattered and his eyes fluttered with fatigue. Upon seeing the barrel of the "Uzi" aimed at him, he raised his arms in supplication and immediately sank back in complete exhaustion.

It soon became clear that the man had been lying in this place for three days after his friends had deserted him. They had left him there without a drop of water on the assumption that Zahal would discover him. Somehow he had managed in spite of his desperate wound.

There was no need for his supplication that I should spare his life. I knew immediately that I would not dare to cut it off. There were too many corpses lying around, and the man—the odor of decay already came from him. I had no greater desire than to return him to life. It was not "one soldier less," the slogan of battle, but "one corpse less," the rule of life. After six days of destruction and killing, now suddenly the desire grew in me to create again.

My friends came quickly. In an old leather case we found on his body we discovered pictures of his family: his wife, three children and his house in Alexandria.

The wounded soldier groaned, "It's been five months since I've seen them. They're waiting for me . . ."

We carried him in our arms and laid him down on a mattress which we spread on the back of the command car. He looked at us as if he could not believe. His eyes said: "Are you going to kill me?"

We offered him water. He held the water canteen and drank wildly, in huge gulps, four water canteens one after the other. We looked at him closely.

We drove him slowly, avoiding rough spots, a nearby camp where there was a regional clinic. We did not move away from him until the doctor with his staff came. They sterilized his wound, bandaged it well and gave him "battle rations." The wounded soldier swallowed everything with the hunger of an animal. After he had stilled his hunger a little he stared at us with a look not of this world.

Suddenly he burst into tears, his large shoulders heaving. He asked to kiss the hand of each one of us and did not cease murmuring, "Thank you, my dear brothers! God will bless you, courageous warriors."

We prepared to leave. The desert sun again burned on our heads and the sandstorms flogged us like many whips. Not one of us spoke a word.

Three days later we found ourselves on one of our tours in the same regional clinic. We remembered our wounded soldier and went to visit him, as human beings do. The doctor was very busy. "He was turned over to the Red Cross," he told us hurriedly. "Soon he'll be returned to his country." We turned to go when suddenly he remembered. "Wait a minute. He really asked me to give this to you."

It was the case of the Egyptian and in it the pictures of his wife, his children and his house. On the back of each picture there was written in tiny handwriting: "To my brother fighters, restorers of life, keep this as an everlasting souvenir. Thanks to these pictures I held out until you came and freed me and thanks to them I can return now to my children and family. Who will come and bring an end to wars? Who will come and bring us peace and we shall meet together so that I can pay you your just reward? Yours, friend and brother eternally. Ahmad Abdul Rachman Issah."

Uri Oren: Prisoner of War; *Yediot Aharonot,* 14.7.67

The fighting in Sinai had ended, and the soldiers were trying to get over the deep shock of the war. Yael Dayan described the feelings of the soldiers returning home from the battles.

The sound of the cannon stops. The news broadcasts announce a cease-fire. Soldiers and officers alike turn to after-battle thoughts, to re-arranging the knapsack, shaving, casual conversation. The military machine continues to operate. Fuel and water are dropped to us, the half-tracks and tanks enjoy some oiling and overhauling. The units are regrouped in concentrated areas and special orders are issued for their behavior. Reconnaissance units survey the axes of movement to confirm that the area has been absolutely cleared. Postcards written home finish with a "be seeing you soon," which is assured and cheering this time.

On Thursday afternoon an Egyptian armored brigade was destroyed here along the Thamed–Nakhl axis, with Air Force support. After the battle was over we moved along the axes with a motorized infantry unit which carried out the final stage of the operation.

A valley of death. All of a sudden even the commanders of the force become simple human beings who are liable to show their feelings. There is silence. Not because of the price we paid but because we can see what happens when an army does not fight. Boots are scattered all over the area, corpses are dispersed along the whole track. The young Egyptian soldiers lie fallen, filthy and tattered, the magazines of their weapons still full. They did not shoot. Some of them are still hiding in the low brush, running towards the hills, with our half-tracks chasing them. The aim of war is to destroy the enemy—but here the enemy has been destroyed. At first sight an enemy corpse looks like a lifeless doll, an object and nothing more. But these sights spread sadness among the veteran fighters as well; even though they know all this is inevitable.

"Today I killed a man for the first time," said an 18-year-old soldier to me. "At first I didn't think about it. Now that things are quiet I'm thinking about it again. I don't regret it. We had no other way. But I'm not proud of it either. I'm proud of the victory but not about details like that."

For our army, including its commanders, is not a professional army. Professional it is in respect of technique. It fights but it has no animosity, desire for bloodshed or pleasure in pressing the trigger.

By the morning the major problem is looting. The stores are full. There are stern and explicit instructions not to loot, and the Military Police supervise the implementation of these instructions with full severity. In conversation nobody now asks any longer where we are moving, what forces lie ahead or what battles have been prepared for us. Instead it is—what's happening in Tel-Aviv, where shall we go after the war, what should the first meal be, how's the girl at home getting on, and what is happening with the wounded.

Nakhl. Miserable houses, officer's quarters. A grayish wood, cars that have been burning all night long. Now the communication sets are coordinating the axes of movement for supplies, parking arrangements. The five-day war in Sinai is over and we are halfway. East of us lies Eilat, and west the Suez Canal, and we are surrounded by our forces. The general issues an order to all units—shave! So through the layers of dust that have collected the face of this army emerges once again, smooth and clean. Faces of lawyers, drivers, clerks, professional men and office men, faces of the young soldiers of the regular army after the first battle.

The commanders have a strange feeling. They have already been through three wars. "This is my last war, it's strange to think that way," says the brigade commander to me.

For many this was the first war; and maybe the last for them all.

Yael Dayan: The Battle Dies Away; *Army Press Release,* 9.6.67

Chapter Six

Jerusalem Forever

MAP OF JERUSALEM (4.6.67)

JERUSALEM IS USED TO WARS AND CONQUEST. IT SAW MANY A BATTLE in the 4,000 years of its existence. In the past 19 years, when the city was split in two, with barbed wire and fortified positions in its very heart, it also got used to frequent shooting, to a no-man's-land which made a wasteland of places where life used to throb. Nevertheless, only a handful believed that Hussein, king of Jordan, who was considered as the most moderate of Arab rulers, would do anything more than pay lip service to Arab unity, in case of war in the Middle East. Therefore many were surprised when, at ten o'clock on the morning of June 5th, the Jordanians started a heavy shelling of western Jerusalem.

The aide to General Uzi Narkiss, Commander of the Central Front, kept a diary during the battle of Jerusalem, noted down the development of the fighting for the Holy City and its surroundings, and quoted General Narkiss' communications with his fellow-officers. (Parenthetic remarks have been inserted for readers' convenience).

0911: Jordanian troops were in position. Amman radio declared that Jordan was being attacked.

0927: Hussein declared on the radio: "The hour of revenge has come . . ."

0930: "I spoke to the Commander of the Jerusalem area and asked him if he had enough tanks. These were being held well to the rear as there were restrictions under the Armistice on what we could have in Jerusalem itself. I reminded (him) that he should be prepared to take Abdul Aziz Hill (one mile from Castel) and perhaps Government House as well."

0933: "I talked to Rabin and told him: "My forces are ready to take Latrun, Government House and Abdul Aziz.'"

0955: "I ordered the trains (from Tel-Aviv to Jerusalem, which for nearly ten miles of their journey pass within 200 yards of the Jordanian border) to continue running—but empty."

1030: Cairo radio announced that Government House had been taken.

1130: "There was fire all along the line. I spoke with Rabin (Chief-of-Staff) and asked his permission to occupy the places mentioned. He said: 'No.'" Moments later Mount Scopus came under bombardment by 25-pounders and artillery, as did Ramat Rachel.

1150: Narkiss again called Rabin and suggested action. Again he was told: "No."

1200: The UN asked for a cease-fire. Narkiss agreed.

1210: Narkiss spoke to Barlev (Deputy Chief-of-Staff) and told him: "I think we must act. I consider the Jordanians would merely like to be able to say that they have fought, then they will shut up. But I would very much like to get in and take the positions mentioned."

Barlev: "Niet!"

1220: "The Jordanians were bombing and shelling our positions and Hunters strafed a village near Netanya. The shelling continued."

1230: "I spoke with the Commander of the Jerusalem area to tell him: 'If Mount Scopus is attacked, Uri (commander of the mechanized brigade) will penetrate to the north.' I canceled the movement of the trains."

1240: Jordanian Hunters bombed near Tel-Aviv. (Little damage sustained and no loss of life.)

1245: Radio Amman declared: "Mount Scopus has been occupied."

1250: "Immediately afterwards I received authorization to order the mechanized brigade near Ramla to move towards positions near Castel."

1300: "I have ordered Uri to be ready to move. He is to use three roads from Ramla to reach his positions close to Jerusalem." (All the tank transporters were in the Southern Negev where by far the greater part of the Israeli armor was deployed. The transporters would be needed if it proved necessary to rush tanks from the southern front to the Jordanian or Syrian fronts.)

Uri asked that he be allowed to go in to the attack as soon as he reached his access point. He did not want to have to stop and wait at the border and reform his tanks but wanted to go straight in with momentum. Narkiss spoke with Dayan who said that if Mount Scopus was in danger he could go. Dayan proposed that the mechanized brigade should go by a more direct route passing just north of Jerusalem. Narkiss told him he preferred to stick to his original plan as he believed that he would reach the Ramallah–Jerusalem road sooner this way even though it was farther.

Uri's mechanized brigade began its climb up the road towards Jerusalem.

Narkiss told the Infantry Commander to be ready to shell the Police School.

1400: The General Staff informed Narkiss he would receive one battalion of paratroopers to fight in the Jerusalem area.

1405: Uri arrived at Narkiss' HQ. Narkiss: "This will be a revenge for '48. We had both fought here—that time we had been defeated." (Rabin had also fought for Jerusalem in '48. All three had been born there.)

Narkiss told Uri to get to Mount Scopus as quickly as possible.

1410: The Brigade Commander of the Jerusalem area informed Narkiss that Government House (the UN HQ) had been occupied by Jordanian forces.

"We had begun at 0800 in a defensive posture. By 1200 hours this was all changed."

Narkiss asked authorization to counter-attack.

1415: A second battalion of paratroops under their commander, Mota, was committed to Narkiss' command. Narkiss decided to use them for the attack on the Police School and Sur Bahir.

1425: Narkiss was ordered to counter-attack. Meanwhile General Odd Bull (UN Commander) asked again for a cease-fire.

1430: Narkiss asked Intelligence for the location of the Jordanian 60th Armored Brigade. Dayan telephoned and said he was on his way to Jerusalem. Narkiss told him to go by a southerly route.

As Uri left Narkiss' HQ, Mota, the Paratroop Commander, arrived to be briefed.

1550: Government House, together with the fortified zone behind it, was taken by Israeli forces at the cost of eight Israeli dead.

Narkiss asked permission to take Latrun—permission not granted.

1600: Narkiss went with three vehicles to his advance command post at the Castel.

By now the whole paratroop brigade (three battalions) had been committed.

1645: Narkiss gave orders that the Israeli flag be flown from

Government House. At the same time he instructed his Operations Officer to equip Mota with flags for the capture of the Police School so that it would not be shelled by Israeli forces once it had been taken.

1700: A village near Castel was shelled.

1715: The Air Force was ordered to attack the Jordanian 60th Armored Brigade.

1730 "Uri was ready to go—he entered Jordan. None of the tanks was equipped with flails for dealing with mines. (They were all in the south.) Uri had men walking in front of his tanks to detect and uncover the mines. Because of the rapid speed of his advance forty of his men were injured by exploding mines."

1920: Abdul Aziz Hill was taken.

"Uri reported that the Radar position was in our hands. But he reported that without mine detectors or flails the going was slow."

Beit Iksa was also taken.

Narkiss decided that it was likely that the Jordanian 60th Armored Brigade would try to set an ambush for Uri at the junction of the Ramallah–Jerusalem Road but he reckoned that Uri would get there first.

2000: Narkiss arrived in Jerusalem.

"Sur Bahir is in our hands; but there are signs of a counter-attack."

Narkiss went to the Knesset to see Dayan who was to have gone there to be sworn in as Minister of Defense. Dayan was not there and the ceremony was postponed. (He was, in fact, not sworn in until after hostilities had finished.)

Narkiss met Mota who told him that he planned to attack after midnight.

Narkiss told his HQ to press the General Staff for permission to take Latrun.

Narkiss requested that the Air Force continue its strikes against the Jordanian 60th Brigade.

He had a dispute with Barlev on the timing of Mota's attack.

Mota's troops had left for Jerusalem at 1900 hours and would be ready to attack at 0200 hours (Tuesday). The General Staff wanted to make the attack at 0800 the following morning coupled with artillery bombardment and air-strikes. Narkiss told them that it was too close to Jerusalem for air-strikes and persuaded them to agree to the 0200-hour timing.

2400: The Chief Army Chaplain, General Shlomo Goren, visited Narkiss at midnight and told him: "Your men are making history—what is going on in Sinai is nothing compared to this."

Narkiss told him to prepare his ram's horn.

0140: Narkiss accompanied Mota to his command post not far from the Police School. All of the Israeli part of Jerusalem was under artillery and mortar fire. As the two commanders were taking stock of the situation from a nearby roof, a shell from a 25-pounder hit the roof on which they were standing. Fortunately for them it hit the parapet and neither was hurt.

0345: The Police School was taken: "This was the heaviest fighting of all (40 men were killed out of 500 in the paratroop battalion). The Police School was held by more than 200 of the Arab Legion. You should be at least three times as strong as the enemy for an attack against a heavily fortified position."

"The Arab Legion fought like hell. It took us several hours of street-to-street fighting before we took the Police School." When the Police School was finally taken, 106 Arab Legionnaires lay dead in and around the building.

The Israeli forces were given supporting fire by 120-mm mortars and by artillery from the vicinity of Castel. Two searchlights on top of the Histadrut (Federation of Labor) building were used to illuminate the area and enable air-strikes to continue during the night, the Police School being their principal objective.

0600: Uri with his armored brigade reached the crossroads of the Ramallah–Jerusalem road shortly before the Jordanians and prepared an ambush for them in which he destroyed at least fifteen of their tanks. The Jordanian armor was too close to the Israelis for them to use air-strikes against the Jordanians.

Soon after midnight Narkiss told the General Staff that he wanted Mota and his paratroops to enter the Old City in the morning, but the General Staff said he must wait.

0700: A mechanized force of paratroops attached to Uri's command entered and took Latrun (an enclave of Jordanian territory jutting into Israel from the south-western corner of the West Bank area.) The Israelis had terrible memories of it from the war of '48 when hundreds of their comrades had died trying to seize this strongly defended Arab position. (In the war of '48 6,000 Jews out of 600,000, or one in every hundred of the population, were killed. In 1967 the figures were to be incomparably lower; just under

700 out of a population of 2,600,000, or one in 3,700.) This time Latrun fell easily and the Israeli paratroops were able to advance quickly along the road towards Ramallah. Before they reached Ramallah, the towers and minarets of Jerusalem suddenly came into view. As one of them put it: "We had never seen Jerusalem from this side before. It was a fantastic feeling, knowing that the rest of our brigade was fighting there, to think that after all this time Jerusalem would once again be ours. We wished we could be there."

0922: Narkiss asked his own staff to tell the General Staff that if they didn't authorize him to take the Western Wall it would be their mistake. Meanwhile he ordered Mota to try and penetrate the Old City.

1200: Uri joined up with the paratroops on French Hill after a fierce fight in the gully below where the Israeli attack had initially been repulsed by the Jordanians. A few moments later Dayan arrived.

1225: Narkiss and Dayan went to Mount Scopus by half-track. Dayan said: "On this day, June 6, '67, what a fantastic view!" He told Narkiss that he must seal off the Old City of Jerusalem by taking the heights behind it to the east.

Dayan feared that the UN Security Council might impose a cease-fire before the Israelis had achieved their objectives and had obtained a satisfactory and lasting result. He wanted the Israeli forces to be in as commanding a position as possible.

1300: Narkiss gave the order to take the heights behind Jerusalem but warned Dayan it would be difficult. Mota had only one tank company assigned to him; Narkiss gave him another. After one hour Mota reported that he was having difficulty and he was sustaining losses. Dayan returned by helicopter to Tel-Aviv.

Narkiss decided to postpone the taking of the hills until dark.

1715: Uri headed north towards Ramallah leaving behind a company of tanks for Mota. Meanwhile the paratroops slept and organized themselves for the assault. H-hour was set for 2300 hours.

2220: Troops on top of Mount Scopus heard the clanking of tanks coming up the road towards Jerusalem from Jericho. It seemed likely that the Jordanians were about to counter-attack. Narkiss cancelled the night attack planned for 2300 hours and told his men to prepare instead for a Jordanian counter-attack.

0500: Barlev telephoned authorization to take the Old City and said: "We are already being pressed for a cease-fire. We are at the Canal. The Egyptians have been carved up—don't let the Old City remain an enclave."

0830: The paratroops began their attack to the accompaniment of a half-hour aerial bombardment and artillery barrage.

Augusta Victoria was found to be empty and Mota reached Isoric with his tanks.

0950: Mota entered the city by way of the Lion Gate.

1000: Narkiss, following close behind Mota, arrived at the corner of the 'Stork's Tower' where a battle with snipers was in progress.

1015: Narkiss was near the Western Wall with the Chief Chaplain, Barlev and Mota. "Operation Old City" was almost over.

1400: Dayan entered the Old City accompanied by Rabin and Narkiss. They made their way to the Western Wall where Dayan, following an old Jewish tradition, scribbled a prayer on a scrap of paper and slipped it between the stones of the wall. It read: "Let peace reign in Israel."

The Diary of Central Front Command; 5–7.6.67

As in the case of many Zahal commanders and soldiers, this was not the first battle of Jerusalem in which the Commander of the Central Front had participated. 19 *years before, almost to the day, Narkiss had led the last attempt to break into the besieged Jewish Quarter of Old Jerusalem. Now that victory was won, the General was flooded by the bitter memories of those days.*

". . . And finally the light of morning, even though many had not believed that they would get to see it. Eternal Mount Zion saw, on that same spring day of Iyyar 5608, how the Jewish fighters had to retreat, broken-hearted, and how the gates of the wall of the Old City closed behind them, for 19 long years."

Brigadier-General Uzi Narkiss put his hand over his eyes as if trying to block out the memories. From a window of his headquarters, Jerusalem was spread out in the quiet of the Sabbath eve, calm and peaceful, The Jerusalem Front Command was like a sleeping giant. The maps, the vehicles, the telephones and the signals apparatus were silent. Runners did not come and go. The only voice in the street was the singing of the Hassidim on their way to the synagogue. A girl soldier put her head inside the door and said: "*Shabbat Shalom* (a peaceful Sabbath to you), Brigadier."

Uzi Narkiss still stood by the window, immersed as always in the

Jerusalem where he was born and where he had passed the best years of his life. His voice dropped to a whisper: "I was the commander of the last force to retreat from the Old City. We couldn't hold the City of David, and the feeling of helplessness and bitterness has gnawed at us for 19 years. Jerusalem is not the citadel of the forgotten God of the Arava or of the desert. Jerusalem is the Jewish people. The senior officers in Jerusalem have forgiven neither themselves nor each other for that withdrawal. There has been a difficult relationship between me and the former commander of Jerusalem, David Shaltiel, down through the years. But on the day Jerusalem was liberated, Brigadier Shaltiel came to my office, we embraced and the weight of years was lifted from us."

Uzi Narkiss the last to leave the Old City and the first to return to it. How did he feel on his return to the Old City?

"Unfortunately, I am not sentimental. I did not weep. Only once was I close to tears. This was during the paratroops' victory parade. In the rows of the families stood a boy of nine whose father had fallen in Latrun. The boy knew everything and felt everything and I could not bear his expression of loss and grief. I left the stand; otherwise I would have burst into tears in sight of the whole parade."

Uzi Narkiss leafed through the yellowing calendar of battles of 1948. "The Lord of Victory who was with us on all the fronts turned his face away from us in Jerusalem, as if proof were again needed to show that Jerusalem is to be acquired only by suffering. Every Jew, even if he is not religious and has ceased directing his prayers toward Jerusalem, has a place in his heart for the city. There are no words to describe the sorrow and humiliation we felt then, on seeing Jerusalem in its defeat, and there are no words to describe the fall of the Etzion Sector, which was one of my last commands. It was the most difficult command of my life. I was 23 years old, commander of civilians, stubborn Jews who believed that the small chronic incidents with the Arabs would remain small in the future as well. I won't mention the arms that we had. There is nothing to talk about. At night we froze from the cold and we stamped around in the snow, and during the day we dug trenches and sympathized with ourselves a little bit. On January 14 in the morning, 1,000 Arabs attacked the sector. They approached Kfar-Etzion from three sides. The attack was repelled; we went out on a counter-attack. We surprised them and caused them heavy losses. At the end of the battle we were without ammunition. We asked for reinforcements. This was the platoon of the 35, under the command of Danny Maas, which was wiped out to the last man while on its way to us in the sector. His image is clear to me, as though it were only a week since I last saw him. Before he had set out he had given me a skull-cap for luck, but in Jerusalem, luck, like water, was scarce."

January 15, 1948. Message No. 20. District commander to Uzi: A platoon set out on foot from Hartuv to you this evening. It is bringing explosives for blowing up the bridges between Hebron and Kfar Etzion. You should be able to carry this out tonight.

January 16, 1948, 10:30. Message No. 31. From Uzi to the District Commander: Reinforcements not yet here.

January 16, 1948. Message No. 29. From the District Commander to Uzi: Unclear information about massacre of Jews near Beit Safafa. This is close to you. Do the best you can.

January 16, 1948. Message No. 40. From the District Commander to Uzi: This morning 80 men went out to search for platoon. Has platoon reached you?

January 17, 1948, 20:10. From Uzi to the District Commander: Send urgently names of the killed."

The Central Regional Commander said with a gloomy look: "The platoon of the 35 was annihilated near Kfar Tsorif by its people. When we now conquered the village, all its inhabitants ran away because they believed that the time had come for us to settle the account. Not only did we not touch them but we even called to them to return to their houses. They're lucky to be dealing with Jewish Cossacks.

"If I could only assemble the members of my command of those days and the time preceding, you would see how the ranks have thinned out. They fell in every assault, in every battle. Sometimes—even if it isn't logical—I feel guilty because nothing had happened to me. In war you owe your life to blind chance; one is killed and someone else in the assault, right beside him, subjected to the same fire, is not even scratched.

"Let's go back to the Old City. Today I can talk about that battle with less heartache. Briefly, the plan for taking the Old City was this: Units of the field forces of Jerusalem would break through Jaffa Gate, the Etzel force would capture the Rockefeller Museum, and the Lehi group would break through the New Gate opposite Notre Dame. I was then deputy battalion commander of the Fourth

Battalion of the Palmah. The battalion, consisting of two companies, was ordered to carry out a mopping up action in the direction of Mount Zion in order to enable the force to break into the Old City and to the besieged Jewish Quarter, through Jaffa Gate. The 'Har'el' brigade commander, Yitzhak Rabin, called me to his command headquarters: 'If you can take Mount Zion' he said, 'so much the better; if not, be satisfied with mopping up.' The battle began in a burst of fire such as Jerusalem had never heard. In the morning we found ourselves, almost unintentionally, on Mount Zion. It was as if we were dreaming. But the main part of the action failed. Jaffa Gate was not broken through. The other gates were also blocked. Over the wireless we heard the despairing calls from the defenders of the Old City. Hearts grew tight. We promised them that very soon we would reach them. My men were so worn out that they could hardly stand on their feet. For the first time in the history of the Palmah, we asked for volunteers for the force which would break through the Zion Gate, still blocked, and connect up with the Jewish Quarter.

"At 2:40 p.m. the sky was reddened from the blowing up of the explosives laid at the Gate. It collapsed. The signals apparatus announced: 'We are inside.' Later we heard: 'We have reached the Jewish Quarter.' Then we heard blurred noises over the wireless. These were the sounds of kisses which the defenders of the Quarter were showering on their saviors. The Gate did not stay open for a long time. The platoons under my command were exhausted. We were required to hold the Gate, the houses opposite, and the area between the Gate and the Jewish Quarter. Since I had expected this, I asked and was promised that adequate forces would be reaching me. Instead of the forces I had asked, 80 recruits arrived. I ordered them to go inside and join the besieged. The rest of the forces retreated and the Gate was blocked. From that time until the day that the Old City was liberated, I have turned over and over again in my mind what I could have done then but did not do. The military tactics had been flawless, but the lament of generations came into being instead. Old Jerusalem had fallen.

"This time, when the battle broke out in Sinai, I had an undefined feeling that we would be returning to the City of David and to Temple Mount. And so it was. Not only I returned. Many of those who had retreated then were with me now. Colonel Uri Ben-Ari was commander of a platoon in the Fourth Battalion of the Palmah in 1948 and was nicknamed 'The Assault King' because of his courage. In this war he was commander of the armored brigade which gouged out the Legion piece by piece. Also, the brigade commander of Jerusalem, Lieutenant-Colonel Eliezer Amitai, was in those days commander of a platoon in the 'Har'el' Brigade.

"And this time we returned with the strength of our bitter memories and the cemeteries in which our comrades are resting—everything which we suffered then at Latrun and in the Old City, on the Radar and in Mar-Elias, in Nebi Samuel and in Sha'afat, in Sheikh-Jerrah and in the Police School. The spirit of 1948 surged through the fighters of 1967. However, the latter were aggressive and inflexible combatants who liberated Jerusalem and its suburbs and the West Bank entirely through fire and a mighty arm. I told the combatants that from the times of Bar-Giora and Yohanan of Gush-Halav, no Jewish sword had fought on Temple Mount. Nevertheless, the war of the Zealots was a desperate defensive war in which everyone was finally annihilated. This time this was a war of liberation, arousing every possible hope in the Jewish people and in the State of Israel. I told them that no task was beyond their power and that they should fight like the Lions of Judah. And at the same time I said to myself: 'Who am I to be telling this to them?'"

Eli Teicher: After 20 Painful Years; *Dvar Hashavua,* 14.7.67

The most precise, touching and thrilling account of the swift and terrible battle for the liberation of Jerusalem, was given after the war by Colonel Mordecai ("Mota") Gur, Paratroop Commander, one of the heroes of the Sinai Campaign and a veteran of dozens of battles and deep retaliatory raids into enemy territory.

When the war broke out on Monday we were ready waiting near one of our airfields in order to execute an airborne operation. Carrying out a combat airborne operation is the highest desire and aspiration of paratroops, and we were all simply burning to set out for the objective. The units were dispersed over the area and the brigade command was waiting for orders to move. But until a decision is finally taken to carry out an airborne operation we have to go through whatever hells there are. So we were waiting for orders all the time. Towards noon the paratroop instructors were brought in. We again checked the equipment to be dropped. Instruction sheets were distributed to all the troops, down to the last man. But actually we were all busy guessing whether we were to jump or not.

About 2 p.m. we received orders to send one battalion to Jerusalem. I drove to the brigadier and found that it was not going to be a matter of one battalion but of two. By the time we were back at the airfield it turned out that the whole brigade was required. We had been given the objective which we knew was one of the most difficult possible. Our task was to break through in a built-up area, which every army regards as a very difficult kind of combat area. It is particularly suitable for defense and requires high-quality fighting on the part of each individual soldier in the attacking force. Here it is impossible to look out over great distances, and equally impossible to coordinate and direct. Here an order has to be given, and then the men dash forward and carry it out to the end.

The mission required us to link up with Mount Scopus and also bring about a situation which would enable us to break through conveniently into the Old City. "The Old City!" I do not think I need to say more than that. The green light had been given. This was a mission we were prepared to carry out with the same enthusiasm as we had for the jump.

Only a few days earlier, when the situation was warming up, I had gone to inspect the area, the positions, the fortifications, and check the disposition of the enemy. But the unit commanders were not up to date. So instructions were issued for unit commanders to proceed to Jerusalem at once, while the men were to follow.

In Jerusalem the fighting was already at its height. There had already been a counter-attack on Government House. Since the morning there had been sniping and shooting. The area from which we had to observe was under constant enemy fire. I found to my great regret that the unit officers were less familiar with the sector than I had hoped. So in the early stages we had to use the help of the Jerusalem District Brigade men, who were perfectly familiar with the sector.

We improvised a command group in one of the rooms of a building where, I should remark, all the residents promptly volunteered to help us. They placed the telephone at our disposal, they began to brew tea and coffee and cook other things. The intelligence set up their point for the distribution of intelligence material. And there, in brief, we sat down to work.

As twilight fell, the unit commanders approached the frontier line and succeeded in getting a glimpse of the positions. They fixed the routes of movement and decided on the various stages of the operation. As soon as I had presented the plan on a brigade scale all further steps were taken over by the unit commanders. Each battalion was allocated its sector, and each battalion knew precisely to which specific sector it had been assigned. When it was a question of Jerusalem, each commander knew quite clearly that he had to take the precise section that had been assigned to him.

Meanwhile the forces had reached the neighborhood of Bet Hakerem. Most of the troops, I may even say all of them, had never before seen the whole spread of this sector. Maybe they had seen part of it here and there when they were in the regular army, but they had never viewed it as a break-through sector. Nor had they ever inspected it with the eyes of somebody who is going in to attack. For there is quite a difference between the gaze of sitting and looking out and the gaze of someone who knows that in a little while he is going to make his break-through here.

Brief and improvised instruction sheets were written on the backs of maps and by the light of flashlamps, and the forces began to move. The additional loads, the extra ammunition and precise composition of forces for this operation had to be improvised *ad hoc,* while we were in motion and while instructing the forces in the actual field of operations.

We had hoped that we could attack about midnight. But the attack was delayed because of difficulties that resulted from unfamiliarity with the terrain itself, as well as insufficient familiarity with the sector of Jewish Jerusalem. The routes of movement to the objectives were difficult. We knew that we would have a very large number of casualties here. So we had to prepare the evacuation system in advance, in order that the wounded should be brought to the central hospitals as swiftly as possible. Each step of this kind needs another few minutes and a few more minutes, and by now it was almost 1 a.m. Then the question arose whether we should attack that night at all, or wait for the morning and obtain more support; air support in particular.

We preferred to attack at night. I say "we" because I also asked the battalion commanders and all of them to the last man expressed their wish to advance at once, by night, in spite of the deficiencies in our knowledge of the sector. What they had succeeded in learning seemed enough for them, and they preferred to make a night passage from the area which had been Jewish Jerusalem till now to the sector of the barricades and the fortifications. Then we made the final decision: To begin at night. At about 2:20 a.m. we went into action.

The brigade command went up on one of the roofs in the middle of the sector. This was done under shell-fire. During the first stage the shell-fire was not particularly heavy, but as soon as we released a number of explosive charges a real bombardment began. From that moment we began to suffer casualties, even before contact had been established. The reason was that the area was familiar to the Jordanians and had been ranged for artillery in advance. So from the very first bursts of shell-fire our casualties were numbered in the dozens.

One of the complaints of our first casualties was that they never even had a chance to raise their Uzis or fling a grenade, but they had to go and be wounded and evacuated to the rear before they had managed to do anything! Who could call that taking part in the fighting? But it happened to several dozens of the men. At the points of entry into the area artillery fire from 25 pounders and 81 mm. artillery was turned on them. Here and there 120 mm. guns were also used. So in actual fact our very first operation was to evacuate the wounded to the rear.

At 2:20 a.m. we began to provide artillery support. The tanks advanced down the street-slope and took up positions. As soon as the rattle of the tanks was heard the enemy opened fire all along the line. The bombardment increased. About five minutes after commencement of operations a shell fell on headquarters. Luckily for us it struck the roof. Splinters of stone flew on two signalers but once again, luckily for us, only the communication sets were damaged. I do not know whether it had been planned or not, but the area where we were stationed was hit by a great many shells. In actual fact most of the forces came under fire at once. The tanks advanced from their positions and opened fire to silence the positions they knew. A large proportion of the tankmen belonged to Jerusalem and had surveyed the enemy emplacements in daylight. They now began to crack the positions. We opened up with strong artillery fire and began to move, advancing with two battalions. One battalion operated in the sector of the Police School and "Ammunition Hill," and the other in Nahlat Shimon–Sheikh Jerrah.

Now I have been through a no small number of combat battles and battles to conquer a fortified area. In our exercises at Hussan we had quite a number of casualties. At Nuqeib on the Syrian sector we had had quite a considerable number of casualties and there had been heavy fighting. But I must admit what I heard in the field today —I have just come straight from a reconstruction of the action on the ground itself—was simply unbelievable. We moved around with all the commanders from position to position and from trench to trench and from rock to rock; and one of the commanders finished his story by saying: "When I came away from there to move to the cross-roads there were four soldiers of my company with me." Another unit that completed the occupation of Ammunition Hill from its southern side finished the operation with seven men in all. The company that fought in this area fought along the whole line. It is enough if I say that in the trenches, in the limited area of Ammunition Hill, the enemy left more than 50 dead.

This is fighting of a kind I have never experienced, neither in intensity nor in length—of trenches and time alike. The men had to demolish at least five fences before they reached the emplacements. They had to break open the first line of emplacements, which absolutely dominated the open area. In our plan we had specified that penetration was to be effected at a spot concealed from Ammunition Hill, and from "Giv'at Hamivtar," the Cleft Hill, in order that fighting should be restricted to a narrow stretch. Yet in this sector as well there were dozens of positions from which the enemy fired. They had a vast amount of ammunition beside each emplacement. And judging by the number of cartridge cases they left, it is clear they made full use of it.

Well, our men passed the first line of emplacements and entered the trenches. There the battle was fought in trenches, in rooms, on roof-tops and in cellars. This was total warfare, everybody fighting everybody. Two companies advanced—Deddi's company and Dudik's company. In spite of all the attempts to flank one position or another they finally had to take the bunkers one after the other. This post consisted entirely of bunkers upon bunkers, one on top of the other. The headquarters basement happened to be a pleasant place because it was cool and airy, situated in a long cave with many openings, rather like the caves of Sanhedria. Almost all the bunkers were constructed of concrete. Today we went from position to position and inspected the hits scored by our artillery, which had been remarkably accurate and effective. A few bunkers had received direct hits and were destroyed. Yet bunkers which had been hit at intervals of 10 or 20 centimeters were intact.

This battle in the trenches continued until about 7 a.m. It was a four-hour fight in the trenches, and during all this time ammunition was being passed up from the rear. The main work fell on the commanders, who felt it their duty to know what was happening all the time and to lead the mopping-up of the trenches. As for the men, I shall give only one example. We reached a bunker with two heavy machine-guns, which we had not known about. (It was difficult to site it from the air photos.) The company commander was right on top of it and did not know there was a bunker there. It had a wall that projected into the trench. Then David Shalom, one of our men, jumped on top of the bunker and dropped in a grenade, though he was completely exposed to enemy fire. The grenade exploded but firing continued from within. One of the other men flung him three charges of explosives. He jumped back into the trench on the other side and exploded the three charges. The bunker blew up; three soldiers were killed and two more were left who continued to shoot. David came from the other side, flung in another grenade, and that was the end of it. There were other soldiers there who carried out heroic deeds. One lad named Naphtali was standing at an observation post and saw the beginnings of a flanking movement. He ran above the trenches shooting and reconnoitering until he was wounded. He has now recovered.

Fighting went on this way, with soldiers and commanders dashing off all the time to fetch back more ammunition and urging on additional forces. Nobody ran away during four hours, though they were returning to the rear all the time whenever they were short of anything. Meanwhile we in the brigade headquarters had not the slightest idea that the fighting was so bitter and savage. We knew there were casualties, but we did not know exactly what was happening. Nor was that all. The battalion commander was moving ahead according to plan, and swiftly reached the Ambassador Hotel area. He asked Deddi and Dudik "What's going on?" And they answered: "Everything will be in order here soon." They did not ask for anything, and finished the fighting with four soldiers left in each unit. This was fighting indeed. I think it will be a most remarkable story of combat in a fortified area, namely, the Police School sector.

The second sector was Sheikh Jerrah, which is also dominated by fire from the Police School sector, and the Mandelbaum Gate sector as well. We at headquarters might have thought there were no battalions or platoons operating there, that they were not under fire and that units had not been driven back from there to begin with.

Everything seemed to be calm and quiet except for the exploding shells. There was not a word, not a report. They breached fence after fence, evacuated their casualties and continued to advance. Every time we dared to cut in on communications and ask what was happening, the reply came: "Everything is O.K. It's going according to plan." The only thing they worried about was that we should evacuate the casualties in time and as required.

We have visited the wounded and have already questioned each one of them. All their evidence has been taken down, and from it we find that the medical orderlies were unbelievably heroic. So far I have seven recommendations for mentioning orderlies in dispatches, all given by soldiers; and they keep on insisting on this. For example, this is what I was told by Nir, Dudik's deputy commander. He had reached a junction of two trenches and was running forward when he saw that one of his machine-gunners had been hit. This man was keeping up with him beyond the trench on the right all the time and did not notice that he had been wounded. Suddenly he asked Nir: "What's happened to me?" And Nir relates it as follows: "I looked at him and saw a hole at this place, just above the hip. I stuck my finger in, stopped the blood and yelled: 'Orderly!' The orderly arrived and shouted: 'Nir, it's O.K. I have him. Go ahead!' Then I went on running forward. He was the only orderly left, and he was looking after all the company during the whole of the attack."

That was how they advanced, from fence to fence, from house to house. Finally they crossed the road and entered the American Colony and went on mopping up. So far we had plenty of wounded, and a number of the surgeons had been hit as well. I was told about a civilian woman orderly who arrived with an ambulance at one of the evacuation points. When she saw what was going on there, she refused to return and stayed until the end.

The two battalions continued to advance. The Ambassador Hotel fell into our hands about 6 a.m. I do not remember precisely, but the whole of the American Colony was in our hands a little later. It seems, though, that some of the Legionnaires who had retreated from the front line entered the houses. House-to-house and court-to-court fighting began, and several times we fought twice in the same house. Since the men were advancing at a run there were wounded in the streets. The Legionnaires went on fighting from the houses that had not been damaged, and some of our men were fired on from the rear. So it was necessary to go back and clear up those houses. When day began to break after 4 a.m. we brought our tank battalion forward. The tanks were distributed among the various units and fighting in the courtyards began, in order to clean up the main axes as far as the Rockefeller Museum. Before it was fully light we brought in the third battalion, which had been operating in the Mandelbaum Gate sector. Its orders were to reach Herod's Gate. This was a very important objective, for we planned to introduce our infantry into the Old City through it.

The commander of this battalion, which I joined in the morning, was at his forward post in the Rivoli Hotel with 17 fighters, two of them wounded. The rest of his force was dispersed in several other posts as well. Some were at the Rockefeller Museum according to plan, while quite a number had already been evacuated. These men had advanced along the main streets, so they and those with them had suffered most of all from the shelling.

Near the Police School our engineers unit was taking steps to clear the ground for tanks. As this had to be done quickly they worked at least four hours under constant artillery fire. After every volley or two they came out and went on clearing the minefields. By the time the tanks arrived the way was already clear and they could enter the area.

The mopping-up stage was over by about 10 a.m. We were in control of all the objectives designated and were now prepared to make the leap and breakthrough into the Old City. During the day we did a little more mopping up. From this stage onwards the impetus of our attack declined somewhat through no fault of our own. To be sure, we had gone into action swiftly, but the situation was complicated. On open ground it is difficult to maintain speed with infantry troops and without armor. The advantage lay here with the enemy and it was impossible for us to move. When our men entered certain streets they were wounded at once. It grew clear that as long as the city wall had not been cleared it would be impossible to move along the streets. There was a similar situation in the Augusta-Victoria area, where every movement was dominated by two ridges. So the tank unit attached to us required considerable regrouping. It had also been brought into action in a hurry and had many wounded, so regrouping took a long time. Finally we decided to renew the attack towards evening, and during the day we did a little cleaning-up in the areas we were holding.

When it became dark, we went out to continue the attack. This time our objective was the Augusta-Victoria ridge. The plan was to operate with two reduced tank battalions, one to provide cover, the other to advance up the road straight to the Augusta-Victoria compound.

Our information was quite vague, but towards evening we verified a number of enemy positions and our tanks opened fire. When the tanks opened fire we saw men running from a number of the positions at which we had aimed. We were not fired on, but we had learned our lesson from the previous evening. On account of the quiet during the evening hours we had supposed that the enemy had been weakened by the mutual shelling which had continued all day long. Although we did not count on this we proved to be wrong, for the moment fighting began we met with heavy artillery fire. So I had reason to believe that this time as well we would come under fire only when we approached the enemy positions.

Well, we sent the tanks forward and one of our infantry battalions began to move. But the forces near the wall came under heavy anti-tank fire from the wall. One of our tanks went up in flames at once, and so did a number of the reconnaissance jeeps that had joined us. We had casualties from the first moment, and therefore introduced some changes in the plan. Amos took one group of tanks up-hill. Arik took another group and began dealing with the evacuation. The infantry regiment also began to climb upwards. Information had been received meanwhile, however, that armor was advancing at A-Tur, so we decided not to bring the infantry up until the situation was clarified. We spent the night regrouping for defense in the built-up area, and preparing for the continuation of the operation next day.

In the morning General Uzi Narkiss phoned and informed me that time was running short. The faster we did the job the better it would be for the State of Israel. Thereupon we set to work on all three plans at once. I sent one battalion to Mount Scopus immediately, in order to break through to Augusta-Victoria. The enemy knew the route very well, but by now there was no choice. We suffered a great many losses in this operation—far more than we should have done—and those who fell were among the best we had. But one thing was clear: This time things were moving. And this I say explicitly: No matter how many losses there might be, it was perfectly clear to all commanders that this time the Augusta-Victoria ridge and A-Tur and the Old City must be ours, no matter what it cost.

In this situation we permitted ourselves to take all kinds of risks, which we would not have done, probably, under ordinary conditions. One battalion was to advance straight from Mount Scopus to Augusta Victoria. A second would proceed to a daylight frontal attack, with the Old City wall behind them and capable of hitting them all the time. The third battalion was to advance along the wall from Herod's Gate, break through the wall in spite of the heavy fire from above, and reach the Temple Mount.

We did not know precisely what the state of the enemy was, but we decided that here things were moving according to plan, whether we had information or not. At 8:30 a.m. the air attack began, and the battalion that had to break through on Mount Scopus asked for 15 minutes. We had no 15 minutes, so I told them: Proceed to frontal attack, begin climbing. Then I ordered the tanks to begin the ascent and see at what point we'd establish contact with the enemy, in order to fix the battle plan accordingly. We laid down a heavy artillery cover. The tanks advanced firing in every direction. I sent a mechanized unit with recoilless cannon immediately behind them.

At this stage everything began to flame up. We jumped into the command half-track and dashed ahead. We reached the cross-roads and saw that matters here were simpler and easier than we had supposed. We knew that there were tanks higher up in the direction of A-Tur and the Azariya cross-roads. We promptly turned the column right along the ridge and swept it with heavy fire. This same push brought us to the New Hotel, which we had already passed in our half-track. After this we mounted again and found ourselves in the square that faces the Old City, with the Temple Mount lying open before us and the radiant domes, one of gold and one of silver, and the entire New City before us. Then I gave the brigade the order to proceed to the Old City. The plan was to advance with the tanks along the road to the gate. Three infantry regiments received orders to advance as fast as possible. Whoever was luckiest would get there first.

We began with a very powerful bombardment of the Moslem quarter of the Old City, which lies behind the wall and might have prevented the battalion at Herod's Gate from breaking through. The shelling lasted about 10 minutes. It was effective. We opened fire from all tanks and the recoilless guns, sweeping the whole wall. But not a single shell was directed at the holy places or hit them.

The break-through area underwent concentrated fire. The whole wall shook and some of the stones bounced a bit. But all the firing was directed to the right of the Lion Gate.

When I saw that the tanks were advancing to the wall we mounted the half-tracks and started to catch up. All this time we were ordering the tanks to move faster, and the infantry to move faster as well. I broke off the artillery fire for a moment. After the tanks had located one of the enemy positions we renewed artillery fire and reached the bridge under the Lion Gate. Here it was more difficult for the tanks to maneuver, but it was impossible to check our impetus.

Beside me sat my bearded driver, Ben-Zur. In his time, during the War of Liberation nearly 20 years ago, there was a custom in the Negev of "leaving a ribbon." "Leaving a ribbon" meant pressing on the gas pedal with the full weight of the body and then "leaving a ribbon," which meant getting away fast. Here it was the exact opposite. This Ben-Zur must have weighed 90 kilos at least (about 200 pounds or more) with his beard. "Ben-Zur, travel!" I said to him, and he traveled. We passed the tanks and saw the gate before us. In front of the gate stood a burning car, with very little room to pass. "Ben-Zur, move!" So we passed the burning car and in the gateway we saw a half-open door, and there could well have been grenades above the gate. There should have been grenades. But "Ben-Zur—move!" He pressed the gas, flung the door sideways and to the devil, and we crunched on over all the stones that had fallen from above and blocked the way. As soon as we came in there was an Arab on our right. Would he fling or not? He did not fling a grenade and we went past. We turned left along the road and reached the third gate. In this gateway a motor-cycle was standing before us, right in the middle. Booby-trapped or not? we asked ourselves. Ben-Zur went right over the motor-cycle and it was not mined. We passed and reached the Temple Area.

The moment we reached the Temple Mount we saw we had achieved our objective in all respects. There was no firing here. It is a holy place. And sure enough in this sector nobody fired—neither our men nor theirs. The tanks could not enter, but behind us came all the infantry and in effect the operation of taking the Temple Mount was completed. We prepared the regiments for going on with the mopping-up of the city.

At this point the mayor of the city approached with the Kadi, and informed me that there was a solemn decision not to offer resistance in the city. The army had withdrawn, said he, and he was sure there would be no further resistance. I assured him that we would begin mopping-up without firing, but if there were any resistance we would open fire. He went on to say that he could not be responsible for all kinds of bandits who might shoot. And he was right. Taking things all in all there was no resistance within the city, although we paid with four men while cleaning up.

That, to all intents and purposes, was the end of the battle for Jerusalem, with one regiment stationed hard by Damascus Gate, another stationed at the corner of the wall facing Yemin Moshe and the third stationed near the Dung Gate, on the corner of the wall near Mount Zion. And I must say that this was not at all bad.

Who are the men of the brigade?

I said before that our casualties included the cream of our units. But it is indeed hard to classify. Where are you going to find the best in such a group? Well, when I spoke of the best I was thinking of those who had taken part in reprisal operations, almost all of them. Some of them had been wounded more than once and returned. They had participated in the Sinai operations. They had passed retirement age for paratroops and when we told them that they had to leave there was a general revolt, and they all signed on special waiver forms declaring that they were volunteering to continue their service in the paratroops. It is needless to mention that now when we visited hospitals they caught us by our hands and made us swear. They made us take oath on two things. One was to take the Syrian Heights. They were lying wounded, it was hard for them to breathe, they were barely alive, yet that was what they asked. Nor were they the only ones. When the battalions mounted the broad steps to the Temple area I asked them how they felt and they were the happiest people in the world. They only had one question: When are we going up against Syria?

The second request of the wounded was: Heaven help you if you don't take us back from here into the brigade!

With these men you have to ask yourself: What is driving them? What makes them run? In everyday life, in general conversation, it seems you do not know with whom you are dealing. Yet even in battle and even in their behavior when wounded it is really above and beyond all that you can think. It is far more than a commander deserves, to command such men. These are not men who take orders. These are men who take the responsibility on themselves in each and every decisive moment of battle. They decide for themselves, they act for themselves. One decides to withdraw now and dashes off to fetch a tank. So he dashes off to fetch it, fetches it, reports and says: Here I am. I've arrived.

Well, those are the veterans, the old guard, so to say. Maybe there is nothing surprising about them. And yet, most of the men had never engaged in a single action before. They are paratroops, but we know that during recent years there have not been many actions. Among them were some who had been standing by for action many times and might even have carried out one or two operations. But they have not had much battle experience. And you know that paratroops are usually thought of in special operations or minor actions; and are not accustomed to this kind of fighting in urban areas, which takes a lot of time. That is a business for regular troops rather than paratroops. Yet you should have seen how swiftly they organized and arranged matters. These are youngsters who had never fought before in their lives. They were using weapons they did not know. They advanced and they also bandaged the wounded. These are men indeed!

The Taking of Jerusalem; *Statement by Colonel (Mota) Gur at Press Conference,* 13.6.67

After the Six-Day War, Colonel Mordecai Gur, better known to everybody as simply "Mota," was appointed to the Israel delegation to the UN General Assembly, which was gathering for the political fight over the military achievements. During his stay in New York, he was interviewed by Author Eli Wiesel (who writes his books in French, essays in English, and articles in Hebrew), in order to find out about the feelings of the man who had the privilege of liberating the Mount of the Temple, the Western Wall and all of the Old City, after 2,000 *years of separation.*

"No, I'm not religious. Certainly not, really not." Religious? Him? As though he looked it! "Why do you ask?"

"Oh, nothing special."

Colonel Mota Gur was obviously not born yesterday. He gives me a quizzical glance. My "no special reason" didn't convince him.

"Why do you ask?"

"I heard your radio broadcast—twice."

"Did I say anything about God?"

"No."

"Did I mention religion, or soul, or anything of the sort?"

"No."

"Did I say anything about 'man and his Creator?'"

"No."

"You see? Your question is off the beam. I told my own story—and that's all. Right?"

. . . Right. But what a story! Many generations did not have the privilege of telling or hearing this story. Do you remember? The feverish preparations, the high tension, the last night: waves of flame swept through the division when it learned that it was destined to deliver Jerusalem from bondage. Do you remember the enthusiasm of the men who charged the wall, the insistent orders of the commander to his driver: "Drive, Ben-Zur, drive!" The motor-scooter that could have been—and should have been—booby-trapped? The casualties that fell along the way. The race into the Old City and on to the Temple Mount. The weeping at the Western ("Wailing") Wall. There was something special about these casualties.

"Don't tell me this is just another war story for you."

"All right, I won't tell you. But it was on account of Jerusalem."

? ? ?

"Don't you see? Jerusalem isn't just another objective, some town on a map. Jerusalem is Jerusalem. What are you grinning about?"

"'Jerusalem is Jerusalem.' How?"

"What do you mean how? In her history."

"Jericho also has a history. And Hebron. And Bethlehem, too."

"Don't make me laugh! There's a difference . . ."

The time: three weeks after the conquest of Jerusalem. The place: a restaurant near Rockefeller Plaza in the heart of Manhattan. Mota, a temporary member of the Israel delegation to the UN, is dressed like a professional diplomat: dark summer suit, elegant tie. He took his assignment to the Emergency Session seriously: he listened to the speeches, took part in the consultations, delivered speeches at mass rallies of the United Jewish Appeal and also at closed leadership meetings. Meanwhile, he has also turned into a television personality. All the major networks are after him. If he were only willing, he could spend fully a year here in broadcasting studios. His every appearance evokes sympathetic curiosity and enthusiasm. For some reason, he is shy to speak of his successes, but they are well-known. Countless Jewish communities want him to visit them. Many people are sending him money for the Israel

Defense Forces. "Colonel Gur" is the talk of the country, from coast to coast: millions of TV viewers who saw the telecasts of the paratroopers weeping at the Western Wall identify him with the men he commanded.

"Tell me the truth, did you cry too?"

"At the Wall? No."

"How come?"

"I don't know. Maybe it's because I was a bit late in getting there. The fighting was still going on, and I didn't have time for ceremonies."

"But you were the first up on the Temple Mount, weren't you?"

"That's right."

"Were you excited?"

"What do you think?"

"Did you cry?"

"No, I didn't cry."

"Why not?"

"I don't know. I don't like tears."

"Did you feel any?"

"Of course. Like all the others. But I didn't cry."

"What *did* you feel?"

"I don't think I can put it into words."

"Try."

"No. I don't think people should discuss their feelings."

"What should people discuss?"

"Who says you've got to discuss anything? You don't have to."

"I beg to differ: it's a duty—and a privilege—to talk about this. Every word, every little detail, every incident. Future generations won't forgive us if we leave out anything connected with this war."

Mota muses for a moment, then smiles. "Maybe you're right."

"Then what did you feel when you reached the Temple Mount as—well, as its liberator?"

"I won't tell you. All I'll say is that what I felt was something very deep."

"What did you think of?"

"A dream."

"A dream *you* had?"

"A dream. A very remote dream. And a very persistent one."

There is no need to ask. It is easy to guess what he is referring to. What Jewish soldier didn't dream of fighting for his forsaken capital, which was so near yet so far through so many long days and years of forgetfulness and indifference stemming from political expediency and resignation to the *status quo*?

But Mota's was a double-dream, with an added element of pain. Throughout his service in the Israel Defense Forces he hadn't been able to live down the fact that in the period before the establishment of the State, he had not taken part in bringing "illegal immigrants." He had been too young. That is why, in Paris in the 1950's, when he was already a senior officer, studying at the French War College, he asked the then Chief-of-Staff, Zvi Tzur, to allow him to do something in connection with Jewish immigration to Israel. But he was turned down. Mota still can't live it down. It bothers him that he did not bring any Jews to Israel, that he did not go to them in their places of exile in order to bring them to their homeland.

But his big pain, his deep, prolonged pain, had to do with Jerusalem. It hurt him that he had not participated in the Battle of Jerusalem in 1948. He had fought in the Negev, only in the Negev. He had made a resolution then: If the occasion ever arose, he would be the one to lead the men in the conquest of his city and theirs. He had once told the Chief Chaplain to the Forces, Brigadier Shlomo Goren, that if he wanted to be among the first to enter the liberated capital, he should stick close to him, Mota Gur. Brigadier Goren reminded him of this when they met at the Western Wall. Mota Gur kept the promises he had made to himself and to the Rabbi.

"Maybe you'll laugh," Mota Gur said, "but somehow I always believed that in the end I would get to Jerusalem. And that's the way it turned out. Two days before the war, I went to the capital and toured the forward positions, even though I knew the set-up like the back of my hand."

"Did you know then that your brigade would get the assignment?"

"How should I know? The whole thing hadn't been planned yet."

"Then why did you go?"

"To be ready. Just in case."

"When did you know the zero hour?"

"Monday morning. I told my battalion commanders to be on the alert. I didn't get much sleep, even though we didn't know till the last minute. Then we heard and saw the planes taking off. I contacted the Chief-of-Staff and asked him: 'Is this it?' He said: 'This is it.'"

He still didn't know, didn't even guess, that the privilege he had been dreaming of for some 20 years was so close to realization.

Nobody could tell in advance whether King Hussein would be foolish enough to enter the war. Mota Gur got an order to prepare one battalion. Then two. Then again: just one. Finally, it was three battalions. Then he knew for sure: the objective was Jerusalem.

"Who decided for Jerusalem?"

"Someone."

"Who?"

"It doesn't matter. The important thing is that the order was given. And it was carried out."

"Did you know that you would make it, and that everything would go off well?"

"Of course I knew. Only a fool could think otherwise."

"You didn't have the slightest shadow of a doubt?"

"No. Look: anybody who knows the enemy's power and our power as well as I do could feel pretty safe in taking a guess at what would happen and how long it would take. I gave Egypt three days. The same for Jordan—maybe a little less. That's why I think this war should be called the 'Foolishness War'—the foolishness of the Arabs. Because the Arabs really thought they had a chance of winning; that was their undoing."

Mota explains: the Jewish fighter is superior to the enemy in every respect: his fighting ability and readiness, his spirit of self-sacrifice, his devotion to his commanders and his comrades. It has not yet happened that Israeli soldiers should abandon a tank, a vehicle, a position without having exhausted every possibility, without having fired the last bullet.

"Does this mean that the Jewish soldier isn't a coward, while the . . ."

"Maybe. There may be something in that."

"Weren't you ever afraid? Didn't you ever say to yourself that victory might be achieved without you?"

"And how I did! Plenty of times."

"In Jerusalem, too?"

"In Jerusalem too. The shell that landed on my command post. The bullets whistling overhead. The sniping. There was something to be afraid of. Every man gets scared: it's a very human emotion."

"Wouldn't you like to get rid of this emotion?"

"No."

"You don't think it's easier when you're not scared?"

"No. Fear is the price you have to pay, the price I want to pay.

It's much, much harder to be in the command post back behind the lines and send people into the firing line. And it's harder yet when the people you send into the fire are your friends. And then you get flashes that they've been hit, killed. You'd give a great deal to have been at their side, to have been there instead of them. It happened to us. This time. During the first night attack. I sent six tanks from a certain direction. They went the wrong way. They went right into an ambush of Jordanian armor. The first tank went up in flames, crew and all. The others realized what was happening, but they were so stunned they couldn't budge. I rushed over some staff officers to get them out of there, to literally pull them out. Luckily for me and for them, my military brain was working just then. At the same time, though, I couldn't shake the picture of my friends lying there as casualties. At that moment I envied the men in the front line. I envied them for the fear they felt."

He fell silent, as though reliving those moments. His glance softened and his voice hardened.

"I'm thinking of suggesting some changes. The men shouldn't be allowed to become too attached to each other. We shouldn't get to know each other so intimately. It isn't healthy. It opens the door to emotional challenges. And this is dangerous: war isn't a matter of emotions."

But it is for him. His brain hasn't stilled his heart. At the height of the fighting he thinks of the personal problems of some of his men. For example, while racing to the Temple Mount, he suddenly remembered that one of his company commanders was Orthodox. He immediately passed back an order that the man should be sent to the Western Wall. And sure enough, he got there before his Division Commander.

"At first the whole thing looked like an ordinary military operation, the sort of operation for which we had been preparing for years. But then the whole character of the thing changed, and maybe our character, too. Suddenly we saw it all in a different light. We fought differently. A queer and ancient sensation enveloped us. You felt as though you were going to redeem not a place but history itself. We walked holding our breath. Walked? What am I talking about: We ran! And how we ran!"

But don't you dare tell Mota Gur that his story has a religious quality. That will get his dander up. What has he got to do with

Judaism? To be sure, he drops in at a synagogue now and then, because of his children. What does that prove?—that he's a good father?

No—Mota Gur, whose destiny it was to give Jerusalem back her crown, isn't religious. In any case, not in the accepted sense of the word. He doesn't even look religious. Is it his fault if his descriptions sound like legends and prayers, as though they had been transmitted to him, to us, by all the Dreamers of Redemption of bygone days.

"Come on. Get off it. All I've told you is my own story." That isn't true: you've told their story, too.

Eli Wiesel: The Dream of Col. Gur; *Yediot Aharonot,* 14.7.67

The key to the conquest of the Old City were the well fortified positions around and above the Wall: Mount of Olives, A-Tor, Augusta-Victoria, the wealthy quarter of Sheikh Jerrah. One of the fighters of the paratroop unit, Dan Arazi, reviewed the fierce fighting over one of the most fortified positions: the Police School.

The baptism of fire was quick and sharp as a razor. We set out from the formation center in the concrete houses of the Shmuel Hanavi (Samuel the Prophet) Quarter to the border fence. Under continuous fire we began to cut it with wire cutters. Ariel the bazookist, who was wounded first, tried to overcome his pains by strangled shouts. Then an unknown thrill passes through you which the realization of war instills in you; a personal war which awakens in you the desire to live. It seemed to you that you cry out, "I want to live," but your thoughts were expressed in one way only: to carry out the mission in the best and quickest way possible.

The first squad lays the first bangalore. We wait for the fence to blow up. For twenty seconds the fuse burns with maddening slowness. You bend over close to the earth and pray for the strength to have your body cling to it. "Explosion." The second bangalore squad gets up. Unknown power lifts you from the earth. The enemy locates the direction of the breakthrough. Fire is directed at you and even so you go and with you ten other people, each one holding a section of metal pipe whose length is ten meters and which, upon exploding, can destroy another ten meters of barbed wire fencing spread over a mine field. The friend beside you suddenly collapses, wounded.

Platoon commander Buki, with a calmness that arouses in you an incomprehensible confidence, examines the field of activity and quietly whispers, "All right." He pulls the lighter. We jump backwards and wait again for the explosion. You look forward and suddenly you realize that from every window and every corner of the concrete fortress located above you a burning barrel is opening its mouth in fire. "Explosion." We took another ten meters. We crawl forward. They locate the narrow breakthrough which was made in the sea of barbed wire fence and mark its place with a searchlight.

You are again on the earth and your friends are moving above you, continuing forward. The shells falling about light up their faces. The words "Fellows, it's all right" gets an answer in the shape of a smile from under the steel helmet strap.

We get up and go on. Several strenuous steps on the dirt road and you have reached the first communication trench lying by the wall of the monstrous Police School looming above you. A slight shiver goes through you when you see the concrete bunkers from which only the narrow gun slits protrude above the ground. The knowledge that Dudik's forces have already passed here calms you but several short bursts fired at you from the distance of three meters puts an end to the delusion. Another two friends, on the right and left, fall. There is no time to take cover. Exposed to fire you stand and shoot. Eliezer, the company sergeant-major, jumps in a flanking movement with a grenade in his hand and "lays" it on the heads of two figures which were standing and firing at us. You see the two crumple and for the first time you see the faces of the enemy soldiers.

The company commander Giora calls out to re-group the company. Slowly, slowly, we return, count off and go on. Someone whispers to his friend as they walk, "Have you seen Amos?" He answers, "Yes. He was wounded at the fence." "What about Abner?" "He's also not with us." Shivers go over you. We have only begun and already so many have become casualties. "Has anyone seen Mayer or Hanan?"

The next target is identified outside the area of the Police School and we continue to move, crouching. The sounds of the shots and explosions from the cleaning up operations, still going on in the rooms of the building, continue. Suddenly shooting from the rear is heard. A machine gun squad which was hidden in a small house which we had just passed opened fire on us from the back. We spread out with grenades and finish them off. The barrel of the "Uzi" is against the body of the soldier you are shooting.

We reach the first building in the Sheikh Jerrah Quarter. Several soldiers take up positions around it. Two go up to the door and knock. Someone shouts in Arabic, "Aftah el-bab" (Open the door). Voices from inside are heard but the door is not opened. There is no choice; a demolition brick is placed by the iron door. A few seconds go by. Explosion—and the door flies off. We jump forward. Some frightened civilians come outside with their hands up. We comb the house. There are no soldiers. One of us climbs out on the roof, pulls a wrinkled Israeli flag out of his pocket and raises it on the pole.

First light of day. Suddenly all around we see houses, streets, well-tended gardens and the faces of your tired friends bent under the full knapsacks of explosives, ammunition for machine guns and grenades. The first battle has come to an end.

Now you are sitting at home. Your mind reviews quick pictures, as they keep rising before you, of this battle and of the battle against sharpshooters who had remained in the Sheikh-Jerrah Quarter, of the battle the next day, of taking Augusta-Victoria when Giora, the admired company commander who was beside you, fell. You remember the return to the combat area which we made at the end of the battles: how surprised you were when you saw the deep bunkers and the crowded communication trenches, numerous arms, mountains of ammunition and shells which they had there, their many corpses which were still spread out—and most of all, the question keeps coming back of how, anyway, did we do it.

And then, you recall your friends who got up and went forward under heavy fire, fell and again got up and went on. No one imagined that it could be otherwise. It was not said—not in instructions, not in forming up and not during the fighting—that perhaps it is impossible or perhaps it is necessary to retreat.

You recall Dan Shiloah who got a bullet which split his steel helmet but descended from the fifth storey of the "Ambassador Hotel" under his own power, was transferred to hospital and in the evening suddenly appeared saying, "I've come back."The next day, while deploying around Augusta-Victoria he got another bullet in his shoulder and when he was taken out he asked the fellows: "What's the position? Did we make it?"

Dan Arazi: The Battle for the Police School; *Dvar Hashavua,* 14.7.67

The evacuation of the wounded from the battlefield is one of Zahal's most inviolable duties, and an important factor in the faith of the soldiers in their comrades. In the Six-Day War, there were several magnificent examples of mutual help and self-sacrifice, regardless of cost and consequence, in the best tradition of the Israeli Army. One of these is the story of the paratroop reconnaissance unit headed by Major Micah Kapusta–Ben Ari. (His deputy was Meir Har Zion, whom Moshe Dayan describes in "The Fighter's Spirit," p. 128*).*

When the fog of war had dispersed, Colonel Mordecai Gur said about Micah Kapusta (Ben-Ari):

"Fighters like Micah set the pace of this war, and they made this victory possible." And Dannie Matt, a paratroop commander who has also known many heroes in the course of his military career, stated: "Micah is one of the most courageous fighters the Israel army has ever known." Yet in spite of this Micah came back from the war looking gloomy.

"We didn't fight. The operations of my unit can't be called real fighting," he insisted.

The preparatory days were hard for the paratroop reconnaissance unit, just as they were for every other unit in the army. But on June 5th, when Micah realized that no specific objective had been allocated to him, he felt all broken up. Then he went to the one address on which he thought he could rely: Mota, beloved commander and friend ever since the old days of the retaliatory measures. "I'm looking for a job," said Micah in his hoarse voice. "We're both in the same boat," explained Mota. The reserve brigade of the paratroops had been given only protective and reserve tasks.

But the picture changed within a very few hours. Jordan attacked Israel and it was decided to remove the silk gloves with which it had been hoped to deal with King Hussein, and pass from a stone-walling policy to a counter-attack. Mota's brigade was called on to strike at the Jordanian forces around Jerusalem. And within this major objective, room was found also for Micah's unit.

"Go, take your force to Yossi's Battalion in the Police School and Ammunition Hill, and give help to anyone who needs help," Mota told Micah. And the scout unit, riding jeeps equipped with recoilless cannon and machine-guns, set off like a sheriffs posse that has been instructed to catch an outlaw. Among the jeeps that forged ahead there was one that stood out on account of the identity of two people in it: One being Micah, the commander himself, and the other Meir Har-Zion, the reconaissance paratrooper who had become a legend during the retaliatory operations, and had set up the first paratroop scout unit which he commanded until he was severely wounded in the assault on the Al-Rahwa Police Station. (He had been saved there when the unit's surgeon had cut his throat open with a penknife, which enabled him to breathe through his damaged windpipe.)

Since his recovery Meir had not fought any more, though he had returned to his full physical fitness. Micah, his former assistant, had become unit commander, and now Meir chose to fight shoulder to shoulder with him.

When the unit reached the battle-ground the men jumped off the jeeps and began operating "like old times" with professional coolness and without any hurry. "We obtained information from the troops on the spot and acted accordingly. We approached the building which showed opposition, dropped a demolition brick through a window, flattened out until after the explosion, burst in, cleaned up and continued the advance."

The *modus operandi* of the unit was the fruit of ample experience in retaliatory measures, in most or all of which they had participated. The scouts evacuated casualties, removed the bus of a mortar unit under heavy fire and relieved the pressure on part of Yossi's battalion which was bottled up in the Rockefeller Museum. "We approached quietly, silenced the Jordanian power with accurate hits, and at 2 p.m. took up positions in three houses opposite Rockefeller. All in all four of my men were wounded, and all of them were bandaged up and wanted me to leave them with the fighting force," Micah subsequently reported. Since the fighting in the vicinity was dying down except for sniping, Micah returned to Mota in order to obtain a fresh objective.

"It has been decided to take the Mount of Olives, A-Tur and the Hotel," Mota said to him. "The tanks will go ahead and if they do not meet with heavy resistance you'll follow behind them and clear the way for the paratroops."

By evening the force had regrouped and the order to move was given. The advance to A-Tur should have taken less than an hour. Micah's unit made it in 12 hours. When Micah's force behind the tanks reached the embankment bridge at the foot of the north-east corner of the Wall near the Lion Gate, an overwhelming fire opened on them by the light of flare shells which made the whole area as bright as day.

One of the tanks was hit in the first salvo. After the crew had escaped it burst into flames. Most of the jeeps moving in advance were also hit. In the first jeep was Yishai, one of the commanders of the sub-units of the force. He was among the first to be wounded.

Benno the driver kept his presence of mind. He swung the jeep around and began to withdraw. The two men seated behind were wounded at the start of the maneuver. Benno gripped the wheel with his left hand, flung his right arm round the shoulders of the wounded man beside him and reached Rockefeller like that. There he handed the wounded over to the dressers and the surgeon. He learnt that his jeep was also a casualty. Bullets had split the radiator open. But he did not abandon the vehicle. The boys filled it with water from time to time and blocked the holes with bits of wood; and so the jeep continued to function.

Micah, seated in the fifth jeep, saw what was happening. One jeep had escaped from the infernal fire while two jeeps had remained at the foot of the wall. One of them burst into flames from a shot in the fuel tank, and apparently its men had been finished off. Those in the second jeep were almost all wounded, but not one of them proposed to withdraw. They returned fire as long as they had ammunition. "Our men stay in the field and fight as long as they have any prospect of striking the enemy and helping the other fighters to achieve the objective," remarks Micah.

Uri Levitan, in the stuck jeep, had been wounded by the first bursts. One of the bullets had cut off one of his toes. Other bullets struck his upper thigh while one hit him in the waist. Controlling the pain, Uri realized that the enemy fire was being directed from behind. He could not return fire from the place where he was sitting behind the jeep machine-gun, which was aimed ahead. He left the jeep, stretched out on the bonnet, swung the machine-gun round 180 degrees and shot at the Jordanians on the Wall. But after he had been wounded again by a bullet in the shoulder and by fragments of a mortar bomb in the face he could no longer shoot, so then he abandoned his weapon and vehicle and tried to get away. He managed to reach the Embankment Bridge by himself, but fell off it. As the bridge is about seven meters high he was badly hurt. But he reached the casualty station.

The forces were not evenly matched. The enemy had the Wall and many men and varied arms. The scouts had a "soft skin" and a mere handful of fighters. Micah and his assistant commander saw clearly that they had to retreat. "But," explains Micah, "in the lightning census I conducted I found that about half a dozen of my men were missing. They had to be found and extricated from the field."

From that moment forward, and for another six hours, Micah's unit was engaged in an obstinate rescue operation. It was so obstinate that it stupefied the enemy and led to unforeseen results.

"I sent the platoon behind me to provide cover, and sent the flank platoon to get the wounded out," Micah related. "A few were evacuated but I was still four men short. I knew that one had died in his comrade's arms. But I had to know what had happened to the other three."

A burnt-out tank blocked the road for the other tanks, which otherwise might have helped to provide cover. Micah sent one of his men, carrying an anti-tank gun, to the corner of the wall to silence the enemy shooting posts. The fighter was hit after his first shot. An Israeli tank advancing cautiously to the corner of the wall with its gun at the traverse managed to shoot a shell or two as soon as it turned the corner; but it was promptly hit by an enemy bazooka shell. In trying to swing round and withdraw the tank fell from the Embankment Bridge. The crew escaped through the emergency exit, and took shelter among the stones.

Acts of bravery came one after the other. Captain Ya'acov Eilam entered the field of fire twice in order to bring wounded men out of the immobilized jeeps. Then he returned to remove the casualties on the bridge. There the enemy fire caught him. He wanted to find shelter beyond the side of the bridge, gripped the edge of the parapet but was mortally wounded and dropped below. Captain Dubbie Hellman tried to steal onto the bridge after Ya'acov Eilam. While in motion he called the names of the missing but there was no response. By the light of the blazing tank he distinguished three motionless paratroopers. "They're done for," he reported to Micah, but the commander wanted to confirm this with his own eyes. After a brief consultation with Meir Har-Zion,who never moved away from him during all those terrible hours of battle, he reached the conclusion that the only prospect left for reaching the casualties was "by the old infiltration method." This method he afterwards explained with much simplicity: "When I have to steal quietly I stop even my own breathing. Every rustle interferes with me. I'm all ears. We acquired the technique in the paratroops over the years, by dint of much toil and sweat and mortal peril."

The two veteran reconnaissance men crawled between the bullets, calling out the names of their brothers-in-arms. Micah swarmed down into the ditch beside the bridge, straightened up here and there and shouted the names of the missing. Not one was breathing. Five killed and 14 wounded—that was the total of the losses of his unit underneath the Wall. The wounded and the others returned to their vehicles. It was two o'clock in the morning. Micah contacted Mota by wireless and asked permission to continue towards A-Tur.

"Stay where you are," answered Mota. "The Legion has sent more tanks to A-Tur. There's no point in arriving there exhausted and running into Jordanian armor."

The scouts fell asleep wherever they were. Meanwhile the fire from the Old City died away. The Legionnaires, who had faced steadily mounting pressure all day long and had then fought a savage six-hour battle against Micah's scouts, had been broken and evacuated the city under cover of the dark; maybe because they thought that this force intended to drive through into the Old City.

Arieh Hashavia: The Unit that "Did not Fight"; 7.67

Captain Ya'acov Eilam was one of the officers in Micah Kapusta's reconnaissance unit. "Twice he walked into the fire in order to rescue the wounded. The third time, he was hit by enemy fire," says Micah. Captain Eilam's comrades—all of whom used to call him "Hubi," got together after the war, in order to piece together this shining image and ease somewhat their great pain. The following is part of their reminiscences, as recorded:

These are the stories which friends tell about Hubi—Captain Ya'acov Buchman-Eilam, born in Jerusalem on May 1, 1937. He fell in the battle for its redemption, 30 years later, in the Six-Day War, in the act of rescuing three wounded comrades.

Hubi was a captain in the paratroop brigade patrol unit. His commander, Major Micah Kapusta described the action:

"At seven in the evening of June 6, the second day of the war, after a full day's fighting, we received orders to go up and capture

Augusta-Victoria. We did not find the road going up the hill and continued along the wall toward the Mount of Olives. As we reached the bridge at Gat-Shemanim, heavy fire was opened at us from atop the wall. The entire area became illuminated with flares, sent up from the moat at the base of the wall, and all the Jordanian positions opened fire at the bridge with rifles and machine-guns, from both the wall and the monastery. The jeeps were immediately caught in the cross-fire. The first one, whose driver remained unscathed, succeeded in turning around and going back. Of the others in the jeep, two were wounded and one was killed. Three jeeps remained, unable to extricate themselves, with two dead and ten wounded among them.

"The unit under Hubi's command, immediately behind the leader, set about rescuing the wounded. Hubi ran along the bullet-swept road. Seeing that his gear was going to hamper him in the operation—and since he was not in position to shoot, anyway—he evidently decided to discard his belt. He ran down to the first jeep, got hold of a wounded man and came back with him, then, went down once more and, again, returned with a wounded man. Meantime, he was shouting instructions to the other wounded how to find cover. He went on to the other jeeps, almost to the point where we later put up the monument. Some of the men tried to jump off the bridge, and Hubi yelled to them not to do it because the drop was too great. They were hanging onto the railing. When the shooting abated somewhat, the others made it back, but Hubi remained where he had been hit. We brought tanks so that we might use the armor as protection while we were rescuing the wounded. This didn't work; five of the tanks were hit.

"Hubi was killed about midnight. The battle ended about two in the morning. We returned, re-grouped, and at five o'clock, we went up a different road. We captured A-Tur and the Mount of Olives and reached the Pan-American Hotel. We continued on to the Silwan crossroads, and there, actually, Jerusalem began to fall. Not every victorious action had to be in the form of conquest; at times, it is sufficient to break the enemy down. I think that the night battle broke the Arabs. I might add that the first attack on the jeeps cost us four dead and ten wounded. In the rescue operation, Hubi was killed and eight others were wounded. Hubi, himself, rescued three wounded under fire, a feat which we, using the tanks' protection, could not achieve."

When Hubi was a year old, his family moved to the Ramat-Rachel Quarter, and there he went through primary school. Then he was sent to the academy of Kibbutz Mishmar Haemek for his high school education. Following his stint in the army, he returned to the kibbutz and remained there for two years before returning to Jerusalem with the intention of studying medicine at the Hebrew University. Failing to pass the qualifying examinations, he took up philosophy and biology, then, in his second year, entered medical school and studied medicine and philosophy concurrently. He received his B.A. in philosophy and, this year, completed his fourth year in medicine.

Elisha Amir, his foster-parent in the Kibbutz, said: "Hubi's dean at the academy once told my wife, Ziva, that he had some kind of anarchist who should fit very nicely into our family. I met Hubi next morning in the potato patch. I asked him who was his favorite composer; Brahms, he replied. I invited him to our quarters. He showed up two days later. The radio happened to be playing some bizarre new piece, full of dissonances. Hubi thought it was a magnificent work. This was the first of the contradictions I noticed in him; there were others. He played the oboe. When he entered the army, I did all I could to get him into the Zahal orchestra. I told him he would find that the army would give him the best opportunities for playing, but he didn't agree to it. He wanted to be a combatant.

"Whenever he came on week-end leave, I would ask him what he had been doing. He told me that he was interested in geology. I found him reading the Bible—at two in the morning. When I tried to get below his surface, I found a very strange world, full of strange things—just as was his library at home. When I would come into his room after midnight, to hear him play, he would put down the instrument and say that now, he was going to study. I couldn't understand why he didn't choose one course and follow it, or at least be interested in related matters, instead of spreading himself in so many directions.

"Hubi always wanted to do everything better, more thoroughly, more quickly. He would come to us 'on the double.' When I asked him to sit for a while, his reply was that he had a full day's program. At times, he would drop in late at night for a snack. We would sit outside on the porch; these were the few moments we spent together, over ten years, when we could chat as equals, or even as a teacher and a pupil—with me as the pupil. He always had strange and unexpected things to tell me. He had an insatiable desire for more and more knowledge.

"Once, I came to Jerusalem and rang him up. He said: 'Wonderful of you to come. Today the visibility here is at its best.' We went up to Sheikh-Marzuk ridge, the symbolic crest of Hubi's dreams.

"Music, nature, landscape—all were as one for Hubi, as though they complemented each other and could not be enjoyed separately. He used to carry a Bible in his pocket, even when he worked on irrigation. Everyone was perplexed by this strange combination; it should be either—or, said the others.

"Once a group of us started out on a trip, at three in the morning. After we ate, sang and played the accordion, everyone went to sleep. Hubi took a small volume out of his bag and began to read. I wondered what he would be reading this time. It was Kant. I was prepared to discuss Kant with him, but Hubi said that he was doing homework. I had no choice but to go to sleep.

"Again, we made a trip to the Judaean Desert. Just before we left, Hubi suggested that I talk about the flora and he would talk about everything else on the way. I agreed. In the course of the trip, he recited, by memory, entire chapters from Vilnai and from books on geology and history, then delivered lectures on the economic problems of the Middle East. This was the strangest trip we ever took.

"All of these—older companions, music, studies—made up an indivisible entity. On our trips, Hubi used to bring along enormous quantities of food, when obviously there weren't enough people to eat it all. But he saw to it that nothing was left. In consuming food, he had no peer. He held that a successful trip called for good company, good surroundings and good food. I must admit that no other trips were as entertaining and satisfying as those with Hubi.

"I don't know if Hubi ever realized that he was so well-liked, especially, for his readiness to bring so many and such varied people into his own life. His many-faceted personality made him welcome everywhere. When we last met at the Abu-Gosh Festival, he said to me: 'See, once I knew how to play the oboe. Now, I no longer know.' 'I told you so,' I remarked. 'Still,' he said, 'it was worth it.'"

Hubi's best friend was Donny Gil, whom he knew from childhood. For many years they lived together. Donny, now a geology student in the United States, returned to Israel on the last day of the war. He was the most emotional among those who came to talk about Hubi.

"Every letter he wrote was a literary masterpiece. He wrote penetrating articles on music and keen evaluations of current issues. It was incomprehensible how Hubi could get to the bottom of things and describe them with such clarity—whether it was philosophy or history or music, Israel's geography or landscapes. He also knew sports and engaged in them with the same enthusiasm that he had for everything else. I have his letters from various periods. I shall start with sports, although this is not a major topic:

'During recent weeks I have been training intensively. I do not know what kind of demon has gotten into me and is pushing me to take training so seriously. Anyway, I have plunged into it headlong, recognizing no obstacles and determined to score achievements. On these blue-sky mornings, after the rain, when the cold air is at its most crisp, you put everything you have into every movement, simply to get the full enjoyment out of the sport. I have set up a more or less orderly schedule. Two laps around the track, some setting-up exercises, then short-distance runs, especially dashes. Then I do a lap on one foot, and wind up with the hammer and discus.'

"Hubi kept a diary in which he had noted the birth and death days of all the composers. Half of those were unknown to anyone but him. Once he had noted them down, he would remember them always. It was his custom to devote the entire day to that composer—Haydn, let's say: he called it 'Haydn Memorial Day.' He played a good deal of chamber music with the Mishmar Haemek Orchestra, the joint orchestra of the Kibbutzim and Gadna. He ferreted out musicians from Hefzi-Bah and Bet-Alpha for two hours of playing together, then he'd come back home.

"The most outstanding aspect of this mixture was that Hubi could combine it into one entity. All these varied topics became interwoven. He would talk about Brahms, then go on to discuss the history of the period and tie it in with a trip he had taken or some landscape which had impressed him.

"Two days before he was to enter army service, Hubi wrote: 'The army is a test for the individual, a test of his nature and characteristics. All of his education and upbringing either passes the test or is completely repudiated. You see, I can retain my easy-going smile but still be very serious. Be well and take care of yourself—for others, too.'

"There followed one of the finest periods in Hubi's life; this was when he was in the Golani border patrol cruising unit. He devoted himself to this task as he did to everything else. I wasn't a member of this unit, but many stories came back to me about his dedication, his planning and the physical strength he gave to his work.

"Here's a letter from Tel-al-Saffi. I have such others from the top of Massada, Sheikh-Marzuk and other points:

'I have a growing feeling that my ties with patrol cruising are stronger than the mere fact of participating. This holds true, especially, for the Judaean Desert, where I am familiar with every trail and which I love very dearly.'

"I think that I ought to close. I just want to quote one sentence, from one of the letters I have already read, on the meaning of friendship:

'I have recently been thinking of you quite often, for almost no reason at all. At times, it was during take-off or just before the door opened for our jump. It gave me a strange feeling, but a genuine one, nevertheless. Keep well.'"

Gideon Spilt of Kibbutz Hazorea was another of Hubi's childhood friends. They were together in the Mishmar Haemek school and went into the army at the same time. He related:

"We were insanely eager to become paratroopers. We went to the assignment center and found that we were too late; the paratroop quota had already been filled. We tried to make the best of it by applying for the Golani and the cruising unit. Hubi ran here and there, made all sorts of contacts and arrangements, and all of a sudden we were on a truck en route north. We went through boot training express-style, and two months later we took part in the Sinai Campaign. We took a course for junior commanders, then tried to make the cruising unit. One day, Hubi said that a company commander was about to visit the base. He made an appointment for both of us. The commander took us to a course for cruising sergeants, but it was full. The same night we wakened somebody who knew somebody who could pull the right strings and get us in. It worked. That same night we made a quick transfer to a Nahal camp, from which we worked ourselves into the cruising unit. We served with it quite a while.

"In this unit there was keen competition on the subject of familiarity with the countryside. Among us were many kibbutzniks, and they knew the country inside out, but Hubi led the pack even in this distinguished company. Once, I recall, I came to Jerusalem and went out with him to look over the Herodion. He was champing at the bit to break loose of the narrow confines of Israel and to see everything, rove about and inspect things for himself. Now the borders have changed, but Hubi is no longer with us."

Major Kapusta, Hubi's commander in the paratroop reserve unit, said: "I truthfully don't know how he got to us. All I know is that when he came I welcomed him with open arms, having heard about him from others. He turned out to be exceedingly talented. He was with us for seven or eight years. He could have left us on several occasions, but he had become attached to us, and we to him. He wouldn't leave us under any conditions. He was prepared to do anything in order to remain with the company, and he never missed going out on maneuvers. At times, during these periods, he asked me for a half-day leave to take an examination."

Ruth Mann knew Hubi from their studies in medical school. They often prepared for their exams together. "I really came to know him while we were preparing for our exam in organic chemistry. It was really a pleasure to work with him and even to be subject to his penetrating questions. Studying with him always brought out something new about his personality. The school usually prescribes for the students what and how to study, but Hubi didn't follow the prescription. He always felt sure that he had not covered the subject quite completely, and he was always the last to enter the examination hall. But he always came through."

Binyamin Gedalyahu, another long-time friend: "No one has, as yet, said here that he really knew Hubi. We were hoping that we would learn more about him this evening, but we find that what has been said still falls far short.

"We had many *kumzitz* sessions together. Food was Hubi's dependable pre-occupation. Once we went up to Sheikh-Marzuk. Hubi brought along a vat, like the one that masons use for mixing mortar. He set three of us to cutting up vegetables into it, 'for a salad.' We didn't expect to see the last of that salad, but it went.

"During the first year or so in Jerusalem, we used to kid him by asking him what it was that he was studying. And, in fact, we didn't know. He used to wander from one department to another. When he tried to explain to us what he was studying, he succeeded in confusing us even more. It was only when he entered medical school that we felt we could safely assume where he was heading.

"Hubi's famous state of preparedness was also something of which we made sport. We once rang him up and said: 'Buchman, this is your brigade headquarters. In two hours you are to present yourself at Nahshon Circle.' If we hadn't called him again in a few minutes to 'rescind the order,' he would have gone to keep the appointment.

"I want to add that, for all his seriousness, Hubi was full of life. We would ask him to join us in a *kumzitz* and bring his accordion. He, in turn, wanted to know who was going to be there and what was going to take place. It didn't take us much to convince him to come, though. He came and stayed and played."

Zadok Binno, a friend from Jerusalem, related: "Hubi came to the last Independence Day *kumzitz* at half past three in the morning, with his wife Ruthie and with little Alon on his shoulders, plus the accordion. He played for us until seven o'clock. 'From now on,' he promised, 'I shall bring Alon every year to the Independence Day *kumzitz.'*

"Hubi found it difficult to study at home. Alon would be sleeping in one room and Ruthie in the other. He would therefore go the the bunkhouse to study. I found him there one night at three, bent over a book in the light of a lamp.

"He liked to work, to put his shoulder really to the wheel, but he didn't like to be told what and how. He wanted to do things and to get to places all on his own. He didn't want to be *told* to bring ten pounds to the next *kumzitz*, but when he got there and saw money was needed, he would contribute a hundred pounds or even more."

Ati Padan, a friend from Mishmar-Haemek, recalled: "Hubi's passion for orderliness and punctuality amounted to an obsession. His clothes locker could have served as a model for any man's closet. His clothes were neatly folded, his pencils always carefully sharpened. He noted down everything he had to do, and checked things off as he did them. On the other hand, there were times when he would do things completely without any system at all.

"Hubi had another paradox in him—he liked company, yet he also liked to be away from everybody. He mingled with people very easily, yet when he came back from the university, he chose to live in the remotest shack on the place. True, he turned it into a beautiful home and surrounded it with a garden. This he accomplished in his usual way, concentrating on the project, day and night, until it was done. At the same time, he had the spirit of adventure in his heart. He liked to do things which had a measure of risk. He made trips to places where a human foot had hardly ever trod. He was a great morale builder, the life of the party. At a graduation ceremony of an officers' training course, it suddenly developed that Hubi was a songwriter as well. Once, when the noted 'cellist Piatigorsky was appearing in Haifa, we bought tickets, took our knapsacks and sleeping bags, and in this fashion attended the concert. On our return we stopped near Jalmi, unrolled our sleeping bags, and slept on the ground till daybreak."

Thelma Linn, a friend from Mishmar Haemek: "Hubi carried his idealism to the extreme. With all his constant striving to achieve more and more, he nevertheless felt the lack of a goal, as though, when everything was said and done, nothing had any real value. At times he would undertake something, then drop it because suddenly it seemed empty of content. He tried to work out some kind of a crutch inside himself on which he could lean. He tried doing it by giving value to everything. He used to note down, in his well-known diary, what he had to do that day, half-hour by half-hour, then, once it had been done, draw a line through it. He peopled his world with composers; they were his best friends. To them he revealed his innermost secrets. His attitude toward music and composers went far beyond what we would call love of music. It was more personal, as though they had been members of his family.

"Hubi always seemed to feel that he had to prove himself; this, I think, was his motivating force in courting danger, to put himself to test, to prove that he was a fighter, strong, capable, brave. I could never understand this; after all, he knew so much, accomplished so much, and he had so many friends who loved him.

"I did have the feeling that, of late, things were become clearer for him, more tranquil, as though he had finally begun to understand that the purpose of life may be life itself. Had Hubi been given the chance of becoming a creative thinker or researcher, which he really wanted to be, he would have surely found answers to most of the questions which had been bothering him."

Michael of Mishmar Haemek was Hubi's friend from school days; for a while, the two shared the same quarters. "Hubi's readiness to be of help came to the fore when we went on trips. He never found it too heavy to carry still another knapsack. He used to sing and keep up the spirits of the gang. He helped us with our lessons, trips, adventures. He was our metronome, setting the beat."

Another friend from Mishmar Haemek: "After the capture of the Old City, we passed through Ramallah, Nablus and Jenin on our way to the re-grouping area. We said to one another: 'For whom was this territory taken, now that Buchman cannot walk the length and the breadth of it, climb a hill and spot on his map every rise and dip in the ground until he was satisfied he knew every inch of it.'

"When he came back from the army he wanted to go in for medical research. Meanwhile, on the farm, he did everything to which he was assigned. When he decided to take the matriculation exams, he worked during the day and studied at night. After matriculation he felt that he didn't know English well enough, although he had received a good grade in the subject. That was the way he worked. On one occasion an irrigation pipe burst during the night. Hubi woke me up. I protested that the matter could keep until morning, whereupon he practically dragged me out of bed. We worked on the pipe for three hours, until the sprinklers were working again and Hubi could go back to sleep in peace."

Yitzhak Cohen, a neighbor in Jerusalem, told about a stormy night in the city. A cat had become trapped high up in a tree in the yard. Its meowing was heart-rending. "The tree was some eight meters high. Hubi and I were in despair. We thought of waiting until morning for the rain and wind to die down, but Hubi couldn't sleep. He took a saw and an iron poke and, long after midnight, was able to get the drenched cat down."

Ben Golan of Mishmar Haemek: "As far as I am concerned, Buchman was like a phenomenon of nature. When I was told that he was dead, the news just didn't sink in. It didn't make sense, any more than if somebody had told me that the wind had been killed.

"Once we were harvesting vegetables. Buchman's job was to cart them away. I saw him coming with a tractor but without the trailer. 'Where's the trailer?' I yelled. 'Right here,' he yelled back, then turned around; the trailer had slipped off the hook somewhere. We came to changing shifts, and he warned me that he couldn't plow straight furrows. 'Somehow I make parabolas.'

"Hubi was beset by contradictions, but you tended to overlook the fact because of the interesting way he discussed them. When I read his letters I advised him to drop medicine and go in for writing, which I felt to be his natural talent. He was the kind you like, in a warm, personal sense. At the gathering around the monument near the bridge in Jerusalem, I found myself feeling irritated by the presence of the others there. 'What are all these strangers doing here?' I asked myself. 'Hubi was *my* friend.' But I wouldn't have been surprised it everyone had felt the same way.

"I liked to listen to his stories of what he had been doing, or of what was going on in general. He talked as entertainingly as he wrote. I loved to listen to his stories, especially those which involved him personally, like the one about the time when he and others, while traveling by car in the fjord region of Norway, became stuck in the snow in some village. They decided to sleep in the car. In the morning, Hubi heard strange noises and stepped out of the car, in his underwear, to find himself in the middle of a school yard full of children. 'They must have thought I came from Mars,' he wrote. 'They fled in all directions.'"

To his foster-mother at Mishmar Haemek, Ziva Amir, Hubi wrote: "Alon is growing up nicely, He is making his first attempts at long-distance toddling, much as Engels describes a person's progress in the family—a pace sufficient to prevent constant falling down—except that Alon, being as yet unfamiliar with dialectics and antagonisms, keeps falling down all the time. We shall be celebrating his first birthday, two weeks hence—perhaps up at Sheikh-Marzuk.

"Ruthie has not yet begun working, but she may do so soon. My affairs have not changed. I work hard at the oboe and make my living with the sweat of its mouthpiece. I am still not a soloist, but I am at that stage of chamber music which borders on it. Apparently my attachment to music is stronger than I had thought. Perhaps I shall take up formal study of counterpoint and conducting, now that I have my first degree in philosophical studies and mathematical logic. Of course, I still have four years of medical school hanging over me—if all goes well. Shalom."

This he wrote in 1964. Exactly a year ago he wrote again to Ziva: "I had intended to pay you a flying visit, together with Ruthie and Alon. However, the university sprang a special course in genetics on us, and we had to stay put. I am withered with longing for your village. We are under such pressure. My curriculum is at its maximum; everything else comes at its expense. The intensity cannot be eased for even one day, and I am still a long way from discovering the magic formula which would bring all of my consonant elements into balance—my family, my music, myself. Shortly I shall be arriving at the crossroads where one has to decide, not only which direction he should take, but also the pace at which he should proceed. If I can do this, just once, I shall deem it a great achievement. Meanwhile, yesterday I played Mozart's Divertimento and excerpts from Ibert with our woodwind quintet, at a public performance."

•

Micah Shagrir, Hubi's friend from their youth movement days: "During the last few months I found it possible to chat with him dispassionately on any topic. We talked about serious political issues, the world situation in general and Israel's position in particular, plus bits of nostalgia. Little things, really. How he kept his bicycle even after he had bought his car. Or the abiding love he bore toward Mishmar Haemek. Hubi always tried to arrange marriages between his Jerusalemites and prospective spouses from Mishmar Haemek. He remained attached to the kibbutz, not like so many others when they leave their kibbutz for good.

"One day, as I recall, Hubi, Ruthie and I drove to Haifa to see a play by the Haifa Theater. We came early because Hubi drove like mad. This was also typical of him—he was always in a hurry. Hubi decided to use the time for a visit to Mishmar Haemek. We thought that he must have an important appointment there. When we arrived, we found the gang sprawled out on the lawn. Hubi greeted them all —and back we went. That was all he wanted—to be in Mishmar Haemek. Once, when he was still studying philosophy, I accompanied him to the home of Prof. Samuel Hugo Bergmann. After the high-spirited meeting with this distinguished personality, Hubi suggested that we go to Abu-Shaul for shishlik. He ate the shishlik with the same enthusiasm which marked his conversation with Dr. Bergmann."

Just before the outbreak of the war, when Hubi's unit was already deployed in Jerusalem, he asked Major Kapusta's permission for a half-hour leave to go to the university, where he had several mice under observation. Also, the last time he was in Jerusalem he dropped in to see his friend Malka and found her and her neighbors filling sand bags. She related: "He was in his paratroop uniform and looked wonderful. He laughed at us and said that the sandbags wouldn't be of much use. Then, regretting his action, he went and bought ice cream for all of us. He calculated the shell trajectory and admitted that the bags might be useful, after all. Then he went home. I remember how worried Ruthie became when she learned that the paratroops were in Jerusalem. She was afraid that Hubi might come back from the fighting a changed man . . ."

Two days before the outbreak of war, Ruthie received the following letter:

"Dear Ruthie and Alon,

"No price would be too high for my seeing you, even just once more. I feel a tremendous desire that this wish should be granted. Will it be? We are still sitting in the shade of the trees in the orange grove, waiting for the next orders. Each of us is deep in thought about his own home. No one is thinking about war; this is too awful to consider, but we know that the worst is not just a matter of mere possibility. I feel deep turmoil and agitation within myself. War's lack of purpose has been tormenting me for days. Again destruction, ruin, the loss of dear ones. In the cemeteries the tombstones are increasing, and each one is a question mark: Why did this have to be? If we could only be assured that this would be the last war between peoples, regardless who is 'right' and who is 'wrong,' I would dedicate my entire being and all my means to it, just to be able to leave a legacy of peace. But here I am going into probable war and my heart is still rent with disillusionment, the pain of despair in humanity, of the so-called better tomorrow, because there is no hope of a better humanity and therefore none for a better tomorrow. And the compass which each of us creates and imbeds in his soul, and which should be functioning on so-called cultural and ethical values, does not get to function at all. It remains hidden, mute, motionless, atrophied, buried under forces which operate above and beyond human nature. These forces set aside for themselves all the roles, and we are but the spectators; or else we are forced to be the actors, the audience, the financiers, without having a hand in writing the script. Be well, my dears, I shall always love you wherever I go. No matter what comes, be strong and well.

Yours, Hubi."

Micah Shagrir went to pick up Hubi's personal effects. There was a briefcase stuffed with his beloved maps, Yehuda Amihai's poetry and S. Yizhar's stories, which he had brought specially from Jerusalem to read aloud to his companions. "Yizhar describes, exactly, the very orange groves where we have been stationed," he had told Malka when he last saw her. There was also a book about the Spanish Civil War, *From Berlin to Madrid,* and Flaubert's *Madame Bovary*. There was a photograph of Ruthie and Alon, and letters which he had begun writing to Donny and others. There were songs which he had copied for his own use and for community sings. And there was the accordion. All of these went back home, without Hubi.

Friends Talk About Hubi—*a recording, Davar,* 4.10.67

"Who is this female medical orderly?" That was what Israel Army commanders asked themselves in Jerusalem. Who was this slender young woman with the quick hands and the smiling eyes? The question was asked by the wounded paratroops whose injuries she bandaged with high courage and expert knowledge, while mortar shells exploded all around. She came, she did a wonderful job, and she vanished without leaving any traces.

Maybe Mr. Haim Vigolik, director of the Red Shield of David in Jerusalem, could remember who she was? But he shrugs his shoulders. No, he does not remember. We had so many volunteer women, he explains, that I'm simply incapable of remembering which one it was that came to the paratroop brigade.

Doctor Jack, the paratroop surgeon, does happen to remember her. "About 30 *years old, with hair down to her shoulders, short, with lively eyes, slender figure, not more than* 45 *kilos." (Say* 100 *pounds.) Who is she? What is her name? He does not know. Who had time to ask?*

The ambulance drivers also remembered her, but not one of them was capable of giving details that could help to identify her.

The daily Ha'aretz *published an account of the mysterious orderly under the heading: "Who knows? Who has met the unknown female orderly?" Telephone messages began to reach the editorial offices from all parts of the country. People reported: "The unknown woman? I know her! She is my neighbor, my acquaintance, my friend, my girl, my cousin, etc."*

All information was checked, but the real unknown medical orderly was not revealed and continued to keep silent.

Later a woman phoned the Ha'aretz *editorial offices in Jerusalem: "My name is Esther Zelinger, and I am the person you are looking for. I live in Bet-Hakerem, in Jerusalem." When the information was checked, it turned out that Esther Zelinger was indeed the medical orderly in question, but she was not the person who had phoned the paper. One of her friends had wanted to do her a favor. As for Esther Zelinger, it seems as though she would have preferred to remain anonymous.*

Dear Mrs. Esther. We have received Arnon's postcard which you enclosed in your letter, and we are very, very grateful to you. We hope that you will have a chance to visit us in Sarid, so that we will be able to thank you in person. There is an Egged bus from Haifa every hour, through the Valley Road.

Respectfully yours,
Gisa and Ernest Plaschkes

Esther Zelinger's eyes browsed over the few lines. She read the letter a second time, and a third time, and then laid it atop a huge pile of letters and postcards that covered the table. Except for the telephone bill, all were letters of appreciation and gratitude which had been streaming to her home in the Bet-Hakerem Quarter of Jerusalem, after she had been identified as "the nurse," the only woman who actually took part in the liberation of Jerusalem, who had earned from wounded soldiers and doctors alike the title: "The Saving Angel of the Paratroops." She suddenly turned up, without having been summoned, just worked devotedly under fire for 52 hours, and then vanished again without anyone having managed to say "Thank you" to her.

The first to tell about her was the commander of the paratroop unit which liberated Jerusalem, Colonel Mordecai ("Mota") Gur, when he described the battle in a broadcast over Kol Yisrael. The doctors and the wounded men who wanted to thank her wondered who she was. The newspapers asked about her.

At last she was located. It was when she telephoned to the headquarters of the paratroop unit to ask how to return the equipment which she still had—a windbreaker, a sweater, and some medical equipment. She asked to be allowed to keep the helmet.

Esther Zelinger (nee Arditi) is certainly not an average woman, and it turned out that her activities in the Six-Day War were not her first of this kind. She is petite, barely five feet tall, with a pair of brown, smiling eyes. Until a few months ago she drove an ambulance for the Magen David Adom station in the capital. Now she is a housewife. Evenings, she is attending the course for guides at the Tourism School in Tel-Aviv.

Here is her story.

"When the first alarm came on Monday morning, followed by the roar of the cannon and mortars, the children were a bit frightened. But that didn't prevent them from scolding me. They said: "What are you doing here, mother? Why don't you go and help the soldiers?" I got in touch with Nurit's teacher, and she agreed to take care of the children. Then I went to the Magen David Adom station and offered my services. Immediately I was given an ambulance, and I started to pick up wounded civilians.

At about 11 o'clock that night, I saw the throngs of paratroops crowding the roads around Mount Herzl, and I decided to join them if possible. At exactly midnight the paratroops left the area, and I went back to the station. At that time, the shelling had let up somewhat. But in the area of the border dividing the two parts of the city the guns were rattling and roaring. No more wounded were being brought to the Magen David Adom station, and there were no more calls.

Early in the morning, a soldier arrived at the station, panting, and told us that ambulances were needed immediately; there were many casualties. I sensed that this was my moment. I got into my ambulance and raced towards a casualty station in a *yeshiva* on Shmuel Hanavi Street."

The division medical officer, Dr. Jack, was taken aback by the sight of the female figure in black slacks and a dark shirt. As the doctor later told it: "At 2:30 a.m., a Medical Corps unit arrived in the area under heavy fire. At that time the casualties started streaming in, including many who had been hit by shrapnel while waiting in the staging area. The stream of casualties mounted rapidly. I realized that we did not have enough ambulances handy, and I sent a soldier to the Magen David Adom station to ask for more vehicles. Esther came with the ambulance and started treating the wounded men. I told her in no uncertain terms to get right out of there. After all, she was a woman, a civilian, under fire. What is more, I was afraid that she would be more trouble than help. But she refused to leave and went on treating the wounded men. In spite of the terrific load of work, I saw immediately that she was doing her work in a professional and most efficient manner. 'If that's the way it is,' I told her, 'then at least put on a helmet.' "

Wounded men were bandaged and removed, and new casualties kept coming in. Most of them had been hit by shrapnel or had been knocked down by the strength of the blasts, while some were suffering from potentially fatal shock. All of them needed immediate bandaging, or tourniquets, or plasma transfusions, or morphium injections. It was clear that time was of the essence.

The stretcher-bearers and quartermaster men helped her, even though they were not experienced in that sort of work. They prepared the bandages, handed her scissors and hypodermic needles, and carried the wounded men according to her instructions.

In the morning, when the unit started moving into the captured area, Esther was left behind. She had to drive some couriers to the Pagi Quarter.

She was looking for us when a half-track stopped beside her, and someone told her: "We're carrying casualties, and we can't find any doctors or medics."

"I'm coming," she said.

They refused to take her, saying the area in which they were operating was right at the front.

"That O.K.," she said, pointing to the Magen David Adom armband she was wearing. "I'm the unit doctor's nurse."

The men in the half-track had no choice but to take her word for it. She got in, and the half-track rode right into the fire, its treads raising dust.

It stopped near the Jordanian Police School. All around the shells were exploding and bullets whistling. The men in the half-track jumped out and took shelter behind a wall. For the first time in her life, Esther found herself right in the thick of a real war. For some reason there came to her mind a movie about the Marines which she had seen a long time ago. She saw the paratroops charge forward in waves. They came out of holes, sprawled on the ground, dashed forward, dropped down on the rough stones, and poured heavy fire into the positions of the Jordan Legion. The Legionnaires were also busy firing away into the charging waves of paratroops, many of whom kept falling. Stunned, Esther would see men suddenly drop in mid-dash, their hands clutching the area where they had been hit.

She left the defense wall and ran towards the fallen men. All around bullets whistled as they flew in search of living targets. Feverishly she dashed from man to man, bandaging wounds, stemming the flow of blood, injecting morphium, hastily scrawling on slips of paper the time of the injection, and giving instructions to the soldiers beside her how to carry the wounded men out of there. Many of the wounded were in a semi-faint, and they gaped incredulously at the hazy feminine figure that had treated them. "Mama, mama," they groaned over and over.

All the while the paratroops were taking position after position by leaping rapidly from house to house in a mopping-up operation. Esther went with them. There was still considerable resistance, though it weakened gradually towards evening. When night fell, the advance was halted. The force went into radio silence and regrouped. Meanwhile, the roar of explosions came from the direction of the Augusta-Victoria Hospital, where a battle was still raging. The men took advantage of the hours till dawn, curling up in their coats for a deep sleep. One of the soldiers gave Esther his heavy heavy sweater. "I'm from Safad. I'm used to the cold," he said.

She did not sleep, using the lull in the fighting to treat the lightly wounded. Among these were officers with their green field insignia, who had suffered wounds in their arms and legs but had continued fighting, refusing to be treated. Now they came one by one, their wounds already swelling from infection, in need of immediate treatment.

When dawn broke on Wednesday morning, everyone got into half-tracks, and the order was given to advance. The vehicles took off in a roar. This time Esther attached herself to a mopping-up unit moving behind the charging force. From time to time, as they approached narrow, twisting lanes, soldiers leaped from the half-tracks and proceeded on foot, tossing grenades into the nests of resistance and then blasting away at them with their sub-machine guns. Esther stayed with them, treating the casualties left behind by the charging force.

"It was late in the morning when we reached the Lion Gate," Esther relates. "At the Gate stood a burning Jordanian bus, and at the side of the road stood a scorched tank, one of ours. Inside the Old City rose thick clouds of smoke, and we could hear the sound of sniper fire. We got inside the Gate and moved forward slowly. Suddenly I heard a cry from one of the houses. A moment later an Arab woman came out towards us, carrying a bleeding baby; it had obviously lost a lot of blood. I guess it was the baby's serious condition that had impelled the woman to risk going out into the street. I took the baby from her arms, almost by force. I stopped the flow of blood immediately and gave it something to drink. In the Via Dolorosa I saw a monastery with a white flag flying from its turret. I ran to it. Inside there were some French-speaking monks, who eyed me with undisguised hostility. I handed them the baby and ran back outside to rejoin the force. Suddenly I found myself in a strange and unfriendly city. It was really a very frightening feeling.

I didn't know which way to turn, and then I started moving off just in any direction. Suddenly an old Arab ran towards me, carrying a huge cake wrapped in a yellow ribbon. He handed me the cake with a grateful look. I gathered that he was some relative of the baby's, probably the grandfather. Then the silence was broken by a burst of fire. Plaster fell from the wall behind me. I felt that my situation was an eerie one indeed. A bloody battle was raging inside the city, bullets were flying overhead, and there I stood in the middle of the Via Dolorosa holding a cake nearly as big as I am."

At first Esther wanted to jettison her colorful burden. But on second thought, she decided to hold on to it. An Arab boy came out of a doorway and spat at her. She walked quickly, then started running through the deserted streets. A few minutes later she caught up with the paratroop unit and with it reached the Temple Mount a little later. There, in a copse, amid the stretchers and the wounded men, she found Dr. Jack, hugged him tight as the tears ran from her eyes, and with an exaggerated curtsy and flourish handed him the cake.

Her work wasn't over. She went on treating the wounded men. Late that evening, when she got home, utterly exhausted, she picked up the telephone receiver and did not put it back on its cradle again until she had conveyed the dozens of regards she had taken along with her on cigarette boxes and slips of paper, for the families of the paratroops in Eilat, Haifa, in the Jezreel Valley, and many other parts of the country.

When the dozens of letters of gratitude started arriving at her home, Esther could not hold back her emotions.

She had felt a similar joy when she served as a nurse at an air base some years ago.

"It was a particularly difficult night. I was duty nurse in the control tower. Outside there was an electric storm, when suddenly a short circuit turned out all the lights on the base. Up above, five Mosquitoes were circling the field, unable to land. They were given an order to land at another base. Just then one of the planes, containing the flight commander and a navigator, went into a spin and fell into a plowed field near the base. I got right into an ambulance and went dashing off together with the fire engines. The vehicles stuck in the mud, and everything seemed lost. Besides, the plane was carrying live bombs which were likely to go off at any moment. The plane's machine-gun suddenly went off, firing spurts of bullets at 90 degrees.

I was stunned. Suddenly, through the driving rain I saw a huge flame erupt and I heard groaning. I ran towards the burning plane. I heard people shouting, but I paid no attention. My shoes got caught in the mud, so I ran on barefooted. Finally I reached the plane. I forced the door open and found the navigator still conscious. I dragged him outside. The fire was spreading, and I knew that the plane was going to explode any minute. I didn't realize then that there was another man inside the plane, but then I smelled burning flesh from the cockpit. I ran back and saw the pilot, Ya'acov, unconscious. The cockpit was full of flames which were scorching him. Finally I managed to free the pilot from the seat-straps and drag him outside. One of the bullets from the machine-gun grazed my head. I dragged the two wounded men a few more yards, and then I heard a hissing sound. I flung myself down on top of the two men, and the plane exploded. I heard someone cry: "Poor soul. She's gone too." But I was not. I put the wounded men in the ambulance, and I stepped all the way down on the accelerator and drove off towards Kaplan Hospital in Rehovot. To this day I don't know how I avoided a smash-up. I drove the ambulance into the hospital yard, told the doctor in the emergency ward what it was all about, and fainted. The two men were operated on. The navigator died 60 days later, but the pilot, Ya'acov, survived."

Some time later, she got a merit citation from the Chief-of-Staff, for "displaying extraordinary courage in a rescue action." She is the only female soldier to have received such a citation.

When Esther was introduced to the Chief-of-Staff at the time, Moshe Dayan, he looked at the skinny little girl and said: "What? Is that all there is to her?!"

Shimon Manueli: An Angel Named Esther; *Bamahane,* 18.7.67

When the news about the liberation of the Western Wall was received, the whole country wept—both religious people and free-thinkers. Ever since May 15th, 1948, there hadn't been a time of such deep emotion for the whole nation. There is something mystical about the Wall of big rectangular stones, something transcending religion, logic and historical fact. (It is only part of the outer wall of the Temple court.) All the longings of the Jewish people for Jerusalem were embodied in those ancient stones.

We enter the city, passing tanks and half-tracks on the way. The streets are empty, on the eve of war. The place: Paratroop units staff headquarters on Zephania Street. From all around come sounds of explosions. The combat room is in the stair-well, which also serves as the prayer-room. A woman of the flat where the staff is housed keeps crying and praying. "The Lord be with you, the Lord be with you." All night she has tended the little wick stove, boiling tea for the soldiers. In the next yard, an infant is crying. "This noise isn't for children," comments the commander. A junior officer mutters: "Tomorrow the child will sleep peacefully." Runners come and go.

Only a short while until the assault. The commanders go over their plans, call for additional ammunition, scan the area from the roof, coordinate every last detail. Every tree outlined against the reddened sky has its individual place in the planning; every building is pinpointed on the large-scale map. Residents are leaving the border area for the center of the city. An old man is pushing a baby carriage. His wife struggles along after him, pausing to embrace a soldier. "You are our Messiahs."

The final briefing. A dimmed flashlight illuminates the map. Reports come in from other sectors in Jerusalem: Sur-Bahir is ours. Mortars are firing in the southern sector. The battle is spreading.

Dawn. The battle for the Old City is under way. "The operation has begun," says paratroop unit commander Mota Gur. The Israeli mortars are in action. Shells fall on the Legion positions. The tanks have opened fire. The air is rent asunder in all directions at once. The other side replies, and shells fall in Jerusalem like hail. Giant searchlights light up the area. Every conceivable type of weapon is firing away—mortars, cannons, short-range automatic weapons, rifles, machine-guns.

One of the units is inside the break-through area. Shells rain down, 120 mm. messengers of death which, according to the books, should break up the ranks. But not these ranks. The long, explosive-stuffed bangalores take care of the fences. The barbed wire disintegrates into minute metal splinters. We are spread out on the ground, firing our sub-machine guns, bazookas, grenades. Step by step we approach the trenches. Hand-to-hand fighting—bayonets, fists. We follow the sounds of the grenades from trench to trench. The decisive moment is at hand. Yossi, on the walkie-talkie, asks for another portion of "iron" on the Police School. The barrage does the trick. The paratroops sweep inside, There is firing from the rear. Bullets and grenades come from all directions.

Young paratroops brave the fire to get a wounded comrade to some kind of shelter. Smoke envelopes the Police School. On to Ammunition Hill. The area is heavily fortified. Hard fighting on every step, for every house and block, just to stay alive.

The sun goes up over a battle-charred Jerusalem. The road to Temple Mount has a long way to go. Houses, stores, shacks are aflame, windows shattered, doors caved in. A "No Trespassing" sign is ground under the cleats of a half-track. Death lurks in every yard. The paratroops are now atop the Police School roof.

There is bitter fighting in the American Colony, on the way to the Rockefeller Museum. Eight Legionnaires are standing on the steps of one of the houses, hands high in the air, unarmed. An officer named Meir and the two soldiers with him tell the Legionnaires to come forward. The eight suddenly drop to the ground, and behind them three Legionnaires open fire with sub-machine-guns. Two of the paratroops are hit. Three Legionnaires lie dead on the steps. A tank turns the corner, fires a shell. The Legionnaires are no more. The battle moves up the street. A dead Jordanian hangs out of a Hotel Ambassador window. Another is spread-eagled on the floor, and two are folded over the balustrade. Weapons are scattered all over the floor.

The city is quieting down. Paratroops clatter from corner to corner, along the walls of the fortified Rockefeller Museum, through the blasted gates. Paratroops and Legionnaires are meters away from each other, and the Legionnaires come out second best. An Israeli paratrooper climbs up the Museum tower and, defying snipers' bullets, plants the Israeli colors. The snipers try to shoot the flag down. The unit commander reports: "Rockefeller is ours."

The prisoners are seated in the courtyard, faces black with defeat. Many have succeeded in discarding their uniforms and are wearing striped pyjamas. One is an exception. "I am a captain," he says. He is commended for not having stripped himself of his uniform, and is taken for interrogation.

At a turn in the road, a paratroop patrol jeep is stuck at the base of the Old City wall. Hard to get to it. A burning tank lights up the area.

Air Force planes are strafing Augusta-Victoria. The paratroops have taken the last Legionnaire positions in the sector. The staff command is stationed on a hill opposite Temple Mount. Everyone is dead tired, but everyone's eyes are glistening. The paratroop commander issues his orders, the last before the conquest of the Old City. The tanks drive on Lion Gate. The paratroops dismount and rush headlong toward Temple Mount, with history in their wake. The paratroop commander pauses by the square in front of the Mosque of Omar to report on his signals communications: "Temple Mount is under my control! I repeat: Temple Mount is under my control." Somewhere the snipers are active. The paratroops run along the maze of alleys, heading for the Western Wall. How do you get there? Suddenly a hoarse yell rises above the clattering of feet. "I see the Western Wall!" They squeeze through the narrow opening, throw themselves on the large worn stones. Red-eyed, bearded paratroops weep aloud like children, embrace each other, shout "Jerusalem is ours!" The second in command of the unit appoints an honor guard for the Wall. The standard-bearer, an officer with a skull-cap, clambers up to the top of the Wall and plants the Israeli flag. A salute is fired. Again the embracing. The mission has been accomplished. Other paratroops keep pouring into the square. Overcome with fatigue, hardly able to stand only a moment earlier, they lock arms and dance the *Hora* until they sink down in exhaustion.

10 a.m. June 7, 1967. The Western Wall is again the possession of the Jewish people.

To the Western Wall; *Based on Army Press Releases*

The Chief Army Chaplain, Brig. General Shlomo Goren, said at the Western Wall:

Soldiers of Israel, beloved of your people, crowned with valor and victory!

God be with you, valiant warriors!

I am speaking to you from the Western Wall, remnant of our Holy Temple.

Comfort ye, comfort ye My people, sayeth your God.

This is the day for which we have hoped, let us be glad and rejoice in His salvation.

The dream of all the generations has been fulfilled before our eyes. The City of God, the Temple site, the Temple Mount, and the Western Wall—symbol of the Jewish people's Messianic Redemption—have been delivered this day by you, heroes of the Israel Defense Forces.

This day you have redeemed the vow of the generations: "If I forget thee, O Jerusalem, may my right hand wither." We did not forget thee, Jerusalem, our Holy City, home of our glory. And it is your right hand, the Right Hand of God, that has wrought this historic deliverance.

Whose is the heart that will not exult at hearing these tidings of redemption? Henceforth the gates of Zion and of Old Jerusalem, and the paths to the Western Wall, are open for the prayers of their children, their builders and their liberators in Eretz Israel, and to the Jews of the Dispersion who may now come there to pray.

The Divine Presence, which has never forsaken the Western Wall, is now marching in the van of the legions of Israel in a pillar of fire to illuminate our path to victory, and is emblazoning us with clouds of glory before the Jewish people and the entire world. Happy are we that we have been privileged to earn this, the most exalted hour in the history of our people.

To the nations of the world we declare: we shall respectfully protect the holy places of all faiths, and their doors shall be open to all.

Beloved soldiers, dear sons of your people! To you has fallen the greatest privilege of Jewish history. There is now being fulfilled the prayer of the ages and the vision of the Prophets: "For Thou, O God, didst destroy her in fire, and Thou wilt surely build her up again in fire, as it is written (Zechariah 2:5): 'For I, saith the Lord, will be unto her a wall of fire round about, and will be the glory in the midst of her.'" Blessed art Thou O Lord, consoler of Zion and builder of Jerusalem.

And to Zion and to the remnant of our Temple we say: Your children have returned to their borders, our feet now stand within thy gates, Jerusalem: city bounded together once more with New Jerusalem; city that is perfect of beauty and joy of the whole earth; Capital city of the eternal State of Israel.

In the name of the entire community of Jewry in Israel and in the Diaspora, and with joy sublime, I herewith pronounce the blessing: Blessed art Thou O Lord our God, King of the universe, for having kept us alive and sustained us and brought us to this day.

This year in rebuilt Jerusalem.

With God's Help; *The Chief Chaplain, Brig.-Gen. Shlomo Goren, to the Forces,* 7.6.67

An immense human current started surging towards the Western Wall, in order to see it, to touch its stones, to weep and pray, to insert a piece of paper between its stones, to rejoice. The Prime Minister Levi Eshkol and the Minister of Defense, General Moshe Dayan, said at the Wall:

I consider it a great historic privilege to be standing here at the Western Wall, remnant of our Holy Temple, and reminder of our historic past on this spot. I regard myself as the emissary of the entire Jewish people, the emissary of many generations of our people which had yearned for Jerusalem and its sanctity.

To the residents of Jerusalem who underwent so much suffering in 1948, and who with heroic calm withstood the criminal shelling of these past few days, I say: The victories of the Israel Defense Forces, which will keep danger away from the capital of Israel, will be a source of encouragement and consolation to you and to all of us. In the consolation of Jerusalem be you consoled.

And from Jerusalem, the eternal capital of Israel, may the blessings of peace and security come to all the citizens of Israel and to our brother Jews wherever they may be.

Blessed is He who has kept us alive and sustained us and made it possible for us to reach this time.

Prime Minister Eshkol at the Western Wall, 8.6.67

We have returned to the holiest of our sacred places, never to be separated from it again. To her Arab neighbors Israel extends her hand in peace. And to the adherents of other faiths we promise full religious freedom and rights. We have not come here to take away the holy places of other people or to interfere with their rights, but to safeguard the integrity of the city and to abide in it together with others in unity.

Defense Minister General Moshe Dayan at the Western Wall, 8.6.67

The summer sun rose gaily, for the first time in more than 19 *years, over Israeli soldiers posted on the battlements of the wall of Jerusalem. Dozens of Jewish boys, guns in hands, are standing at attention on the stone wall.*

The time is 5:30 a.m.

"How was it last night, fellows?"

"It was cold outside," they said, "but inside . . ."

Morning begins to stir in the conquered city. The residents of the

Old City muster up their courage and go out to their conquerors. Eyes dazed from lack of sleep, faces smiling fawningly, hands holding white flags or handkerchiefs:

"*Shalom, Shalom* to you."

This word, this word that we had been repeating for years to their deaf ears. How did they manage to learn it overnight?

"*Shalom* to you. *Shalom* to all of you. Please come in. Have some coffee." All of it spoken in Hebrew.

Outside sits a dignitary surrounded by a cluster of soldiers. "We don't want war. What are Nasser and Hussein to us? We want to live in peace with you."

Veiled women pass through the street. Jet-black garb. Forgotten scenes of long ago.

A woman weeps bitterly, wringing her hands, running up and down the Via Dolorosa. "My son, my son! Has anybody seen my son?" An old woman, who has not yet taught her tongue smooth talk, speaks her heart: "*Yalla*—go on, beat it! Go back to your own city!"

Our soldiers go into the houses and herd the young men out to the prisoners' lockup. Some of them are wearing pyjamas, trying to look harmless. A man of about 20, wearing a Red Cross frock, whines that all he wants is peace. An Israeli soldier of the same age, whose buddy fell in battle yesterday, rips off the white frock—and a bloodstained khaki uniform is revealed.

Groups of prisoners march through the streets, hands up, led along by a soldier. He has some trouble finding his way through the narrow lanes, and they help him: they lead themselves to the lockup.

The war still hangs heavily over the city's lanes. Thousands of empty cartridges, shrapnel, fragments of stone that showered down from house walls, ripped electric wires, pools of vomit and excreta everywhere. But the city looks richer than it did a generation ago, when we last saw it. American cars everywhere. Some of them scorched, some of them new and intact, glossy red.

An abundance of hotels.

Our soldiers sit in the hotel doorways, handing our their cards to all takers. At the entrance to the Al-Ahram Hotel hangs a portrait of King Hussein. Clusters of soldiers hand us bunches of letters home. The envelopes bear the legend, in Arabic and English: "Al-Ahram Hotel, Wood St., Jerusalem."

They're laughing, our soldiers. They're high with elation. "Imagine

—spending the night in a Jordanian hotel, between white sheets, wearing your boots and ammunition belt."

We head for the Western ("Wailing") Wall. A soldier comes to escort us. "Keep close to the house walls," he warns. "There are still snipers loose." We hear shots here and there.

These are the narrow lanes we remember from our boyhood. The stairs ascend and descend, countless stairs. Local Arabs show us the way. They know where we are headed without our asking. Very quickly we find ourselves walking with other groups of soldiers. Officers, non-coms, privates—everybody walking, running, to the Wall.

Here it is!

The massive stones, smooth from the touch of lips and tears of the generations. Still suffused with devotion. Did anyone shed a tear on them during the 19 years just gone by?

The moss between the huge stones. That so familiar green growth cropping out of the Wall's heights. Nothing has changed.

Dozens of soldiers standing here. Some of them put on phylacteries and pray devoutly. Others, who had never before in their lives uttered a prayer, cuddle up to the Wall. A young major silently kisses the stone. A soldier of Moroccan origin sounds a ram's horn.

"Lehayim! Lehayim!"

A bottle has appeared from somewhere and passes from hand to hand. The soldiers recite the blessing aloud: "Blessed art Thou O Lord our God . . . Who created the fruit of the vine."

We look for the way back. We stray. "How do we get out of here?" we ask.

"Where to?" ask two bearded soldiers in a jeep.

"To Jewish Jerusalem."

"This *is* Jewish Jerusalem." They laugh and offer us a lift. "Hop in. But we only know the lanes of this city. In *that* Jerusalem you'll have to show us the way."

Uri Oren: Inside the Old City; *Army Press Release,* 8.6.67

The buildings of the first Hebrew University and the Hadassah Hospital on Mount Scopus had been deserted ever since the creation of the State of Israel. Despite the fact that the armistice with Jordan gave Israel free access to these places, only a fortnightly convoy of policemen and a few university workers occupied the beautiful stone buildings on the mountain, overlooking all of Jerusalem and the great expanse of the desert of Judaea stretching to the slopes of Jericho and the mountains of Gilead on the road to Amman. When the fighting broke out, there were 120 *people on Mount Scopus, and only after a day of shelling was the road to the mountain opened. The way to the former pride and glory of the small Jewish community was open again.*

"Egged" Cooperative in Jerusalem yesterday renewed the route of the Number 9 Bus Line to Mount Scopus after a break of 19 years.

The operation of this line was stopped in 1948 because of Arab machinations. The number was not given to any other bus line in Jerusalem in the hope of resuming the bus line to Mount Scopus some day. This day has arrived.

Avraham Ferrara drove the first bus which went to Mount Scopus yesterday. His father was killed in 1948 by an Arab bullet while driving a bus on this same line.

Bus to Mount Scopus; *Jerusalem Post*, 9.6.67

Even though opinions differed about some of the territories held by Israel, one thing was beyond any dispute: the unified Jerusalem is the capital of Israel, and no power on earth will tear the Jewish people away from the Eternal City.

On June 27*th, the Israeli Government adopted a resolution regarding the official unification of both parts of Jerusalem, and on June* 29th, *the gates were opened to traffic in both directions. The residents of the Jewish city of Jerusalem, and the Arab residents of Jerusalem, became inhabitants of the same city just three weeks after they had been fighting each other. Poet Haim Guri (who commanded a battalion in the Battle for Jerusalem), described that historical moment.*

From the early hours, a long time before 12 noon, we saw them in the streets of Jewish Jerusalem, in groups and more groups. We knew them at once by their faces, the way they walked, the clothes they wore. They moved round the streets, standing in front of the display windows, looking around, talking quietly and moving on.

We did not know that the invasion of Old Jerusalem by Jewish Jerusalem had commenced at that hour. We hurried to the Mandelbaum Gate and met two streams. Thousands of Israelis were moving on foot or by car towards the Damascus Gate, and thousands of Arabs were flowing towards the New City.

For a moment we stopped the car, observing the scene before our eyes as though in a dream.

I had thought that only a handful would exploit their right on this first day; the brave ones, the curious ones whose inquisitiveness was stronger than their apprehension and uncertainty.

The sight we saw filled us with quiet astonishment if not stupefaction. The currents moving west and east grew stronger from moment to moment, causing whirlpools and stoppages, while with our own eyes we watched the unbelievable.

They came out of the gates, the maze of alleys; boys and men and women in black. Some in *Frangi* (Western-style) hats and some in *kefias,* young and old. They hurried towards the city which had been blocked off to them for about 20 years. Among them were many who remembered it from those times and many who could not possibly have seen it at all.

At the sight of the rush of movement this way and that I could feel that a hundred megatons of expectation and a hundred megatons of curiosity were exploding before our eyes.

The city was exceedingly quiet, as though it had made up its mind to live through this strange meeting between its two halves with a soul-shaking casualness.

For a moment you forgot that a terrible war had been raging here 25 days ago. Only as we passed towards the Damascus Gate did we see a memorial, a heap of Jerusalem stones and upon them strips of bullets and pieces of rusty weapons, red wings of a paratrooper like the crimson of blood, with names and a date.

People froze for a moment at these improvised memorials, then continued on their way. The farther they moved the harder they found it to believe what they saw. For a moment it seemed to me that I was witnessing a stormy movement of desire, strange motions of love, as though the two parts of the city were dashing towards one another.

What was actually happening here? Where was the hatred? Where was the fear of the conqueror? Where was the dread of the defeated? What traces were there of Shukeiry? Where were the 20 years of siege and the mined and bloody border? Where were the traces of the last battle for Jerusalem?

Its traces were clear in the houses, the roofs, the roadways. It was hard to identify them in the faces of these people as they hurried towards Jewish Jerusalem, as they hurried towards the Old City.

Later I learnt something. They had been told that Jewish Jerusalem had been destroyed by the Legion's bombardment, that it did not exist. Some of them had hurried to see her ruined face, while others were looking for their one-time homes.

When evening came they all returned.

Thinking to myself, and talking over with friends this wonderful scene we saw, we were swept away in the mighty streams of the Israeli invasion of the Old City.

We saw a strange fair. Thousands of Jews and Arabs were mingled together. *Tarbushes* and *kefias* and *tembel* hats and black *Meah Shearim* hats. Arab village women in embroidered coloured dresses. Jewish girls in tight-fitting jeans and tricot blouses, with all the charms of young Israel, ambitious, conquering, swaggering, to be seen beneath the thin material, all the heart-breaking glowing Sabrism, to coin a word, as they hurried to see and buy. With them were hundreds of soldiers with weapons and astonished tourists who could not grasp what was happening, and foreign correspondents frozen where they stood, and nuns and monks and young Arabs yelling and selling and beseeching and busy, and shrewd Arab merchants who had grasped the exchange rate on the spot, and taxi drivers yelling "Ramallah!" And Jewesses with market baskets in their hands swiftly slipping past the historic monument and hurrying into the gloomy alleys of the Old City, hurrying to the exotic markets to buy cheaply no matter what! And United Nations cars like orphans whose homes had been destroyed and who had chanced into a country that was not theirs, villagers with sunburnt faces and large hands, and porters yelling at the tops of their voices and forcing their way through the crowd that was becoming as solid as a rock. All moving noisily in the crazy group fraternity of a moment without barriers or bounds to be broken down, with that stupendous curiosity that drove them forward.

Within a short time we had passed through the Damascus Gate and found ourselves in the world which lies beyond the wall, in that world which we had never imagined we would reach except in dreams.

We reached the old roofed bazaar, the market covered with vaulted stones and mortar and faded colors. We reached the reticulated alleys, the bewitched labyrinth in which one can wander as in an oriental dream fragrant with spices and ancient long-forgotten forms and shapes.

We moved slowly along, heel and toe, through the dreadful crush, catching beginnings of scenes that rose out of forgotten abysses, initials of dust-covered, long-dead memories.

We saw the shops and the niches, the shopkeepers and the craftsmen, the olives and the cheeses, the saddles and the straps, the bracelets and the nose-rings, the dresses, the *kefias* and the shoes, the colored sweetmeats and the heavy *halwa,* the cakes dipped in oil, covered over with almonds and hazel nuts and green pistachios of Aleppo, and boiling *felafel* and black coffee, and the copper and earthenware vessels; and the mementoes and the piles of fruit and greenstuffs.

We saw our brethren of Israel in the lust of purchase as though they were possessed. We saw the wonder of all-conquering commerce, the force of the worth-while, the astounding capacity of the defeated to conduct an ancient oriental war of chaffering and bargaining, the desire of the victors to reach the defeated, to start noisy gay negotiations with them; and the inquisitiveness, the insatiable inquisitiveness of those who were ceaselessly moving and discovering the long-forgotten, those who were for the first time seeing this thunderously colorful scene; for it is impossible to imagine the noise with which this meeting was celebrated yesterday in these alleys.

There was also one other, a carefully-dressed young man who owned a shop for beaten copperware and wooden mementoes and crosses. "I shall never accept Israeli money," cried he. "Never, never, never!" Then he went on quietly: "You have come to an Arab country." I told him that I was born in Tel-Aviv. "Tel-Aviv is also in an Arab country," said he in English.

I expect that he will be accepting Israeli money in a day or two. I thought of the metamorphosis of animosity. These were silent in their depression, but smoked the *narghile* with apparent indifference. Some view us as an episode, others hurry to meet us, disregarding their ruined honor, and others again receive us with a strange and twisted kind of "that's how it is;" while there are some who seem to be glad to see us, as though this were an interesting change which promises all kinds of opportunities.

A long day, an endless day. The first day of our meeting. In a day or two we shall understand it, we shall grasp the whole range of problems involved in living together within the one Jerusalem.

Today we saw them in their thousands, moving about in our streets as part of the Israeli victory. For a moment Jerusalem seemed to have returned to the days of the Mandate. But this is the year 1967, and the one Jerusalem is the capital of Israel.

Now Jerusalem is different, so different it makes you glad, it makes you strangely apprehensive. That dreadful war which burst out so suddenly has passed. Now the Arabs are moving to and fro in the streets of the city, citizens of the future, in an endless and quiet procession. And now we are in their streets as victors offering our hand.

Nimrod, Nimrod, why did you never see all this?
Robert, Shmaryahu, you died so near this vision.

Haim Guri: A Hundred Megatons of Expectation; *Lamerhav*, 30.6.67

The first encounters between two worlds, separated by a border 19 *years long and* 100 *prejudices wide were often surprising—the things in common between an Israeli university graduate and his Arab counterpart were more numerous than ever imagined.*

It was hard to get used to the idea that only a few weeks ago we were ready to kill one another. Now we sat in a little café in Jerusalem, the city where we had both lived our lives for a generation. We were both born in Israel, almost in the same place: he in Jaffa and I in Tel-Aviv. Our formal education is about equal. He is a student of political science at Oxford University, while I have taken a degree in the same subjects at the Hebrew University in Jerusalem. Even our fields of activities are similar. He edits a students' organ and writes essays from time to time, while I am a journalist.

We never met until last week, when we took our respective measures with much curiosity because I am an Israeli citizen while he, Abd el Kader Yassin, is a Palestinian refugee, an inhabitant of Jerusalem and a citizen of Jordan. I met him by chance in Mamilla Street in Jerusalem, half an hour after he left the Old City for the first time and came to visit the Jewish State. He had not yet had occasion to wander around or see what the New Jerusalem looked like, when I saw him stopping at the doorway of a shop and trying to have a conversation with the owner:

"What are the daily wages of workers in Israel? What is the price of a loaf of bread? How many people live in Jerusalem?"

I relieved the confused shopkeeper and gladly took over the burden of the conversation. Abd el Kader immediately agreed to my condition: Open and honest conversation, and an answer to every question.

His questions were many and frequent, and most of them were about facts. He clearly wished to fill a large vacuum of ignorance, to check the reliability of his information about the State of Israel. We talked while I was driving him round in my car, showing him the city. He was astonished when he saw that among us there are no women with veiled faces. "I thought that the women of the oriental communities at least went like that." He was surprised that the city was scarcely damaged in spite of the heavy shelling, and wondered to see that we have scarcely any high buildings. The beauty of the University campus really surprised him: "This is the most beautiful university in Europe."

"This isn't Europe," I remarked.

"Of course, geographically speaking."

At the social sciences building he paused and asked: "Do you think that they would allow me to continue my studies here?"

After that he volleyed countless questions at me: "What is the age-limit of compulsory education in Israel? What is the women's cultural level? What is the difference between the cultural level of the Jewish and Arab populations in Israel? Is it true that the Arabs are not allowed to join the Israel Army? Have you changed the names of the Arab villages you took in 1948? What is the democratic system like in Israel? Is the Opposition really free in its activities?"

Little by little he went deeper with his questions: "Are there really equal rights for women here in actual practice? Does this also find expression in their social status and the field of freedom in love?" Finally he allowed himself to ask about the strength of the Israel Army. About conscription, about service in the reserves, the nature of the system of command and the fighting spirit of the soldiers. He seemed quite shaken even before my turn came to ask questions.

Abd el Kader Yassin, aged 22 years old, born in Jaffa. His father was killed in the War of 1948 ("We call it the War of Calamity"), and he went to live with a cousin in the Old City. None of his family stayed in Jerusalem after the Six-Day War. They all ran away to Jordan and he does not know anything about them. "I decided to wait and see what would happen."

He is a third year student at Oxford. Last year he was elected Chairman of the Arabs Students' Organization in Western Europe. 22,000 students from all Arab countries belong to this organization, including 3,500 from Jordan and more than 10,000 Egyptians.

"Did you work against the State of Israel through that body?"

"Naturally. We held discussions and meetings against Israel, and just before the war we arranged for a large blood-donation drive among the students."

"Where were you when the war broke out?"

"Here in Jerusalem. I arrived from Oxford at the beginning of May."

"Did you come to fight?"

"No, I came on vacation. Students aren't conscripted into the army in Arab countries."

"Are the students the only ones exempted?"

"Everybody can be exempted from military service in Jordan if he pays 100 Dinars—about 800 of your pounds."

"Did you believe that war would break out?"

"It was hard not to believe it. The city was crowded with Legionnaires and the army was moving on a large scale. We were expecting war every day."

"Did you believe that you would win?"

"Once the treaty had been signed between Hussein and Nasser I believed it. We never thought that Jordan could fight against Israel alone. But the united strength of the three countries appeared to be a guarantee of victory to all of us."

"What was the guarantee?"

"Chiefly the strength of Egypt. We trusted in her. The continuous propaganda prepared us for that. About a year ago I visited Russia for a five-month tour, and there they were telling us all the time about the vast amount of military equipment that was sent to Nasser. His collapse stupefied us all."

"Was there any atmosphere of fear in Jordan on the eve of the war?"

"No, there wasn't. We were sure of ourselves."

"And were you personally happy at the approaching war?"

"Naturally. I'm a Palestinian refugee. I was educated towards this moment all my life long."

"And what did you think you would do with us after your victory? Destroy us?"

"No, we never thought of total destruction. The world would never agree to go back to the Hitler period. We thought that the Jews would all return to the lands were they were born."

"Which lands?"

"Germany, Russia, Rumania, France, After all, Israel is a country of refugees."

"Do you think that all those countries would take the Jews back?"

"I assumed so."

"And how about the million Jews who came to Israel from the Arab countries? Would you have received them as well—in Egypt, Morocco, Syria and Iraq?"

He was confused. "I admit, I never thought of it. I always thought of the Israelis in terms of European refugees."

"And your press never dealt with this question?"

"Never at all."

"And this wasn't because it was clear to your leaders that the solution was extermination?"

"It may be . . . It is hard for me to believe . . . "

"Your students are exempt from military service. People with means also buy themselves out. Then who remains in the army?"

"The simple people."

"And who heads the Legion?"

"The leaders of the Bedouins."

"Abd el Kader, you know quite well that a modern army and modern weapons require people of a high intellectual level. How did you believe that you could defeat us with an army like yours?"

"The truth is that we would never have believed that your army is so strong. If it was a surprise for the whole world who know you better, why shouldn't we also have been surprised when we were fed on false propaganda?"

"Who in your opinion began this war?"

There was a smile which as much as said: "I put it to you."

"Nasser began it the moment he closed the Strait of Akaba. This was a definite war operation, and I am surprised that you didn't succeed in explaining this to the world. But your story about his military attack on the 5th of June is not correct. You attacked first, and it was a well-planned attack."

"And in the war against Jordan—who began it?"

"We did."

"How do you know?"

The same smile again.

"I was here, wasn't I? My hotel is 100 yards from the Wall. We were shelling for hours and there was no reaction."

"And how do you view Hussein's statements about this at the United Nations?"

"As a lie."

"And you accept it so simply?"

"I'm a student of Political Sciences, and I accept it as a political step. You also lied about your attack on Egypt. Political lying doesn't come within the field of morality."

"In your opinion, is another war possible between Israel and the Arab countries?"

"Under no conditions. You'll win against us in every war."

"What solution is possible now?"

"I read Abba Eban's speech at the United Nations from beginning to end, and I agree to almost every word of it."

"Where did you read it?"

"In the *Jerusalem Post*. I read it in England as well. It is clear to me that the solution now is to return the occupied areas under the conditions of a peace arrangement, or else to set up an Independent Palestine State."

"Do you say that for lack of choice, because of your military inferiority?"

"It's true that we have no alternative, but I say this as a matter of choice. Now I know that peace will be good for both sides."

"What do you know now that you didn't know before? What did the six days of fighting do to make such a fundamental change in your views?"

Abd el Kader moved uncomfortably in his chair.

"I'll tell you the truth, and I find it hard to say it. I know many people claim that we Arabs have a tendency towards exaggeration and even towards flattery. So I find it hard to say these things to you, but they are the truth: The six days turned me into another man. I discovered you are a different people. Entirely different from what I thought. Half of this truth I discovered during the fighting. Then I realized your military wisdom and battle spirit. The bragging declarations of Nasser, the man I revered, simply made me feel ashamed.

"I discovered the other half after your occupation, when your forces entered the Old City. That was the most dreadful day of my life. The shame of collapse and the fear of the results. We were sure that you would destroy us or expel those who were left. They taught us to think that you are a cruel and aggressive people. And what happend you know as well as I do. Now, a week or two later, I'm sitting with you and chatting like a friend. Only a courageous people is capable of such generosity. With a people like that it is well worth-while to live in peace."

Uri Oren: Abd el Kader Changes his Mind; *Yediot Aharonot,* 14.7.67

Chapter Seven

To the Jordan

WEST BANK (4.6.67)

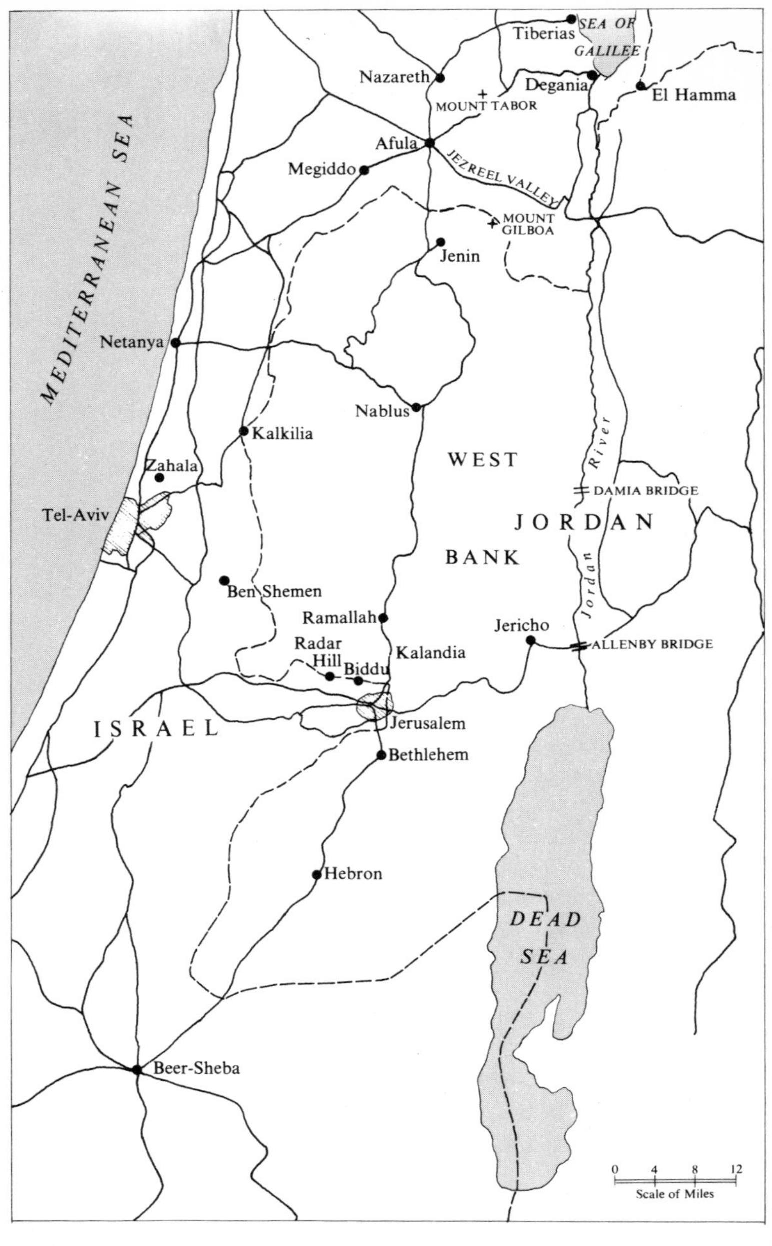

THE JORDANIAN ARMY, UNDER EGYPTIAN COMMAND, OPENED GUN and mortar fire on the first day of the war all along the 530 kilometers of the Israeli border, shooting at dozens of settlements on the narrow coastal strip of the Mediterranean. Zahal counter-attacked from two directions. The units led by the Northern Front Commander, General David Elazar (who later on was assigned the conquest of the Syrian Heights) struck from the north, and the troops led by the Central Front Commander, General Uzi Narkiss, conqueror of Jerusalem, struck at the center. The force from the north advanced southward, in the direction of the town of Jenin, which was taken the following morning, after a fierce battle and despite the stubborn resistance of the Jordanians, who had at their disposal battalions of Pattons and modern American equipment.

After the conquest of Jenin, the troops received orders to move southward, to Nablus. A night battle of armored forces was waged on the outskirts of that city. When the first Israeli soldiers entered the city, they were amazed to see its inhabitants giving them a warm welcome, waving their handkerchiefs and applauding. The Israeli soldiers smiled back, but when one of the officers tried to take away a rifle from an Arab standing at his side, the Israelis found out that the welcoming reception was not intended for them. Since the Israeli troops had outflanked the city and arrived unexpectedly from the rear, from the east, the inhabitants of Nablus concluded that these were the Iraqi reinforcements which were expected to come from the direction of the Damia Bridge on the Jordan. After the first volley the civilians disappeared from the streets, and the fighting started. Later on, a great battle was fought against the Jordanian tanks positioned at the western entrance to the city, where they had been waiting for the arrival of the Israeli troops. The city capitulated in the evening of the third day of the war. An armored brigade advanced at the same time from the approaches to Jerusalem towards the area at the north of the city, on the road to Ramallah. This was a key zone to the whole West Bank. The troops moved in three axes, in a mountainous terrain rising to a height of 700 meters, along narrow roads and mine-fields.

On the following morning, the second day of the war, a fierce battle was waged in the fortified position named Hamivtar, north of Jerusalem, as well as a battle of armored forces in the vicinity of Tel-el-Fuhl. An infantry brigade from Jerusalem advanced simultaneously towards Mar Elias–Bethlehem–Mount of Hebron. On the evening of June 6th (the second day of the war), Ramallah was conquered by the armored brigade, which climbed down the slopes of the Mountains of Ephraim towards Jericho (equipped with several trumpets) and northward to Nablus, where it joined the units of the Northern Command. An additional detachment of the Central Command conquered the Latrun enclave, on the Jerusalem–Tel-Aviv road. Cruel, bloody battles had taken place at this spot in the war of 1948, ending with an Israeli defeat. Another detachment advanced through the axis Kalkilya (the Arab town which for many years had been the center of raids against the Israeli coastal settlements)—Tul-Karem. Three days later, when the cease-fire with the Hashemite Kingdom was imposed, Zahal had in its hands the whole West Bank of the Jordan—which up to 1948 had been part of Eretz Israel. All the Israeli commanders commented that the Legionnaires had fought stubbornly and well during the first stages of the battles, but collapsed after the break-through.

The campaign which took Zahal cross-country from Latrun to the Jordan and from the "Large Triangle" down to Hebron differed from the action in Sinai in two important respects. Although the points of combat were far more numerous here, the distances were much shorter, so that the physical aspect of the fighting resembled an unbroken chain of combat. Also, the progress involved a considerable population and the inevitable confrontations on the human level—a significant factor when viewed in the light of the enemy's acts of brutality in the region less than two decades ago.

In these confrontations, as elsewhere, Zahal displayed the uniqueness, as a conquering army, which has gained for it the reputation for high moral standards as well as an unsurpassed morale.

Colonel Uri Ben-Ari is one of the few brigade commanders participating in the Six-Day War who is not in the regular army. Like the rest of his brigade, he is a civilinn doing reserve duty.

My brigade (armored brigade of the reserves) was located in the plain for defensive duties. At 1:00 p.m. on Monday we received an order—to break through in the Ma'ale Hahamisha–Motza area and to seize the mountain ridge between Ramallah and Jerusalem.

The posts in this area had long been known. Radar Ridge opposite Ma'ale Hahamisha—I remember it from 20 years ago, when I attacked it several times. Once we took it, but later it was lost. It was a concrete post, as was Sheikh Abdul Aziz, while Beit Iksa was a fortified village. There was another axis of movement, through Beit Likya, which is very difficult but the shortest way to the top. If anybody had taught at the Command and Headquarters School that it was possible to go into an attack with an armored brigade within four hours, from the plain to the Jerusalem positions, he'd have been thrown out, but my men did it. The order was carried out.

The problem in these positions is the bunkers, and one tank was detailed to each bunker. Its task was to silence the bunker by direct fire, from five to seven. The bunkers were silenced and the armored infantry went up to those posts. They removed the mines with probes, one by one, with great persistence, in the darkness. In any event, those two positions fell. The problem was to clear the axes and to put the armor onto them. This was completed by 12–1 at night. A third force moved along the Beit Likya axis, and this completed the break-through. Both Sheikh Abdul Aziz and Radar Ridge were in our hands.

The next battle was against Biddu. This was also a fortified locality which we had to take at night. A heavy fight, with many casualties, but when it was finished we had an open road—the force passed through Beit Likya and reached the rear of the mountain at 4 in the morning. There a hill opposite Tel-el-Fuhl was seized and the rest of the force moved on. Nebi Samuel fell in an easy fight, and at dawn the brigade gathered together on the top of the mountain, blocking the road to Jerusalem coming up from the Jordan. At this spot a tank-vs.-tank battle took place. There were about 30 Pattons on the heights. Six or seven of them were destroyed, while 13 escaped to Jericho.

This whole height is dominated by Tel-el-Fuhl on which Hussein had built his palace. Fortunately for us the construction had not been finished, otherwise it would have been held by a far larger force. This threatening hill was taken against medium resistance.

The orders were to take the gully and French Hill. We moved southwards. Sha'afat fell quite easily. There was a lot of sniping, but that doesn't affect armor. One battalion went against the two objectives—both the axis and the gully. The assault was terrible. I remember one of the battles of the Sinai campaign, about which much had been said of the night attack on the dam and the murderous fire there. This assault was many times worse, and in fact we didn't take it at first. We were forced to retire and attack again, whereupon the Legion ran. There were many casualties whom we evacuated (with the aid of helicopters) to the hospitals down on the plain. French Hill fell more easily. The Legion abandoned it after a light battle. Two battalions advanced on Ramallah. Atarot and Neve Ya'acov were freed. For the first time in my life and in that of my brigade we had to capture a city almost in the dark—and that's a problem. We decided to go into Ramallah with a battalion of tanks, shooting on all sides as fast as possible. We crossed and recrossed the city several times and it slowly fell silent. There was some resistance from bazookas, etc., but within three quarters of an hour the town was silent. We cleared out of it at night and took up positions to the north and to the south. By morning there was no resistance and the town was mopped up.

We continued on to Jericho. We had a few trumpets—everything that was needed. When you go to Jericho it's a long time before you see it. The routes are pretty difficult. There was no resistance en route, but the scouts and look-outs which moved ten kilometers ahead, in advance of the brigade, discovered the rest of the Pattons in the distance. Whoever knows the road knows that suddenly there opens up before you the entire Jericho landscape and the Dead Sea. We moved along two axes. One battalion attacked the police station—the most important part of Jericho. Another battalion used the "Ramallah patent"—went through Jericho and back again, wiping out all resistance on the way. Sniping and enemy movements continued throughout the night. When morning came we "washed up" the town again, and it fell silent.

We went down to Beit Ha'arava (on the shores of the Dead Sea), where not one stone of the kibbutz remains. This actually completed the operations of the division. One battalion went north and seized the Chabara camp which lies before Nablus, where it linked up with other units which had taken the town. To sum up in a few words—we had two enemies. One was the Legion, which fought hard and seriously all along the road. The second enemy was the terrain, and it became apparent that not the vehicle and its armament are the fundamental factors but the commanders and the soldiers who operate the equipment. I did it with a regular brigade in Sinai. This time it was done by reservists no less well—maybe better—since they were older, more serious, more devoted to the objective.

Statement by Colonel Uri Ben-Ari at Press Conference on 13.6.67

Colonel Uri Ben-Ari (Banner) stands for something in the Israel Army. He has taken part in three wars. He first fought at Jerusalem in 1948, and later his battalion also took Eilat. During Operation "Kadesh" (Sinai Campaign), in 1956, he commanded the armored brigade which captured all those points that have come back to us now: Abu Agheila, Gebel Libni, Bir Gafgafa, Bir Hassna, and as far as Ismailia. During the Six-Day War, Colonel Ben-Ari commanded an armored brigade of reserves which took Radar Ridge, French Hill, Nebi Samuel and the Mivtar (Cleft Hill) from the Jordanians, then went on to Jericho and as far as Beit Ha'arava.

General S. L. A. Marshall and Colonel Robert Henriques both found occasion to heap praises on the tactics used by Colonel Ben-Ari in the Sinai Campaign. I contacted him in order to hear what he had to say, incidentally, on various points about reserves, both in action and when, uniforms off, they return to their daily routine.

Question: Colonel Ben-Ari, you are now managing a large printing concern. Did you worry about what was happening there while you were called up?

Answer: (quietly) There was someone left at the plant who took over my job. I went off without having to worry too much. Anyway, war grips you so quickly that you simply don't have time to think about what's happening at your civilian job. *(concentrates)* A senior officer enters into such a maze of problems and responsibilities so swiftly that he really doesn't think about what he was doing before. In general, this is because you are coming to a reserve brigade, whose headquarters must wait a day or two for the gears to begin to mesh, and you must put a lot of work into it. This is far more so in armor, because of the numerous problems of equipment. As a result you find yourself head over heels in work. Once again, it may be that this is something personal, of course, and I assume that if a brigade goes off to ordinary reserve duty, to exercises and maintenance, then undoubtedly there is also room to think about the work; *(decisive)* but in this case our men went off to war.

Question: Did the men of your brigade talk over their personal problems with you after the fighting ended?

Answer: They didn't have time to speak about that at all. They didn't manage to worry about it because the experiences and impressions were far too deep. People seem to think that this war was the most difficult of all. But as far as I can remember my personal impressions, the War of Liberation was far more difficult because of our lack of resources and the long time it lasted.

The Six-Day War involved a far greater number of men and much more equipment. Developments followed one another in quick succession. Still, it was a tension of only six days, while the War of Liberation lasted more than a year. In the War of Liberation I served in the Fourth Palmah Battalion at Jerusalem, the sector where my brigade has been operating now as well, at Radar Ridge, at Nebi Samuel and at Beit Iksa. We then spent 74 days from the time we went up to Jerusalem and until the first cease-fire, when we went down to the coastal plain. During those 74 days we engaged in 68 night operations. I went up to Jerusalem with a company of 200 men in sound condition and came down with 15 in good condition, 100 wounded and 85 dead. That's why it seems to me that, psychologically speaking, the War of Liberation was much harder. Maybe it was also because of our absolute faith that this time we would win, while then we could not even be certain that we could hold out. *(sighs)* People forget. 20 years have passed and people forget what had happened.

Question: How does the human material of 1948 compare with the troops of 1967?

Answer: The material of 1948 and that of the Six-Day War are identical. In the War of Liberation the battle-cry of the officers was, "After me!" *(emotional)* and that's how it was now as well. The remarkable thing is that this spirit has remained. Then the commanders were veteran Hagana and Palmah men, ideologically imbued over a long period, while that is the civilian spirit of the entire people now.

Question: And all the talk about "the Espresso Age" and "the Discotheque youngsters?"

Answer: (waves it away) That's all nonsense. You can sense it clearly. Among my battalions was one in which I had served in the War of Liberation, while another consisted of youngsters. Yet you could spend the whole day with them in battle without feeling the slightest difference in spirit, in morale. I think that we have assessed our youth incorrectly. We thought that all kinds of external trifles which appeared out of order to us, things that are part of the younger generation all the world over—would affect their being. But they did not touch it! The same verve, the same volunteer spirit and courage and maybe above all, the knowledge that if they did not fight to a finish they would be wiped out. It was not the youngsters who were mistaken; it was the parents who were wrong in their assessment. The older generation simply did not understand or grasp what is contained in Israeli youth.

Question: How did you feel this time, when you went back and fought in all those places where you had fought in 1948?

Answer: (enthused) It was an exceptional feeling, and an experience that is hard to describe—to go back to the same place where you fought 20 years ago, and which was not included in the area of the State because of the insufficient forces. Take Radar Ridge, for instance. This is the British Radar Station that lies north of Ma'ale Hahamisha, a locality that dominates the entire neighborhood. The British abandoned it when they left the country, and it was occupied by the Legion. We captured it during a savage battle in May, 1948. Then our forces moved over to fight at Mount Zion; Radar Ridge was assigned to one of our other forces and was recaptured by the Jordanians.

At the time we had a feeling of severe loss. Ma'ale Hahamisha all but fell as well, as a result of the capture of Radar Ridge by the Legion. We were summoned back to Ma'ale Hahamisha and we managed to save it; but four additional attacks of my company were repulsed with a loss of our best commanders and men—the best of my comrades. So it was an exceptional experience to recapture it now. Just a little sign: Since the end of the Six-Day War and until now, hundreds of members of my Battalion of those days have contacted me and expressed their joy with handshakes and embraces. The same thing goes for a position called Biddu and Nebi Samuel.

Question: Don't you sometimes have a strange feeling, when men who were under you in 1948 and in Sinai have climbed up in rank and now give you orders?

Answer: Many of the present brigade commanders were under my command at various stages, either in 1948 or in Sinai. I was happy to see them commanding and winning in this war, and felt a little personal pride to think that something of my spirit and approach had been implanted in them. The man who was my assistant in the 1948 attack on Rạdar Ridge is now Commander of the Northern Sector, General David Elazar (Dado). I was happy to receive orders from him in the attack on the Syrian Heights.

Question: When a leading officer returns to civil life, don't his army habits interfere with him in his relations with men at work?

Answer: Anybody who was a senior officer in the army knows how to adapt the positive things of the army to civilian life and, vice versa, to transfer the important things of civilian life to correct use when he commands military formations. *(laughs lightly)* Character remains character, of course. It is obvious that an army man who has so many years of experience behind him will have certain methods of organization, certain fundamental ways of assessing a situation and thinking. But if you lack these things in civil life, you will certainly go bankrupt. The basic difference may be that in civil life you operate only by intuition and what may happen can cause you material loss only.

On the other hand, if you operate only by intuition in the army, it will become plain in a very short time that you will never get to be a high-ranking officer.

Question: In your opinion, is it possible to revert to everyday life after a war with such stirring experiences as these six days of ours, or is there something like a crisis of transition?

Answer: (knitted brow) There is a crisis of one kind or another that is experienced by everybody who took part in the war, among the fighters at the front and also among the wives of the fighters. Undoubtedly the crisis should be split into two. First of all, it is a crisis of personal experience and tension. A man continues to be tense and ready for weeks and months, until the crisis vanishes and you seem to go back to being the same man you were before. On the other hand, I think that there is a second crisis, far more prolonged, which is liable to bring about deep-seated changes in Israeli society as regards the education of the Israeli youth and the opinion people have of it, and the hope that something of the unity we all felt will remain; that maybe the subconscious side of all the people will more firmly sense that security for the State of Israel must be given priority. And maybe the thought of that distant day, when we shall have to fight for life again, will help to shape people's behavior, even in daily life and at times of crisis that are not necessarily military in character.

Raphael Bashan: A Brigade Commander Looks Back; *Ma'ariv*, 14.7.67

Movie-goers suspect sometimes that life imitates stage-craft. Hundreds of movies have been made about the lonely hero, surrounded by enemies, fighting single-handed a desperate battle and beating them in spite of their numerical superiority. There is only one difference between script and reality: the heroes do not look like movie-stars.

And then, suddenly, two big Patton tanks appeared, pouring shell-fire on our half-track. One fired on us from the right, and the other from the left.

And then we noticed, two or three more Pattons joining them. Four or five Pattons against one half-track, and we were in it!

We beat a retreat, and they gave chase. They were still at a distance, but getting closer, closer, five frightening monsters . . .

Then Abu-Kassis took his 0.3 machine-gun, and started firing, firing at the tanks, one shot to the left and one shot to the right . . .

A few seconds later, Abu-Kassis jumped up from his seat, and, like a man possessed, climbed on the engine hood. He stood there on the hood and fired away . . .

We shrank and flattened ourselves against the floor of the half-track, trying to protect our heads with our hands. Abu-Kassis was still standing on the hood, erect, exposed to the fire, returning the fire of the Pattons with his 0.3 with incredible arrogance!

The half-track races, careens, swerves, and Abu-Kassis still stands on the hood. Every now and then he falls, but he gets back to his feet, and calmly takes aim with his machine-gun. Machine-gun fire is completely powerless against a tank, but he aims his 0.3 over our heads and returns fire from the retreating half-track, as though he were their equal . . . He calmly stands there, under fire, and keeps shooting at the Pattons . . .

Thus went the saga of Avraham Abu-Kassis, as told by the crew of his half-track. Their excitedly incoherent words slowly delineate the image of the fabulous Abu-Kassis—and here he is, that Hercules, so courageous, strong, powerful, heroic . . .

A few minutes later I was facing the man—short and skinny like a boy, ill at ease, staring around him with big eyes, speaking in a thin voice, very quietly, in simple words.

On the second night of the war, the armored brigade broke through the fortifications of Jenin in order to crack the Jordanian defense line running along the Dothan Valley, sweep into the Triangle, and then swing southeast, to the Damia Bridge across the Jordan.

It had been a long day of fighting, of rescue-forces which needed rescue themselves, of Pattons lying in ambush and attacking our half-tracks and the few Sherman tanks. In the pandemonium of the rescue half-track of the engineers unit, at 2 p.m. of Tuesday Junes 6—that is where Private Avraham Abu-Kassis was to be found. He is not clear about the overall picture of the battle. All he knows now is that his half-track, together with other half-tracks of the engineers unit, had been sent to the field—and this time, not to clear minefields nor to breach barbed wire nor to lay mines, but to rescue tankmen stranded in enemy territory.

All he knows is that he, Avraham Abu-Kassis, 23 years old, from Kiryat-Shemona, tractor-driver in peacetime, scout in wartime, was now a half-track machine gunner, although his is a technical half-track, without an installation for his machine-gun, which meant that, if the need arose, he would have to improvise a better shooting position.

He has never been under fire before.

The half-track moves toward one of the stranded tanks. All is quiet. Suddenly—the roar of cannon. And one second later Abu-Kassis realizes that his half-track is caught between the jaws of two Pattons.

Another thing that Abu-Kassis immediately realizes is that his weapon is perfectly ridiculous against a tank, and even more ridiculous against two tanks, but he uses it, and the weapon shoots, shoots fire, useless fire perhaps, but fire nevertheless . . .

The third thing to sink into his consciousness at this moment is, that it is really difficult to maneuver a machine-gun which has no place set for it in the half-track . . .

And while he is digesting these facts, Abu-Kassis' half-track is attacked by the two Pattons, and then by five . . .

"Over us, on the hills around the valley, there were olive groves, and the tanks were firing from the groves; we, on the other hand, were exposed to the fire in an open terrain, in a wheat field. I rose a little from my seat, so that I could handle the machine gun more easily, but it didn't help much. I fired a shot to the right and one to the left. A sergeant was sitting at my right, and every time I swung the machine-gun to the right, I bumped into him. I gave him a good push, and went on firing . . ."

Abu-Kassis' half-track started retreating with the rest of the force. On the way they found another half-track, which had suffered a hit, and the crew was milling round. Abu-Kassis' half-track raced on. Private Abu-Kassis, still busy with his machine-gun, noticed the crew of the damaged half-track and ordered the driver to pick them up. The driver, frightened by the shells pouring all around him, kept moving. "So I shouted at him and ordered him to stop."

The crew of the damaged half-track was picked up. Abu-Kassis' half-track raced on. Abu-Kassis kept firing from his seat. Now he had to stand with his back to the driver and his face turned back, towards the tanks, and fire with his machine-gun over the heads of the men squeezed in the half-track. "It was not very comfortable," he says. He jumped and climbed on the engine-hood, and stood there, in the half-track, retreating in an open field, exposed to the fire of five Pattons, returning their fire with a machine-gun.

"I fell several times, but I got back on my feet. One shell hit the half-track between the chains, and the half-track reeled with the impact. I flew several meters in the air, and then fell back in the half-track. I got a good blow in the chest. It took my breath away . . . It still hurts. But I went back right away and stood on the hood, there was not a moment to lose. I was not afraid of falling. I fell from time to time and stood up again. I didn't think of falling. I didn't think of fear . . . I only knew that I was in the midst of fighting, that some of the boys were in my half-track, and that I had to save them and save myself . . . That was the only thing I thought about."

In spite of everything, in spite of the rain of fire, Abu-Kassis had enough coolness of mind to notice whenever anybody in the half-track raised his head. He would stop firing for a moment and order the soldier to keep his head down. And he had sufficient self-control not to be exasperated by the dazed soldier trying to feed his machine-gun with the ammunition belt turned upside down. Abu-Kassis took the belt, turned it around and fed the machine-gun himself, without stopping fire for an instant.

"And didn't your fingers get mixed up?"

"No, my fingers didn't get mixed up. I worked the way I work on the tractor. My fingers don't get mixed up there either."

"The engine exploded the moment the half-track reached the edge of the open field. Perhaps it was the heat. I don't know exactly. Luckily it was the edge of the olive grove, and we could jump down and take cover. When I jumped down, I saw on the ground the magazine of an Uzi sub-machine gun. I thought, maybe one of the boys lost it, and he'll miss it. I almost touched it, when a bullet whistled right over my hand, and struck the magazine. I gave up the whole thing and ran. On the way I met a buddy of mine. Before I climbed on the hood, I had asked him to hold my Uzi for me. "Give me the Uzi now," I told him. "I forgot your Uzi in the half-track," he said. So I ran back to the half-track, took my Uzi, and ran back to the grove."

"And weren't you afraid at all?"

"No, I felt no fear at all."

Commented one of the men in the half-track:

"I saw Abu-Kassis sprawled on the hood, holding the machine-gun and firing it from that position. My first thought, I remember, was that it was no easy task to hold the hot and heavy 0.3 in your hands. Generally, this machine-gun is fired while mounted on legs. You need quite a lot of strength to hold such a heavy weapon and fire—especially when you are exposed to tank fire."

Lieutenant-Colonel Moshe, commander of the brigade:

"At first glance, Abu-Kassis' action appears absurd—a soldier, exposed to the fire of five tanks, shoots at them with a machine-gun. But then, it becomes clear that this feat is not only daring but very useful.

"Even a monster like a tank has its vulnerable points. A tank commander stands up in the turret, the upper part of his body exposed. Machine-gun fire can hit him, or, at least, force him to stay inside the turret, which reduces the efficiency of the tank itself. Machine-gun bullets are also liable to hit the directional instruments on the tank (the antenna, for instance), which also impairs its operation. Abu-Kassis may not have damaged the tanks themselves, but he certainly kept their commanders distracted. We also have to remember that the firing of a Patton is very accurate; were it not for Abu-Kassis and his bothersome machine-gun, the Pattons would have had no difficulty in hitting the half-track practically at will.

"Certainly his action, calling for rare coolness and daring, is no everyday occurrence. It demonstrates the fact that a soldier, trapped by superior enemy fire, stands a better chance if he uses his weapons, however inferior, with judgment and resourcefulness."

"That hour and a half was a bit long," is the way Abu-Kassis puts it, careful as ever to conceal his emotions. He doesn't say "the longest hour and a half of my life" or "it was a nightmarish hour and a half."

Now that we have heard all about the long and amazing 100 minutes of Abu-Kassis, on that Tuesday afternoon at the Kabatya crossroads, it would be interesting to know Abu-Kassis, just as he is, outside and beyond those minutes.

First, then, a few milestones:

Avraham came here from Rabat, Morocco, when he was seven and a half years old. He was one of the ten children of a destitute family, four sons (all fought in the Six-Day War, one was wounded) and six daughters. He attended an agricultural school in Magdiel, up to the tenth grade, then left school because he wanted to help support the family. He got a job as a tractor driver, and, except for his military service as a path-clearer in the engineers corps, he has been working at this job ever since. He and his wife live in Kiryat-Shemona.

The engineers company commander who recommended Abu-Kassis for a citation said: "He protected the men with extraordinary courage. He activated that machine-gun with frightening efficiency."

The traits of resourcefulness which were revealed in this feat did not seem to characterize Abu-Kassis prior to the event. His fellow-servicemen knew him as a disciplined but non-descript soldier, by no means an extrovert and certainly far from a hero.

How come, then? Here is the probe:

Q.: Does this act of yours amaze you, or can you recall other instances where you faced severe tests?

A.: I can't remember such a case. Never in my life did I ever do such a thing. I always sat on the side and kept quiet. This was really the first time in my life that I acted so unusually.

Q.: Were you a mischievous child?

A.: No, never. I was always obedient. I listened to my parents and to my teachers at the children's home. I obeyed my commanders in the army.

Q.: Try to remember, anyway. Were you *always* obedient? Didn't you ever have arguments with your parents?

A.: I'm trying to remember, but I can't think of any. Whatever my parents said, I always found acceptable. After all, parents are parents.

Q.: When you were a youngster, did you ever beat up any other kids?

A.: No, never.

Q.: Really, not ever?

A.: That's right. Once a kid hit me, but I didn't hit him back. I decided not to, so that it shouldn't lead to a quarrel. Other than this, no one ever hit me.

Q.: In that case, you have extraordinary luck.

A.: That's not luck. It's a matter of nature. This can happen to a person like me, who likes to live quietly. I prefer to give in.

Q.: In that case, would you say that giving in should be the policy of our country, in the crisis which it underwent a month ago?

A.: No, it's different for a state. There, it's not a matter of inconveniencing an individual. This is a threat to the entire state. In such a case, a state cannot give in.

Q.: Did you ever lift your hand against any of your younger brothers?

A.: Never.

Q.: Would you have been capable of striking an enemy in hand-to-hand fighting?

A.: Yes. I would attack him with or without a weapon, with my hands and feet.

Q.: Have you ever quarreled with your friends?

A.: No, I always yield.

Q.: Have you never quarreled with anyone?

A.: The Moroccans of my community are hotheads and get angry easily. Sometimes I feel that I, too, am getting upset, but I immediately calm myself. Everything can be settled quietly and with good-will. It's not pleasant to yell at people.

Q.: On that Tuesday, you showed resourcefulness and leadership. You were in command of people. You issued orders. You shouted. How do you explain it?

A.: I really don't understand. But that was war.

Q.: How did these traits of yours come out? Did you ever want to be an army commander?

A.: No. That's not for a quiet man like me. I've always lived quietly and I don't want to be someone big. Even in civilian life, I am glad to work a tractor. I love physical labor. I love to work hard. I get up at four in the morning and come back at seven in the evening. I was offered a job as a clerk in a bank. I didn't take it. They offered me a job as a foreman in the Jewish National Fund, to handle 40 people. I didn't accept. They should work and I should look on especially, when there are, among them, people older than I? No, that's not honorable for me!

Q.: If you work that hard, when do you rest?

A.: There's less work with the tractor in winter. Also on the Sabbath; then I go swimming at Horshat-Tal (Dew Glen). At times, I play on a recorder. I am sorry that my recorder was smashed during the battle, otherwise, I would play it for you.

Rachel Halfi: Abu-Kassis and the Five Monsters; *Bamahane*, 11.7.67

War has many faces, and every fighter mirrors them according to his own feelings. Menahem Shelach, member of kibbutz Mishmar Ha'emek—one of the oldest in the country—stared in the face of war and saw it was clad in mourning.

Many times during the war, I imagined that I had already seen all this in some awful movie. Exactly like this, four jeeps were parked in a field of ripe corn and, like this, shots were cracking and bullets were whistling, and this scene (low hills hugging a drowsy village in the hot morning hours) had at some point appeared on the screen with the same dialogue: "Cover us; more to the left, towards the pink house." All this while I am still sitting in the darkened hall. Everything appeared strange, fanciful.

Before dawn, when the convoy, lights out, crawled along the Hasargel Road, the transistors played martial tunes and the calming voice of news-analyst General Haim Herzog explained to us the progress of the situation. We, with week-old beards, red-eyed, half asleep by the 0.3 in. machine-gun, listened.

By the Hill of Almonds a bearded sapper officer (Gregory Peck? Burt Lancaster?) passed us, leaning on his long rod as on a hiking stick, striding jauntily along to the mine field on the border of our country. Slowly a rosy light appeared, and from the hill we saw the boundary barrier.

Gideon said, "Go down there and remove the barrier."

The minute I touched the barrier I wanted to feel the touch of history, but instead I felt a sudden thirst. I rolled the border marker into the thorns lining the road, deserted for 19 years. Shaya opened his eyes for a minute and said, "What next?"

"Next is war," I wanted to say, but between the hills two airplanes appeared. We all lay down in the almond grove.

"Hunters," Ijo shouted.

There was no time to be afraid because the second-in-command of the brigade now drew us after him into enemy territory. We hastened along the road in the water jeep of Ein Harod, in the field crop jeep of Beit Alpha (two days earlier they had been mounted with machine-guns in the machine shop of Beit Hashita). We passed a village and took it. Three old men had their pictures taken with the conquering second-in-command (his pistol at his waist, commando knife on his hip, and American carbine in his hand), and still not one shot had been fired. From far, far away came the sound of explosions. Ours? Theirs? Only farther away. Only Ami noticed the two Hunters which came down over us and opened machine-gun fire 0.5 in.—ta-ta-ta-ta—on us. He took up his "Uzi" lying on the seat and joined in, laughingly saying afterwards, "I hit them." Shaya almost believed him because he hurried to oil his own machine-gun, in case another chance came up.

"Spread out," Gideon called.

We jumped into a ploughed field. From afar we could see the houses of the same village.

"Have you ever been in Jenin?" asked Shaya.

"I was there in '46." I remembered the smelly bus in which I had ridden from Jerusalem during my summer vacation. Now Jenin stood silent. Four blue buses approached the police station building and figures got out. Then the shooting began. At first it was hard to believe that everything was really happening. A burst was shot at us from the pink house. A nice house, a large porch, three straight cypress trees.

"Cover us!"

All of us together and, after us, Maier's recoilless cannon. Boom.

"Stop, you're shooting our fellows." But Maier was in an ecstasy. Since taking the course he had not fired a recoilless cannon; he had to take advantage of the opportunity. Higher, higher.

A new and shiny Mercedes stood at the entrance to the village. "Some standard of living," commented Ezra.

When had we seen an abandoned city, so silent? Not a creature. Shots. The driver of the commander of the brigade lay on his stomach in the doorway of a house. "Theyre shooting at me," he said. "I have a flat, tow me," he said, but did not get up. When we tied the cable, he left the Arab mosque on bloody legs and ceaselessly murmured an unintelligable prayer in a tearful voice.

Three soldiers were standing in the doorway of the mosque, smoking quietly.

"What's going on here?" I shouted.

"Nothing," one of the soldiers answered, "Just snipers."

Farther up the street, by an electric appliance shop, where a notice advertised a Syrian airline "Fly to Kuwait and Enjoy Yourself," several figures were running. The second-in-command gathered us together and called while in motion: "After me. They have set up an ambush in the orchard."

Where was this orchard? We left the car with the flat tire in the central square and went on, guided by the fresh smell of orchard and fertile clay soil. Three bursts and the ambush disappeared.

"Jenin is in our hands," the signalman of the second-in-command said into the signals apparatus.

"Maybe now we can get some sleep," Ezra pleaded.

Two television writers stood by a huge Sherman tank and photographed the tired conquerors. Maier stopped by them and suggested: "Pikcher, ha?" They smiled and took pictures. In the courtyard of the police station everyone was milling around and pushing up to the Shekem canteen car. At the back door, wounded with closed eyes lay in the sun. No one paid attention to them.

"Why are they in the sun?" I asked.

"They will be evacuated right away," answered a beardless officer. ("Disgraceful to go home like that," I thought).

I lay down by a wall in the shade and went to sleep. Yehuda wakened me. "Are you here?" he asked.

"No, I'm there," I answered, opening one eye, "In the world of dreams."

"Take care of yourself," he said and gave me half a bottle of Tempo.

"From what?" I asked.

"There was one wounded among us," he said. "This isn't a game."

As though I had thought it was a game! They shoot in the air—sheer fantasy. Only the wounded man lay quietly, the blood stains showing through the bandages.

"He's going to die," someone said.

"Nonsense."

"Really, he might die," I thought but did not believe it. Again I fell asleep.

At night, when we entered Nablus we were ordered to wait for the rest of the force.

"Let's eat," I said. We took out a can of halvah, a can of grapefruit sections and two cans of sardines. In the field, by the side of road, three forms lay wrapped in white sheets.

"Dead?" Shaya asked.

"Killed," I answered.

"Ours?" asked Shaya.

"Ours," I said.

"Go on, slice the bread," Ezra said. I took the knife and cut six slices. We ate sardines, and the dead slept. No one approached them, they lay in complete rest, as if around them a desert had been carved out, completely detached from the bumps and tumult of the moving convoys, from the thundering, crawling lines of tanks, from the rising dust, from the sound of explosions in the city.

"Is there a doctor here?" a young lieutenant asked us.

"We don't know," we said.

"I need a doctor," he said. "Give me the jeep. I have to find a doctor."

"Give an order," we said.

"Are you crazy?" he exclaimed. "People are dying here and you ask for orders."

"But we are forbidden to move," Shaya said.

"Give me the jeep," the lieutenant repeated in a tired hoarse voice. We cleared the cans off the road and Ezra drove off to find a doctor. The wounded were sitting in a bus, some of them lying on stretchers in the aisle. Shaya went over to take a look, went up the steps and asked the driver, "Why don't they evacuate them?"

"Impossible," the driver said, "The road is blocked, everyone is riding to war."

Shaya got off and asked, "Did you leave some compote?"

Damn it, I had thought all the compote was for me. "Three sections are left."

"Do you want halvah?" I countered.

"I hate halvah," he said. The lieutenant returned with the jeep, and Ezra said, "We found a doctor." The doctor apparently was very tired but the lieutenant dragged him after him into the bus. We heard him say, "What can I do? They have to be evacuated."

"But that's impossible," the lieutenant said. "Do something."

"What am I?" asked the doctor, "God?"

Ezra asked, "Is there any compote left?"

"No," I said.

"Hell," said Ezra and turned off the motor.

"Coffee, tea, or tea with milk," asked Shimon. At every stop he would light a fire, put the blackened tea-kettle on the flames and ask sweetly: "Coffee, tea, or tea with milk?"

"I want cream," said Maier.

"Why cream?" we asked. He came over to us and threw on the ground a handful of large pink berries.

"What a flavor, what a flavor! Paradise. Only cream is missing. That's what we're missing in life." Absolutely correct. In the shade of the gnarled and twisted olive trees, in the shade of Mount Gerizim, after a sleep of four faultless hours ((what luxury!) we did not lack for anything. Life was a gift. In the nearby vineyard, smoke was still rising from a Jordanian Patton. Shaya urged me, "Come on, let's see what's happening there."

"Wait," I said. "First let's drink something; tea with milk." The thick milk in blue-yellow cans is a legacy from the Jordanian Army, or rather from American aid to countries on the brink of collapse. I hurried to take out of the jeep the thin glass cup which we had been using since we had entered the police station (deserted, disordered, full of pillows thrown about, colored silk clothing rolling about like rags with nothing inside them). The former occupant was a police sergeant of the police force of His Majesty, King Hussein of Jordan.

A good drink, tea with milk—a lot of essence, a lot of tea, and the sweet heat goes down the throat to the stomach, making you forget sleep and thirst, fear and sensitivity. Afterwards you could take a handful of berries and fill your mouth while listening to the babbling of the brook where five enemy tanks had taken up positions but were then abandoned by their crews. The city was behind us, the war was behind us. Now all we could do in the peace and quiet, was to look at the dead, who were lying open-eyed by the side of the roads, inside the vineyards, by the houses and in the gates. Shaya urged us on. We walked. I would have preferred to go to sleep, but it was forbidden to go off by yourself; there was no telling who might be playing innocent.

"This must be the tree," I said as we came to a marvelous berry tree, spread like a green canopy.

"What tree?" Shaya asked.

"Where Maier got the delicious berries." I picked two or three and held them out in my hand.

"Quit it," Shaya said. "Come on, let's go." Two, three, four, more and more, the ungainly tanks arouse pity in their downfall. Giant toys painted yellow and green, open turrets, some of them scorched, some of them lying on their sides. Shaya put out a hand, not quite touching the cannon head, extending like a threatening finger towards the road, towards the stone houses on the slope of Mount Ebal. The sight of this destruction was something apart from the shock of the shooting, apart from the movement of the armored trucks, something which belonged to the very nature of this heavy equipment. The sun was already shining and the road was empty. We were the advance units for the brigade leaving from Jerusalem. The reeds rustled in the wind, a song, a real song, God is in His heaven—impossible, no, impossible to understand how we were here, but no one sang, no one shouted for joy. Shaya looked for his first dead man, Maier gathered berries, Shimon boiled water, I asked for an answer—everything in the same frame, even the scorched body on the road. In Shaya's opinion, this body did not count because it was no longer a casualty; it was a piece of carbon and smelly, very smelly, but the lad lying on his stomach with nose pressed into the crook of his arm, he was a real casualty. Here Shaya could make his first experimental attempt to solve the mystery of the universe. Death, my friends, and the frightened soldier. Therefore, the first step bringing you into the forbidden area was the fateful one. Shaya did not throw up, was not nauseated; Shaya was disappointed. He could not derive any philosophy from what had been a body a few hours ago and now resembled a picture in a sensational afternoon paper. At home, it would be possible to answer, nonchalantly, a sweet young girl who asks, "Did you see any killed?" "I saw." Later she will certainly ask, with a slight shiver, "And did you kill?" and then you can say, "It's hard to know; it's possible." And you can also lie and say, "Yes," because this will add spice to the coming lovemaking, even awaken and encourage it: the power in the contrast between life and death.

After the first casualty came the second, the third, the fourth, the tenth, because this valley, the gateway to Nablus, was full of bodies; no, no bones as yet, but this would also follow in a short time by multitudes, perhaps together with Shmulik and Danny, with

Ahmed and Mussah and Shukry, each to himself. Also a prophet will stand there and shout from Mount Ebal and Mount Gerizim to the four winds to come and then it will be clear to all that there is a God in heaven and all His deeds, including the most evil, like the sweet stench on the descent to Jericho, are part of the great wisdom which has no end.

Enough, enough theorizing this morning. Even Shaya had enough of casualties. Later, when we will drink another glass of sweet tea with milk, after we will sleep a little, after the brigade from Jerusalem will arrive and we, the conquerors, will be discharged, we shall fall on each other's necks, only then shall we begin to listen to the bad news.

No newspaper had arrived for many days. "What day is it today?" we asked, and no one knew; some watches gave the date but no one knew what day of the week it was. When the newspapers did arrive, we made fun of the headlines, of the stories of glory and events of heroism and wisdom, and we hastened to the black columns. There, inside black frames, were the names of Giora and Shmulik (the hoarse voice, the tremendous stride, the hand holding the shovel for cleaning out the chicken coop) and Ezekiel (the last kiss in the dining room, "Ma, really, let me go, I have to hurry") and Hubi and Mulah. There they were, all written down. We passed quickly over the columns but we did not miss one single name. Just names, We said, "Him, too." I asked, "Where?" In Jerusalem, in the Old City, in Sinai, here in Nablus. Perhaps by the side of the road, while we were eating the sardines. After this we saw the newspapers every day. The war was ended, but the names kept on coming in. Soon we shall be commemorating them. Someone very frankly said, "His voice will be forgotten, the hug we envied him, his jokes and his anger, only the nation of Israel will remember the best of her sons." Very candid.

I received a letter. They called my name and I held a piece of paper in my hand and read: "I am at peace, my whole being is at peace; you are alive and well. Alive and moving. Tears of happiness are flowing from my eyes, tears of tranquility, tears of joy. First I was afraid to write, only God knew on whom the weight of war would press."

Yes, only God knows, He the All-Knowing, for not the dead will praise Him, nor those who came out of it alive.

Menahem Shelach: Impressions of War; *Hotam,* 6.7.67

Few are the wars in the annals of mankind—and mankind has seen many wars—in which two generations fought side by side. Zahal's peculiar structure often threw father and son together on the battlefield.

Tired and worn out, I approached the outskirts of Jenin in the evening. I parked the Volvo at the side of the road and waited for the convoy.

Jenin. Only 24 hours since it has come into our hands and already our soldiers come and go as though it belongs to them. There is no more shooting from the hills. Members of the gangs and the soldiers of the Legion have put on disguises and look like calm and peace-loving citizens. I should have felt free to rejoice with the victory after all the fatiguing weeks. But my heart, my silly heart . . .

I haven't heard a word from my son, a tankman. For him these battles were his baptism of fire. He is probably on the northern front; certainly a postcard from him is on the way.

A roaring noise is approaching. Apparently our convoy of machines is arriving. The noise increases. Not machines but tanks, heavy ones, churn the road. They lift one's heart. Here they are passing by me. They are clanking along in pride, with purpose. The faces of the drivers are not seen. Too bad . . . maybe Amiram? . . . what nonsense!

I get out of the Volvo and wave my hand. The tank slowly stops—and so does the entire convoy. A curly head and a dusty face peep out of the turret.

"What's the matter?"

"Oh, do you know Amiram by any chance?"

"Which Amiram? From Kfar Saba?"

"Yes! Yes!"

"Sure. He's at the end of the convoy. He's towing a tank."

I want to shout with joy. To ask questions. To wave my wide-brimmed hat. Amiram at the end of the convoy! He's all right! He's untouched!

Horns blow from behind.

"What's going on? Who's holding up the convoy?"

"Shut up, what's the yelling? He's asking about Amiram."

"Who's asking?"

"How do I know? Maybe his brother or his cousin."

"Not his brother and not his cousin," I answer, "but his father."

"Hey, fellows! Amiram's father is here. Knock off the honking and yelling!"

A sergeant jumps out of one of the tanks. He's an older man, evidently a reserve. "Are you Amiram's father?"

"Yes."

"Who told you that we would be passing by here?"

"No one. I didn't know. I'm also in a convoy going to Jenin."

"Oh, that's what I call luck! You'll have to wait till the end of the convoy."

In the meantime our trucks have arrived. The load has to be taken down and then we return to the base. What can I do?

The tank convoy is enormous and moves slowly. It will still take a long time until the last tank will pass. I talk it over with my sergeant and tell him why I am waiting. The excitement that grips him and the rest of the drivers—all of us reserves—is as if they had come across their own sons.

"What's the problem? We'll transfer your load to other cars and you'll stay here."

In the twinkling of an eye my load was transferred by many willing hands to other cars. Baruch, the sergeant, came over to me. "How will you get back alone in the middle of the night?"

"Don't worry. I'll get back. My 'Uzi' is with me."

Time passes and the line of tanks goes on. I decide to go along with it and in this way I drive along the length of the tank line and I know that Amiram is driving the tow tank. Rumor flies on wings. I hear my name over the intercoms. They are most probably passing it to the rear, to Amiram.

A sergeant approaches me and says, "Ten minutes stopover for your sake!"

Both the tow tank and the towed one stopped. The fellows jump out and dust themselves off.

I can't remember how, but in a second Amiram is hugging me and saying: "By God, this war isn't normal. Here, one o'clock at night, meeting my dad! It's not normal, by God . . ."

"Three cheers for Amiram's father!" someone calls out.

Uri Oren: Brief Encounter; *Yediot Aharonot*, 28.7.67

The Arab broadcasting stations and the Arab press had for years painted the "Zionist enemy" across the border as a monster in human disguise, but the first encounters between the Israeli soldiers and the

Arab civilian population were very different from what the frightened inhabitants of the West Bank had imagined.

Actually the enemy defeated us before the battle even began. The convoy was moving past the Arab village, but we were taken prisoner immediately at the entrance.

The enemy force stood at the side of the road and sobbed. He was barefoot. Flies were resting on his nose. His only garment was an undershirt.

"Be careful of that kid!" Zvika called to the driver of the half-track. "He'll fall into the cleats." The driver stopped, and so did the entire convoy.

"What's the matter?" came from all sides.

"An Arab kid is stranded here in the middle of the road."

"Get him off! Are you crazy?"

"Where should we put him? He'll be run over."

There was not much time for discussion. In a twinkling Zvika jumped down, grabbed the youngster around the waist and there we were, on our way to battle, with a three-year-old Arab child in tow. At the same minute we were all transformed into nursery maids; Avraham stuffed the kid with mint drops and Yossi neglected his signal apparatus and tried to win him over by strange facial contortions. The child stopped crying and smiled. "See?" said Yossi, "All kids are the same."

"What?" Shlomo yelled in order to be heard above the noise.

"I said that all kids are the same; they change only when they grow up."

"You're crazy!" yelled Shlomo. "We're all completely crazy. We are on our way to kill his mother and father and here we are wiping the nose of this little Araboosh!"

The child suddenly began to howl as though he had understood Shlomo's words. At the same instant the shooting began. Live ammunition, as is known, is not a pleasant thing; but when one is in a half-track taking care of a small child, it becomes many times more difficult. The shooting became more violent; several bullets and a shell splinter hit the armored plates of the vehicle.

One of the "nursery maids" took off his steel helmet and put it on the kid's head. The helmet covered his frightened face, revealing only the pale lips and trembling chin. Not one of us thought any longer about himself. The question was: What would happen to the child? Somehow the rumor spread through the entire convoy and the signals apparatus began to sound with jokes on our account.

"Zvika," someone yelled, "Diaper him. Don't you see that he is wet?"

"That's not the kid, that's me . . ." a whining voice imitating Zvika's broke through on the instrument. All at once the voice of the commander came over the signals: "What's going on in your half-track? What child are you keeping there?"

We told him and waited for the reprimand. Instead of the reprimand came a terse order: "Leave the head of the convoy at once and go to the rear."

We did as ordered. We went off to the side of the road and let the convoy pass us.

About an hour later we reached Kfar Tubas. At the sight of the Israeli force rolling through their gates, the inhabitants moved aside to let an old woman in the street come forward and wave her hand in a sign of peace. We stopped near her. Zvika jumped out and put the child in her hands. While she was still trying to comprehend what it was all about, the vehicle sped off—to the next target.

Uri Oren: A Kid on the Road; *Yediot Aharonot*, 11.8.67

The first instinctive reaction of part of the population of the West Bank, was to flee. The great exodus eastward, across the Jordan, started even as the battles were being fought, and increased with the conclusion of the battles and Zahal's victory. In trucks and in shiny Mercedes-Benz limousines, on donkeys and on foot, thousands of Arabs, old people, women and children, streamed with their bundles to the half-ruined Allenby Bridge near Jericho, in order to cross the Jordan, which in the heat of summer looks more like a narrow ditch. The refugees had many explanations for their precipitate flight: fear of acts of retaliation by the conquering troops, the wish to join relatives in Jordan, the fear that the financial help of relatives working in Kuwait would be cut off for those in Israeli territory, the assumption that there is not much to lose anyway: the UNRWA doles would be available to them in Jordan too.

Within one month, the stream of refugees had dwindled to a trickle, and within two months, there was the beginning of a westward movement: many thousands of refugees returned to the territories held by Israel, with the assistance of the Red Cross. Poet Haim Guri was an eye-witness to the double exodus.

I went to see the refugees returning from the East Bank. It was a fine summer day, wide-open spaces all around and an Israel-blue sky above. Time has not as yet dimmed the glow of victory. One keeps riding, and finds the distances shorter than expected. Here is Al-Izriah. I draw up at the local council building and go inside to see the council chairman, Mahmoud Abu-Rish, but he isn't in.

I had come with my company to this village, on the Jericho highway, several days after the conquest. We planned to take up quarters in the school building, located at the eastern end of the village, opposite the Greek monastery, but found the doors locked. As the commander of the unit, I went to seek out the head of the village or the principal of the school, in order to get the keys. Someone finally summoned Abu-Rish. "The principal is gone," he said. "Break down the doors and have done with it."

One of our soldiers, a good and hefty fellow, put his shoulder to the doors; they yielded with hardly a protest.

Abu-Rish, a ruddy, blue-eyed man of 55, represented the village, by virtue of his position. He didn't look as though the world had tumbled down over his ears. He chain-smoked and consumed considerable whisky, to which he attributed his good health.

The village seemed all but deserted; four out of every five of its inhabitants had fled, explained Abu-Rish. But they were starting to return, seeing that the devil was not as black as he had been painted. Quite the contrary.

Why did they flee?

Said Abu-Rish: "The Legionnaires came through and told the people that the road to Jericho was still open. Rumors had been circulated that the Jews were killing, burning, raping. The people were frightened. There was some shelling. The villagers saw fire and smoke, and they fled."

We used to meet every now and then to handle current matters. One of the monks, with whom I had become friendly, told me that Abu-Rish was alright, "but that tall one, with the *kaffiya,* beware of him."

One time I told Abu-Rish that we were going to spot-check the houses in the village for firearms.

"There are no firearms in the village," insisted Abu-Rish.

"We've been pretty fair with you," I told him, "but if we find firearms we're going to be pretty harsh."

Abu-Rish declared that if we would find firearms in the village, we had his permission to blow up his house. He and a handful of village dignitaries, chosen by him, went along with us. We proceeded through the place, knocking on a door here and there, searching in closets, under mattresses, in the kitchen, in the attic, down in the cellar, in the wells. It took us quite some time.

Thank God, we found no firearms. I hadn't relished the task in the first place. "You see," said Abu-Rish. "The Legion didn't hand out arms to the Palestinians. Didn't think much of them."

Maybe yes, maybe not. After all, the British searched our homes for firearms and didn't find any either.

Abu-Rish's house is still standing up the road, but in neighboring Abu-Dis village five houses had recently been blown up, after a young villager had fired on an Israeli car and on the soldiers sent out to arrest him.

Before we left the village, Abu-Rish presented us with flags and photographs of the king. The facts of life kept him smiling.

This time as a civilian, I wanted to see him again, to see what changes had taken place since then, but, as I said, he wasn't in. I went on and, as I came to the school, I slowed down.

This was where we had stayed for several days, checking the area, roving through the Judean Desert, looking for war remnants and souvenirs.

We found encampments loaded with equipment, vehicles, weapons and documents. We found the remains of stricken caravans, desiccated by the sun. We saw scores of Jewish tombstones from the Mount of Olives cemetery which had been used for paving storehouses and tenting-grounds. We found no Legionnaires, but we did come across the refugees.

They were headed east, toward the Jordan, or were returning home, westward, to the Jerusalem area.

I recall the Jericho highway in the blistering heat, the refugee caravans heading home—a donkey with an old man or an old woman astride, then a man with a child on his back and a woman carrying an infant, and an older brother dragging a younger one plus several other urchins—barefoot, ragged, shuffling along in the desert sun, red-eyed, hoarse, near fainting. Then more men and women and children, one holding a plastic canteen and another clutching a primus and a woman balancing a copper pot on her head. At intervals. someone with a white flag. People with rolled-up blankets. odd-shaped bundles, people in long files by the score, by the hundreds, climbing wordlessly up the boiling asphalt highway which snakes across the wilderness.

You pass by them and they keep moving on, dry lips parted. They already knew that they wouldn't be harmed, but they were yet to learn to hope that someone would deal with them kindly—as though they had renounced all rights to compassion.

The sight of the youngsters, dragging themselves with their last remaining strength, was heartbreaking. I knew that if we wouldn't give them water, they would simply shrivel up in the sun. I wished there were a bit of shade somewhere, and that we could feed them and drive them to their homes.

We stopped. They kept on moving, their faces expressionless. Those among us who spoke Arabic called out to them. They came to a halt, waiting for some calamity to befall them.

"Water! Come and get water!" we said. Slowly they understood. They clustered about the truck. We poured water from our jerricans to their pitchers and tins and aluminum cups.

They let the children drink first, then the old folks, and finally the men and the women drank. I don't suppose that a gulp of water on the burning highway can put out the fire of hatred in a person's heart, but then, that was not our intention. We did it because we couldn't do otherwise. Still, I think that a person will always remember the hand which gave him water.

We continued abreast of the caravan and gave water to the thirsty. Very soon there wasn't a drop left in the jerricans.

"Commander," one of the men said to me. "We have some room in the trucks. We might take some of the children to Al-Izriah."

I made a quick decision. "We'll take as many as we can."

We beckoned to a man who seemed to be the leader and offered to take some of the younger children aboard. The offer confounded them. They huddled in the hot sun for a discussion. I could see they were undecided.

"Tell them that a few of the mothers and two or three of the men may come along."

This seemed to quiet them somewhat. After a few seconds, they began thrusting their children up into the trucks. The mothers followed—abashed and trying to smile; finally, an old man who looked like a hundred, eyes shut.

We went on westward, a bizarre caravan if there ever was one. An Arab aboard, about 60, from Silwan village, still remembered some Hebrew and used it to thank us profusely, though it must have cost him a measure of gall.

We dropped them off at the outskirts of Al-Izriah and went on to the mess hall for a midday meal served out of cans.

I went back to my room. About four o'clock I got word that some colonel wanted to see me. I got up and saw colonel B., an old friend. We talked about things for a while, then he said to me: "Listen, I have no authority over you right now, but I would ask you that if you have vehicles available, you send them out with water to the Jericho highway for these refugees. I have a child of two myself. It's horrible how those kids are drying up in the sun."

We loaded up the trucks with water tanks and several loaves of bread, and set out again.

The lines of refugees were still just as long. In the setting sun they looked like grotesque shadows plodding along a dark road to a black eternity. We distributed the bread and the water, took on the young ones and drove them home, until night fell. On the way we saw trucks with paratroops returning from the desert to Jerusalem. They, too, had little Arab children aboard.

And now I am driving along the same road and thinking of that incident. A few moments later I come within sight of Jericho, city of palms and water, then past it to Allenby Bridge. The asphalt highway runs between mounds of gray soil, into which the wind and shifting temperatures have carved amazing designs.

A blue-and-white flag is fluttering above the building adjacent to the bridge. In a nearby grove and on the road itself there are convoys of empty trucks, ambulances, and a lean-to stacked with cases of soft drinks and plastic bags filled with rolls and tomatoes. Red Shield of David nurses and orderlies. soldiers, policemen, foreign correspondents, photographers, Arab porters move among groups of returning refugees. A "Kol Yisrael" reporter is holding a tape-recorder, ready for action-words. Blond, blue-eyed Red Cross workers go back and forth.

The hour is 10 a.m. Very hot. I come near the collapsed bridge.

The beautiful iron bridge (on the way to Amman, only 45 minutes away by car) is mired in the murky water, its sides twisted and broken. The greenish Jordan trickles through the wreckage on its way south to the Dead Sea. A makeshift wooden bridge now connects the two banks. On this side, in a stone building, are the headquarters of Jordanian Lieutenant-Colonel Talal—a decent fellow, our people say. Next to them are three tents; one for the Red Crescent, another for the Red Cross and the third for the four officials of Israel's Ministry of the Interior. One ambulance. Several luxurious red and blue cars. Policemen, soldiers, porters. In the middle of the wooden bridge a group of our soldiers and Red Shield of David people are waiting for the refugees.

It is now 10:45 a.m. By this time some 150 Arabs have crossed over, I am told. As I am listening to the account, I see an elderly woman being helped down the steps. She shuffles toward the center of the bridge, followed by a family of husband, wife and seven children. Jordanian porters put down their parcels and bundles on the wooden planks at the center of the bridge, and other porters—Israeli and West Bank Arabs—take them up and carry them to the trucks waiting in the glade.

The Red Shield of David people help the old woman and pick the children up in their arms. Cameras click. The mother turns away her head. The father walks by without a word.

I kept seeing similar scenes which were not photographed. The cameramen and the reporters went back to Jerusalem, but the Red Shield workers keep helping the elderly and the children, take them to the eucalyptus glade and give them soft drinks and sandwiches.

It is a kaleidoscopic crowd—one returnee, about 30, in European dress, tall and sporting a neat moustache (a teacher? merchant? UNRWA official?) strolls across in the company of his pretty blonde wife and their children. Weatherbeaten men with broad and lined palms. Farm workers from Nablus and Hebron in *kumbaj* and *kaffiya* attire. Women dressed in black, carrying drowsy and fly-covered children on their backs. A porter, carrying a giant load of mattresses and blankets. A woman, carrying a brass pot. A young man with a valise. Porters sweating under burdens of household goods. Someone with a Singer sewing machine, a primus, and a kerchief containing *peetah* bread and onions. Some faces show gladness, others are glum and painful. The Red Shield of David people shuttle back and forth, taking the children to the glade, where good-hearted women fill them with food and drink. An ancient-looking Haj comes along, looking like one of those old picture postcards of days gone by.

Whenever the stream slows down, the porters sit by the collapsed bridge, smoke, laugh. Near them stands an Israeli Arab policeman, at attention.

Several French Jews come along. They take pictures and discuss, in low voices, the lot of the refugees. The Red Cross people move about.

I look up Lieutenant Ben-Aryeh, liaison officer for the Red Cross. "How many have crossed till now?"

"About 300."

"How many do you estimate will cross by the end of the day?"

"About 500 here and some 300 at Um-Shurt Bridge."

"Why so few? The transit points will be closed in a few days."

"There are several reasons. One, they are not in control of the situation, just not organized properly; the project keeps on dragging. Two, not all the refugees want to return. Some have relatives on the East Bank, and others have members of their families working in Kuwait. They are afraid that if they go back, no more money will be remitted to them. Then again, some of them are going back to see what the new set-up is; if they like it, the others will follow. If not, well—they're getting their allocations where they are; why should they care! Finally, the Jordanians don't care to cooperate. They don't treat the refugees like brothers; if anything, they make things tough for them."

"For instance?"

"On Friday afternoon, last week, a busload of refugees came to Um-Shurt Bridge. The Jordanian guards wouldn't let them get off the bus until Sunday morning."

"Why was that?"

"They didn't want to bother. The refugees remained in the bus without water. When we got them on Sunday, many were faint. One of them said to us: 'Why didn't you take Amman?' "

"But these refugees are their brothers."

"That's the way it is. If a man has no money or social standing, they treat him like dirt."

"But you yourself told me that Lieutenant-Colonel Talal is a decent fellow."

"That he is. But the officer in charge of the other bridge, even though he is subject to Talal's orders, does whatever he pleases there. You wouldn't believe it, but more than once the Jordanians made the refugees give them their Red Cross parcels and the money they had received, five dinars per person. You see this ambulance of theirs? It is used to bring food and drink and cigarettes for the Jordanian soldiers. The officers eat in Amman. The sick and the wounded are hauled here in buses. Only we take them right away by ambulance to clinics and hospitals."

As we are talking, two dust-covered Israeli officers appear. They have come from Damia Bridge. They tell us that they came across many Arabs crossing east to Jordan. These Arabs sign a document in which they state that they are leaving of their own free will and that they have no complaints to make.

This, then, is the picture. Some are returning to the West Bank, while others are crossing eastward. Each one is doing what he thinks is best for himself. Many who had crossed over to the East Bank are waiting there to see how things work out. They are aware that, should they want to return, they would be able to do so under the "family reunification" program. The entire vociferous discussion about the subject going on all over seems, here at the Allenby Bridge, quite out of proportion. Only a few have taken advantage of the permission to return.

I meet Yussuf Muhammad Abdul Hadi of Hebron. "Why did you flee?" I ask.

Replies the Hebronite: "I was afraid we would be massacred."

The same refrain. "We make mistakes," the old man says sadly. "We see that the Jews are good. They give us bread and soda-water and deal with us kindly."

I don't know if all Jews are kindly, but one of them is the essence of kindness. I refer to Joel Schechter of Yeshiva University of New York. This young fellow moves ceaselessly among the refugees, gives them food and drink, takes care of the children, gives advice and encouragement. Somehow he tied in with the Red Shield of David people and is working with them.

I think that this Hebrew-speaking young man belongs to that category of Jewish youth throughout the world which has always pursued "humanitarian causes," going to all the unfortunates and the storm-tossed in all generations, to help them and to bring to them the light of brotherhood and understanding and compassion. Such young people, if I am not mistaken, went down South in the United States to fight for Negro civil rights, and they paid for it dearly. They are a sort of a Jewish "Peace Corps." Joel probably got here as a volunteer, "dying" to do something, and when he discovered that the war lasted less time than he had expected it would, he got to those whose suffering seemed to him to be longer than it should. He found these rootless people on Allenby Bridge and has been doing for them everything he can. At times he seems somehow out of place, but if we were to set up an American Jewish "Peace Corps" to solve the refugee problem, I'm sure that we would discover thousands of such Schechters.

Allenby Bridge, Israel's eastern boundary. Here meet the facts which make up reality. Many falsehoods are turned to ashes in the blazing sun.

What is the truth? We are here and so are they, many and increasing. We can also increase, if we so desire. We and they in this land. All the Arab rulers, down the generations, used the Palestinian Arabs for their own advantages. We are destined to live with them or to return to within the small pure Jewish State, a foreign body amongst the Arabs. The danger here is great, and the opportunity is great. Allenby Bridge symbolizes both.

We have nothing to do with the Arab states. Our preoccupation is the Arab people in the Land of Israel. The day we shake hands in brotherhood and co-existence here, we shall be immune to all the Boumediennes and the Nassers and the Husseins. Let us not be hasty in giving up on them, nor on the land which they are populating. The time has come for a new, daring experiment.

A chapter in the history of the Land of Israel has come to a close, Chapter 1947–1967. The hour has come for a new chapter. Even the peace with Damascus and Cairo must take into account this child and this dark-eyed woman and this elderly man, leaning on his staff.

Haim Guri: Allenby Bridge; *Lamerhav,* 1.9.67

There had been six Jewish settlements in the eastern part of Eretz Israel, taken in 1948 *by the Jordanians: four in Gush Etzion, on the road to Hebron; the kibbutz Beit Ha'arava, on the shores of the Dead Sea, near Jericho; and Atarot, north of Jerusalem. Beit Ha'arava was reluctantly abandoned by its members, because there had been no possibility of defending it, but the inhabitants of Gush Etzion fought desperately against the Legionnaires and the Arab gangs, trying to defend their homes.* 270 *people, including most of the men of the four settlements, gave their lives defending the place. After the conquest of the West Bank, the remaining members of Gush Etzion returned to the place where their homes had been—after a* 19*-year-long separation.*

A pick-up truck pulled up on a rocky,hill. A group of civilians in white shirts, Sabbath khaki trousers and embroidered skull-caps got off and dispersed, to wander among the abandoned corrugated iron barracks.

They had come to look for Kfar Etzion as they knew it 19 years ago, but they never found it. There was not even a memory of the houses that once stood here. The bunkers had been filled up, the defense trenches covered over and even the trees that were planted in this rocky soil were not their trees. They passed between the heaps of ammunition boxes with their Arabic inscriptions, between the yellow lorries, the speckled artillery pieces, the padded armchairs from the officers' club, and the Legion uniforms that lay about in heaps between the barracks. Until a fortnight ago the spot had served as the camp of a regiment of Arab Legion gunners. They themselves were all that was left of the Kfar Etzion of 1948.

On top of the hill, amid tanks and half-tracks, stood a number of soldiers belonging to a Jerusalem reconaissance group that had raced down to the Etzion Bloc while on their way from Bethlehem to Hebron. They watched the civilians wandering round between the buildings, with a certain dissatisfaction.

"The tourist season has started," said one of the soldiers.

"What are you looking for over there?" a young soldier called to one of the travelers in the truck, who had picked up a stone and was inspecting it at close quarters.

"I'm looking for Kfar Etzion," said the man.

"This is it. You've found it." The soldier called back, and his companions in the shadow of the tank burst out laughing.

"I know," said the man and flung the stone away. "I know the place. Once I stood here with four grenades and a Sten."

The soldiers grew quiet. The man went his way, bending down from time to time to pick up a stone or some other trifle. He was searching for something that would remind him of Kfar Etzion. He was looking for something that would bear witness to those terrible days when he was lying here together with a handful of fighters who were members of Massuot-Yitzhak, Revadim, Ein-Tzurim, Kfar Etzion, the Palmah and the Hish (Field Force), in the most advanced outposts of this area of Jewish settlement; when they had tried with their Stens and their grenades to block the assault of the villagers who came against them yelling *"Itbah al Yahud!"* (massacre the Jews), and the armored cars and tanks of the Legion which were beginning to surround them.

The man went up the hill and joined his fellow travelers, who were standing on the veranda of one of the buildings. He lit a cigarette which somebody handed him and said: "It's hard to believe." The men of Ein-Tzurim and Massuot-Yitzhak who stood by nodded their heads in agreement. So many years they had thought of the day when they would return to the Bloc. Now they were standing here and their hearts were empty.

They ran their eyes over the surroundings and tried to identify the more distant posts and emplacements which had fallen on the first day of the attack. The Russian Monastery, Khirbet Sawier, the Hill of the Tree, the Yellow Hill, Khirbet Zakariya. In the last fight 151 fighters had fallen at Kfar Etzion. Only four men remained alive. Two had been saved by an old Arab who handed them over to the Legion. One had succeeded in hiding himself in a vineyard, wounded; and a girl had been saved by an officer of the Legion. All the rest had fallen, in a bunker blown up with all those in it, or in trenches. Even the last, who had surrendered after their ammunition had given out, had been shot by the Arab mob.

Only a handful of the members of the settlements in the Bloc had been taken prisoner and remained alive. Of these a few were now standing on the hilltop, and still seemed to hear the yelling and the shrieking of the shells.

"Maybe our sons in the army will want to come back here," said one of them. "I would also come back," said another. "We owe that to those we left here."

Dan Ben-Amotz: Return to the Village; *Bamahane*, 21.6.67

Chapter Eight

The Threatening Heights

GOLAN HEIGHTS (4.6.67)

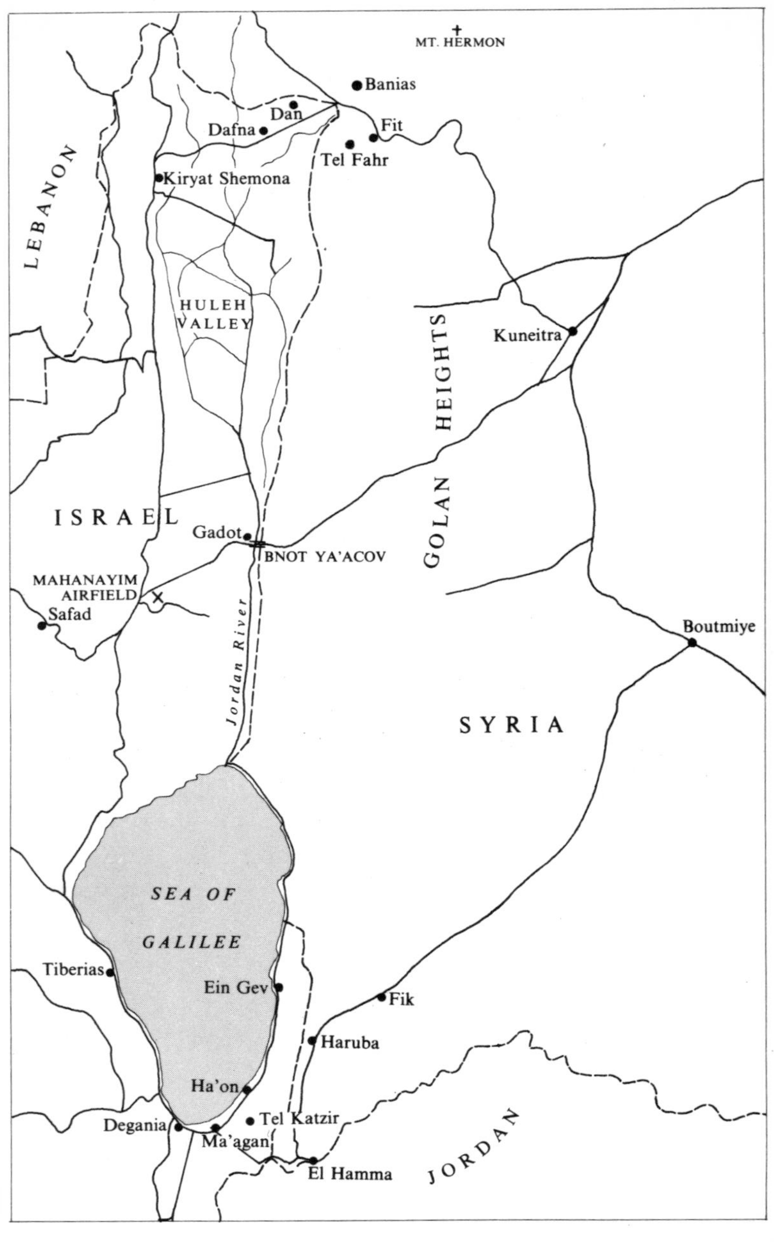

IN RECENT YEARS THE SYRIAN BORDER HAD BEEN ISRAEL'S MOST threatening, troublesome and strife-ridden frontier. From the fortified positions on the Heights, the Syrian Army took advantage of its topographical superiority to turn the lives of the Israeli farmers in the valley below into a living hell. Hardly a week passed without the Syrians shooting at an Israeli tractor; hardly a month went by without shelling of kibbutzim and mining of roads in the north. The Syrians constantly kept igniting the frontier, and the settlers along the northern border became accustomed to hurry to the underground shelters as soon as the Syrians started spraying the valley with fire.

In Tel Katzir, Haon, Almagor, Gadot, the children grew up in the nightmare of guns which kept them in their sights around the clock, and Israeli farmers would look every morning at the Syrian positions at Tawafik, Jelabina and Tel Azaziyat, wondering whether the day would end as peacefully as it had begun. The following was written two months before the outbreak of the Six-Day War.

One stormy winter night, when the air was rent by thunder and lightning, the night watchman of Kibbutz Haon had a strange experience. He came to the childrens' quarters in order to check the shutters—and froze with fright. All the beds were empty.

The youngsters had been aroused from their sleep by the turbulent elements. Well-trained and disciplined, they reacted to the roll of thunder by trooping down into the shelter; the Haon settlers had built an underground tunnel leading from the children's building directly to the shelters. Such are the things—a tunnel playgound, for instance—which leave an imprint on the mind of a child.

In Tel-Katzir a high wall had been erected along the northern length of the dining hall, to ward off sniping and shelling. The wall obscures the mountain on which are located the village of Tawafik and the Syrian tank emplacements. But the mountain itself cannot be blocked out of the people's consciousness. The children divide the kibbutz area in two—the "quiet side" and the "mountain side."

The "quiet side" maintains an almost normal course of life, except that in times of tension no one is to be far away from an entrance to the shelters. The "mountain side" is the one fraught with danger. At one time, when a period of quiet created an illusion of peace along the borders, a basketball court had been laid out in that area. They no longer play basketball in Tel-Katzir.

Kibbutz Gadot suffered 16 wrecked buildings—the children's quarters among them—in the "40 terrible minutes" on April 7. The kibbutz educators subsequently made a study of the effect of the shelling on the children. They went over the pictures drawn by the children in the course of the week immediately following. Only one child had given expression to his feeling of fright by drawing a "war scene" of planes and cannons. The others chose their regular subjects—flowers, a meadow, cows—as though the shelling had never happened.

Benny of Haon and Gideon of Tel-Katzir feel sure that children can be raised "normally" even in the shadow of the Heights. "The children know that the shelters afford them complete security," says Benny. "There is less bed-wetting here than in settlements farther away from the border, or in the cities."

Says Gideon: 'When my child was in the shelters for the first time he was only six days old. Now it's part of his daily life. The shelters are not very comfortable, especially when you have to sit there nine hours on end, like last Friday. But the tension is the result of congestion and discomfort, not of fear."

The same Friday, April 7, when all the children in the Kinneret (Sea of Galilee) Valley were sent into the shelters, was the eighth birthday of Ronen, in Ma'agan. A party had been prepared at school, and the teacher explained to Ronen why it would have to be postponed. Ronen wouldn't think of it. Thereupon, all the decorations were transferred to the shelter. The walls were festooned with gay balloons, the birthday cake was brought in, and while the shells were already falling in nearby Tel-Katzir, Ma'agan celebrated indomitable Ronen's birthday—underground.

War and all, life goes on.

On the following Monday, the Gadot children were host to a group of school children from Acre, who came to congratulate them on their miraculous escape and to express their solidarity with the youngsters of the bombed kibbutz. The guests brought gifts—chocolate bars. The hosts reciprocated with souvenirs—chunks of shrapnel gathered from all over the kibbutz yard.

The Syrian Heights, rising steeply from the eastern bank of the Jordan River, are studded with Syrian artillery emplacements and with tanks imbedded in the earth. They dominate the entire region. There is no escaping them.

"When we make up our work sheets," says Gideon, "and the matter of who should be sent to work 'that side' comes up, we are tempted to stop writing down the names. You can decide when the men should go out to work, but not when they should come back, if they do at all. Who are we to decide the fate of others?"

Tel-Katzir, Haon and the other settlements owning "controversial" tracts have adopted the principle that no one should be compelled to work those areas. A man is allowed to get up and say: "I am not up to it," and he is replaced, without any discussion. And truly, how can anyone determine another man's breaking point? He may go out with a tractor and be pinned down by enemy fire once, twice, three times and still bear up under it and even joke about the terrible hours he had undergone, in that exposed field. The next time his nerves—or his wife's—may snap, and he has had enough.

There is no discussion, says Gideon, because "we have come here to live, and a man of Tel-Katzir has the same right to a quiet and peaceful existence as does a man of Shefayim, who has it." At the same time, never had the cultivation of a controversial tract been abandoned or even postponed because of the lack of men willing to go out there and do the work.

When the Prime Minister visited the shelled settlements, on the following day, he was besieged with demands that the tracts continue to be worked. Each settlement worded it almost identically: "This is our home. Every bit of destruction is painful for us. But we settled here in order to confirm the sovereignty of Israel along these borders. We therefore accept all the risks and ask the Government that the work be allowed to continue."

The readiness of the settlements to risk further shelling doubtlessly influenced the decision to continue cultivating the area.

When you stand on the northern slope of Tel-Katzir and look

out across the valley separating it from the Syrian Heights, you can clearly see the houses in the notorious village of Tawafik.

"On that Friday," related a member of the kibbutz, "we saw two Syrian tanks moving among the houses. They would fire a shell, then retreat behind a house; another shell, back again. When they saw our shells falling close, they understood that we were ready for them. In fact, one of them was hit before it could escape."

The tracts to which the Syrians had been paying such violent attention have special names: "The Nose," for instance—as the population well knows from the official communiques about the incidents.

"The Nose" is a comparatively small tract, shaped like an irregular triangle with sufficient resemblance to a large proboscis, pointing north. The tract is wholly under cultivation, fresh and deep-green in the spring of the year. South of it is another square tract, also under cultivation. Between the two is a narrow strip of untilled land, bare except for two trees growing out of its soil. For some reason the Syrians had decided that this strip had to remain inviolate. Whenever a tractor would cross the strip, the Syrians would invariably open fire, only to cease firing when the tractor would reach the other side.

"Why is that?" I ask. "Where is the boundary line around here?"

"There isn't any. During the Mandate, the International Line ran along the foot of the Heights, but the Syrians didn't recognize it. At that time El-Hamma village was in Palestine territory, but ever since seven men of the border patrol were killed from ambush on the way to the village, in 1950, no Israeli has set foot there. Nuqeib village, on the shore of Lake Kinneret north of Ein-Gev, also used to be in Palestine and even had a Palestine Constabulary border post, but ever since 1951 it has been under Syrian control, and, except for a few hours on 'Nuqeib Night' in 1962, no Israeli has been there."

The valley at the foot of the Heights, east of the Lake, has three boundary lines: International Line, long forgotten; the "Zaro Line," a furrow plowed through in the days when General Zorea was in charge of the Northern Command, and "The Black Line," a strip set by the unsympathetic head of the UN observation unit, Karl von Horn. Each line went farther back than its predecessors, but the Syrians disregarded them equally.

The operational boundary line was eventually established by a row of furrows and patrol trails, "The Plow-and-Rifle Line," and this line now became the point of conflict.

Remarked one of the regional security staff: "One way to look at the entire issue of cultivation in the sector is to see it in color. Today, following a good rain, the valley is all green. We then plow it and 'paint' it brown. Comes harvest time, and the valley turns yellow. Then the Syrians burn it and it turns black. Even if the field escapes burning and we get to harvest it, the cost of the kernel we reap here is higher than if we would have imported it from the United States, each wrapped separately in cotton and cellophane."

"Is it worth it then?"

The comment brings Gideon to a boil. "What if we were to plant watermelons in a controversial tract and invite a major incident. would you not also say: 'The entire nation is being endangered by a watermelon; is it worth it?' Then why stay here at all? We could have been in Shefayim."

The settlers who founded Haon and the city folk who came out there to build Tel-Katzir chose their sites precisely because they are on the border. Most of the settlers could have found life easier, and certainly safer, in the city, as witness the long string of cars which came from Tel-Aviv, on the day after the shelling, bringing grandparents anxious to see their grandchildren. By that time, the settlers were already preparing to cultivate the bean patch.

"We are not doing this out of the spirit of adventure," say the settlers. "Even from a purely economic standpoint we cannot give up the controversial tracts. These comprise 250 out of Tel-Katzir's 525 acres, 200 out of Haon's 775. Still, the issue is not one of economics alone. Past experience has shown that making concessions to the Syrians does not further the cause of peace. We would only invite them to challenge our rights to the next tract."

"For instance," adds Gideon, "some time ago it was decided that, for the sake of achieving peace, we forego cultivating 'The Table' and 'The X's.' Did we get peace? The Syrians merely turned the bean patch into the bone of contention."

In Haon, tracts 51, 52 and 53 (so designated by their elevation on the map) were never controversial until this year. Actually, they are located alongside the road to Ein-Gev—across from the yard of the settlement. When we passed the spot, we saw storks calmly pecking at the fresh furrows in search of worms. Only a week ago, this strip was an inferno of shell-fire; the driver of the armored tractor called into his transmitter: "The shells are landing ten feet away. What should I do?" Came back the answer: "Keep going as long as you can."

On that Friday, history wrote an important chapter in the "Book of the Border," not only in that six MIG's were felled and decisions were taken, on our part, not to be bound, in the form or extent of our retaliation, by Syria's action. The Syrians also wrote a new chapter on that day. They no longer restricted their attack to one sector of the region at a time. Previously, when they created an "incident" in the northern sector (Dan–Dafna area) they concentrated on that area alone. When they decided to "heat up" the southern sector (Kinneret Valley region) they stuck to that area.

On that Friday, Haon proceeded to work tracts 51, 52 and 53, which the Syrians had shelled earlier that week. Then the MIG's appeared again. Elsewhere along the border, farmers went out to cultivate their tracts.

That was when Gadot received its battering.

The incident began as did all the others. Machine-guns opened fire on Haon tractors. The fire was returned. The Syrians then brought up tanks from their emplacements and sent them between the Tawafik houses. One of the tanks was hit by the accurate fire from below, and the other fled. The Syrians then drew up 120 mm. mortars which had been stationed on the other side of the Heights. Most of the shells missed Haon and Tel-Katzir, dropping into the Sea of Galilee, but some 50 shells fell along the shore and among the buildings of Ein-Gev. One hit the barn. Anat Steinberg was the only one working there at the time. She opened the gate and let the cows out before making for the shelters.

Our Air Force went into action, first against the Syrian mortars, then against the Syrian planes. The planes could be seen and heard from Gadot, some 25 miles to the north, but the settlers there, accustomed to the previous Syrian pattern, did not feel that Gadot was involved in the fray. But with their mortars silenced and their planes smashed, the Syrians still felt that they had to make a good showing somewhere. Their artillery opened fire from above B'not-Ya'acov Bridge.

The story was told by Avik, a virile young man whose turn it was to serve as Gadot's "public relations and liaison department." He had just completed taking a school group from Kiryat-Shemona on a guided tour of Gadot's demolished premises.

"It began on Friday at 2:55 in the afternoon, when most of our people were about to return from the fields and the small children were geting up from their afternoon naps. The yard was full of people, watching the action at Tawafik. Then the first shell landed, about a hundred yards north of our most outlying building. For a moment we debated whether it was a shell or a supersonic boom. The debate was cut short by the landing of the second shell. The third almost hit one of the children's houses.

"During the next 40 minutes, more than 300 shells landed within the compound. In its intensity, the shelling of Gadot was no less than any action on a battlefield.

"As soon as we realized that Gadot was the target, everyone made a dash to the children's quarters. Each grabbed a child or two and headed for the nearest entrance to the shelters. Three minutes later all of us were underground. Not all, actually. Yehoshua and Ziva Ilan were in their room when the shelling began. Ziva was lying ill. Yehoshua tried to lift her, but her pain was too great. She just couldn't be moved. Yehoshua put a mattress on the floor, and they both lay there, shrinking close at every explosion outside. Finally, their senses became so dulled that they didn't even feel the shell which tore away a corner of their house."

Another couple—Gal and Osnat—were stuck in a connecting trench. They were only some 40 yards away from an entrance to the shelters, but the shelling was too heavy to risk even that short a distance. They lay face down in the trench and listened to the shells whining overhead. Fifteen yards away, Esther Banas crouched in the same trench, all alone. She, too, couldn't make it to the shelters in time. Thick smoke and the acrid smell of gunpowder descended upon her. Desperately fighting back a feeling of panic, she waited for a lull in the shelling, then made a dash for the nearest entrance.

Swedish Jani, one of the eight "International Brigade" students and tourists working at Gadot, had never known what a shell was. Like the other "Brigade" members—Swedes, Swiss, and a lone Canadian—she came from a country which had not felt the impact of war for generations. "Even my father wouldn't be able to tell me anything about it."

"It was probably our fault," admitted Avik. "We should have told them what to do in such a case. But then, we hadn't experienced it ourselves for several years, and one forgets such things quickly."

When the shells began to fall, Jani and her two companions were in their room, in the south-eastern corner of the settlement. They rushed outside and saw swirls of smoke all around them. A nearby wooden hut was hit and set ablaze. Fragments pierced the walls of their own building.

"We were terrified," related Jani. "We didn't know what to do. Then we remembered about the shelter next to the office and we ran there." The presence of the others and the obvious security of the shelters allayed their fears. Aside from a slight scare hangover, they were actually proud of having "passed the test." In the evening they joined the others in clearing away the debris, and on the next morning they gave up their Sabbath rest to do the same—as did everyone else.

"To tell the truth," remarked Avik, "we were sure that they would leave. After all, why did they have to stay here? They aren't even Jews. But up till now, none has said a word about leaving."

Sam, the only Jew among the eight, had been assigned on that day to work in the truck farming area. He was on his way in from the fields when the shelling began. With him was a member of the kibbutz. They immediately dropped to the ground, and from this position saw "how the settlement was being destroyed before our eyes."

The shells began getting nearer, as though the Syrian artillerymen had spotted the two figures lying in the field and were now trying to hit them. Sam couldn't stand it any longer. He dashed across the fields to Ayelet Hashahar, barely got there, and gasped: "Gadot is finished!"

His companion, Omer Bagadi, lay in the field and kept his eyes on the smoke enveloping his kibbutz. "A heap of ruins. Where is the Air Force?"

The same question was being asked in the shelters.

First came the checking of the people clustered there. Via the inter-shelter communications telephone, it was soon established that all the children were accounted for. There was some uncertainty about the adults. Several evidently had not come back from the fields. There were also the residents of nearby "Campsite" quarters, built where an army encampment had once been. Its shelter had just been completed, but it was still not connected to the underground telephone system.

The "Campsite" shelter was in a state of utter confusion. Several parents had come there in search of their children. "There was one mother," said Avik, "whom we had to restrain by force from running out to look for her child. During a lull in the firing, a runner came to 'Campsite' to check the people there, and he told us that all the children were safe below ground."

The children's shelter, built right near their quarters, was very crowded, since many of the adults who had brought the children had no alternative but to remain there. As in the other border settlements, the children's shelter was equipped for a long siege. There were cribs for the infants, equipment for preparing meals and, most important of all, toys galore. The older children were immediately drawn into a community sing. The little ones cried a bit, but there was hardly any commotion.

Outside, the shells continued to multiply. The people, sensing that the entire settlement was being demolished, asked repeatedly: "Why aren't they here?"

Then, at 3:30, Esther Banas, the last person on the kibbutz grounds to have remained outside, darted into the shelter with the tidings: "They have come!" And indeed, at that very moment the shelling seemed to grow weaker. In its place came the muffled sound of bombs exploding in the distance. Ten minutes later, all was quiet.

The sound of a motor vehicle outside broke the stillness. The "Egged" bus was there, with just one passenger for Gadot in it.

What happened in Gadot and other border settlements, during that hour and other days, is part of the story of life in the shadow of the Heights.

"At 4:30," said Avik, "we were still in the shelters, since our instructions were to remain there until nightfall, but already people were beginning to come from Mahanayim and Ayelet Hashahar to see what had happened and to be of help. Right after them came the service crews of the Electric Company and the electricians from the Jordan Valley settlements. Volunteers came to help prepare the Sabbath meals; actually, all we had to do is warm up our own food, which we had prepared earlier in the day. On Saturday morning, the volunteers pitched in to help us repair the damage. Telegrams offering aid came from the stevedores in Haifa. The atomic reactor workers in Dimona offered to send 50 men for two or three days."

At Tel-Katzir, among the first help to arrive was the speedy "Impala" of Amcor, to see whether any of the electrical appliances needed servicing. Each of the Jordan Valley settlements contributed a diligent cow to Ein-Gev, so that the kibbutz should be able to fill its milk-quota. Laborers from Hatzor, themselves on part-time work, contributed two hours of labor, "the same length of time the people of Gadot spent in the shelters."

That Sabbath Eve, the regular Sabbath gatherings were held by Tel-Katzir and Haon. Ein-Gev threw a party in honor of marathon runner and kibbutz member Yosef Batzri, who had placed second in the "Tabor Run." In Gadot, where the electricity didn't go on until eleven at night, the settlers entertained their guests with shell-by-shell description of the "40 terrible minutes."

Four days later, signs of the shelling were still visible in Gadot. Houses were still in ruins, and piles of broken glass had been raked together everywhere. The ugly yellow blemishes of shell cartridges were on the lawns, and branches snapped off by the force of the shelling lay strewn all about.

The telephone operator was busy. "Gadot here . . . Yes, we're fine. Let me speak with Avraham. Gadot calling . . . the spirit is fine . . . let me talk to the Settlements Committee, please. This is Gadot . . . everything is in order . . . no need to worry . . . may I speak with the electrical engineer. This is Gadot . . ."

This is the border land.

No need to worry.

Aviezer Golan: In the Shadow of the Heights; *Yediot Aharonot*, 14.4.67

During the last two years, and especially during the half-year preceding the war, the aggressiveness of the Syrians kept constantly increasing. The Syrian Government, headed by the Ba'ath Party, was the most extremist of all the Arab countries. It declared a popular war against Israel and recruited, trained and armed the Al-Fatah infiltrators, sending them to perform acts of sabotage and subversion in Israeli territory. The Syrian Army, sheltered in reinforced concrete bunkers dug deep in the Golan mountains, intensified its shelling of the Israeli settlements. Therefore, when the Six-Day War broke out, the shelling along the Syrian border with Israel came as no surprise. The people of the border settlements went into the shelters. This is the diary of a shelter in the Ayelet Hashahar kibbutz, as recorded for a week by one of its young members.

Midnight, Monday, June 5, 1967

We receive a notice to go to Shelter 14 and set ourselves up there "with all the comforts." We take over mattresses, blankets, books, games. The girls bring embroidery and other handicrafts. In the shelter we find all its "tenants" there—Grades Two and Three in Room No. 1 and the rest in the other room. We are told that the young people will be serving as runners and will help man the positions. We of the Seventh Grade should make ourselves at home. Toward evening we get a notice to put the children in the shelter to sleep. The older ones stretch out in sleeping bags and blankets outside, near by. The transistors and the mosquitoes function in the sector with equal zest. The atmosphere is like that of a large encampment.

The night is unusually dark. Only the bright stars wink at us from afar. Such a beautiful and quiet Galilean night. Sort of a calm before the storm. Flashlight in hand, I pass along the rows of children; they had finally fallen asleep, close to midnight. The flashlight casts long shadows. Peaceful children, torn away from their beds and forced to huddle together in the bowels of the earth. Everyone knows that in a few hours it will be our turn, and we dread to think what may happen to the settlement, and especially to the children, our treasure. And what about the children of yesterday; where are they? We try to think of their faces, to listen to their faraway voices. We pray for their safety, for their success, for their return to their homes, shelled and destroyed and rebuilt 19 years ago, in the War of Independence. Those who claim to know say that the Syrians "like" to shell at dawn, when the sun is at their backs and the valley settlements are like sitting ducks below them.

Someone says: "Jews really don't have luck. This year, after the abundant rain we've had, we expected to harvest full-measure crops, and we find that we can't do any harvesting in peace." We are beyond sleep. Our ears are glued to news from Sinai and the Strip. "Hello, Headquarters; what's new?" Perhaps they know more than the hazy news we get from "Kol Yisrael."

Tuesday

The shelling of our sector began at 5:45 a.m. Here in Ayelet Hashahar the first shells land at 6:10. The shells, falling so close, cause momentary confusion, but then we burst into song so loudly that we can hardly hear the phone ringing. "Hello, Shelter 14? Everybody inside? Don't let anyone sit on the steps. Two shells just fell on the central lawn, and someone sitting on the steps was lightly wounded by a fragment." It's easy to issue orders, but people are bursting to go out and see what is going on. We understand them. We, too, would like to go up. The older ones organize a "discipline unit," block the exit bodily, and everyone stays put. We continue singing and clapping. "Jerusalem the Golden," the old Palmah and war songs. We pause only to listen to the news and to the sound of our planes on their way to reply to the shelling. The fellows inside the shelter identify them: *Vautour, Mirage, Mystère . . .*

At 10:30 the shelling dies down, and the rumors begin to roll. We smell smoke. We learn that the barn containing the fruit-gathering crates is going up in flames. There is a smell of smoke from the fields as well. Soon nothing is visible. The entire Galilee seems to be in flames. Later a member of the command comes and tells us that Gadot, Hulata and Rosh Pina were shelled even worse than we were, and that there were casualties because people didn't stay in the shelters. The command has decided to remove the youngsters from our shelter. We are to prepare for a long stay below the surface.

Lunch arrives at 11:30. One of the women old-timers goes from shelter to shelter to see whether we need anything. We receive her with the song "Hats off to You" and marvel at the tasty hot meal, prepared while the shelling was going on.

Spirits rise when the news comes that Jenin and the Valley of Dothan have been taken. Someone suggests that we call headquarters to find out whether they found, in the Valley, the pit into which Joseph's brethren had cast him.

Night falls again. The smell of smoke persists. Everything is quiet, except for the radio. We listen, with pent-up emotions, to the "News Diary"; we marvel at the human and considerate expressions voiced by General Haim Herzog, the military analyst, who concludes his broadcast with Kamzon's poem about the gates of "Jerusalem the Golden;" any army whose military analyst mentions a poem like this certainly cannot but emerge victorious.

"This is Shelter 14. What's going on?"

"Hello 14. You better get some sleep. Tomorrow things will probably be kind of hot."

We try to fall asleep. Between naps we dream about tomorrow, about our men, peace, the good bed, the routine life which seems suddenly far away.

Wednesday

The morning turned out to be quiet, after all. We even managed to clean up the shelter and wash the dishes in hot water. We listen to the radio. For the sake of variety we tune in to Damascus, and we hear, between military marches, that "the praiseworthy Syrian army had taken Kfar Hannassi, Rosh Pina, Shear Yashuv and Kfar Kibbutz." "Hello, headquarters? This is 14. Tell Kfar Hannassi that they were mentioned on the Syrian radio." The fellow on the other end of the line doesn't get the joke and proceeds to interrogate us. We give up, but it's a lot of fun.

At 1:30, after lunch, we get a call: "Hello 14! Old Jerusalem is ours. I repeat—Old Jerusalem is ours!" We don't believe it. The adults stare at each other, in tears. We turn to the radio for confirmation. Nothing there, just news about Ramallah and Tubas, the Tebetz of ancient days. We suddenly remember that we have phone contact with the outside world. We run to the schoolhouse and put a call through to Jerusalem. Yes, it's true. We return to the shelter. People embrace and kiss one another. What a day . . . what a day! At seven in the evening comes a stirring broadcast, perhaps the most stirring in Israel's history, from Old Jerusalem, from the Wall. The sound of the ram's horn. Now no one is ashamed to cry. As one we stand at attention while *Hatikva* comes over the air.

Thursday

3:30 a.m. The early risers steal out of the shelter for a peek outside. All the others are asleep. A smell of coffee. Again dawn rises above the hostile Heights. We all feel that its hour is approaching.

At 7:00 our air force is already at work above the Heights. The radio tells us how the war had come to a close in Sinai, the Negev, Jerusalem, in all of the West Bank.

At 8:30, with the shelling outside going full blast, we hold an orientation session in up-to-the-moment geography. We "travel" from one point to the next, through yesterday's "Triangle" and today's Land of Israel. Time is too short to devote even a few words—at least the Biblical reference—to the roads by which we are proceeding. We pass by in a flash, but now everything is clear. This land, dissected until yesterday, was and will remain the land of the Bible, the Maccabees, the legends—our land. The children are amazed. "How come we haven't yet been to Rachel's Tomb and the Cave of Machpela and the City of Palms?"

The shelling goes on all morning. "Hello headquarters! What's going on outside?"

"14? Take good care of the kids. The entire sector, from Hulata to Gadot, is being shelled again." We fear for our battered neighbors, even though now we are getting it as well. We feel the impact in the shelters. Our experts claim they can distinguish between "their boom" and "our boom." The electricity goes out, but soon a group of electricians arrives from Haifa. They are on a repair tour in the area, although they didn't expect to find the war still going on here. We compel them to have a bite, and they move on to their tasks. In the afternoon comes a brief lull. We use the opportunity to wash up well, the first time in three days.

Friday

They say that there is cease-fire in our sector, but we are still in preparedness. "Hello headquarters! What's the state of affairs?" "14? Stay put!" And indeed, at 8:00 a.m. a new barrage is laid down, then is repeated intermittently until evening. The battle for the Heights in on. Our hearts are filled with apprehension. Will our soldiers be able to take the Heights, which have been spewing fire like that legendary dragon? We welcome the Sabbath midst the noises of mosquito and plane squadrons. Candles and chants and hope. Who does not pray at a moment like this?

A runner, gasping for breath, comes from headquarters. "Sharm-a-Sheikh is ours. The fellows are bathing in the Canal!" What a crazy day. We cluster about the map on the wall of the shelter, go over the names of places mentioned in the news, not knowing, as yet, that they had all been taken: Hebron, Gush Etzion, Beit Ha'arava—all of them. The children demand that we alter their annual excursion routes to take in Jenin and Nablus and Jericho and Sinai. A second-grader doesn't think that all this can come about in a hurry. "I'll be 14 before I will get to bathe in the Canal," he complains.

Our planes again rake the Heights. When will we get to hear that the Heights are ours, too? We argue about the official name of the Heights—Golan? Bashan?

At 6:15 we see one of our planes, hit by ground fire. An eternity-long second later we see a lone white parachute against the fading sky. We can see the pilot, pulling at the parachute strings to head it west. Our hearts stop beating. The descent seems to take forever. What if he lands in enemy territory? The Syrians will shoot him.

Our planes cover him like a mother hen. The Syrians keep firing at the plane until it goes down in smoke.

The phone rings. "Hello 14! This is headquarters. Is the doctor with you? The pilot came down in our area. He's alright. Hello?" We are so excited we can't answer. The doctor has already come and gone, and we send a runner to find him in one of the other shelters. In the meantime we are informed that there is no need for a doctor; the pilot is already with the armed forces. We give him a loud cheer. The phone rings. The battle for the Heights is over. We can leave the shelter—and never come back, we hope.

The children decide to set up a settlement on the Heights. "We will protect you from up there, just as you protected us. We mean it."

Ruth Geffen-Dothan: This is Shelter 14; *Dvar Hapoelet,* 7.67

The first day of the war went by, and the second, and the third, and the fourth. The news about victories in the southern and the central front followed each other, but in the northern sector nothing had changed. The Syrians continued their shelling and tried to attack Kibbutz Dan and the Shear Yashuv village. This was apparently a diversionary move, designed to hide their real intentions, which, according to the files found at the headquarters of the Syrian intelligence at Kuneitra, were to attack the Mishmar-Hayarden area. The people of the northern settlements sent a delegation to the Prime Minister. "What is the matter?" they demanded. "Have you forgotten about us? After all those years of suffering? This is impossible! You must free us from the Syrians—this is our chance!"

Their demand was fulfilled.

Yugoslavia-born General David ("Dado") Elazar, the man who headed the fierce and stubborn fighting on the northern front, is a dark-skinned, dark-haired, energetic and tough man. During the last three years, as C.O. of the Northern Command, it had been his task to retaliate against the Syrian provocations under unequal conditions: the enemy always fired from the Heights, and Zahal was forced to return fire from the plains. The time had come to change the situation.

The battle of the Heights lasted 27 hours, and when it was over, General Elazar summed it up as follows:

Our forces were drawn up for defense, and particularly anti-artillery defense. The Northern Command deployed a considerable number of tank regiments and anti-tank emplacements, and our armored force was spread out in a typical defense distribution. It was the objective of our force to minimize the extent of possible damage by firing on the batteries of the enemy and, to the extent in which there might be a ground attack, to prevent the capture of any position or settlement of ours.

Despite our preparations, all through the period from June 5th through the 8th, and to a limited extent, on the 9th (the day of the attack as well), the Syrians poured a ceaseless hail of artillery fire into our settlements, which were repeatedly hit. As a result of this shelling 205 houses, nine chicken-coops, two tractor sheds, three clubs, one dining-hall, six barns, 30 tractors and 15 motor cars were hit and some 175 acres of fruit orchards and 75 acres of grain and other fields were burned down. Our losses in men were two killed and 16 wounded (in the main superficially). This is, naturally not a pleasant statistic but it is not necessarily negative, in view of the concentrated power of the Syrian artillery shelling. In fact, this being the result of three days of staying put under enemy fire, I believe that at this stage, too, we can chalk this up as a minimal achievement.

After these days of uninterrupted provocation, on the morning of the 9th, we received the order to attack. Our forces proceeded from distant assembly points which were generally fixed outside the range of Syrian artillery, came to the grouping-points and went out into battle.

The Syrian army had taken up defense positions along the heights, disproving our estimates of recent years when we believed that part of their forces had been retained for the defense of Damascus. The fact that all forces were thrown forward shows not only a defensive objective, but also one of aggression. The armored units constituting their reserve were not deployed on the heights and did not take up defensive positions, as noted before; they were concentrated partly on the axis from Kuneitra to the bridgehead (the Customs House), with the obvious intention of attacking.

Their defensive force was built up, first, of the three regular brigades which had manned the lines throughout the year—the 8th, 11th and 19th. Deeper in the rear, two infantry brigades were added; the 90th north of Kuneitra, and the 32nd south of Kuneitra. Since we estimated that our action would take place mainly at the "edges," we engaged, from June 5th, in deceptive action in the Korazin sector.

As a result, another brigade appeared in that sector to reinforce the one already stationed there.

As for armor, each of the five Syrian infantry brigades had a battalion of T-34 and C.U.-100 tanks. In the forward positions, they had drawn up the same Panzers which had been situated there in peacetime (some 30 in number). The armored striking force was composed of two armored brigades, and two mechanized brigades, reinforcing the build-up before June 5th through the addition of an armored brigade. Later a mechanized brigade was added. In my estimate, these two brigades—one armored and one mechanized—remained in the Kuneitra sector, and, since this was the only force not seriously damaged, I believe that these were the forces that retreated towards Damascus in order to defend it after the collapse of the entire army.

Operating against these forces, whose strength we had estimated with some certainty, we had made the following plan: a break-through at a comparatively soft place, although difficult from the viewpoint of the terrain, somewhere near Giv'at Ha'em, i.e. south of Tel Azaziyat. From here there entered an armored force which took up a position on the ridge in the vicinity of Ein Feit Ze'ura, its task being to proceed southwards in the direction of Zuwaib el Meiss Kala'ah. An infantry force from the Golani Brigade—in this case reinforced by tanks—was to take the difficult posts at the corner of Tel Azaziyat, Tel Fahr and Burj Buvil, and afterwards Kafr Banias. You will be hearing about Tel Fahr. I estimate the battle of Tel Fahr as the most difficult we experienced on all the Syrian Heights, and if you visit the Rambam Hospital you will hear a great deal of testimony about this battle. At the post and in the trenches there were at least 60 bodies spread about. There was hand-to-hand fighting there, fighting with fists, knives, teeth and rifle butts. The battle for the objective lasted three hours.

The task of another infantry force was to open a number of additional breaches in the areas of Gonen, of Darbashiyeh and of Jelabina with the object of providing us with more break-though points in case we wished to bring in armor and to prevent the enemy from locating the focus of our main effort until too late. An additional armored force came in from the direction of Gonen via Kafr Awiya to reinforce our attack. All this took place on the 9th. We crossed the border at about 11:30 hours and our advance towards the objectives proceeded all through the afternoon. Towards evening, having succeeded in scaling the Heights up to about Bakala, we had taken the enemy positions at Azaziyat, Fahr, Burj Buvil and had broken through at Darbashiyeh. We now had two bridgeheads on the heights. In my opinion this was the maximum measure of success attainable that first night, and it augured well for the action to come. We did not exploit our success any further that night, for the break-through had been made along steep and narrow routes. We had encountered many serious difficulties in the scaling operation—difficulties in operating the tanks and in bringing up supplies. We needed the night in order to regroup, so as to be able to continue the following morning with our second blow.

This we did. The following morning, with very heavy air support—and our air force played an important part in smashing the Syrian Army—we embarked on the second stage with our forces on the heights attacking in the direction of Kuneitra. An additional armored force arrived in the course of this attack, having grouped during the night, and attacked at dawn in the direction of Tel Hamrah, thus assisting in the taking of Banias and mopping up the whole northern area of Nuheila and Abasiyeh—i.e. the whole of the Syrian–Lebanese frontier. This task was carried out rapidly and our force broke through in order to take part in the attack directed towards Mass'ade to the north. This was the force commanded by Moshe, and the first force which carried out the regimental armored break-through was that commanded by Albert, which was also the first to push on to Kuneitra. The force that sped onwards towards Ruweyeh along very difficult mountainous terrain that morning encountered anti-tank emplacements which it overcame and managed to descend towards the central axis, pushing on from there towards Kuneitra: this was Uri's force. The objectives of Golani, under Yona, have been described in connection with the first stage—the break-through effected in the forward positions followed by the taking of Banias. After this action Golani turned towards Kuneitra in order to mop-up inside the town. The additional forces taking part in this action, after it was felt that we had completed the break-through stage, with the Syrian forces beginning to collapse and retreating precipitately, were infantry regiments conducting mop-up operations.

An additional force, operating on June 10th, in the area where the enemy collapse had not yet taken place, was the one commanded by Aluf (Brig.-Gen.) El'ad Peled. Its task was to cut in among the enemy positions so that our achievements should not be limited, and it consisted of an infantry force which climbed up the cliffs of Tawafik, an armored force which, to our surprise, pushed on through ground not initially prepared, and a paratroop force flown in by helicopter to attack the enemy's positions in the rear, thus cutting across enemy lines and preventing troop movements. Its area of operation extended from Tawafik up to Butmiyeh. An additional armored force arriving on the 10th pushed on through Darbashiyeh, mopping-up and effecting junction with Peled's force at Butmiyeh. Kuneitra was in our hands at 14:30 hours, some 27 hours after the operation started.

After we took Kuneitra, as you can see, we did nothing but put a few finishing touches to the borders of the territory we had taken. The road to Damascus was almost entirely open, and I believe we could have been in Damascus in 36 hours.

We disengaged our troops long before the cease-fire deadline (at 6:00 p.m. on June 10th) and all the complaints and stories disclaiming this are utterly fallacious. There was no need for us to advance any further. We had attained our objectives in the time limit set—i.e., before the cease-fire deadline.

This battle against the Syrian Army which fell into the three stages mentioned above (break-through, fighting and exploitation of the enemy's collapse) was very bitter and hard. The Syrian Army had occupied its reinforced concrete bunkers and covered stone emplacements for many years—and it was difficult to expel them from these positions during the first stage. The actual fighting following upon the break-through was brief. This was mainly due to three factors: The first was the efficient action conducted by our air force; the second was our initial impetus which threw the enemy off balance; and the third was the fact that the commanding officers of the glorious Syrian Army were the first to turn tail—which is the reason why among the hundreds of prisoners in our hands there are so few officers. Due to these three factors the fighting was brief, the enemy was routed and fled, leaving behind most of his heavy equipment.

While the Syrian Army was not totally destroyed in this war, it suffered very serious losses. About one-third of the enemy tanks were lost—of the 300 or so they had before the fighting started, some 40 are now being driven by our men, and another 60 or 70 have been put out of action. Over 50 percent of the Syrian artillery which was in the nature of eight regiments was lost, and half of it is in our hands. We also have very large numbers of vehicles and small arms of all types. Of the Syrian infantry, two brigades suffered heavy losses and fled in utter disorder. Of the four armored brigades we estimate that one brigade suffered very heavy losses, and half of another brigade suffered lighter losses; the tank and infantry regiments suffered heavy losses.

On the Syrian Heights our losses totalled 115 killed and 306 wounded.

Brig.-Gen. David Elazar, Commander of the Northern Front; *At Press Conference*, 16.6.67

★

I have seen the Maginot Line fortifications; I have also seen the fortifications atop the Syrian Heights, and I consider the latter not to be inferior to the former. Of course, the Maginot Line was much better organized, infinitely cleaner, and contained enormous quantities of concrete. On the other hand, it was not situated along such a commanding height and, in my opinion, it was poorer in its defensive potential. The Syrians spent ten years constructing the fortification lines along the Heights. They built bunkers in the depth of the earth, mined vast areas, filled open gaps with barbed wire and stones—all this extending almost 20 miles east from the border. We fought very bitter battles on the Syrian Heights, and some of our best men paid with their lives for their capture. I think that if these positions would have been occupied by a better fighting force, our losses would have been infinitely greater.

As long as the Syrians were inside the positions, they fought very well, since they had been trained for ten years to operate from within them. But once these positions began to crumble, they lost their wits completely. Their control and mobility patterns had already been confounded by the scope of our bombing from the air, but even this does not explain their total lack of operational flexibility. As soon as they had to deploy, transfer forces and exercise resourcefulness—as soon as they had to make decisions and improvise on the command level—it was evident that they could not stand up against pressure. In 24 hours their entire structure gave way. For them this was an absolute shock. On Saturday, when the Syrian leadership realized that Zahal could reach Damascus in a matter of hours, they were seized with panic. In fact, to date they have not recovered from the blow.

Individually the Syrian soldier fought well. He is very unsophisticated, and years of digging and working on the fortifications did not advance him culturally. But, on the whole, he carried out his duties. The basic failure of the Syrian army lies with its commanders. These commanders, incapable of utilizing, to its fullest advantage, the complement of modern arms at their disposal, spent huge sums on their own comforts and paid little attention to their men and to their obligations. One should see the officers' club in Kuneitra, the lounges and the easy chairs. One cannot hoist himself from such lounges and readily participate in a shooting fray.

Of the 300 tanks brought up to the front by the Syrians, about 100 fell into our hands. We have most of their 18 artillery battalions, including 300 anti-aircraft shafts and a good deal of equipment. Assessment of manpower is somewhat more complicated. I have read in some foreign publication that the Syrians suffered about 3,000 dead and 8,000 wounded. To me these figures appear plausible. In general terms, the Syrian army was hard hit but not destroyed. It is now in a stage of rehabilitation, and is engaged in building a defense line for Damascus—an hour away by my car. I imagine that the feeling in Damascus is not overly joyous.

In January of 1965, the Syrians came up with the doctrine of a "people's army" to wage war against Israel. This doctrine contended that Israel could be destroyed by such an army plus acts of sabotage. The doctrine led us to believe that, sooner or later, it would cause a direct clash with Zahal, but we felt that they who would set off this war might not end up as they had anticipated. We therefore repeatedly warned the Syrians that, in case of a direct clash, we could be in Damascus in 48 hours. The Syrians obviously did not give our warning the attention it merited. Now we are intimating to the Syrians that we are half-way there. They must now surely understand that a direct clash is no solution, and that the only way to achieve a solution is to agree on a border which both sides would honor.

Speaking about a border, there is one, actually, between Syria and Israel. I am not referring to the "International Border," which is in reality a demarcation line between the French Mandate and the British Mandate boundaries; this border never served the purpose, nor was it ever approved by the UN or accepted by the Arabs. On the other hand, the border which exists today between Syria and Israel is the cease-fire boundary line. This is a good, natural boundary for both states—a broad "no-man's land," no bunkers or points of friction in the area and consequently no grounds for daily clashes. Without spelling it out as an agreement, we say to the Syrians that this boundary is acceptable to us as it is.

The Golan Heights differ from other regions in that they are sparsely populated. Only some 10,000 Druses and several hundred Circassians and Arabs live there. The Military Government, under my direct supervision, is responsible for all activities within the civilian administration, in which all government ministries are represented, each functioning in its own field.

While the military is setting up this region with posts, lookout points and reconnaissance systems, the Military Government is doing everything necessary to restore civilian life to its normal course. Among its activities are the marketing of farm produce, import of supplies, and the employment of local residents in public works, mainly repairing and building roads. It is expected that Heights residents will soon be leading their daily lives regularly and normally.

Now that we are on top, I recall what the border settlements and Zahal had undergone while we were down below, and I realize that this nightmare must never be allowed to return.

Who is supervising the Syria–Israel border right now? I suspect it is three servicemen with a machine-gun; one is probably taking a sun-bath. That's what the Syria–Israel border should look like—no opposing fortifications, friction points, or compromises which may tempt an enemy to strike and bait. There is a natural border between us and Syria—and we are straddling it.

My most difficult hour was on Thursday night, when there was a question whether Zahal ground forces should attack the Heights or not. It was a most distressing situation—to sit in command headquarters and feel that an historic opportunity was slipping through your fingers.

My most gratifying moment came on Saturday morning, when I sensed that the Syrian fighting force was falling apart. I studied the map as I listened to the reports coming in; I heard how the Syrians were retreating and from where they were firing—and suddenly the intimation came to me that the Syrian army was disintegrating. That's a professional point, something which every trained commander can actually feel. I was highly pleased; at once I knew that we had won, and even though we still had to finish the job, the atmosphere changed completely. For the first time, the command allowed itself to relax.

Benjamin Landau: Interview with Brig.-Gen. David Elazar; *Bamahane*, 1.8.67

The fiercest battle in the north, and perhaps even in all the war, was the battle for the Tel Fahr position.

Tel-Fahr dominates the entire region in front of it. The post itself is some kilometers inside and before it are two posts along the access route: Burj-Buvil, which is a relatively small post; and Tel-Azaziyat—a name familiar to the public from previous incidents. Part of our forces attacked the posts of Tel-Azaziyat, Burj-Buvil and others, whilst at the same time a task force moved to outflank and attack Tel-Fahr.

The battle for Tel-Fahr started long before our force reached the hill. On its way the force was shelled and a few vehicles were hit. It was also subjected to shelling from anti-tank guns and tanks positioned inside the post. The force itself had artillery cover, as well as tank cover from tanks moving along with it.

During its advance—both because of the topographical conditions and because fighting had started at such an early stage—the company commander decided to attack from a slightly different direction from the one which had originally been decided upon. He therefore shortened the outflanking movement and attacked immediately in an endeavor to avoid further delay under enemy fire and further damage to his forces. As a result of this change, the force had to attack from a very inconvenient position.

I wish to relate certain parts of this attack.

Three double-sloped fences surround the post. The force, which had been partly disrupted whilst on its way, arrived quickly at the fences, jumped off the half-tracks and broke through to the target. Instead of using bangalores, they lay down on the fences. There were mines in the fences. The men knew there were mines but continued their attack without hesitation. Some of the soldiers lay on the fences whilst others passed over them and penetrated into the trenches.

The target was built in two sections—the southern section and the northern section. The force which attacked first broke into the southern section. This force was led by a company commander. They swept through the entire post and mopped it up whilst continuing to fight face to face and whilst being subjected to localized enemy counter-attacks and bursts from within the bunkers. Many of this force were hit on their way to the target in order to make possible the advance of the second force coming in the same direction.

The second force moved along the northern section, which was also the roughest section, and broke into the trenches. The first section advanced halfway along the target. There they suffered a counter-attack and it became necessary to send additional forces into the battle. At approximately this stage, both the battalion commander and his second-in-command were wounded. I realized the necessity for an additional action in order to compel the enemy to a quick capitulation at this spot.

I pushed a further outflanking force to the rear of the target. I sent out my second-in-command with this force in order to try and take command over all our forces in this direction. In other words, the force that was already in the southern post and the force that had been sent out to outflank. I, myself, moved towards the main force which was at the northern section and which appeared, from my observation post, to have been considerably disrupted during the attack. My second-in-command arrived with his outflanking force and the battle that ensued was more than a face-to-face battle. There were almost no faces. Pressed as they were against each other, there was no space between the faces. One of the commanders of the force—the second one to move—Ruvke by name—was hit on the head with a butt when he ran short of ammunition and a Syrian officer appeared in front of him ready to shoot him. He could not have changed the magazine of his gun in the same second and therefore hit the Syrian officer with his hand with such force, that he dislocated his shoulder in doing so. He and the Syrian officer, practically glued to each other, fell into the trench. I do not know what would have been the outcome, but at this very moment one of our officers appeared from behind and killed the Syrian.

They continued to advance and had six or seven encounters, one after another, within a section of trench 20 meters long.

At the same time I was moving in another section. I arrived to the west of the post. I succeeded in grouping a force of tanks and infantry and we assaulted the target. We penetrated whilst the force that was already inside was mopping-up after having finally overpowered it. During the mopping-up, it was necessary to go from position to position and wipe out the enemy, who had fought with extraordinary stubbornness.

There are many examples of soldiers who continued to fight after their commanding officer was hit, in order to fulfill the objective. Some of them fought until they reached their assigned targets. There are many soldiers who continued to fight after they themselves were wounded. And it is only because each and every one of them persisted stubbornly to complete his assignment that we were able to overpower the enemy and break his resistance.

In conclusion I would like to present you with enemy casualty figures from only one post—a company post reinforced by fire cover. In this post we found 50 to 60 enemy corpses and we took about 20 prisoners.

Finally, this was a very difficult assault, executed by a good unit of men and officers, full of loyalty, steadfastness and comradely examples of mutual help between the soldiers, not only when wounded, but during the battle. All this gave us the great advantage of being able to overpower a difficult target which had dominated all its surroundings as well as the access routes which we were unable to avoid in order to reach it.

Brigade Commander Colonel Yona; *At a Press Conference*, 21.6.67

115 *men, half of them officers, were killed within one day of fighting in the north, and* 306 *were wounded. The struggle to save their lives was as desperate and stubborn as the battle itself.*

On a Sabbath, a month after the war, a small car climbed the heights of the Golan. On the left side of the windshield a red Magen David was pasted, emblem of the Israel Association of Physicians. Dr. Yitzhak Glick, released from his military reserve duty two days previously, was returning to the once bloody battlefield. It was a clear and beautiful day and the mountain above the winding dirt road was green, as if one of the bitterest and most difficult battles of the war had not taken place a few weeks earlier at this spot.

Dr. Glick had entered this battle completely by accident and through a misunderstanding. On Friday morning, the fifth day of war, Dr. Glick was stationed with his brigade at Kfar Szold. He had been attached to the reconnaissance company which, the day before, had been ordered to remain inactive. Therefore, he was trying to reach a medical unit. All Thursday he wandered about the Galilee together with the orderly attached to him, Ronni Ben-Dror, and looked for the company. In the morning, after his first sight of the war, he continued his search. "We left our equipment with the idea that everything was over. We set out as if for an excursion. Suddenly it became clear that there was much tumult of preparation. We came to brigade headquarters where there was much excitement and no one could tell us where the medical army unit was. They told me: 'Listen, just join any unit.' They were stationed in a green clover field among trees and by water—a real paradise. We were almost talked into it. But we decided to go on. It turned out that there was some sergeant major who was riding around looking for his bangalore unit. I joined him and on the road, just a little before Kfar Szold, I saw a tank unit standing. I knew the people. I saw Biro the officer and Mokady, the reconnaissance company commander. I recognized through them that this was the force of a brigade. They told me to join as an additional doctor. The doctor of the unit was Dr. Leron, a friend of mine at work. He sat me down in a free half-track. We divided the equipment and as we sat down the half-track began to move."

Straight brown hair, long dark face, very tired smile and cigarettes—that is Dr. Glick after the war. He is a graduate of the Herzliya High School in Tel-Aviv, 34 years old and father of two children. He completed his medical studies before his army service, during which he served as battalion doctor of the "Golani" Battalion. "The Heights were a little bit mine. I sat opposite them a lot. I had heard about the battle arrangements and fortifications there but from where I used to sit the view was innocent and picturesque." In 1962 he was released from the army and decided to specialize in gynecology and obstetrics. Today he is a gynecologist and obstetrician in the Tel-Aviv Municipal Maternity Hospital.

Five minutes after the force began to move it came into the Syrian shelling range. The ascent route was so narrow that the tanks and half-tracks actually stood in line. To get off the road was impossible because of the danger of mines. "These were the hardest moments. I sat still inside the half-track without anything to do. There was a terrible shelling and I did not know what was happening all around. I didn't know where we were going to, what force was going up, what was happening 100 meters ahead or behind."

After the first few minutes, Dr. Glick, who had joined the unit by chance, remained the only doctor. Dr. Leron, the unit's medical officer, was wounded when a shell hit his half-track. The medical orderly and the signal man were wounded with him and the three were taken to the rear. More wounded began to arrive. Because it was impossible to treat them in the half-track the whole team got out of it and set itself up by the road side. The brigade tanks continued going up to conquer the Syrian positions carved in the living rock. Parallel to the ascending advance there was a flow of men and material descending to the rear. These were the wounded and casualties. After an hour of fighting, Biro, the company commander, was also wounded. "My communications didn't work. The shell that hit the medical half-track hit the communication instrument. I didn't know what was happening. We received the wounded who flowed in all the time and we didn't even have the time to look around, to see how they were going forward. I only remember that everyone asked me if everything was all right, if we were still going up. Suddenly I saw Biro reach his jeep. He sat straight up like another antenna. His head was bandaged. I found out later that the minute he was wounded they asked by radio to send a vehicle to take him out. We hadn't heard the call. An ambulance ascended to look for him and didn't find him and then they apparently sent up a jeep. I didn't see the jeep come up and therefore I was so surprised when I saw it descend with Biro. Biro, who didn't stop commanding the unit and who didn't agree to leave his tank even though his mouth was lacerated, couldn't talk then. I remember that he really spoke with his eyes. His face was covered with blood. I took cotton wool and wiped it and he showed me through his eyes that I was making him feel better. Later I told him to lie down but he shook his head negatively. I bandaged him again, closed the safety chain of the jeep and that's how he went down, upright."

The Syrian shelling did not stop for a minute. The tanks were slow and vulnerable. The line began to lengthen and to thin out. The first tanks had already passed the first positions and those behind were held up because of bottlenecks and by disabled tanks which blocked the road. Dr. Yitzhak Glick and the medical orderly Ronni Ben-Dror, on their knees by the small emplacement they had made for themselves, were taking care of the wounded without the protection of helmets. They had left them behind with the rest of their equipment when they had gone out to look for the medical unit which had left no trace. Shells fell a few meters from them, throwing up splinters, rocks and sand. "Near us there was a destroyed anti-tank emplacement. There were some sandbags and a small trench there. I wanted to go over there, spread out the instruments and work in quiet. From all the war stories I've ever read I got the impression that two shells don't fall in the same place. I remember that in the middle of my work the desire to go forward penetrated my brain, to cross these few meters between me and the emplacement and to find cover but from overwhelming fatigue I couldn't move and change the situation and the place, especially since I would have to transfer the wounded who lay by me as well as the equipment. Ten minutes later this emplacement with sandbags, the focus of my dreams, got a direct hit. There had been a cannon barrel there before, afterwards it wasn't there any more."

A field of thorns caught fire from the shells and the flames began to reach Dr. Glick's private hospital. Soldiers passing by, the wounded and the driver told him: "Doctor, come on, let's move. The fire is getting near," but he continued to care for the wounded. "Compared with the horrible fire of the shelling the field fire was like water."

It was about three o'clock in the afternoon and the sun was already beginning to go down. The road cleared. Intact tanks burst through the first row of emplacements and afterwards the second one and went forward to the main top emplacement, the final target for the same day, Kala'ah. The first stage of treatment and clearing of the casualties came to an end, and the medical unit of the force got into the half-track and went forward to Na'amush, a conquered Syrian emplacement. A little lower down, at a distance of about a kilometer, the difficult battle of Tel Fahr was then going on. "I saw it as if it were on the palm of my hand. I had the feeling that all the fire that had been directed towards us a few minutes before had gone over there. We had comparative calm."

The second round of wounded began to arrive. Ilan, the tank company commander, was brought in severely wounded in the lower abdomen. He was fully conscious in spite of the terrible pain. Dr. Glick's operation under fire, on the ground, took about 30 minutes with the help of equipment which was running out. Three injections of morphium dulled and quieted Ilan, who propped himself up and watched the doctor operating on him. "Everything will be all right. I'll be coming to visit you yet," the doctor spoke to him and lay him down again. "Afterwards they told me that when Ilan's tank was hit he jumped out of it wounded. Outside he saw that two of his crew had remained inside the tank. With these severe wounds he returned to the tank, turned the cannon and saved the two members of his crew. He also didn't stop asking me if we were going forward and breaking through. What fellows!"

During the operation, Dr. Glick noticed a man working beside him with unusual devotion. "I didn't recognize him. I asked him if he was a medical orderly and if he belonged to my group. Then he answered me: 'No, I'm a driver.' Later he told me that he is a physical education teacher and had had a course in first-aid at the Wingate Institute. When we finished the treatment at this stage of the battle, I saw the driver standing and shooting with his 'Uzi.' I began to shout at him: 'Are you crazy? Now you've found the time to play?' I thought that he had gone into shock." This was during a period of a few minutes quiet. "We felt that we were going up, that we had passed the difficult stage of the breakthrough and the climbing, that we were on the plateau." The valley behind seemed unreal. Disabled tanks stood around and men were milling about. Dr. Glick's clinic was at a crossroads. Casualties were brought for treatment and immediately after were taken down below to the medical unit. The infantry of the "Golani Brigade" began to ascend after the armor had broken through. "The driver-orderly kept on firing and said that the emplacement over us wasn't clean. He said that he heard voices inside the bunker. I placed two orderlies to shoot inside the bunker and Eddy, the driver, stole over to the other side and threw in a grenade. It was intended for the inside of the bunker but he missed and it hit a tank. Suddenly we saw five Syrians come up with their hands raised. They'd been sitting there all the time under us—while we'd been taking care of the wounded. We made them lie down and we bandaged one whose eye had been wounded." The medical team of the battalion headed by Dr. Glick noted to its credit, as incidental, five Syrian prisoners.

When night began to fall, Dr. Glick and his aides were half a kilometer from Kala'ah. "We were a small screw in the whole affair. In the morning they told me to join the force and I joined. I didn't know at all what was going on, what the alignment of the forces was, where we were going. In Kala'ah I saw several isolated tanks in the darkness. This was one of the saddest sights that I saw. Only one thing made me happy. This was when I heard that, above us, there was transfer of the wounded by helicopter. We advanced slowly because we treated people on the way and because the supplies of our medications were running low. Up above we found another five wounded and one dying. When I came the fellows actually cried. They felt themselves isolated and abandoned with the few tanks that remained to them, with the wounded and with their dying mate. When they saw me they asked: 'Doctor, why did you get here so late?' Then I couldn't control myself and I yelled: 'What do you think I was doing, playing all the time?'

"On this casualty I worked in the light of lamps for almost an hour. I tried artificial respiration, injected directly into his heart, I did external massage. They walked around and said: 'Just half an hour ago he was still talking, still telling us all kinds of things.' They had the feeling that I had arrived too late, that they'd been abandoned. I remember I was massaging his heart and then putting my ear down to hear the beats which appeared and disappeared until they disappeared completely. When I told them they cried. They'd been hoping that I would perform a miracle. This was the hardest time for me. There was also a terrible feeling of isolation—we were alone in all the world. It was quiet and completely dark. What were we doing here alone? Did anyone know that we were here? The case of medications was completely empty and I had to go down to refill. I was certain that the next day more battles like those of this day were awaiting us. I was sure that we were going forward to self-destruction, to make war with a few tanks and a few tired and nervous people. When I told them that I was going down they actually clung to me like small children and said: 'Doctor, you will come back, you will come back, you will.'

"The descent took more than an hour and a half. Halfway I came across forces preparing to ascend after us. Suddenly I saw that everything would be all right. Below I took on a supply of new material and before dawn I was back on the Heights and then I saw them tending to their wounds. They were lying under the tanks, fixing and oiling them. Then I already knew that this day would be different, that the plateau would be taken. These children conquered it," said the old doctor of 34 and added in a half voice: "How charming they are."

Edith Zertal: Dr. Glick, Gynecologist; *Bamahane*, 18.7.67

On Saturday, the day called by the people of the north "The Great Saturday," it was at last possible for the settlements of the

Upper Galilee, the Huleh Valley and the Sea of Galilee to breathe freely. The Syrian Heights had been conquered. The diary of the Kibbutz Dafna tells about the change.

The Syrian Heights are in our hands. Zahal is in Kuneitra. The alert is still in force, but a large crowd had been gathering at the gates since the early morning hours to watch, with fast-beating hearts, the convoy of armored vehicles and tanks moving along the road. The soldiers told us that the highland of Banias and Tel Hamrah are ours.

One of the soldiers, wearing a red *Kaffiya* (an Arab head-dress), shouted in our direction: "That's it. We've conquered everything. No more troubles for you." It was thrilling to hear it, and it was marvelous to see them—the growth of beard on their fatigue-lined faces, but smiling and waving their hands in greeting.

We listened eagerly to the stories told by the soldiers about the seemingly endless five-day week.

Here, by the gate, you could meet friends whom you had not seen for a week, children and grown-ups who had emerged from the shelters, members who had been stationed at their posts, and soldiers. The spectators at the gates are searching for familiar faces, inquiring about members of our kibbutz. Our womenfolk went ahead and set up coffee and cakes, turned the porch of a house near the road into a "coffee shoppe" and invited passing soldiers to refresh themselves.

Whenever a convoy passed along the road, our women, helped by the children, would run towards it with drinks and cakes. Others threw packets of cigarettes into the hands of the soldiers riding by. Seven armored cars raced by, flying the red-green-black-and-white Syrian flag. A soldier blew a Syrian trumpet. Portraits of Nasser were waved about by our soldiers. "Good thing that the picture is upside down. It serves him right," remarked one little boy. A soldier, standing on top of a tank decorated with flowers, shouted: "Hey, you can now turn your shelters into museums."

From Kibbutz Dafna Diary; 10.6.67

It was strongly rumored in Israel that Russian officers and experts had participated in the fighting over the Syrian Heights. According to General Elazar, the Russians had trained the Syrian Army, instructed them in reconnaissance, armor, artillery and communica-

tions and took part in the drills, but they probably did not participate in the fighting itself.

An Israeli soldier, Rafy Kotser from Kibbutz Hagolan, found in one of the bunkers at Nuqeib on the Golan Plateau the works of Balzac in Russian.

I met Rafy Kotser in Jericho. He told me about this and added that it is apparent that one of the soldiers of the Syrian army is very erudite if he could find time, between finding the ranges of the artillery across at Ein Gev, to learn Russian and look through the works of Balzac.

Balzac in Russian; *Al Hamishmar,* 20.6.67

The Israeli soldiers behaved like gentlemen, as compared with any other victorious army in the world, even though they could not always resist the temptation of helping themselves to booty in the deserted villages. Some would take a souvenir, others took more and were court-martialled, others got away with it, and many would not touch the abandoned property as a matter of principle. One of the fighters told the following story:

This happened after the battle. The unit was preparing to descend from the Heights. The soldiers were rushing and were still collecting from here and there all sorts of things for souvenirs. The troop leader did not pay any attention.

I remembered very well the warning my mother had given to my older brother on the occasion of the War of Independence and the Sinai Campaign. She always repeated that he should not bring her anything. She did not want any presents. She did not want any souvenirs. She only wanted him to stay alive.

But a small clay jar, really miniature, stuck in the ground caught my eye. All the soldiers kicked it in passing and for some reason it did not break. I picked it up and thought that I would bring it to my girl friend for a souvenir.

We descended from the Golan Heights and drove away. When we reached Jericho we stopped to rest. There the troop leader took out his Bible from his pocket and read to us the chapter on looting from the Book of Joshua. When he finished all the soldiers in silence pulled out the things they had collected, made one pile, poured petrol on it and burned it.

From there we went on to the Western Wall. The excitement was great. I was also excited and put a slip between the stones of the Wall: "Let there be peace."

I. Bella: Story of a Warrior; *A Kibbutz Bulletin*, 7.67

For days after the battles had ended, it was impossible to put through a telephone call to the north. Worried parents in the center of the country kept asking day and night: Are you all right? Day and night, the soldiers who had fought on the Heights sent messages to their families at the rear: We are safe. And those who failed to hear from their sons at the front were in the grip of terrible fear.

In a small village near our army car depot, an old woman raises her hand asking for a hitch. She is small, withered, with a kerchief tied round her head and a plastic shopping bag and money purse in her hand. When we stopped it turned out that she isn't old in years but only in suffering.

"Where to? What are you doing here alone on this road?"

"Take me to B'not Ya'acov Bridge. I'm in a hurry."

Hitch-hiking on the Syrian plateau!

When we explained to her that we were not going to the bridge, she was ready to go with us to any place from which she could get to Tel-Aviv.

Her tight lips, as if she wanted to force back her words, suddenly opened. "I'm looking for my son. He hasn't come back. No one knows anything about him. He's disappeared. I'm looking for him. He fought here, on the plateau, in a tank. No one wants to talk to me, no one answers me. They think: she's an old woman, crazy, uselessly looking for her son. But I know that it isn't crazy. I'm an old fighter from the days of the English. I'm a member of a moshav. My son went, he was called up. He didn't even manage to come home to say goodbye to us. And I'm now tracing back his way from talking to his officers. They don't want to answer me. They say, "If all mothers went out looking for their sons what would we do!" But I'm not giving in. I have to know what happened to him. Let them search the area! With helicopters! I've traveled around, I've looked, but how much can I look! I spoke to the Medical Officer who treated the wounded. His name did not appear on his lists. But I'll find him, I'll find him . . ."

She takes out papers, slips, a small notebook from a nylon bag.

"Here, I've written everything down, every detail, every name. I've been to see everyone I could think of. Here, on the Heights, he last fought. I'll go back there and turn over every stone until I'll find him!"

This is modern warfare: recoilless cannon, concrete fortifications, electronic rangefinders and radio-given commands. And a mother searching the fields looking among the stones for her son.

Masha Shapira: A Hitch-Hike from Kuneitra; *Al Hamishmar,* 23.6.67

The people of the northern settlements spent six days in the shelters, and emerged on the seventh. They went up the mountains towering over them, looked at the vacated positions, at the deserted bunkers, at the gutted Syrian tanks strewn along the roads. For the first time in years they knew the meaning of peace.

Beyond the eucalyptus grove, tree-tops shaven by Syrian artillery, you catch a glimpse of the houses of Kibbutz Dan and the adjoining moshav, Shear Yashuv. These two have thoroughly drained the concept of frontier. 19 years on the firing line, with the Syrian sights trained on your back and the barrels of the machine-guns pointing straight into your windows. You never knew when the guns would roar and the rain of shells would open gaping holes in the walls of your home; you could never tell if your fields would go up in mushrooming smoke, and if your children would spend the night in a subterranean tunnel—all because the first war, which elsewhere terminated in the spring of 1949, ended here only on the Tenth of June, 1967. Done with.

Dan and Shear Yashuv have now lost their special halo of the frontier. Zahal took the enemy hills and freed the valley. The enemy nests were crushed and the frontier was pushed back to the far peaks. Genuine quiet reigns in the country of the Jordan tributaries. No longer a feigned stillness. The car climbs the pot-holed road, among the hulks of charred tanks, their invasion blocked by the bodies of the men who climbed the mountain, the men who forged ahead through minefields, under the rain of shells, across bunkers spitting hellish fire. They climbed from the valley, from the paradise down here, to the hell up there. They pushed back, conquered, liberated.

Forty-two blood-drenched hours silenced the dialogue between gun and field which had been going on for 19 years, a dialogue between instruments of destruction and creation, between a scorched and barren hill, impudent in its brazen claim to superiority, and the green abode of the farmers. You climb a hill which is one big military fortress, excavated and entrenched in boulders of basalt. You travel across a country of tough and hostile barrenness. Wherever you look, for kilometers around, all along the ridges of the Golan, you see barbed wire, trenches, fortifications, positions excavated in the basalt, reinforced with steel and concrete. Tunnels vein the mountain. The gun-slits surround you on all sides. One bunker leads into another. You catch a glimpse of a tank half-hidden behind a bend of terrain; and over it, on a sharp slope, guns raise their muzzles. The Syrian war machine had ploughed up every inch of the mountain.

The valley spreads below, like a gigantic fresco conceived by an artist. A cubist painting, executed in burning color. Brown and green and yellow and ochre mingle riotously. Everything is within reach, at your choice; from this spot you can fire at the dining room of Kibbutz Dan, or shoot straight into the nurseries in the Shear Yashuv homes.

You stare in amazement at the war effort and means invested by the Syrians in these unyielding hills. They excavated the mountain and fortified every inch of the soil, they armed the inhabitants of the hillside and turned their villages into military camps. The valley is inhabited by civilians. The mountain was occupied by the military. Down there—a chain of settlements. Up here—one military camp leads to the next. The valley is green, yellow, ochre. The mountain is gray, scorched, barren. Even its civilians lived by the army and for the army. It has only miniature pockets of cultivated land, and you won't find a single flower in the isolated green patches. This is the land of aggression, the reign of absolute militarism.

The sound of running water and the voices of the Israeli soldiers splashing in the Banias pool help you overcome your somber thoughts. The hills of aggression are in Zahal hands now; the valley is free.

You can't help feeling the absolute tactical supremacy which imparted a sense of security to three Syrian brigades, reinforced by armor and artillery, equipped with unlimited quantities of modern arms, the pride and glory of the Soviet and Czechoslovakian industry!

Kuneitra, the headquarters of the Israeli front. 1,000 meters above sea level. The high and mighty Syrian had the Israeli valley in the palm of his hand.

"They knew very well that every shell, every bullet would hit civilians, not military men," says Colonel M., commander of a reservist infantry brigade which conquered the fortifications of the first line of defense along the routes of attack and assault on the mountain, shattering the centers of resistance in the positions of Jelabina, the Customs House, Murfa'at, and Durijat (in the Gadot sector); Urfiya and 8100 (the Gonen sector), and pushed back the attempts of Syrian invasion from the direction of Tel Hamrah and Tel Azazyiat (the sector of Dan and Shear Yashuv).

Colonel M. had the pleasure of sending the wireless message to the headquarters bunker in Gadot about the liberation, when, at noon of the "Great Saturday," he was standing on the crest of the mountain above the fortified village of Jelabina, which had sent 3,000 shells into the courtyard of the kibbutz. He spoke little of the Syrians, much of the Israelis. "Now it can be told," said Colonel M. "Throughout all these years, we faced three Syrian brigades with a handful of soldiers. The Syrian Army kept on the plateau every type of weapon known to the ground forces: machine-guns, light mortars, heavy mortars, anti-tank guns, tanks and artillery of every description, including Katiushas and 112 mm. guns. The biggest weapon we had at our disposal against all this Syrian might—until the clouds of war started gathering, that is—was a 81 mm. mortar. All these years a duel was fought between three armed and armored brigades, straddling the hillside about 1,000 meters above us, and a handful of Israeli soldiers with a mortar battery. Imagine that," chuckles Colonel M. "We silenced them nevertheless."

"How?"

Colonel M. shrugs.

He had been on a military tour of Europe, and visited the Maginot Line. "Look," he says, "I am not exaggerating when I say that what you saw this morning on the Golan Heights, with your own eyes, is a miniature Maginot. We succeeded in circumventing their Maginot, even when we were down in the valley, and the fortified heights were above us. Nevertheless, we never imagined what we found here. You may ask how the miracle took place on the morning of Friday, 9th of June, the first day and the one before the last of the Syrian–Israeli war. In the morning we took the positions of Tel Hilal and Dardara; in the evening, Urfiya and its suburbs were ours, as well as Darbashiyeh and 7175. On Saturday morning we conquered the fortified village of Jelabina. Let me tell you, the name of this miracle is—the Israeli fighter. Examples? Let me give you just one. The brigade was already mobilized, when one morning one of our former soldiers showed up. He came to volunteer. We tried to persuade him, to talk him into going home. But he insisted; he wouldn't budge until he was given some task. He wanted a pistol, because you can use a pistol with only one hand. He had lost an arm during the annual drill of the brigade. We didn't send him home. He was a symbol; he stood for everything—the heroic spirit which imbued all our reservists—the whole nation."

On Saturday, the reservists of the brigade stormed the approaches to Jelabina. They fought for each house, and cleared one trench after another in hand-to-hand combat. At dawn, the force had already reached the plateau, and when the tanks raced through Jelabina, the brigade advanced along three routes toward the position of the "Customs House," which was being thoroughly strafed by the air force.

The reservists of this brigade were mobilized when tension started mounting. Its units encamped in the main defense positions in the northern front. The kibbutzim on the front opened their homes and their hearts. The merger of army and agriculture was kept up until the fighting in Sinai started. Farmers in uniform and soldiers in work-clothes mingled so that it was hard to tell one apart from the other. They worked together in the fields of the kibbutzim, drained of its working hands by the mobilization. The war broke out on June 5th. And the merger became a fighting combination: the civil population in defense positions, the brigade units in combat assignments. At dawn of June 6th, a Syrian brigade attacked the houses of Ashmura. The invaders came from Tel Hilal and Dardara, only one kilometer away. Under cover of the dense morning mists, they reached the protective fence. They placed their weapons facing the windows of our bunkers. The attack was repelled, but was renewed on the dawn of the next day. Now two Syrian infantry companies tried their luck on the northern end of the front. They descended from the lower ridge and assaulted Kibbutz Dan, crossing the fields of the Shear Yashuv village. The invaders were received with intense fire. The fighting population fired from the bunkers, and infantry units lashed out and repelled their attack. At the time of the second attack, that very day, the commander of the brigade sent a battalion of tanks to help the settlements. The measure was justified but superfluous. When the armored column arrived, the invaders had already been repulsed.

A report came at night: Suspicious movements in the Customs House area. The sound of tractors and bulldozers had been detected. Orders were given to light the area with search-light. The suspicion proved to be well-founded. The Syrians were trying to open roads of access to the Jordan, apparently in order to repeat their feat of 19 years before, when they had used this tactic in order to conquer Mishmar Hayarden. The area was lit up, as we said, and a heavy fire smashed the heavy equipment to smithereens and repelled another attempt at invasion. This was the end of the operation designed to open routes of invasion to the Jordan banks.

Commanders, soldiers and tankmen alike scanned the skies during the fighting for the conquest of the mountain. "Each of our airplanes gave us new strength," says Colonel M. "The men felt emotionally close to the pilots. The scream of jets was like sweet music to the assaulting force, exposed to fire on the slope."

"And then, a 'Mystère' was downed by anti-aircraft guns. The pilot jumped from a height of 4,000 feet. Heavy fire was directed at him from the Customs House positions. Hundreds of fighters held their breath on the battle-field. For a few moments, the Syrians were forgotten. The fate of a single pilot became one of the dramatic high points of the battle. In order to rescue the pilot, we sent an infantry battalion with its weapons, and an armored force which deployed in front of the Syrian positions to silence the fire they were pouring on the air-borne parachute.

"The fire from the Customs House was silenced. Several detachments, motorized and on foot, were sent to the spot where the pilot had presumably fallen. A jeep with the deputy-commander of the battalion, Uzi, and the operations officer, Uri, raced under Syrian fire from the Gadot sector. The pilot had been shot down, but they reached him on the crawl, rescued him, dragged him out and brought him safely to the headquarters bunker. That was an exemplary feat carried out by the many for the one.

"Lieutenant-Colonel Yitzhak Halfon, commander of one of the battalions of the brigade, sacrificed himself for the many.

"Friday morning, when the general of the Northern Command told me that we were moving to attack, Dardara and Tel Hilal were designated as the first targets. The task was entrusted to Halfon's battalion. I called the commanders, spoke to them and sent them forward. The difficulty in the conquest of these targets was in the crossing of the two bridges on the Jordan canals. The attack was carried out in broad daylight, and the battalion advanced under Syrian fire. As soon as the battalion had arrived and set up the auxiliary arms, a slow but effective fire was opened on them. A shell falling on the tree-tops produces a rain of splinters. The men were under the trees. The fire from Dardara and Tel Hilal, as well as the heavy artillery fire coming from deep in the Heights, was increasing. Halfon's battalion, defying the fire, regrouped and moved to attack both targets by two routes; one leading to Dardara and the other one to Tel Hilal. The battle of Dardara was swift. The enemy fled in terror, leaving behind both casualties and weapons. The battle with the positions of Tel Hilal was a different matter. The enemy fought fiercely. Our men crossed barbed wire. They swept in broad daylight through mine-fields, under artillery fire. Finally the Syrian resistance weakened. The enemy soldiers who didn't flee were killed. The targets were in our hands, but immediately after the conquest, the Syrians started shelling the conquered positions, and sniping began from the upper ridges. The force had walked into a fire-trap. In order to rescue them from annihilation, we had to locate the Syrian firing positions and silence them. That was our main task for that moment. Yitzhak Halfon, the battalion commander, did not assign it to any of his soldiers, but took it upon himself. He rose over the trench, exposing his head, and had time to locate the direction of the Syrian shelling and to order fire, when a sniper's bullet hit him in the forehead, over his glasses, and he fell dead in his soldiers' arms. Yitzhak Halfon, the battalion commander, 36 years old, was the best soldier of his battalion. The Syrian fire confronted him with a personal problem—the survival of his unit within the conquered target. He solved the problem, and paid for it with his life."

At 11 o'clock in the morning of Saturday, June 10th, Colonel M. stood on the ridge overlooking the upper Customs House, and called his assistant on the transmitter: "Call Gadot on the telephone, and deliver them the following message from me. 'To Gadot. The nightmare is over. When seen from the Heights, you look ten times more impressive. Over.' "

Within a few seconds, the transmitter set at the feet of the brigade commander was squeaking. The assistant was on the line. "Answering message from Gadot. To Zahal and the brigade, congratulations from Kibbutz Gadot! Over."

The hills hoisted a white flag.

A large three-storied building stands on the outskirts of Kuneitra, a market-town surrounded by military camps. This is the headquarters of the Israeli front. The Israeli flag is flying on the headquarters' roof, and quantities of military equipment taken by our forces are piled in the open square. The headquarters of the Syrian front are occupied by our soldiers. Somebody wrote in French "Vive Israel," and "Long Live Zahal" in Hebrew and Arabic. The Syrian command had fled, leaving everything behind: depots full of equipment and ammunition, and loads of materials. Lieutenant Uri is ensconced now in their intelligence room.

"This was the office of Ahmad Al Amir, with the rank of Akid, which is equivalent to our chief-of-command," says Uri. "The whole building was the nerve center of the Israeli front. A separate military state. Apart from three infantry brigades, supported by armored and artillery battalions, they had Mahal soldiers (National Guard), recruited from the civil population. The luxurious room of the front commander, furnished in oriental taste, is crowded with chairs upholstered in crimson velvet. The front commander saved his skin by taking to his heels, quite precipitately it seems, since he did not even take along the plan of the overall attack against Israel; the plan was found by the conquerors. A map is hanging on the wall, studded with arrows to indicate the lines of attack, the grouping and size of Zahal units, as well as the size of the Syrian forces which were supposed to storm all of the Israeli territories, in addition to many other variations on the theme."

Eighty babies, tots and children, emerged from the shelters in Gadot after six days of subterranean life, and filled the air with their excited voices. Parents came out from bunkers and trenches. The fighting population came to appraise the destruction. Gadot was licking its wounds. 3,000 shells had been showered on Gadot, and half of them fell in the courtyard of the kibbutz. Installations were destroyed; buildings were in ruins; not a single house had been spared. In the nursery, big holes gaped in the walls; the ceilings sagged, doors had been torn off their hinges. A sign warned: "Danger! Entrance forbidden!"

"Difficult days ahead," says Abik Malcon, 32 years old, the man in charge of the reconstruction. "We must rebuild the ruins. The kibbutz has suffered terrible damage. Not a single building is intact. Our production system was hit. The hen-coop is completely lost. 24,000 dead chickens. The three cattle-pens are destroyed, and the heavy shelling played havoc with the cotton plantation. 900 fruit-trees were uprooted; the electricity network is shattered; the irrigation system is a shambles; the tractor-shed is ruined, all the tractors have been damaged. We must start from scratch."

How many times can you start from scratch?

"We must prepare for the future. It's not so simple. Our lives and the lives of our children have been endangered for too long. Our homes and our fields provided tempting targets for the enemy. Yesterday we went to have a look at the Customs House positions. We saw from that vantage point how we must have looked to them. Luckily we couldn't see that before. The very thought of the Syrian Army entrenched on that hill, makes you shudder. Perhaps this is what's changed."

Aharon Dolav: A View from the Mountain; *Ma'ariv*, 23.6.67

For the youngsters in Kibbutz Tel Katzir, on the shores of the Sea of Galilee, practically on the threshold of what used to be the Syrian frontier, constant preparedness was a way of life. Ten-year-old Opher, the oldest boy born in Tel Katzir, summed up his views on the war and the time preceding it in an interview with the correspondent of Bamahane, *the Zahal weekly.*

I went to Tel-Katzir, a settlement once on the Syrian border and now at the country's center, and asked Opher Chen (not quite ten) for an interview. Opher pulled out his notebook, ran down his list of activities for the day, scratched his head, and said he could make it between seven and eight in the children's room. Half an hour later we met there. He turned on the air-conditioning unit and plunged into vital statistics: Two sisters (eight and eleven); he is a graduate of the fourth grade; he is the first-born male in Tel-Katzir, a title which he is not inclined to share with anyone else.

For the interview, Opher wore short blue trousers and a light shirt. Strands of unruly hair wisped across his smooth, tanned face. "Well," he said, with gracious maturity, "how can I help you?"

"To begin with, how did you spend last Independence Day?"

"That was a long time ago. This year we had a festive meal. Then they gave out tickets for prizes. I won a pen and a sharpener. We also had entertainment and fireworks."

"When did preparedness begin at Tel-Katzir?"

"Right away—or maybe two days afterwards. I saw the men in the kibbutz oiling their guns, filling bullet clips, then they went out to the firing range. They also dug trenches and stood watch at night. In school, before the lesson, each of us told about what he had heard. On Sunday we talked about news from all over the world. I said De Gaulle wasn't on either side, but I think he helped Egypt."

"What else did you talk about?"

"Say, that was a long time ago. Oh yes, when Egypt took five of our men prisoner, this one boy said that one of them was, I think, a lieutenant-colonel, I mean, an Israeli commander."

"How did he know?"

"I . . . look here, I don't know if I should tell you."

"Why not?"

"It's a secret. There are secrets which you shouldn't tell."

"Alright. How did you know that war had broken out?"

"On Monday morning the teacher came into the room, all red in the face, and said that war had broken out. We weren't afraid, but we were very excited. During recess the teacher brought a transistor and all of us listened, then we went down to the shelter."

"Why do you think war broke out?"

"One of the main reasons was the closing of the Straits of Tiran. There was also a big gathering of Egyptian armies in Sinai."

"Are you really only ten?"

"Sure. Why?"

"How do you know all these things?"

"Whaddyamean, how? I read newspapers and listen to the radio."

"Do you read children's newspapers?"

"No. Those don't interest me."

"What do you know about Nasser?"

"He's the ruler of Egypt. He's a blowhard. He doesn't think enough about what he does, and he doesn't know enough about Israel's strength. What takes him ten years takes us ten minutes. Besides, I think he's an evil man. Everybody in Israel thinks so."

"You think the Syrians are bad people?"

"There are Syrians who are bad and there are Syrians who aren't bad. I know the villagers wanted to work their land in peace, but their army didn't let them. My father went up to the Syrian Heights on the first day after the war, and he told me that the bunkers are like fortresses. They spent all their money on bunkers."

"Do you hate the Syrians?"

"Yes. Did you see what they did to the kibbutz? All the time they kept shelling us and shooting at us and wouldn't let us live in peace."

"But why did they shoot at you all the time?"

"What! You mean to say you don't know?"

"I want to know what you think."

"The Syrians claim that we drove them away from the fields during the War of Independence. I don't think so."

"Did Israel want war?"

"No. Israel never wants war."

"Would you like to take part in a war?"

"No, I don't, but if they will need me, I will."

"During the war, were you at any time afraid that you would die?"

"How could I die? I was in the shelter all the time."

"What did you do all the time?"

"I read a lot. I read 'The Heart' and 'The Secret Seven.' They also taught me shash-bash and rummy."

"You probably play rummy very well."

"Just so-so. It's hard for me to hold the cards."

"Now, Opher, I want you to tell me how the Syrian Heights were taken."

"Well, it was a very hard battle. Our planes bombed their positions, the tanks went up, and the soldiers attacked. The Syrians kept shelling all the time. Did you know that a shell hit the cooking gas tank and burned down the whole dining-room? It's true. Since then we get our food every day from the other kibbutzim around here. Many of the houses were also hit."

"When did you leave the shelter?"

"When they said that the tanks were going up to the Syrian Heights, everybody went out of the shelter, without permission. My father raised the flag above the pool. Then the helicopters came, and we were allowed to leave the shelter."

"What would you like to be when you get to serve in the army?"

"I want to shoot the cannons in the Armored Corps. When the tanks were here, before the war, I made friends with the Centurion gunners, and they showed me how to work the cannon."

"Do you know that tank gunners eat a lot of dust?"

"Dust is nothing. We eat a lot of dust when we ride to the Kinneret, every Saturday."

"Are you happy, now that the Syrian Heights have been captured and you won't be shot at any more?"

"Yes, but I don't want it to get boring here."

Benjamin Landau: Opher of Tel-Katzir; *Bamahane,* 1.8.67

Chapter Nine

On the Seventh Day

THE FIGHTING WAS OVER, 130 HOURS AFTER THE WAR HAD ERUPTED. On Monday, 12th of June 1967, one week after it had all begun, the Chief-of-Staff, General Yitzhak Rabin, read at the Western Wall the Order of the Day announcing the end of the war.

"Soldiers of Zahal! Now, with the cease-fire, there comes to an end the struggle we have waged against those who would have shrouded us with oblivion.

"The Israel Defense Forces, on land, sea and in the air, have shattered the armies of four Arab states. Undivided Jerusalem is free. The West Bank is in our hands. The entire Sinai Peninsula is under our control. The Syrian threat to the northern settlements has been banished.

"The war was not an easy one. It was waged by Zahal—and Zahal alone. The battles spread over wide areas. All the forces of Zahal, the regulars and the reserves, the border settlements and the home front—all have a share in this great endeavor.

"Many of our commanders and soldiers have fallen in battle. We shall remember them with sorrow—and pride.

"Zahal has now achieved all of its objectives, in virtue of the supreme effort on the part of its commanders and soldiers—and the pace of its operations.

"The struggle may not yet be over. I want to state here, at the Western Wall, with full confidence, that as we went forth to fight for these objectives, so we shall know how to safeguard and protect them in the future.

"Commanders and soldiers—we salute you!"

Gen. Yitzhak Rabin: Message to the Soldiers; 12.6.67

The Minister of Defense, Moshe Dayan, had said the day before:

Soldiers of Zahal:

At 6:30 in the evening of the day before yesterday, Syria accepted the cease-fire. The war, the Six-Day War, has ended. In those six days we liberated the Temple Mount, broke the shipping blockade and captured the heights commanding our villages in the Galilee and the Jordan Valley.

The Arab forces which had gone forth to overcome us lie shattered at our feet. From Sharm-a-Sheikh in southern Sinai to Kuneitra in Syria, the earth is strewn with the remains of tanks, planes and artillery pieces; charred embers and twisted steel of the armies of Egypt, Syria and Jordan, a host which banded together to annihilate the State of Israel.

We have vanquished the enemy. We smashed their battalions and frustrated their connivings. But deliverance came to us at a high price. The best among our comrades, the most daring among our fighters, the most precious of our sons fell in this war. The sands of the desert and the boulders of Galilee are steeped in their blood. We achieved victory, but our homes are in grief.

Soldiers of Zahal! The battle has died down, but the campaign is far from over. Those who rose up against us have been defeated but they have not made peace with us. Return your swords to their scabbards, but guard and take care of them, for the day of beating them into ploughshares is not yet at hand.

Minister of Defense: To the Soldiers; 12.6.67

No information was given during the war on the number of the wounded and the dead, but this was never far from people's thoughts. How much is this war going to cost? Tens of thousands? Thousands? Hundreds? Is it going to be the dearest one? An official announcement appeared on June 12th.

Zahal stands at attention in memory of its fallen in the war now ended, thanks to whom victory was achieved. Our losses in this war, up to June 11, 1967, were 679 dead and 2,563 wounded. Of the wounded, 255 sustained serious and medium injuries; the others suffered light injuries.

Zahal Announcement

According to the experts and commentators, the number of casualties was far smaller than estimated, as far as figures went. But when the figure was broken down into units, into names, into familiar faces, into young men, fathers, husbands, brothers, sons and comrades, a heavy pall of mourning descended on the country.

A young soldier, turned old in one week, yesterday sat in a fine restaurant, surrounded by members of his family, celebrating his safe return. He tried to do what was being expected of him—to entertain them with tales of valor and miraculous escapes, in the saucy vocabulary used, but a week earlier, by his fellow-*sabras*.

But his heart was not in it. Every once in a while his eyes would drift into space, as though he were seeing his comrades, there at his side in the assault on the hill, then crumpling and rolling down the slope. And he would whisper, more to himself than to the others: "It was worth it. It would have been worth it at any price."

Any price. But he wanted to be convinced.

This morning, the entire nation stands beside the fresh graves of those who statistically make up the "comparatively low" number of those who fell in battle, but a dreadful number nevertheless, whose every figure stands for a son, a husband, a father, a friend. The nation stands and seeks to be comforted, to be convinced: "It would have been worth it at any price."

The nation prays: "Let not the sacrifice have been in vain."

Aviezer Golan: At the Open Grave; *Yediot Aharonot,* 12.6.67

This is a small country—its population does not exceed that of a small metropolis. Everybody knew at least some of the 700 dead. Lieutenant Ilan Yekuel, however, was known to hundreds of thousands: a long and detailed interview with him had appeared just two weeks before his death in the large evening paper Ma'ariv.

Three weeks before the war I went down to Beer-Sheba to interview one of the thousands of soldiers stuck in the sands of the south, growing restless, getting a tan, and waiting for the order to attack. I asked myself: How will the army be able to select, from among all its soldiers, the right man, the one who will be truly representative of the extraordinary spirit of the Israeli tankman? After half an hour with Lieutenant Ilan I was certain that this was the right man. When we had finished the interview I asked him: "What is your surname, come to think of it?" He smiled and answered: "What difference does it make? The censor will pencil it out anyway. Just say Lieutenant Ilan, commander of a Centurion unit. That will do."

Three weeks later, when it was known that he had fallen in combat, the black boxes of the obituary notices framed his name and surname: Ilan Yekuel, officer and philosophy student. Now he will never find the answer to the problem he was investigating at the Tel-Aviv University: Does God exist?

He reached Beer-Sheba, brimming with good spirits, from one of the concentrations of Israeli striking power in the south, his uniform and high black shoes dusty with travel. He laid down on the table his personal gear—an Uzi sub-machine gun, ammunition belt, compass and field-glasses, quenched his burning thirst with a cold soft drink. He wiped the sweat away from his brow and rubbed his palms to get rid of the clinging layer of yellow dirt. Now he was ready for the interview.

Name: Ilan

Post: Commander of a "Centurion 105 mm." tank unit.

Age: Twenty-one.

Home Address: Tel-Aviv.

Civilian Job: Student at Tel-Aviv University, philosophy and psychology, first year.

Distinguishing marks: Tall, slightly wavy black hair, large brown eyes, reserved, confident, direct.

Parents own furniture store on Allenby Road. Father is fourth generation in the land. Mother came from Bulgaria, at the age of 12.

Q.: How were you called up to the reserves, and when?

Ilan: (simply) I received a phone call at three in the morning to report at the meeting point.

Q.: What was your first thought when the telephone wakened you? Had you been expecting this call?

Ilan: Frankly, no—but I knew immediately what it was all about. I took my father's car, drove it to the place, and left it there. My father came by later and took it home.

Q.: What did you take along for your trip?

Ilan: I always have my gear packed for this occasion—my uniform, a change of underwear, goggles, high shoes, socks, shaving things, shoe polishing stuff, my army documents. That's it.

Q.: How about cigarettes?

Ilan: (smiles) No. I don't smoke.

Q.: What did your Mom and Dad say?

Ilan: What could they say? They know I don't like it when they begin worrying. *(embarrassed)* Mom tried to cram in things to eat. I said to her: "Let it go, Mom. Do you think they starve us in the army?" *(graciously)* You know mothers. I had a business with my kid brother, a fifth-grader. Insisted on coming along with me, even threatened that he'd find some way to go south with us. Some youngster!

Q.: What happened at the meeting point?

Ilan: The unit cars were waiting for us. Mobilization was in full swing. Everything clicked a hundred percent, just like we say: "Armor tempo."

Q.: What is "armor tempo"?

Ilan: It sounds like just a phrase, but it isn't. "Armor tempo" is a very definite term for fast organization, exact and thorough execution, fast thinking and resourcefulness.

Q.: How was your meeting with the other reservists?

Ilan: It was great. The men slapped each other on the back, called one another by their nicknames, joshed. "How come they called *you*?" or "How did they manage to break into your sleep?" They know each other well. *(appreciative)* Some got to the meeting point even before they received the official call. This just goes to show you how sensitive the fellows are to the situation. Some of the men weren't enthused while they were serving as regulars, but now they came forward eagerly, ready to serve all the way.

Q.: It has been said that some of the reservists were in such a hurry that they came in their civilian clothes. Did that happen in your unit?

Ilan: It sure did. Men went down in their everyday clothes and went to work on the tanks. *(empathizes)* Many a suit was ruined with grease. But the fellows didn't mind—even joked about it. "In town we run to the dry cleaners every time the suit gets a spot on it. Now there isn't one clean spot on the whole suit!"

Q.: Is it possible for a personal relationship to develop between the men and the steel monsters you call tanks?

Ilan: No doubt about it. Each crew becomes attached to its own tank. They don't let you paint names on the tanks any more, but the crew can identify its tank down to the last detail. When a Zahal "tankist" works on the same tank over a period of time, and especially if he goes through a few battles with it and it does the job right, *(heartily)* he really becomes attached to it. You can see that in many ways. He doesn't just maintain it in good working order. He gives "his" tank all kinds of attention—he paints it, burnishes it, practically blows off every speck of dust. He couldn't be more careful if it were really his own property. And if you think that all tanks look alike, let me tell you that the tank crewman has a sixth sense for identifying his particular tank, even when it is jammed in among a host of others.

Q.: How is the morale among the men of your unit?

Ilan: It's very high. The men are not eager for war; they'd rather be with their families. But if we have to fight *(clenches fist)*, every man will carry out his duties a hundred percent. And when I tell you that morale is high, I'm not just talking. So far, not a single man in my unit has asked for leave, even though most of them left everything in the middle—their shops, their businesses. One of the boys was about to be married; he didn't even think of asking for leave. Now how do I know that he had been about to be married? Well, he came to me for permission to phone his folks and tell them to postpone the wedding.

Q.: There is a saying that "armor eats sand." What's the situation in the south; are you really "eating sand"?

Ilan: (happily) Armored units do eat sand—not only through the mouth. Your eyes get it, your nose, everything. Tank crewmen are used to it, and some—you'll laugh at this—even like it. Their first request is for permission to take their tank just a little way into the desert, churn up enough sand for a good mouthful—to get the taste of it back again.

Q.: Have you established any traditions down below? I have heard, for instance, that you boil up tea inside the tank.

Ilan: (practical) The situation is this: The fellows do make tea inside the Centurion—wonderful tea. Perhaps even better than what you get at home. There's no water shortage, thank God. Some of the men went and estimated their need for water, and they figured out that in the conditions of Negev heat and dust, they use up a full jerrican each day. But we have plenty of water, and food, too. As for our traditions—well, there's always the fat fellow who has trouble getting into his pants. Naturally we ask him how he expects to get into a tank. But he has the answer: With the help of a shoe-horn.

Q.: Do you get many complaints about the tough life you lead?

Ilan: None at all. The men take everything in fine spirit.

Q.: Then it is true that some reservists actually love to be called up?

Ilan: (thinks about it) Some do—not because they have trouble with their wives *(laughs)*, although there are such cases—but because they are attached to their friends in Zahal and they like the atmosphere in the army. And those who aren't glad when they're called up, it's not because they dislike it but because it uproots them from their daily life.

Q.: What about fear? Does a "tankist" fear anything at all?

Ilan: (frankly) Every soldier, a tank crewman as well, feels fright every now and then. People think that we are never afraid because we are protected by a heavy steel shell. That's not true. Generally, though, the "tankist" knows how to get over his fear and to adapt himself to any situation which may arise. Manipulating a tank is a special problem. The crewmen don't see what's doing around them—not even the reassuring presence of other tanks moving along with them. In our Corps you can't hear the commander when he shouts: "Follow me!". We get our orders by wireless: "Attack!", and every "tankist" pushes the accelerator down to the floor, and forward we go. The men have great faith in their commanders. Also, we don't go in for superstitions. Our business is with concrete things. We know that the guns will fire, the cannon will hit the mark, the motor will function in direct proportion with what we put into them. Our faith—in the commanders, in the tanks—is built on solid sentiment. It's the same way with the crewmen. *(gratified)* Their faith creates lasting friendships. Even in civilian life they continue meeting each other, take the families to the movies together.

Q.: What were you studying at the University?

Ilan: (exact) In Dr. Shuval's group it was Freud and philosophy. With Prof. Sharfstein we discussed the matter of whether there is a God or not—is there or isn't there a Divine Presence.

Q.: What is your personal opinion?

Ilan: (hesitates) I think there isn't, but it's good to believe so. The fact that this subject has been debated down the centuries shows that it isn't a simple matter.

Q.: Are you taking up philosophy and psychology with the aim of teaching the subjects or will you be going in for research?

Ilan: (shrugs) I haven't decided as yet. Right now I am taking them up because I am interested in them.

Q.: Isn't the changeover from Freud to commanding a tank in the south rather sharp?

Ilan: Not for me. I am familiar with that kind of life. The first day you feel strange, but you get used to it. *(romantic)* I do want to tell you that at first I dreamt about joining the Air Force, but after spending some time in the Armored Corps I fell in love with it—with the sands, with the grease and maintenance. In general, every soldier who gets to know armor falls in love with it. Now you might well ask me: If you love the Armored Corps so much, how come you didn't sign up for regular service? I'll tell you. I obtained my release six months ago in order to know another side of life, but I can tell you that the release was sort of conditional, and I may yet come back to armor.

Q.: What do your parents say?

Ilan: They wouldn't object to my remaining in the army.

Q.: How would you describe courage?

Ilan: When you are facing enemy tanks and keep going forward at full speed despite his shooting at you—that's courage. As you know, we don't abandon a tank as long as it functions in some way; if it can't move on but the guns are still working, we're still in the battle.

Q.: What's going to be with your studies?

Ilan: (strokes his sub-machine gun) I'll have to make up what I've missed. I feel sure that they will understand. What I am worried about are the exams in psychology and philosophy. They are coming up at the end of this month.

Raphael Bashan: A Tank Commander; *Ma'ariv*, 26.5.67

★

The telephone rang.

"Remember Lieutenant Ilan Yekuel? You interviewed him about a month ago?"

"Sure."

"He was killed in battle."

Lieutenant Yekuel had come to our appointed meeting in Beer-Sheba some two weeks before the war broke out. I enjoyed the interview. He phrased his words clearly and spoke them with quiet self-confidence.

We talked about the relative fighting spirit of the two sides. He had a definite opinion on the subject. "About a year and a half ago,

I took part in reprisal action against the Syrians at Korazin. We put three of their tanks out of business, but not before one of the tanks simply turned right around and fled from the field. Now I am not saying that the Egyptians will run away, but with us it has never happened—nor ever will—that a crew should turn its tank around and run away, or even abandon the tank before getting the last shred of usefulness out of it. Then there is the matter of leadership on the battlefield. When our commanders are given an assignment, they don't just follow the instructions that go along with it. They study them down to the last detail and figure out every possible development that might take place in the course of their fulfilling the task."

Ilan knew how to handle his men. Although only 21, he could still understand the feelings of the married men and their concern over their families and livelihood. "Most of the men in my unit are married. They can't communicate with their homes by telephone, only by letter, but at least they are already receiving replies. I know that my gang has problems, and I tell the men to come with them to me, but they don't—not because they feel that I can't help them, but because they understand what's going on in general and don't want to aggravate matters with their personal problems. They take everything in stride, although there are always some fellows who must be convinced that everything is right before they get into the spirit of things. But then, you can't deal with soldiers as though they were robots. They are people, and they react like people...

"In the Armored Corps, you won't find any distinction between the regular serviceman and the reservist. Each of them does his job with equal thoroughness, efficiency and discipline. At times, when you see all of them in the same khaki uniform, you are tempted to think of them as one mechanism, but inside each uniform there is a different personality, various beliefs and opinions—all fused, however, into singleness of purpose."

So spoke Lieutenant Yekuel, only a month ago.

I went to see the commander of the Armored Corps, Brigadier-General Yisrael Tal. The General tried to conceal his emotion, but there was no mistaking the deep anguish in his eyes. "I knew many of the officers and men who fell in the war, but I want to tell you about Ilan because he was the one we sent for the interview, and since the public read about him when he was alive, I want people to know more about him and how he was killed.

"Ilan was truly a blessed young man—handsome, very talented, extremely intelligent. His family was well-off. As a young man of 21, he had everything his heart could desire. He could have followed any course of his choice. But he was always troubled by the question of what is actually right—what *must* a man do with his life. When he had completed his stretch in the Corps, he turned to study. I encouraged him in this, but it seemed to me that he didn't find peace in learning; he was more interested in values. I think that, for the past few months, he was seriously considering enlistment in the regular army.

"He was one of my Centurion unit commanders, then Battalion Operations officer. Because he was so talented, we tried to pressure him to sign up permanently. But he had made up his mind to continue his studies in the United States; in fact, his passport already had the US visa stamped on it. Just then the trouble with the Syrians broke out. They were trying to divert the Jordan waters and, not content with that, made incursions into our territory. Ilan was in charge of one of our tanks, which on that occasion destroyed three of the enemy's, but the action almost cost the life of the battalion commander, to whom Ilan was very much attached. He was at the commander's bedside in the hospital for days and nights on end. One evening he said to the commander, as a sort of an impulsive pledge: 'If you get well, I'll stay in the Corps.' Well, the commander did recover. When he told me what Ilan had said, I called the young man in and said: 'Ilan, I've heard about your statement. Will you redeem your promissory note?' Without a word he signed up for a year. I appointed him to be the head of my office, but he was more than that. He was my friend, my right hand.

"When the year was up he enrolled at the Tel-Aviv University for courses in philosophy and psychology. Before doing this, though, he made sure that he was on the list of active reserves, on call, with a tank unit. He passed the course for company commanders in the Armored Corps School and was appointed tank company commander in the reserves. When we moved into Sinai, he led his company to head off enemy tanks moving from Gebel Libni against our positions at Bir-Lahfan. Ilan thrust his head out of the tank turret so that he might direct his men more effectively, and that was when a piece of shrapnel pierced his cap—the same thing that happened to his battalion commander in the battle with the Syrians. Ilan was not attached to my Division at Gebel Libni, but the success of his blocking action opened the way for us to penetrate farther into Sinai.

"I was informed about Ilan's death as soon as his company joined up with us. He went the way so many of our officers have gone, exposing themselves to the worst dangers in order to lead their men better—and to victory. This, I tell you again, is the secret of our superiority—but the price is so very, very high."

Raphael Bashan: Requiem to a Tank Commander; *Ma'ariv*, 23.6.67

The little black boxes of the obituary notices on the soldiers killed in combat filled many pages of the newspapers throughout the month of June. As the battles were raging, the casualties were given temporary burial in several military cemeteries in various parts of the country. The official ceremonies took place 30 *days after their death. The Prime Minister, Levi Eshkol, said on that occasion:*

Dear parents, wives, sons and daughters, friends:

Head bowed, the entire nation stands with you at these fresh graves. Sons, husbands, fathers and friends have given their lives in bitter battles so that we may live on, so that the State may survive.

They all knew what the war was about, what was at stake. They therefore gave their all—their devotion, their loyalty, their unsurpassed courage. They made the difference. They and their comrades decided the outcome of the war—for life, for security.

The fighters inspired the entire nation to bring forth courage, devotion and fellowship. In the crucible of conflict we became fused, from segments and sections, into one unified nation.

Our debt to them is beyond payment. While we cannot restore them to life, we must together do everything within our power so that the nation and the State will, by their way of life, deserve all that which they have given us in their death.

Let us continue to show the same spirit of willingness, of self-sacrifice, of mutual help and loyalty which they had shown in their lifetime and by their death. There can be no consolation for this deep grief, only the nation's gratitude to its heroes, a gratitude mingled with sorrow and pride.

The Prime Minister at the Thirtieth-Day Memorial Observance for the Fallen; 5.7.67

★

They have enlarged the military cemetery in Afula, the resting place of the fallen in the War of Independence and the Sinai Campaign and, now, the newly-dead of the Six-Day War.

All day long, the weeping of the bereaved, the sobs and the tears rise into the still air. While the fighting was yet going on, earth-moving machines cut through trenches along the rows, and, when darkness set in, the bodies of the fallen on the northern fronts were interred, in the spotty glare of floodlights. The silence of death shrouded the burial crews, the Zahal honor guard and the chaplains.

140 young fighters from all over the country were buried here, temporarily, in a new section where, only recently, there had been a few solitary graves. Small wooden markers bear the names and serial numbers of the remains beneath them, with the words "fallen in battle." Each grave has been marked off with a border of white brick and flower-pots. Within the year every family would have to decide whether it wants the body transferred elsewhere or left in the Afula cemetery, in which case a permanent monument will mark the grave.

At the end of the row, a mother from Nahariya is slumped over the grave of her son. Her husband and daughter, mute and tearful, try to sustain her. From a distance you can see her fingers entwined in the carnations on the grave, then falteringly move among the flower-pots on the white bricks.

In the next row, a large family which had come from Egypt and now lives in Kfar Ata is visiting the grave of the youngest of its sons. The others—sons, daughters, relatives—try in vain to keep the father and the mother from throwing themselves, again and again, on the grave of their child. Finally the father takes hold of himself, brings forth a large sack and, from it, hands out copies of the Psalms to the male members of the family. All recite the prescribed verses, in the traditional chant of their community, and the strains of the Kaddish memorial prayer float out over the graves. When they are done, the father from Nahariya comes up and asks them to accord to his son, too, the "grace of eternal truth" of reciting the Kaddish over his grave. The Kaddish is pierced by the wail of the unconsolable mother.

Mourners throng the cemetery all through the day, coming alone or in groups from all over the land. They bring flowers and plants and vases, prostrate themselves at the graves of the fallen, adorn the fresh earth with the favorite blooms of their dear ones, plant small bushes along the border, drawing the water from the font near the purification chamber.

Each mourns in his own fashion. A young woman stands at her

husband's grave; her lips move, but no sound comes forth. Near by, an Iraqi-born family from Kfar Yona is mourning for its son. Eleven women, identically dressed, sit around the grave. The mother sits at their head; in her hands she holds a photograph of her fallen son, and on the grave are the new clothes which she had prepared for his wedding day. For hours the family sits there, mourning for its son, in its own way.

Comrades from army units who have taken time off from their leaves to meet at the graves of the fallen, stand there, heads bowed, and talk about feats of bravery which the dead had left behind them. On one of the graves there is an additional marker, a piece of gray cardboard on which, in crude letters, are the words: "Zalman, you are one of us. We shall always be with you."

A. Mash: Mourning has Many Faces; *Davar*, 6.7.67

The possibility that a dear one might be killed in combat, is never far from the thoughts of anybody living in Israel. In case of war and conflicts—and these have been far too many for such a small country—worry emerges from the recesses where it has been lurking, and becomes apprehension, fear—or reality.

"I loved him, and I long for him. What a terrible feeling this is—to have this longing, yet to know that it will never be fulfilled. I have always dreaded death. Now it has come as something new; I no longer fear it, but now I don't understand it. I visited his grave on the thirtieth day of his death. I stood there and didn't understand it. The grave itself is the only thing that is real, in all this nightmare. Again and again, I find myself waiting for him to return, to ask for me."

The grief is all within her. The house is clean, tidy, everything is in its place, as always. Sima Lamkin, 31, war widow. White mesh blouse, blue skirt, silvered sandals, rings. The imprint of the tragedy is upon her and upon her three-year-old son. His little heart is aware of something, but he has all kinds of little doors to close behind himself.

Little Roy was with his mother when she received the news. He saw the shock, the burst of tears, and couldn't understand what had happened. He looked on and was filled with fear. He understood one simple thing; something had frightened his Mommy.

"That is why I mustn't cry. My tears worry Roy. When I received the notice, he was standing behind me. I felt the child's presence even before I could make out the meaning of the news, and I knew that I had to control myself, for his sake, only for his sake. He knows that something has happened to me, but he still doesn't know that his Daddy will not be coming back."

Donald Lamkin had been called up on the Thursday before the war broke out. The days preceding his call-up were filled with tension. A native of South Africa who had cast his lot with Israel, Donald could not remain quiet. "They should call me, too," he kept repeating. When he left home for work he told his wife: "The minute they call me, ring me up. Let me know right away." Small talk was out of the question. Uncertainty filled every room like a fog.

Then he was called up, a week before the war. Two days after it broke out, he was dead. His comrades put up a rough monument to his memory, on the spot where he had fallen between Kalandia (Atarot) and Jerusalem. On it they wrote. "Donald Lamkin. Fell on June 6, 1967. Reconnaissance unit."

Eliezer Peled, Donald's comrade-in-arms, was an eye-witness to the incident:

"I met him eight years ago. We spent many hours together in the reserves. Both of us were with a recoilless cannon unit. He drove the jeep and I was in charge of the crew. He was quiet, modest, a really nice fellow. Donny was first in everything; he had an extraordinary sense of responsibility. When the situation became serious, just before the war, his employers, Olympic Airways, allocated ten tickets for the foreign citizens in their employ, in case they wanted to leave the country. Donny was offered a ticket, but he spurned it. We were together when we took Latrun and Kalandia. When we went on toward Jerusalem we ran into an ambush. We were up front, with the unit commander. We took cover, but the commander felt that enemy reinforcements might be coming from Ramallah. He therefore decided to have a road-block set up, back on the road we came. Before he could say another word, Donny was already driving away to set up the block. In the meantime the firing from the ambush became so heavy that our commander decided to move off in another direction. We signalled to Donny, but as he was returning a sniper's bullet got him in the back and right through the chest. He died instantly. We didn't announce his death because everybody loved him, and we didn't want to depress the men's spirits. Later, when the news became known, the entire company was grieved."

"I saw him just before he left for the front," related Sima. "This was on the Friday before the war. They let me come very close to the staging area. Donny had never told me what, exactly, was his work in the army. When I saw him in the jeep, with the cannon mounted on it, I became terribly frightened. 'Donny,' I said to him, 'this is a suicide army. Is this the way they let you go, with a cannon in an open jeep?' Donny tried to laugh my fears away.

"He first came here during the Sinai Campaign. Then, too, he volunteered. He was taken into the Navy and was on the scene when it captured the Egyptian frigate *Ibrahim el-Awal*. I once asked him: 'Why did you come?' He told me that he felt his place was in Israel. In South Africa he had everything—wealthy parents, an estate, sports, comforts of every kind; here he had to start from the bottom. But that was what he wanted—to strike out for himself, rather than live on what his father had earned. He spent 20 months in Israel, then went back to South Africa and came back three years later, for good. This was in 1960. When I first met him I tried to match him up with my younger cousin, but I didn't get anywhere—except that Donny decided he wanted to marry me, which he did. This was in 1962, in Haifa."

That was the story. Five years of married life; one child, whom Donald loved passionately. As for his work, he did indeed start at the bottom, but quickly worked himself up to the position of assistant manager of Olympic's offices in Lydda. He was crazy about flying. Every screech of a jet and the smallest innovation in flying excited him no end. Two weeks after his death came new flying instruction manuals which he had ordered abroad.

"Four months after 'Roy-Boy' was born I went back to work," continued Sima. "We couldn't afford either a full-time maid or a nurse. A good deal of the responsibility fell on Donny. He worked the night and morning shift, and we arranged things to fit our schedules. Roy went out with his Daddy, played with him; the two of them would stretch out on the floor and do exercises. I never saw such love between a father and his little son. I left the house at seven and returned at four, completely worn out. Donny took care of Roy, washed and dressed him. He even did all the cooking. I can't imagine where he could have learned it—certainly not in his elegant home in Cape Town, where there were plenty of servants.

"Roy-Boy and flying were the two things he loved best. He liked to go to parties, drink and dance and flirt a bit. He loved tennis and books. He was 30 years old, full of energy, his life before him. Everybody expected him to go far. Now I am emptied of everything. I no longer jump when the doorbell rings. I don't know what I would do, were it not for Roy. I will just have to keep on going. My friends are still with me. I have not been neglected.

"I went with Roy to a psychologist. I wanted some advice so that I shouldn't make too many mistakes. I was told that Roy must continue waiting for his father to come back; under no circumstances was he to be told that his Daddy would never return. His anticipation will be his hope and protection. I said to him, 'Daddy went far, far away.' I told him that I, together with him, was waiting for Daddy. He has to feel that I am his partner in this waiting, and this will reassure him. But this is not enough. Yesterday he picked up the telephone and said into it: 'Daddy, are you working? Why don't you speak to Roy?' The other day a mood of deep grief fell on him. He threw himself to the floor and bit his own arm. 'Mommy fooey!' he screamed. 'Where is Daddy? Why did you take him away from Roy?'

"The doctor told me that in eight months he won't remember his father's image any more. That is why I must keep Donny's photograph in his room, so that the image should remain with him, even dimly. In a year or two the other children will be asking him about his father, and I shall have to tell him."

Sima Lankin's lips smiled sadly. "Six must be our number. The number of our first apartment was Six; so was the second. We were married on the sixth of February. He fell on the sixth day of the sixth month, at the age of 30—five times six. I shall visit his grave on the sixth of every month. My personal tradition."

Nurit Khalif: War Widow; *Ha'aretz,* 4.8.67

Perhaps this was the reason, that at war's end there were no victory parades nor raptures of joy; perhaps it was because of the sorrow for those who paid for the cost of the war with their lives, and because of the regrets of those who were spared.

Death has a permanent contract with the People of Israel; never has he allowed us a single hour of greatness without exacting his price for it. We have been paying him his full price, in blood, for our soil, our rejoicing, our festivals, our independence. The soldiers were aware of it, even as they chafed against the long wait. As the soldiers rode forth, Death rode with them alongside, and we could see his shadow. Yet we accepted wartime as something which we had been expecting, much as we would a moist wind after a suffocating dry spell. All of us felt it, the men who said "Let's go!" and the others who said "Farewell," for it is better to fall in battle than to disintegrate in peace.

Death is not like taxes. It cannot be divided equitably among the citizens, granting to each man his due portion of so many years of life. To us he gave everything—victory, hope, pride, life; to them he gave a few grains of sand on their eyelids. One would like to imagine a gathering of the warriors, somewhere on high slapping each other on the back, telling stories, listening to the sound of the Shofar at the Wall, seeing the flag flying above Sharm-a-Sheikh, and joining us for a trip to Jericho. If only they could enjoy the life which their death has made possible!

The radio announced glorious battles and dazzling victories, but above the words we heard the whining bullets and the exploding shells and the dull thunder of cannons. The raucous voice of Death was counting his spoils. And they who shook like a leaf every time the doorbell rang, lest they find there two stony-faced bearers of the evil tidings; and they who went down to the mailbox ten times a day—perhaps there *was* a card from the military post-office; and they who, for hours and days on end, sat by the telephone—perhaps a comrade would call, with regards . . . *they* will tell you that, in time of war, there are but three words in the vocabulary of those who wait: "Let them return."

Foreign correspondents and military analysts throughout the world have duly noted that Israel's losses in the Six-Day War were "relatively low"—relative, that is, to the gains and the conquest, and in view of the numerical superiority of the enemy. But the theory of relativity does not hold true for us, at this hour. Past wars can be evaluated calmly and dispassionately, but right now one death carries more weight than all the statistics put together. Yes, there are those who say: "Look here, in one year more people are killed in traffic accidents than were killed in the war," and no one really knows why. What bothers us now is that we have our lives—and we know that it is at the cost of theirs.

We have just one way of paying our debt—to pledge to ourselves that no power will uproot us from the soil which they had won for us—no Security Council and no world power, not UNEF nor sanctions or embargo, no boycott, no threat, no promise. No, not this time. We went in with force of arms, and only with force of arms will we be compelled to surrender what we wouldn't give up even in return for peace. The experience of other nations has shown that, when one does not yield to pressure, the pressure yields to will. We have now gained the goodwill of the nations—and this is very gratifying—but even if they should hate us, condemn us and sever relations with us, it would make no difference. Israel did not come about because of the goodwill of the nations, nor will it thereby survive.

This preoccupation with what the world powers are hatching for us contains a good bit of irony; since the Arabs were not able to annihilate us, one should apologize to them for their failure. In ministerial offices and presidential suites, calculations are being made by the guardians of the world to see what they would stand to gain at the expense of our concessions, and what advantages would accrue to them if they would assume the role of spectators on the sidelines. But, if diplomacy means flexibility in negotiating and readiness to compromise, let us change it to mean stubbornness. It is far better that the world consider us crusty and hidebound, crude and uncivilized, rather than allow ourselves to be thrust back into the nightmare of the borders. Let us be bastards rather than well-bred children whom the world's mentors commend for their good behavior.

We have been abiding with Death all along, and after every holocaust we would say: Perhaps this was the last struggle, perhaps now peace will come. This time, more than ever, we would want to believe that this was the final war—if not absolutely, then at least for the time being . . . if not unto eternity, then at least for generations . . . and if not for all generations, at least for this one. Let us, just once, get to know the feeling of peace.

Because we knew full well that ours has not been a generation of golden dreams, that our rose-colored glasses were smashed long ago, we are now, in the wake of those six days, as dreamers—after so many years of not allowing ourselves to dream, of forcing ourselves to be realists, of seeing life as it was and things as they were really meant to be. Today our views still have to catch up with reality, but when they do, and when we comprehend what has happened to us, we shall include dreams in our *realpolitik*. If our generation was able to fight for its survival, it should also be able to withstand partisan politics, long-winded theories of social structure, pettiness and idylls which became mired in the mud of bygone pioneering days and which no tractor can extricate. Perhaps it is not by chance that our prowess has showed itself in agriculture and warfare, in which we were not engaged in the Diaspora and where we had to begin at the beginning, while our weakness is showing itself in politics related to Jewish congregations and Zionist Congresses.

All of us became old in these six days, and each day was reckoned in years. Time has a force and weight of its own. It did not pass us by; it penetrated into our very marrow and left its impress on our entire being. We are not the same as we were a week ago, even though our identification cards bear the same names and describe the same distinguishing personal features. These six days have altered our own lives, our children's lives, the lives of millions of Arabs and perhaps of the entire world. For within the jockeying on the part of the major powers for positions of strength, there persists a stubborn struggle on the part of the small nations to conduct their own existence, and not to be hangers-on, serving-pieces or toys, nor children under the protection of Big Brother, nor rungs in the ladder of someone else's ambitions; to be small, insignificant, rejected, but to live.

During the six days, the news broadcast beep of "Kol Yisrael" was, for us, the muezzin's call to prayer. Like believers adhering to their faith, we put aside all work and gathered about the voice that emerged from the little instrument, our important fighting weapon—other than the really important ones. This was a war of transistors, the first and perhaps the last in history; previous wars did not know this small battery-charged apparatus, and those in the future will surely be waged on television. This was the shining hour for the transistor. In due course, when tension disappears and we are sufficiently recovered to do things calmly, we shall give the transistor the acclaim it deserves, perhaps build a small monument in its honor and write songs about it, for its having been on our side in all the battles.

Despite the modern armaments involved—radar, Mirages, Pattons—this was still, in a way, an old-fashioned war, almost primitive, the kind of war the world may yet recall with longing, a war marked by personal courage, individual resourcefulness and self-sacrifice, a war in which man fought with his heart and did not push a button with his finger. And we, on the home front, still felt the privilege of volunteering and working, of being brave in our own fashion, of scanning the skies for shells, not a mushroom cloud.

When a person is happy he is bound to be self-centered; otherwise he would not be content. In times of danger, a nation is self-centered, otherwise it could not endure. During those six days, the world disappeared as though it had never existed, except where it had some connection with our struggle. Earthquakes, air crashes, changes in governments, the war in Vietnam, the extradition of Staengel, the death of Dorothy Thompson, the London theater, Gina's latest movie, the cosmopolitan and the human—none of these existed; there was nothing but us, only us, in the egocentricity of a nation fighting for its life.

The warfare of man against man is terrible for both conqueror and vanquished, but he who fights for his life cannot afford the luxuries of considerateness and compassion. Only after the storm will have subsided and the ache over our fallen will have dulled, shall we be able to summon pity for all of us—Jews and Arabs, soldiers and farmers, women and children, scorched fields and demolished homes, false promises and heady rhetoric. Perhaps human compassion is not such a worthy trait, since it always has a tinge of the supercilious. Compassion is in the domain of the strong. Compassion is the possession of the Almighty, since He is always in a superior position—but we should not attribute it to ourselves. Happy is the man who is privileged to pity others but is not the object of their compassion. When the wave of goodwill toward Israel will blow over—and it will blow over—and the time for compassion for the Arabs will be at hand, we shall not begrudge it to them. Let them have the compassion and us the victory, rather than the reverse.

We tend to pursue an old and worthless tradition which will simply not learn from experience. We seek justice. Easy-going Tel-Aviv emerged from the war without hardly a scratch. It was again Tel-Katzir that got it, again Kibbutz Dan, again Nahal-Oz and Jerusalem, in the course of those six days as in the past. Tel-Aviv got away almost scot-free—three shells, six air raid warnings, a bit of a blackout and some inconvenience. On the other hand, it was bombarded with rumors. According to rumor, everything conceivable happened, except perhaps the landing of Martians on Shalom Tower and the appearance, in the skies, of flying saucers laden with export-quality "Telma" soups. The notion that the rumors were intentionally disseminated by the enemy in order to create confusion shows a lack of familiarity with urban powers of imagination—speculation grows into fact, fancy becomes "information from reliable sources," fears emerge like genii from a bottle and blossom into giants. Psychiatrists may hold that rumors are an escape from tension, but we know that mental disturbances are peacetime luxuries. Would that we were again neurotic to our hearts' content, confused well over our heads, full of eccentricities as a pomegranate is full of seeds, and steeped in fears like Kafka—the sooner the better.

At present, one cannot write a story, an article or a report without involving some manifestation of the Almighty, some miracle which He has brought to pass. The stock of the Divine rose immeasurably, during those six days, among the non-believing Israeli public. Agnostics became believers, and even atheists yielded. The reasoning behind this is simple: If there is a God, then He must be Jewish. Since He is, obviously he is not going to be neutral and stand aside like a mere spectator. Since He won't be neutral, then let Him grant us what we have been asking all these years—not Zionist funds but Jewish immigration, not the sentimentalities of the elders but the strong will of the young. Plus the aforementioned peace. Then He can go on vacation, along with the rest of the country. Then, when all tension is gone, we shall festively declare a "Let-Your-Hair-Down Month," fold up like pocket knives, totter about like reed huts, crumble like a stale cake, throw ourselves down on the beach and languidly wave the flies away.

Since wartime passed before we could acclimate ourselves to it, no name has been given to this experience. Now we are wondering what name to give to the infant. No, not the "War of Victory"; this smacks of arrogance and is likely to arouse resentment. Also, there have been many victories in the world. Nor the "Last Round"; there have been so many wars to end wars. Nor the "Battle for Jerusalem," since the outcome was decided in the air and in Sinai. The "War of the Sons of Light?" No, that would commit us too much in the future.

The windows we have taped with paper we shall now wash off with soap and water. The black cloth which covered the windows we shall put away. The shelter we cleaned out will again be cluttered with a variety of junk. The Civilian Defense workers will go back to their unglamorous tasks. And we, so recently a glorious nation, will now become everyday, as always.

Ruth Bondy: The Ages of a Week; *Dvar Hashavua,* 16.6.67

The soldiers returning from the battle brought back with them a load of pain, of rage, and nights of sleeplessness. They also brought back the clear conviction that life can never again be as it has been.

Your familiar ring of the door-bell. A storm of kisses from your wife and daughter greets you at the threshold, and the unavoidable tears.

"First of all, go over me with a vacuum cleaner. Wipe the war off."

Running water and a snow-white bathtub.

"You don't have to clean up when you're finished."

The mirror reflects your pre-war face. And on the following day: "You must continue from where you left off. Go and have the fitting for your suit."

When did it all happen?

The glare of rockets and shell-fire rips through the darkness, bullets pierce their way, stars split in the explosion of battle, and the hoarse voices of commanders are heard over the two-way radio.

We did not see the border line. The sky is the same sky, and so is the slim moon, looking as if it had been taken off a Turkish flag. Only the emotions have changed. It is not the physical border that matters. It is the border between peace and war. Now it is difficult to forecast the return home. Life is a closed deck of cards.

A voice calls into the night: "Good evening. You are now entering a mine-field. Proceed along the trail. Don't turn aside. Watch for the white marking strips."

On the third or fourth day of war, you could hear Lily Levy's voice on the wireless. The only voice of a woman in the whole of the Sinai Peninsula. A soft, feminine voice of a communications operator —like the dove that came back to Noah's Ark with an olive leaf in its bill. From that point, the war turned into a triumphal march.

Our communications half-track continues to roll southward ahead of the news. Unlike the Sinai Campaign style, we advance with transistor in hand, and thus see ourselves as the home front sees us.

A transistor lets you examine your action in the perspective of time and space and attach to your action its real value, not in terms of the effort, the emotions and senses you've put into it, but in relation to other actions.

Without a transistor, in Sinai of '56, every soldier saw the war in the light of his own operation. With the transistor, it is possible to see the whole operation, to be inside the incident and outside of it, at the same time, to hear suddenly the deed translated into words— and you wonder how small they are. Thus, for instance, after having watched a few sunrises in the desert, after Um-Katef, Gebel Libni, Abu-Agheila and Bir Hassna, we learned about the greatest sunrise of them all, the capture of the Old City of Jerusalem. And everything else assumed other proportions.

The highway from A-Nakhl, in the center of the Sinai Peninsula, to Bir-Gafgafa, presents a horrible sight of destruction of man and metal and their conversion into scrap. Miles of conflagration and disaster. Destroyed tanks at all sorts of angles, charred trucks burnt down to the tires. Russian half-tracks cut in two, crippled field-guns, tow-trucks blown to smithereens. Not a battlefield but a field of slaughter.

Iron that turned into ashes, flesh that turned into coal, and the smell of death rising from the corpses, carried by the wind, and the sand and the flies buzzing the buzz of death. Faced with the very power of the defeat and the disaster, your head starts spinning. This cannot be the result of your fire-power—it's a holocaust of nature. It cannot be the handiwork of man. Some mythological creature must have interfered here. You are speechless; daily language is far too inadequate, and only the Bible could describe it all.

Then come the abandoned encampments. Again the corpses, the scattered papers, letters, photographs, documents, newspapers, *Al Ahram* with its screaming, inflated headlines all over the page. Nasser's pictures on every page; his arrogant, confident declarations, warning that "the war against Israel will not be a limited war, but a total war of annihilation."

What terrible irony! Crude cartoons, depicting Israel's destruction —a brute of an Egyptian soldier thrusting his bayonet into the heart of the Star of David.

The farther we advance southward, the more recent become the dates of the newspapers. In A-Nakhl we found *Al Ahram* dated May 23, and in Bir-Gafgafa we found even that of June 3rd. After that date no more Egyptian papers arrived in Sinai.

The column "Whereto To-night?" in Cairo could only have been meant for us. "The Palace of the Nile" was showing the film "Viva

Maria," with Brigitte Bardot and Jean Moreau; at Almoricha was "Rasputin." The Abu Simbel Hotel offered luxurious accommodations at a low price, and at the Alhaj Zahi Bar you could enjoy the performance of belly dancers. Moshe Siprut of Yahud prefers the Alhaj Zahi; he says we can pay the bar bill with our battle rations. "If the bartender refuses we shall give him promissory notes."

When the war broke out we decided that if we came home alive and well, we would meet at the Ariana Night Club on the 5th of the month immediately following and start telling our tales. All the communications men would be there, all of them brothers-in-arms. They promised to create a little "earthquake" at the club with their merrymaking, without any distinctions of rank.

Maybe it would be worth-while, after all, to go and be fitted for that suit.

Gabriel Ben-Simchon: You Can't Go Home Again; *Ma'ariv,* 30.6.67

Brave (and pretty) girl soldiers, holding Uzi sub-machine guns, were very much in demand as export merchandise. Consequently, it was something of a disappointment when at the end of the war the army let it be known that there had been no girls in the fighting units. And then Ma'ariv *published the above article.*

We were all set to believe Zahal's statement that "there were no women serving with the army in this war," when Gabriel Ben-Simchon happened to make some remark about "the only female wireless operator whose voice was to be heard in all of Sinai."

Who was this operator—a regular soldier. . . perhaps "an angel with earphones?"

Now that Lily Levy is back, neat and tidy, in her parents' home in Holon, she is a far cry from the dust-covered girl, near collapse with thirst and fatigue, who turned up at the Bir-Gafgafa military encampment, soon after the site was captured.

Lily's voice is pleasant and she did her job well, as did all the operators, but to the dusty and tired men on the move along the desert war routes her voice, in those days, held "something special."

In civilian life, Iraq-born Lily is a secretary; in the reserves she operates the wireless communications system. Her last tour of duty in the reserves was during the "Great Drill." This time she was called up while the days of preparedness were at their height, exactly two weeks before the war broke out.

The air alert, on the first day of the war, found her at work near the southern border. She didn't mind being in the thick of it, but what could a girl do?

She found herself and her instruments moving into Sinai, in the wake of the Zahal conquerors, with shooting and explosions marking the route. "At times it was just like in the movies."

Lily's communications station was in a half-track. She was on day shifts and night shifts, sending messages into the teeth of sandstorms, fighting valiantly to keep the tons of fine dust from caking her hair and clothes beyond recognition. "I was thoroughly camouflaged." She recalls with affection the staff of workers with whom she went through the war. Though shy by nature, "we were all comrades," she said, "after just two days." At A-Nakhl, on the third day of the war, she met her brother, who had been mobilized three weeks earlier, and gave him an earful for not having written home during all that time. "June the first was my 26th birthday. I never thought that I would be celebrating it within sight of Sinai. The fellows rounded up bottles of juice and cakes. They also sang birthday songs to me."

Her experiences in Sinai: "When we first came across Egyptian dead, we ran to see what they were like. After that I wouldn't look any more. We were glad to see our victory—the burnt-out armor, the demolished fortifications. I was excited over our success. Then we saw letters scattered all about, pictures of smiling families. After all, they, too, had once been living people."

Lily talks about her war experiences quietly, without bluster. She doesn't even have photos of herself in the war. But in a few days there will be many photos taken, and she will appear in all of them, wearing a white wedding dress. On Tuesday, July the 11th, a date set before the war, Lily will stand under the wedding canopy, and all her comrades of Sinai days are cordially invited to attend.

The Lily of Sinai; *Ma'ariv*, 7.7.67

Most Israeli journalists of military age followed the fighting units to the front as military correspondents, but more than a few participated in the war as regular fighters, irrespective of their profession. Ya'acov Ha'elyon, Ma'ariv *correspondent, served as a tankman, was wounded in the battle of the Syrian Heights, and his leg was amputated. This is his account, written in the hospital, after the first shock had worn off.*

A black abyss. You float out of it, slowly, slowly, up to the surface. At first—nothing but a dense, almost liquid emptiness. Suddenly, at a certain point, you are sucked into a crazy whirlpool of changing scenes, whipping by like frenzied phantoms—the stir of battle, the cry of a wounded comrade, the acrid smell of gunpowder, the helpless animal look on the face of the man in the half-track, no more than an arm's length away from you; the shell had landed at his feet—and amputated both of them.

Then, all at once, the whirlpool regurgitates me into reality and consciousness. I hear my wife's voice, warm and soothing, a sound that a man hears perhaps once in a lifetime: "I am here, with you." Of all the beautiful words that should be spoken in reply, all I can get out is a faint "Shalom." I try to open my eyes. They stay shut, as they had been for a whole day, from the moment the anti-tank shell scored a direct hit on the turret of the tank I was commanding. I sink back into a sort of pleasant stupor. Something inside me has just given me a playful pinch and whispered eagerly: "See! You're alive, in spite of everything." I drift off into sleep.

The massive, unearthly force grabbed me by the hair and rattled me back and forth with frightening strength. I became enraged. What kind of trick is this to spring on a fellow! I tried to open my eyes to see what kind of a brute was toying with me. They didn't open. My anger grew. For 12 years I had been a close friend of the tanks. I had never failed to spend some time with them, every year, whether it was for a few days or long weeks. I was certainly familiar enough with anything that could possibly happen to me inside a tank. But this force which was making sport of me, which had blinded me, was something I hadn't expected. Not for a fraction of a second did it occur to me that the thing most likely to happen in battle had happened to me—I had been wounded.

Desperately, again and again I tried to open my eyes. Then I heard voices; it could have been seconds or minutes after I had been hit. Voices came at me: "We are wounded! Help us!" I recognized the voices of my crew men: Shimon the cannoneer; Albert, loading and communications; Avraham the driver, Amram the machine-gunner. Two thoughts surged through my brain, one slow, almost impersonal: "Looks like I've been hit, too." By God, this thought didn't upset me at all. But the second hit me with a shock. The crew has been wounded, and the tank can explode at any moment and be turned into a burning hell; the men may become burning torches. I lowered myself down, groping for the wireless equipment in the turret. I found the connection and called for help. My hand moved to the steel helmet on my head; strange that it should have been so completely splintered. I thanked God for my last-minute decision to put it on, rather than enjoy the comfort of not wearing it.

I heard voices approaching me, but could not identify them or even tell from what direction they were coming. Suddenly a thought struck me: "I wonder whether the men had seen the magic scenery of the Huleh Valley, as we were traveling along the Syrian oil highway, an hour or two earlier." I know I had stopped the tank and said to them: "Fellows, this is an historic moment! You can see the Huleh Valley from a point you had never seen it before!"

The voices were now speaking to me. "We came to get you." I wondered how they could take time out from the battle to care for me. Stopping their own tanks meant that they could easily become prime targets for the anti-tank shells.

They laid me down on the ground by the tank. I was still in a state of shock, but conscious. Suddenly I heard a thunderous noise, followed by dead silence. Then I felt it—a mortar shell. I counted the splinters as they cut into my leg: one break—two breaks—three breaks. The pain was horrible. I heard outcries around me. I tried to hold back, but my own cries were churning up through my throat. Suddenly, irrationally, I became angry. The first wound, I said to myself, was legitimate, as in a duel; score—0:1 for the Syrians. But why this?

The pain in my leg was unbearable. I had almost forgotten the wound in my head, except that the trickle of blood annoyed me. My senses remained clear, and I heard my company mate, Meir Zuck of Sha'ar Ha'amakim, talking to his men. I tried to make it easier for them to pick me up, and apologized for being "such a fat slob." But the moment they lifted me I felt a sickening pain; the men had taken hold of my leg without knowing that it had been broken. I yelled with my last bit of strength: "Not by the shin—by the thigh!" A strange thought occurred to me; what if they didn't know the difference between a shin and a thigh! "Take hold of the upper part, not the lower," I cried.

The Medical Corps jeep drew up, but now I had sunk into deep depression. My comrades had bathed my face, and I heard one of them exclaim: "Take it easy! Careful! All his brains will ooze out!"

I said to myself: "This is beginning to sound serious." However, it was my leg which was getting most of my sympathy, perhaps in reply to the painful messages that it kept sending to me. At the same time, my ears caught the cry of someone yelling: "My leg! Oh, my leg!" Was that I? No, it was—as I learned later—the soldier in the half-track, the one I had seen (was it only moments ago?) just after the shell had hit the vehicle. He was bewailing his truncated limbs, and around him were the bodies of the others in the half-track. Gone.

A familiar voice was asking for me, by name. I replied, automatically. "Ha'elyon?" Yes, I said. "Ya'acov, this is Don Shilon."

I felt a tingle of pleasure. Here was someone I could lean on, without hindering the advance of the others. A battle has no time for the wounded. Gross as this may sound, the wounded hamper the others, keep the soldiers busy, even endanger them.

My meeting with Don, a "Kol Yisrael" reporter assigned to cover the assault on the Syrian Heights, was a series of coincidences. I had seen him first by chance, when the attack was about to be mounted. He sped by in a jeep and we exchanged a quick "Shalom." When we were already moving, I spied him through my field-glasses in the command car of the infantry, which had joined us for the drive. He saw me and we jerked "thumbs up" together. The third time I saw him was just before I was hit; he was standing by his disabled command car. Now, this fourth time, he was on his way to Kiryat-Shemona to file his story, in the ambulance half-track which had now stopped to pick me up. He did not move from my side, except to plead with the driver to go slowly. During the ride he kept giving me water which, as far as I was concerned, came from the purest stream in the Garden of Eden.

Then began the series of transfers from hospital to hospital. After repeating the story of what had happened, again and again, I grew proud of the fact that my sanity was still with me. Finally I was taken to Rambam Hospital in Haifa. Again the doctors ran their searching fingers over me. One of them said something—and here I felt fear, for the first time—that "this is a job for the plastic experts." Plastic surgery, no less. Now my dreams about resembling Apollo would have to be stowed away in the attic. Only later did I learn that I had exaggerated the situation. The sculptors of human limbs and features were really doing a fine job, considering their working conditions.

Thus I rejoined the realm of the living, ascending in a haze of pain and sedatives, through the whispering of worried voices around me—the voices of friends and comrades. I felt my hold on this world growing stronger. I could feel the bandages on my head, face, eyes, knees, the cast on my leg, the bandage on my right foot, where skin had been expropriated for the graft on my head. An intravenous tube was attached to my arm. My thoughts, too, were now clearer. I pretended not to be awake and took inventory. At war's end, combatants are divided into two groups. The larger consists of the physically well; the smaller consists of war casualties. I was in the latter group, but I was also alive. I wondered how I could evaluate things so rationally when in fact I was feeling such grievous pain.

A wound, it seems, induces new worlds which remain sealed unless some part of you is injured. Nightmares, for one. Depressing insomnia. You drop off to a few moments' sleep, then the sight of your comrades, lying dead or wounded, awakens you with a sharp fear which lingers on even when the nightmare is gone.

I awoke one night to find the nurse at my bedside, her soothing hand on my arm. "What is troubling you, Ya'acov?" "I dreamt that my best friend in the company was wounded," I sobbed. Funny how a physical hurt can open the floodgates of tears and emotion.

The nurse. You become attached to her with all your heartstrings. In some ways, she is the pillar of your world in the hospital. She is the one who, when the pain becomes unbearable, brings you the blessed injection or sedative. She straightens your mattress, washes the blood and mud from your body. Early in the morning you call out: "Nurse!" All you want, really, is something to warm your heart. You fall in love with the nurse—not necessarily the prettiest one, but the one with the softest touch, the warmest smile, the one who knows how to insert the needle so gently that all you feel is the slight prick.

In the hospital you find that wonderful segment of humanity called the "one-time" and "regular" volunteers, whose eyes seem to beg you: "Help us pay the debt we owe you for suffering on our behalf." There are the quaint and kerchiefed grandmothers who come along with baskets filled with bottles of juice and practically force you to have one, even though all you want, at that moment, is to depart from the earth and its pains. But when you tell them, for the fifth time, "No, thanks, I am not thirsty," they disappear for a moment and come back with a bulging bag of candy: "So have a few sweets." Then there is Deli, the girl from Kfar Yarok, who left her studies and hasn't missed a day fulfilling the task she had set for herself—to bring newspapers to the wounded servicemen. High school girls come from Tel-Aviv daily to make tea and sandwiches for the wounded. All this warms your heart, and you simply wonder: "Why do *I* deserve this?"

Then the sadness sets in again, especially at night, when the minutes refuse to move and the thoughts keep piling up. For months, you will be separated from your family, your work. Your little daughter probably won't recognize you when you come home. You begin longing for the simple, almost nonsensical things, like going down to the grocery store, taking the stairs two at a time, driving your car, and a furtive hop-and-skip in the "potsy" boxes, after having made sure that no one is looking.

I get to feel genuine pity for the visitors who look at me with eyes that are goodness itself, who sympathize with me and who, with nothing else to say, murmur: "The main thing is patience. You must have patience."

Yes, of patience I have a great deal, but how does one go about making the long days go by faster?

Ya'acov Ha'elyon: The Wounds of War; *Ma'ariv,* 7.7.67

Physicians, medical assistants, nurses, volunteers, anybody who had tended the wounded, reported the same thing: the wounded never cried out in their pain. They were as brave on their stretchers as they had been on the battlefield. Sometimes it takes more strength to bear the lifelong wounds of the war than to fight in battle.

And if physicians and nurses alike were full of the wonders of the wounded, the latter could also tell a thousand and one tales about the courage and supreme devotion of doctors and medical orderlies, who performed their duties under enemy fire at the risk of their lives. Zahal has no medals, only commendations; and among the many candidates for those, there are quite a few members of the Medical Corps.

". . . I have seen the thunderous valor of the battlefield," said a worn-out white-haired doctor, "yet the quiet heroism you find in a military hospital is not inferior. The courage of a wounded soldier, bearing up under his pain with silent suffering, is not inferior to the courage of his comrade who, in the darkness of the night and under fire, crawled up to the fence and blew it up."

This is a military hospital in wartime—coagulated blood, broken bones, reddened bandages, a dangling shoe, a pierced shirt—red and white in a nightmarish mixture. Among them are the plasma bottles, the blood transfusion tubes, swaying stretchers, morphine injections, and nurses in white moving among heads of unruly hair and beards.

They reached the hospital on stretchers only when they had to. As long as they could keep on their feet, they made themselves temporary bandages and went on fighting with their units. Lieutenant-Colonel Moshe was hit by a bullet in the shin-bone while leading his armored brigade against Jenin. He went on fighting for the next two days until he met Commanding General David Elazar of the Northern Command. The General noticed his blood-drenched trousers and immediately ordered him to the hospital. There he tried to convince the doctors that he had to be back in half an hour. They tried to persuade him to stay, but he wouldn't listen. They finally administered local anesthesia and operated to remove the bullet. Half an hour later he was gone. He rejoined his brigade in time to participate in the assault on the Syrian Heights.

". . . Among our first casualties was a pilot named Ya'acov. He had been hit by a bullet in his instep. When we began taking care of him, he demanded that we be quick about it, because he had to be back with his unit. We tried to get him to stay and kept a sharp eye on him, but to no avail. He succeeded in sneaking out, then disappeared in one of the helicopters. Three days later he dropped in for a change of bandages. 'See,' he said, 'I told you I'd all right.' "

The wounded were put out with themselves for having had to leave their comrades to finish the job. "The wound becomes more irritating," said a young officer, "when I think of them fighting, while I am stretched out on a white bedsheet." A wounded kibbutz man was beside himself. "What a feeling! On Friday and Saturday, while the gang was fighting up north to protect my own kibbutz, my own home, I had to rot helplessly in the hospital and even listen to my praises—as though I were some unfortunate orphan!"

The doctors had a good deal to say about the behavior of the wounded. "I found it strange to see the serenity on the faces of scores of wounded about me. Some were severely wounded, and they had an idea of what was awaiting them. You try to soothe them, stroke their heads, and secretly you hope to hear some outcry of pain from them; a sob, a curse, some sign of suffering or at least some resentment—nothing! The nurses do all the sobbing. We never had such wounded, not in the War of Independence and not in the Sinai Campaign."

There was one wounded serviceman whom the hospital staff will never forget. His medical record reads: "Unit commander leading a charge on fortified target on Golan Heights was severely wounded in his jaw, face and neck and was in danger of suffocating. Tracheotomy was called for in order to prevent immediate death. It was impossible to lay him face down because of the severe wound in his jaw, and he therefore had to forego anesthesia. The operation was performed with the patient fully conscious, but despite the terrible pain he did not utter a single sound."

All the wounded made the same demands of the doctors: "Take care of my comrades first." "Doctor, let my hand alone! It's doing fine." "What about the others in the tank?" "Doctor, do what you have to and don't waste so much time thinking. I'll get by. Look at the long line behind me." "Look, doctor, I don't care how badly I'm hurt. I was their commander. Take care of them first, then you'll come back to me."

Said a young doctor: "There just aren't suitable words to describe the exemplary behavior of the wounded. I say this as a physician who handles similar cases every day. At times there were 25–30 wounded at the evacuation point, some of them quite badly, but there wasn't a sound to be heard. One of the orderlies had his forearm smashed by a shell. He lay quietly and wouldn't allow me to take care of him—not even to give him a morphine injection—until I had finished taking care of all the others. His forearm was later amputated. The orderly, Yedidya, begged me to see that he be allowed to return to his paratroop unit as soon as he recovered."

This fear—of being forced by the wound to transfer from a fighting unit to a supporting unit—is common among the wounded. A hefty paratrooper of 19, on crutches after having sustained a severe wound in his thigh, said: "I'm rejoining my unit as soon as they let me. If they down-grade my health rating and have me finish my service just as an ordinary soldier, I'll go crazy."

His commander, a paratroop lieutenant of 21 from Netanya, said: "I've always regarded the army as my career. I am an officer by profession, and my home is the paratroop brigade. If I remain disabled and they discharge me, I'll be through."

Another paratrooper was put out because he had been wounded, not in face-to-face combat with the enemy, but from a distance; an Egyptian MIG-21 hit him, in a dive, with a 20 mm. bullet. "You see," he said to his wife, in her fifth month of pregnancy, "the bullet tore through here"—he held up an X-ray—"for about nine centimeters. I was really lucky. The bullet went through the right side, not the left, where the heart is." The wife was not overjoyed, but thankful none the less.

A stroke of fortune also befell an armored corpsman of 20 from Kiryat-Ono. A sniper's bullet in El-Arish pierced his chest, a few millimeters away from his heart, and came out through the back. "It was really a bull's-eye to the heart," he remarked, "but I guess I was lucky. They flew me by helicopter from El-Arish to Tel-Aviv and operated on me, and here I am alive. Born again."

The wounded re-live the battles in the hospital. Nurses tell that even in their sleep they cry out the battle calls: "Forward! Attack them from the rear! I'm all out of ammunition! Hit them hard! Don't let them advance! Give it to them! They're running!"

They don't want praise. "Write about *them*—those wonderful doctors and nurses. How can they stay on their feet? They are the real heroes."

The courage of the doctors and their resourcefulness during battle is a chapter in itself.

The commander of an armored battalion had been badly wounded. Both of his legs were shattered. He had lost a lot of blood. When he was brought to the evacuation point it looked as though he didn't have the slightest chance of surviving. Dr. Martin Moses, in charge of the evacuation, realized that the wounded man would not reach the hospital in the rear alive. In order to save his life, something had to be done—immediately. Unfortunately, the blood bank at the evacuation point was empty. The doctor decided to take blood directly from the veins of a soldier-donor. In his satchel he found a plastic bag of anti-coagulation fluid. He attached tiny tubes to the soldier's veins, and the blood began to flow into the plastic bag. At the same time, the fresh blood began to flow from the bag into the tubes which the doctor had attached to the veins of the wounded man. After a few seconds, the officer began to revive. He recovered consciousness and was then taken to the hospital.

An impressive medical achievement was attained by a physician in an underground hospital in the north.

Several hours after the outbreak of fighting, a wounded soldier was brought to the hospital, unconscious from the loss of blood as the result of a shell fragment in his right thigh. The fragment had cut through the main veins and arteries. Dr. Amitai Barzilai, the surgeon, had two alternatives—to try ligaturing the severed vessels or to amputate the limb.

"This type of operation," explained Dr. Barzilai, "must be conducted under perfectly sterilized conditions and with special surgical instruments. In the bunker I had neither. I succeeded, in an operation lasting an hour and a half, in ligaturing the vessels, and the limb came back to life."

The wounded themselves reconstruct the action. "I was one of the men assigned to cut a path through into the enemy encampment. Fellows who go on these missions usually say that they don't know whether they would make it back. We cut through the barbed wire quickly. Four of us went through, and just as I was about to follow I was hit. The battalion was right behind us. The path ran right through a mined strip. I braced myself on the ground, and the fellows stepped on me and kept going. The commander later told me that more than a hundred pairs of feet had done that; nobody knew, of course, that I had been hit. I tried to reach for my canteen but couldn't manage it. Then I yelled for an orderly. He came, tore off my uniform, and brought a doctor to give me morphine. Everything became confused, but I remained conscious all the way to the evacuation point. A helicopter later took me to the hospital. I guess I'll be spending a few months in this cast. The doctor said one leg will always be shorter than the other. But it's alright. The main thing is we beat them."

An army doctor relates: "On the first day of the war, an ambulance arrived at the central hospital in Beer-Sheba with four soldiers inside. The driver said that three of them were badly wounded and the fourth was dead. I placed my stethoscope on the man's chest, as a matter of course, and was astounded to hear a faint beat. The soldier was taken immediately to the admitting room, was restored to consciousness, then taken to surgery, where both of his legs were amputated. Now he wants to know if we can help him play soccer again."

A well-known ophthalmologist can hardly hide his emotions. "The most outstanding examples are those set by men who sustain eye injuries. Young boys who lost one eye in battle told the doctors that they don't want to have an artificial eye; they'd rather wear a black patch like the Minister of Defense, so that everybody will know that they are Dayan's boys."

The most amazing story, without a doubt, belongs to Moshe Shar'abi, a 21-year-old teacher, of Rosh-Ha'ayin. Moshe is a Yemenite, dark and Arabic-speaking—two facts which saved his life. This is his story:

"We were charging ahead in a half-track toward Khan-Yunis. On the way we were halted by a tank to pick up a wounded officer. We bandaged him and took him up into our half-track. Our armored column had in the meantime gone on; we figured on catching up with it later.

"We had gone just a few meters when a hellish fire was opened on us from both sides of the highway. We had an 0.3 machine-gun, which suddenly stopped working, and a few Uzis. We kept firing until we ran out of ammunition. A shell hit the half-track and killed the driver. We kept changing drivers as we went on, until all of us were wounded and the half-track remained stuck in the desert, without ammunition, surrounded by the enemy.

"I decided to try to make it to the rear and bring up our tanks, which were following the half-tracks. I had a smoke grenade left. I threw it in the direction of an almond grove nearby, then made a dash for it. Bullets were still coming at me. I took off my uniform and buried it together with my tag and prisoner's card. I ran, in my underwear, without knowing where I was running. Suddenly I heard voices speaking Arabic, and I knew that I had stumbled on an Egyptian position.

"The Egyptian soldiers got a hold of me. I pretended to be in a state of shock. I heard the Egyptian officer say, 'He looks like a Sudanese; probably ran away from the Jews.' When the officer tried to revive me, I murmured: *'Ya akhai, ya akhai!'* This helped. They took me to a house and placed me in the hands of an old woman to bind my wounded thigh.

"I lay there for several hours. At night I heard our artillery and the echo of the battle of armor at the gates of the town. The old woman fled from the house, and I after her. I crawled back to the almond grove, rested a bit. My wound was very sore. Then I continued crawling until I reached the road. There I saw our armored columns, moving ahead. I stood up in my underwear, like an idiot, and yelled to the fellows. They thought I was an Egyptian and didn't pay any attention. Suddenly a half-track went by and somebody shouted: 'Stop! This is no Egyptian. He's one of ours. I know him.' So everything turned out alright. I'm still wondering how that fellow could identify me in my underwear, right in the middle of the desert!"

Eli Teicher: Wounded in Battle; 7.67

After the war the Israelis felt dazed, stunned, unable to believe what had happened in such a short time. The war had been too swift, and it was hard to grasp its significance so soon after it had ended. Nathan Alterman, one of the foremost Hebrew poets, wrote the following:

I. We should not say that "there are no words" to express what has happened during these days. There are words; and words are still the primary instrument for expression and thought. But they also seem to be blinking and pinching themselves, in order to be sure that they are speaking in a wakeful state and not in dream. Only little by little have they come to know that they are actually describing the situation as it is; and that they are not illusionary. Their confusion can be understood. The unique transformation, that which changed the situation from danger of destruction to incomparable salvation, has come about in less than a week. This was a war that was unprecedentedly swift, possibly increasing the difficulty of finding oneself amid this amplitude of all that Israel has achieved. Yet this speed, although it has left us breathless, was actually an absolutely necessary condition and the sole assurance of victory.

If victory was to come about, it had to be as swift as lightning. The world powers that supported us with kind words before the fighting would not have moved a finger on our behalf if we had become bogged down in prolonged battles, whereas the hostile forces would have done all they could in coming to the aid of the enemy.

And yet, while we now stand gasping at the speed of this war, let us not forget what lies between the hour before it and the hour after. Between one and the other stretch endless moments of highest effort and strength, strained to the utmost; a tank halting momentarily, then gradually and with incredible effort overcoming the obstacle in its way; soldiers rolling over and struggling with their enemies; the eternal seconds between the leap and the blood;

the harsh, ponderous movements of an all-out, tooth-and-nail fight. These things are not swift. The everlasting slow-motion character of these moments is what determines the speed of the struggle; and those moments have a common character, whether they are part of six days or part of a whole year. They constitute an absolute value. These are the eternal minute details out of which grew the sweeping surge. This we must remember in order not to begin viewing this terrible war, as time goes on, as though it were one single comprehensive leap which removed the threat of destruction from us with a wave of the hand. This we must know in order that we should always see the achievements of the Six-Day War in their proper perspective.

II. The point of this victory is not that it has restored to the Jews their most ancient and loftiest sanctities, all those places which are engraved in our memories, and in the depths of Jewish history more than anywhere or anything else. The significance of this victory lies in the fact that it has actually obliterated the distinction between the State of Israel and the Land of Israel. For the first time since the destruction of the Second Temple the Land of Israel is in our hands. Henceforth the State and the Land are a single identity; and what is now missing from this historic unification is only the People of Israel which, together with what is already on the spot, can weave "the threefold thread that cannot be snapped." If the gates of immigration continue to remain unused now as heretofore, this victory may remain a feat which has not yet become merged with the deepest roots of our history. For without this, the Land of Israel will remain the possession of Jewish rule but not of the Jewish People. For this reason, when we say that this victory gives us a position of strength for negotiating with the Arab States and the world powers, we must remember that, come what may, we also have to transform it into a position of strength for our negotiations with the Jewish People. The response of the nation to this great hour, and not merely a response of financial contributions, is a necessity, an inescapable condition for safeguarding the historical logic of these great days. This has to be the main thought and purpose of our efforts now and henceforth.

III. Along with the expanded time and spacious landscapes that have now been revealed to the people who dwell in Zion, another important and fundamental fact has become manifest. Our own face has been revealed to us in the mirror of these days. During this brief period the people displayed its visage not only to enemies round about but also to its own self. The storm of the times seemed to sweep all that was secondary and irrelevant from our image and essence, leaving only that which counted. And what counted was faith and discipline, and a quiet tense readiness, and a specific and practical and ready courage. These qualities were revealed clearly and strikingly everywhere; in the streets of the towns, in the hamlets and villages, in workshops and fields, at the front and behind the lines. This visage was also reflected in those pages of greetings to soldiers which were regularly printed in the press and which became an inseparable part of the news and the front-page headlines.

Seeing those pages, it was just as though the husks and shells surrounding the kernel had suddenly been removed and the true living tissue of the nation revealed—the vital tissue of ties and bonds, of apprehensions and loves and worries and nervousness and weariness, so tense yet quiet in the hour of trial. It was as though the top of a giant piano had suddenly been raised to show taut strings, whose throbbing is the throbbing of that stuff from which life is fashioned, from which nations and their histories are wrought.

Reading those pages of good wishes, you felt that actually the headlines in the papers describing assumed proposed steps and second-guessed meanings of this Prime Minister and that United Nations delegate were no longer important, possibly even less significant than the news the wife sends her husband that all is well with her and the children, and father is feeling better and everything is in order but they are longing for him and want him to write.

Reading this, you suddenly felt that as far as the security and life of our people was concerned, this was very probably the essential news. You felt that the difference between the statement by such and such a UN delegate and Mrs. Simona's information to her husband that grandma had come to live with them, or Violet (Segolit's) message to her fiancé that she was looking after the engagement ring and waiting for him, was in that such news is not transitory and is more reliable. This is material that does not spoil. From it all things are made: History, Language, Literature, Knowledge and Faith, Industry and Cities, Country and State. The character of the nation that has been revealed to us these days is one of the greatest sources of wealth that has come to us; and when we demand that the gains of the fighting should not be squandered, let us also bear this great asset in mind.

Nathan Alterman: A Situation Without Parallel; *Ma'ariv,* 16.6.67

For a few moments, for a few days after the fighting, people lived with the illusion that this had been the last war, and that it would be followed by the long-awaited peace.

Daddy, what did you bring us from the war?

I didn't bring anything—not a Russian rifle and not a Jordanian *kaffiyah* . . . not a commando knife nor a portrait of Hussein; no gold buttons and no insignia . . . not a transistor nor a camera; no American cigarettes and no playing cards . . . no bolts of silk cloth and not even a Syrian flag. No, I didn't bring any souvenirs. But I do have a story for you:

We had taken a village, and now our battalion was moving on. I was with the supply trucks, carrying ammunition, fuel, field rations.

On the outskirts of the village we caught sight of two figures, dressed in the green of enemy uniforms. We jumped down from the trucks. I cocked my rifle, hooked my finger around the trigger. We came near, running and weaving. Then I saw them . . . two scared children, staring into the muzzles of our guns.

I stood as if turned to stone. I barely heard the order to go back to the trucks. We continued on our way.

Many times my thoughts returned to what had happened to me. More than once did my imagination put you, my children, in the place of those two.

This was the only time, during the entire war, that I was about to shoot someone. I promised myself that if I come back to you I will bring you this story—and flowers. Here, then, take these flowers, in blossom despite the war.

Kibbutz Revivim Bulletin: War Flowers; 7.67

Chapter Ten

Summing Up

THE WAR ENDED SO QUICKLY THAT THE ISRAELIS HAD NO TIME TO think of a fitting name for it. The Minister of Defense, Moshe Dayan, suggested calling it "The War of Victory," but the name did not sound right to the Israelis, who were less concerned with the victory than with the ensuing peace. Perhaps it was because of a superstitious fear of the "evil eye," or because of the demands inherent in a name such as "War of the Sons of Light," mentioned by the Chief-of-Staff, that a prosaic and unassuming name like "The Six-Day War" became popular. After long debates, this was proclaimed as the official name of the war.

After six days of fighting and a week of elation and entranced feeling, the like of which the State of Israel had not known since its creation, it was possible to start reviewing summarily the lessons of the war, analyzing its development and its influence on the area and all of the world.

The Chief-of-Staff, General Yitzhak Rabin, discussed the lessons of the war and sketched out Zahal's plans for the future in an interview, the first granted after the war. The interviewer was Y. Livni, editor of Bamahane, *the Zahal weekly.*

Q.: Let us begin with the present and the future. Zahal now controls new territories, much larger in area than Israel itself. How is Zahal set up for the tasks which it must now carry out? How will quiet and order be instituted in the conquered areas?

COS: With the addition of areas acquired through the Six-Day War, we shall have to reconstitute ourselves in line with the new tasks. On the other hand, it should be borne in mind that the defense of Israel now requires less stringency than previously. The common borders with the enemy are shorter. The Jordanian border is today along the Jordan. The Egyptian boundary is today a natural and easily defensible line—the Suez Canal. We have also gained in depth—the whole expanse of Sinai, the West Bank, and the Golan Heights stretches. Obviously these are not boundaries which have been set by mutual agreement, nor have any relevant political decisions been made as yet. We shall therefore have to employ larger forces to defend them than in time of peace.

Q.: What do we propose doing in order to restore normal life in the conquered territories?

COS: The term "normal" is somewhat premature. Up to now we have been trying to re-establish, as quickly as possible, the daily life of the civilian population—its economy, public transportation, municipal structure, health services, water, electricity, food supplies—and to prevent confusion from entering into it.

Q.: Newspapers abroad have been accusing Israel of banishing Jordanian citizens and destroying residential areas. What is your comment?

COS: It should be remembered that a war has taken place. In the course of the war, and especially in areas of armed concentration, there were battles, destruction, flight of residents. At the same time, our forces received orders to be careful not to harm residents or their property.

Q.: Every army is faced with the danger of fighting a war in the pattern of the preceding war. How will Zahal avoid this?

COS: The recent war proved that Zahal was not preparing for it along the lines of the previous war. Indeed, this marks the philosophy of Zahal and all its commanders. Zahal arrays itself for the future. But before any step is taken in this direction, certain conclusions must be reached and tested, and certain questions must be answered. What is the probable "look" of the next war? Against whom are we likely to be fighting? With what means would the war be waged? And these matters always fluctuate. What had appeared perfectly clear three or four years ago did not hold true two months ago. What is true today may not be true a year or two hence. Zahal's uniqueness lies in its foresight and in the adaptation of its structure and concepts to developments. In this war, since no basic changes had taken place in the composition of the Arab armies, none was necessary in ours.

Q.: What, to your knowledge, is the nature of the unrest in the Egyptian army and of the stability of Nasser's regime today?

COS: Nasser is certainly in a much more difficult situation today than he was following the Sinai Campaign; he now cannot gloss over his defeat. This is why he faked a resignation before the populace and arranged "public pressure" to get him to rescind it. But he had to find a scapegoat, which he did—the Egyptian officer cadre.

Q.: Do you believe that the Egyptian army is the chief reason for Egypt's defeat?

COS: Not the army alone, although it was a determining factor. Nasser certainly based his decisions on his officers' evaluation of the ability of the Egyptian forces to carry out their assignments. It was therefore to be expected that he should dismiss the top echelon of the officers' cadre, beginning with his personal friend, Assistant Chief-of-Staff Amer, Egypt's only Field Marshal, down to commanders of air, sea and ground forces. In all, a wide stratum of the officers' cadre in all the services was purged. I am sure that the combination of a military defeat, extensive purges and economic depression, though not emanating entirely from the war, has created a situation which Nasser does not relish. He is certainly at one of the most critical junctures in his career.

Q.: Is there not a danger that Egypt will attack us again in the near future?

COS: In this war, Egypt was defeated in the air, on the ground, and, to some extent, on the sea. Its air losses were primarily in planes and not so much in pilots and maintenance men, without whom no modern air force can operate. On the ground, much Egyptian equipment was destroyed and many Egyptian soldiers fell in battle or were taken prisoner. It is true that, if Russia so desires, the Egyptian army can replenish, in a relatively short time, the stocks of equipment it has lost in the war—and this equipment may be even better than the other. But one cannot overlook the impact of the defeat on the morale of the Egyptian army. This time, the Egyptians cannot claim that they were the victims of a surprise attack. Egypt was all set for war. The shaken confidence of the Egyptian army in its ability to destroy Israel is a more important factor than its ability to rehabilitate itself in physical terms. The restoration of Egypt's military morale will take some time, to be measured not in months but in years—and many years at that.

Q.: What is known about the armaments now being airlifted from Russia to Egypt?

COS: The airlift has political and military aspects. Russia wants to stress its assistance to Egypt because Egypt's defeat was also Russia's defeat. The volume of the equipment is considerable, although it is far below that which Egypt had at the outbreak of the war. It is possible that the armaments it will be receiving will be newer and more efficient. We do have information that Egypt now has ground-to-ground missiles.

Q.: To what extent will the presence of Egyptian missiles affect the situation in the region?

COS: The advantage of the missile lies in its being independent of the human combatant. Instead of sending a plane into enemy territory, you fire a missile. Of course, this calls for a high degree of technical skill; on the other hand, a missile can be of great value to an army whose weakness lies in a lack of will to fight—missiles do not need morale. Now, as long as the missile is equipped with a conventional warhead, it is no more effective or accurate than a bomb released from a plane.

Q.: It is being said that the Russians will be much more involved in training the Egyptian army than they had been previously. How can this affect the level of the Egyptian army?

COS: The Russians have been having a hand in the intensive training of the Egyptian army for some time. For instance, all of Egypt's naval personnel received its training either in Russia itself or in its satellites, as did a notable part of the Egyptian command and air pilots, especially those flying late model planes. In addition, hundreds of Russian instructors and advisers of all kinds have been and still are active in both Egypt and Syria. Thanks to them, the Egyptian army was probably better than it would have been otherwise. On the other hand, since this activity has been going on for ten years, it may not make much of a difference. Even if the Russians were to have a direct hand in giving battle orders, there is still no guarantee that their orders would be properly executed. The chief test of an army in battle is not in issuing the right orders but, essentially, in carrying them out, down to the lowest ranks.

Q.: What about the Soviet military doctrine? Did it fail?

COS: Insofar as the Egyptians understand this doctrine, they followed it only in part. From the Soviet viewpoint, the defeat in Sinai did not disprove the Soviet doctrine of military deployment as much as it represented the loss of a ten-year investment in the Egyptian military structure. This investment went down the drain fast—the air force in three hours, the land forces in seventy-two.

Q.: What are the details of the booty which fell into our hands? How much of it will Zahal be able to use?

COS: The materiel which fell into our hands came from two sources. From Jordan we "received" Western equipment, while the Egyptian and Syrian materiel abandoned on the battlefields came from Russia and Eastern Europe. Some of the booty, such as construction materials, fuel and food can be used regardless of the source (although we would not consider giving all of the Egyptian rations to our soldiers—and *kashrut* is not the sole reason). As for Soviet arms, I think we shall be able to incorporate considerable quantities of artillery and vehicles. Should the number of salvaged tanks justify it, and if the spare parts we found in the larger depots be usable, we may absorb these into Zahal as well.

Q.: Only some of the prisoners we took have been exchanged for Israeli prisoners. What is the policy there?

COS: Israel's policy is to exchange prisoners with the Arabs. Since the Iraqi troops were stationed in Jordan, we held the Jordanians responsible for the return of the two pilots captured by the Iraqis. These two—the only ones captured by either Jordan or Iraq—were eventually exchanged for more than 400 Jordanians taken prisoner. As for Egypt and Syria, negotiations are still going on. Egypt has returned to us, until now, one prisoner, and we have been sending back wounded prisoners, unconditionally. We are holding 5,000 Egyptian prisoners as against eight Israelis in Egyptian hands. We have more than 400 Syrian prisoners, while they have one pilot of ours. However, Syria is still holding several Israelis whom she had abducted and imprisoned prior to the war. We regard these as part of the prisoner issue.

Q.: During the war and its aftermath many rumors were circulated, to the effect that one family had lost four sons in the war, that we had taken several Russian prisoners. How valid were these rumors?

COS: War times do give birth to rumors, and it follows that most of them are inaccurate. No family has lost four sons. Two families did lose two sons each. Zahal is not holding a single Russian prisoner. It is difficult to combat rumors, and it would be much better if we were to rely on official statements. We do not falsify facts.

Q.: Among the rumors circulated by the foreign press there was one which said that the Israel Air Force possesses a secret weapon.

COS: The Western press, especially the American, is inclined to look for a technological answer to every success which it cannot explain otherwise. Obviously, the excellence of IAF marksmanship and execution level was quite a puzzle.

Q.: Zahal's victory is being regarded by the world at large as the greatest and swiftest military campaign in history. You yourself stated, several days ago, that Jewish history has known no greater triumph. What, in your opinion, were the outstanding causes of such a decisive and smashing victory?

COS: The overall power of Zahal; the realization on the part of every soldier and civilian that "there's no alternative," and that the war would be not only over the Straits of Tiran but for plain, simple survival; Zahal's innate ability to carry through with the tasks presented before it; the ability of Zahal commanders to find solutions, in action, to problems as they develop; the low Arab fighting capacity, which has not improved noticeably since the Sinai Campaign, even though the Arabs had far more and better weapons.

Q.: Are there any other characteristics which set this war apart?

COS: This was the most important war in Zahal history. Never had Zahal produced so much power. Never had we put into the field such contingents of armor—in fact, the tank battles in Sinai overshadow the battles at El Alamein in the Second World War. I believe that this was the first war in which no task assigned to any unit remained unfulfilled. Many units achieved much more than their assignment called for. And there are few instances in warfare where the side which eventually triumphed won all the victories, in all the battles. In many respects this was a hard war, as witness our own losses and those of the enemy. Still we won, with speed which amazed the entire world.

Q.: How would you describe the part played in the war by the Israel Air Force?

COS: The IAF victory was fast and thorough. It created the basic conditions for the success of the ground forces in doing their jobs with incredible speed. Our air supremacy gave us freedom to maneuver, without fear of attack by enemy planes, and at the same time deprived the enemy of this advantage. Of course, it would have been impossible to reap full victory on the basis of air strength alone.

Q.: Analysts have stressed the role of the intelligence service in the war. Of course, the subject is generally avoided. Even so, can you say anything about it?

COS: It is a subject which is generally avoided.

Q.: Newsmen who visited the Syrian Heights were impressed by the fact that the fortifications there were stronger than the French Maginot Line. The Maginot Line was flanked but not broken through. How do you account for Zahal's ability to break through such fortifications and at such a pace?

COS: Since I haven't been at the Maginot Line I cannot make comparisons, but I can say that the Syrian defense layout was formidable, due to the combination of topography and the work put into the fortifications—concrete trenches, mines, pillboxes—tanks and artillery and all the rest. True, there were fortifications also at Rafiah and Um-Katef, including subterranean officers' clubs, but Syria had the advantage of topography. The fact that we were able to smash through this array was due to precise planning and, more important, the fighting spirit and diligence of our men. For example, Tel-Fahr on the Syrian Heights was attacked by a battalion of Golani troops. The battalion commander was killed and most of the company commanders had been wounded. Still the battalion fought on. The men followed unit commanders and fought on their own.

Q.: Were there any noticeable differences in the fighting levels of the three armies arrayed against Zahal?

COS: Comparisons are difficult because the circumstances in each of the sectors were not alike. I would say that all the forces we encountered were good in defense. The level dropped when the battle became mobile and initiative passed on to the lower ranks.

Q.: Recently the theory was advanced regarding the regularity of the re-occurence of war between Israel and the Arabs—a war every ten years. What is your opinion of this theory?

COS: In the first place, this theory is not new; I heard about it some time ago. It encompasses the riots of 1921–22, the disturbances of 1936–39, the War of 1948, the Sinai Campaign in 1956 and now the Six-Day War. So far, it is the past which has substantiated this theory. It carries no guarantee that the spacing of the repetition will hold in the future.

Q.: You call it the Six-Day War. Others call it the War of Victory, the War of the Sons of Light. No official name has as yet been given. Do you have any preference?

COS: I don't think that this war needs a special name. Those suggested until now—the War of Daring, the War of Deliverance—are too presumptuous. The simplest and most forceful is the Six-Day War, paralleling the six days of Creation. True, our six days have not been followed by a Sabbath of peace and rest; on the other hand, a new week is before us.

Y. Livni: From Kuneitra to Kantara; *Bamahane*, 5.7.67

President Nasser, on the other hand, had his own version of the results of the war. In a message to the nation, in which he also tendered his resignation (withdrawn the same day "bowing to the voice of the people"), the Egyptian ruler said, among other things:

Brothers, it has always been our custom, in times of victory and in times of stress, in the sweet hours and in the bitter hours, to speak with open hearts and to tell each other the facts, confident that through this alone we can always find our sound direction, however critical the circumstances and however dim the light.

We cannot hide from ourselves the fact that we have met with a grave setback in the last few days. But I am confident that all of us can in a short time overcome our difficult situation. To do this we shall need much patience, much wisdom and moral courage, and ability for devoted work.

We all know how the crisis began in the first half of last May. There was an enemy plan to invade Syria, and the statements by his politicians and all his military commanders frankly admitted it. The evidence was ample.

The sources of our Syrian brothers and our own reliable information were categorical on this.

Even our friends in the Soviet Union told the parliamentary delegation which was visiting Moscow early last month that there was a calculated intention. It was our duty not to accept this in silence. In addition to it being a question of Arab brotherhood it was also a matter of national security. Who starts with Syria will finish with Egypt.

So our armed forces moved to our frontiers.

Following this came the withdrawal of the United Nations force, then the return of our forces to the Sharm-a-Sheikh position which commands the Tiran Straits and which the Israeli enemy used as one of the results of the tripartite aggression on us in 1956.

The passage of the enemy flag in front of our forces was intolerable and so were other matters connected with the most precious aspirations of the Arab Nation.

Our estimates of the enemy's strength were precise. They showed us that our armed forces had reached a level of equipment and training at which they were capable of deterring and repelling the enemy.

We realized that the possibility of an armed clash existed, and we accepted the risk. There were several factors before us, nationalist,

Arab, and international. These included a message from President Lyndon Johnson of the United States which was handed to our ambassador in Washington on May 26, asking us for restraint and not to be the first to open fire, otherwise we would face serious consequences.

The same night, at 3:30 the Soviet Ambassador asked to see me urgently, and told me that the Soviet Government strongly requested we should not be the first to open fire.

On the morning of last Monday, June 5, the enemy struck. If we say now it was a stronger blow than we had expected we must say at the same time, and with assurance, that it was much stronger than his resources allowed.

It was clear from the very first there were other forces behind him which came to settle their accounts with the Arab Nationalist movement.

There were significant surprises:

1. The enemy we expected to come from the east and north came from the west. This showed he had facilities beyond his own resources and exceeding the estimate of his strength.

2. The enemy attacked at one go all the military and civil airfields in the United Arab Republic. This meant he was relying on something more than his normal strength to protect his skies from any retaliation from us. The enemy was also fighting on other Arab fronts with other assistance.

3. The evidence of imperialist collusion with the enemy is clear. It sought to benefit from the lesson of the former open collusion of 1956, this time concealing itself cunningly. What is now established is that American and British aircraft carriers were off the enemy's shores, helping his war effort.

Also, British aircraft raided in broad daylight positions on the Syrian and Egyptian fronts, in addition to operations by a number of American aircraft reconnoitering some of our positions. The inevitable result was that our land forces, fighting a most violent and brave battle, were inadequate in face of decisive superiority.

It can be said without fear or exaggeration that the enemy was operating an air force three times its normal strength.

This was also faced by the forces of the Jordanian Arab Army which fought a valiant battle under the command of King Hussein who, to be just and honest to him, adopted a fine attitude. I confess that my heart bled as I followed the battles of his gallant army in

Jerusalem and other positions on the western coast on a night in which the enemy and the powers plotting with him massed at least 400 aircraft to operate over the Jordanian Army.

There were magnificent and honorable battles.

The Algerian people and their great leader, Houari Boumedienne, gave without reservation to the battle.

The Iraq people and their loyal leader, Abdel Rahman Arif, also gave without reservation.

The Syrian Army fought heroically, supported by the forces of the great Syrian people and under the leadership of their nationalist government.

The peoples and governments of Sudan, Kuwait, Yemen, Lebanon, Tunisia and Morocco adopted honorable attitudes.

The peoples of the entire Arab nation, without exception throughout the Arab homeland, struck an attitude of determination; an attitude of insistence that Arab rights will not be lost nor will they dwindle, and that the war their defense would continue whatever the sacrifices and setbacks along the road of inevitable definite victory.

There were great nations outside the Arab world which gave us moral support which cannot be estimated, but the conspiracy was bigger and stronger. The enemy's concentration on the Egyptian front, to which it pushed all its main force of armor and infantry, was backed by an air superiority the dimension of which I have already described to you.

The nature of the desert did not permit a full defense, particularly with the enemy's air superiority. I realize that the development of the armed battle may not be favorable to us. I tried with others to use all resources of Arab strength. Arab petroleum played its part. The Suez Canal played its part. And there is still a major role required of Arabs everywhere and I am fully confident they will be able to perform it.

Our armed forces in Sinai had to evacuate the first defense line and fought their terrible battles with tanks and aircraft along the second defense line.

Then we responded to the cease-fire resolution following assurances in recent Soviet draft resolutions to the Security Council and following declarations by the French Government that no one could achieve territorial expansion as a result of the recent aggression, and in view of international public opinion, particularly in Asia and

Africa, which watches our position and feels the ugliness of the world-dominant powers which pounced on us.

We reach now an important point in this soul-searching by asking ourselves: Does this mean we do not assume responsibility for the consequences of this setback?

I tell you truthfully that I am ready to assume the entire responsibility. I have taken a decision with which I want you all to help me.

I have decided to give up completely and finally every official post and every political role and to return to the ranks of the public to do my duty with them like every other citizen.

President Nasser's Broadcast to the Nation: Israel Alone did not Defeat Us; 9.6.67

For all their efforts to find and publish any trace of a rumor which might prove detrimental to Israel, even the Russians could not believe the fantastic version of the events which Nasser tried to foist on the world after the debacle, according to which the Americans and the British helped Israel in the Six-Day War. The Israeli Intelligence Services scored an unparalleled coup when they succeeded in recording a radio conversation between Nasser, the Egyptian President, who tried to concoct together with the Jordanian King, Hussein, the story of the Anglo-American airplanes. The Israelis recorded and released the conversation held by both Arab leaders. The world listened and heard a classic example of political conniving.

In the primary stage Nasser checked the story with King Hussein in a radio-telephone conversation which was held on June 6 at 4:50 a.m. This conversation was recorded by Israel.

The result of the Nasser–Hussein conversation was apparent two hours later when Cairo Radio began to claim at 6:45 a.m. that foreign forces took part in the campaign on the side of Israel.

Hello, is His Majesty ready?

Hello, Amman, is His Majesty ready?

Hello, His Excellency, the President is ready.

How are you? I hear Your Majesty. The brother wishes to know if the battles are continuing all along the front.

(Questions and answers are missing.)

Yes. Should we also include the United States? Do you know about it? Should we declare that the US is participating with Israel?

Hello. I don't hear. The connection is extremely bad.

. . . Yes . . . Yes.

Hello. Good morning. Oh brother, no matter, be strong.

Yes, I hear.

Your Excellency, the President, if there is anything, or any idea . . . at any time . . .

We are fighting with all our strength in our battles on all the fronts all night and if there was something at the beginning, it's not important. At any rate, we shall overcome, Allah is with us.

Hello, let's say that the US and England or only the US?

The US and England.

Does England have aircraft carriers?

(Answer missing.)

Good. King Hussein will make an announcement and I will make an announcement.

Will His Majesty make an announcement concerning English and American participation?

(Answer not clear.)

Long live Allah! I say that I will make an announcement and you will make an announcement and we will see to it that the Syrians will make an announcement that American and English airplanes from aircraft carriers are fighting against us. We'll make an announcement, emphasize it and intensify it even more.

. . . Good. All right.

Does Your Majesty agree?

(Answer missing.)

A thousand thanks. Be strong and brave. We are with you with all our heart. Our planes are over Israel today; our planes are pounding the airfields of Israel since morning.

Be strong and brave—Amman.

A thousand thanks. Let there be peace.

Conversation between Nasser and Hussein: Radio-telephone Cairo-Amman; 6.6.67

Never have so many Israelis been busy writing so much as after the Six-Day War. People started writing poetry, songs, sketches, memoirs, long letters to the editors, in order to give vent to their feelings, to share with other people experiences which they thought unique. Even school-children—as usually happens after a momentous event—settled down to record their experiences. The following compositions were written by the pupils of the fourth grade of the Arnon elementary school in Tel-Aviv, and by the pupils of several grades of the

Luria school in Jerusalem. They prove one thing: the children grasped fully the meaning of the war.

"From the mouths of babes" and their immediate elders come these comments on the events and circumstances attending the Six-Day War, related and written in most styles known to literature—and a few besides.

Danit (Seventh Grade, Luria School, Jerusalem):

We stay close to the radio, hang on every word. Has it come? Tomorrow, says somebody; next week, say others. Never, perhaps. But this is too much to hope for. It must come, and everyone is tense. Let it be bad, horrible—but over with.

The war is here.

Shelling. Shooting. A darkened shelter. Children crying. Will we ever leave these shelters and return to normal life? The days before the war seem so far away, so strange. The little sister is told: Daddy has gone to defend the land. Daddy is strong, a hero. He will beat the Arabs. Will it really turn out that way, you wonder. And you worry, a great deal. Are we really that strong—to stand up to the armies of four Arab states? They are larger and more powerful. Daddy may never . . . no, heaven forbid! This cannot happen. God will not allow it.

Then—victory.

Out of the shelters and into the open air. You see the blue skies and the shining sun. You feel the breeze on your face, and you know it: We have won. We sing, we dance in the streets, we weep with joy. We tell one another: "We have won! We have won!" The heart still questions, but the mind has no doubts; the blue and white flags on the buildings bear joyful testimony.

You recall the war, only a few hours ago, and you rejoice. Now you can go anywhere and not be stopped by barbed wire and the threatening yellow sign: "Halt—the border is before you!"

You look about. The Old City, Hebron, Bethlehem—all ours! You can ride and ride and still be inside the boundaries of Israel. It's wonderful! You try to understand how this miracle could have happened. Then, bursting with joy, you run toward the tired, begrimed man coming slowly up the street. "Daddy!"

Later we think of those who won't be embracing their wives and children and whispering: "We have won!" Those who won't see this day of victory and will never be aware of it. They will lie in their graves, cold and lonely, and we shall keep telling them: "We want you to know that we have won—because *you* have won."

Tammy (Seventh Grade, Luria School, Jerusalem): The war as seen by my five-year-old sister.

Yael comes home from kindergarten. "Mommy, Bathsheba said the Arabs won't let us pass."

"That's right, dear. Now go to your room."

"Tammy, why won't the Arabs let us pass?"

"Don't know. Be quiet. I'm doing homework."

Yael broadcasts the news. The Arabs won't let us pass. Bathsheba brought paper and pasted it on the windows. They took the big door out of the shelter. Why did they all of a sudden put the new mattress into the scary storage room?

"Shmulik, my father is a soldier."

"O.K. So what?"

"Your father is not. Mommy, how come they took Daddy? Sharoni's daddy is still here."

"Don't you want your Daddy to be a hero?"

"I do, but I—I don't want them to take Daddy."

"Silly girl," laughs Shmulik (he's six). "You say yes, you say no."

Mommy lowered all the windows and bought candy. Ophra said they took her daddy, too. Bathsheba says the Arabs won't let us pass.

Today there was a big "boom," right in the middle of the kindergarten. Then there was another "boom" and another. Bathsheba said, "Woe is to anyone who goes out." She said the Arabs were shooting. "Why are they shooting?" "Because they are bad."

Bathsheba put sacks on the windows. The door opened and a tall man came in. He said something to Bathsheba, and Bathsheba said we should go home. "Run! Quickly!"

Mommy was waiting in the hallway.

It was dark in the shelter. Shmulik was there, and Sharoni and Yossi. Mommy gave me my Ruthie Doll and a cookie. She asked me: "Are you afraid, Yael?"

"No . . . where's Daddy?"

"In camp."

"Where's Tammy?"

"In school."

"And the Arabs?"

"They are in their own countries."

"Then how are they shooting?"

"They can. Bullets fly very far."

It's dark in the shelter. Bullets all the time. But I'm not afraid!

Tammy comes. "Tammy, I have my Ruthie Doll."

I can't go out. I must not climb on the mattress with my shoes on. I must not hit Shmulik. I must be a good girl—not make any noise. No running, or you will fall down. Don't open the door. We sleep on the sloping mattress and keep sliding down all the time. Mommy tells me to take off the skirt and put on slacks, to keep warm.

Miriam says: "Oh, Ethan!"

"Mommy, why does Miriam talk that way??"

"She is worried about Ethan."

"Mommy, Sharoni is pushing me and won't let me sleep."

"Sharoni, you're going to get it."

"She's pushing me, too."

The Arabs are shooting and the children have to stay in the shelters. Daddy is a soldier. He's shooting at the Arabs.

"Mommy, what if they shoot at Daddy?"

"No, they won't shoot at him." Then she talks a lot to Miriam. She doesn't talk to me at all. Tammy all of a sudden becomes good and tells me a story. Maybe she is afraid. Why are the Arabs shooting? Because they are bad. But why are they shooting? Mommy kisses me and says that we captured Sinai and Hebron and Gaza and Bethlehem . . . Where's Sinai? What does capture mean? This "boom-boom" makes me mad.

All of a sudden we are sleeping in the house. Daddy comes and goes away. All day we make tea for the neighbors. They all come and they laugh. Mommy sighs sometimes, and Miriam worries about Ethan.

"Mommy, I don't want to stay in the house . . . Why can't I? It's all right now."

"Daddy will be here soon," says Tammy.

"I wasn't talking to you!"

Mommy says that now the Arabs are letting us pass.

Nurit (Seventh Grade, Luria School, Jerusalem):

Now it is here—the war which has been hanging in the air for such a long time, about which so much has been said and thought, which always seemed so strange and far away. Strange that it should have started. It doesn't sound like any war we have read about.

We sit in the shelter with the others. We feel like one family; there is a warm atmosphere. Outside it is dark, and we can hear the shelling. The little children have a game; they call it "Let's Say There's a War Going On." The sky is full of stars. The street is silent and empty, a rare experience.

The horizon glows with shells. There is a slight breeze. Tension is in the air. Everyone is huddled about the transistor. The newscaster repeats the same news.

It is frightening to think that there can be someone whom we shall never see again.

Nahum Eisenthal (Fifth Grade, Bar-Ilan School, Tel-Aviv).

A person undergoes many happenings in his life, but there are occasions which deserve to be called "historic moments." The soldiers, the nation, the Jewish people abroad, all as one waited for it with the trepidation of sanctity. Then it came, like an unfolding miracle: "Old Jerusalem is in our hands!"

Victory can be of many kinds.

There is a victory that arises from technical superiority, good organization, resourcefulness and understanding. And there is a victory of the heart. The deep yearning of nation and individual for the triumph of historical justice. The crown has been won—Jerusalem, the crown, is ours, and in it are the pearls of our ancient and eternal crown: Bethlehem, Rachel's Tomb, Shechem, Hebron and the Cave of Machpela. Gibeon, Anatot and Samaria are ours.

We have indeed shown that "not by might, nor by power, but by My spirit, said the Lord of Hosts."

Dubby Cutler (Ramla):

The radio fell silent and everything grew still, but I could not be calm as I thought about Zahal's magnificent victory.

I found it strange that our little land of Israel could overcome the Arab countries. I always found it hard to imagine—it is like a legend—that the few can triumph over the many. I am therefore happy that I have been privileged to see it come to pass.

Ayal (Seventh Grade):

Suddenly it grew quiet. The plums in the yard were the only ones happy about it; the birds no longer peck at them. Mama says that birds always fly away from a war. Mama always knows what she is talking about.

I remember what she said a week before it began. "This time we won't be led away as lambs to the slaughter." Of course not, but I still saw fear in her eyes. She was again picturing to herself the evil days under the Nazis.

It was still peaceful in the house, at first. Dad was still home, but I could feel the tension in the air. On Saturday there came a knock on the door. We all looked at Dad. When Mama came back with the call-up notice I could see a tear in her eyes. Dad didn't sleep home that night.

In the morning, I saw Mama with the big kitchen knife in her hand. Her face looked as though it was saying: "Good, let them come!" Mama is not a heroine, but once was enough for her. She didn't run, like the others, to buy a kilo of flour.

Outside, the women were building a big shelter. We went to help them. Better be prepared.

Dad came home on leave Saturday and said we might not need the shelters. I hoped he was right.

Monday. Suddenly everything was still. Mama began crying. I knew that the war had come. The air raid sirens began wailing. The radio said they had started it. They probably don't understand that here it isn't Germany. They don't know that we are not frightened Jews but Israelis. This time they will know.

Now the plums in the yard are having trouble again. The birds are back.

Collected by Uri Oren: Children and the War; *Yediot Aharonot,* 9.7.67

The feelings of the Israeli public were mixed: joy over the victory, and apprehension because of the possible developments in the international arena; regrets for the great days which were passing so quickly, and reluctance to go back to the ordinary, daily life.

It really doesn't take much to win a war—ask anyone who has a first-rate army, A-1 fliers, an on-the-ball intelligence, armor trained razor-sharp, a top-level officers' cadre, the ultimate in weapons, a magnificent fighting spirit and other such inconsequential details. To be the victor, on the other hand, is a much more complicated matter; for this, you must have nerves of steel. You'd expect that victory would bring an end to all problems. We have won, vanquished, conquered—that's it! We should be able to go home and take it easy. But here we are, our brow crowned with victory, yet our troubles are just beginning—refugees, world powers, the UN, finances; problems are zooming about and at us like those monstrous Sinai flies.

It's simply not fair. Only a month ago we were the noble candidates for annihilation, and the entire world was with us, on our side. Now that we chose to reject annihilation (for purely selfish reasons), the esthetes are beginning to grumble: "Fooey, it's not nice to win. Only the brute are strong, the militarists are ever victorious. Our hearts go out to the weak, to poor Hussein, to confounded Nasser, to the face-losing Arab states."

We shall have to adapt ourselves to this sorry state of being a winner. The world was all agog (it didn't do much, but exceedingly agog it undeniably was) while threats hung over our heads, but as victors we blundered into a category which does not draw political solicitude. People might acknowledge us, perhaps accord us respect, but no longer will they pinch our cheeks and fondly call us *bubbah-leh* (baby-doll).

We cannot deny it. For two weeks it was a pleasure to read the foreign press, the heart-warming articles about David's joust with Goliath, the informally dressed people's army, heading for the front in commercial vans smeared with mud, the marvellously disciplined restraint on the part of the home front, the cultural life going on midst the shelling. We had just about convinced ourselves that we were, indeed, the favored child of the Western World. Then, disaster! With this businesslike victory of ours we have ruined everything. Perhaps we had made a blunder by winning so quickly, so decisively. Psychologically it might have been much better, more refined, to have barely managed to scrape through.

We shouldn't take it to heart if political columnists the world over have become disenchanted with us. The press has an ironclad rule: When too many people voice the same opinion (let us say, hypothetically, that Israel had fought a glorious war), it must necessarily follow that the international commentators, each viewing the situation through his personal prismatics, should disagree with the facts. Real newsmen don't follow the beaten path, lest their readers stop reading their material. After a week of unbridled enthusiasm, the time came for thoughtful reservations: "Yes, but . . ."

On the other hand, were we now in Nasser's power, with *fedayyeen* running wild in Tel-Aviv, what a wave of sympathy would be ours! Our children would have been compassionately evacuated overseas. Those of us still sufficiently alive to receive mail would be enjoying food parcels, vitamin pills and instant coffee sent from abroad. Conquered Israel would be tendered eulogies such as no country, RIP, had ever received in the annals of mankind. We would be like Republican Spain; everybody simply adored her and wrote the most touching stories about her, even though the pacts and trade agreements were being signed with Franco.

Moreover, had Nasser conquered Israel, he would, no doubt, have behaved in the finest traditions of Mother Russia, that outstanding example of largesse on the part of a conqueror. The *fedayyeen* would have distributed candy in military hospitals, *El-Fatah* members would have put on benefit shows for "Malben" Rehabilitation of the Elderly Association, not a hair of the Finance Minister's head would have been harmed, and within a matter of days the Egyptian dictator would have withdrawn to his previous boundaries—but not before he had visited the Holocaust Cellar on Mt. Zion and toured the kindergarten network of the Working Mothers Association.

Our trouble is that we are primitive barbarians. It is only days since we won the war, and already we are shying away from living under threat and danger. A truly cultured people would have shown greater understanding. We *know* that we are the winners. Why should we not let Nasser have a bit of gratification by announcing that the whole thing was an error in cartography and proceed immediately to evacuate the area in favor of the really valorous Egyptian troops? (Incidentally, in the Gaza Strip, they still have left over a few arches of triumph commemorating their victory in the Sinai Campaign.) We can also state that what looks from the plane window over Mitla Pass like a Flit-hit column of ants is really not the twisted wreckage of Egyptian half-tracks, tanks and vehicles, but an immense traffic jam caused by the malfunctioning of the signals at the crossroads; after all, such jams do happen. Yes, if we would only be able to restore Nasser's prestige, he would readily and willingly grant free passage through the Suez and the Straits of Tiran—if not to our ships then at least to De Gaulle's.

This victory is not all sheer enjoyment. We are especially adept when it comes to absorbing blows. Disasters—we are Ph.D.'s in being the victims, having been marvellously trained in the art over a two-millenia semester. But to be the *victors* in a *war*—fooey, it doesn't even sound Jewish. For generations our lives were measured by curfews, our movements were restricted, our houses were ransacked—and suddenly we have become rulers and governors. Were we to act in accordance with the universally-loved Jewish heart, we would say to the Arabs in the Gaza Strip and the West Bank: "Look, dear friends, we don't enjoy this business of being your governors; we have enough Jewish troubles of our own. Stop hating us, and everything will turn out well. We are an amenable people, more amenable (any way you look at it) than the Russians or the Chinese, whom you adore. That much we can guarantee. We have hospitalization, milk stations, free-of-charge compulsory education, national insurance, social services, trade unions, WIZO, solar heat tanks, gas ranges, insecticides, a Philharmonic Orchestra—whatever you want is yours, but please, *please,* make peace with us and do not hate us more than is absolutely necessary."

War is cruel to everyone involved. War is blood and suffering and wrecked dwellings and dead poultry strewn about disintegrated yards. War is the sickly sweetish smell of bodies rotting in the sun. War is bullet-riddled cars and looted stores. War is many hard and evil things, but when all is said and done, war can be nutshelled into four words: Kill or be killed, and no victory in war has ever been achieved with white silk gloves. And now that we have come out of it alive, we would like to remove, as quickly as possible, all traces of this war, to beat swords into spades and melt down cannon into sculpture, to make peace with the Arabs, rehabilitate the refugees. Instead, we must prepare for renewed struggle and pressure and rearmament on the part of the Arab states. On my word, if this dawdling peace ever does get here, it should be roundly punished for reporting late.

In the days of preparedness, each of us was a military strategist, with a power of perception which somehow evaporated when the actual fighting began. When it was over, we became political analysts. We assumed the burden of Israel's future personally, each of us carrying it on his back as though it were his exclusive problem. We took it for granted that the Foreign Ministry was waiting, with bated breath, for our solutions to the refugee problem and our advice on international relations. We flooded press editors with sage epistles; we published declarations and statements as paid advertisements; we circulated petitions, pulled strings and used connections—instead of stretching out on the grass, looking up at the sky through the treetops, dreaming golden dreams and leaving everything else to our man at the UN.

If, some thousands of years hence, an archaeologist (should such still exist) will unvault the hidden records of the UN, he will never believe that this State of Israel, which had kept the UN busy throughout most of its lifetime—year after year, condemnation after condemnation—was just a flea on the globe. Aside from the big names who come to the UN when the occasion calls for their presence, there sit, in that international glass cage, thousands of UN professionals through whose frames the mere mention of the words "Israel" and "the Middle East" sends a horrendous shudder. These words conjure up the same speeches in agonizing variations, sessions on end; the same charges and counter-charges, the same impotent decisions, the same convolutions of rhetoric, the same squabbling in the corridors. Why should this be so? The globe is large and spacious, even without outer space. Upon it are important and exotic countries, replete with natural wonders and interesting customs—still the UN must chew the cud called Israel, year after year! O peoples of the world, spare these UN servants, these guardians of mankind's last hope! Forget Israel! Take it off the agenda. Give other nations a chance; let *their* entrails be turned inside out, and let *their* lives be internationally regulated. Really, we are not selfish.

In this past month, our way of life has turned a new corner. We can still continue with this new direction. We are still like artificial snowflakes in a glass ball; someone shook us and we go on floating in the air. As yet we have no desire to sink back into routine, to do things in an orderly and considered fashion, to keep an appointment diary and live according to the clock. Now is the time for decisive exuberance—change living quarters, switch to another job, settle in the Old City, set up a kibbutz on the West Bank, open a snack bar at Sharm-a-Sheikh—things we never thought we'd do—so long as we keep going, as long as the sparks keep flying.

The willingness to run risks, which led us to victory, is an aspect of Israeli character which must contend with another aspect—the tendency toward "showing-off." It is difficult to reconcile the two—the readiness to sacrifice your life when the call comes and the timidity of everyday life. It's unthinkable to say: For six days don't give a hoot about your lives, but on the seventh and thenceforth be sure to cross the road carefully, halt your car at all intersections, swim only where a lifeguard is present. The Council for the Prevention of

Traffic Accidents and the other agencies which try to teach the Israelis the rules of caution and safety will have to augment their efforts, because this war has penetrated into our marrow.

Still, "Kol Yisrael" has gone back to its regular schedule; newscasts are back at the old intervals, beginning at six and ending at eleven. Parking on Rothschild Boulevard is again unavailable, hitchhikers within city limits don't get lifts (unless they are in battle fatigues and look very tired). Again people bake cookies and stop to window-shop, give house parties and go to the beach, and life begins to draw away from the days which had given it history. You feel like embracing those six days, rough and translucent like chunks of diamond with every hour imbedded in them, the wild heartbeat and the body stretched taut as a cord, the sleepless nights and the dizziness of victory, the pride you had that you were here, in Israel, and nowhere else, and *now*, not sixty years ago nor eighty years hence. You want to pry them away from the cycle of days, so that they remain exclusive and do not vanish, that they stay with us, always within arm's reach, that they should not be buried under the dust of time, that they remain as pure as they once were.

We may have flown over Sinai and visited the West Bank and climbed the Golan Heights and convinced ourselves that they are indeed in our hands, but we haven't yet grasped the new map. Only the small things refer to the new reality—the forecast of weather at Solomon's Gulf and the Sinai Desert, direct dialing to the Old City, the train going to Gaza, the ride to Jerusalem via the Latrun highway, names of places like Bir-Gafgafa and Kuneitra rolling off our tongue like Raanana or Gedera, a dip at Coral Beach beyond Eilat, a snap decision to hop over to the Western Wall, for just a few minutes.

We never had it so good. We were here, right in the middle of things. Those to be pitied were the friends and relatives elsewhere. They almost went out of their minds—and Jews are proficient worriers all the way down the line—as witness the frantic cables, letters, telephone calls, flight tickets (one-way) for the children. In normal times, Diaspora Jewry may be short-tempered with us for being Levantine or provincial, too pious or not sufficiently so, show-offs and rude of behavior, for charging too much for hotel accommodations and for the low level of our restaurants, but when danger loomed they realized that, without this pesty, irritating, tremendously expensive Israel, world Jewry would lose its props, its self-respect, its hobby and its pride.

The war has done away with many things other than certain Arab ambitions. The Canaanite separatist cult is gone; we are bound to world Jewry, and world Jewry is bound to us; this is now the cardinal point of Jewish existence. Oh yes, host countries where Jews now abide may remind them, should evil times come along, of their having placed Zion above all other considerations. They will say: "We told you so—it was an international Jewish plot" or "It happened because of Jewish pressure on the rulers of the world." What may seem to us as the shining hour of Jewry may in time be interpreted negatively, for anti-Semitism has many faces, Slavic and Chinese, intellectual and votary, nationalistic and socialistic.

Right now it's wonderful. No spirit of Tashkent, no illusions, no mouthings of brotherhood. We can call the Soviet Union anything we want—anti-Semites, cynics, imperialist war-mongers—and even the leftist leadership won't rebuke us. And we can listen with equanimity when people call us Nazis, militarists, criminals, murderers. We can take all this guff, especially when those who dish it out are themselves acknowledged masters in these arts. But to call General Haim Herzog a *Gauleiter*—for heaven's sake! If he is the *Gauleiter* type, then what they have in Russia is genuine socialism . . .

Ruth Bondy; It's Hard to be Victorious; *Dvar Hashavua,* 23.6.67

The concern for the safety of the State of Israel and its security coincided with the proclamation of the victory and the onset of the cease-fire. Thousands of letters flooded the editors, each of them suggesting the best possible solution for the problems the State was facing; advertisements by groups of citizens, urging the Government not to give back an inch, or else to give back everything; articles by hundreds of people who were not professional writers, analyzing the situation created when the fighting ended, and debating in periodicals and newspapers the future of the State. All of these gave clues to the deep apprehension of the citizens of the country: Shall we be able to win the peace?

Physics Professor Yuval Ne'eman, who served during the Six-Day War as a colonel in the Intelligence, published an article in Ma'ariv *after his return to his scientific work. In this article, he lucidly exposed some of these feelings.*

I have just taken off my uniform. From now on I shall be free again to engage in Physics as much as I like. But it is hard to make the transition. These were tense days in which I was one of thousands of reservists called up to defend their country. My scientific work, on the other hand, is so abstract and requires a contemplative mood, intense concentration and therefore complete isolation from one's surroundings. For three weeks all my thoughts have dwelt upon the problems arising from the need of safeguarding the People of Israel and their State. First I had to span the information gap which had developed during the seven years that had passed since I last participated in this permanent concern. My comrades in uniform, who had continued to bear the burden of defense all the time, extended a helping hand. After a while I was able to contribute my share in the effort. Now, before retiring once again into my scientific ivory tower, I feel it my duty to sum up several lessons. I have to warn my fellow citizens and describe the dangers lying ahead during the days of peace that will follow this War of Our Resolution.

In a piece of research which I did some fifteen years ago, I made the following observation. The first time the Arabs as an organized body tried to liquidate the Zionist enterprise by force was in the Disturbances of 1920 and 1921. They tried again in 1929. Their third attempt was made in the years 1936–39; and the fourth in 1947–48. In all these cases the intervening periods were spent in licking wounds, forgetting defeats, reorganizing and regrouping one's forces. These intervals all lasted about nine years. I added the same period to 1948 and got 1957 for the next onslaught. Sure enough, in October 1956 the organization of the Joint Arab Command was completed with Egypt in charge and Syria and even Jordan coming under it. It's declared purpose was the destruction of Israel. On October 29th., 1956, we set out to strike at Egypt and succeeded in dispelling the threat just before the general Arab offensive could materialize. In 1964 when General Rabin was appointed Chief-of-Staff, I sent him a brief message of congratulations from Pasadena in California, where I was staying at the time. I reminded him that on the same calculation, the next war could be expected to occur during his period of office. I wrote that I was especially pleased that he should be in charge. Note that with this nine-year interval, hostilities should have broken out early in 1966. The war in Yemen interfered with the sequence and led to a delay. I was beginning to believe that the series might break after all. It turns out, however, that all the Yemen War did was to extend the interval by slightly more than a year.

This is why I can't help but think of 1977. Will the process continue so that we shall then have to face the same threat once again? Or is it possible, in spite of everything, to break the sequence altogether—or at least to decelerate and settle for longer periods of peace—like in the times of the book of Judges when "the land was quiet for forty years?"

Let us not delude ourselves into thinking that the apparatus which sets off these regular bursts of animosity is going to run down naturally, through some falling-off in hatred and in the will to wipe us out. Anybody who wants to believe in a "spirit of Tashkent" should be given the facts. The prospect for a fading away of Arab animosity is roughly the same as were the prospects for a weakening in the Antisemitism of Eastern Europe about a generation ago. In the early stages, to be sure, the conflict between the Arabs and ourselves represented a clash between two nationalities that had crystallized in the same geographical region and had repelled one another; but nowadays the situation is different. The Arabs have undergone a process of sublimation of their enmity. Instead of considering us as a circumstantial enemy or a dangerous neighbour, they have come to regard us as a sub-human (and occasionally super-human) factor which must be destroyed by all means, like some dangerous bug. The Arabs now hate us bitterly, and the ideologic basis of this hatred is expressly based on the Antisemitic theses of the last century and the days of the Nazis: On the Protocols of the Elders of Zion (a bestseller in Egypt) and the Jewish domination of the world (Capitalism when speaking of USA, Communism in speaking of USSR). Jews are loathsome on the one hand and demonic on the other. In these circumstances the sheep can come to terms with the wolf only at the cost of their lives.

The only prospect for an effective, lasting peace lies in the creation of conditions that will deprive the Arabs not only of the possibility of overcoming us but also of any hope of doing so. The Arab's arrogance, their capacity for self-delusion, their lack of discrimination between the word and the deed, all these easily lead them to an incorrect assessment of ratios of strength and make them eager to assault us even when they really have no prospect of achieving our destruction. Their's not the bravery of a David prepared to do battle with some Goliath. It is the self-excitation, almost the spontaneous combustion, of nations and leaders who are more than certain of their own superiority. They love to mention numerical ratios, and recently they have been repeating the refrain of the "hundred million Arabs" who will sooner or later overcome us—disregarding their actual weakness, all the time. Whenever Arab power increases and displays some numerical superiority, they convince themselves that they are indeed in a position to attack and exterminate us, and we witness such sudden hostile acts as the closing of the Straits of Tiran and the recent threat.

The natural strategic frontiers which have come about as a result of this War of our Resolution can break the vicious circle. As compared with the former situation, where the Egyptians could freely brace for a leap straight into the heart of Israel, they will henceforward have to contemplate first a crossing of the Suez Canal, the setting-up of a bridge-head on its eastern bank, and an advance across the Sinai Desert. Only then can they re-establish a base which will permit them to threaten Tel-Aviv in the next phase of their offensive. If we retain some armour and air forces in Western Sinai, we can prevent these initial phases or delay them enough to remove every prospect of the threat materializing. An operational depth such as we have never known before has now been established on every side. There is no longer any reason to fear the development of another such hair-raising situation in which a large enemy force (Jordanian with the addition of some Iraqi, Egyptian, Saudi or Syrian Expeditionary Force) might establish itself amid the Mountains of Ephraim and so directly threaten Jerusalem or Tel-Aviv, as well as possibly cut the country in two. After all, the Iraqis almost made it to the ridge this time. The Gaza Strip and the El-Arish oasis on the one hand, and the Triangle and the Hebron Mountains on the other—these bases, which have been in the enemy's hands ever since the War of Independence, have constituted the gravest danger for the existence of Israel. Together with the geographical weaknesses of the old Armistice lines, the narrow corridors of the Coastal Plain and the Jerusalem Approaches, the fact that Jerusalem and Tel-Aviv were on the border itself—all these facts *constituted an invitation for aggression*. For anybody nursing a powerful destructive urge, there could be no reason to refrain from fulfilling such a dream. How could they resist the temptation to hit at a state which looked as if it could so easily be carved in two, and whose centres could so lightly be crushed.

Depriving the Arabs of these bases and setting up an appreciable operational depth in all directions, ended their excuse for aggressiveness, an excuse which was formerly offered by Israel's impossible and artificial geography. Moreover, the frontiers now held also offer prospects of liquidating the one painful human problem which was exploited against us: That of the Refugees. We are now in a position to organize their orderly migration or to settle them in empty areas as we decide.

Hence the preservation of our military-cum-geographical gains is vital for our future. In order to prevent a repetition of the menace and losses we must now fight our political campaign as skilfully as the military one, and with an identical readiness for sacrifice. We have to be prepared for condemnations at UNO, sanctions, the breaking-off of relations, expulsion from UNO, etc. It will all be worth while if we can succeed in consolidating our gains. What is more, we may quite possibly succeed in preventing the worst of these blows by skilful political manoeuvering. It will lean upon the facts we have created in our reaction to the aggressor, upon our strength and upon the absolute bankruptcy of the political substitutes. The UN Force, international guarantees, demilitarized zones—none of these were able to safeguard our right to pass through the Straits of Tiran and certainly not our right of passage through the Suez Canal. Of course they did not prevent the onslaught on our frontiers. Indeed, the Jordanians chose to attack right through a dimilitarized zone. There is no solution for safeguarding our maritime rights except through our military hold on Sinai. Any and every factor in the world which may wish to prevent the renewal of the crisis that began on May 23rd, will have to accept our continued presence in Sinai for a long time to come.

There will be however another decisive factor upon which much will depend in these fateful developments—the robustness and stability of our political leadership. We won the war after our public opinion compelled the Government to alter its composition. The entry of Dayan and Begin into the Government were an injection of strength and a directive on the part of the people to their Government to choose the most daring solution.

It is now often stressed that we gained much good-will in the world thanks to the dreadful waiting period of the crisis weeks. It is true that since the war has ended as it did end, we may as well congratulate ourselves on those weeks of waiting. What has not been said is that were it not for the overwhelming pressure which came from all parts of the public, that waiting period might have lasted until this very day and could have ended with moral, political and practical bankruptcy for which the Minister for Foreign Affairs would have borne the main responsibility. Anybody who claimed as he did that it was worth waiting for the maritime powers' actions, was actually hiding behind the fine-sounding words and ensuring that nothing effective would be done to open the Straits of the Gulf of Eilat while at the same time risking our very existence. Fine words and logomachy dominated the Government and led to shameful votes.

Now that the fighting is over, a campaign has begun to stress the marginal value of Dayan's entry into the Government. After all, the country and army were ready, and what could he have accomplished in two days? I shall try to shed a little light on this subject, although it is hard to go into details for obvious reasons.

To begin with, there is no room to confuse the functions of the Minister of Defense with those of the Chief-of-Staff. The General Staff worked wonders. I am convinced that the Israeli Army is the best in the world. At the top level, all Chiefs-of-Staff in the past contributed to this; three of them did in particular, namely, Yigael Yadin, Moshe Dayan and Yitzhak Rabin.

Yadin established the framework according to which the Army was shaped and organized, after growing like a weed out of the "Hagana" during the War of Liberation. Dayan built up its wonderful fighting tempo, based on commanders who were trained to exhaust their objectives to the utmost. I remember a Meeting of Commanders held in 1953 following a number of failures in retaliatory operations, the last of which, at Falameh near Kalkilya, was the most disappointing of all. Then it was that Dayan, who had at the time been appointed Head of the "G" Division, began his educational campaign towards a hard-punch army. This is the kind of army, imbued with a sense of mission and readiness for sacrifice, in which the Commander marches first and thereby ensures the speed and drive which characterized the Sinai Campaign and the Six-Day War. Dayan directed the Israeli Army towards a fighting objective, renouncing all activities such as absorbing immigrants, operating hospitals, etc., which were of much benefit for the State, but diverted the Army from its principal purpose.

I saw the Israeli Army in operation after having been away for seven years, and I could see what Rabin had contributed. The Military Machine had been greatly improved. Operational planning, instruction and organization had all achieved a level of perfection, to which the swift victory bears best witness.

Rabin has a better balanced and more rounded personality than his two predecessors, also less brilliance. But he is a man of ideas, balanced, solid and experienced. His ascent up the ladder of command had been slowed down for various reasons. This gave him an advantage over his predecessors. He gained experience in many functions at every level of command and instruction. When he finally became Chief-of-Staff he had a better feel than any of his predecessors as to what makes the military apparatus tick. The military achievement as such is that of a Chief-of-Staff and a daring yet well-balanced Staff who continued and developed the organizational doctrines received from Yadin together with the fighting principles of Dayan. Rabin also built himself up an excellent Staff with three outstanding operational aides, Haim Barlev, Ezer Weizmann and Rehaveam Ze'evi. Such an operational staff did not exist in the War of Independance, where Yadin was the only officer at that level, or in the Sinai Campaign. We also possess an intelligence service the like of which I do not believe is to be found in any other army in relation to its threats, as regards both information and quality of evaluation. This was mainly achieved by the two last heads of Intelligence, Meir Amit and Aaron Yariv. Logistics were in the capable hands of Matty Peled. Much has already been written about the field and arms commanders.

Now for the Minister of Defense.

Dayan's role in the War is at the level of defense and war policy—grand-strategy—rather than the military level. His appointment to the post of Minister of Defense gave everybody—from the Ministers to the last of the soldiers—a feeling of security which they had not felt before. The Chief-of-Staff could not have infused this sense of security beyond the Army itself. It is the task of the Chief-of-Staff to operate the military machine and not to decide whether this should be done or not. It is also impossible to expect the required resolution and determination to originate in the Minister for Religious Affairs, the Minister of Trade and Industry, or any other Minister except for the Premier or the Minister of Defense. They alone are in a position to weigh the perils against the military resources available to the people. They alone can give the signal. If the Prime Minister and Minister of Defense are hesitant, how can we be surprised when the other Ministers do not regard themselves as entitled to demand military action? This was the key to the negative votes between May 23rd and June 3rd.

The situation changed with the entry of Dayan. The assurance he spread permitted a change in the general stand. This was no foolhardiness. He had spent the waiting period in visits to army units and making a study of the enemy; he spoke from a knowledge of the facts. His inclusion in the government made all the difference in reaching the final decision to take up the enemy's challenge at the next provocation.

Obviously my description omits all the other processes which led the Government to harden its stand; particularly the final realisation that it was hopeless to count on any results from diplomatic activity. Yet in spite of this I am convinced that the knowledge that "there is someone on whom we can rely," was the most important of all. When the enemy began moving towards our frontiers, there were none who hesitated any more, and there was nobody to suggest that we should wait again and try to swallow yet another pill. We entered upon this War of our Resolution.

Prof. Yuval Ne'eman: How to Safeguard the Achievements of the War; *Ma'ariv,* 18.6.67

✶

THE ISRAELI VICTORY IN THE SIX-DAY WAR FIRED THE IMAGINATION of millions all over the world. People considered it as a surprising turn of the wheel of historical justice, where, in spite of everything, David defeated Goliath. On the other hand, there were many politicians who could not stand the fact that the Israelis, members of the persecuted Jewish race, no longer needed compassion nor help, but stood up and beat their enemies. Therefore, when the guns stopped roaring, Israel found itself facing a new struggle; a hard, involved and difficult battle in the international arena, whose purpose was to rob Israel of the fruit of its victories, and force it—by stratagems, by vague promises and even threats—to retreat from the conquered territories. This struggle was headed by the Soviet Union, whose Premier, Alexei Kosygin, and Foreign Minister, Andrei Gromyko, went to the UN for this specific purpose. Together with the Arab countries, with the active assistance of several countries of the Afro-Asian bloc and with the aid of France, they formed a powerful front, which for many long weeks tried, both in the General Assembly and the Security Council, to push Israel back to the frontiers of June 5th.

A lucid and comprehensive analysis of the Israeli position in the international arena after the Six-Day War, was given by the Foreign Minister, Abba Eban, in a brilliant speech at the General Assembly in New York.

In recent weeks the Middle East has passed through a crisis with many consequences but only one cause. Israel's right to peace, security, sovereignty, economic development and maritime freedom —indeed its very right to exist—was forcibly denied and aggressively attacked. This is the true origin of the tension which torments the Middle East.

The threat to Israel's existence has been directed against her in the first instance by the neighboring Arab States. But all the conditions of tension, all the temptations to aggression have been aggravated by the one-sided policy of one of the Great Powers which under our Charter bear responsibility for international peace and security. I shall show how the Soviet Union has, for 15 years, been unfaithful to that trust.

The General Assembly is preoccupied by the situation against which Israel defended itself on the morning of June 5. I invite every peace-loving state represented here to ask how it would have acted if it faced similar dangers. But we must understand that great events are not born in a single instant. It is beyond all doubt that between May 14 and June 5 Arab governments, led and directed by President Nasser, methodically mounted an aggressive assault designed to bring about Israel's immediate and total destruction. My authority rests on the statements and actions of Arab governments themselves.

During Israel's first decade the intention to work for her destruction by physical violence was part of the official policy of Arab States. But many members of the United Nations hoped and some believed that relative stability would ensue from arrangements discussed in the General Assembly in March, 1957. An attempt was then made to inaugurate non-belligerency and coexistence between Egypt and Israel. A United Nations Emergency Force was to separate them in Sinai and Gaza. The maritime powers were to exercise free and innocent passage in the Gulf of Akaba and the Straits of Tiran. Terrorist attacks against Israel were to cease. The Suez Canal was to be opened to Israel shipping, as the Security Council had decided six years before.

In March, 1957, these expectations were endorsed in the General

Assembly by the United States, France, the United Kingdom, Canada, and other states in Europe, the Americas, Africa, Asia and Australasia. These assurances induced Israel to give up positions which she held at Gaza and the entrance to the Straits of Tiran and in Sinai. Egypt expressed no opposition to these arrangements.

Yet as we look back it becomes plain that the Arab governments regarded the 1957 arrangements as a breathing space before a later assault. At the end of 1962, President Nasser began to prepare Arab opinion for an armed attack to take place in a few years. As his armaments grew his designs came more blatantly to light. On 23 December 1962, Nasser said: "We feel that the soil of Palestine is the soil of Egypt, and of the whole Arab world. Why do we all mobilize? Because we feel that the land of Palestine is part of our land, and are ready to sacrifice ourselves for it."

The Foreign Minister of Egypt, Mahmoud Riad, echoed his master:

"The sacred Arab struggle will not come to an end until Palestine is restored to its owners."

In March 1963, the official Cairo radio continued the campaign:

"Arab unity is taking shape towards the great goal—i.e. the triumphant return to Palestine with the banner of unity flying high in front of the holy Arab march."

The newspaper *Al-Gumhuriya* published an official announcement on the same day:

"The noose around Israel's neck is tightening gradually . . . Israel is no mightier than the empires which were vanquished by the Arab east and west . . . The Arab people will take possession of their full rights in their united homeland."

Egypt is not a country in which the press utters views and opinions independently of the official will. There is thus much significance in the statement of *Al-Akhbar* on 4 April, 1963:

"The liquidation of Israel will not be realized through a declaration of war against Israel by Arab States, *but Arab unity and inter-Arab understanding will serve as a hangman's rope for Israel.*"

The Assembly will note the imagery of a hangman's rope or of a tightening noose in the macabre vocabulary of Nasserism. He sees himself presiding over a scaffold. In June 1967, in Israel's hour of solitude and danger, the metaphor of encirclement and strangulation was to come vividly to life.

In February, 1964, Nasser enunciated in simple terms what was to become his country's policy during the period of preparation:

"The possibilities of the future will be war with Israel. It is we who will dictate the time; it is we who will dictate the place."

A similar chorus of threats arose from other Arab capitals. President Aref of Iraq and President Ben-Bella of Algeria were especially emphatic and repetitive in their threat to liquidate Israel. They were then far away, but the Syrians affected a neighboring frontier. In 1964, the Syrian Defense Minister, General Abdulla Ziada announced:

"The Syrian army stands as a mountain to crush Israel and demolish her. This army knows how to crush its enemies."

Early last year Syria began to proclaim and carry out a "popular war" against Israel. This was a terrorist campaign which expressed itself in the dispatch of trained terrorist groups into Israel to blow up installations and communication centers and kill, maim, cripple and terrorize civilians in peaceful homes and farms. Often the terrorists were dispatched through Jordan or Lebanon. The terrorist war was formally declared by President Al-Atassi on 22 May, 1966, when he addressed soldiers on the Israel–Syrian front:

"We raise the slogan of the people's liberation war. We want total war with no limits, a war that will destroy the Zionist base."

It is a strange experience in this hall of peace to be sitting with a delegate whose philosophy is: "We want total war with no limits."

The Syrian Defense Minister, Hafiz Asad, said two days later:

"We say: We shall never call for, not accept peace. We shall only accept war and the restoration of the usurped land. We have resolved to drench this land with your blood, to oust you, aggressors, and throw you into the sea for good.

"We must meet as soon as possible and fight a single liberation war on the level of the whole area against Israel, imperialism and all the enemies of the people."

From that day to this not a week has passed without Syrian officials adding to this turgid stream of invective and hate. There has not been a single month without terrorist acts, directed from Syria against Israeli citizens and territory. I would have no difficulty in swelling the General Assembly's records with a thousand official statements by Arab leaders in the past two years announcing their intention to destroy Israel by organized physical violence.

We were able to limit our response to aggression so long as its scope appeared to be limited. President Nasser seemed for some years to be accumulating inflammable material without an immediate desire to set it alight. His speeches were strong against Israel. But his bullets, guns and poison gases were used to intimidate other Arab States and maintain a colonial war against the villagers of the Yemen and the peoples of the Arabian Peninsula.

But Israel's danger was great. The military build-up in Egypt was designed to enable Egypt to press war plans against Israel while maintaining violent adventures elsewhere. Israel was forced to devote an increasing part of its resources to self-defense. With the declaration by Syria early in 1965 of the doctrine of a "day-by-day military confrontation" the situation in the Middle East grew darker. The Palestine Liberation Organization, the Palestine Liberation Army, the Unified Arab Command, the expansion of military forces and equipment in Egypt, Syria, Lebanon, Jordan and more remote parts —these were signals of a growing danger to which we sought to alert the world.

In three tense weeks between 14 May and 5 June, Egypt, Syria and Jordan, assisted and incited by more distant Arab States, embarked on a policy of immediate and total aggression.

June 1967 was to be the month of decision. The "final solution" was at hand.

Egyptian and Soviet sources claimed that an Israeli invasion of Syria was expected during the second or third week in May. No claim could be more far-fetched. It is true that Syria was sending terrorists into Israel to lay mines on roads and, on one occasion, to bombard the settlement at Manara from the Lebanese border. The accumulation of such actions had sometimes evoked limited Israeli responses. All that Syria had to do to ensure perfect tranquility with Israel was to discourage the terrorist war. But she gave it every moral and practical support. The picture of Israeli troop concentrations for an invasion of Syria was a monstrous fiction. Twice Syria rejected simultaneous and reciprocal inspection of the frontier. On one occasion the Soviet Ambassador complained to my Prime Minister of heavy troop concentrations in the north of Israel. When invited to join the Prime Minister that very moment in a visit to any part of Israel, the distinguished envoy brusquely refused. The prospect of finding out the truth at first hand seemed to fill him with profound disquiet. But by 9 May the Secretary General of the United Nations from his own sources had ascertained that no Israeli troop concentrations existed. This fact was directly communicated to the

Syrian and Egyptian governments. The excuse had been shattered, but the allegations still remained. The steps I now describe could not have had any motive or justification in an Israeli troop concentration which both Egypt and Syria knew did not exist. Indeed, the Egyptian build-up ceased to be described as the results of a threat to Syria.

On 14 May Egyptian forces began to move into Sinai.

On 16 May the Egyptian Command ordered the United Nations Emergency Force to leave the border. On 17 May, 1967, at 6 in the morning, Radio Cairo broadcast that Field Marshal Amer had issued alert orders to the Egyptian armed forces. Nor did he mention Syria as the excuse.

This announcement reads in part:

"The armed forces are to be in full preparedness to carry out any combat tasks on the Israel front in accordance with developments."

On 18 May, Egypt called for the total removal of the United Nations Emergency Force. The Secretary-General of the United Nations acceded to this request and moved to carry it out, without reference to the Security Council or the General Assembly; without carrying out the procedures indicated by Secretary Hammarskjöld in the event of a request for withdrawal; without heeding the voices of some of the permanent members of the Security Council, and of the Government at whose initiative the Force had been established; without consulting Israel; and without seeking delay to enable measures to be concerted for preventing belligerency by sea and a dangerous confrontation of forces by land.

This decision was disastrously swift. Its effect was to make Sinai safe for belligerency from north to south; to create a sudden disruption of the local security balance; and to leave an international maritime interest exposed to almost certain threat. I have already said that Israel's attitude to the peace-keeping functions of the United Nations has been traumatically affected by this experience. What is the use of a fire brigade which vanishes from the scene as soon as the first smoke and flames appear? Is it surprising that we are resolved never again to allow Israeli interests and our very security to rest on such a foundation?

The clouds now gathered fast. Between 14 May and 23 May, Egyptian concentrations in Sinai increased day by day. Israel took precautionary measures, though nothing could be more uncongenial to peace than large armies facing each other across a narrow space, with one of them bent on early assault. For the purpose of the concentration was not in doubt. On 18 May, at 24 hours, the Cairo Radio *Saut El Arab* published the following Order of the Day by Abdul Muhsin Murtagi, the General then Commanding Sinai:

"The Egyptian forces have taken up positions in accordance with a definite plan. Our forces are definitely ready to carry the battle beyond the borders of Egypt.

"Morale is very high among the members of our armed forces because this is the day for which they have been waiting—to make a holy war in order to return the plundered land to its owners.

"In many meetings with army personnel they asked when the holy war will begin—the time has come to give them their wish."

On 21 May General Amer gave the order to mobilize reserves.

Now came the decisive step. At an air force base at 6 o'clock in the morning, President Nasser announced that he would blockade the Gulf of Akaba to Israeli ships, adding: "The Jews threaten war and we say by all means we are ready for war."

On 25 May, Cairo Radio announced:

"The Arab people is firmly resolved to wipe Israel off the map and to restore the honor of the Arabs of Palestine."

On the following day, 26 May, Nasser spoke again:

"The Arab people want to fight. We have been waiting for the right time when we will be completely ready. Recently we have felt that our strength has been sufficient and that if we make battle with Israel we shall be able, with the help of God, to conquer. Sharm-a-Sheikh implies a confrontation with Israel. Taking this step makes it imperative that we be ready to undertake a total war with Israel."

Writing in *Al Ahram*, on 26 May, Nasser's mouthpiece Hassnein Heykal, wrote, with engaging realism:

"I consider that there is no alternative to armed conflict between the United Arab Republic and the Israeli enemy. This is the first time that the Arab challenge to Israel attempts to change an existing fact in order to impose a different fact in its place."

On 28 May, Nasser had a press conference. He said:

"We will not accept any possibility of coexistence with Israel."

And on the following day:

"If we have succeeded to restore the situation to what it was before 1956, there is no doubt that God will help us and will inspire us to restore the situation to what it was prior to 1948."

The troop concentrations and blockade were to be accompanied by encirclement. The noose was to be fitted round the victim's neck. On 30 May Nasser signed the defense agreement with Jordan; and described its purpose in these terms:

"The armies of Egypt, Jordan, Syria and Lebanon are stationed on the borders of Israel in order to face the challenge. Behind them stand the armies of Iraq, Algeria, Kuwait, Sudan and the whole of the Arab nation.

"This deed will astound the world. Today they will know that the Arabs are ready for the fray. The hour of decision has arrived."

On 4 June Nasser made a statement on Cairo Radio after signing the Protocol associating Iraq with the Egyptian–Jordanian Defense Pact. Here are his words:

". . . We are facing you in the battle and are burning with desire for it to start, in order to obtain revenge. This will make the world realize what the Arabs are and what Israel is . . ."

Nothing has been more startling in recent weeks than to read discussions about who planned, who organized, who initiated, who wanted and who launched this war. Here we have a series of statements, mounting in crescendo from vague warning through open threat to precise intention.

Here we have the mass of the Egyptian armies in Sinai with seven infantry and two armored divisions. Here we have 40,000 regular Syrian troops poised to strike from above at the Jordan Valley. Here we have the mobilized forces of Jordan, with artillery and mortars trained on Israel's population centers in Jerusalem and along the narrow coastal plain. Troops from Iraq, Kuwait and Algeria converge towards the battlefront at Egypt's behest. 900 tanks face Israel on the Sinai border, while 200 more are poised to strike the town of Eilat at Israel's southern tip. The Southern Negev was to be sundered in a swift blow. The Northern Negev was to be invaded by armor and bombarded from the Gaza Strip. From May 27 onward Egyptian air squadrons in Sinai were equipped with operation orders, now in our hands, instructing them on the manner in which Israel's pathetically few airfields were to be bombarded, thus exposing Israel's crowded cities to easy and merciless assault. Egyptian air sorties came in and out of Israel's southern desert to reconnoitre, inspect and prepare for the attack.

Those who write this story in years to come will give special place to the decision to close the Straits of Tiran. It is not difficult to understand why this had such a drastic impact. In 1957 the maritime nations, within the framework of the United Nations General Assembly, enunciated the doctrine of free and innocent passage through the Straits. Now when that doctrine was proclaimed—and incidentally, not challenged by the Egyptian representative—it was little more than an abstract principle. For Israel it was a great but still unfulfilled prospect; it was not yet a reality. But during the ten years in which we and the other States of the maritime community have relied upon that doctrine and upon established usage, the principle has become a reality consecrated by the establishment of a whole complex of commerce, industry and communication. A new dimension has been added to the map of the world's communications, and on that dimension we have constructed Israel's bridge towards the friendly States of Asia and Africa.

Surely the closing of the Straits of Tiran gave no benefit whatever to Egypt except the perverse joy of inflicting injury on others. It showed a total disregard for the law of nations, the application of which in this specific case had not been challenged for ten years. And it was an act of arrogance, because there are nations in Asia and East Africa that trade with the Port of Eilat, through the Straits of Tiran and across the Gulf of Akaba. Other sovereign States from Japan to Ethiopia, from Thailand to Uganda, from Cambodia to Madagascar, have a sovereign right to decide for themselves whether they wish or do not wish to trade with Israel. These countries are not colonies of Cairo. They can trade with Israel or not, as they wish.

Blockade is by definition an act of war, imposed and enforced through armed violence. Never in history have blockade and peace existed side by side. From May 24 onward, the question who started the war or who fired the first shot became irrelevant. The moment the blockade was imposed active hostilities had commenced. If a foreign power sought to close Odessa or Copenhagen or Marseilles or New York harbor by the use of force, what would happen? Would there be any discussion about who had fired the first shot?

Less than a decade ago the Soviet Union proposed a draft resolution in the General Assembly on the question of defining aggression. The resolution reads:

"In an international conflict that state shall be declared an attacker which first commits one of the following acts:

(a) Naval blockade of the coasts or ports of another State."

In the Soviet view this act constituted direct aggression, as distinguished from other specified acts designated indirect aggression. Here the consequences of Nasser's action had been fully provided for. On March 1, 1957, my predecessor announced that:

"Interference, by armed force, with ships of Israel flag exercising free and innocent passage in the Gulf of Akaba and through the Straits of Tiran, will be regarded by Israel as an attack entitling it to exercise its inherent right of self-defense under Article 51 of the United Nations Charter and to take all such measures as are necessary to ensure the free and innocent passage of its ships in the Gulf and in the Straits."

The representative of France declared that any obstruction of free passage in the Straits or Gulf was contrary to international law, "entailing a possible resort to the measures authorized by Article 51 of the Charter."

The United States, inside and outside the United Nations, gave specific endorsement to Israel's right to self-defense against any attempt to blockade the Gulf. Nasser was speaking with acute precision, therefore, when he stated that Israel now faced the choice either being choked to death in her southern maritime approaches or awaiting the death blow from northern Sinai.

Nobody in Israel between May 23 and June 5 will ever forget the air of foreboding that hovered over our country. Hemmed in by hostile armies ready to strike, affronted and beset by a flagrant act of war, bombarded day and night by predictions of our approaching extinction, forced into total mobilization, her economy and commerce beating feebly, her main supplies of fuel choked by a belligerent act, Israel faced the greatest peril to her existence since her resistance against aggression at the hour of her birth. There was peril wherever she looked and she faced it in solitude. On May 24 and succeeding days, the Security Council conducted a desultory debate which sometimes reached the point of levity. The Soviet representative saw no reason for discussing the Middle Eastern situation at all. The Bulgarian Delegate uttered these words:

"At the present moment there is really no need for an urgent meeting of the Security Council."

This was the day after the imposition of the blockade!

Multitudes throughout the world now began to tremble for Israel's fate. From Paris to Montevideo, from New York to Amsterdam, tens of thousands of people of all ages, parties and affiliations marched in protest against the approaching politicide—the murder of a State.

Writers and scientists, religious leaders, trade union movements, even the Communist parties in France, Holland, Switzerland, Norway, Austria and Finland asserted that Israel was a peace-loving State, to whom peace was being wantonly denied.

On the fateful morning of June 5, when Egyptian forces moved by air and land against Israel's western coast and southern territory, our country's choice was plain. The choice was to live or perish, to defend the national existence or forfeit it for all time.

From these moments Israel emerged in five heroic days from awful peril to successful and glorious resistance. Alone, unaided, neither seeking nor receiving help, our nation rose in self-defense. So long as men cherish freedom, so long as small states strive for the dignity of survival, the exploits of Israel's armies will be told from one generation to another. The Soviet Union has described our resistance as aggression and sought to have it condemned. We reject this accusation. Here was armed force employed in a just and righteous cause; as righteous as the defense of freedom at Valley Forge; as just as the expulsion of Hitler's bombers from the British skies; as noble as the protection of Stalingrad against the Nazi hordes. Never have freedom, honor, justice, national interest and international morality been so righteously protected.

While fighting raged on the Egyptian–Israel frontier and on the Syrian front, we still hoped to contain the conflict. Even after Jordan had bombarded and bombed Israel territory at several points we still proposed to the Jordanian monarch that he abstain from general hostilities. A message to this effect reached him several hours after the outbreak of hostilities on the southern front on June 5.

Jordan answered with shells. Artillery opened fire along the whole front, with special emphasis on the Jerusalem area. This responsibility cannot fail to have its consequences in the peace settlement. Death and injury rained on the city. Jordan had become the source of Jerusalem's fierce ordeal.

I have spoken of Israel's defense against the assaults of neighboring states. This is not the entire story. Whatever happens in the Middle East is affected by what the Great Powers do or omit to do. When the Soviet Union initiates a discussion here our gaze is drawn to its role in recent Middle Eastern history.

There was in Soviet policy a brief but important episode of balanced friendship. In 1948 the USSR condemned what she called "Arab aggression."

Since 1955 the Soviet Union has supplied the Arab States with 2,000 tanks, of which more than 1,000 have gone to Egypt. The Soviet Union has supplied the Arab States with 700 modern fighter aircraft and bombers, more recently with ground missiles. Egypt alone has received from the USSR 540 field guns, 130 medium guns. 200 120 mm. mortars, 695 anti-aircraft guns, 175 rocket launchers, 650 anti-tank guns, 7 destroyers, a number of Luna-M and Sopka-2 ground-to-ground missiles, 14 submarines and 46 torpedo boats of various types including missile-carrying boats. The Egyptian army has been trained by Soviet experts. This has been attested by captured Egyptian officers. Most of this equipment was supplied after the Cairo Summit Conference of Arab leaders in January 1964 had agreed on a specific program for the destruction of Israel; after they had announced and hastened to fulfill this plan by accelerating arms purchases from the Soviet Union. The proportions of Soviet assistance are attested to by the fact that in Sinai alone the Egyptians abandoned equipment and offensive weapons of Soviet manufacture whose value is estimated at two billion dollars.

Thus, a Great Power which professes its devotion to peaceful settlement and the rights of States has for 14 years afflicted the Middle East with a headlong armaments race, with paralysis of the United Nations as an instrument of security, and with blind identification with those who threaten peace against those who defend it.

It is clear from Arab sources that the Soviet Union played a provocative role in spreading incendiary reports of Israel's intentions.

On 9 June President Nasser said:

"Our friends in the USSR warned the visiting parliamentary delegation in Moscow at the beginning of last month that there exists a plan of attack against Syria."

Similarly an announcement by Tass of 23 May states:

"The Foreign Affairs and Security Committee of the Knesset have accorded the Cabinet, on 9 May, special powers to carry out war operations against Syria. Israeli forces concentrating on the Syrian border have been put in a state of alert for war. General mobilization has also been proclaimed in the country . . ."

There was not one word of truth in this story. But its diffusion in the Arab countries could only have an incendiary result.

Cairo Radio broadcast on 28 May (0500 hours) an address by Marshal Gretchko at a farewell party in honor of the former Egyptian Minister of Defense Shams ed-Din Badran:

"The USSR, her armed forces, her people and government will stand by the Arabs and will continue to encourage and support them. We are your faithful friends and we shall continue aiding you because this is the policy of the Soviet nation, its party and government. On behalf of the Ministry of Defense and in the name of the Soviet nation we wish you success and victory."

This promise came less than a week after the illicit closing of the Tiran Straits.

The USSR has exercised her veto right in the Security Council five times. Each time a just and constructive judgment has been frustrated. On 22 January 1954 France, the United Kingdom and the United States presented a draft resolution to facilitate work on the West Bank of the River Jordan in the B'not Ya'acov Canal project. The Soviet veto paralyzed regional water development for several years. On 29 March 1954, a New Zealand resolution simply reiterating UN policy on blockade in the Suez Canal was frustrated by Soviet dissent. On 19 August 1963, a United Kingdom and United States resolution on the murder of two Israelis at Almagor was denied adoption by Soviet opposition. On 21 December 1964 the USSR vetoed a United Kingdom and United States resolution on incidents at Tel Dan, including the shelling of Dan, Dafna, Shear Yashuv. On 2 November 1966, Argentina, Japan, Netherlands, New Zealand, Nigeria joined to express regret at "infiltration from Syria and loss of human life caused by the incidents in October, November 1966." This was one of the few resolutions sponsored by member States from five continents.

The Soviet use of the veto has had a dual effect. First, it prevented any resolution to which an Arab State was opposed from being adopted by the Council. Secondly, it has inhibited the Security Council from taking action in disputes between an Arab State and Israel because of the knowledge that the veto would be applied in what was deemed to be the Arab interest. The consequences of the Soviet policy have been to deny Israel any possibility of just and equitable treatment in the Security Council, and to nullify the Council as a factor in the Middle East.

The position becomes graver when we recall the invective against the Permanent Representative of Israel in the Security Council. In its words and in a letter to the Israel Government the USSR formulated an obscene comparison between the Israel Defense Forces and the Hitlerite hordes which overran Europe in the Second World

War. There is a flagrant breach of international morality and human decency in this comparison. Our nation never compromised with Hitler's Germany. It never signed a pact with it as did the USSR in 1939. To associate Israel with the tyrant who engulfed the Jewish people in a wave of slaughter is to violate every canon of elementary taste and fundamental truth.

In respect to the request for a condemnation, I give a simple answer to the Soviet Representative. Your Government's record in the stimulation of the arms race, in the encouragement throughout the Arab world of unfounded suspicion concerning Israel's intentions, your constant refusal to say a single word of criticism at any time of declarations threatening the violent overthrow of Israel's sovereignty and existence—all this undermines your claim to objectivity. You come here not as a judge or as a prosecutor, but rather as an object of international criticism for the part you have played in the events which brought our region to a point of explosive tension. If the Soviet Union had refrained from exploiting regional rancors and tensions for the purposes of its own global policy, the crisis which now commands our anxiety would never have occurred. To the charge of aggression I answer that Israel's resistance at the lowest ebb of its fortunes will resound across history, together with the uprising of our remnants in the Warsaw Ghetto, as a triumphant assertion of human freedom. From the dawn of history the people now rebuilding Israel has struggled, often in desperate conditions, against tyranny and aggression. Our action on the 5th of June falls within that tradition. We have tried to show that even a small state and a small people have the right to live. I believe that we shall not be alone in the assertion of that right, which is the very essence of the Charter of the United Nations.

Similarly, the suggestion that everything go back to where it was before the 5th of June is totally unacceptable. The General Assembly cannot ignore the fact that the Security Council, where primary responsibility lies, emphatically rejected such a course. It was not Israel but Syria, Egypt and Jordan, who shattered the whole fabric of interstate relations which had existed since 1957. That situation has been shattered to smithereens. It cannot be recaptured. It is easier to fly to the moon than to reconstruct a broken egg.

The Arab States have come face to face with us in conflict. Let them now come face to face with us in peace.

Address by Foreign Minister Abba Eban in the United Nations, 19.6.67

The State of Israel had kept friendly relations with the US ever since its creation. In spite of certain vicissitudes, they had never been substantially damaged. The US policy during the Six-Day War, and especially its sober and firm stand in the international arena after the Israeli victory, strengthened the relations between both countries, and brought forth in Israel a wave of warm feelings for the powerful nation across the ocean.

"My Favorite Uncle" was written by Davar *Editor Hanna Zemer when the US Embassy in Israel postponed its Independence Day celebration because July* 4, 1967 *coincided with the "Sheloshim" (Thirty) Day of Mourning for Israel's fallen in the Six-Day War.*

Of all my uncles, the one I like best is Uncle Sam. Heaven is my witness that this love does not stem from any ulterior, practical motives. I love Uncle Sam, not because he has sent me and my sisters a lot of presents (something the rest of our uncles haven't done), or because we always could and still can go and cry on his shoulder and ask for his help and encouragement, or because he allows us to get fresh with him—which is what I like to do, but which our other uncles don't allow because they are terribly sensitive about their dignity and they immediately punish the slightest show of disrespect. No, that isn't why I love Uncle Sam; I love him because he's just plain marvelous, kind, and understanding.

I must confess that I didn't always feel this way about him, and there were even times when I simply couldn't bear him. But that wasn't his fault, or mine either, but the fault of those other uncles, who had prejudiced me against him. They didn't care for him, because he was stronger than they, and more successful. They avoided him even when they maintained political relations with him, because he was very rich and famous for his philanthropy and he often helped them, and so they had to compensate themselves somehow for being poorer than he and accepting his help. So they tried to boost their self-esteem by looking down on him as a *parvenu* and emphasizing all his human frailties.

When I first met Uncle Sam at his home, to which I had come with all my prejudices, I didn't care for him one bit. He seemed materialistic, simple, and rather vulgar. And all my first impressions of the way he went about doing things and the way he lived strengthened my prejudices.

But I stayed with him quite a while, and gradually I came to appreciate and admire him. Uncle Sam is the sort you learn to appreciate only after you have come to know him very well, because he is a much more complex creature than you might expect of an overgrown boy like him.

When I left his house, I was very sorry for having wronged him in my former superficial judgment of him. Now I took every opportunity to defend him against the slurs of my brothers and sisters, who had also been influenced by the other uncles. I had no qualms at all about speaking up for him, because I knew that his motives were pure—for the most part far purer than the motives of the uncles who sniped at him.

Strange as it may seem, Uncle Sam, rich and influential as he was (and still is), needs somebody to stand up for him. Because, while he is unbeatable in the way he advertises his products, he isn't very good at selling his image.

Thus, for example, many people think he is rich because he was born with a silver spoon in his mouth, and is rich in natural resources, and because money matters to him more than anything else. But they forget that money counts very much to others, as well, and that others also have natural resources—while Uncle Sam is industrious as an ant and efficient as a computer. They forget that he is rich first and foremost because he takes work very seriously, and there is no such thing as an "unimportant" task for him. He has transmitted this almost moral attitude to work to his entire household, and all of them take it for granted that work has to be planned, organized and carried out efficiently. When you see the way they work, you can't help taking your hat off to them—that is, if you wear a hat.

And Uncle Sam works so hard and so well that his entire family lives well—though not all to the same degree, of course. The latter fact may disturb you, because you were brought up on the idea of equal division of wealth, or at least to strive for equal division, and Uncle Sam doesn't aspire to this. But when you remember the *purpose* of all economic activity, which aims at the humanitarian ideal of freeing mankind from want, then you must admit that Uncle Sam has come closer to the fulfillment of this ideal than anyone else, and you must admire him for this.

You might say that this doesn't necessarily make people happy, because money can't buy happiness and all that, and the fact is that Uncle Sam isn't happy—he has turned the psychiatrist's couch into a virtual shrine, and the analysis of complexes into a cult. But I don't think that any of this proves unhappiness. It is only a sign of a lack of other problems. After all, Uncle Sam is the only one in the world for whom the pursuit of happiness is a declared aim and a sacred tenet.

And it isn't true that he lives by bread alone, or by steaks alone. He also lives by love of liberty and respect for liberty, and the members of his household are free men in every respect—in some respects far freer than anybody else anywhere in the world, because this materialistic Uncle Sam is a true idealist, sometimes to the point of naiveté. He loves people and believes in Man—and if he lacks the sophistication of those older uncles across the sea, he is also free of their moral degeneracy. Uncle Sam still has many moral inhibitions of which others have long since freed themselves.

That is why I learned to respect him and love him, without any connection with his attitude to me. And when I come to wish him well on his birthday, I should like him to know that these good wishes have no connection or correlation with the present he gave me in New York this week. It is a very precious present, and a very useful one, and God only knows how I would manage without it. But my birthday wishes are not by way of thanks for his latest present or previous ones; it is an expression of gratitude to Uncle Sam for being what he is and for the inspiration he has given to the world since the day he was born.

My birthday wishes to him are that his house should always know happiness and serenity, and that he should always overcome his adversaries—because I believe implicitly that he is better than they, and worthier, and nobler.

I am happy to count myself among his friends, and these birthday wishes of mine will stand even if we should one day quarrel—and that can happen, because a man's own interests come first. But the question is whose interests does he place after his own. As for me, Uncle Sam is my favorite uncle.

Hanna Zemer: My Favorite Uncle; *Davar,* 7.7.67

Chapter Eleven

The Aftermath

RETURNING TO EVERYDAY LIFE AFTER THE UPHEAVAL OF WAR IS A more difficult process than to go out and fight. Things of import before the war seem small and insignificant, relations with friends and family take on a different dimension and tension suddenly vanishes.

The aftermath of a war is hard on each individual separately and on the nation as a whole; new problems loom and old ones remain, forgotten hopes reappear and new disappointments come up unsolved.

Israelis started to dissect a miracle with the scalpel of logic. They looked close by at the victory on their hands, wondering what would grow out of it.

All our thoughts run ahead like horses with blinkers over their eyes, in one single direction—the fighting. You pick up a book, a detective story or a novel, a biography or a volume of poetry, and after a few pages your thoughts have strayed from the adventures and loves and memories of others, and run back to the same old stable. Whatever you may want to write about, you finish up by writing about the war and what went before and what will come after. You meet friends and want at last to talk about something else, but the conversation about food or the theater, about Jayne Mansfield or Sammy Davis, comes back to the same subject: what has been and what will be. At work and in the bus, in the bath and in bed, the war looks in through every window. The war is in the marrow of our bones, lies like a weight on our eyelids, weighs like lead on our brains.

As long as the actual fighting went on, we did not permit ourselves any superfluous thoughts, and there was no point in them anyhow: the events themselves, hour after hour, supplied enough food for thought for the next 60 minutes. But now we are no longer afraid and sad and tired; now we want to understand, to consider, to draw conclusions; now we want to know what really went on in the Government before the war broke out, what is really happening behind the scenes, what are really the plans for the future, what's up with Dayan and with Eshkol and with Abba Eban and with Yigal Alon, and what to do with the refugees and what with the volunteers; how we shall overcome unemployment and farm surpluses, what Hussein will do and what Nasser and the Russians and De Gaulle are up to. There are a hundred question marks against one exclamation mark: Let this be the last war! At least for 20 years. Until the kids grow up. Until the boys are out of the army. Until we make room on the parking lot of life. And deep within ourselves we know: We'll never have a rest, not in this country. Israel is not the place where peace will dwell forever; it feels more at home in Switzerland.

These last few weeks we have learned to say "thank God" where we used to say "God forbid." Thank God, we said, only shells and no bombs. We thanked Heaven that there were only ordinary bombs and no gas bombs; that only houses were destroyed, only fields burned down. Thank God, we said, they're only wounded (being wounded seemed a reprieve of fate compared with the final sentence). It is a reprieve that wears different faces: sometimes smiling—a broken shoulder or a splinter in the knee, a crushed finger or a bullet in the thigh—and sometimes colder than death.

Life weighs heavy when one sees the columns of little black boxes in the newspapers, health seems pilfered when one looks at a pale face on a white pillow. And you tell yourself what has been written so often and still is true: that our wounded soldiers get the best treatment modern medicine can provide; and you add that the soldiers of the IDF are no less courageous in the hospital than on the battlefield, and that is true too; and you see them sitting in the lobbies of the hospitals, laughing, arguing, smoking, joking with the nurses, eating cake mother has baked, counting the days until they get out—and you say thank God once more, and you relax.

But then, by mistake, you open the door of the wrong room, and on the only bed lies a body with two lumps for hands and scraps of skin for a face and a white dressing where the eyes were—a body that looks too small for a soldier—and only the little radio that lies on the pillow and softly plays folk songs lets you know that there is still some life there. So you close the door, quietly, and you feel terribly ashamed, as though you were the cause of his tragedy.

Every single one of us is a certified hero: whoever lived in Israel during the war is a hero: he has it in writing, signed by a dozen of friends abroad. Who ever was in the rear, that is not actually on the border, knows that the real heroes are the people of the border settlements, who lived and brought up children right on the border. The people from the settlements know that the real heroes are the soldiers who freed them from 20 years of nightmare; and the soldiers know that the real heroes are the people in the front line, who took part in the actual attack. And those who were in the real fighting say: the real heroes are under ground. But when you stand at the grave and see the figures in black, shrunk with sorrow and bent with pain, you know that courage means going on living.

Anyone who is not about to publish a victory album or writing a book about the war, or a film script for a great adventure film against the background of the events of June 1967, or collecting an anthology of eyewitness stories, or planning a series of lectures about "the war of David against Goliath," has either really been at the front and so missed the right moment, or lacks all commercial, literary or other talent—and then he can always write newspaper articles. War may bring out the best in man, but it certainly produces the worst of prose.

The trouble is that words are such a poor tool when it comes to events and emotions that are bigger than ourselves, but what shall one do—they are the only way of communicating something of the essence of these days to the future. And also, one must get rid of at least some part of the rubbish pile that has collected internally. The advantage writing has over speech is that for a conversation one needs at least two, while one is enough for writing: someone who is prepared to publish.

In this world of specialization and narrow professional know-how, it is good to know that there is at least one field of public life that is open to all comers and demands no vocational training: Information. It's like sex: everyone learns it in course of time, more or less. After all, what is difficult about information? Truth does not need talking about, it speaks for itself, so all that is needed is a little makeup for lies. If only those foreign journalists and those bothersome television people wouldn't stick their noses in other people's business, and the Arabs wouldn't rave with their noisy propaganda, and the world would show more understanding for the troubles of our political parties, our information campaigns could be the best in the world.

And if here and there in our information effort there are little things that could stand some improvement, it is only because we haven't used the right experts. It is no more than common sense that being a spokesman or press officer is something any retired *halutz* or any quartermaster no one knows what to do with can handle, as long as he detests journalists, and with good cause. Still, it may well be that for information on a nation-wide scale one needs, not only a couple of advertising men who know exactly what the people have decided and what is on every tongue—and that is why they were able to sell the country what it lacked according to market demand—but also a few assistants: an experienced housepainter to do the whitewashing and cover dark outlooks with a lighter tint, a plumber to get rid of the smells from the drains, a skilled mathematician to reduce ministers' broken promises to a common denominator—and if it is still unsatisfactory, one might always try a brain, electronic or other.

As if we did not have enough trouble handling ourselves, the volunteers from abroad come in masses, all cocked for action. True, the people who volunteered must have done it out of some irresistible inner impulse and of their own free will, and no one can hold us responsible for their overly hasty actions, but it is just too embarrassing to tell them that they had best lie on the sand of the Herzliya beach and get a bit of a tan. If the volunteers had a little sense, they would not have crowded the airfields and jumped on the first plane, but would have waited patiently until all the proper agencies would have given the problems of their absorption all due consideration and reached conclusions and drawn up detailed plans and referred them through the accepted channels and come to an agreement about the division of authority. Then it would have been easy enough to handle a few hundred volunteers a month without excessive trouble. But when they come in their thousands, just now when we have barely recovered from the war, it's plain irresponsible of them.

Luckily we have at least invented the kibbutzim, where one can always get rid of some of the volunteers who are spoiling for action. But what to do with all the others? The suggestion of building a road by hand, the way people did in the good old days, without bulldozers or steamrollers, is the sort of idea only someone deeply rooted in the labor movement could have conceived, and it gives us ground for hoping that we shall manage to keep at least half of those frail university students busy handling spades and pick-axes, carrying stones, and stirring tar in empty kerosene barrels. For the remainder we shall have to find some other make-work employment. We can be frank about it, they do not read the Hebrew papers anyhow, and the English translation of "we need you like a headache" is "we are very happy to have you here."

So we need not stop at building a road by hand. There are many other fields where Jewish hands can replace Gentile machines. One could strain sewage with a plastic strainer and a wooden spoon; one could use volunteers as rickshaw boys on our town bus lines; one could use them as runners when the telephone has broken down; one could shut down the air conditioning in the Jewish Agency offices and let the volunteers wave paper fans over the perspiring heads of the poor officials who plan their absorption and who have not yet become used to the silly idea that there are people who want to come to Israel without being card-bearing Zionists, while they could remain faithful members of the Zionist Organization for the remainder of their natural lives and live nicely in countries with a moderate climate.

Wherever the Israeli goes, he brings civilization with him; traffic bottlenecks in Jericho, scrap paper in the Church of the Nativity, empty cans in the water of the Banias, autographs on Rachel's Tomb. One of the great mysteries Israel's best investigators have not yet been able to solve is this: in order to visit the Occupied Territories, one needs a permit from the Military Administration, and this is hard to get. One needs a reason, a destination, justification, and on the permit they write your name and trade and the number of your car and a stamp and a signature and a date—and the Sabbath comes, and half the country is on the Golan Heights and the other half on the West Bank. And they all have valid permits: blue, green, yellow and white permits, and none remains in Israel itself but a few Orthodox Rabbis and military policemen at the checkposts. Either the Movement for an Undivided Land of Israel prints the permits underground, or the Almighty lets them rain down from heaven instead of manna, for He knows the needs of His people Israel.

Instead of putting obstacles in the way of a Greater Israel, let them make the trips compulsory. It should be compulsory to go up to the Golan Heights and stand in the withered grainfields and see Israel's real conquests: the Huleh Valley and the Jordan Valley, green, flourishing, cared for; to see the settlements of Upper Galilee just as the Syrians saw them, from above, as if you could hold them in your hand; to see the bunkers and the forts, the trenches and the ammunition dumps and the rifle emplacements stretching out for miles—first line and second line and third line; to see the routes on which the soldiers of the IDF scaled the Heights in broad daylight, straight up the barrels of the Syrian guns. For then you cut the formula "to give the Heights back in return for . . ." right out of your dictionary. No treaty and no peace and no nothing—we won't give it back. We're lucky, at that, that the Syrians cooperate with us on this point.

If they throw stones on Sabbath Square again, it means that life is back to normal. If the police write tickets again, it means life is back to normal. If you get a headache because of a quarrel at the hairdresser's, life is back to normal; if the cars race past people waiting for a hike, life is back to normal; if we settle political accounts again, if a minister issues a statement and another minister denies it, life is back to normal.

Back to normal, but not quite: we are still full of the great tension, and every day adds to it: someone killed, a mine, a threat, a demand. What we need is to stop the world for four weeks for a globe-wide annual holiday: no Assembly and no Security Council, no Fedorenko and no De Gaulle, no border incidents and no shelling on the Suez Canal, no refugees and no deficits. To cancel and annul all problems: military, political, financial or other. We want a rest, we want papers with headlines about a murder or bank robbery again, we want newscasts starting "this year's sugar beet crop will reach . . ." We want a country where nothing of historical interest happens for a whole month except for the divorce of an actress and surprises in the football league. We want a month of being b-o-r-e-d. After that we shall be ready to go on making history.

Ruth Bondy: Post-War Pangs; *Dvar Hashavua;* 14.7.67

For the writers and self-styled writers, the real fighting started only when the war was over. This was the war of books and albums.

Let's take off the uniform and, with hearts beating a martial march, join the parade of they that gather the fruits of victory. Such is life:

soldiers win the victory on the battle-field, but others gather the spoils.

15 albums on the fighting. 12 collections of war memoirs. Six pocket books. Five medallions. 150 key-holders on military subjects. Eight Israeli dinners celebrating the liberation of Jerusalem, catered by Chef Nicolai at IL9 a plate.

To victorious Zahal, congratulations from Israel Ice Cream Enterprises. Hake-fish join the cheering. When you come back from the fighting, don't forget to take along anti-mosquito spray. Lola the Beautician offers all soldiers, men and women, a free beauty treatment for IL15.

Tour the Holy Places with "Culture and Education Publications." New geography books. New wall maps. New calendars. All hail Zahal . . . we are the sole agents for guided tours. The soldiers' choice—instant coffee "Elite."

On the west platform of the bus station, Fat Lily draws pictures of Rabin and Arik Sharon—one pound each. On the east platform of the station, a man wearing an eye-patch draws Dayan's portrait in three minutes flat, at a pound and a half. Pieces of "Tupolev" for mementoes are sold at half a pound apiece.

Everyone I meet, it seems, fought in the Old City. This means that we had two million fighters in the Old City. Work accident casualties, road accident casualties and bar brawl casualties draw admiring glances. New collection boxes tinkle in the new Holy Places.

The newspaper industry has a field day. One petition asks for the creation of a Federation; another calls for the creation of a Canton; a third demands the creation of a Confederation. Then there is a petition against the creation of a Federation, against the creation of a Canton, against a Confederation. And then Harry Salzman and Jules Dassin arrive and turn all this into a co-production, co-starring Mandy Rice-Davies.

I don't care what you think, but except for defeat in battle, nothing is more saddening than victory.

Ziva Yariv: Fruits of Victory; *Yediot Aharonot,* 29.6.67

It will take years for the Israelis to grasp fully the significance of this war, but one thing was clear to them as soon as the battles were over: something within them had changed. A 21-*year-old student at the Hebrew University in Jerusalem expressed the feelings of many other people.*

In the midst of our pride and joy we have become thoughtful in Israel, even sad. There seems to be a fatigue and exhaustion in everyone to whom I speak. When I ask, I get uncertain answers—we do not know how to describe our feelings. One mentions something about a friend he no longer has, another simply states that he can't carry on any more; he cannot concentrate, he cannot find his way back to normal living, interest has gone out of everything.

Inwardly something has happened which reaches beyond all events. Events can be stated; they are measurable in units of time and in numbers. But inside, it is immeasurable. In a letter from abroad I read: "I am very glad . . ." Can one be very glad after a war? And what about the pain?

A deep restlessness has come over us all. The war did not even last seven days and yet there is no one today who can determine its consequences in the decades to come. An explosion has taken place, and the Israeli stands on the brink of the crater he has opened. He is facing new formats and somewhere inside he is deeply shocked.

We are not at all doubtful of our own courage. We knew our position exactly when war broke out—we could not but win, and we did win. Our army achieved unimaginable feats and we sense this rather than know it. The miracle of it has lifted it beyond the bounds of our comprehension. Meeting the soldiers coming home from the battle-field we feel simple feelings of relief because this one is still alive and that one was not injured. More than this we cannot offer.

They all have a great name now—*Giborei Israel*—the heroes of Israel. Zahal is the modern name. *Giborei Israel*—those were the warriors under King David, those were the Maccabees, those were the people of Massada and the rebels of the Warsaw Ghetto. That is what we call them today. There is a greatness in the name and the mouth that utters it is not important.

When the Hebrew University resumed its work, an English teacher asked his class to end the sentence—"The liberation of Jerusalem is like . . ." with an appropriate English expression. For some minutes the class sat in silence and no one offered a suggestion. There is no synonym for this pride.

And there is no synonym for the pain. A boy from the kibbutz where I had been staying was killed in action. His folks are my best friends there. News of his death crept into the kibbutz and everyone knew of it long before my friends did. Nobody told them. Everyone was waiting for the official statement from the Army.

I was supposed to give a lesson that afternoon, but my pupil and I spoke about Avi all of the time. Towards evening she went to her room to dress for supper, which is eaten together in their communal dining hall. I lay on the green and waited for her.

I saw my friend from far away. Maybe he was walking fast, or maybe everything in me was slow. He stood over me suddenly:

"Why are you lying around, like dead?"

Chaim did not know yet. His eyes were tired as they had been before. They had been waiting for news every day.

I got up. I do not know if I answered. Something strange happened during these seconds. Part of life seemed suddenly covered by a curtain; it sank out of my consciousness, I spoke to Chaim as on any other day. We were laughing.

Then my pupil came out of her room. With a sudden movement she turned back to the door, but, when she faced us again, she said simply: "Will you come and eat with us, Chaim?" Her voice sounded natural.

I did not go to see my friend that evening, for the first time in many weeks. Later, in my room, I smoked a bitter cigarette, inhaling the smoke deeply. My head started to turn and I felt ill. Only then did I fall asleep.

A few days later we went to the funeral. A long line of vehicles left the kibbutz; heavy trucks, moving very slowly.

An old man gave the funeral sermon, and he was crying. I still remember one sentence:

"Avi, we loved you very much . . ."

We cannot comprehend the greatness and we cannot comprehend the pain. Maybe this is the shock. When I came to Israel three years ago, I wrote to a friend of mine, a few weeks after my arrival:

"Describing an experience may be done in stages. First you give the outward features. Then you try to give your personal outlook. And then comes the third stage. The relation of a person to his experiences is a matter of chance, for no one can choose his experiences. But whether the experience is a genuine one, whether there was a response to it deep down in the personality, is no longer a matter of chance. It will be a long time before I try to decide on this question. Only then will I discover the innermost core of my journey—the understanding of my own self as a Jew . . ."

Maybe that is it. Maybe I have experienced it, they with me and I with them. Maybe it is the sudden realization of the fact that has always been there—the Jewishness of the Israeli.

"Nationalism" would be a ridiculously simple name for the deep ties that bind us, the ties we did not know were there. A superficial observer may see nationalism . . . an ordinary state . . . parliamentary democracy . . . people striving to reach a European middle-class standard . . . local problems caused by the complexity of the population . . .

All this is not Israel. Not deep down. Unexplained is the unbelievable unity with which the people rose to the threat. Incomprehensible is everyone's readiness to take upon himself duties foreign to his normal way of life. As soldiers, they went into battle, as civilians they worked in strange unfamiliar places for the simple reason that they were needed. There was a strange spirit, such as people attain only when the alternative is total destruction—the Greeks in the fight against the Persians, the English in their resistance to Germany.

This was a Jewish battle, not just an Israeli—ours is the only nation in the world to face an enemy who declared destruction as his program. And history has taught us more than any other people to recognize the writing on the wall.

But Judaism is ingrained even more deeply in our bones. Not only the Jewish nation but world Jewry as a whole was suddenly endangered. This absolute and limitless identity of all Jews everywhere is an unmatched phenomenon. It cannot be compared to the solidarity which was expressed by millions of non-Jews. The two are on different planes.

Solidarity stems from a moral feeling for justice, from historical uneasiness, from admiration for the enormous achievement. These sources belong to the rational sphere of human existence or correspond to it. But identity is the nucleus, the center of us all, that from which we came to be what we are, the law by which we started.

Identity is an origin—an origin of existence which hence forth shall bear the title: "Jewish."

We heard that Jerusalem was liberated and I saw the eyes of the kibbutzniks as they spoke about it. They are not religious in my kibbutz, and for them the Western Wall is not a symbol of our belief; still their eyes were shining. Their happiness derived from the same source that had once given them the strength to go into a desert and to build a new existence.

It is perhaps symbolic that Yitzhak Rabin is the victorious general of war. In his speeches he could have shouted fiery words, as other generals have done before him in similar situations. But he spoke always with unprecedented modesty and simplicity, and also without hate or rancor.

That is it—the background of our war is too great even for the greatest men of our nation. It is the sudden realization of the nucleus which a few weeks ago one would have assumed to be existent in a different spot—if at all. It is the illumination of our innermost being, and it leaps at us from a thousand mirrors.

Perhaps it is a feeling Franz Kafka once described—a deep suffering, a pain that takes complete possession of him, but is nevertheless the greatest truth he can discover. "Today I constantly felt my depth," he says. Since June 5, and actually for many weeks before that, we have been constantly feeling our depth. Our own self is constantly staring at us, and we are afraid of the stare. But it also uplifts us and welds us to the chain we are part of—the image of the "Eternal Jew" is there again. It is painful as usual—but it also is infinitely proud. The touch of eternity has passed over us, leaving everything it passed a-tremble.

Jacob Hessing: Something has Changed; *Jerusalem Post;* 14.7.67

At the end of June, after 19 *years of neglect, the amphitheater on Mount Scopus became the scene of a symbolical event. The Chief-of-Staff, General Yitzhak Rabin, received an honorary Ph.D. degree from the Hebrew University. In his acceptance speech, he bridged the apparent contradiction existing between such widely dissimilar fields as the army and philosophy. It seems that in Israel every military commander must also be something of a philosopher, and every philosopher must be a soldier.*

I stand in awe before you, leaders of this generation, here in this ancient and magnificent spot overlooking Israel's eternal capital and the birthplace of our nation's earliest history.

Together with several distinguished persons who are without doubt worthy of this honor, you have chosen to do me great honor by conferring upon me the title of Doctor of Philosophy. Permit me to express my feelings on this occasion.

I regard myself here as the representative of the entire Israel Defense Forces, of the thousands of officers and tens of thousands of soldiers who brought victory to the State of Israel in the Six-Day War.

It may be asked why the University saw fit to award the title of Honorary Doctor of Philosophy to a soldier in recognition of his military activities? What do soldiers have in common with the academic world, which stands for civilization and culture? What is there in common between those whose profession is violence and those who are concerned with spiritual values? I am, however, honored that you have chosen through me to express your deep appreciation of my comrades-in-arms and of the uniqueness of the Israel Defense Forces, which is no more than an extension of the uniqueness of the Jewish people as a whole.

The world has recognized that the Israel Army is different from other armies. Although its first task is the military one of maintaining security, it has numerous peace-time roles, not of destruction but of construction and of strengthening the nation's cultural and moral resources.

Our educational work has been widely praised, and it received national recognition in 1966 when the Israel Prize for Education was awarded to the Israel Defense Forces. The Nahal, which combines military training and agricultural settlement, also provides teachers for border villages who contribute to their social and cultural development. These are only some examples of the Israel Defense Forces' uniqueness in this sphere.

Today, however, the University is conferring on us an honorary degree in recognition of our Army's spiritual and moral superiority, as revealed precisely in the heat of war. For we are all here in this place only by virtue of the war which, though forced upon us, was forged into a victory which has astounded the world.

War is intrinsically harsh and cruel, and blood and tears are its companions. But this war which we have just waged brought forth rare and magnificent instances of courage and heroism, and at the same time humane expressions of brotherhood, comradeship and even of spiritual greatness.

Anyone who has not seen a tank crew continue its attack though its commander has been killed and its track badly damaged, who has not watched sappers risking their lives to extricate wounded comrades from a minefield, who has not witnessed the concern and the extraordinary efforts made by the entire Air Force to rescue a pilot who has fallen in enemy territory, cannot know the meaning of devotion among comrades-in-arms.

The entire nation was exalted and many wept when they heard

of the capture of the Old City. Our *sabra* youth, and most certainly our soldiers, do not tend to be sentimental and they shrink from any public show of feeling. But the strain of battle, the anxiety which preceded it, and the sense of salvation and of direct confrontation with Jewish history itself cracked the shell of hardness and shyness and released well-springs of emotion and stirrings of the spirit. The paratroops who conquered the Western Wall leaned on its stones and wept—in its symbolism an act so rare as to be almost unparalleled in human history. Rhetorical phrases and cliches are not common in our Army, but this scene on the Temple Mount, beyond the power of words to describe, revealed as though by a flash of lightning truths that were deeply hidden.

And there is more to be told. The joy of triumph had seized the entire nation. Nevertheless, a strange phenomenon can be observed among our soldiers. Their joy is incomplete, and their celebrations are marred by sorrow and shock. There are even some who abstain from celebrations entirely. The men in the front lines saw with their own eyes not only the glory of victory, but also the price of victory—their comrades fallen beside them soaked in blood. I know, too, that the terrible price paid by our enemies also touched the hearts of many of our men. It may be that the Jewish people has never learned and never accustomed itself to feel the triumph of conquest and victory, with the result that these are accepted with mixed feelings.

The Six-Day War brought to the fore numerous instances of heroism far beyond the kind manifested in the daring, one-time assault in which the attacker goes unthinkingly forward. In many places there were desperate and lengthy battles. In Rafiah, in El Arish, in Um Katef, in Jerusalem, on the Golan Heights and elsewhere, our soldiers displayed spiritual courage as well as bravery and tenacity to a degree to which no one who has witnessed this great and inspiring human phenomenon can remain indifferent. We speak a great deal of the few against the many. In this war, perhaps for the first time since the Arab invasions of the Spring of 1948 and the battles of Negba and Degania, units of the Israel Defense Forces stood few against the many in *every* sector. In other words, relatively small units often entered seemingly endless networks of fortifications, surrounded by hundreds and thousands of enemy troops, and had to force their way, hour after hour, in this veritable sea of dangers. Even after the momentum of the first attack had passed and all that remained was the overwhelming necessity of believing in our own strength and in the goal for which the battle was being fought, since there was no alternative, we summoned up every spiritual resource in order to continue the fight to the end.

Thus our armored forces broke through on all fronts, our paratroops fought their way into Rafiah and Jerusalem, and our sappers cleared minefields under enemy fire. The units which penetrated the enemy lines and reached their objectives after hours of struggle, continuing on and on while their comrades fell to the right and left of them, were carried forward by great moral force and by deep spiritual resources far more than by their weapons or the techniques of warfare.

We have always demanded the cream of our youth for the Israel Defense Forces. We coined the slogan *Hatovim l'Tayis*—"the Best for the Air Force"— and this became a meaningful phrase. It referred not only to technical and manual skills. What it meant was that if our airmen had to be capable of defeating the forces of four enemy countries within a few short hours, they had to be imbued with moral values and human values.

Our airmen who struck the enemy's planes so accurately that no one understood how it was done (all sought technological reasons in terms of secret weapons); our armored troops who stood their ground and defeated the enemy even when their equipment was inferior to his; our soldiers in all the various branches of the Israel Defense Forces who overcame our enemies everywhere, despite their superior numbers and fortifications—all of them revealed not only coolness and courage in battle but a burning faith in the justice of their cause, and sure knowledge that only their personal stand against the greatest of dangers could bring victory to their country and to their families, and that if the victory were not achieved the alternative was annihilation.

Furthermore, in every sector our commanders, of all ranks, far outshone those of the enemy. Their insight, their understanding, their preparedness, their ability to improvise, their care for their men and, above all, the fact that they went at the head of their troops into battle—all these are not matters of equipment or technique. They have no rational explanation, except in terms of a deep consciousness of the moral justice of their fight.

All this springs from the spirit and leads back to the spirit. Our warriors prevailed not by their weapons but by their sense of mission, by the consciousness of the rightness of their cause, by a deep love for their country and an understanding of the difficult task laid upon them: to ensure the existence of our people in its homeland, to protect, even at the price of their own lives, the right of the Jewish people to live in its own state, free, independent and in peace.

This Army, which I had the privilege of commanding through these battles, came from the people and returns to the people—to a people which rises to great heights in times of crisis and prevails over all enemies by virtue of its moral and spiritual strength.

As the representative of the Israel Defense Forces, and on behalf of every one of its soldiers, I accept with pride this token of your appreciation.

Address by the Chief-of-Staff Major-General Yitzhak Rabin; 28.6.67

Almost all of the university students and many of the teachers took part in the fighting.

The administration of the Technion Library decided to exempt the student Aviv Hadari, first-year student in Agricultural Engineering, from payment for the book, "Calculus" by Bacon. The decision was reached following receipt of a letter from the student. It said: "On June 6, 1967, during a battle in Sinai, the tank in which I fought caught fire from a direct hit by the Egyptians, and all my personal equipment was burned. My belongings included "Calculus" by Bacon, lent to me by the library at the beginning of the current academic year. Therefore, I cannot return it."

This student took the book along with him to prepare himself, in his "spare time," for the examinations due at the end of the year.

Book Fallen in Battle; *Ha'aretz*, 26.7.67

What now? The Russians are stepping up their armament shipments to Egypt, the Syrians keep up their bellicose declarations, Arab leaders meet in summit conferences, politicians from east and west circle the globe to attend conferences on the future of the Middle East. And the Israelis are looking for solutions for the myriads of new problems which make up the aftermath of victory.

The transition from war to everyday life is not easy.

Within a short period of time we experienced apprehension and anxiety, a sigh of relief when a united government was established, tense preparedness before battle, the rage and fury of war, the joy of victory, sorrow and mourning for lost friends, and a slow acceptance of the thought that this is not the end and that we stand before a new, quiet but prolonged struggle. These have been days of glory, days during which this nation of sworn individualists all had one strong pulse. Those who were not with us during those days will never be able to understand what it was like.

It is not easy to abandon those days. It is not easy to go back to everyday life while we are bearing within ourselves the sights of the war and the memory of those who but yesterday were still with us laughing and cheerful and who have now become names within a black frame.

What will remain of all this? How are we going to translate the memory of those days into the future?

Israel has emerged from the war more definite in mind than it was ever before. Once again it became clear to everybody, in the most dramatic fashion possible, that the primary issue is that of assuring our physical security. Above all other problems rises the question: shall we live? If anybody supposed that this question had been invented by army officers and the staff of the Ministry of Defense, the war has removed every trace of doubt from his heart. The war has increased the sense of common responsibility we all feel for the existence of Israel and its people.

Israel has emerged from the war more united. Years of controversy, bickering, splits, divisions, quarrels and mutual recrimination did not weaken us in time of crisis. The foundations remained firm, though the roof seemed to be caving in. The democracy of Israel, in spite of all its faults, stood the difficult test and came out victorious. The raw material from which Israel is constructed again proved its quality. Service in the reserves brought together different kinds of Israelis and gave them the feelings of a family.

Israel emerged from the war younger. Now we can speak in praise of young Israelis without any note of apology. Where are now the professional lamenters who so recently charged the youth of the discotheques with so many faults? How hollow, miserable and ridiculous now sound all those endless discussions in the Knesset and elsewhere about the careerist, cynical, nihilistic youth who dance "ballroom" dances, (heaven protect us)? What has happened to all those vocal heroes who had declared so absolutely that "the volunteer spirit is at an end among us?" The war ended the lamentations and put a stop to the empty verbiage.

Israel has emerged from the war more mature. Boys have seen death for the first time, while their fathers discovered that they are still strong and capable. The unprecedented victory was not accompanied by any intoxication of the victors. Never was there such a smooth conquest: without hate, without ill will, with so much largesse towards those who were ready to massacre all of us. The war has not blunted but has strengthened the will to peace.

However, one should not exaggerate the influence of those glorious days on our future. War is different from the kind of struggle we can expect now. The war was short and required a tremendous one-time effort. The new issues will require patience, persistence, strong nerves for a very long time. In the war we were all united against the foreign enemy who rose to destroy us. In the new struggle no such unity will be possible. Here the questions are harder and more complicated, and differences of opinion about the answers will be unavoidable.

Furthermore, there is a danger that we may run to superficiality and shall try to draw a parallel from the army's victory and try to apply the same methods in other, entirely different fields. There is no greater mistake than that of comparing a military campaign with an economic one. An army operates within the framework of orders and discipline. The same men who were ready to die for their country are not prepared to renounce a material interest. This may be illogical and regrettable, but the experiences of 1948 and of the past weeks go to confirm it. The severe orders issued against purchases in the new areas were disobeyed by thousands of Israelis who swooped down on the shops of the West Bank in a search for "bargains." This is regrettable and annoying, but it is a fact. The wheels of economics are chiefly set in motion by egotistic instincts. The war machine operates by the force of the volunteer spirit and self-sacrifice. The transfer of military methods to the economy is liable to produce grave results.

Furthermore: The art of internal government is a compromise between conflicting social interests. This is far harder than the work of an army, which is directed entirely against an external foe. In a certain sense more strength and firmer resolution is required to manage the Israel Port Authority than to command an armored division. Stronger nerves are necessary to withstand a wave of exaggerated wage demands than an air attack. The Israel experience proves this fact.

On the other hand, certain lessons ought to be learnt from the war. First and foremost, the war dramatically proved once again the need for a change-over in all branches of government. This need is so obvious, so immediately comprehensible—that it is difficult to find reasons supporting it. Why should our affairs be run by people whose outlook was formed in pre-First World War Eastern Europe? Who decided, arbitrarily, that death alone releases politicians from their office? Who decreed that the generation of Israelis who serve in the army and reserve forces should scarcely be represented at all in the leadership of the State?

These words are given double force in the light of the difference between the founding generation and its sons. This difference finds expression in form and content. Anybody who listened to the gripping broadcasts of "Kol Yisrael" during the war—and who did not listen?—could clearly sense this difference. How simple, direct and comprehensible were the words of the army commanders and generals! How they spoke to our hearts in our Hebrew, in our own terminology, in our concepts! How our spirits rose when we heard the Minister of Defense, Moshe Dayan, and the Chief-of-Staff, General Yitzhak Rabin! And what a distance separates them from the speeches of the old leadership which spoke out of the past, in the language and thoughts of the past.

Yet it is not merely a matter of language or style. Behind these also stand differing approaches to fundamental problems. For a large part of the founding generation, the Party comes before the State. This can be understood: For them the Party preceded the State, chronologically speaking. The parties of the Jewish community of Palestine came into being before the State and engaged in vital governmental functions under a foreign rule. As far as we are concerned, that period is so much history. For them it is an ever-present reality that has set a deep stamp upon them. They can be understood, but it is impossible to agree that these people should lead us. Their world is not our world. Theirs is a world of petrified doctrines and dogmas. Mr. Meir Ya'ari, leader of Mapam, declared on the eve of the war that the appointment of Moshe Dayan to the post of Minister of Defense would be "a black day for the workers of Israel." In his conceptual world, this declaration is significant. The class war, on which he was brought up at the beginning of the century, is a more concrete reality than the Israel of today which he does not know. Yet for many Israelis his is simply a hallucinatory world. For most Israelis, Mr. Ya'ari's "black day" was a great day, a day of high spirits.

As against the petrified doctrines of these men of yesterday, the contemporary Israeli is marked by a pragmatic approach. The Israel Army is led by young men of this type. These are men who set themselves an objective, attacked it effectively, rapidly, skilfully, and reached their objective by the best possible means. All the deficiencies to be found in the veteran political leadership—historic rights, petrified dogmatism, lack of contact with the people, language and style dating from the past—do not exist in the Israel Army leadership. Only in the army is the new Israeli generation permitted to talk its own language, to do its job in the way it understands. And we may say that the results of this attempt are not so very bad.

For the sake of the peace and well-being of Israeli society it is urgently necessary that this generation should express itself in all branches of public life. The days of glory have given us a time of opportunity. It is possible to distinguish between the privileges of the past and the needs of the present. There is no real necessity for the future to be dictated by archives and archivists. There is no real reason why we should have a dynamic and effective army while the information apparatus, for example, should be laggard, paralyzed and dormant. It is possible to increase the speed of action and capacity for decision of our democratic rule. It is possible to give Israel the young leadership we deserve. These laudable days have given us the opportune time for doing all this.

Dr. Amnon Rubinstein: Days of Glory, Hour of Opportunity; *Ha'aretz*, 30.6.67

★

The war came. The victory was overwhelming. The smashed Arab armies are licking their wounds. The Israel Army stands along the Suez Canal, on the West Bank of the Jordan and on the shores of Birket-Ram in the Golan, which is the real Waters of Merom of Bible days.

What more can you ask for?

Just—not to lose the sense of truth, of reality; just—not to lose your sobriety about everything. Just—not to hide yourself away from the Voice!

Not to allow yourself to be seduced by the argument that the delay in the Army's proceeding to action has helped to improve the outcome of the fighting and has made our present political situation easier. If the delay in going out to fight changed anything, it is possible to prove that it was a change for the worse at least as much as it can be claimed to have been for the better.

But the chief thing to remember is the ineffectiveness of the leadership during those days, when it came to seeing the truth and showing it to us. All you need is a good memory, without any special sources of information, in order to determine quite definitely that the delay and hesitancy, the absence of any spirit of leadership at home and the bent back abroad were not the fruit of any planning, understanding of processes, or secret and well-weighed strategic considerations. They were the fruit of confusion, they derived from a refusal to recognize a reality that did not match theoretical assumptions. They became worse and worse because of an absence of inspiration. And they were presented to the public day after day in great doses of silence and stammering. God Almighty, what is a leader after all? "Speak to the people!"... "Go and say to them!"... "Then it was that Moses sang . . .". . ."And David raised his voice and said!"

Leadership is essentially a power of expression, and power of expression is composed of a two-fold, simultaneous rhythm, the rhythm of listening and speaking. Leadership first and foremost involves listening—listening to the inner seething of the realities, of the processes of life, of the ceaseless changes; and naturally that also includes listening to the people, to their murmurings, achings and aspirations. If anybody has lost this capacity for listening, his leadership is undergoing calcification. And in addition to this, leadership means speaking. Speaking in the highest sense of the word, which is the raising of the reality to an essence that is capable of leading to experiences and deeds. If anyone loses the quality of being able to express what is going on and summing problems up so as to make the way clear and set people moving along it, his leadership has lapsed.

Our leadership did not listen in the days of trial. It evinced no capacity for pointing and saying and making clear: This is what is going on, here is the source of danger, this is what things are like. And it was even less capable of speaking to the people in the language of the time and the speech of the generation, with a force and inspiration that would be capable of preparing the people to face the most extreme tests and trials.

Now why do I come back to this again and again in spite of the fact that obviously we have won a war, we have a victorious army and a victorious government?

Very simply indeed, because we have not yet won a victory.

War is not a game of football, where you record the results and go home cheerfully. Our war has only just begun. Everybody says this but nobody acts accordingly. We fought against three or four Arab countries. Now we have to be prepared for war against most of the nations of the world, against great powers, international institutions, public opinion and the press. In another few weeks the final vestiges of the honeymoon intoxication will be over. In the political part of the war we must be prepared for the most extreme isolation possible, with almost all the states of the world supporting the defeated aggressor in one form or another. In any case there is no way to prepare for war, for any war whatsoever, other than on the assumption that the worst possible, the harshest possible may very well happen.

Just as our military victory was greater this time than anything that went before, so it is this time with our peace objective. Here it is, we say, take it or leave it. Speak about withdrawal as much as you like—this time there will be no retreat from full and absolute peace. And what this means is a political, economic, moral struggle, the longest and most exhausting that we have ever had. Shall we be able to withstand this with the public, social and moral alignment and leadership of the past two years?

The answer is: No.

"And he sent him forth from the Garden of Eden . . . And the flash of the whirling sword to guard . . ."

There is no way back. A few hours before flying abroad for a lightning visit to Jewish centers, on a trip to rouse Jewry and mobilize financial resources, one of the victorious and laurel-wreathed generals dropped in to say *Shalom* and exchange a few everyday words with his usual modesty and warmth. At the last moment, and without the slightest humorous intention, he happened to say the words: "Listen, don't you go handing back even one centimeter meanwhile!"

This raging torrent, which has come from all parts of the people and is sweeping all parts of the people along, did not begin after the victory. It began during our gloomiest moments, during the most bitter nadir of the political debacle which preceded the war. It was that torrent which compelled the leadership to stop stammering. It is the identical torrent which set the fighting units moving and is still today what it was to begin with: Not the rejoicing of victors but the unyielding grimness of those fighting for their existence and their right to breathe.

If the Oder–Neisse frontier is an expression of historic justice and a security for peace in Europe (and that it is, 100 percent), then our cease-fire frontiers today with Egypt, Jordan and Syria are no less so in respect of justice, humanity and the assurance of peace.

The demand not to give anything back, the declaration that there is no way back is the most pacifist position today. It is the clearest expression of our aspiration towards peace and the assurance of peace. It is even more than that: The demand not to give up even a single foot of ground contains within itself not only a healthy sense of self-preservation and the sober political instinct of a people done with illusions once and for all. It is also the quintessence of thousands of never-expressed yearnings not to go back in a thousand other senses too; not to return to the recent past in any field, in any sense, in any fashion.

There is no return. Today that is the realistic, sober and effective principle for shaping foreign and home affairs alike, and for the awareness that they depend on one another more than they ever did before.

Today the most realistic step in our political struggle is to resolve and state that our Army will not vacate a single foot of ground unless it is absolutely clear and certain that the area will remain open to us, precisely as it was open to any other nation in the region or the world. We do not enjoy having to keep military units on the Canal. But if their withdrawal means the canceling of our clear and recognized and full presence in that area, we shall continue to maintain that presence by a military force. Presence means right of passage by every waterway and land-way, possibilities of taking part in economic development, equal rights with everybody else to share in the exploitation of minerals and trade routes; and over and above everything else: Absolute, bilateral demilitarization of all the areas in question, on the basis of a full and honorable bilateral peace treaty and relations based on mutual goodwill.

It has to be made absolutely plain that not a single Israeli soldier will withdraw from even one square meter if the day after, when he has taken his uniform off, he will not be permitted to return there as a worker, an engineer, a businessman, a driver, a ship's captain or a tourist. If the Arab countries—or any other force in the world, or the whole wide world together—decide that for the future as well there are to be frontiers that are closed to us, frontiers beyond which the "Judenrein" principle is law—then we shall retain the prerogative of deciding precisely where those frontiers are to be.

Moshe Shamir: No Way Back (II); *Ma'ariv,* 30.6.67

Calendar of Events

IN 1966 THE ARABS BEGAN STEPPING UP THE TEMPO OF MARAUDING, mining roads and points of habitation, especially in the northern sector. One of these incidents drew the sharp reprisal action at Samua. The Arabs lost no time carrying their activities into 1967.

January 1	Syrians try to obstruct sowing of Haon fields.
January 2	Syrians open fire on Korazin; one Israeli soldier wounded.
January 3	Syrians fire on Zahal patrol near Notera.
January 4	Syrians fire on Ein-Gev settlers.
January 7	Syrian tanks shell Almagor and Tel-Katzir sectors.
January 8	Syrian tanks and machine-guns fire on Zahal patrol; one tractor operator and two jeeps are hit.
January 9	Two Syrian tanks destroyed at Tawafik.
January 10	Syrians open light arms fire on Ashmura and Tel-Katzir.
January 11	Syrian tank destroyed in Ashmura sector battle; two Zahal soldiers hurt. Prime Minister warns Syria.
January 14	One young man killed and another wounded by Syrian shoe-mine in Dishon settlement.
January 16	Aqueduct blown up near Adamit. Three shoe-mines uncovered near Tel-Katzir.
January 18	Three Zahal soldiers wounded by Jordanian fire near Eilat.
January 26	At U Thant's initiative, Israel–Syria Mixed Armistice Commission begins meetings.
February 25	Two border guards wounded in gun battle with Jordanians.
March 12	Train sabotaged near Jordan border. Shots exchanged with Jordanian position in May-Ami sector.

March 16	Two saboteurs of Arad water works killed.
March 20	Syria refuses to renew deliberations of MAC on the basis of scheduled agenda.
April 3	Syrian artillery fires on Haon tractors; total of 770 Syrian penetrations in two months.
April 5	Foreign Minister Abba Eban warns Syria.
April 7	IAF downs six Syrian MIG's; war scare in Damascus.
April 8	Prime Minister reviews reasons for air action against Syria; "Let this be a lesson to Damascus on Zahal's combat power," says Chief-of-Staff; "Zahal is superior on all levels and with all weapons," says Northern Command General.
April 9	Two sabotage attempts foiled on northern border. Syria rushes reinforcements to border.
April 10	Cultivation of tracts near Syrian border resumed. Syria complains to Security Council: "72 Israeli planes took part in the bombing."
April 11	Syrians direct heavy mortar fire at tractor of Tel-Katzir.
May 2	Syrians again refuse to participate in MAC sessions.
May 6	Syrians shell Manara from Lebanese territory. Pumping station near Kinneret blown up. Armored vehicle hits mine at Bar'am.
May 9	*Al Fatah* man, who planned to place bombs where Independence Day celebrants were to gather, caught.
May 10	Prime Minister warns Syria: "We have no other alternative but to take action against sources and supporters of sabotage." Jordan protests to U Thant against holding of Independence Day Parade in Jerusalem. Gideon Rafael warns Security Council: "Israel has right to defend itself if Syria does not change its aggressive policy."
May 14	Prime Minister Eshkol: "In view of 14 incidents during past month alone, Israel will have to take more drastic steps than on April 7."
May 15	19th Independence Day Parade is held in Jerusalem. Egyptian army parades through Cairo on way to Sinai. Egyptian and Syrian army commanders meet in Damascus. Israeli forces put on alert.
May 16	Egypt declares state of emergency. All Egyptian forces

are on war footing and "have taken up defense positions along Israeli border." Chief-of-Staff General Fawzi informs UNEF Commander, General Rikkie: "I have instructed my forces to take action against Israel in case of aggressive action on its part against any Arab state; in order to safeguard UNEF, I request all your forces along Israeli border be withdrawn at once." Zahal spokesman: "We are watching developments in Sinai."

May 17 Egyptian forces arrayed along border. Egyptian army on full alert. Jordan announces deployment of forces along border. Levi Eshkol: "Positioning of Egyptian forces in Sinai has dangerous implications."

May 18 Egypt gives UNEF 15 minutes to evacuate Sharm-a-Sheikh. U Thant accedes to Egypt's demand to evacuate UNEF. Egypt continues pouring troops into Sinai. Iraq and Kuwait announce troop mobilization. Zahal takes "adequate steps" to meet new situation.

May 19 UNEF evacuated from Israeli border. Israeli spokesman states Israel is considering representations to UN General Assembly *re* U Thant's acquiescence to withdrawal of UNEF from Israel–Egypt border.

May 20 Egyptian force occupies UNEF positions at Sharm-a-Sheikh. Palestine Liberation Organization troops occupy positions along Gaza Strip border. Egypt calls up reserves. 12 Arab states support Egypt's preparations for war. Israel completes partial mobilization.

May 21 Egypt calls up all its 100,000 reserves. Ahmad Shukeiry announces that all 8,000 PLO men have been placed under various Arab commands. Cairo, Damascus threaten increased sabotage activities. Syrian charge of explosives kills 14, wounds 28 in Jordan.

May 22 Nasser announces blocking of Tiran Straits to Israeli ships and to foreign ships with "strategic material" for Israel. "If Israel should threaten war, it is welcome to it." Levi Eshkol: "Blocking of Tiran Straits is an aggressive act against Israel." The Soviet Union announces: "The USSR will strongly oppose any aggression against Arab states." Levi Eshkol says: "Egyptians have increased their forces in Sinai from

35,000 to 80,000 men;" demands return to former positions along both sides of border. Britain and France withdraw from tripartite agreement.

May 23 President Johnson declares blocking of Tiran Straits is an illegal act; deplores UNEF's hasty withdrawal from Sinai border and Sharm-a-Sheikh.

May 24 Egypt mines Tiran Straits. Saudi Arabia, Jordan and Lebanon declare full mobilization. Jordan allows Iraqi and Saudi Arabian troops to enter its territory. 20,000 Saudi Arabian soldiers concentrated along Jordanian border at Akaba. Abba Eban meets with General De Gaulle and Prime Minister Harold Wilson. Washington proposes compromise plan: An association of "Eilat Gulf Users"; the US does not wish involvement in military intervention. US Sixth Fleet is positioned in Eastern Mediterranean. Israel prepares for eventualities: Emergency committees set up in urban centers; shelters are prepared. Food stock-up increases; Government warehouses open at night for convenience of shopkeepers. Transit system reduces routes. Foreign citizens begin leaving country. World Jewry aroused.

May 25 Russia rejects French proposal to have four powers settle controversy. Pressure increases on Prime Minister not to use force to open Tiran Straits. *Al-Fatah* saboteurs resume infiltration. Civil defense, medical centers prepare for emergency. Young people, women, elders volunteer to aid services.

May 26 Abba Eban sees President Johnson, after day's wait. Nasser speaks in Cairo: "If war breaks out it will be total in scope; the objective: annihilation of Israel; we are confident of victory and are prepared for war."

May 27 Nasser speaks further: "We now await the opportunity to destroy Israel; military confrontation is inevitable." U Thant reports to Security Council: "Outbreak is at hand." Egypt places economy on war footing. Seven soldiers hurt by mine at Gaza border.

May 28 Prime Minister tells nation: "Government has decided to continue preparedness and political action for free passage." Nasser tells press conference Russia supports

Tiran blockade; threatens to close Suez Canal in case of war. General mobilization in Sudan. Three senior Egyptian officers captured by Zahal patrol near Nitzana. Wave of volunteering grips Israel's communities. World Jewry demonstrates solidarity with Israel.

May 29 Prime Minister tells Knesset: "No retreat from position on free passage." Nasser announces all military plans completed by Egypt and allies to liberate Palestine; Soviets have promised to thwart any intervention on part of US in Israel's favor. At Security Council session, US proposes that Egypt open Tiran Straits "for a breather," so that UN may have time to handle crisis. Egypt objects. Egypt opens fire on Nahal Oz and Zahal patrol along Gaza border.

May 30 King Hussein of Jordan pays surprise visit to Cairo and signs defense pact with Nasser. Ahmad Shukeiry in Amman: "PLO may well be the one to fire first shot; after Arab conquest of Israel, all Jews left alive will be helped to return to lands of origin, but I say that it is unlikely that anyone will be left alive." Abba Eban tells press conference: "Israel is prepared to accept any proposal which will assure free passage for all shipping through Tiran; however, diplomatic action must come within days or weeks." Russia informs Turkey of its intention to send 10 warships through Bosphorus to Mediterranean. Chief-of-Staff to troops in south: "Current task and test—a bit of patience."

May 31 Britain, Holland, Portugal support US initiative to test Egyptian blockade. Cairo threatens with "blitzkrieg." Moshe Dayan offers Prime Minister his services in any military post under Chief-of-Staff, preferably as Southern Front Commander. Volunteers arrive from abroad.

June 1 National Unity Government formed: Moshe Dayan—Minister of Defense, Menahem Begin—Minister Without Portfolio; third ministry reserved for Gahal Party. Brigadier-General Haim Barlev—Assistant Chief-of-Staff. Iraqi planes leave Habaniyeh Air Base near Baghdad and arrive at Base 3, near Israel border.

June 3 — Moshe Dayan to press: "We don't want foreign troops fighting for us; I shall be happy with diplomatic success." Commander of Egyptian forces, General Murtagi issues order of the day: "Outcome of this fateful moment is of historical importance to Arab people and to the liberation of ravished Palestine." Israel's industry shifts to emergency lines. Two Zahal soldiers and one Syrian saboteur killed in Galilee skirmish. Many Israel soldiers are given leave; photos of soldiers at seashore appear in foreign press and on TV.

June 4 — Government worried by slow pace of powers. Iraq joins Egypt–Jordan pact. Israeli Arabs volunteer for service. Security levy approved. High school students participate in emergency preparations.

June 5 — *The Israel Air Force*. War begins at 7:45 a.m., when first wave of IAF planes crosses border to strike at Egyptian forces set to attack Israel. IAF strikes at 24 airfields in Egypt, Sinai, Jordan, Syria and Iraq. Within less than three hours, 300 of Egypt's 340 air force planes are destroyed, among them all 30 long-range TU-16 bombers. Knocked out of use are all air-fields except El-Arish, preserved by IAF as advance base for its own planes. Egypt announces major air victories; alleges downing of 86 Israeli craft. *Israel Navy:* Port Said and Alexandria harbors attacked and two Egyptian submarines and two torpedo boats damaged; Egyptians remove warships from Port Said to Alexandria. *Southern Front:* 12 hours after outbreak of war, Zahal isolates Gaza Strip by capturing El-Arish. *Central Front:* Jewish Jerusalem and Mount Scopus shelled incessantly by Jordanians. Hussein on the air: "The hour of revenge is at hand." 10:30 a.m.: Legionnaires capture "Government House." UN proposes cease-fire, but Jordanians go on shelling. Netanya plant is bombed by Jordan planes. Jordan announces capture of Mount Scopus. Toward evening Zahal takes "Government House," Radar Ridge and Beit-Iksa. Knesset holds session in shelters.

June 6 *IAF:* At end of second day, total enemy air force losses come to 309 planes for Egypt, 60 for Syria, 29 for Jordan, 17 for Iraq, one for Lebanon—416 in all, of these 393 destroyed on the ground. Bomber attacking Netanya downed by Zahal anti-aircraft fire. Lebanon claims downing of IAF plane. *Southern Front:* Gaza and Abu-Agheila taken. Armor units of Generals Yisrael Tal and Avraham Yaffe join forces at Gebel-Libni, trapping all Egyptian forces in Sinai. Annihilation of Egyptian forces begins. *Central Front:* Capture of Police School opens way to Mount Scopus. Northern Command forces take Jenin and Nablus. Latrun, Ramallah, Jericho, Tul-Karem and Kalkilya are taken. With capture of Bethlehem and Hebron all of West Bank comes into Zahal hands. *Northern Front:* Syria heavily shells settlements and troop concentrations in the north. Three Syrian attempts to capture Israeli settlements are foiled. Security Council votes cease-fire. Egypt accuses US, Britain of active air collaboration with IAF. Nasser breaks off diplomatic relations with US and blocks Suez Canal. Arabs stop oil flow to US and Britain.

June 7 *Southern Front:* Sharm-a-Sheikh captured. Zahal reaches Suez, goes back 20 kilometers at Government's request. *Central Front:* Old City is captured; Dayan at Western Wall: "We have returned to our most sacred sites, never again to be separated from them." *Northern Front:* Syria continues shelling Israeli settlements; IAF attacks Syrian positions. Israel accepts cease-fire order, on condition that Arabs do likewise; Hussein accepts, Nasser rejects.

June 8 *Southern Front:* Israeli forces are entrenched on eastern bank of Canal. Six Egyptian divisions are trapped in Sinai. Egypt accepts cease-fire. *Northern Front:* Syria continues shelling Israeli settlements. US communications vessel, the *Liberty,* is mistakenly attacked by Israeli planes and torpedo boats; 34 sailors and officers are dead and 75 wounded. White House announces that "hot line" between Washington and the Kremlin has been busy these days.

June 9	*Northern Front:* 11:30 a.m.—Israel launches attack on Syrian fortifications above Kfar Szold. Nasser resigns, then retracts on the following day.
June 10	*Northern Front:* With capture of Kuneitra, conquest of Syrian heights is complete. Syrian losses: 1,000 dead, 500–600 taken prisoner; Israeli losses: 115 dead, 306 wounded. War ends officially at 7:30 p.m. with cease-fire order set by UN going into effect.
June 11	Israel makes official announcement of losses in Six-Day War: 679 dead, 3,563 wounded. Jordan announces 15,000 dead. Nasser fires army heads and top commanding officer.
June 12	First Israeli ship passes through Tiran Straits on way to Israel.
June 14	Security Council rejects Soviet motion to condemn Israel. Russian demand for convening emergency session of General Assembly is accepted.
June 19	Abba Eban addresses emergency session of General Assembly. President Johnson outlines five principles of US policy in Middle East.
June 24	USSR head Aleksei Kosygin and President Johnson meet at Glassboro.
June 25	Two leaders continue meeting.
	Emergency session rejects Soviet-supported Yugoslavian proposal to force Israel withdrawal, as well as the Latin American proposal, supported by US and Britain.
July 8	Five Zahal soldiers are killed and 3 wounded by Egyptian shelling from across Canal. Egyptian MIG is downed. Israeli soldier killed and two wounded by mine near Canal.
July 11	"Sukhoy 7" plane is shot down in Kantara sector.
July 12	Two Egyptian torpedo boats are destroyed in a night battle in Canal.
July 15	Heavy battle in Canal sector: 10 Zahal soldiers killed and 22 wounded; Egypt suffers 44 dead and 133 wounded. Six MIG's downed.
July 22	Emergency session of General Assembly ends without any practical resolutions.

Contributors to the Anthology

ALTERMAN, Nathan—One of Israel's noted men of letters: poet, essayist, playwright. Has translated many of Shakespeare's works into Hebrew, as well as other classics originally written in English, French and Russian. Columnist for *Ma'ariv*.

ARAZI, Dan—Geology student at Hebrew University. Fought with paratroop reserves under Col. Mota Gur in Battle for Jerusalem.

AVIDAR, Tamar—Editor of *At,* illustrated women's monthly.

BARKAI, Mordecai—Holds rank of Major in reserves. Past editor of *Bamahane* and now spokesman for Ministry of Defense.

BASHAN, Raphael—Feature writer for *Ma'ariv*, specializing in interviews, a collection of which has appeared in book form. Winner of Sokolow Prize in Journalism for 1962.

BELLA, I.—Writer for kibbutz publication.

BEN-AMOTZ, Dan—Prominent broadcaster and journalist.

BEN-ARI, Colonel Uri—Commander of an armored brigade of reserves which took part in the Battle of Jerusalem, Ramallah and Jericho.

BEN SIMCHON, Gabriel—Poet, journalist on *Ma'ariv* staff.

BONDY, Ruth—Outstanding feature writer for *Dvar Hashavua*. Winner of Sokolow Prize for Journalism for 1967.

COHEN, Geula—Author, journalist on *Ma'ariv* staff. Won fame as member of LEHI underground during British Mandatory regime.

DAYAN, Major-General Moshe—Israel Minister of Defense, Zahal Chief-of-Staff during Sinai Campaign, author of "Sinai Diary."

DAYAN, Yael—Author. Holds rank of Lieutenant in Zahal and was military writer during service.

DOLAV, Aharon—Senior feature writer on *Ma'ariv* staff.

DOTHAN, Ruth Geffen—Member of Ayelet Hashahar Kibbutz.

DUDAI, Yadin—Military writer for *Bamahane.*

EBAN, Abba—Israel's Foreign Minister and its foremost protagonist on the international scene.

ELAZAR, Brigadier-General David—Head of Northern Command and the campaign against the Syrian Heights.

ELGAT, Zvi—Feature writer, *Ma'ariv.*

FRENKEL, Erwin—Journalist, on *Jerusalem Post* staff.

GAVISH, Brigadier-General Yeshayahu—Commander of the Southern Front (Sinai).

GILLON, Philip—Journalist, editor of *Junior Jerusalem Post.*

GOLAN, Aviezer—Senior feature writer for *Yediot Aharonot.* Author of "Six Days of Glory."

GOREN, Rabbi Shlomo—Chief Chaplain of Zahal, with rank of Brigadier-General. Trained with paratroops.

GUR, Colonel Mordecai ("Mota")—Commander of paratroops who liberated the Old City.

GURI, Haim—One of Israel's foremost authors and poets. Columnist for *Lamerhav.* Served with Palmah and in Six-Day War (rank of Captain) participated in Battle for Jerusalem.

HA'ELYON, Ya'acov—On editorial staff of *Ma'ariv.* Was wounded in battle for Syrian Heights.

HALFI, Rachel—Journalist for *Bamahane.*

HASHAVIA, Arieh—Free-lance writer on military affairs. Member of Institute for Strategic Studies (London).

HESSING, Jacób—Student at Hebrew University.

HEYKAL, Mohammed Hassnein—Editor of *Al-Ahram* (Cairo). Close friend of Col. Nasser.

HOD, Brigadier-General Mordecai—Commander of the Israel Air Force, directed Israel's most decisive blow of the Six-Day War.

KENAN, Amos—Author and journalist, columnist for *Yediot Aharonot.*

KHALIF, Nurit—Free-lance journalist.

LACHISH, Carmela—Writer for *Al Hamishmar.*

LANDAU, Binyamin—Military writer for *Bamahane.*

LIVNI, Yitzhak—Editor-in-Chief of *Bamahane;* director of Zahal Broadcasting Network.

MANUELI, Shimon—Writer for *Bamahane.*

MASH, Avraham—Journalist for *Davar.*

MEGGED, Aharon—Prominent author and playwright.

MOSSINSON, A.—Free-lance writer on military affairs.

NADEL, Baruch—Journalist and public relations man.

NARKISS, Brigadier-General Uzi—Commander of the Central Front (Jerusalem, and Jordan West Bank).

NASSER, Col. Gamal Abdul—President of Egypt.

NE'EMAN, Prof. Yuval—Lecturer in Physics at Hebrew University. Winner of awards in U.S. in recognition of his work. Was head of Israel's military intelligence.

OREN, Uri—Short story writer and journalist.

PORAT, Uri—Journalist on *Yediot Aharonot* staff.

RABIN, Major-General Yitzhak—Chief-of-Staff, led Zahal to victory in Six-Day War.

RUBINSTEIN, Dr. Amnon—Lecturer in Jurisprudence, Tel-Aviv University; editorial writer for *Ha'aretz.*

SAYAR, M.—Pen name of Menachem Talmi, journalist for *Ma'ariv;* known for his Israel travelogues.

SHAMIR, Moshe—Prominent author and playwright ("King of Flesh and Blood").

SHAMIR, Shlomo—Free-lance journalist.

"SHMULIK," Col.—Commander of armored brigade, first to reach Suez.

SHAPIRA, Masha—Editor of *Al Hamishmar* women's section.

SHELACH, Menahem—Writer, *Hotam.*

TEICHER, Eli—Author and attorney-at-law.

TEVET, Shabtai—Senior military writer for *Ha'aretz.* Winner of 1967 Italia Award for radio script. Author of books on Sinai Campaign and the U.S.

WIESEL, Eli—Journalist for *Yediot Aharonot.* Author in Hebrew, French and English ("Gates of the Forest," "Jews of Silence").

YAFFE, Brigadier-General Avraham—Director of Nature Reserves Authority and division commander in Sinai in Six-Day War.

YARIV, Ziva—Writes satire column for *Yediot Aharonot.*

ZEMER, Hanna—Associate Editor-in-Chief of *Davar;* featured radio program participant.

ZERTAL, Edith—On staff of *Dvar Hashavua.*

Press Sources

Al Hamishmar (On Guard)—Daily organ of MAPAM, left-wing labor party.

Bakibbutz (In the Kibbutz)—Weekly inter-kibbutz publication of AHDUT AVODA (left-of-center labor party).

Bamahane (In the Camp)—Illustrated Zahal weekly.

Davar (Word)—Israel's first and leading labor daily (morning).

Dvar Hapoelet—Women's labor movement monthly.

Dvar Hashavua—Illustrated weekly magazine supplement of *Davar*.

Ha'aretz (The Land)—Independent daily (morning); the country's oldest newspaper.

Hotam (The Impress)—MAPAM young people's weekly.

Israel Magazine—Monthly, published in New York.

Jerusalem Post—Israel's only English-language daily (morning).

Lamerhav (To the Open Spaces)—Daily organ of AHDUT AVODA.

Ma'ariv (Evening)—Independent daily (afternoon); largest circulation in Israel.

New York Times Magazine.

Yediot Aharonot (Latest News)—Popular Independent daily (afternoon).

TRANSLATED FROM THE HEBREW BY:

ISRAEL I. TASLITT, TEL-AVIV

MOSHE COHEN, JERUSALEM

I. M. LASK, TEL-AVIV

MRS. NEOMY OFRY, TEL-AVIV

DAVID SARATH, RAMAT CHEN

MRS. GOLDIE YEVNIN, RAMAT CHEN

ENGLISH TEXT EDITED

BY ISRAEL I. TASLITT